BARRY LYNDON R-5
YNDON R-2 REFERENCE
NDON R-1 REFERENCE
LYNDON R-3 REFERENC
SHUT" REEL 4 A/B C/COPY AC
EL 3 A/B C/COPY ACTION
SHUT" REEL 2 A/B C/COPY AC
SHUT" REEL 1 A/B C/COPY AC
ATHS OF GLORY
DR.
DR. STRANGELO
DR. STRANGELOVE

PATHS OF GLORY REEL 1AB
EL 3 REFERENCE PRINT FROM
S OF GLORY REEL 4 REFERENC
ANGELOVE REEL 1 B+W MARRIED
DR. STRANGELOVE REEL 2
REEL 3 B+W MARRIED PRINT
EEL 4 B+W MARRIED PRINT

THE STANLEY KUBRICK ARCHIVES

Stanley Kubrick

S. Kubrick
Corrected 22 Nov. 1968

IMPORTANT
RETURN AT ONCE

NAPOLEON

SK
SCRIPT No. 1

S.KUBRICK
COPY

MADE IN COOPERATION WITH JAN HARLAN, CHRISTIANE KUBRICK, AND THE STANLEY KUBRICK ESTATE

THE STANLEY KUBRICK ARCHIVES

EDITED BY
ALISON CASTLE

TASCHEN
Bibliotheca Universalis

Contents

Early Work

DAY OF THE FIGHT
1950 / BLACK AND WHITE / 16 MINUTES

CAST
HIMSELF WALTER CARTIER
HIMSELF VINCENT CARTIER
HIMSELF NATE FLEISCHER
(Boxing historian)
WALTER CARTIER'S OPPONENT
BOBBY JAMES
RINGSIDE FAN JUDY SINGER

CREW
PRODUCED AND DIRECTED BY
STANLEY KUBRICK
SCREENPLAY STANLEY KUBRICK
EDITOR JULIAN BERGMAN
ASSISTANT DIRECTOR ALEXANDER SINGER
NARRATION SCRIPT ROBERT REIN
NARRATOR DOUGLAS EDWARDS
PHOTOGRAPHY STANLEY KUBRICK
ORIGINAL MUSIC GERALD FRIED
SOUND STANLEY KUBRICK
2ND UNIT DIRECTOR, ADDITIONAL PHOTOGRAPHY ALEXANDER SINGER
(uncredited)
EDITING, SOUND STANLEY KUBRICK
(uncredited)

FLYING PADRE
1951 / BLACK AND WHITE / 9 MINUTES
Distributed by RKO RADIO

PRODUCED BY BURTON BENJAMIN
DIRECTED BY STANLEY KUBRICK
NARRATOR BOB HITE
EDITOR ISAAC KLEINERMAN
MUSIC NATHANIEL SHILKRET
SCREENPLAY, PHOTOGRAPHY
STANLEY KUBRICK (uncredited)

THE SEAFARERS
1953 / COLOR / 30 MINUTES
Distributed by THE SEAFARERS INTERNATIONAL UNION / AFI

AS TOLD BY DON HOLLENBECK
WRITTEN BY WILL CHASEN
DIRECTED AND PHOTOGRAPHED BY STANLEY KUBRICK
TECHNICAL ASSISTANCE STAFF OF THE SEAFARERS' LOG
PRODUCED BY LESTER COOPER

FEAR AND DESIRE
1953 / BLACK AND WHITE / 68 MINUTES
Distributed by JOSEPH BURSTYN INC.

CAST
MAC FRANK SILVERA
SIDNEY PAUL MAZURSKY
LT. CORBY & THE GENERAL KENNETH HARP
FLETCHER & THE CAPTAIN STEVE COIT
THE GIRL VIRGINIA LEITH
NARRATOR DAVID ALLEN

CREW
ASSISTANT DIRECTOR ROBERT DIERKS
UNIT MANAGER STEVE HAHN
DIALOGUE DIRECTOR TOBA KUBRICK
MAKEUP CHET FABIAN
ART DIRECTION HERBERT LEBOWITZ
SCREENPLAY HOWARD SACKLER and STANLEY KUBRICK
ORIGINAL MUSIC GERALD FRIED
PRODUCED BY STANLEY KUBRICK
ASSOCIATE PRODUCER MARTIN PERVELER
DIRECTED, PHOTOGRAPHED, AND EDITED BY STANLEY KUBRICK

Early Work

by Gene D. Phillips

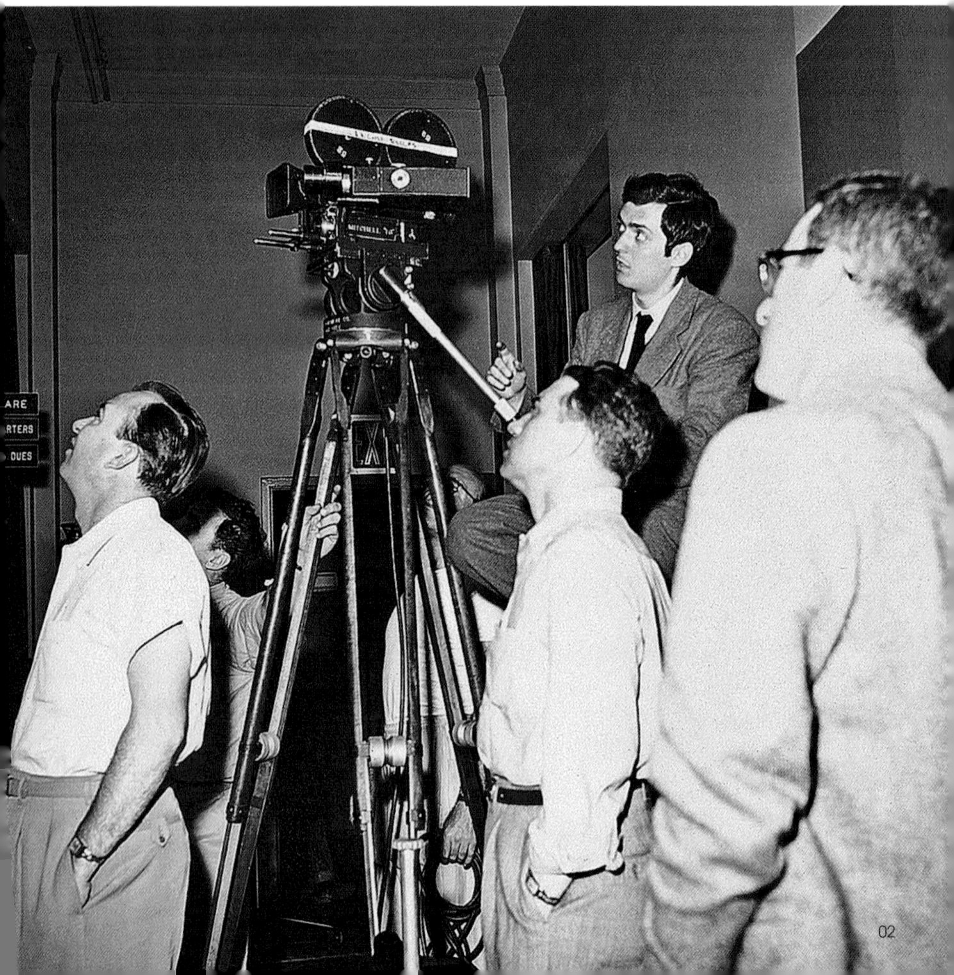

02

Stanley Kubrick was born in the Bronx section of New York City on July 26, 1928, to Jacques (Jack) and Gertrude Kubrick. Jack Kubrick, a professional physician and amateur photographer, gave Stanley a Graflex camera when he was thirteen, and Stanley soon became a photographer for his school newspaper. Marvin Traub, a neighbor who was the same age as Stanley and shared his passion for photography, had a darkroom in his bedroom, and together they developed their pictures. Photography was manifestly not a hobby for the two boys, for they were on the road to becoming professional photographers. They began embarking on picture-finding expeditions around New York City.

Kubrick was enrolled in William Howard Taft High School, but seldom attended classes. Instead, he often played hooky by attending matinees at the Loew's Paradise movie palace just off the Grand Concourse near his home. It was there that he first thought of becoming a movie director. Meanwhile he made a name for himself around school by getting his photos frequently published in the Taft newspaper; but when it came to his academic performance his teachers generally thought of him as an underachiever and an incorrigible truant. Although Kubrick's overall performance in high school was poor, an IQ test proved that he was brighter than most of his classmates. He was simply bored by most of his classes.

01 ***Contact sheet showing Kubrick's photographs of Walter Cartier for the* Look *picture story "Prizefighter" (1949).***
02 ***On the set of* The Seafarers.**

Although he was probably not aware of it at the time, Kubrick began building toward his life's work as a moviemaker during his high school years. While still a senior at Taft—and not yet seventeen years old—he sold his first photograph to *Look* magazine. It portrayed a dejected newspaper vendor surrounded by headlines declaring the death of President Franklin Delano Roosevelt on April 12, 1945. Kubrick, who often had his camera hanging from a cord around his neck, noticed the newspaper stand while on his way to school; he instantly saw the makings of a telling photo in the scene. Sitting in his vendor's stall, with newspapers in front of him and hanging above his head, the news dealer is framed by the sad headlines. Kubrick's carefully composed shot captured the nation's grief over the deceased leader. Kubrick said at the time that it was just a lucky happenstance that he caught the decisive moment on film; but he later admitted privately to friends that he had to coax the elderly newsagent to look suitably despondent. This incident presages Kubrick's method in working with actors on a movie set to get them to generate the right emotion for a shot.

By this time Kubrick had a darkroom of his own set up at home, so he developed the picture soon after taking it. He had the gumption to venture into the editorial offices of *Look* magazine on Fifth Avenue in Manhattan and offer the picture to Helen O'Brian, chief of the photography department. O'Brian saw the haunting photo not as a snapshot taken by an amateur but as the work of a promising newcomer to the profession; she bought it for $25. "It's hard not to detect the self-confidence that would mark the film-maker in this ballsy school kid," *Sight and Sound* has observed.[1] As he left the *Look* offices, Kubrick noticed "the bull pen" where freelance photographers awaited assignments. It would not be too long before Kubrick would himself join them.

Stanley Kubrick's first professional photo ran in the June 26,1945, issue of *Look.* He continued to submit pictures to *Look* while at Taft, including a shot of a string of motorists lined up as they waited for their share of gasoline, which was rationed during the war; that picture netted him $100.

Kubrick went on to sell a picture story to *Look* that was inspired by one of his English teachers at Taft, the only person who ever managed to interest Kubrick in studies while he was in school. Aaron Traister stimulated his students to appreciate Shakespeare by acting out scenes in class, playing all the parts himself. Kubrick took a series of photographs of the animated teacher doing a rendition of a scene from *Hamlet* for his students.

"This sequence of photographs looks like a montage in a film," Kubrick biographer Vincent LoBrutto told me in conversation. "Kubrick was already looking toward movies. He always took more shots than he could use for one of his photo essays and then chose those that were most impressive for use in the photo sequence.

03–08 ***The Taft high school magazine,*** **Portfolio.**

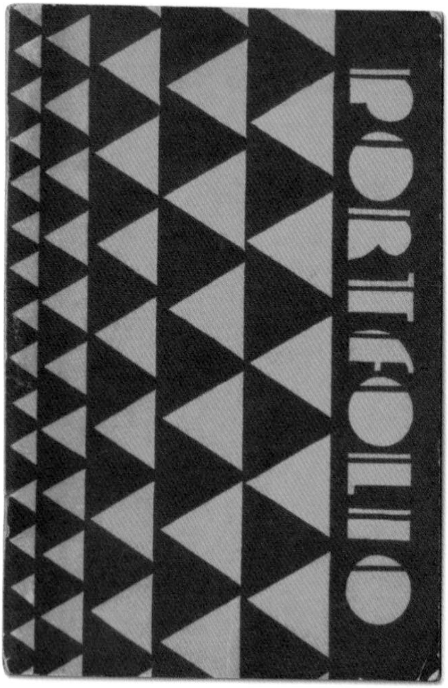

03

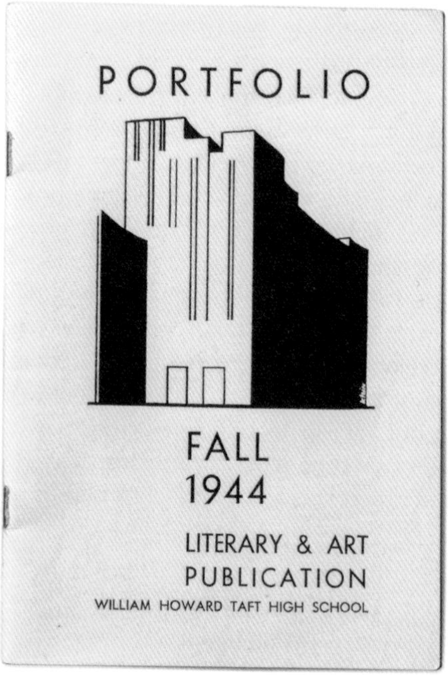

04

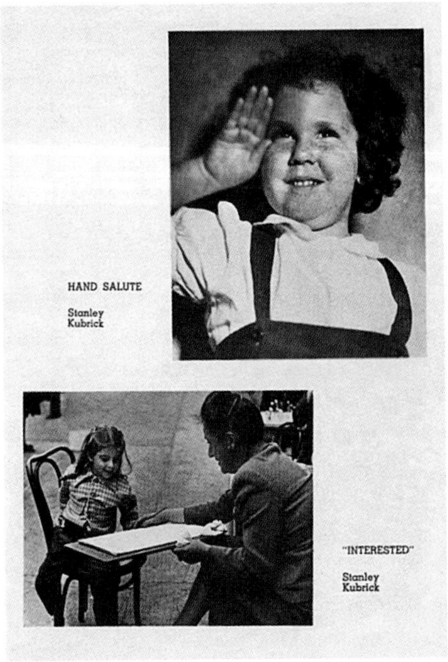
HAND SALUTE
Stanley Kubrick
"INTERESTED"
Stanley Kubrick

05

WELCOME HOME
PORTFOLIO

06

PORTFOLIO
FALL
ISSUE
1945
LITERARY-ART
PUBLICATION
W. H. TAFT H. S.
THE BRONX • NEW YORK

07

CENTRAL PARK
Stanley Kubrick

08

There are no throwaway shots in a Kubrick photo essay; each shot is carefully composed; he made every shot count." He was already proceeding like a film director, who selects the best takes from the footage he has shot for a scene, in order to give the best coverage of the scene by including all of the most significant details. "The photo sequence sits at the door of cinema," LoBrutto continued. "Kubrick's photographic essays for *Look* were already propelling him toward motion pictures."

Kubrick continued selling pictures to *Look* until he graduated from Taft in January, 1946. His high school average was a flat 70—just barely passing; it precluded his pursuing a college career, since no reputable college would accept him. Helen O'Brian accordingly hired him full time as an apprentice photographer. Kubrick stayed with the publication for four years, until he was twenty-one. "From the start I loved cameras," he remembered. "There is something almost sensuous about a beautiful piece of equipment."

In shooting pictures on assignment for *Look*, Kubrick sought to add a little drama to a subject whenever he got the chance. For an article on hypochondriacs (September 17, 1946), Kubrick contributed a photo of a harried woman who constantly worries that she will be stricken with some threatening disease. He portrays her opening a telegram about a relative's operation that she fears may have been fatal. Kubrick photographed the woman from a low angle, with high key lighting (sharp blacks and whites, no grays). "This gives a threatening tone to the picture," LoBrutto comments, "and anticipates the moody, dark shots in Kubrick films like *Killer's Kiss.*"

Kubrick presented a two-page spread of eighteen photos, portraying individual patients in a dentist's waiting room, for the issue of October 1, 1946. His picture study portrays a cross-section of the individuals ruefully contemplating their impending fate and wishing they were somewhere else. Of special interest is the fact that Kubrick moves his camera around the dentist's waiting room, covering the entire setting and all of the people present. The effect is similar to a tracking shot in a film, when a movie director maneuvers the camera around a movie set, gliding from one character to another, closing in to capture a key gesture or facial expression. The influence of cinematography is undoubtedly beginning to manifest itself in the photographer's work in this artfully photographed picture story.

The young Kubrick was greatly impressed by the tabloid journalist Arthur Fellig, known as "Weegee," who was adept at catching New Yorkers off guard in his deft photo essays. In the photo sequence "Life and Love on the New York Subway" (March 4, 1947), Kubrick caught his subjects unawares in the way that Weegee liked to do: a woman sleeping in her lover's arms; a woman nursing her baby; and a young man holding flowers intended for his girlfriend above his head, to keep them from being crushed by his fellow passengers. These character studies exemplify not only Kubrick's technical competence, but also his increasing experience in adroitly capturing an individual's personality in a facial expression or gesture. As LoBrutto puts it, "Kubrick was expressing his capacity to record on film the totality of a scene: the atmosphere,

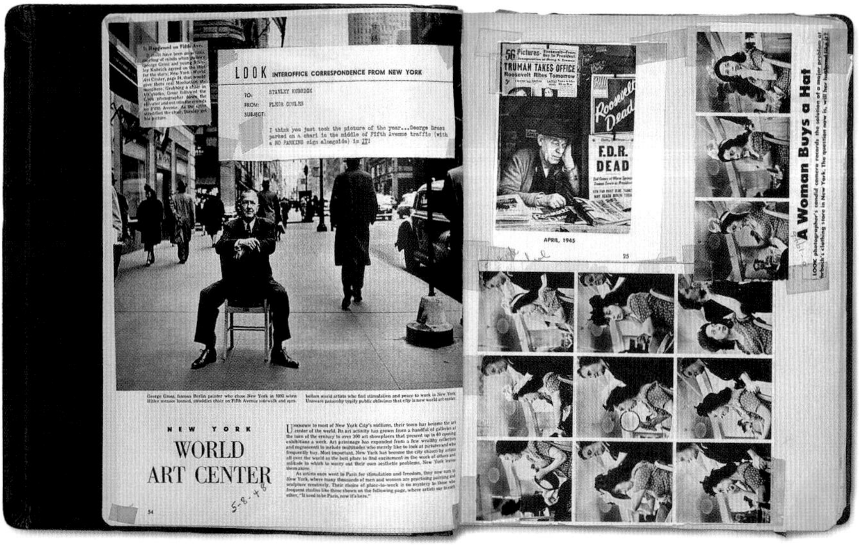

09

the environment, as well as the various types of people present. He was becoming a photographer-storyteller.

The May 11, 1948, edition of *Look* was a milestone for Kubrick. It not only included his nine-page photo feature on Columbia University and its new president, Dwight Eisenhower, but also carried an article profiling the young photographer himself. The essay noted that the quiet nineteen-year-old photographer, who had spent two weeks at Columbia working on his photo story, was "an experienced photographer who knew exactly what he wanted." At that point he had been with the magazine for two years.

Kubrick's fellow photographers were aware of his increasing interest in cinematography, the article points out. Although "his preoccupation with photography remains unchanged," it concludes, "in his spare time Stanley experiments with cinematography and dreams of the day when he can make documentary films."[2]

The editors of *Look* began giving Kubrick some more ambitious assignments. Moreover, one of his photo sequences for *Look* in particular brought him one step closer to the director's chair. For the January 18, 1949, edition Kubrick did a picture story on middleweight boxer Walter Cartier entitled "Prizefighter." Kubrick

09 ***Kubrick's mother kept this scrapbook of his* Look *picture stories. Left: a photo of painter George Grosz (1948) with a congratulatory letter from* Look *editor Fleur Cowles. Right: the first photo Kubrick sold to* Look*, of a newsvendor reacting to the death of President Roosevelt (1945), shares the page with a photo story Kubrick later shot about a woman buying a hat.***

10–11 ***Portraits of anxious patients waiting in a dentist's waiting room (*Look*, 1946).***

Should she wait — or run? It's a hard choice to make.

It hurts, and probing finger shows exactly where.

Resigned to his fate, he placidly sweats it out.

That thumping jaw keeps him oblivious of everything.

Okay, so it'll hurt! That tooth's got to come out.

He's enjoying a book, but she frowns unhappily.

He can concentrate on jaw and magazine at same time.

She can't see a thing, but that drill sounds awful.

Her composed face reflects patience and fortitude.

Dentist's Office

Americans visit the dentist more often than any other

Photographs by STANLEY KUBRICK

Picking old nail polish keeps her mind off pain.

Nothing he can do but wait, so he settles to read.

She's worried. Outgoing patient didn't look happy.

Dejected, she slumps in her chair. Hope seems gone.

On the alert! He keeps a sharp lookout at the door.

Restless, she broods – wonders whether it will hurt.

Something tells him that no good can come from this.

Well! What's the use of fretting about a tooth.

He seems to think it's all in how you look at it.

people. But in the dentist's waiting room, they always look as if they want to be somewhere else.

had been a boxing fan throughout his teen years and was eager to do a photo study of a prizefighter. Kubrick ran across Cartier when both of them were living in Greenwich Village, where Kubrick had moved after he left high school.

The striking shot of Cartier that fills the entire first page of the seven-page sequence indicates how Kubrick had matured as a photographer. Cartier is portrayed waiting with his manager Bobby Gleason for the fight to begin. He sits on a bench with his gloved hands in his lap, leaning his back against a cinder-block wall. Cartier gazes upward, gathering his strength for the bout. The single ceiling light shadows his eyes and emphasizes his broad, hairless chest. "Shooting from his favorite low angle, Kubrick turns him into an icon of masculinity," writes John Baxter.[3]

The photo sequence that follows is headed "Day of the Fight." Walter Cartier is shown as he awakens at 9:30 a.m.; then he and his twin brother and manager, Vincent, go to church to pray for a successful outcome to the fight. Kubrick records the pre-fight rituals, such as Cartier weighing in and being examined by a physician; then, before the bout, Gleason gives him a pep talk and Vincent adjusts his boxing gloves.

The photo story climaxes with Cartier knocking out Jimmy Mangia at Roosevelt Stadium in Jersey City. The victorious Cartier is pictured standing in the ring while Mangia lies on the mat, out for the count. This photo spread, which comprises nineteen pictures, pushes the limits of the photographic sequence, indicating how Kubrick was moving toward cinema.

Recalling his early career as a photographer for film historian Michel Ciment, Kubrick reflected: "I worked for *Look* magazine from the age of seventeen to twenty-one. It was a miraculous break for me to get this job after graduation from high school. I owe a lot to the then picture editor, Helen O'Brian, and the managing editor, Jack Guenther. This experience was invaluable to me, not only because I learned a lot about photography, but also because it gave me a quick education in how things happened in the world. To have been a professional photographer was obviously a great advantage for me.... It was tremendous fun for me at

12–13 *Subway passengers were caught unawares by Kubrick for the photo story "Life and Love on the New York Subway"* (Look, *1947*).

It's not so crowded later in day. So this 15-piece orchestra, complete with instruments and girl vocalist, travels by subway to a late show.

Flowers for my lady. They may be a bit battered by the time they reach her, but this lad's doing his best to keep them above the crowd.

Subway etiquette. When should a gentleman give a lady his seat? Not, as picture shows, when he can hide his face behind a newspaper.

(Continued on page 62)

12

14

that age, but eventually it began to wear thin, especially since my ultimate ambition had always been to make movies. The subject matter of my *Look* assignments was generally pretty dumb. I would do stories like: 'Is an Athlete Stronger Than a Baby?' photographing a college football player emulating the 'cute' positions an 18-month-old child would get into. Occasionally, I had a chance to do an interesting personality story. One of these was about Montgomery Clift, who was at the start of his brilliant career. Photography certainly gave me the first step up to movies. To make a film entirely by yourself, which initially I did, you may not have to know very much about anything else, but you must know about photography."[4]

While he was working for *Look,* Kubrick and his friend from high school days, Alex Singer, who was working for The March of Time, used to discuss filmmaking as a career. Kubrick learned from Singer that *The March of Time* documentary shorts were budgeted at $40,000 apiece, and he speculated that he could produce a documentary for a fraction of that cost. Drawing on the Walter Cartier picture story, Kubrick made a sixteen-minute short called *Day of the Fight* (1950), documenting the boxing match between Cartier and middleweight boxer Bobby James held in Newark, New Jersey, on April 17, 1950.

Kubrick did everything himself, from writing and shooting the film to dubbing in the punches and the slams of car doors

14 ***Kubrick staged these photos of his future wife, Toba Metz, pretending to kiss a friend in Manhattan's 81st Street subway station.***

on the sound track. One of the employees at the camera store where Kubrick rented his equipment taught him each step of the technical side of filmmaking as he went along. Based on this experience he said, "Perhaps it sounds ridiculous, but the best thing that young filmmakers can do is get hold of a camera and some film and make a movie of any kind at all."

Day of the Fight opens with a neon sign proclaiming "Boxing Tonight!" and cuts to a middle-aged man scrambling for a ticket at the box office and being ushered to his seat. "What do fight fans—or rather fanatics—seek?" asks narrator Douglas Edwards. "They seek action, the triumph of force over force." Kubrick illustrates this remark with a quick succession of shots of knockout punches from several different fights. "But why do they—the fighters—do it?" Edwards continues. "There is the prestige of the winners; but also it is a living."

The movie then zeroes in on Cartier, "one fighter out of the record book. This, then, is the story of a fighter and of a fight." On the bleak dawning of the day of the fight the camera cuts from a poster announcing Cartier's bout, to be held at 10 p.m. that same night, to the apartment house where Cartier lives. "At 6 a.m.," says the narrator, "begins the waiting." Walter Cartier and his twin brother rise to go to make their way through the deserted streets of New York for early morning Mass at a nearby church because "Cartier doesn't place all of his faith in his hands."

Kubrick quickly takes Cartier through his day, showing the various preparations, such as the weigh-in, that lead up to the impending bout. Yet the director still manages to communicate that restless sense of interminable waiting that the fighter experiences all day long. This feeling is best conveyed in the shot in which Cartier stands in his dusky living room in late afternoon staring down at the street below, and in the one in which the boxer contemplates his face in the mirror just before leaving for the boxing ring, wondering what kind of image the glass will reflect the following morning.

Then the tempo of the film picks up as Cartier reaches the arena and begins the final stages of getting ready for the fight in his stuffy dressing room—a scene which Kubrick would draw on in making his second feature, *Killer's Kiss.*

"The first really important book I read about filmmaking was* The Film Technique *by Pudovkin. This was some time before I had ever touched a movie camera and it opened my eyes to cutting and montage."

—SK/1960 (to Charles Reynolds/*Popular Photography*)

It is time at last to go into the ring. The crowd cheers as the fighters are introduced and this noise carries over into the next shot, that of a young man standing on a street in downtown New York City, intently listening to the fight on his portable radio—someone who looks very much like young Stanley Kubrick.

While the two fighters sit in their corners waiting for the bell to sound, Cartier is

photographed at the opposite end of the ring through the legs of his opponent—a shot that would be repeated in *Killer's Kiss.* Kubrick used a handheld camera to shoot the bout that climaxes the documentary. He shot the fight from a variety of angles and edited them together in rapid succession, thereby imparting to the viewer the intensity of the battle, which culminates in Cartier's kayoing the other boxer. As Cartier's manager leads the winner through the ropes and down into the smoke-filled auditorium toward his dressing room, the narrator concludes, "A day in the life of a man who fights for his existence, the end of another working day."

Day of the Fight was scored by Gerald Fried, who grew up in the Bronx with Kubrick; the latter remembered Fried as a budding composer from those days and asked Fried to write background music for the movie. Fried composed "The March of the Gloved Gladiators" as the short's principal motif; the theme is built around a stirring fanfare, which Fried employed as a big buildup to the fight. He orchestrated the music and conducted the group of nineteen musicians whom he

15 ***This photo from the set of* The Naked City *(1947) captured Kubrick, photographing for* Look, *as he enjoyed a piece of watermelon.***
16 ***A jazz ensemble performing in Greenwich Village.***
17–25 ***This selection of photographs taken for* Look *between 1946 and 1950 reveals the young photographer's versatility and sharp eye for composition.***

brought together for the recording session at RCA's New York studios. "I hired the best musicians I knew, all of whom were about my age, twenty-two, which was also Stanley's age," Fried recalled.[5] It was the youngest group of musicians that the RCA staff had ever encountered.

To make *Day of the Fight*, Kubrick spent the $3,900 that he had saved while working for *Look;* he sold the distribution rights for $4,000 to RKO for its *This Is America* series, netting himself a $100 profit. By the age of twenty-two Kubrick had made a film on his own (for one-tenth of the cost of a *March of Time* documentary) and it had shown a profit, however modest. Stanley Kubrick was hooked for life on moviemaking. By this time he felt that he had outgrown his interest in still photography and consequently quit his job at *Look*.

There are marked affinities between *Day of the Fight* and Kubrick's second feature film, *Killer's Kiss* (1955), which focuses on a young prizefighter named Davy Gordon (Jamie Smith). As John Baxter opines, the movie recycles some of the images from *Day of the Fight*, "even repeating the shot of a fight poster dangling from a lamp post."[6] Davy narrates the film. "That's the way it began for me, just before my fight with Rodriguez," he muses, and we cut to a poster advertising Davy's fight, then to Davy examining his face in the mirror of his cheaply furnished room—a shot which clearly recalls the similar image in *Day of the Fight*.

Kubrick's photographic sequence on Cartier and his experience in making *Day of the Fight* undoubtedly helped him to give to the arena scenes in *Killer's Kiss* a ring of authenticity. Referring to a comment made about Josef Von Sternberg, Kubrick told Alexander Walker, "When a director dies, he becomes a photographer. *Killer's Kiss* might prove that, when a director is born, a photographer doesn't necessarily die."[7] In fact, perhaps due to his experience as a photographer, Kubrick developed the habit from the beginning of his film career of participating actively in photographing his films.

Like "Prizefighter" and *Day of the Fight*, *Killer's Kiss* gives a frank, unvarnished account of the life of a struggling boxer. When one traces the continuity from the photo essay to the documentary to the feature film, one understands why Kubrick said at the time, "Cameras and the stories they can tell have been my hobby, my life, and my work."[8]

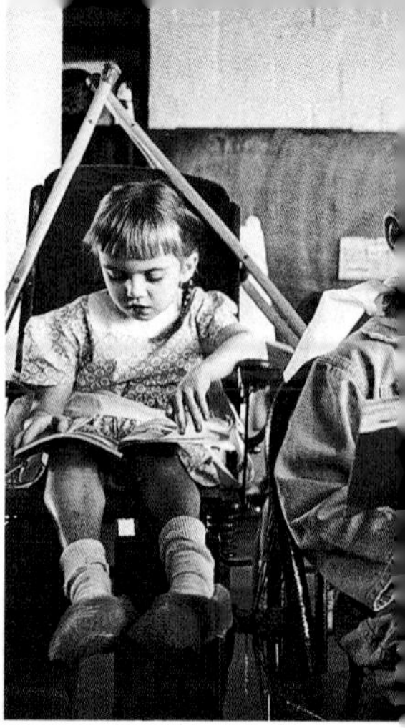

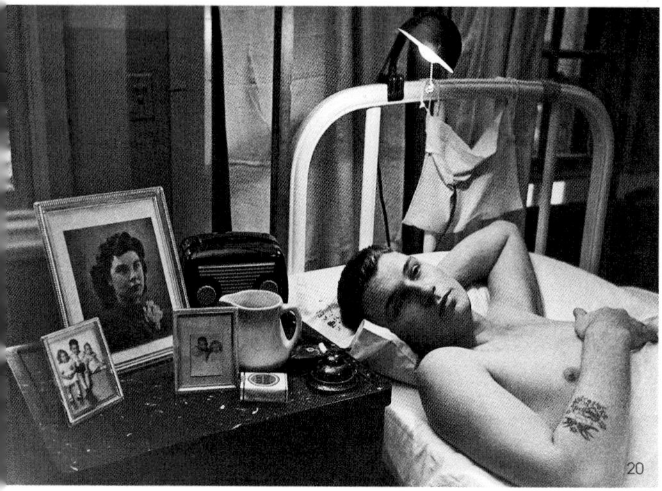

20

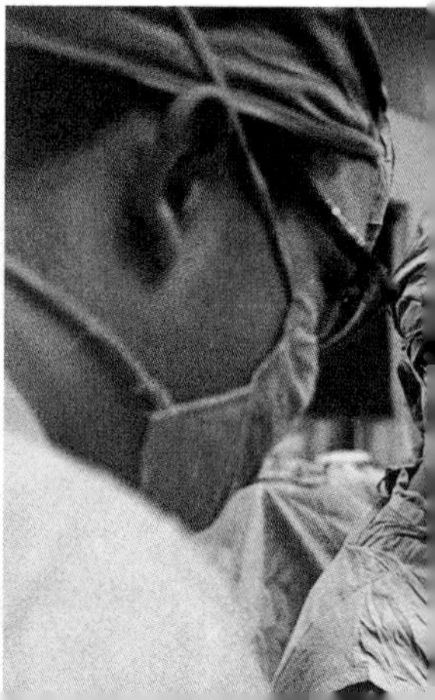

18

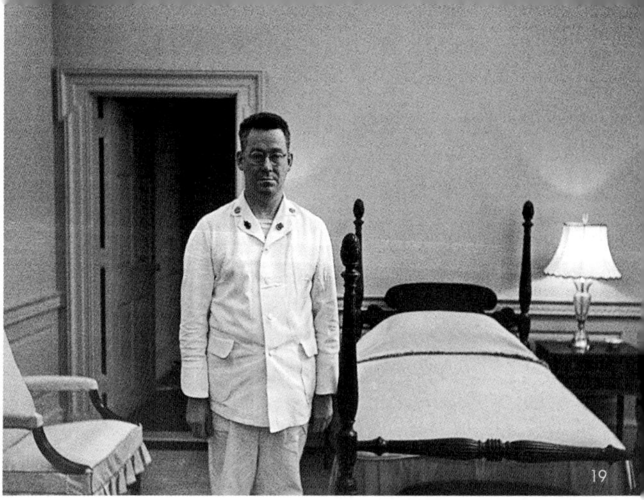

19

21

22

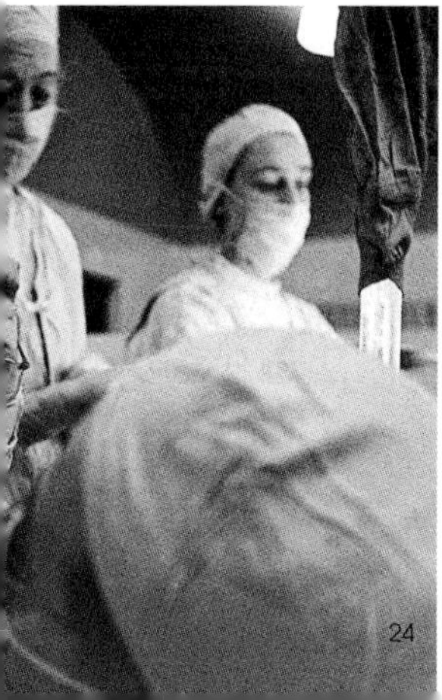

24

25

RKO advanced Kubrick $1,500 for a second short, *Flying Padre* (1951), for its RKO Pathé Screenliner series. "It was about Father Fred Stadtmueller, a priest in New Mexico who flew to his isolated parishes in a Piper Cub," Kubrick later told me. The opening shot is a pan over the vast plateaus and canyons of New Mexico, after which the camera tilts upward to encompass the little plane coming in for a landing on a prairie. Two lone cowboys on horseback await the priest to escort him to a funeral service that he is to conduct.

Even at this early stage of his career Kubrick was interested in bringing the viewer into the action as much as possible. He photographed Stadtmueller inside the cockpit of his plane from various angles, even shooting upward at one point from the floor through the controls. He was also aware of the importance of catching significant details that would bring a scene to life. Hence the burial scene is punctuated with close-ups of an aged man and woman watching the ceremony as the little group of mourners huddles together around the grave. Later, when the priest has to fly a mother and her child to a hospital, Kubrick again puts us in the cockpit of the plane with the priest, showing the land below rushing by and finally disappearing as the Piper Cub gains speed and takes flight.

26 ***Montgomery Clift eating breakfast (1949).***
27 ***Middleweight champion boxer Rocky Graziano (1950).***
28 ***A painter and his model.***

Although Kubrick did not make a profit on *Flying Padre* as he had on *Day of the Fight,* he did break even. As a result, he made one final documentary short, *The Seafarers* (1953), before moving on to features. The Atlantic and Gulf Coast district of the Seafarers International Union commissioned Kubrick to make a half-hour documentary about the life of men who sail American cargo ships. One might be tempted to dismiss the movie as a mere industrial documentary except for the fact that it contains several instances of a young filmmaker reaching to photograph in an inventive and creative fashion what could otherwise have been a perfunctory film done as a routine assignment. It was also Kubrick's first film in color, though he would not make another color film until *Spartacus,* seven years later.

In an early sequence in the hiring hall, Kubrick moves among the men with his camera, photographing their intense expressions as they vie for good berths on their favorite ships. In fact, Kubrick, who as usual served as his own cameraman, constantly moves his camera about in each scene, whether on ship or off, to keep visually alive what could so easily have been a static documentary. He is forever looking for—and finding—interesting images to punctuate the film. The scene in the seamen's bar starts with a close-up of a mermaid carved out of wood to look like an ornament on the prow of a ship, and then the camera pulls back to show the men grouped round it at the circular bar. The sequence at the Marine Hospital begins with a shot of the flower garden in the grounds, filling the screen in stunning color before moving on to show the convalescents enjoying the view and the sunshine.

Only rarely does the film fall into looking like a conventional documentary, as when a group of seamen are pictured spending some of their shore time reading and writing letters in the union library. There is a somewhat stagy quality about the way that they are self-consciously "arranged" at the tables from foreground to background. Conversely, one shot in particular hints at the promising things to come for the young director: several seamen are grouped round a table discussing grievances with a union representative while a single lamp above their heads sheds light on their conference. This lighting and composition would be

Miss Sacha Lawrence, right, script clerk, tries translating between cameraman Marcel Reviere, left, and director Stanley Kubrick, in center.

29

repeated to great dramatic effect in *The Killing* three years later, in the scene in which the thieves plan their strategy for the racetrack robbery.

After completing *The Seafarers,* a worthy piece of work for a filmmaker still finding his way and gaining experience, the young director then decided to make his first feature film. He borrowed $10,000 from his father, who cashed in his insurance policy, and his uncle, Martin Perveler, a Los Angeles druggist, and added $3,000 of his own money. Then he went on location to the San Gabriel Mountains near Los Angeles to shoot *Fear and Desire* (1953), a drama about a military patrol trapped behind enemy lines in an unnamed war.

The script for *Fear and Desire* was written by Howard Sackler, another friend of Kubrick's from high school days, who later wrote the award-winning play and film *The Great White Hope*. Other friends helped out during the location shooting in the mountains, assisting Kubrick in setting up and putting away the equipment each day; three Mexican laborers were engaged to transport the boxes of materials to and from the location site. Kubrick's first wife, Toba Metz, served as dialogue director. But it was Kubrick himself who carried out all of the jobs associated with shooting the film: he was director, cinematographer, prop man, and general factotum.

Kubrick designed the film as an allegory, and the intent is clear from the beginning, as a narrator sets the mood of the film: "There is a war in this forest; not a war that has been fought, nor one that will be, but any war. And the enemies that struggle here do not exist unless we call them into being. Only the unchanging shapes of fear and doubt and death are from our world. These soldiers that you see keep our language and our time, but have no other country but the mind."

The four men who make up the military patrol on which the film focuses are Lieutenant Corby (Kenneth Harp), Mac (Frank Silvera), Fletcher (Steve Coit), and Sidney (future director Paul Mazursky). Their plane has crashed behind enemy lines and Lt. Corby suggests that they build a raft and float down the river out of enemy territory. While they are moving through the woods, the quartet comes upon a group of enemy soldiers, whom they summarily ambush and kill. Next they happen upon a girl, whom they tie to a tree and gag, fearing that she would

29 ***Kubrick working on location in Hogdenville, Kentucky, as second-unit director for a television series on the life of Abraham Lincoln*** **(Courier-Journal Magazine, *October 26, 1952*).**
30 ***Up close with Frank Sinatra (1950).***

otherwise turn them over to the enemy. Sidney, who has been on the verge of hysteria ever since the plane crashed, becomes more and more upset as his craving for the girl grows inside of him. He says plaintively, "I know you hate me. Please try to love me." He hugs and kisses her, then unties her, intent on raping her. When she struggles to escape him, he shouts, "You're going to tell on me!" The hysterical young soldier then shoots her dead. As she lies face down in the dirt, Sidney disappears into the forest in a panic.

When the others return, Mac persuades them to kill an enemy general whose headquarters they have come across nearby. Mac, who is an angry, primitive type, is determined that they should exterminate the general; as he explains to the others: "I'm thirty-four years old and I've never done anything important." When the war is over, he continues, he will spend the rest of his life fixing radios and refrigerators. Hence he wants to do something significant for once. Mac, comments Norman Kagan, is a "burning, chaotic jumble of hatred and self-hatred." Mac raves: "You try every door, but the knobs come off in your hand; it's better to make your life all in one night!" They agree that Corby and Fletcher are to move in on the general and his aide and kill them while Mac employs diversionary tactics to preoccupy the general's guards. When Corby focuses the general and his aide through his binoculars, he discovers that the general is

30

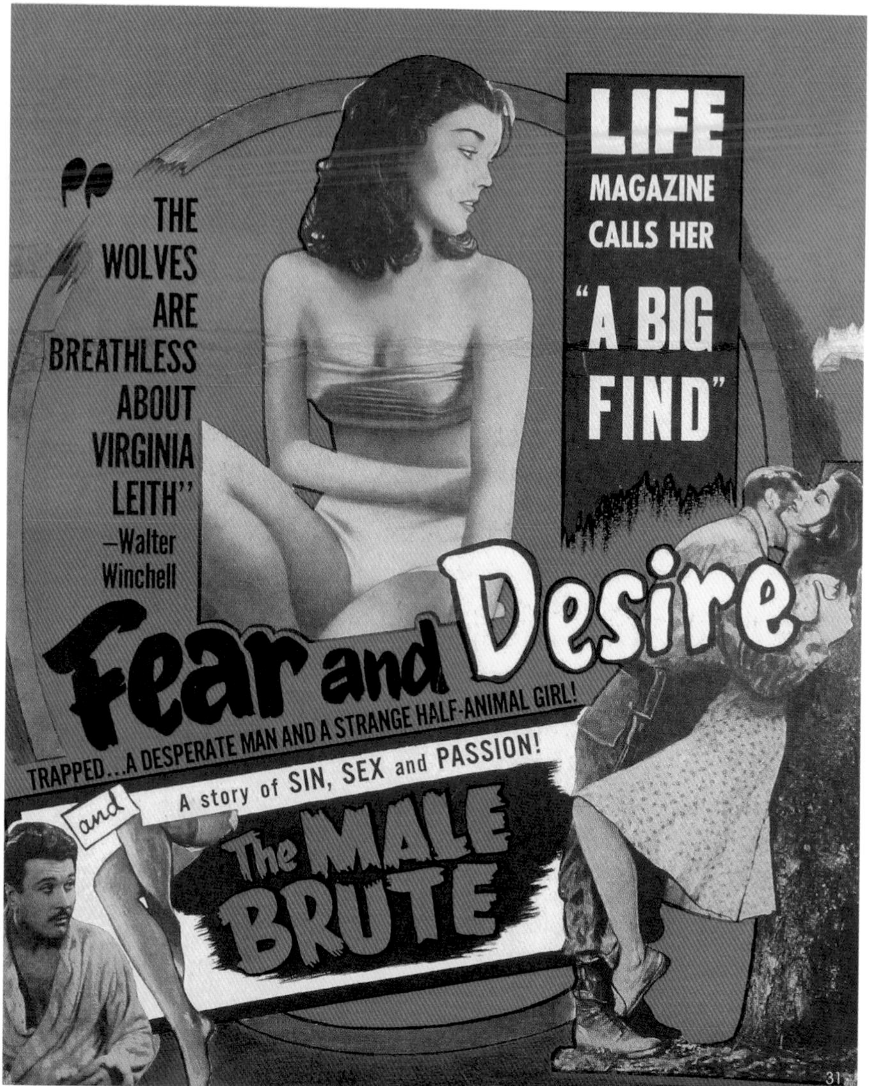

31 Fear and Desire *was released as a double bill with* The Male Brute.
32 *Mock-up of an advertisement for* Fear and Desire.

a double for him and the general's aide is a double for Fletcher (the general and his aide are played by the same actors who enact the roles of Corby and Fletcher). Fletcher shoots both of the men, but the general does not die immediately. He crawls toward the edge of the porch and Corby fires, finishing him off. As Corby looks into the general's dead face, he sees his own countenance staring back at him.

Although they all get away, Mac is seriously wounded by the guards. Still, he manages to get aboard the raft he and his comrades had built earlier. At the film's end Mac is seen lying on the raft, floating toward the shore. With him is Sidney, whom Mac has picked up along the way. Sidney is still traumatized by what he has done. Standing on the shore waiting for them are Corby and Fletcher; and they escape on the raft back to their own lines.

Fear and desire, composer Gerald Fried points out, are the two dominant human passions. All four of the soldiers fear for their lives while they are behind enemy lines; and one of them, Sidney, desires a native girl whom they have captured. The music which he composed for the movie "had to be profound, meaningful, touching, despairing, but yet triumphant" when two of the four soldiers escape from the ordeal unscathed.

The theme entitled "A Meditation on War" reflects in its inexorable forward motion the dangerous trek of the small squad through hostile territory. "Madness," another theme, occurs after Sidney tries to rape the native girl and then shoots her dead so she cannot report him. David Wishart, in his commentary on Fried's film music, writes, "The blatantly eccentric tonalities and ominous mounting intensity of 'Madness' realizes (Sidney's hysteria) in 'music.'"[9] In his popular column, Walter Winchell singled out Fried's underscore for praise.

Paul Mazursky told Peter Bogdanovich that while working with Kubrick on his first, low-budget feature, he was impressed with Kubrick's determination; the money the director had borrowed to make the picture had run out before the film was finished, "so Kubrick drove down from where we were shooting in the San Gabriel Mountains to see his Uncle Martin in L. A., with me and Frank Silvera," his co-star, in the back seat. Kubrick, who needed $5,000 to complete the picture, said "I'm gonna get the money from him no matter what." Needless to say, adds Mazursky, "he got the money."[10] Silvera, Kubrick told me, was the only experienced actor in the film, so his performance as Mac, a tough brute of a soldier, naturally stands out.

32

Since he had saved money by shooting his documentary shorts without sound and adding the soundtrack to the film afterward, Kubrick tried the same method with *Fear and Desire*. However, because post-synchronizing a soundtrack for a feature film is more complex than dubbing sound for a short subject, Kubrick ran into problems that added $20,000 to the $9,000 already spent on shooting the picture. As a result, *Fear and Desire* never earned back its initial investment, even though independent distributor Joseph Burstyn was able to book the film on the art-house circuit, where it garnered some good reviews.

"When I made my first film, I think the thing that probably helped me the most was that it was such an unusual thing in the early 50s for someone to actually go and make a film. People thought it was impossible. It really is terribly easy. All anybody needs is a camera, a tape recorder, and some imagination."

—SK/1968 (to Charles Kohler/*East Village Eye*)

Kubrick was perhaps too hasty in writing off *Fear and Desire* as a "student film." The movie's amateurish quality, after all, makes its virtues all the more obvious. Chief among those virtues is Kubrick's handling of the camera, with which he creates limpid visual images, particularly in the shadowy forest scenes. As the spoken prologue suggests, the forest becomes a metaphor for the jungle of man's own psyche, the heart of darkness of which novelist Joseph Conrad wrote. In Sidney's case, the border he crosses when he enters the forest represents the boundary between the civilized and the savage; for, in his brutal treatment of the native girl, he has turned savage.

When *Fear and Desire* was previewed in Los Angeles, Kubrick got some negative feedback from members of the audience who thought Mazursky's performance was overwrought. A member of the film's crew who was present recalled that Kubrick wept when some moviegoers had tittered at Mazursky's performance during the film. That only showed, he explained, how much Kubrick cared about his movies. Nevertheless, the film got some positive reviews. More than one critic singled out some scenes, such as the one in which an enemy general is shot, as visually compelling.

It was the respected critic James Agee whom Kubrick recalled as making the kindest remark about *Fear and Desire*. After seeing the movie, Kubrick and Agee had a drink in a Sixth Avenue bar in Greenwich Village in New York. "There are too many good things in the film," Agee said, "to call it arty."[11] Kubrick later told me that he still thought of the movie as inept and pretentious, although it was important in helping him, at age twenty-five, to gain invaluable experience in his craft.

33 ***Kubrick's wife, Toba, worked as dialogue director on*** **Fear and Desire.**
34 ***Kubrick watches as Paul Mazursky performs.***

33

"The ideas we wanted to put across [in* Fear and Desire*] were good, but we didn't have the experience to embody them dramatically. It was little more than a 35 mm version of what a class of film students would do in 16 mm."

— SK/1971 (to Alexander Walker)

In a letter to Joseph Burstyn, dated November 16, 1952, Kubrick describes *Fear and Desire* as a poetic allegory, "a drama of man lost in a hostile world—deprived of material and spiritual foundations—seeking his way to an understanding of himself and life around him." There is, furthermore, "an unseen but deadly enemy" lurking around him—an enemy who is shaped from the same mold that he is.[12]

Indeed, all four of the central characters are prey to the fear of death and to desire for the girl in the woods. Sidney succumbs to both fear and desire by attacking and killing the girl, then withdrawing into a state of shock because of what he has done. His plight underscores, more than anything else, the thought that perhaps one's most deadly enemy is the man within and that therefore, as the prologue would have it, it is in the country of the mind that man's real battles are fought.

35 ***Kubrick crouches down behind the camera; next to him is his wife, Toba.***
36–37 ***Early draft of the* Fear and Desire *screenplay.***

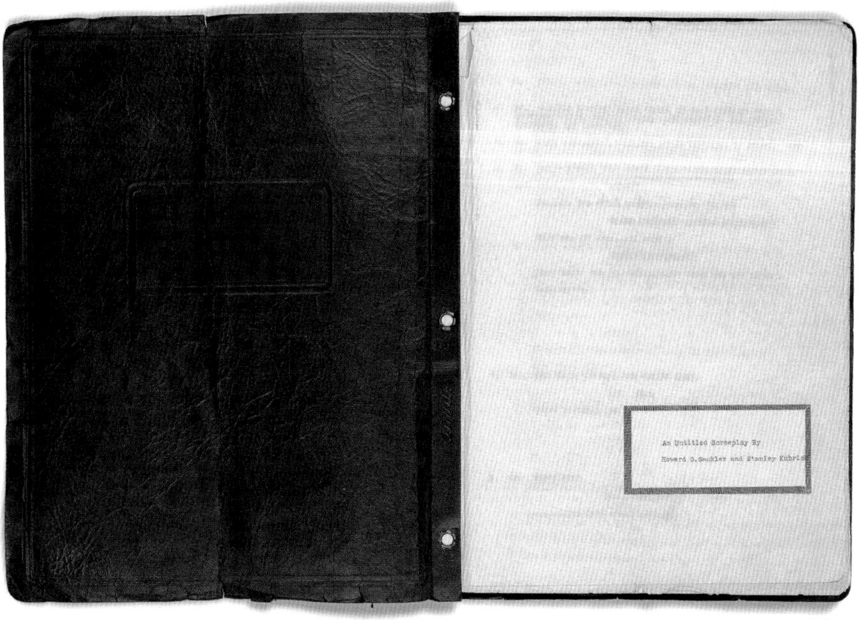
An Untitled Screenplay By
Howard O.Sackler and Stanley Kubric

36

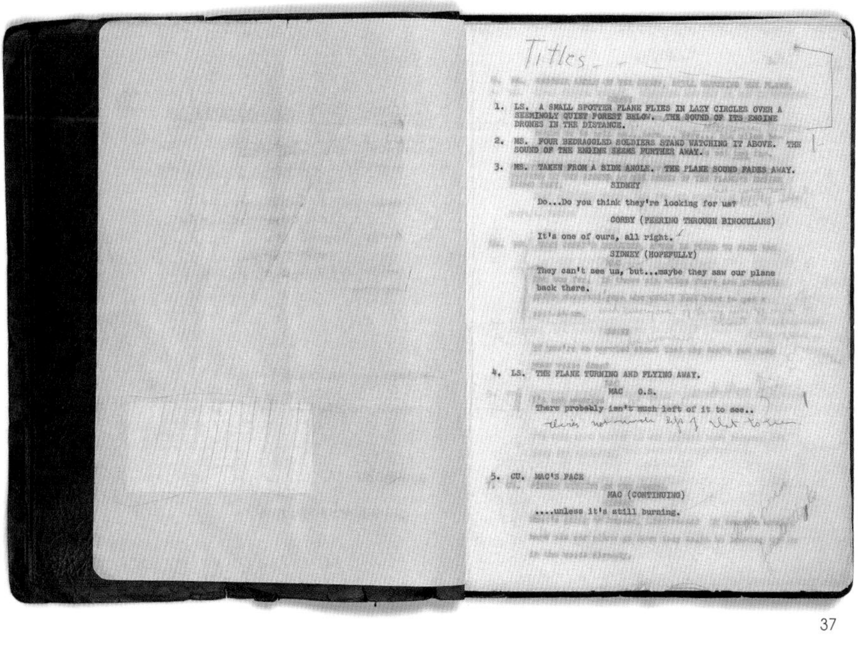
Titles
1. LS. A SMALL SPOTTER PLANE FLIES IN LAZY CIRCLES OVER A SEEMINGLY QUIET FOREST BELOW. THE SOUND OF ITS ENGINE DRONES IN THE DISTANCE.
2. MS. FOUR BEDRAGGLED SOLDIERS STAND WATCHING IT ABOVE. THE SOUND OF THE ENGINE SEEMS FURTHER AWAY.
3. MS. TAKEN FROM A SIDE ANGLE. THE PLANE SOUND FADES AWAY.
SIDNEY
Do...Do you think they're looking for us?
CORBY (PEERING THROUGH BINOCULARS)
It's one of ours, all right.
SIDNEY (HOPEFULLY)
They can't see us, but...maybe they saw our plane back there.
4. LS. THE PLANE TURNING AND FLYING AWAY.
MAC O.S.
There probably isn't much left of it to see..
5. CU. MAC'S FACE
MAC (CONTINUING)
....unless it's still burning.

37

38–42 **Fear and Desire *publicity stills featuring Virginia Leith*** (38, 39)***, Paul Mazursky*** (39, 41)***, and Frank Silvera*** (40, 41)**.**

40

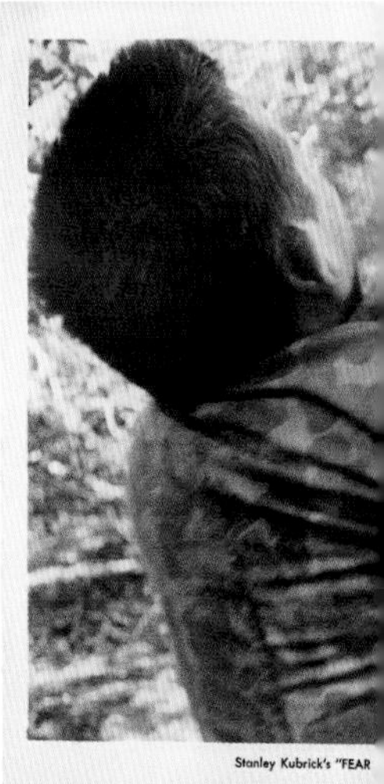

38

Stanley Kubrick's "FEAR AND DESIRE" a Joseph Burstyn Release

39

41

Stanley Kubrick's "FEAR AND DESIRE" a Joseph Burstyn Release

42

"The ideas which we wanted to put across were good," Kubrick commented to Alexander Walker in *Stanley Kubrick: Director*, "but we didn't have the experience to embody them dramatically."[13] Nevertheless, a great deal of the thought-provoking content of the movie does come across, especially in Mac's insistence on lending some meaning to his empty life by doing something courageous while he still has the chance.

Kubrick's own description of the film—as a drama of man deprived of material and spiritual foundations, lost in a hostile world in which he seeks to understand himself and the life around him—could well serve as a keynote for all of the director's films. In each of them Kubrick presents someone who is trying to cope with the tough world in which he finds himself. That description fits the hero of Kubrick's next film, *Killer's Kiss*.

Notes

1. "The Bigger Picture," *Sight and Sound*, (February 2001): 4.
2. *Look* article of May 11, 1948, reproduced in Christiane Kubrick, *Stanley Kubrick: A Life in Pictures* (London: Little, Brown, 2002): 36.
3. John Baxter, *Stanley Kubrick: A Biography* (New York: Carroll & Graf, 1997): 36.
4. Michel Ciment, *Kubrick: The Definitive Edition* (New York: Faber and Faber, 2001): 196.
5. Gerald Fried, CD liner notes from *Music from the Films of Stanley Kubrick* (New York: Silva Screen Records, 1999): 11.
6. Baxter: 65.
7. Alexander Walker, *Stanley Kubrick: Director* (New York: Norton, 1999): 16.
8. Vincent LoBrutto, *Stanley Kubrick: A Biography* (New York: Da Capo, 1999): 53.
9. David Wishart, CD liner notes from *Music from the Films of Stanley Kubrick*: 6.
10. Peter Bogdanovich, "What They Say about Stanley Kubrick," *The New York Times Magazine* (July 4, 1999): 21.
11. LoBrutto: 88.
12. Norman Kagan, *The Cinema of Stanley Kubrick* (New York: Continuum, 1989): 9.
13. Walker: 15.

"Despite everything,* [Fear and Desire] *got an art-house distribution ... and it even got a couple of fairly good reviews, as well as a compliment from Mark Van Doren. There were a few good moments in it. It never returned a penny on its investment."

— SK/1966 (to Jeremy Bernstein/*The New Yorker*)

43 *Kubrick laughs as he watches Frank Silvera apply his makeup.*
44 *Kubrick photographed* Fear and Desire *in addition to producing, editing, co-writing, and directing it.*

Killer's Kiss

1955 / BLACK AND WHITE / 67 MINUTES
Distributed by UNITED ARTISTS

CAST
VINCENT RAPALLO FRANK SILVERA
DAVY GORDON JAMIE SMITH
GLORIA PRICE IRENE KANE
ALBERT, THE FIGHT MANAGER JERRY JARRET
HOODLUMS MIKE DANA, FELICE ORLANDI, RALPH ROBERTS, PHIL STEVENSON
OWNER OF THE MANNEQUIN FACTORY JULIUS "SKIPPY" ADELMAN
CONVENTIONEERS DAVID VAUGHAN, ALEC RUBIN
IRIS PRICE RUTH SOBOTKA

CREW
EDITED, PHOTOGRAPHED, AND DIRECTED BY STANLEY KUBRICK
PRODUCED BY STANLEY KUBRICK and MORRIS BOUSEL
STORY BY STANLEY KUBRICK
SCREENPLAY HOWARD SACKLER and STANLEY KUBRICK (uncredited)
ORIGINAL MUSIC GERALD FRIED
PRODUCTION MANAGER IRA MARVIN
CAMERA OPERATORS JESSE PALEY, MAX GLENN
ASSISTANT EDITORS PAT JAFFE, ANTHONY BEZICH
ASSISTANT DIRECTOR ERNEST NUKANEN
CHOREOGRAPHY DAVID VAUGHAN

Opposite *Publicity brochure.*

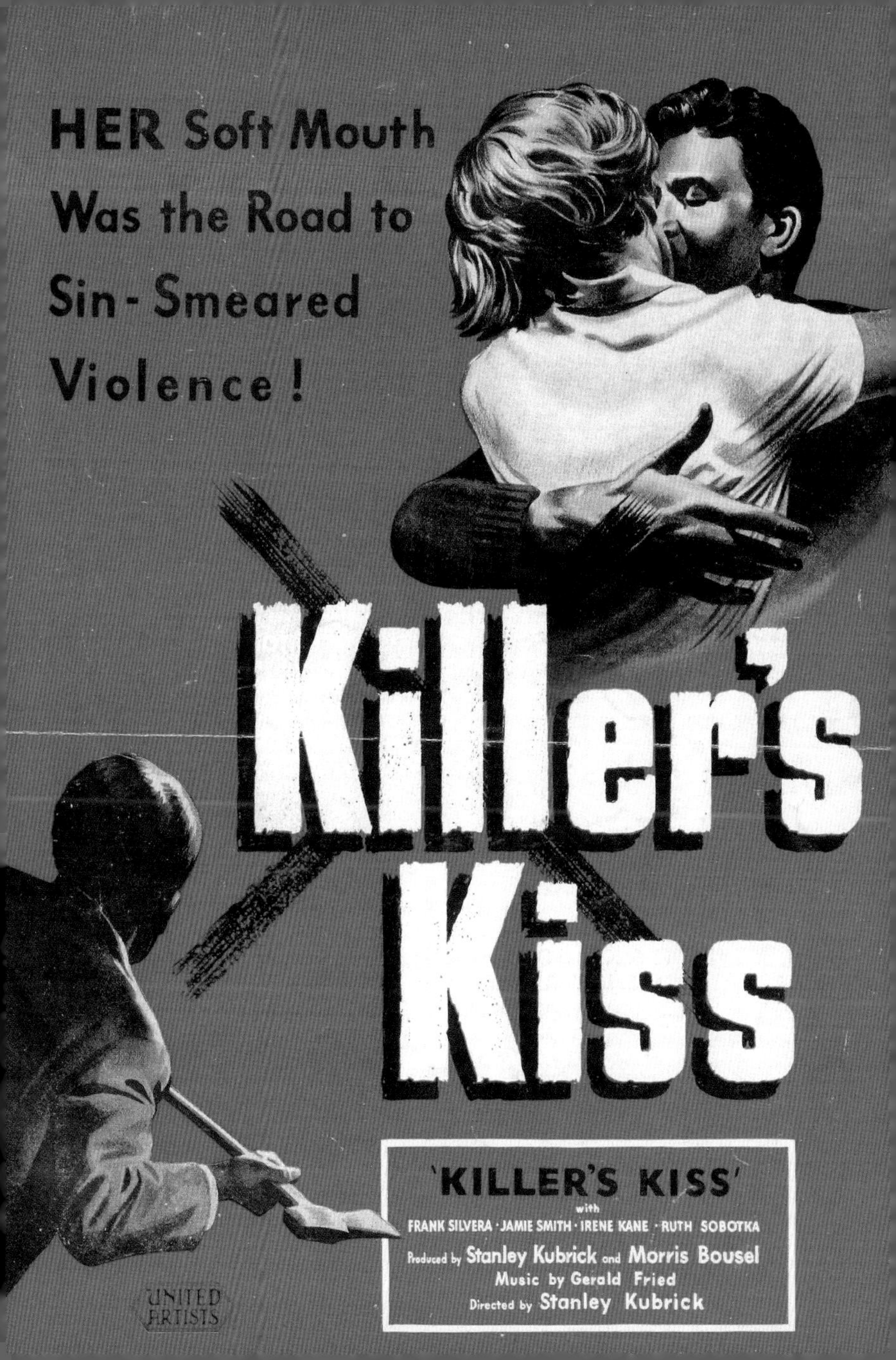
HER Soft Mouth
Was the Road to
Sin-Smeared
Violence!
Killer's
Kiss
'KILLER'S KISS'
with
FRANK SILVERA · JAMIE SMITH · IRENE KANE · RUTH SOBOTKA
Produced by Stanley Kubrick and Morris Bousel
Music by Gerald Fried
Directed by Stanley Kubrick
UNITED ARTISTS

"KISS ME, KILL ME"
Copyright MCMLIV MINOTAUR PRODUCTIONS, INC.

A SLUGGING WELTERWEIGHT NATURAL
CITY ARENA - FRI. OCT. 25
10 Round Main Event
DAVEY GORDON
RODRIGUEZ
DAVEY GORDON
KID
OTHER GREAT BOUT
dmission $1.50 - Reserved $3.00 - Ringsi

WATCH your STEP

LOEWS STATE
COLOR
WHERE TO GO
WHAT TO SEE
BOND

THE END

Killer's Kiss

by Gene D. Phillips

02

"[O]n the strength of* [Fear and Desire] *I was able to raise private financing to make a second feature-length film,* Killer's Kiss. *And that was a silly story too, but my concern was still in getting experience and simply functioning in the medium, so the content of a story seemed secondary to me. I just took the line of least resistance, whatever story came to hand."

— SK/1962 (to Terry Southern)

In *Killer's Kiss,* Kubrick shows us the struggles of a second-rate prizefighter to rise above the tawdry existence to which he is tied. Both *Killer's Kiss* and *The Killing,* his subsequent film, belong to the trend in American cinema that was just nearing its end when Kubrick began making films. French film critics called this cycle of postwar American movies by the name of film noir, indicating the somber, cynical vision of life that was reflected in these movies.

French reviewers had noticed "the new mood of cynicism, pessimism, and darkness that had crept into American cinema," writes Paul Schrader in one of the most influential essays on film noir in English. Never before had Hollywood films "dared to take such a harsh, uncomplimentary look at American life."[1] The new pessimistic tinge exhibited by several American movies in this period grew out of the disillusionment resulting from the war, which would continue into the Cold War. This disillusionment, Schrader maintains, was often mirrored in melodramas in which servicemen return home from the war to encounter a society that has grown corrupt.

It is easy to identify *Killer's Kiss* and *The Killing* as examples of the kind of noir films that exhibited the corrupt postwar world. Moreover, as director Michael Cristofer observes: "Born of the post-World War II culture, film noir owed much to the disillusioned cinematic artists" who began to emerge in Hollywood at the time, such as John Huston (*The Maltese Falcon*) and Billy Wilder (*Double Indemnity*). The American cinema co-opted their pessimistic vision, "married it to the Hollywood gangster films of the 1930s, blurred the edges between good and evil, and created a dark, menacing, paranoid universe in which many a film hero was drawn and then destroyed by forces he could not understand or control."[2] Noir films are often preoccupied with the past and therefore make frequent use of flashbacks intended to show how the characters must confront the past if they are to cope with the present.

The sober look at life presented in these films was in keeping with the movement toward greater realism in the cinema that followed World War II. Audiences had grown accustomed to the realism employed in wartime documentaries and fiction films about the war, and continued to expect this same brand of realism in

01 ***Kubrick lines up a shot of Irene Kane.***
02, 04–05 ***Kubrick shot the boxing scenes himself with a hand-held camera, getting as close to the action as possible to provide a sense of immediacy and obscure the background so the lack of fans in the audience would not be visible.***

postwar films as well—not only in pictures that dealt with the war directly, but in other kinds of movies too, such as crime melodramas like Kubrick's *Killer's Kiss* and *The Killing*. These films were frequently shot on location and called forth more naturalistic performances from the actors in order to match the authentic settings. Furthermore, this air of spare, unvarnished realism was typified by the stark, documentary quality of the cinematography.

Schrader enumerates several elements that were usually evident in film noir, of which a number are noticeable in *Killer's Kiss* and *The Killing*. A noir film takes place almost entirely at night, often in murkily lit rooms, alleys, and side streets. What's more, the sinister nightmare world of film noir is one of seedy motels, boarding houses, shabby bars, and cafés—a night world of distorted shapes, where rain glistens on windows and windshields and faces are barred with shadows that suggest some imprisonment of body or soul. The actors move about in this dark, brooding atmosphere, giving the movie a hopeless mood. "There is nothing the protagonist can do," writes Schrader. "The city will outlast and negate even his best efforts," and this is why the hero and heroine of *Killer's Kiss* flee the city at film's end.[3]

It is a world in which a woman with a past can encounter a man with no future in the isolated atmosphere of a tawdry cocktail lounge. The heroine is often discovered propped against a piano, singing an insolent dirge. The hero is a cynic who has been pushed around once too often by life. As the seductive temptress Mona Stevens says in the 1948 noir film *Pitfall*, "If you want to feel completely out of step with the rest of the world, sit around a cocktail lounge in the afternoon."

Schrader rightly contends that film noir is not a separate movie genre, since it depends on the conventions of established genres, such as the gangster film, the science fiction film, and the western. Hence, it is necessary to "approach the body of films made during the noir cycle as expressions of pre-existing genres."

Noir films were frequently shot on a tight shooting schedule and a low budget, and many noteworthy examples of film noir, including *Killer's Kiss* and *The Killing*, were turned out under these conditions.

Foster Hirsch, in *The Dark Side of the Screen: Film Noir*, writes that the trend prospered between the early 1940s and the late 1950s, the outer limits of the cycle stretching from Huston's *Maltese Falcon* (1941) to Orson Welles's *Touch of Evil* (1958). Moreover, the low-budget, high-quality thrillers that surfaced in the 1940s had a profound influence on the crime film throughout the later 1940s and 1950s.

The term film noir was not in common use in the film industry itself at the time. It was not until the 1960s that the term gained widespread currency. Film actress Marie Windsor (*The Killing*) has since said that, after a number of film noir pictures were made, the term became generally known. At the time she was making *The Killing*, she added, she thought she was just making a routine gangster picture. The term has continued to be applied to certain movies that have been influenced by the noir tradition in succeeding decades,

03 ***Portrait of Irene Kane, a. k. a. Chris Chase.***

03

04

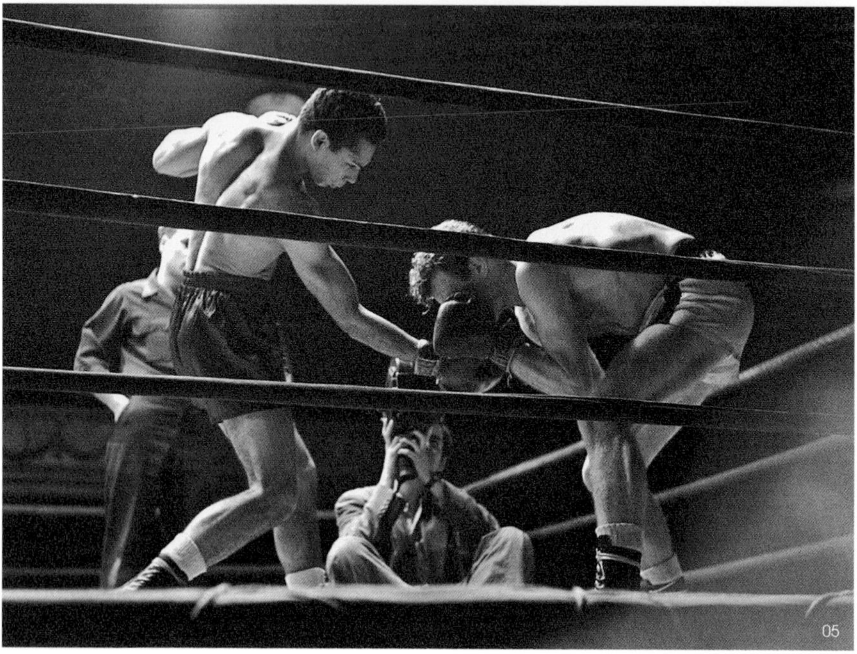

05

such as *Chinatown* (1974) and *L. A. Confidential* (1997).

Killer's Kiss is steeped in noir conventions. Boxing arenas figure prominently in noir films because they provide visual metaphors of enclosure and entrapment. The hero of *Killer's Kiss* is a prizefighter; the packed, smoke-filled arena in which he loses his last bout is an image of his destiny. As Hirsch explains, "The beating that he gets within the tight, fixed frame of the ring reflects the kind of battering that is doled out to him in the outside world." With the eye of a born filmmaker, Hirsch writes, Kubrick chose his settings effectively: "a smoky gym where the boxer trains, a dance hall where the heroine works, a bizarre mannequin factory where the climactic fight is staged.... True to noir tradition, the story begins at the end, and is told in flashback, with the beleaguered hero serving as the narrator of his own downfall."[4]

The hero of the story is a young fighter named Davy Gordon (Jamie Smith), who is already a has-been. We discover Davy pacing in Penn Station, awaiting the departure of his train. Over the sound track we hear his voice as he begins to recount the events of the past few days in an effort to sort them out for himself. "That's the way it began for me, just before my fight with Rodriguez," he muses, and we cut to a poster advertising Davy's fight. We see Davy examining his face in the mirror of his cheaply furnished room, wondering what his face will look like after the fight—a shot modeled on a similar one of Walter Cartier in *Day of the Fight*.

Davy's only companion seems to be his pet goldfish, which he dutifully feeds. Davy is the type of film noir hero who is hard-boiled on the surface in order to hide from the brutal world around him the more human, emotional side of his personality. A shot of Davy seen through the fishbowl as he peers into it suggests that he is, like the typical noir hero, imprisoned in his narrow life—as is the fish in its bowl.

> ***"While* Fear and Desire *had been a serious effort, ineptly done,* Killer's Kiss *... proved, I think, to be a frivolous effort done with conceivably more expertise though still down in the student level of filmmaking."***
>
> — SK/1971 (to Alexander Walker)

In his loneliness, he has taken to staring at Gloria Price (Irene Kane), the girl whose window is just opposite his. That she is also lonely is reflected in the fact that she sometimes snatches looks at Davy from her vantage point. Later they leave their building at the same time, and their paths cross in the lobby as Davy makes for the subway on his way to his fight, and Gloria meets her boss, Vincent Rapallo (Frank Silvera), who is waiting at the curb to drive her to Pleasureland, the dance hall where she works as a taxi dancer. Rapallo's possessiveness is immediately apparent when he indicates that she should stay away from Davy.

There follows a series of shots of Davy in his dressing room getting ready for the fight, intercut with shots of Gloria dancing with a succession of anonymous partners

in Pleasureland to canned music from an old phonograph. Kubrick's adroit cross-cutting between Davy and Gloria demonstrates that he was already mastering the art of editing.

The scene shifts to the arena for what Peter Cowie called, in 1964, "one of the most vicious boxing matches ever seen on the screen."[5] Kubrick's experience in making *Day of the Fight* undoubtedly helped him to give to the arena scenes in *Killer's Kiss* a ring of authenticity. He photographs much of the fight through the ropes to make the viewer feel that he is witnessing the bout from ringside. At crucial moments, the director moves his hand-held camera into the ring, first showing Davy's opponent, Kid Rodriguez, lunging at the camera as if at Davy's jaw, and then showing Davy slumping to the floor in a daze. At this point Kubrick turns the camera upward to catch the overhead lights glaring mercilessly down on the felled fighter.

As Davy lies on the mat and the announcer gives an obituary for Davy's career in the ring, the scene turns to Rapallo's office, where he is busy seducing Gloria. Afterward Gloria wanders along the grubbiest part of 42nd Street toward the subway, while Davy broods in the darkness of his room about his final failure to make it as a fighter.

06 ***Jamie Smith, playing boxer Davy Gordon, listens to advice from Kubrick.***
07 ***Frank Silvera as seedy dancehall manager Vincent Rapallo.***

The next scene establishes that Davy is not above voyeurism. When he sees Gloria enter her room across the way and begin to undress for bed, Davy watches with undisguised interest until his phone rings. It is Uncle George, offering his condolences over the bout. The camera is on Davy as he talks; behind him in the dresser mirror we can see Gloria's reflection as she gets into bed. In a single shot, perfectly composed by Kubrick, the artful cinematographer, we see Davy's erotic interest in the girl registering on his face as he talks distractedly to Uncle George, while at the same time we see the dreamlike image of Gloria in the mirror—the true object of his attention at the moment.

Davy's sexual preoccupation with Gloria in this scene brings into relief the influence of Freudian psychology in *Killer's Kiss*. Kubrick, who had begun dipping into Freud when his works began to be published in inexpensive paperback editions in the early 1950s, was aware that Freudian themes had begun to crop up in movies like Alfred Hitchcock's *Spellbound* (1945). Indeed, by the 1940s, Freud's titillating theories about sex and dreams, and the dramatic case histories he utilized to exemplify them, had captured the public's imagination.[6]

After all, dream sequences provide a shorthand method by which the filmmaker can project the subjective view of reality that the characters nurture for themselves. So Kubrick decided to insert a Freudian dream sequence in *Killer's Kiss,* in which the camera speeds down a narrow

slum street, photographed in a negative image, rendering the scene darkly grotesque. The dream sequence (which has an affinity with the astronaut's ride through the space corridor in *2001*) seems to be a nightmarish premonition of the life-and-death chase through the streets and across the rooftops of lower Manhattan that will be the climax of the film.

Davy is awakened by a scream and sees through the window that Gloria is being assaulted by Rapallo. Her assailant flees when he hears Davy coming, leaving him to comfort Gloria. Kubrick's most obviously Freudian scene in *Killer's Kiss* is permeated with Freud's concept of the guilt complex, whereby individuals can hold themselves responsible for tragic events for which they may not be entirely to blame. The sequence which deals with subjective guilt in the present film occurs when Davy notices some family photographs on Gloria's dresser. He asks her about the people in the pictures. One is her father; the other is her dead sister Iris, who is shown wearing a ballet costume. As Gloria begins her long monologue about the tragedy that enveloped her family, we see Iris (played by Ruth Sobotka, Kubrick's second wife) dancing alone on a dark stage, illuminated by a spotlight. As the vision of Iris pirouetting on the lonely stage fades slowly away, Gloria concludes her monologue by saying that she took her job at Pleasureland partially as a penance for her ingratitude to her dead sister: "I kept thinking at least Iris never had to dance like this."

Norman Kagan comments that "besides being cookbook Freud," Gloria's story, "has little to do with the rest of the film," and speculates that the long ballet sequence was added to bring the film up to the slim feature running time of sixty-four minutes. Kagan, who can usually be counted on to miss the point, fails to see how Gloria's monologue sheds light on her character as surely as the stage spotlight illumines Iris. Through Gloria's memories we learn how a basically decent girl like her became involved with Rapallo and Pleasureland, and why she allows the situation to go on: out of a vague sense of expiation to her dead sister. Kubrick agreed with me in conversation that the sequence, besides being a tribute to his wife's skill as a dancer, adds interest to Gloria's character. Kubrick, who had read Freud's *General Introduction to Psychology* by this time, knew better than to suggest that past traumas can easily be eradicated. Consequently, Gloria continues to be burdened with a sense of what Freud would call neurotic guilt about her sister's death.

In Penn Station once more, we see Davy still nervously awaiting his train for Seattle, recalling now how he told Gloria of his plans to return to the family farm. "Looking back now, I really don't know what her reasons were then, but she agreed to come out to Seattle with me ..." he says to himself. "I should have had sense enough, though, to know that it was no good, and she was so scared that she would have grabbed at anything." Thus the viewer at last learns the source of Davy's anxiety while he paces the station floor: he desperately hopes that Gloria will

08–09 ***Kubrick watches as Sobotka does her hair and makeup.***

08

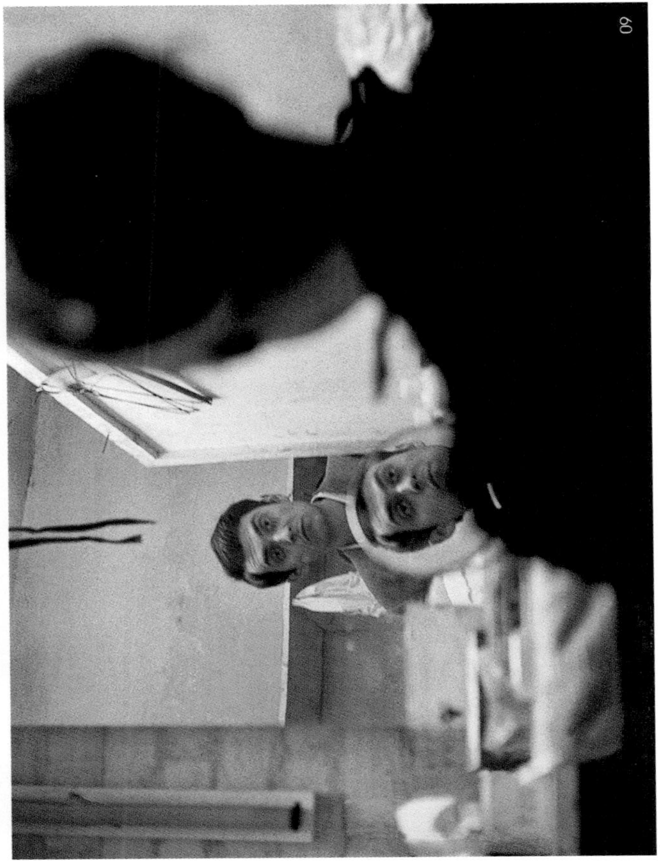

09

10

10 ***Kubrick took this picture of his second wife, Ruth Sobotka, as she prepared to dance for her role in the film.***
11 ***The young director frames a shot with the Arriflex camera.***

12

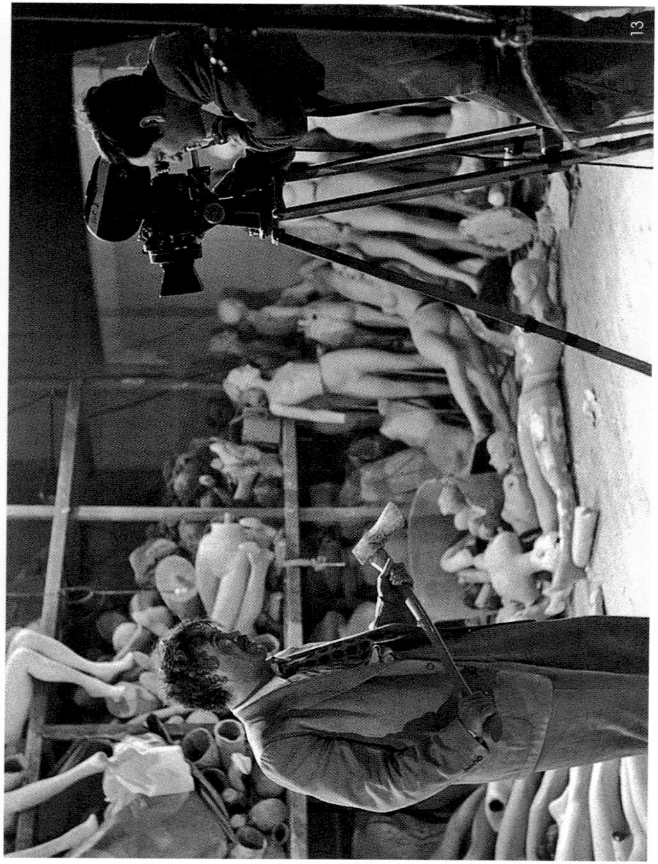

13

arrive in time to go with him as she had promised. This is a suspense hook that holds the filmgoer's interest as Davy goes on with his story.

Davy recalls how he had asked Albert, his manager, to pay him for his last fight immediately, so that he could make the trip to Seattle with Gloria. Albert agrees to meet him at 8:15 p.m. in front of Pleasureland, where Gloria must go to tell Rapallo she has quit her job and to pick up her last paycheck. This situation sets up the intricate and ironic plot twists that lead to the climax of the film.

In Rapallo's office, Gloria turns down his offer to stay on as his mistress. Angered by Gloria's condescending response to his pathetic efforts to keep her, Rapallo throws her out without paying her salary. Gloria goes downstairs to wait for Davy, walking past a sign on the staircase that ominously warns, "WATCH your STEP." This is just the kind of telling detail that one must be alert to, even in Kubrick's earliest films. She stands next to Davy's manager, Albert, who is also waiting for Davy. When Davy does not appear, she departs, and one of Rapallo's hoods takes up a posi-

12-14 ***Kubrick, seen here shooting Jamie Smith and Frank Silvera in the mannequin factory fight scene, told*** The New York Times, ***"The scene took two weeks to film and destroyed fifteen thousand dollars' worth of mannequins." (A. H. Weiler, 1954)***

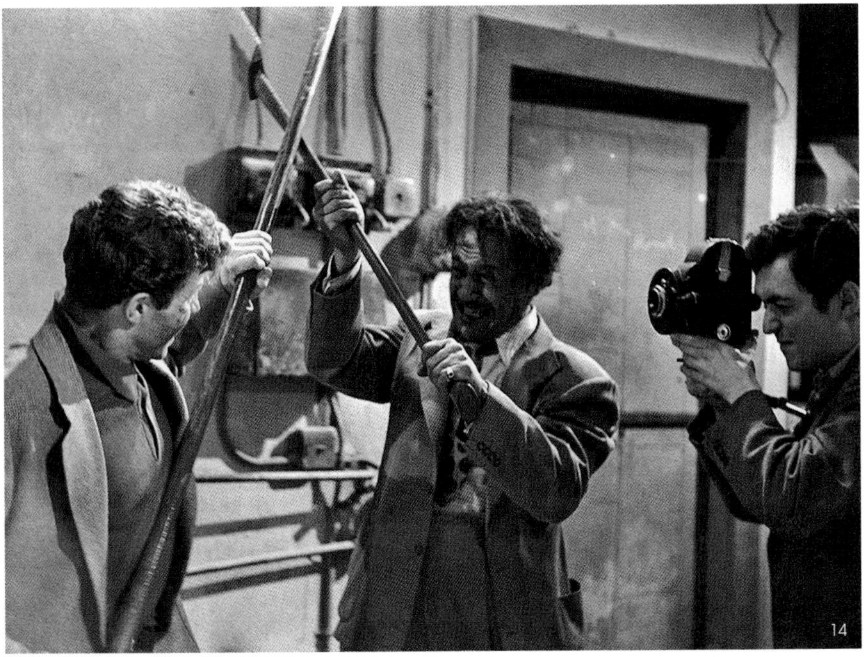
14

15

17

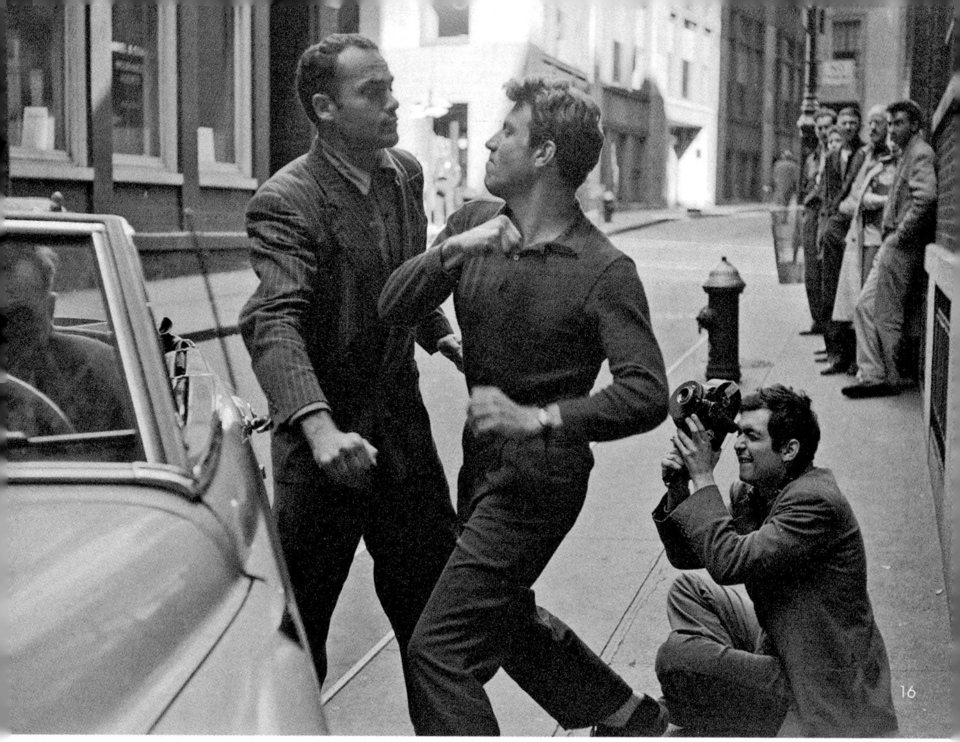

16

18

tion next to Albert, mistaking him for Davy. Rapallo's henchmen back Albert into an alley where they begin to rough him up as a warning to stay away from Gloria. Kubrick employed dim lighting in this scene, making it all the more menacing. The camera peers into the alley from the street, holding on the two thugs; they are pictured in dark silhouettes. While Albert pleads for his life, slatted shadows, cast by a grating in the alley, fall across his cringing form. There is a scuffle in which the two hooligans bash the hapless fight manager's head in. The masterly way that Kubrick has lit and composed the shots in this scene belies the movie's status as a low-budget programmer.

"In my opinion, it's a very amateurish piece. The subject was atrociously bad, and it was badly developed, but still, it allowed me to get some attention."

— SK/1957 (to Raymond Haine/*Cahiers du Cinéma*)

Gloria and Davy meanwhile have both gone back to the tenement to pack. But when Davy goes to Gloria's room to meet her after he has moved out of his room, he finds that she and all her belongings are already gone. This shock is followed by another, as he overhears the building superintendent being informed by the police that Davy is wanted for the murder of Albert.

Davy hunts for Gloria in the dark and forbidding streets of Greenwich Village. Gerald Fried, who had also scored *Day of the Fight* and *Fear and Desire*, employed a restless Latin jazz piece for the scenes in which Davy frantically searches for Gloria in the seedier parts of the Village, as he seeks to save her from Rapallo. Davy finally tracks down Rapallo with a gun and forces him to take him to the warehouse loft where Gloria is being held. At the warehouse, Rapallo's men overpower Davy, but he escapes by jumping through a window to the street below. In the chase scene that follows, Davy's white socks unaccountably change to black; Kubrick told me that that was the only lapse in continuity he was aware of in any of his films.

Davy runs down streets and through alleys, up a fire escape and across rooftops in his efforts to elude Rapallo and his hoodlums, finally taking refuge in a warehouse storeroom filled with department store mannequins. Rapallo finds him, nonetheless, and the two men face each other for what both of them know is going to be a struggle to the death.

The partially dismantled dummies grotesquely prefigure the violence that the two protagonists are likely to inflict on each other. Rapallo hurls a torso at Davy and then grabs a fire ax from the wall. Davy fends off his assailant with the broken bodies of the mannequins until he is able to seize a pike-tipped window pole. The opponents viciously battle among the debris until finally Davy delivers the death blow off camera. For Davy's showdown with Rapallo, Fried composed "Murder 'mongst the Mannequins," an eerie theme scored for high strings and muted brass, with an insistent undercurrent of drums, leading up to the moment when Davy kills Rapallo in self-defense.

There is a close-up of the smashed head of a dummy as the sound of Rapallo's scream of pain blends into the screech of a train whistle in Penn Station. This recalls a similar shot in Hitchcock's *The 39 Steps* (1935), in which the scream of a woman discovering a corpse melds with the whistle of the train which is carrying the hero away from the scene of the murder of which he is falsely accused.

In voiceover, Davy recounts that he was cleared of Rapallo's death because he acted in self-defense, but that he has probably lost Gloria for good. Up to this point in the film the exterior scenes have taken place mainly at dusk, at night, or at dawn, in true film noir fashion. This dark, brooding atmosphere is quickly dispelled as the camera cuts to a bright, sunshiny day outside the station, where a cab is just drawing up to the curb. Gloria gets out and rushes inside to join Davy in his flight from the city to the fresher life on the farm. They embrace and kiss as the camera pulls

15–16 ***These scenes were shot in downtown Manhattan without the required permit; Kubrick staved off the police with $20 bills.***
17–18 ***Chris Chase, the actress who played Gloria under the stage name Irene Kane, said, "Stanley was very sweet and kind to me .... He'd always drive me home. [On one] ride home I said, 'Why are you always so nice to everyone?' He said, 'Honey, nobody's going to get anything out of this movie but me.'" (interviewed for* A Life in Pictures, *2001)***
19 ***Taking the light reading for the famous rooftop chase scene.***

away, losing sight of them in the congested crowd of passersby hurrying through the station.

In their departure from the brutal big city, which has proved a harsh and unpleasant place for both of them, one can see early indications of Kubrick's dark vision of contemporary society. In his films, Kubrick shows us modern man gradually being dehumanized by living in a materialistic, mechanized world in which men exploit one another in the mass effort for survival. One can therefore see early indications of this theme that is elaborated in his later films.

Like *Fear and Desire*, *Killer's Kiss* was financed by Kubrick with the help of his friends and relatives, this time for $75,000. *Killer's Kiss*, originally titled *Kiss Me, Kill Me*, was co-scripted by Kubrick and Howard Sackler (*Fear and Desire*). They built their story around some exciting action sequences that would carry the weight of the film and not be costly to shoot, including two key fight scenes and a chase through some lower Manhattan warehouses. Kubrick saved money by shooting the picture in the shabbier sections of New York, which gave the movie a visual realism that belies the film's meager budget, and throughout the arena sequence, he created the illusion that the darkened area beyond the ring was crowded with fight fans by keeping the camera close to the fighters (in reality the auditorium was virtually empty during the shooting).

Frank Silvera (*Fear and Desire*) agreed to appear as the villain in *Killer's Kiss*, provided that he receive top billing since, once again, he was the only truly experienced actor in the cast. But he, like the rest of the cast and crew, worked for modest salaries. As with *Fear and Desire*, Kubrick handled most of the production chores himself: lighting, camera work, and sound recording.

Kubrick was shooting a scene in a Greenwich Village loft one chilly night, and—already a perfectionist—he took a long time to light the set. The disgruntled technical crew and the actors began to gripe about the cold, the long hours, and the low pay. Silvera complained in particular that he had passed up the chance to do an off-Broadway play to stay with this movie. Kubrick listened patiently to the complaints, and then announced that they would knock off for the rest of the night. After all, he really could not afford to alienate these people who were willing to work for him in such stringent conditions. Every Friday afternoon Kubrick shut down shooting, so that he could go to the unemployment office to collect his weekly check; that is what he was living on.

Money began to run out during the post-production work, and Kubrick was unable to afford an editing assistant. He therefore had to spend four months just laying in the sound effects ("footstep by footstep" as he put it[7]) and Fried's musical score. In any case, Kubrick created his post-synchronized sound track with skill, since he had become more deft in post-dubbing than he had been when he made *Fear and Desire*.

Critics found *Killer's Kiss* the work of a talented amateur, who showed promise of better films to come. But Kubrick himself told me that *Killer's Kiss* was only a notch above *Fear and Desire* in his estimation. When I told him at our first meeting that I had not yet been able to see his first two

features, he smiled and said, "You're lucky," since he regarded both films as amateur efforts. It is significant, however, that Kubrick was able to sell *Killer's Kiss*, a film made completely outside the Hollywood studio system, to United Artists, a major studio, for worldwide distribution. "It made a profit for United Artists," he said laconically, "though it was mostly released as a second feature."[8]

United Artists invited him to make a series of low-budget program pictures for the neighborhood circuits, but he wisely turned down the offer. He did not wish to commit himself to making second features indefinitely. Kubrick was saved from this situation when his friend from high school, Alexander Singer, introduced him to James B. Harris, a wealthy young man who wanted to try his hand at producing motion pictures. Kubrick and Harris, both of whom were only twenty-six years old at the time, formed a three-picture partnership that enabled Kubrick to rise from the rank of promising newcomer to that of major director.

20 ***Kubrick adjusts the sound recording machine.***

Notes

1. Paul Schrader, "Notes on Noir," in *Film Noir Reader*, ed. Alain Silver and James Ursini (New York: Limelight, 1998): 53.
2. Michael Cristofer, "Lost Hollywood: Film Noir," *Premiere* 14 no. 7 (March, 2001): 58.
3. Schrader: 57.
4. Foster Hirsch, *The Dark Side of the Screen: Film Noir* (New York: Da Capo, 2001): 85–86.
5. Peter Cowie, *Seventy Years of Cinema* (New York: Barnes, 1964): 222.
6. D. M. Thomas, "Freudianism Arrives," in *Our Times: The History of the Twentieth Century*, ed. Lorraine Glennon and John Garraty (Atlanta: Turner, 1995): 6–10.
7. Gene D. Phillips. *Major Film Directors of the American and British Cinema* (Cranbury, N. J.: Associated University Presses, 1999): 127.
8. Ibid.

21 ***Kubrick squeezes himself behind the camera on a fire escape to shoot the scene in which the actors climb to the roof during the chase scene.***

The Killing

1956 / BLACK AND WHITE / 83 MINUTES
Distributed by UNITED ARTISTS

CAST
JOHNNY CLAY STERLING HAYDEN
FAY COLEEN GRAY
VAL CANNON VINCE EDWARDS
MARVIN UNGER JAY C. FLIPPEN
RANDY KENNAN TED DE CORSIA
SHERRY PEATTY MARIE WINDSOR
GEORGE PEATTY ELISHA COOK
MIKE O'REILLY JOE SAWYER
CAR PARK ATTENDANT JAMES EDWARDS
NIKKI TIMOTHY CAREY
MAURICE KOLA KWARIANI
LEO JAY ADLER
TINY JOSEPH TURKEL

CREW
DIRECTED BY STANLEY KUBRICK
PRODUCED BY JAMES B. HARRIS
SCREENPLAY STANLEY KUBRICK (based on Lionel White's novel *Clean Break*)
DIALOGUE JIM THOMPSON
ASSOCIATE PRODUCER ALEXANDER SINGER
CAMERA OPERATOR DICK TOWER
DIRECTOR OF PHOTOGRAPHY LUCIEN BALLARD
ART DIRECTOR RUTH SOBOTKA
FILM EDITOR BETTY STEINBERG
ORIGINAL MUSIC GERALD FRIED
SPECIAL EFFECTS DAVE KOEHIER
SET DECORATOR HARRY REIF
MUSIC EDITOR GILBERT MARCHANT
ASSISTANT DIRECTOR MILTON CARTER
2ND ASSISTANT DIRECTORS PAUL FEINER, HOWARD JOSLIN
PRODUCTION ASSISTANT MARGUERITE OLSON
DIRECTOR'S ASSISTANT JOYCE HARTMAN
PHOTOGRAPHIC EFFECTS JACK RABIN, LOUIS DEWITT

Opposite ***Press brochure.***

EXHIBITORS' CAMPAIGN BOOK
These 5 Men Had a $2,000,000 Secret Until
One of them told this Woma
JOE SAWYER as The race track bartender with an ailing wife!
MARIE WINDSOR as The two-timing dame who couldn't keep her mouth shut!
TED De CORSIA as The racketeering racetrack cop
ELISHA COOK as The little man with the big ideas
STERLING HAYDEN as The brains of the mob!
J. C. FLIPPEN as The reformed Alcoholic
see them all in all their fury in
"THE KILLING"
Like no other picture since SCARFACE and LITTLE CAESAR
starring STERLING HAYDEN
co-starring COLEEN GRAY VINCE EDWARDS
with JAY C. FLIPPEN
MARIE WINDSOR TED DeCORSIA
Based on the novel "Clean Break," by Lionel White
Screenplay by Stanley Kubrick • Produced by James B. Harris • Directed by Stanley Kubrick
UNITED ARTISTS

The Killing
© COPYRIGHT MCMLVI
HARRIS-KUBRICK
PICTURES CORPORATION

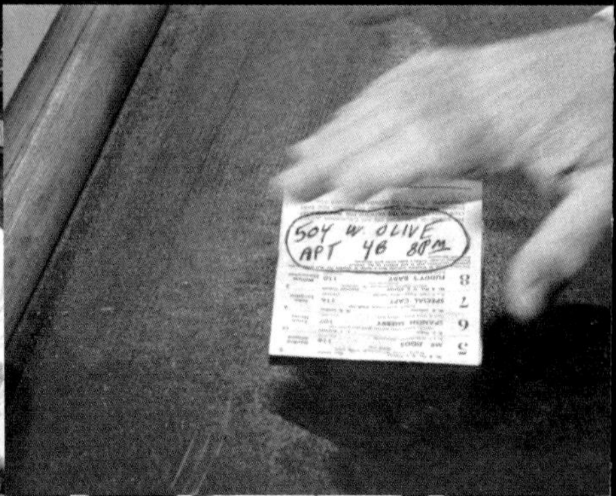
504 W. OLIVE
APT 4B 8PM

PURCHASE TICKETS
FOR
BOSTON

01

The Killing

by Gene D. Phillips

01 *Kubrick directs Sterling Hayden in a scene that was cut from the film.*
02 *Kubrick on the set with producer James B. Harris (center) and associate producer Alexander Singer.*
03 *Left to right: Sterling Hayden, James B. Harris, Kubrick's wife, Ruth Sobotka, who was the film's art director, and Sam Abarbanel, the film's publicist.*

02

Kubrick's first important film was *The Killing*, a far more accomplished work than *Killer's Kiss*. Alexander Singer, a friend of Kubrick's who had worked on his documentary *Day of the Fight*, introduced him to his old high school chum James B. Harris. In 1954, Harris, heir of an affluent East Coast family, had founded Flamingo Films, a movie and TV distribution company. One day Harris met Kubrick on the street in New York, and Kubrick brought him along to an advance screening of *Killer's Kiss*. "I was very impressed with Kubrick," Harris recalls in Vincent LoBrutto's Kubrick biography, because Kubrick had made two features "all by himself," *Fear and Desire* and *Killer's Kiss*. "The guy is going to be a great director," Harris said to himself.[1]

Kubrick and Harris hit it off very well. "We became not only partners, but we became best friends," Harris told Peter Bogdanovich.[2] They soon pulled up stakes in New York and moved to Los Angeles, with the hope of setting up their own production company. Harris reasoned that, with his experience at Flamingo Films, he could help Kubrick with the business end of moviemaking.

Kubrick came across a crime novel entitled *Clean Break* by Lionel White, a

noted author of pulp fiction, about a racetrack robbery. He thought the thriller was terrific, so Harris bought the screen rights to the novel and sought studio backing for the movie. Eventually Harris arranged for United Artists to distribute the film, once they had secured Sterling Hayden, known for appearing in John Huston's *Asphalt Jungle* (1950), to star.

Harris believed enough in the project—and in Kubrick—to put up more than one-third of the film's $320 000 budget, with United Artists providing the rest. UA at this juncture was having second thoughts

04 ***Joseph Turkel as Tiny, Val's partner in crime. Turkel also appeared in Kubrick's next film,*** **Paths of Glory,** ***and later in*** **The Shining.**

about Hayden, however, since Hayden was not considered a major box office draw by the studio moguls. So UA declined to invest more than $200,000 in the film, because, in its view, that was all a Sterling Hayden movie was worth. Max Youngstein, UA production chief, informed Kubrick and Harris that they would have to find the rest of the financing on their own. Harris-Kubrick Pictures was on its way.

The Killing is a tough and tightly-knit crime thriller about a racetrack robbery carried out by a group of down-at-the-heels, small-time crooks who hope to pull off one last big job to solve all of their individual financial crises. Like *Killer's Kiss, The Killing* belongs to the film noir cycle in American cinema. In his book on film noir, Arthur Lyons writes that in *The Killing* "a combination of bad luck and personality flaws brings about the destruction of the gang and foils what would have been the perfect crime. Such fatalism is typical of film noir. Life is unforgiving in noir films.... You can make one mistake, and you're finished."[3] Putting it another way, film director Martin Scorsese notes in his documentary *A Personal Journey Through American Movies* (1995), "There is no reprieve in film noir; you pay for your sins." *The Killing* proves that rule.

The Killing and *Killer's Kiss* came toward the end of the film noir cycle. "After ten years of steadily shedding romantic conventions," Paul Schrader opines, "the later noir films finally got down to the root causes" of the disillusionment of the period: the loss of heroic conventions, personal integrity, and finally psychic stability. The last films of the trend seemed to be painfully aware that "they stood at the end of a long tradition based on despair and disintegration and did not shy away from the fact."

It is Schrader who has pointed out the triple theme inherent in these films: "A passion for the past and present, but also a fear of the future. The noir hero dreads to look ahead, but instead tries to survive by the day; and if unsuccessful at that, he retreats into the past. Thus film noir's techniques emphasize loss, nostalgia, lack of clear priorities, insecurity."[4]

"The Killing was my first truly professional work.... The subject was a fairly bad one, but I tried to make up for it in the direction. Nevertheless, it was shot in only twenty days. The editing —I edit all my films myself— took much longer."

— SK/1957 (to Raymond Haine/*Cahiers du Cinéma*)

This analysis of film noir could well serve as a description of *The Killing*, a sardonic movie that shares with other noir films what Foster Hirsch calls "a bleak vision of human destiny and a sense of man as the victim of forces he is unable to control."[5]

Furthermore, *The Killing* also reflects another element of film noir that Schrader emphasizes as endemic to that type of movie: it utilizes a complex chronological order to reinforce a sense of hopelessness and lost time in a disoriented world. Kubrick's tightly constructed script follows the preparations of the makeshift gang bent on making a big pile of money by holding up a San Francisco racetrack. They have planned the robbery to coincide with the actual running of the seventh race, and Kubrick photographs the heist in great detail with all of its split-second timing. He builds suspense with great intensity by quickly cutting from one member of the gang to another in a series of flashbacks that show how each has simultaneously carried out his part of the plan. All of these parallel lines of action lead inexorably to the climactic moment when the ringleader gets away with the loot. Edward Buscombe remarks, "This early Kubrick picture shows all of the characteristic precision and care in the construction of the narrative, pieced together through flashback and voice-over narration."[6]

"Regarding* The Killing, *I had seen the book mentioned in a column by Jimmy Cannon, a very good sports writer in the States. He said it was the most exciting crime novel he'd ever read. Just out of curiosity, I went into a bookshop and I bought it."

— SK/1963 (*Films and Filming*)

Kubrick was a fan of Jim Thompson, the author of several hard-boiled crime novels dealing with violent and self-destructive behavior, like *The Killer Inside Me* (1952). Kubrick had been particularly impressed by Thompson's ear for dialogue, so he asked this leading author of pulp fiction to work on the dialogue for *The Killing*. In giving us a glimpse into the seedy lives of each member of the gang involved in the robbery, Kubrick and Thompson have lent the film a touch of sleazy authenticity that raises it well above the level of the ordinary crime movie.

Kubrick wanted to introduce a homosexual subtext into the film in terms of one of the older conspirators having a crush on the young leader of the gang. This precipitated a censorship problem. At the time that Kubrick began making films, in the 1950s, Joseph Ignatius Breen, the industry censor, maintained that homosexuality was too strong a subject for American motion pictures. He was backed by the Motion Picture Production Code, which flatly stated that any reference to "sex perversion" was forbidden. Oscar Wilde called homosexuality "the love that dare not speak its name," and the film censor wanted to keep it that way. As Lily Tomlin says in narrating *The Celluloid Closet*, the 1995 television documentary about homosexuality in the movies, "The film censor didn't erase homosexuals from the screen; he just made them harder to find."

Since Breen insisted that the restrictions of the industry's censorship code be upheld, prohibiting Kubrick from depicting homosexuality in any explicit way, Kubrick managed to suggest a hint of homosexuality in *The Killing*. He implies that Marvin Unger, one of the accomplices of

05 ***Sterling Hayden as Johnny Clay, with an expression similar to that of his character at the end of the film.***

05
HK.(R44)-6

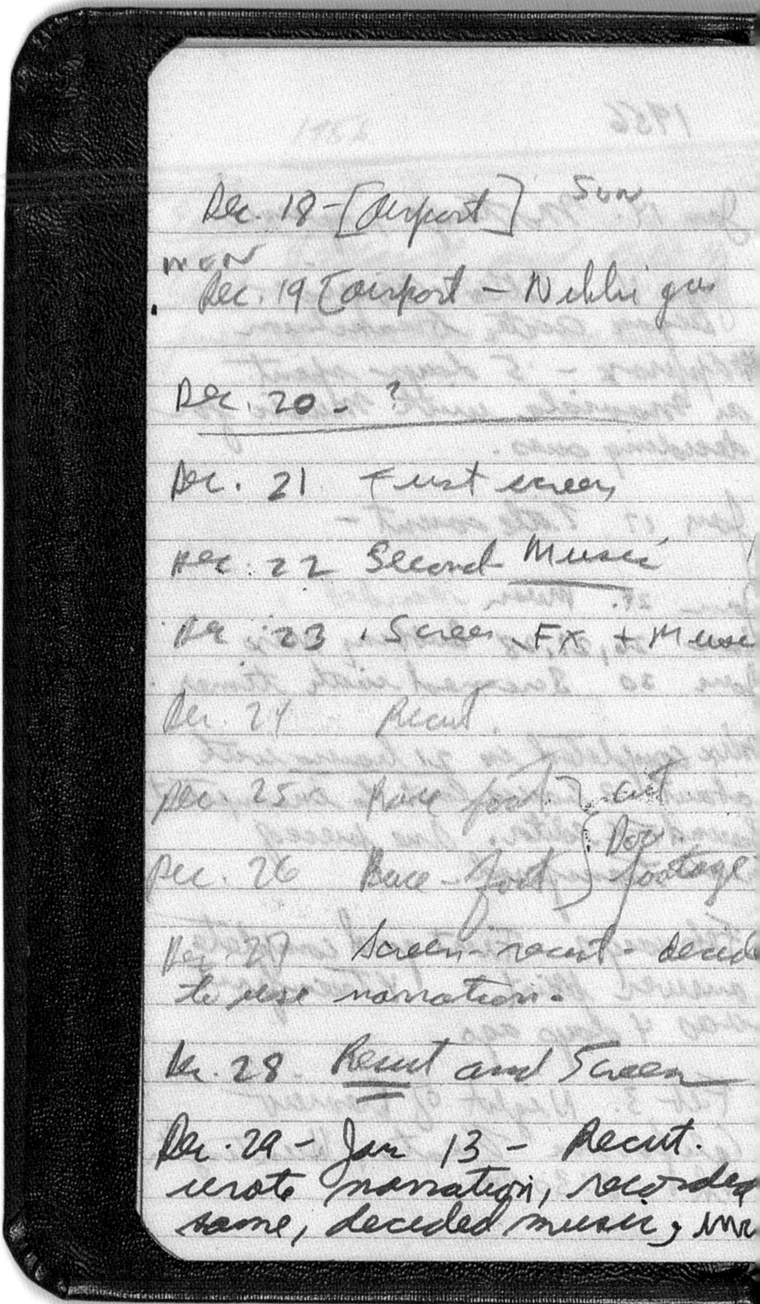

Dec. 18 - [Airport] Sun
Mon Dec. 19 [airport - Nikki gone
Dec. 20 - ?
Dec. 21 First screen
Dec. 22 Second Music
Dec. 23 Screen FX + Music
Dec. 24 Recut
Dec. 25 Have footage cut
Dec. 26 Have footage } Dog footage
Dec. 27 Screen - recut - decide to use narration.
Dec. 28 Recut and Screen
Dec. 29 - Jan 13 - Recut. wrote narration, recorded same, decided music,

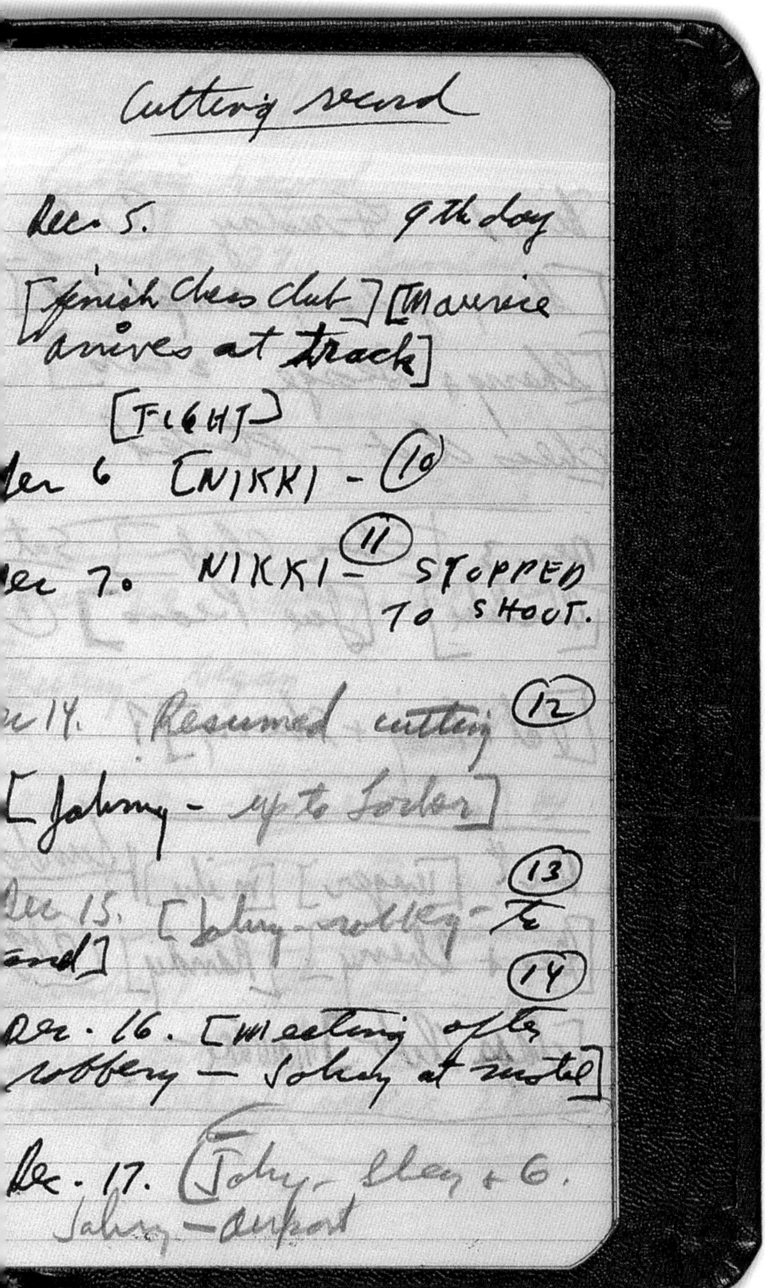
cutting record
Dec. 5. 9th day
[finish chess club] [Maurice arrives at track]
[FIGHT]
[NIKKI - 10
NIKKI - 11 STOPPED TO SHOOT.
Resumed cutting 12
13
14
Dec. 16. [meeting after robbery — Johnny at motel]
Dec. 17.
Johnny — airport

06

"The criminal is always interesting on the screen because he is a paradox of personality, a collection of violent contrasts."

— SK/1958 (to Joanne Stang/ *The New York Times Magazine*)

Johnny Clay in planning the robbery, has a covert homosexual attachment to the much younger Johnny. "There is nothing I wouldn't do for Johnny," he says. In fact, Marvin's participation in the caper seems to be motivated by his need to be near Johnny, rather than by greed for money.

He even suggests that he and Johnny go off together after the heist, "and let the old world take a couple of turns," while they are alone together without any women along, so they can "have a chance to take stock of things" on their own. But his invitation is pointedly ignored by Johnny. As screenwriter Jay Presson Allen says in *The Celluloid Closet*, a clever director like Kubrick could get around the restriction on portraying homosexuality by hints and suggestions. Writer Gore Vidal states in the same documentary, "It was perfectly clear to the cognoscenti who were on the right wavelength" when a character was homosexual.

The budget for *The Killing* was larger than that of the earlier films; as Kubrick told me in conversation, "This time we were able to afford good actors." Hayden saw Johnny Clay as a meaty role, so he was pleased when Harris offered him the

07

lead in *The Killing*. Kubrick elicited a high order of ensemble acting from a group of capable Hollywood supporting players who rarely got a chance to give performances of such substance. Sterling Hayden plays Johnny Clay, the rough organizer of the caper; Jay C. Flippen is Marvin Unger, the cynical older member of the group; Elisha Cook, Jr., is George Peatty, the timid track cashier who hopes to impress his voluptuous wife Sherry (Marie Windsor) with stolen money, since he cannot otherwise give her satisfaction; and Ted DeCorsia is Randy Kennan, a crooked cop. They and other cast members help Kubrick create the brutally real atmosphere of the film.

Each face is right for the part; the features of the social misfits who comprise Johnny's gang are marred with tension and fear of failure. *The Killing* is a film about the end of things, inhabited by crooks that

06 ***The notebook kept by Kubrick during the editing of* The Killing. *On the subject of the film's non-linear structure, James B. Harris said, "Everybody that talked to us said that we should re-cut the picture as a straight line story.... We re-cut the picture as a test and we said, 'Are we crazy? Why did we do this?' ... so we put it back the way it was. I think we learned the lesson... to trust your own instincts." (interviewed for* A Life in Pictures, *2001).***

07 ***The director watches Elisha Cook and Marie Windsor rehearse.***

08 ***Elisha Cook as George, reacting to a slap from a co-conspirator.***

are past their sell-by date, touched throughout by the shadow of mortality.

Coleen Gray, who plays Johnny's girlfriend Fay, had appeared in the vintage noir *Kiss of Death* (1947); she recalled working with Kubrick for Peter Bogdanovich: "He was a small man wearing army fatigues and clodhopper shoes, and had bushy hair and was very quiet." When shooting a scene, "I kept waiting for him to direct me and nothing happened." When was he going to tell her what to do? "He never did, which made me feel insecure. Maybe the fact that I felt insecure was fine for the part—the girl *was* insecure."[7] Fay had good reason to be insecure, as she fretted about whether or not Johnny could bring off the robbery and make good his escape with her to the tropics.

In Jan Harlan's 2001 documentary *Stanley Kubrick: A Life in Pictures*, Marie Windsor recalls that Stanley Kubrick cast her as Sherry because he remembered her playing "the femme fatale in *The Narrow Margin* (1952)," a classic noir. She told Peter Bogdanovich that he was unlike any director she had worked with: "He was a gentle, quiet man, who never yelled at the crew" or the actors. She remembers that "when he had some idea for me to do or change something, he would wiggle his finger at me and we would go

09–10 ***Marie Windsor and Vince Edwards played scheming lovers Sherry and Val. Describing how she was cast in the film, Windsor told Vincent LoBrutto, "Stanley saw a movie I made,*** **The Narrow Margin,** ***and said to Jimmy Harris, 'That's my Sherry!'"***

away from the action and he would tell me what he wanted. He didn't direct you in front of the crew. He was a kid with tremendous confidence."[8]

Hayden likewise remembered Kubrick as always confident about what he was doing, and with good reason. "I have worked with few directors that good. He's like the Russian documentarians who could put the same footage together five different ways, so it really didn't matter what the actors did—Stanley would know what to do with it."[9]

Another thing that attracted Kubrick to White's book, Alexander Walker points out perceptively in *Stanley Kubrick: Director,* is that the novel touches on a theme that is a frequent preoccupation of Kubrick's films: the presumably perfect plan of action that goes wrong through human fallibility and/or chance. "It is characteristic of Kubrick that while one part of him pays intellectual tribute to the rationally constructed master plan, another part reserved the skeptic's right to anticipate human imperfections or the laws of chance that militate against its success."[10] We shall see reverberations of this theme most notably in films like *Dr. Strangelove,* in which a mad general (again played by Sterling Hayden) upsets the carefully planned U.S. nuclear fail-safe system; but this theme asserts itself in other Kubrick films as well, including movies as different as *Spartacus* and *Lolita.*

It is clear from the outset in *The Killing* that the tawdry individuals whom Johnny has brought together to execute the racetrack robbery comprise a series of weak links in a chain of command that could snap at any point. Add to this the possibility of unexpected mishaps that could dog even the best of plans, and the viewer senses that the entire project is doomed from the start. Yet one is fascinated to see how things will go wrong, and when.

During the credits of *The Killing* there are several shots of the preparations before a race: the starting gate is brought into place, the horses line up in their positions, etc. It is a tribute to Kubrick's naturalistic direction that, when the film cuts from these documentary shots of the track to the betting area, few filmgoers suspect that the action has shifted to a studio set. The voice of the narrator further contributes to the documentary air of the picture. He introduces each of the characters, describing why each is implicated in the robbery.

First there is Marvin Unger, who is helping to set up the robbery so that he can obtain enough money to retire with financial security. In a long tracking shot, he walks across the lobby to the racetrack bar, where he slips a note to bartender Mike O'Reilly (Joe Sawyer) on which is written an address and a meeting time. Then he walks to the window of cashier George Peatty and slyly gives him a similar card. "About an hour earlier," the narrator continues, "Patrolman First Class Randy Kennan had some personal business to attend to" with a gambler to whom he is heavily in debt. He stalls his creditor with the promise that he is shortly to come into a large sum of money.

At 7 that same evening, Johnny is describing his accomplices to his girlfriend, Fay, in the kitchen of a dingy flat. "None of these guys are criminals in the usual

11

sense," he explains. He arranges to meet Fay at the airport after the robbery so that they can go away together. Fay reasserts her faith in Johnny as he sends her away.

"Half an hour earlier, at approximately 6:30, Mike O'Reilly ... came home." The bartender greets his bedridden wife, whom he cannot afford to send to a specialist. Mike consoles her with the promise of better days ahead.

Some of the strongest dramatic scenes in the movie are between mousy George Peatty and his wife Sherry. George is hopelessly in love with Sherry and is constantly afraid that she will two-time him with another man—something she has already done repeatedly. Sherry is made up to look slightly tarnished, complete with garish blonde hair and a gaudy frock;

11–13 ***Sterling Hayden with Kubrick on the set. Kubrick admired Hayden's work and subsequently cast him in the role of the mad general, Jack D. Ripper, in* Dr. Strangelove.**

12

Kubrick wanted her to look as tawdry as the shabby apartment she shares with her Milquetoast husband. George comes home from his job at the track as betting-window teller to find Sherry sprawled on the couch reading a magazine.

Their conversation reveals the lack of love and money in their marriage and the obvious disappointments of their life together. Maddened by her constant condescension, George blurts out that he is involved in a big operation that will make them rich. Sherry shrewdly tries to pry more of the details from him, but George, aware that he has already said too much, becomes evasive. "When a woman has been married five years and her own husband doesn't trust her…" Sherry pouts. The two performers breathe a great deal of credibility into their handling of these scenes, particularly Elisha Cook, Jr. (*The Maltese Falcon*), who was the prototype of all sad little men in the movies. Sherry later tells her handsome lover Val Cannon (Vince Edwards) what she has been able to wheedle out of her husband about the caper.

At the meeting Johnny has called with his fellow conspirators, he goes over the intricate plans which he has laid. A single overhead lamp illumines their worn, defeated faces as they talk, leaving them surrounded by a darkness that is almost tangible. It is this darkness that seems to hover around characters in many of Kubrick's films and which they desperately seek to keep from engulfing them—usually without success.

"Three days later," the narrator says, "Johnny Clay began the final preparations." He hires a wrestler named Maurice to start a fight with the track bartender to distract the police from the robbery. Clay next visits sharpshooter Nikki (Timothy Carey) at this farm. Johnny hires Nikki to shoot down Red Lightning, the favored horse, during the course of the seventh race, in order to distract the police. Nikki holds a puppy all the time that he and Johnny discuss the proposition, which explains his hesitation to shoot an animal. The puppy represents another of Kubrick's neat directorial touches.

Once he gets Nikki to agree to his proposition, Johnny rents a motel room where he can hide the loot immediately after the robbery. This is the last item on Johnny's agenda.

Tension begins to mount as the day of the holdup dawns. The narrator says ruefully, "Johnny Clay began what might be the last day of his life." Ironically, it will be the last day of life for just about everyone involved in the project *but* Johnny. At 8:45 a.m. the mastermind of the holdup hides his rifle in a flower box and heads for the track.

From this point onward Kubrick begins to follow each separate strand of the robbery plot through to its completion, doubling back each time to show how each of the elements of the elaborate plan is implemented simultaneously with all the others. Kubrick repeats the shots from the credit sequence of the horses getting into starting position for the seventh race each time he turns back the clock to develop a different step in the complex robbery plan, thereby situating the viewer temporally.

At 4 p.m., Maurice the wrestler starts a fight with Mike the bartender and takes on the entire track police force. At 4:23 p.m., Maurice is finally taken into custody while Johnny, unobserved, slips through the track staff's door, which has been unlocked for him by Peatty. George Peatty takes a gun out of his lunch box and pockets it; Kubrick thereby prefigures Peatty's use of the gun later at a critical point in the action.

Meanwhile Nikki tensely watches the race through his gunsight, as he sits in his car in a secluded corner of the parking lot. At precisely 4:23 p.m., he pulls the trigger and brings Red Lightning down. Thirty seconds later Nikki is dead, gunned down by a track guard as he attempts to leave the lot.

Now the clock rolls back to 2:15 p.m. as we see the robbery from the point of view of its key figure, Johnny. Kubrick has built his film from the beginning toward this peak where all of Johnny's meticulous planning and careful timing suddenly converge on the moment when he enters the cashiers' office and scoops up $2 million: George opens the employee's locker room where Johnny takes his rifle from the flower box and puts on the rubber mask which was also in the flower box. With typical Kubrick irony, the face on the mask is frozen into a perpetual grin.

Thus disguised, Johnny bursts into the cashier's room and orders them to fill his large laundry sack with all the money it will hold. Then he makes his getaway, heaving the bulky bag, which contains the cash, out of an open window. Later we learn that Officer Kennan was stationed below the window to snatch the loot as it hit the ground and transfer it to the motel room where Johnny would pick it up later.

Kubrick begins to draw the last threads of the plot together as Johnny's companions in crime assemble in Marvin's shabby living room to await his appearance with the money. The men sit around drinking nervously. George's hand, anxiously nursing a glass, is in the foreground, suggesting that he especially feels the tension that permeates the room. "Why ain't he here?" George whines. "Everything else runs on a timetable, till it comes to payin' us our share. Then the timetable breaks down."

There is a knock at the door—but instead of Johnny and the cash, it is Val and one of his mobsters. They force their way into the room, expecting to grab the swag for themselves. George opens fire, and a shoot-out ensues that leaves everyone in the room dead—except for George, who is mortally wounded. For a moment Kubrick's hand-held camera lingers on the corpses spread across the room, recalling the clump of mannequins in the climactic sequence of *Killer's Kiss*. The room is silent, except for the sound of bouncy Latin music pouring out of the radio, providing an ironic counterpoint to the carnage of the scene. It has been quite a killing.

Kubrick uses the subjective camera at crucial moments in the picture, in order to remind the filmgoer in the course of the movie that the story is being told from the subjective point of view of various characters. Kubrick employs the subjective camera in the scene immediately following the massacre in the apartment: the fatally wounded George Peatty has enough life left in him to struggle toward the door. The camera, which now assumes his point of view, sways with him in the direction of the door; George's hand enters the frame to twist the knob, the camera's unsteady movements implying that his life is ebbing away.

Johnny has just pulled up outside; the subjective camera now assumes Clay's point of view. The camera peers over Johnny's shoulder, as he watches George come out of the building, sprawl across the hood of Johnny's car, pull himself together, and force himself to continue across the street, where he gets into his own car and drives away. Johnny is dismayed to see Peatty's bloody face, since it telegraphs to him that something has gone horribly wrong.

As we cut to George once more, he is moving with the determination of a man who knows he must accomplish something before he takes his last breath. Once home, he finds Sherry packing to go away with Val, as he suspected he would. "Why did you do it?" he asks plaintively, already knowing the answer. "I love you, Sherry." He then blasts away with his pistol, the impotent husband finally penetrating his wife with bullets. Barry Gifford notes, "Marie Windsor is, as always, the big-breasted blonde who falls for the wrong

13

guy"—in this case, Val.[11] As George himself falls forward toward the camera, he knocks over the birdcage, symbol of his pitifully narrow, constricted existence, which is now at an end. Sherry too has expired; she learned too late that the worm had finally turned.

Although she appeared in only a few scenes in *The Killing*, the part of Sherry Peatty proved the most significant role of Marie Windsor's career. In this regard, Windsor exemplifies the fact that the size of a part does not matter, if one is under the direction of an expert director like Stanley Kubrick. Her riveting portrayal of Sherry Peatty won her a place in film history as a quintessential femme fatale of film noir.

Johnny, aware that something terrible has happened, drives to the San Francisco airport to meet Fay as planned. En route he buys the largest suitcase he can find and stashes the loot in it. He finds Fay and they proceed to the check-in counter. With nervous nonchalance Johnny demands that the airline allow him to lug his huge suitcase on board with him, rather than stow it in the

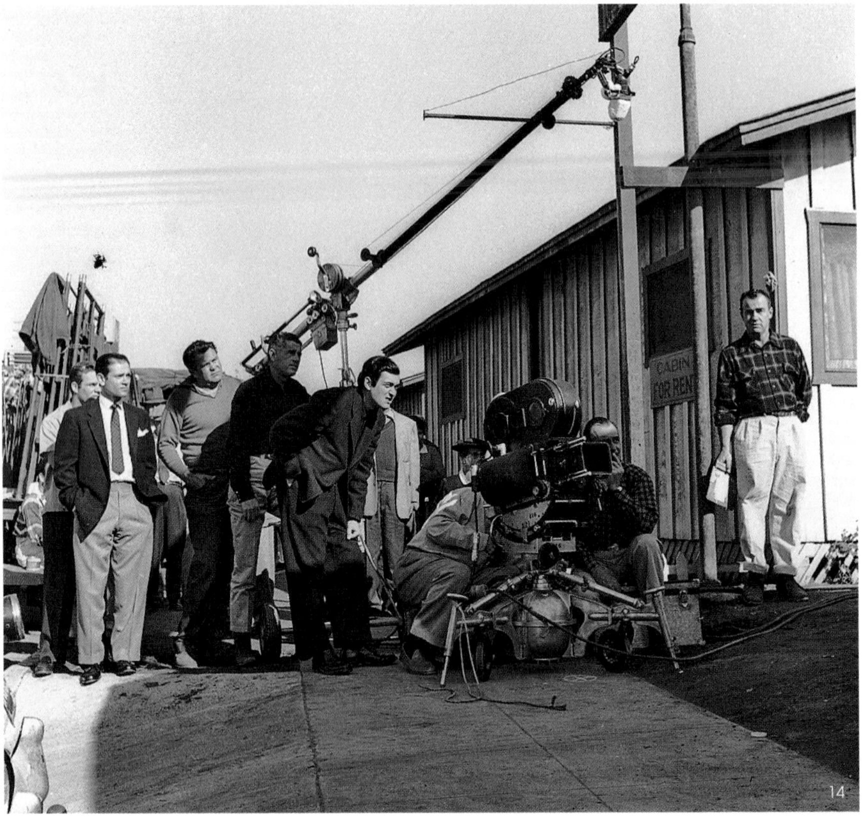

luggage compartment. Throughout his bickering with the airline personnel, which Kubrick records in a single take, the bulky bag stands inertly in the center of the frame, as Johnny futilely attempts to minimize its size.

The scene begins to take on the flavor of the kind of black comedy that will appear in *Dr. Strangelove,* as the obliging clerk suggests that Johnny consider insuring his bag. "If you just give me its estimated value and tell me what's in it," he says with unintentional irony, "we'd be delighted (to insure it)." Realizing that he is causing a scene, Johnny capitulates and watches apprehensively as the bag is casually tossed onto a conveyor belt and disappears from sight.

Johnny and Fay arrive at the departure gate just in time to see the baggage truck drive out onto the windy tarmac. They watch in mute horror as the rickety

14 ***Producer James B. Harris, left, watches as Kubrick directs.***
15 ***Timothy Carey, center, who played the role of gunman Nikki, was cast as Private Feral in Kubrick's next film,* Paths of Glory.**

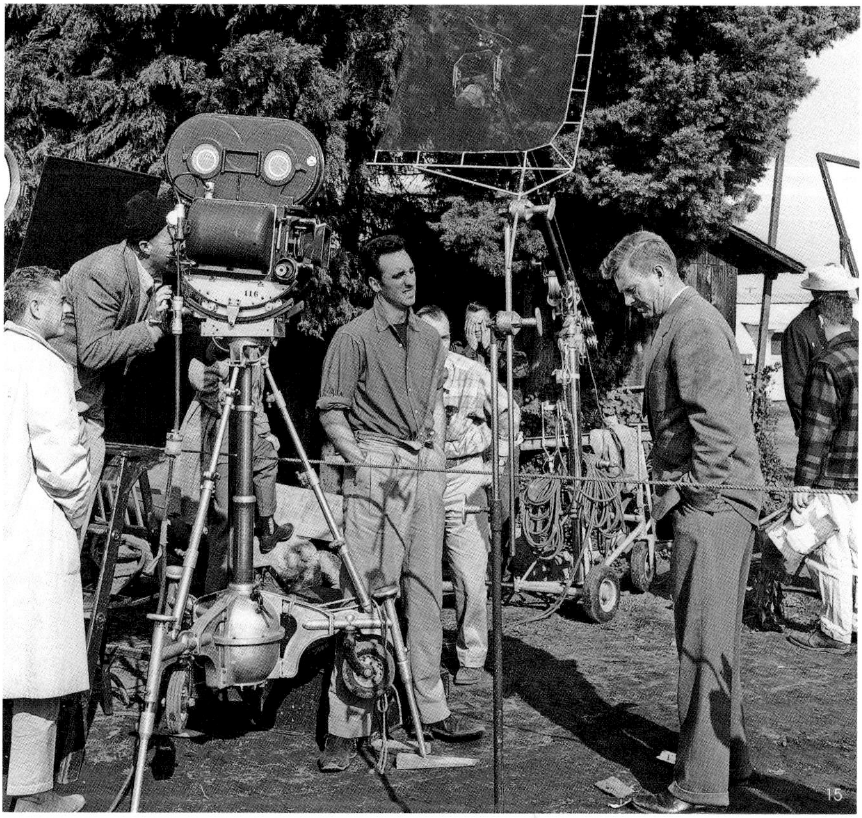

suitcase falls from the baggage truck; the $2 million take is winnowed in aircraft slipstream, flooding the airstrip with stolen bills that blow right at the camera. The fate of the money in *The Killing* recalls how the gold dust in John Huston's *Treasure of Sierra Madre* (1948) blows across the desert sands. In that film the men who had slaved to acquire the gold can only laugh hysterically when they contemplate how it drifted away from them.

But Fay and Johnny are in a daze. She supports his arm as they walk to the street and hopelessly try to hail a taxi before the two FBI agents, who have been watching them all along, can reach them. Resigned to their fate, Johnny and Fay turn resolutely around to face the two men advancing toward them through the glass doors of the flight lounge.

Working out of the grand noir tradition, Kubrick managed in *The Killing* to give a new twist to the story of a man trapped by events he cannot control. The defeat of Johnny and his cohorts, comments Andrew Dickos, "leaves these outsiders with the inevitable negation of their dreams—dreams that they could not buy."[12]

Like Davy and Gloria in *Killer's Kiss*, Johnny and Fay had hoped to escape the corrosive atmosphere of the big city by flight to a cleaner climate. But for Johnny, brutalized by a life of crime, it was already too late.

Surprisingly, most of the film was shot on studio sets, except the exteriors at the track, on the street, and at the airport. Even with the biggest budget of his career to date, Kubrick had to work quickly and economically to bring the film within budget. "During shooting," Harris said, "there was an air of resentment all around us," since there were not very many producers and directors in their twenties working in Hollywood at the time. "Stanley had his own ideas how things were to go, and people resented his encroaching on their contributions."[13]

Because of union regulations, Kubrick could no longer act as his own director of photography, and so veteran cinematographer Lucien Ballard (*Laura*) was engaged to shoot the film. Occasionally friction developed between director and cameraman when they disagreed on how a shot should be set up. Alexander Singer recalls a disagreement between Kubrick and Ballard on *The Killing* in Jan Harlan's documentary.

According to Singer, who was the associate producer of the film, Ballard resented this young director from New York. "The first day on the set," says Singer, "Stanley set up a long, complex tracking shot built around a meeting of Johnny and his accomplices; then he turned it over to Ballard to do the camera setup. When Stanley returned to the set, he found that Ballard had set the camera further back from the action than he wanted." Ballard explained that he pulled the camera way back to a long shot because he preferred to use a 50 mm lens instead of the 25 mm lens that Kubrick had chosen, since it would cause less distortion. Kubrick "realized that Ballard was bullying him," says Singer. So Kubrick quietly told him to put the camera where it was and to use the 25 mm lens "or get off my set and don't come back." Singer concludes, "Ballard changed the camera setup the way that Stanley wanted it, and there was never an argument again."

A mutual respect eventually developed between Kubrick and Ballard, however. Kubrick, after all, was one of the few movie directors who belonged to the cinematographer's union and who sometimes operated his own camera when making a film. In fact, Jeremy Bernstein noticed while *2001* was in production a decade later that Kubrick often took Polaroid shots of a camera setup in order to check lighting effects with the cinematographer, Geoffrey Unsworth. "I asked if it was customary for movie directors to participate so actively in photographing a film," Bernstein records, "and he said succinctly that he never watched any other directors work."[14]

Because Kubrick commanded a bigger budget on this film than on any of his previous movies, this time around, Gerald Fried, Kubrick's usual composer, had a forty-piece orchestra at his disposal. The pulsating theme for the opening credits, comments David Wishart, "both elicits the hustle and bustle of the racetrack" and grimly foreshadows the violent outcome of the caper "with urgently etched staccato tones."[15] Fried was particularly happy with his use of the bellowing, brassy horns in the main title music, which gave the music "a forward thrust," he says. "The movie had gotten started and, like a runaway train, it just never lets up."[16] Among the musicians in the orchestra Fried conducted for the film was the pianist André Previn, whose many film scores also include *Elmer Gantry* (1960).

During post-production, Harris told Jill Bernstein, "We edited the film the way the script was written." Many people said they thought the flashbacks would irritate people. They held a sneak preview in Los Angeles, "with the usual walkouts by filmgoers not interested in a crime picture." Afterward Sterling Hayden's agent, Bill Schifrin, complained to Kubrick that the fragmentary structure of the flashbacks had made hash of his client's performance, and ruefully warned that the film, if released in its present form, would damage Hayden's career. Schifrin's remarks implied a threat of litigation, Harris feared. "If enough people tell you you're sick, maybe you should lie down."

So, Harris continued, "Stanley and I went back to New York, rented an editing room," and, before delivering the picture to United Artists, "broke the whole thing down and started over." When they put all the scenes in chronological order and eliminated all of the flashbacks, they looked at each other and said, "This stinks." After all, it was the handling of time through the use of flashbacks, Kubrick maintained, "that made *The Killing* more than just a routine crime film." Consequently, Harris recalled, "We put it back the way we had had it."

Asked by Jill Bernstein how UA reacted to the film, Harris replied that only one person was present when they screened the picture for UA's Max Youngstein. When the screening was over, Youngstein said, "Good job. Let's keep in touch." Kubrick and Harris had to follow him down the hall to inquire, "Where do we go from here?" Youngstein replied, "What about out the door?" Kubrick then asked, "You have other producer-filmmaker teams. Where would you rate us with all of those people?" Youngstein answered, "Not far from the bottom." Harris concluded, "We never forgot that." Still, "Stanley had absolute awareness of his own talent. He knew he was doing good work."[17]

In fact, *The Killing* has since earned the reputation of a classic film noir and, quite contrary to Schifrin's warnings, gained praise for Hayden's performance. Pauline Kael says in *Going Steady* that robbery pictures tend to be terribly derivative of earlier robbery movies; Kael clearly has *The Killing* in mind when she writes that it is still possible for a director to bring a fresh approach to the project, "to present the occupational details of crime accurately (or convincingly), to assemble the gang so that we get a sense of the kinds of people engaged in crime and what their professional and non-professional lives are like. A good crime movie generally has a sordid, semi-documentary authenticity about criminal activities," she goes on, "plus the nervous excitement of what it might be like to rob and tangle with the law." She sees *The Killing*, in essence, as "an expert suspense film, with fast, incisive cutting, and furtive little touches of characterization."[18] *Time* applauded Kubrick, when the film was released, for showing "more imagination with dialogue and camera than Hollywood has seen since the obstreperous Orson Welles went riding out of town."[19]

"It was a profitable picture for UA," Kubrick told me, "and this is the only measure of success in financial terms." But no new offers were immediately forthcoming

"Jim Harris and I were the only ones at the time who weren't worried about fragmenting time, overlapping and repeating action that had already been seen, showing things again and again from another character's point of view.... It was the handling of time that may have made this more than just a good crime film."

— SK/1971 (to Alexander Walker)

from any Hollywood studio to Kubrick and Harris as a production team, perhaps because word had gotten out that Youngstein had not liked the complex use of flashbacks in the movie any more than Hayden's agent had. Harris-Kubrick then acquired the rights to Humphrey Cobb's 1935 novel about World War I, *Paths of Glory*.

Before Kubrick got started on the script for his next venture, Jim Thompson came knocking on his door to complain that he was listed in the credits of *The Killing* as having only written the dialogue, and not as co-author of the screenplay. Since Thompson had looked upon his collaboration on *The Killing* as his path into the film industry, he complained to the Writers Guild about his credit on the picture. The Guild ruled that Thompson deserved compensation, so Kubrick hired him to work on *Paths of Glory*, along with another writer, Calder Willingham, with co-author's status at a salary of $500 a week.

Because Kubrick has been criticized by Terry Southern and other screenwriters at various times for his "cavalier" treatment of writers, Woody Haut testifies on his behalf in his essay on Jim Thompson that Kubrick and Harris had been kind to Thompson. Because of Thompson's ongoing battle with alcoholism, he had trouble finding work in Hollywood. So Kubrick and Harris "introduced him to their New York agent, advanced money to the writer and supported him through 1959."[20] Meanwhile Thompson was co-authoring with Kubrick and Willingham the script for one of the most uncompromising war films ever made.

16 ***Kubrick using his viewfinder to frame a shot of Marie Windsor and Vince Edwards.***

Notes

1. Vincent LoBrutto, *Stanley Kubrick: A Biography* (New York: Da Capo, 1999): 110.
2. Peter Bogdanovich, "What They Say about Stanley Kubrick," *The New York Times Magazine* (July 4, 1999): 21.
3. Arthur Lyons, *Death on the Cheap: Film Noir and the Low-Budget Film* (New York: Da Capo, 2001): 9–10.
4. Paul Schrader, "Notes on Noir," in *Film Noir Reader*, ed. Alain Silver and James Ursini (New York: Limelight, 1998): 58–59.
5. Foster Hirsch, *The Dark Side of the Screen: Film Noir* (New York: Da Capo, 2001): 139.
6. Edward Buscombe, "The Killing," in *The BFI Companion to Crime*, ed. Phil Hardy (Los Angeles: University of California Press, 1997): 192.
7. Bogdanovich: 21.
8. Ibid.
9. Gene D. Phillips, "Sterling Hayden," in *The Encyclopedia of Stanley Kubrick*, with Rodney Hill (New York: Checkmark, 2002): 153.
10. Alexander Walker, *Stanley Kubrick: Director* (New York: Norton, 1999): 52.
11. Barry Gifford, *Out of the Past: Adventures in Film Noir* (Jackson: University Press of Mississippi, 2001): 100.
12. Andrew Dickos, *Street with No Name: A History of American Film Noir* (Lexington: University Press of Kentucky, 2002): 202.
13. Paul Zimmerman, "Kubrick's Brilliant Vision," *Newsweek* (January 3, 1972): 78.
14. Jeremy Bernstein, "Profile: Stanley Kubrick," in *Stanley Kubrick: Interviews*, ed. Gene D. Phillips (Jackson: University Press of Mississippi, 2001): 42.
15. David Wishart, CD liner notes from *Music from the Films of Stanley Kubrick* (New York: Silva Screen Records, 1999): 6.
16. Gerald Fried, *Music from the Films of Stanley Kubrick*: 10.
17. Jill Bernstein et al., "Stanley Kubrick: A Cinematic Odyssey," *Premiere* (August, 1999): 86.
18. Pauline Kael, *Going Steady* (New York: Boyers, 1994): 183.
19. "The Killing," *Time* (June 4, 1956): 99.
20. Woody Haut, *Heartbreak and Vine: Hardboiled Writers in Hollywood* (London: Serpent's Tail, 2002): 125.

Paths of Glory

1957 / BLACK AND WHITE / 87 MINUTES
Distributed by UNITED ARTISTS

CAST
COLONEL DAX KIRK DOUGLAS
GENERAL BROULARD ADOLPHE MENJOU
GENERAL MIREAU GEORGE MACREADY
CORPORAL PARIS RALPH MEEKER
LIEUTENANT ROGET WAYNE MORRIS
MAJOR SAINT-AUBAN RICHARD ANDERSON
PRIVATE ARNAUD JOSEPH TURKEL
PRIVATE FERAL TIMOTHY CAREY
GERMAN GIRL SUSANNE CHRISTIAN
TAVERN OWNER JERRY HAUSNER
COLONEL JUDGE PETER CAPELL
PRIEST EMILE MEYER
SERGEANT BOULANGER BERT FREED
PRIVATE LEJEUNE KEM DIBBS
CAPTAIN ROUSSEAU JOHN STEIN
CAPTAIN NICHOLS HAROLD BENEDICT
SHELL-SHOCKED SOLDIER FRED BELL

CREW
DIRECTED BY STANLEY KUBRICK
PRODUCED BY JAMES B. HARRIS
SCREENPLAY STANLEY KUBRICK, CALDER WILLINGHAM, and JIM THOMPSON (based on the novel *Paths of Glory* by Humphrey Cobb)
EDITOR EVA KROLL
DIRECTOR OF PHOTOGRAPHY GEORGE KRAUSE
UNIT MANAGER HELMUT RINGELMANN
ASSISTANT DIRECTORS H. STUMPF, D. SENSBURG, E. SPIEKER
COSTUME DESIGNER ISLE DUHOIS
SPECIAL EFFECTS ERWIN LANGE
MILITARY ADVISER BARON V. WALDENFELS
MAKEUP ARTHUR SCHRAMRN
ORIGINAL MUSIC GERALD FRIED
ART DIRECTOR LUDWIG REIBER
CAMERA OPERATOR HANNES STAUDINGER
AMERICAN PRODUCTION MANAGER JOHN POMMER
GERMAN PRODUCTION MANAGER GEORGE VON BLOCK

Produced at Bavaria Filmkunst Studios, Munich.

Opposite *French poster designed by Jouineau Bourduge for the 1976 release of* Paths of Glory, *which was banned in France until 1974 because of its unfavorable depiction of the French military.*

UN FILM DE
STANLEY KUBRICK
LES
SENTIERS
DE LA
GLOIRE
Jouneau Bourduge
KIRK DOUGLAS DANS LES SENTIERS DE LA GLOIRE
"PATHS OF GLORY"
AVEC RALPH MEEKER · ADOLPHE MENJOU · GEORGE MACREADY · WAYNE MORRIS · RICHARD ANDERSON
SCENARIO DE STANLEY KUBRICK, CALDER WILLINGHAM ET JIM THOMPSON D'APRES LA NOUVELLE DE HUMPHREY COBB · RÉALISE PAR STANLEY KUBRICK
PRODUIT PAR JAMES B. HARRIS · UNE PRODUCTION BRYNA · DISTRIBUE PAR
INTERDIT AUX MOINS DE 13 ANS

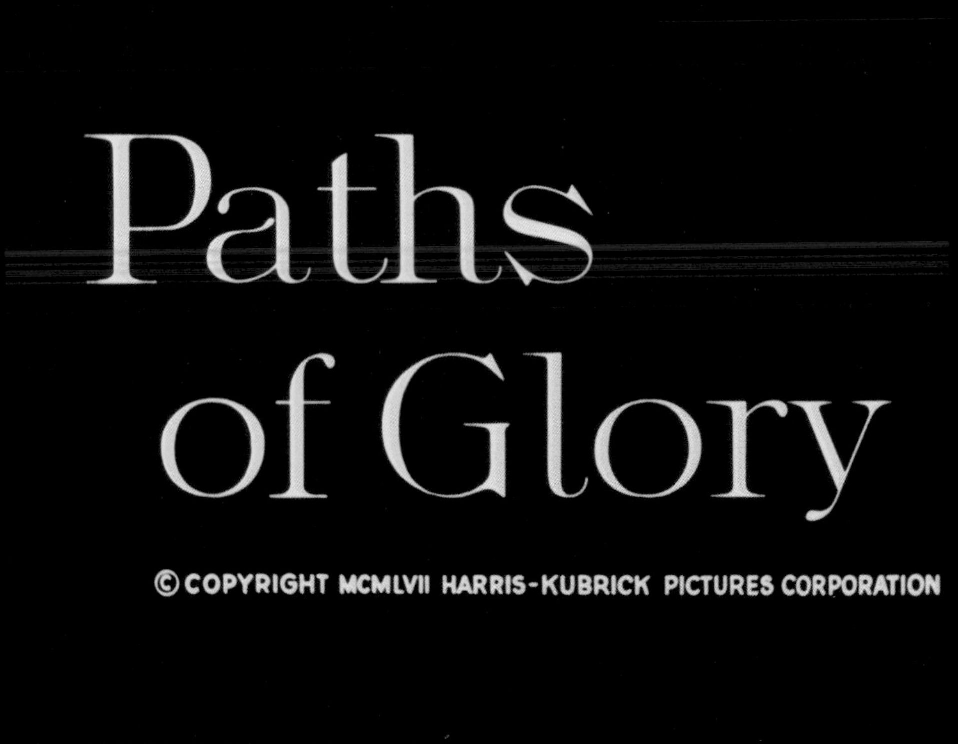
Paths
of Glory
© COPYRIGHT MCMLVII HARRIS-KUBRICK PICTURES CORPORATION

701

40 30 20 10 0 10 20 30 40

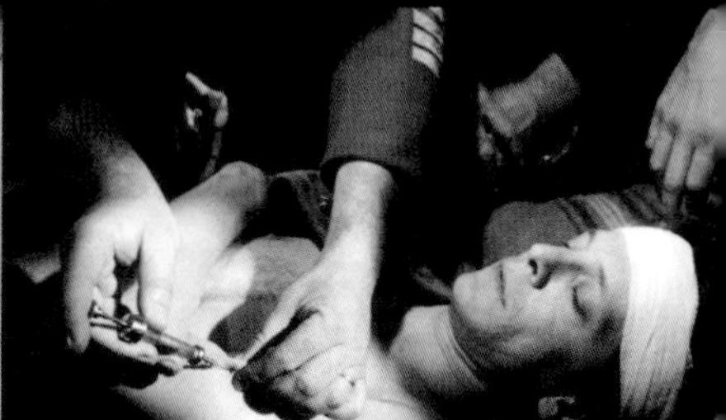

701

Paths of Glory

by Gene D. Phillips

No major studio showed interest in financing *Paths of Glory* (1957), "not because it was an anti-war film about World War I," Kubrick told me, "they just didn't like it." Then Kirk Douglas became interested in playing the lead and United Artists agreed to back the project for $935,000—despite production chief Max Youngstein's brush-off of Kubrick and James B. Harris after *The Killing*. Douglas was, after all, a superstar who would be a calling card at the box office. This was still not a big budget by studio standards, but it was a princely sum compared to the budgets Kubrick had previously worked with. One of the star's stipulations for appearing in the movie was that the film be produced under the banner of Douglas's independent production unit, Bryna Productions. Kubrick pointed out, however, that "although we had to give Bryna a production credit, it had nothing whatsoever to do with the making or financing of the film."

The title of the story is a reference to Thomas Gray's poem "Elegy Written in a Country Churchyard," in which the poet remarks that the "Paths of Glory lead but to the grave." It becomes increasingly clear as the film progresses that the "paths of glory" that the irresponsible French generals are pursuing lead not to their graves but to the graves of the enlisted men, who are decreed to die in the battles that are fought according to strategies which the commanding officers manipulate for their own self-advancement.

01 ***Kubrick watches the actors perform with his characteristic look of concentration.***

Jim Thompson, who had worked on the screenplay for *The Killing*, wrote the first draft of the script. Following the novel, Humphrey Cobb's *Paths of Glory* (1935), Thompson relegated Colonel Dax, Douglas's role, to the status of a marginal character in the action. That, of course, did not sit well with Douglas. Kubrick accordingly brought in Calder Willingham, who worked with him on a second draft that amplified Dax's role in the script. Kubrick continued to revise the script during shooting, as always, so his influence on the screenplay was considerable. However, enough of Thompson's dialogue from his first draft survived in the shooting script for the Writers' Guild to rule that the screen credit "should go to Kubrick, Willingham, and Thompson in that order."[1]

Kubrick shot the movie at the Bavaria Filmkunst Studios in Munich, since making a film that gave an unflattering picture of the French high command in France was out of the question. His two principal location sites, the battlefield and the château where the French officers have set up their general headquarters, were about half an hour's drive away from the studio. Kubrick chose a German palace called Schloss Schleissheim to stand in for the French château in the movie. The director's budget allowed him to assemble as fine a supporting cast as he had for *The Killing*, notably George Macready as the neurotic General Mireau and Adolphe Menjou as General Broulard, the commander of the French forces.

When Kubrick asked the sixty-eight-year-old actor to play General Broulard, Menjou hesitated to do so. As a graduate of a military academy, a veteran of World

War I, and a political conservative, he was chary about appearing in an anti-war film. But Kubrick convinced him that his part would dominate the picture. Kubrick even advised Menjou that Broulard was a good general who does his best in trying to cope with the pressures of command. In fact, Broulard's character is a sly and crafty officer who manipulates his subordinates to his own advantage, but Kubrick knew that if Menjou saw Broulard in this light, he would not have accepted the part. So Kubrick provided Menjou only with the pages of the script in which he had dialogue.

The story has been told that during shooting Menjou grew impatient with Kubrick's desire for several retakes on a scene and became angry when the director insisted on doing the scene yet another time, after Menjou felt he had already given his best reading. In fact, Menjou exploded and made some condescending references to the twenty-nine-year-old director's inexperience "in the art of directing actors." Kubrick listened in courteous silence and then explained in measured tones, "It isn't right, and we are going to keep doing it until it is right; and we will get it right, because you guys are good!" (Addressing the distinguished cast of the picture as "you guys" is a reminder that all his life, Kubrick unconsciously employed the slang he grew up with in the Bronx.) By this time Menjou's anger had abated, and he went on with the scene.[2]

When I asked Kubrick about this incident, he said that a filmmaker must do the number of takes required to get a scene as close to perfect as possible. He believed that "the filmmaker must bear in mind that he has to live with a film for the rest of his life, once he has made it." If the director cuts corners or makes compromises just to avoid conflict on the set, he concluded, "it's still your film to live with for the rest of your days."

For his part, Menjou admitted after completing the picture that Kubrick reminded him of Charles Chaplin, who directed the actor in *A Woman of Paris* (1923), because, like Chaplin, Kubrick always took into consideration the actor's suggestions while working out a scene. But—like Chaplin—Kubrick believed that the director should have the final say. Besides Menjou, Kubrick also experienced difficulties with Douglas, who had the ego of a major star. "Kirk was pretty dictatorial at times," Harris recalled for Jill Bernstein, "but Stanley earned people's respect, and Kirk could tell that Stanley knew what he was doing."[3]

By contrast, George Macready got on well with Kubrick. Macready, trained in the theater, had a resonant voice that was perfect for the role of the power-hungry General Mireau. Furthermore, he had a scar on his right cheek, sustained in an auto accident. Kubrick had the make-up artist accentuate the scar on Macready's face to make Mireau look all the more menacing.

02–03, 09 ***Pages from Kubrick's working script, marked with his notes and sketches.***

RETURN TO S. KUBRICK
BAYER HOF —
1000M REWARD

P A T H S   O F   G L O R Y

Screenplay by

Stanley Kubrick, Jim Thompson

and

[Calder Willingham]

(Third Draft)
Feb.25,1957

Property of Harris-Kubrick Pictures Corporation

BAVARIA FILM KUNST
GEISELGASTEIG

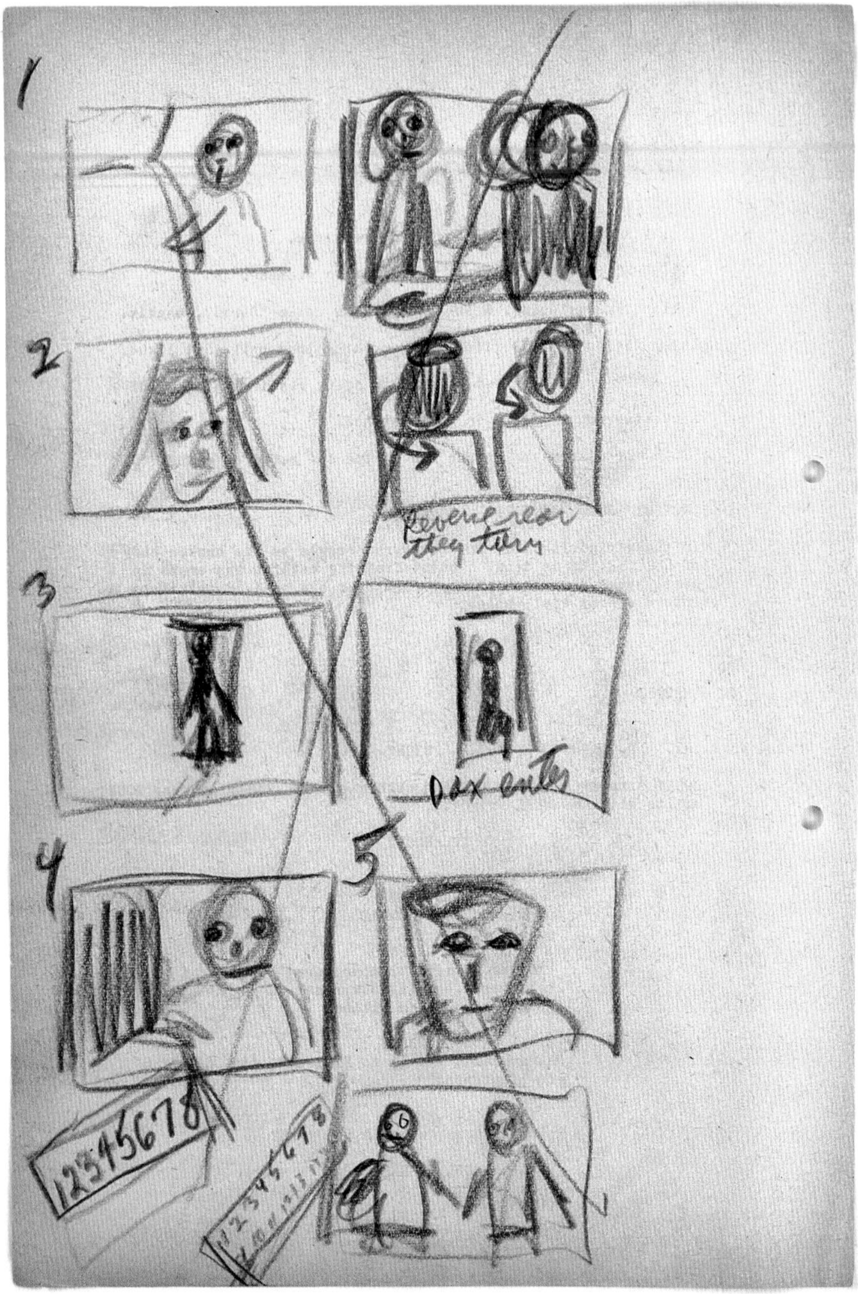
1
2
3
4
5
12345678

For the part of the young German girl that sings to the French troops at the end of the film, Kubrick cast the woman that was to become his wife. Born Christiane Susanne Harlan, she used the stage name of Susanne Christian. "Stanley got his first glimpse of me acting in a German television play in Munich," while he was shooting *Paths of Glory*, she told me in conversation, and he immediately wanted to use her for the role.

The opening credits are accompanied by "La Marseillaise," the French national anthem, played in a foreboding minor key, followed by the pulsating sound of military snare drums. (When the French government subsequently protested the use of their anthem in a film which it considered to be anti-French, a percussion track was substituted for the French national anthem in countries particularly sympathetic to France.)

The novel is divided into three parts: before the attack, the attack itself, and its aftermath, the court-martial and execution. Kubrick followed the tripartite division of the story in his film adaptation of the book. As Anthony Ambrogio notes, Kubrick's film, "true to its source," follows the Aristotelian unities "of action, time, and place; it has a constant, driving rhythm."[4]

The film proper begins with a title: "France, 1916." It is superimposed on a shot of the grand château where French army officers live in luxury whilst the soldiers die amid the mud and the barbed wire of the trenches. Kubrick employs a narrator to set the scene for the audience, as he had in *The Killing*: "War began between Germany and France on August 3, 1914. By 1916, after two years of grisly trench warfare, the battle lines had changed very little. Successful attacks were measured in hundreds of yards—and paid for in lives by hundreds of thousands."

While this commentary is being spoken, a squad of soldiers takes its place in two columns at the front door of the château and an open car drives in the front gate, stopping at the door, where General Broulard gets out. The handsome general's elegant manner belies his callous and ruthless nature.

"Harris and I were looking for a story. I remembered a book by Humphrey Cobb that I had read when I was fifteen and which had made an impression on me, not because of its literary qualities but because of the troubling and tragic situation of three of its characters—three innocent soldiers accused of cowardice and mutiny who were executed to set an example."

— SK/1957 (to Raymond Haine/*Cahiers du Cinéma*)

Broulard seems to belong to the sumptuous setting that the château provides as he lounges in an ornate chair and toys with the ambitious General Mireau's barely concealed hopes for a promotion. With the most adroit coaxing, Broulard is able to manipulate Mireau into agreeing to launch what amounts to a suicidal charge on an impossibly fortified enemy stronghold called the Ant Hill as the first step in an all-out offensive.

The charming, corrupt Broulard patronizes Mireau with compliments, with a view to cajoling him into leading his troops to disaster. Then Broulard gets down to cases, telling Mireau that he has a task he is confident that Mireau can handle for him. Mireau at first hesitates when he hears about the contemplated onslaught on the Ant Hill. Broulard needles him where he is most vulnerable, by promising him the promotion he has longed for if the attack succeeds. Having displayed token concern for his men, Mireau finally agrees to the Ant Hill attack; for, after all, it is not he but Colonel Dax who will have to mount the actual attack.

Mireau marches through the trenches on his way to inform Dax of his mission, stopping awkwardly to buck up the troops' spirits as he passes by. He is oblivious to the squalor in which they live, an ugly contrast to the splendor of the château he has just left. It is a matter of record that the trenches used in World War I, like

04

those in the film, were laid with wooden planks which served as a floor. Kubrick was consequently able to wheel his camera down the length of an entire trench just ahead of George Macready, thereby getting the whole scene in a single, unbroken take.

When he gets to Dax's shabby quarters, which are no better than those of his men, Mireau informs Dax that his men are to take the Ant Hill the following morning. Unlike Mireau, Dax manifests genuine concern for the likely death toll of his men in such an undertaking; but Mireau bullies him into accepting the assignment. Finally Dax capitulates; "If any soldiers in the world can take it, we'll take the Ant Hill." "And when you do," Mireau adds with a flourish, "your men will ... get a long rest."

Just before the battle is to begin, Mireau scans the Ant Hill through his binoculars, which is as close as he and his fellow generals ever get to the field of battle. He speaks enthusiastically of victory. Dax now makes the same journey from one end of the trench to the other that we watched Mireau make earlier, and the contrast is striking. As Kubrick's camera dollies through the trench, sometimes facing Dax as the colonel gives reassuring glances to his men, sometimes looking ahead of Dax, showing his apprehensive troops making way for him to pass down the narrow corridor opening before him, it is abundantly clear that there is a mutual respect between officer and men of which there was no hint when Mireau made his earlier tour. Long, fluid shots such as these reveal Kubrick's mastery of techniques he had begun to experiment with in *The Killing* and which would evolve to his "signature" tracking shots, notably in films such as *2001, A Clockwork Orange,* and *The Shining.*

Peter Cowie has written in *Seventy Years of Cinema* that Kubrick employs the camera in the film "unflinchingly, like a weapon" — darting into close-up to capture the indignation on Dax's face, sweeping across the slopes to record the wholesale massacre of a division, or advancing relentlessly at eye level toward the stakes against which the condemned men will be shot.[5]

Kubrick's deft handling of the camera is exemplified in the battle scene that is the center of the movie. When Dax leads his troops into battle, Kubrick shows the men pouring onto the battlefield in a high overhead shot of an entire line of soldiers, which reaches from one end of the screen to the other. Then he shifts to a side view of the troops sweeping across the slopes toward enemy lines. Prior to shooting this sequence, Kubrick spent several days preparing the landscape for the assault by planting explosives, creating bomb craters, placing tangles of barbed wire all over the terrain, and making it look like what one critic called "the rim of hell." On the day that the battle was filmed, the director had six cameras placed at strategic points along the attack route, while he himself used a hand-held camera with a zoom lens to zero in on Kirk Douglas and record his

04 ***Kubrick and Douglas on the set during shooting of the scene in which Colonel Dax interrupts General Broulard's festivities to inform him of Mireau's order for his troops to shoot at their own men.***

05

reactions to what was happening around him. These shots of Douglas draw the filmgoer into the battle scenes in a way that mere panoramic shots of the battlefield could never have done.

The German extras in French uniforms were actually members of the police force. Kubrick assigned various groups of extras to die in different sectors of the battlefield and told them to fall, whenever possible, near an explosion. Watching the battle as it plays on the screen, one can see that Kubrick's German policemen played the battle scene with great gusto.

Indeed, the effect of all of Kubrick's long-term preparation for the battle sequence is stunning. As bombs explode overhead and shrapnel cascades down on the troops, they crouch, run, and crawl forward, falling in and out of shell holes, stumbling over the corpses of comrades long since dead. The director intercuts close-ups of Dax, a whistle clamped between his teeth, as he sees his men dying on all sides of him and observes the attack turn into a rout and a retreat.

By this time Dax has made it back to the French lines and commands Lieutenant Roget (Wayne Morris) to get the remainder of the men out of the trenches and onto the field. But Roget balks at this, since the retreat is already in progress. As Dax climbs up the ladder out of the trench, exhorting the men to renew their courage and follow him, he is thrown backward into a trench by the body of a French soldier rolling in on top of him. This shot provides

05–07 ***Studio portraits of Adolphe Menjou as General Broulard, Kirk Douglas as Colonel Dax, and George Macready as General Mireau.***

one of the many visual ironies that punctuate the movie.

Mireau searches the horizon with his field glasses for the troops who are supposed to constitute the next wave of the attack "They're still in the trenches! ... Miserable cowards!" He orders Captain Rousseau (John Stein), the battery commander, over the field telephone to fire on the men who are still in the trenches. "The troops are mutinying," the mad general maintains, "by refusing to advance." Captain Rousseau respectfully contends that he cannot carry out the order unless he receives it in writing. Mireau screams at Rousseau in a fury and slams down the receiver.

Mireau is informed that the attack has failed all along the line. His eyes blaze, and light falls across the scar on his face, suggesting a mutilated personality. He roars apoplectically that he will convene a general court-martial for 3 p.m. "If those little sweethearts won't face German bullets, they will face French ones from a firing squad!"

Afterward Dax must stand by while three of his soldiers are picked almost at random from the ranks to be court-martialed and executed for desertion of duty, as an "example" to the rest of the men for failing to attack the enemy

08 ***Kirk Douglas poses with Susanne Christian, a. k. a. Christiane Susanne Harlan, the young actress who would soon become Kubrick's wife and lifelong partner.***

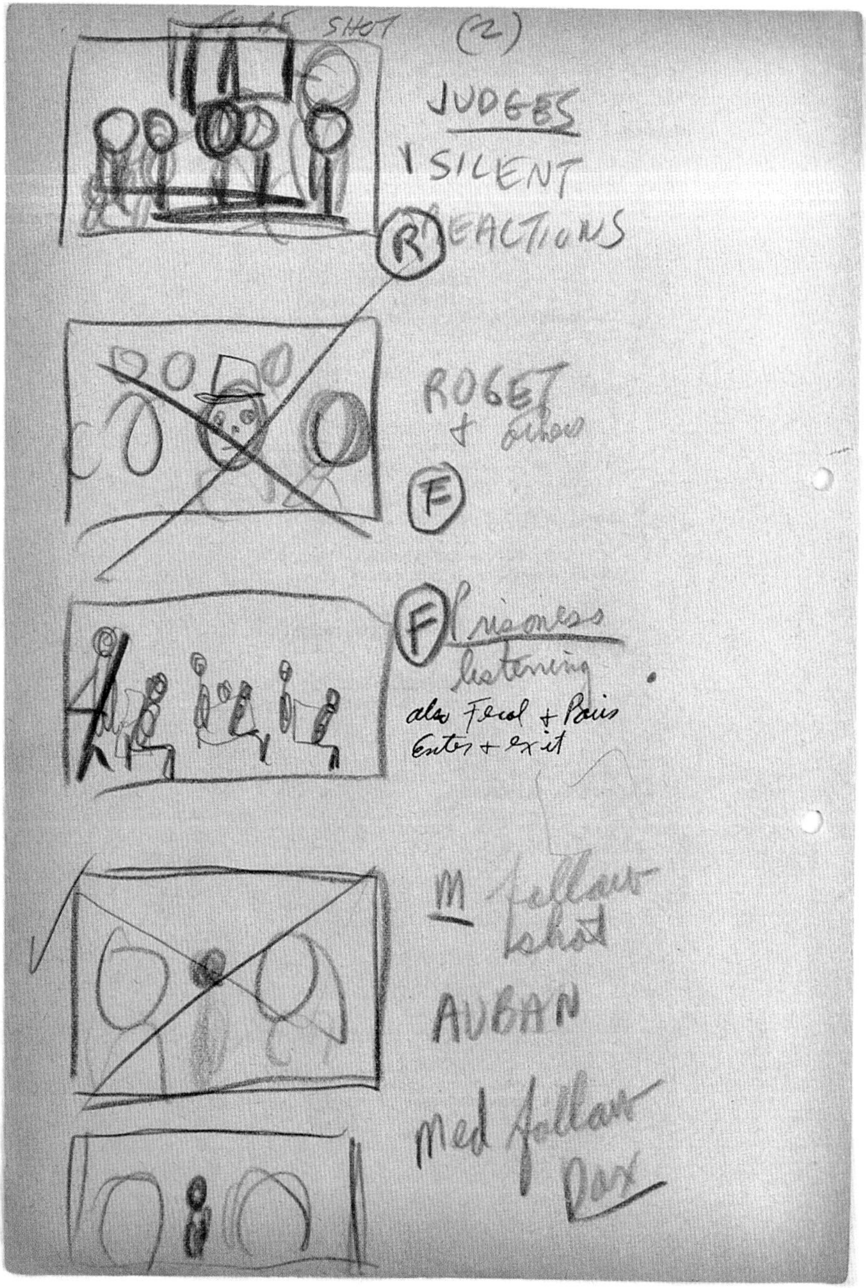
SHOT (2)
JUDGES
SILENT
REACTIONS
R
ROGET
F
F Prisoners
listening
M follow
shot
AUBAN
Med follow
Dax

stronghold as Mireau had commanded. Dax requests, and is given, the task of defending the accused at the trial.

The court-martial proceedings take place in the ornate ballroom of the château. The checkered pattern on the highly polished floor makes the room look like a gigantic chessboard, underscoring the feeling that the three defendants are but pawns in the power plays of their superior officers. Dax vehemently protests the fact that the three defendants were chosen arbitrarily. The president of the court-martial, who addresses Dax as if he were a recalcitrant schoolboy, reminds the defense attorney that it is accepted practice in the French army to choose one enlisted man by lot to serve as an example for the rest of the soldiers. Since not one of the troops succeeded in reaching the German lines, any man who was so chosen could be convicted fairly. The towering illogic of these remarks leaves Dax stunned.

Although some film critics questioned whether or not French officers could be so cruel, Tom Wicker testifies in his essay on films about World War I that the story is "based on an actual Great War incident." *Paths of Glory,* which he believes is the

10 ***This publicity still shows Colonel Dax hurdling dead bodies in the trench during the attack on the Ant Hill.***
11 ***Ralph Meeker as Corporal Paris.***

best film ever made about World War I, is "another true story of individual lives sacrificed to a commander's or a nation's vanity and indifference to justice and humanity."[6] Wicker's remarks are quite in harmony with Dax's defense of the defendants.

"Films deal with the emotions and reflect the fragmentation of experience. It is thus misleading to try to sum up the meaning of a film verbally."

— SK/1959 (to Colin Young/*Film Quarterly*)

When Dax sums up his case, he moves back and forth with his hands in his pockets, as if thinking out loud. The camera is shooting from behind the three prisoners so that they dominate the frame, and Dax can be seen between them. This composition implies that it is concern for them that is in the forefront of Dax's consciousness, and not the favor of his superior officers before whom he is pleading his case.

"There are times when I'm ashamed to be a member of the human race, and this is one such occasion," he begins. "I protest that the prosecution presented no witnesses and no stenographic record of this trial was kept. The attack is no stain on the honor of France; but this court martial *is* such a stain." At this point, the camera is slightly below Dax, shooting up at him in a way that makes his figure more imposing as he finishes his statement: "Gentlemen, to find these men guilty would be a crime to haunt each of you until the day you die. I can't believe that the noblest impulse in man, his compassion for another, can be completely dead here. Therefore I humbly beg you to show mercy to these men."

"The film's anti-war message," Mario Falsetto points out in his Kubrick book, "clearly has its source in Cobb's novel." He further observes that Col. Dax cogently articulates the film's anti-war theme. When Dax delivers his emotional speech to the court, Falsetto states, it is spoken to the camera, which means that "it is a direct plea to the audience."[7]

In their dark, depressing cell the three convicted prisoners speculate about the possibilities of escape or a last-minute reprieve. By this means Kubrick and his co-scripters keep the suspenseful tone of the film from slackening, even after the verdict has been rendered. In addition, the verbal and visual ironies continue to mount up throughout this scene. One prisoner complains that the cockroach on the wall of their cell will still be alive after he is dead. One of his comrades smashes the cockroach with his fist, commenting morosely, "Now you've got the edge on *him*!"

Gradually the hapless scapegoats become resigned to the fact that no last-minute rescue is to take place. Unable to control his despair, one prisoner threatens to start a fight and is accidentally knocked unconscious.

To the incessant throbbing of drums the prisoners are led to face the firing squad down the same avenue that stretches be-

12 ***The iconic Kirk Douglas in one of the most powerful roles of his career.***

fore the château, where the film began. The camera tracks forward relentlessly toward the three stakes against which the men are to be shot, and the drums halt as they are tied to the posts (the injured prisoner, still unconscious, is tied to the stake on a stretcher). There is a final shot of Mireau and Broulard looking on in stern dignity, and then the restless camera moves behind the members of the firing squad to record their blast of bullets, as the three victims in the distance crumble forward in death.

Kubrick cuts from the barrage of gunfire to the clatter of silverware as Mireau exults at breakfast about the wonderful way that the men died—men who were sacrificed to save his vanity. Mireau even feels expansive enough to compliment Dax, who has just arrived, on how well his men died.

13 ***Kubrick in the trench with, from left to right, Richard Anderson, George Macready, and Fred Bell.***

"By the way, Paul," Broulard remarks to Mireau in the most offhand way imaginable, "it's been brought to my attention that you ordered your artillery to fire on your own men during the attack." Mireau, shattered that Broulard has found out, sputters about the falsity of the charge and Dax's effort to discredit him. Broulard continues, still urbane and smiling, "Paul, I'm certain that you'll come through the hearing all right. You have the right to clear your name." As the specter of a public hearing rises before Mireau, he realizes that his career is ruined, regardless of the cheery terms in which Broulard has informed him of it.

Broulard has carefully arranged for Mireau to take the rap for the whole affair, while he goes scot-free. "I have one last thing to say to you, George," says Mireau, throwing down his napkin. "The man that you stabbed in the back is a soldier." He retreats from the camera, stalking toward the door at the opposite end of the room, his diminishing figure a visual metaphor for his irretrievable loss of status.

"It had to be done," shrugs Broulard. "France cannot afford to have fools guiding her military destiny." He then offers Dax Mireau's command, jovially adding with a knowing look, "Don't overdo the surprise; you've been after that job from the start. We all know that, my boy." "I am not your boy," Dax rejoins in contempt. Broulard defensively commands Dax to apologize instantly for telling him what he can do with the promotion. Dax smolders, "I apologize for not telling you sooner that you are a degenerate, sadistic old man."

Regaining his veneer of charm, the general replies, "You really did want to save those men, and you were not just angling for Mireau's command. You are an idealist—and I pity you as I would the village idiot. Those men didn't fight, so they were shot. You bring charges against General Mireau, so I insist that he answer them." Finally, he asks appealingly, "Wherein have I done wrong?"

Dax searches the elderly man's face and gasps in response, "Because you don't know the answer to that question, I pity you."

"[O]ne of the attractions of a war or crime story is that it provides an almost unique opportunity to contrast an individual of our contemporary society with a solid framework of accepted value ... which can be used as a counterpoint to a human, individual, emotional situation."

— SK/1959 (to Colin Young/*Film Quarterly*)

Adolphe Menjou's Broulard is one of the subtlest portraits of evil in all cinema. The filmgoer has to struggle to resist being taken in by the general's suave, engaging manner so as to realize that Broulard is no less ruthless than Mireau, only shrewd enough never to overplay his hand, as Mireau has done; and he is for that reason more insidious. Explaining why he always made his villains charming and polite (in the way that Broulard is), Alfred Hitchcock said: "It's a mistake to think that if you put a villain on the screen, he must sneer nas-

tily, stroke his black mustache, or kick a dog in the stomach. The really frightening thing about villains is their surface likeableness."[8] Menjou played Broulard with all the surface charm the role called for and did a brilliant job, winning some of the best notices of his long career.

Kubrick had made some rather grim movies up to this point. When I asked him if films like *Paths of Glory* implied that he was a misanthrope with contempt for the human race, Kubrick shot back, "Oh God, no. One doesn't give up being concerned for mankind because one acknowledges their fundamental absurdities and weaknesses. I still have hope that the human race can continue to progress. As a matter of fact, the epilogue of the movie ends on a note of hope for humanity."

Despite the unflinching picture of human misery and moral depravity that Kubrick has given us in *Paths of Glory*, the film does nonetheless end on a note of hope. Harris recalls that Kubrick came to him with the concept for an epilogue, which would make the ending of this stark film somewhat less grim. Walking back to his post, Dax hears some of his men whistling and shouting in a nearby tavern, blowing off steam after the ordeal of witnessing the senseless deaths of their comrades earlier in the day. He stands in the doorway and sees that they are coaxing a timid German girl prisoner, played by Susanne Christian, to sing a song to them.

14–15 ***Kirk Douglas during the shooting of the attack on the Ant Hill.***
16 ***Joseph Turkel, who had appeared in*** The Killing ***and would also play the role of bartender Lloyd in*** The Shining, ***seen here as Private Arnaud, unconscious at his own execution.***

16

To make her feel more at ease, the host gives her a merry introduction, presenting her as "a little diversion."

He drags the frightened girl onstage amid a raucous ovation from the troops. Slowly, tentatively, her lips begin to move to a German song, "Der treue Husar" ("The Faithful Hussar"), which is not yet audible because of the general noise. Then the soldiers, most of whom seem either over-age or under-age—a telling comment on the state of the French army—begin to listen to the melody. Though they cannot understand the German words, the plaintive tune stirs their emotions, and they commence humming along with her. Kubrick's camera passes over their faces, finally pausing on perhaps the youngest recruit, whose cheeks are streaming with unabashed tears that match the ones shimmering on the girl's face. Dax turns away, convinced that his men have not lost their humanity, despite the inhuman conditions in which they live and die. Testifying to the power of the epilogue, Tim Cahill writes that this scene, "on four separate viewings, has brought tears to my eyes."[9]

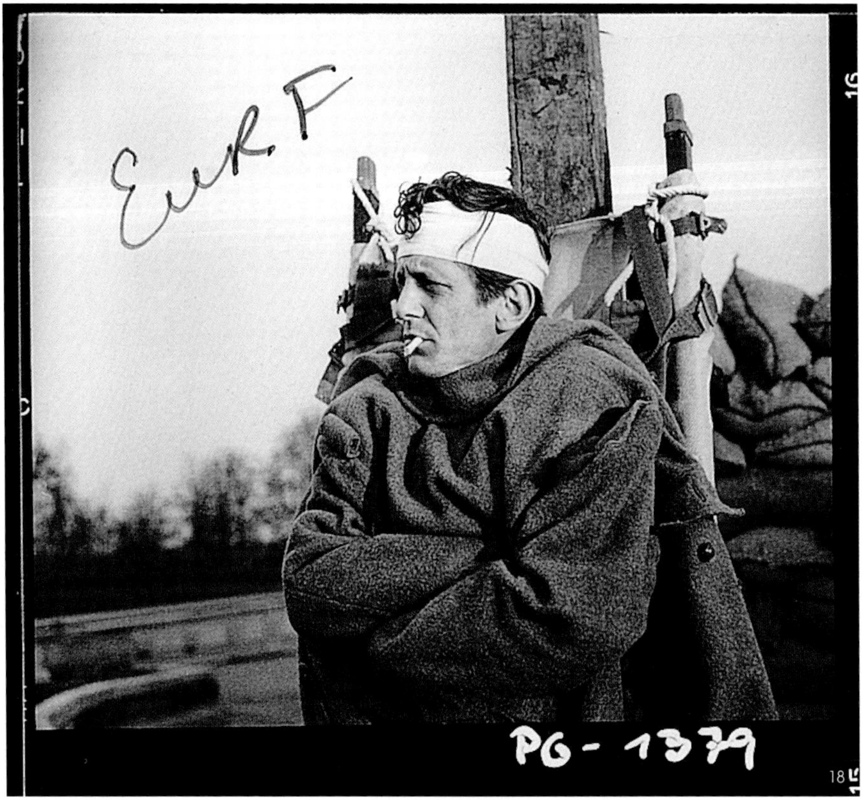

17-18 ***Kirk Douglas and Joseph Turkel take cigarette breaks between takes.***

A messenger delivers Dax's orders to prepare his men to move back to the front. Dax walks away from the scene as a roll of snare drums builds to a climax and the movie ends.

The film's score was composed by Gerald Fried, his fourth and last for a Kubrick feature. Fried relied heavily on percussion for the background music of the movie, sometimes using percussion alone in certain scenes. With no budgetary restrictions, he was able to use the entire orchestra at times, rather than just the percussion section. He remembers, "In Munich we were permitted to hire as many musicians as we wanted." Fried even had the entire Bavarian Philharmonic at his disposal.

Fried relied on percussion throughout the score, he says, because "Stanley and I were both drum crazy." Indeed, Kubrick's experience as a drummer in high school made him partial to percussion, and Fried maintains that "percussion instruments just by themselves are exciting." For example,

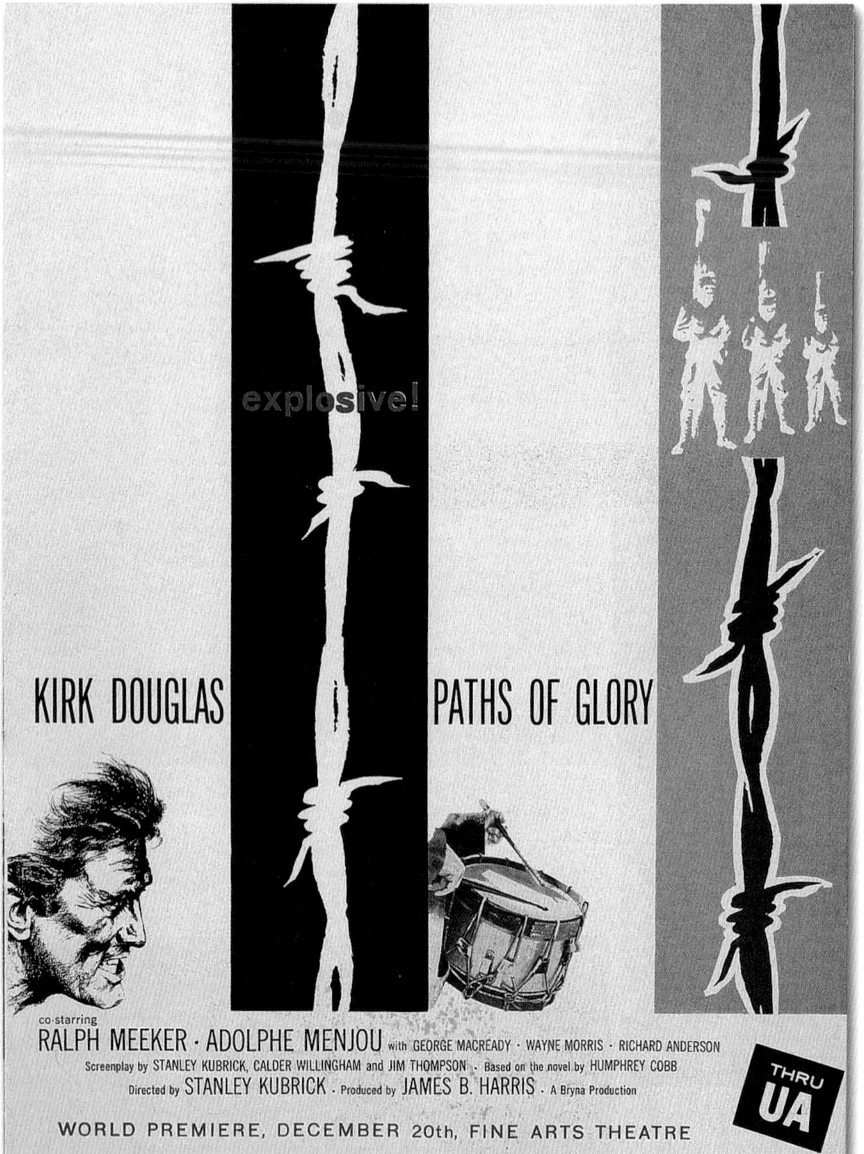
explosive!
KIRK DOUGLAS
PATHS OF GLORY
co-starring
RALPH MEEKER · ADOLPHE MENJOU with GEORGE MACREADY · WAYNE MORRIS · RICHARD ANDERSON
Screenplay by STANLEY KUBRICK, CALDER WILLINGHAM and JIM THOMPSON · Based on the novel by HUMPHREY COBB
Directed by STANLEY KUBRICK · Produced by JAMES B. HARRIS · A Bryna Production
WORLD PREMIERE, DECEMBER 20th, FINE ARTS THEATRE
THRU UA

a suspenseful scene in which a French officer leads a reconnaissance mission into the field on the night before the big battle is scored solely for percussion. The scene with the night patrol, Fried points out, "seemed to be the perfect place for a percussion solo," which sounds in this context very sinister and menacing as the small band of soldiers inches its way toward the enemy lines.[10]

When Kubrick and Harris test-screened *Paths of Glory* in Los Angeles, "the lights would come up and people would just sit there," says Harris. "There was no applause or anything. I think they were just stunned."[11] Reviews of the film commended Kubrick, showing how the film's underlying theme, the dehumanizing effect of war, was portrayed with chilling effect.

The response from the French government was predictably negative, and the movie was banned in France at the time of its release. Specifically, the French government was outraged by the film's depiction of the French army as being presided over by a High Command that would sacrifice innocent lives to maintain the image of the military. (It did not help for Kubrick to point out that the unpalatable story told in the film was based on true events.) It was made clear that *Paths of Glory* would not be released in France, so United Artists canceled its plans to distribute the movie there.

In 1974, however, French President Valéry Giscard d'Estaing stated that there would be no political censorship of films offered for distribution in France, as there had been in the past. Kubrick told me that that was his cue "to announce plans to release the picture in France, in both a subtitled and original version." In due course, the movie was released in Paris in four first-run theaters in 1976.

The film has attracted a large cult following in the decades since it was made. Seeing the film today, it is clear that *Paths of Glory* has lost none of its power in the years since it was made. Its examination of the moral dilemmas that are triggered by war, and which are sidestepped in the film by the very men at the policy-making level who should be most concerned about them, has become more relevant than ever in the wake of subsequent wars.

Reassessing the movie some years later, Judith Crist judged that "this 1957 film has grown in stature through the years, not only as an example of the filmmaker's art, but also as an ultimate comment on the hypocrisies of war." Though the French army in World War I is the subject of the film, she continues, any army in any war could serve for the story. (This statement recalls that in his first feature, *Fear and Desire,* Kubrick deliberately did not specify the actual war during which the story was set, so as to underline the universal implications of the plot.) "It is a bitter and biting tale, told with stunning point and nerve-racking intensity in eighty-seven brilliant minutes. Kirk Douglas has never been better than as the humane colonel caught between generals and privates."[12] Perhaps the universality of the movie's theme helped to make it acceptable to French audiences when it was released in France at long last. Similarly, David Cook states that "Kubrick's best films have always

19 **Paths of Glory** ***premiere brochure.***

been both technically and intellectually ahead of their time. His classic anti-war statement *Paths of Glory*... relentlessly exposed the type of military stupidity and callousness" that Francis Coppola would examine in his Vietnam film, *Apocalypse Now* (1979).[13]

The ultimate accolade to Kubrick's film was paid by Stuart Klawans in his survey of films about World War I. He states emphatically that there has been "only one first-rate film about the First World War" in the last half century, Stanley Kubrick's *Paths of Glory*. "He gave us human disaster, impeccably realized."[14]

Notes

1. Woody Haut, *Heartbreak and Vine: Hardboiled Writers in Hollywood* (London: Serpent's Tail, 2002): 127.
2. Gene D. Phillips, "Adolphe Menjou," *The Encyclopedia of Stanley Kubrick* with Rodney Hill (New York: Checkmark, 2002): 248.
3. Jill Bernstein et al., "Stanley Kubrick: A Cinematic Odyssey," *Premiere* 12, no. 7 (August, 1999): 86.
4. Anthony Ambrogio, "*Paths of Glory*," in *International Dictionary of Films and Filmmakers*, ed. Nicolet Elert, rev. ed. (Detroit: St. James Press, 2000): 777.
5. Peter Cowie, *Seventy Years of Cinema* (New York: Barnes, 1969): 222.
6. Tom Wicker, "World War I," in *Past Imperfect History According to the Movies*, ed. Mark Carnes (New York: Holt, 1995): 188.
7. Mario Falsetto, *Stanley Kubrick: A Narrative and Stylistic Analysis* (Westport, Conn.: Praeger, 1994): 40.
8. Gene D. Phillips, *Alfred Hitchcock* (Boston: Twayne, 1984): 20.
9. Tim Cahill, "The *Rolling Stone* Interview," in *Stanley Kubrick Interviews*, ed. Gene D. Phillips (Jackson: University Press of Mississippi, 2001): 190.
10. Vincent LoBrutto, *Stanley Kubrick: A Biography* (New York: Da Capo, 2002): 148–49.
11. Bernstein et al.: 86.
12. Gene D. Phillips, "*Paths of Glory*," in *Novels into Film: The Encyclopedia of Movies Adapted from Books*, ed. James Welsh and John Tibbetts, rev. ed. (New York: Checkmark, 1999): 321.
13. David Cook, *A History of Narrative Film*, rev. ed. (New York: Norton, 2004): 852.
14. Stuart Klawans, "The First World War Changed Movies," *The New York Times*, November 19, 2000, sec. 2:13, 24.

20

20 Paths of Glory *press booklet.*

Spartacus

1960 / COLOR / 196 MINUTES
Distributed by UNIVERSAL PICTURES

CAST
SPARTACUS KIRK DOUGLAS
CRASSUS LAURENCE OLIVIER
ANTONINUS TONY CURTIS
VARINIA JEAN SIMMONS
GRACCHUS CHARLES LAUGHTON
BATIATUS PETER USTINOV
JULIUS CAESAR JOHN GAVIN
HELENA NINA FOCH
TIGRANES HERBERT LOM
CRIXUS JOHN IRELAND
GLABRUS JOHN DALL
MARCELLUS CHARLES MCGRAW
CLAUDIA JOANNA BARNES
DAVID HAROLD J. STONE
DRABA WOODY STRODE
RAMON PETER BROCCO
GANNICUS PAUL LAMBERT
CAPTAIN OF THE GUARD ROBERT J. WILKE
DIONYSIUS NICHOLAS DENNIS
ROMAN OFFICER JOHN HOYT
LAELIUS FREDERIC WORLOCK
SYMMACHUS DAYTON LUMMIS
EXTRA GARY LOCKWOOD (uncredited)

CREW
DIRECTED BY STANLEY KUBRICK
EXECUTIVE PRODUCER KIRK DOUGLAS
PRODUCED BY EDWARD LEWIS
SCREENPLAY DALTON TRUMBO (based on the novel *Spartacus* by Howard Fast)
DIRECTOR OF PHOTOGRAPHY RUSSELL METTY
PRODUCTION DESIGNER ALEXANDER GOLITZEN
ORIGINAL MUSIC ALEX NORTH
ART DIRECTOR ERIC ORBOM
SET DECORATIONS RUSSELL A. GAUSMAN, JULIA HERON
COSTUMES VALLES
MAIN TITLES AND DESIGN CONSULTANT SAUL BASS
UNIT PRODUCTION MANAGER NORMAN DEMING
SOUND WALDON O. WATSON, JOE LAPIS, MURRAY SPIVACK, RONALD PIERCE
HISTORICAL AND TECHNICAL ADVISER VITTORIO NINO NOVARESE
ADDITIONAL SCENE PHOTOGRAPHY CLIFFORD STINE
EDITOR ROBERT LAWRENCE
ASSISTANTS TO THE FILM EDITOR ROBERT SCHULTE, FRED CHULACK
ASSISTANT DIRECTOR MARSHALL GREEN
SPECIAL EFFECTS WES THOMPSON (uncredited)

Technicolor filmed in Super Technirama (70 mm).

Opposite *One of many versions of the* Spartacus *poster.*

KIRK DOUGLAS
LAURENCE OLIVIER
JEAN SIMMONS
CHARLES LAUGHTON
PETER USTINOV
JOHN GAVIN
and
TONY CURTIS
as Antoninus
SPARTACUS
A
TECHNICOLOR
TECHNIRAMA
LENSES BY PANAVISION
Directed by STANLEY KUBRICK Music composed and conducted by ALEX NORTH Screenplay by DALTON TRUMBO
Based on a novel by HOWARD FAST Produced by EDWARD LEWIS Executive Producer KIRK DOUGLAS
A Bryna Production Released by Universal-International

SPARTACUS

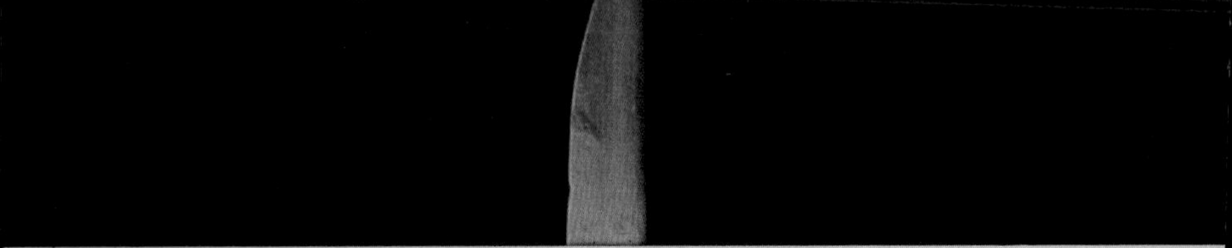

ROME

Spartacus

by Gene D. Phillips

After finishing *Paths of Glory*, Kubrick wrote two scripts, neither of which was accepted for production in Hollywood. Meanwhile, Kirk Douglas had begun production on *Spartacus*, for which he was executive producer as well as star. "Anthony Mann had begun the picture and filmed the first sequence," Kubrick told me, "but his disagreements with Kirk made him decide to leave after the first week of shooting. The film came after two years in which I had not directed a picture," so Kubrick and his partner, James B. Harris, agreed that he should be "loaned out" to Universal to direct *Spartacus*.

"When Kirk offered me the job of directing *Spartacus*," Kubrick continued, "I thought that I might be able to make something of it, if the script could be changed. But my experience proved that if it is not explicitly stipulated in the contract that your decisions will be respected, there's a very good chance that they won't be. The script could have been improved in the course of shooting, but it wasn't. Kirk was executive producer; he and Dalton Trumbo, the scriptwriter, and Edward Lewis, the producer, had it their way."

Douglas had originally hired novelist Howard Fast to adapt his own 1951 novel *Spartacus*, about a slave revolt in pre-Christian Rome. But Fast's screenplay turned out to lack the requisite dramatic punch; Douglas went on to hire Dalton Trumbo. Like Fast, Trumbo had been sympathetic to Communist ideology; at the time of the Red Scare a few years before, both writers had served prison terms for refusing to cooperate with the House Un-American Activities Committee (HUAC). Still they were not "comrades" in any sense of the word; when Fast met with Trumbo to discuss the adaptation of the novel, he pronounced him a "cocktail Communist." In retaliation, Trumbo wrote off Fast as a fanatic. Fast took one look at Trumbo's script and called its author "the world's worst writer."[1] Nevertheless, Trumbo's screenplay was better than Fast was prepared to admit. For one thing, Trumbo scuttled the incident in Fast's book which was pure fabrication—that the Romans sold the corpses of the vanquished rebels for sausage after they were crucified.

Kubrick had never challenged Trumbo's political ideology; he had no reservations about Trumbo slipping veiled political references into the screenplay—as when Trumbo draws an implicit parallel in the script between Spartacus's slave revolt and the Russian Revolution of 1917. Harris has said that Kubrick had good reason to be dissatisfied with Trumbo's script because he believed it had some gaping holes in it.

For example, there was no battle scene portraying the Roman legions defeating Spartacus's slave army, as Harris points out in Jan Harlan's documentary *Stanley Kubrick: A Life in Pictures* (2001). The climactic battle scene, as depicted in the script, was done in a sort of symbolic fashion, "with helmets floating down the river with bloodstains, and battle sounds in the background." Kubrick, of course, maintained "you can't make a spectacle movie and not have a battle scene in it."

01 ***Kubrick (seen here with no less than four cameras) shot still photographs between takes.***

So Kubrick persuaded Douglas to film the battle scenes in Spain, "where he could get all those extras to play the opposing armies" very cheaply. Consequently, Kubrick did manage to make one alteration in the script, and it was a major one.

"Spartacus is the only film over which I did not have absolute control. When Kirk offered me the job of directing Spartacus, I thought that I might be able to make something of it if the script could be changed. But my experience proved that if it is not explicitly stipulated in the contract that your decisions will be respected, there's a very good chance that they won't be."

— SK/1973 (to Gene D. Phillips)

It is evident that Kubrick's problems with the script were not aimed at Trumbo's politics; as he told me, he objected to the overall quality of Trumbo's "pretty dumb script." Kubrick went on to point out that the screenplay was rarely faithful to what is known about Spartacus. Since the known facts about Spartacus's slave revolt against the Roman Empire are few, Trumbo invented a number of subplots in order to create the script for a king-size film of more than three hours running time, making the script top-heavy with plot details. Kubrick explained that he achieved "only limited success" in making the film visually interesting as a way of counteracting Trumbo's pedestrian dialogue.[2] *Spartacus* remains his only film over which he did not have absolute control. "I have since involved myself more and more in the administrative side of film production," he told me, "because it is in this area that many artistic battles are won and lost."

Because of Trumbo's fencing with HUAC, he was blacklisted in the film industry and was reduced to grinding out screenplays under various aliases, including such pseudonyms as "Les Crutchfield" and even "Sally Stubblefield." Howard cites Kirk Douglas's autobiography, *The Ragman's Son* (1988), concerning a meeting between Kubrick, Douglas, and Edward Lewis, in which Kirk Douglas suggested that Lewis be listed in the screen credits as author of the screenplay. Lewis expressed misgivings about being named author of the script, so Kubrick suggested that, if they were unwilling to credit the real author of the screenplay, Dalton Trumbo, they might just as well attribute both the script and the direction of the film to him—"much to the indignation of Douglas and Lewis."[3]

Kubrick's suggestion was not as self-serving as it might at first appear. As long as Trumbo was not to receive an official screen credit for the screenplay, it made more sense for the director, rather than the producer, to be listed as author. As Kubrick told me, "I directed the actors, I composed the shots, and I edited the movie." Kubrick was, after all, on the creative side of the production, while Lewis was strictly on the business end of

02 ***Kubrick's notes and sketches for the slave revolt scenes.***

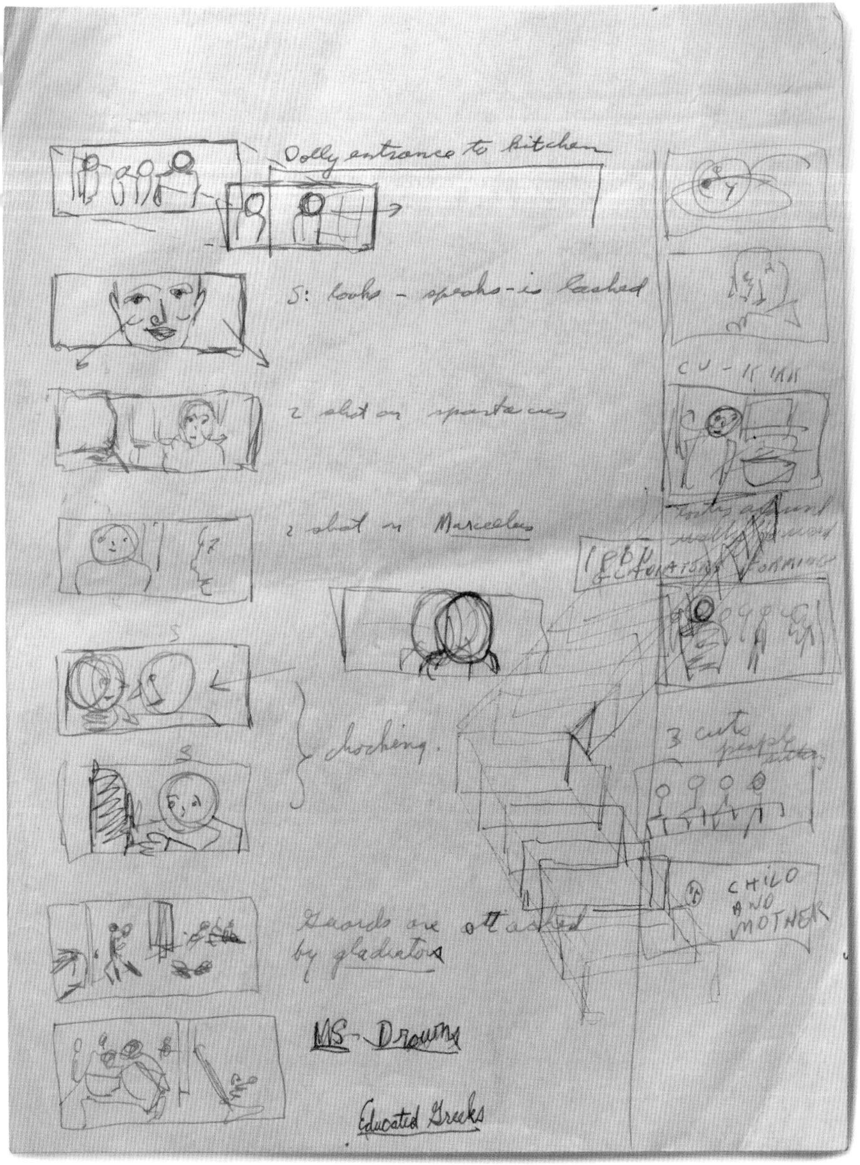
Dolly entrance to kitchen
S: looks - speaks - is lashed
2 shot on spartacus
2 shot on Marcellus
shocking.
Guards are attacked by gladiators
MS - Drawing
Educated Greeks
3 cuts
CHILD AND MOTHER

02

the project. At any rate, as filming progressed, Douglas announced that "Sam Jackson," Trumbo's favorite alias, was to be acknowledged as the screenwriter. He eventually relented, however, when Otto Preminger released *Exodus* (1960) while *Spartacus* was still in production, with Dalton Trumbo officially credited as the author of the script. Douglas decided to follow suit and award the screen credit for *Spartacus* to the script's rightful author. When the name of a blacklisted writer appeared on the American screen for two Hollywood epics, it was obvious that the blacklisting period was, for all practical purposes, over.

Douglas's idea was to use British actors like Charles Laughton and Laurence Olivier to play the Roman patricians, and Americans like himself and Tony Curtis, who appears as Spartacus's friend, to enact the slaves. The polished accents of the English actors make a neat contrast with the more pedestrian voices of the Americans in the cast and nicely reflect the class barrier between the two types of characters being portrayed.

Douglas did not carry through this concept of casting with total consistency, however, since the British Jean Simmons plays a slave girl and the American John Gavin is Julius Caesar. But by and large Douglas's international casting works.

03 ***Photo of screenwriter Dalton Trumbo by Kubrick.***
04 ***Kubrick with Laurence Olivier and Tony Curtis.***

With Anthony Mann in the director's chair, principal photography commenced on January 27, 1959, in Death Valley, California, with the opening scene of the picture, set in a stone quarry where Spartacus and other slaves are laboring. At the end of the first week of shooting, Douglas confessed to actor Peter Usinov and stills photographer William Woodfield, "I need a new director; it's not working out." Mann had implied more than once that Douglas was overacting, particularly when he mauled the actor playing the Roman soldier whom Spartacus attacks. When Douglas asked them to suggest a possible replacement, Woodfield chimed in, "Why don't you get the guy who directed the best picture you ever made, *Paths of Glory*: Stanley Kubrick?"[4]

"The reason [Hollywood] movies are often so bad ... isn't because the people who make them are cynical money hacks. Most of them are doing the very best that they can; they really want to make good films. The trouble is with their heads, not their hearts."

— SK/1959 (to Dwight Macdonald/*Encounter*)

Douglas conceded that Kubrick had been his first choice to direct the film in the first place; it was the studio brass who had insisted that the more experienced Anthony Mann direct. And so Douglas turned to Kubrick, firing Mann on Friday the 13th of February. Douglas phoned Kubrick that evening and told him to be

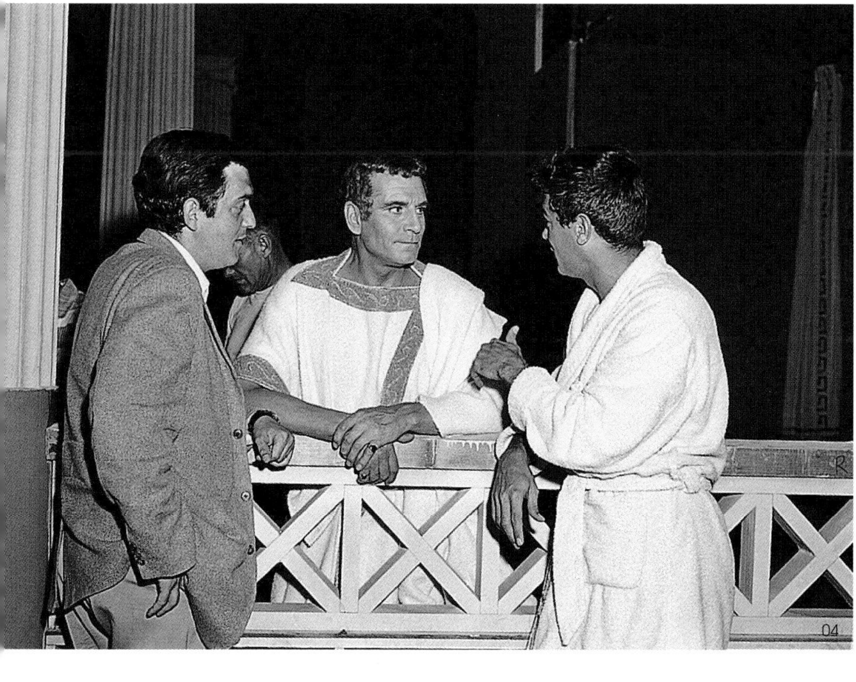

05

ready to start shooting the following Monday, February 16, 1959.

By then the production had moved from the location work in Death Valley to the studio, where Kubrick began shooting the scenes in the school for gladiators presided over by Batiatus (Peter Ustinov). Almost from the beginning of Kubrick's tenure as director, he and Douglas did not have the amicable rapport that they had developed on *Paths of Glory*.

As to the source of the friction between Douglas and Kubrick, the latter maintained a tactful reticence. A person involved in the production, who spoke on condition of anonymity, told me that initially Douglas was disposed to accept Kubrick's suggestions about revising the script and about other aspects of the production. When Howard Fast saw some of the rushes, he reportedly told Douglas that he was lucky to have found such a talented director on such short notice. Douglas was offended by this remark, however well meant, because it seemed to imply that the success of the film would depend largely on the director who had arrived at the eleventh hour.

In all events, Douglas's subsequent references to Kubrick's contribution to the

08

07

film smacked of condescension. Recalling Kubrick's first day on the set with Laurence Olivier, Charles Laughton, Peter Ustinov, and other members of the British contingent, Douglas is quoted by *Newsweek* as saying, "It was a funny scene. Here was Kubrick with his wide eyes and pants hiked up, looking like a kid of seventeen. You should have seen the looks on their faces. It was as if they were asking, 'Is this some kind of joke?'"[5]

Douglas's anecdote seems hardly fair in retrospect, especially since he had enough confidence in the young director to entrust him with steering a $12 million production with a cast of ten thousand extras. Kubrick pointed out that Douglas's attitude was demonstrated clearly when he chose a photograph of Kubrick for the film's souvenir program in which the star-producer was pictured in the foreground, standing over the director.

05 ***Kubrick with Kirk Douglas and John Ireland while shooting the arrival of the slaves at the gladiator school.***
06 ***Kubrick with Laurence Olivier as Crassus.***
07 ***John Gavin (Julius Caesar), Charles Laughton (Gracchus), and Kubrick.***
08 ***Jean Simmons (Varinia) in conversation with the director.***

To make matters worse, Kubrick at first did not get on well with the British actors. Christiane Kubrick told Peter Bogdanovich that Olivier and the other distinguished British actors "treated him, because he was so young, with a certain arrogance."[6] However, Kubrick's real nemesis on the film was not Douglas or any of the other actors, but the veteran cinematographer Russell Metty (*Touch of Evil*). When Kubrick was brought in to replace the older and more experienced Anthony Mann, Metty, like Douglas, scoffed at the director's youth. Tony Curtis, who played the slave Antoninus, recounts in his autobiography that Kubrick would climb up on the camera crane to compose a shot, and Metty, with his gray crew cut, would smirk, "Get that little Jew-boy from the Bronx off my crane." Kubrick simply declined to notice such remarks. Curtis also observed that when Kubrick looked through his viewfinder, Metty would sometimes crouch behind him, holding his Zippo cigarette lighter up to his eye, as if it were a viewfinder. Kubrick was not amused.[7]

Metty was accustomed to working quickly and thus was frustrated when Kubrick lavished great care on each scene and slowed down the rate of shooting. The director of photography particularly fumed at the amount of time and effort Kubrick expended on the scene following the battle, in which the Roman army destroys Spartacus's slave army. It was originally set to be filmed on Universal's back lot; but Kubrick opted to shoot the aftermath of the battle, which shows the hillside strewn with corpses, on a soundstage. In this way he could better control the light, since the scene takes place at sunset.

Actually, the elaborate exterior set which Alexander Golitzen, the production designer, erected inside covered three soundstages. Metty had used an enormous number of crimson and scarlet gels on the lights, in order to create a sunset glow against the cyclorama that served for the sky. According to John Baxter, when Kubrick arrived to survey the completed set, he had a Polaroid shot made by the still photographer, William Woodfield. After studying the photo, he decided that the set looked phony—it was a "typical Russ Metty sunset." He then ordered that the sequence would be shot outdoors after all, on the studio back lot; so the studio had to absorb the expense of the indoor set that Kubrick rejected.

Thereafter Kubrick and Metty developed an uneasy truce: when Kubrick would take exception to the way that Metty would light a shot and suggest an alternative, the camera crew would look to Metty, who would nod in silence. Kubrick had won the day, to the extent

"One of the things I tried to avoid in filming* Spartacus *was the usual thinking that goes into directing epics. We tried to do* Spartacus *as if we were filming a* Marty.*"

— SK/1960 (*Look*)

09 ***Kubrick and James B. Harris in an impromptu percussion jam session at the Kubrick home in Beverly Hills.***

IMAGINATIVE IDEAS, many of them from the fert
of Director Stanley Kubrick, included this one. Kubrick put the n
signs among the "corpses" after the big battle so that he could holle
there, next to number 163, move over or look dead or something." Ot

ld have hollered "you there" and nine guys would have hollered back me?" When he was ready to shoot they took the numbers away and shot. chnique it worked fine but on screen the scene proved disappointing so ot it all over again, this time indoors at Universal's Hollywood studio.

that Universal's hierarchy supported him in his skirmishes with Metty. The cameraman could console himself with the Academy Award that he won for best color photography. By the same token, Alexander Golitzen also won an Oscar for his production design, despite the fact that his indoor battlefield was not used in the movie.

Spartacus begins, like *Paths of Glory*, with a narration that puts the film in a historical context. As we watch a band of slaves toiling in a stone quarry, the narrator intones: "In the last century before the birth of the new faith called Christianity, which was destined to overthrow the pagan tyranny of Rome and bring about a new society, the Roman Republic stood at the very center of the civilized world.... The age of the dictator was at hand, waiting in the shadows for the event to bring it forth. In that same century... an illiterate slave woman added to her master's wealth by giving birth to a son, whom she named Spartacus. A proud, rebellious son... he lived out... his young manhood dreaming of the death of slavery."

After a violent attack on a slave driver, Spartacus is chosen by Batiatus to go to his gladiator school. Spartacus tries to make friends with one of the other slaves at the training center, Draba (Woody Strode), but Draba discourages him: "Gladiators don't make friends. If we're ever matched in the arena together, I'll have to kill you." But Draba and Spartacus do become friends, emphasizing the brotherhood theme that is at the heart of the movie.

Marcus Crassus (Laurence Olivier), a Roman general and senator, arrives at the slave compound to observe an exhibition match. The agitated Batiatus commands a slave, "Second-best wine. No, the best—but small goblets." It is Ustinov's deft handling of such witty lines, in this case showing how Batiatus's desire to please the visiting dignitary is in conflict with his innate stinginess, that no doubt contributed to the actor's winning an Academy Award for his performance. Batiatus entertains the general with his best wine (in small goblets), and Crassus orders a match "to the death" between two of the gladiators. Spartacus and Draba are chosen; so Draba's prediction that one day they might have to fight each other to the death has come true. When they take to the field Draba throws Spartacus to the ground. Crassus, who sits on a veranda above the arena, indicates that Draba should kill Spartacus. Draba, enraged, throws his trident at Crassus but misses, and then climbs up onto the balcony to attack him. A guard spears Draba in the back and Crassus deals him a final blow with his knife.

The next day, when Spartacus learns from slave trainer Marcellus (Charles McGraw) that Varinia (Jean Simmons), the beautiful slave girl with whom he has fallen in love, has been sold to Crassus as his personal servant, he goes berserk and kills Marcellus, thus igniting an impromptu insurrection. He and the other gladiators fight their way into the courtyard and scale the wall that stands between them and freedom. The blue sky suddenly

10 ***The only trace of this famous image in Kubrick's archives are these pages, torn from an unidentified magazine.***
11 ***This photograph of Kubrick in his favorite poncho was taken by his wife, Christiane.***

11

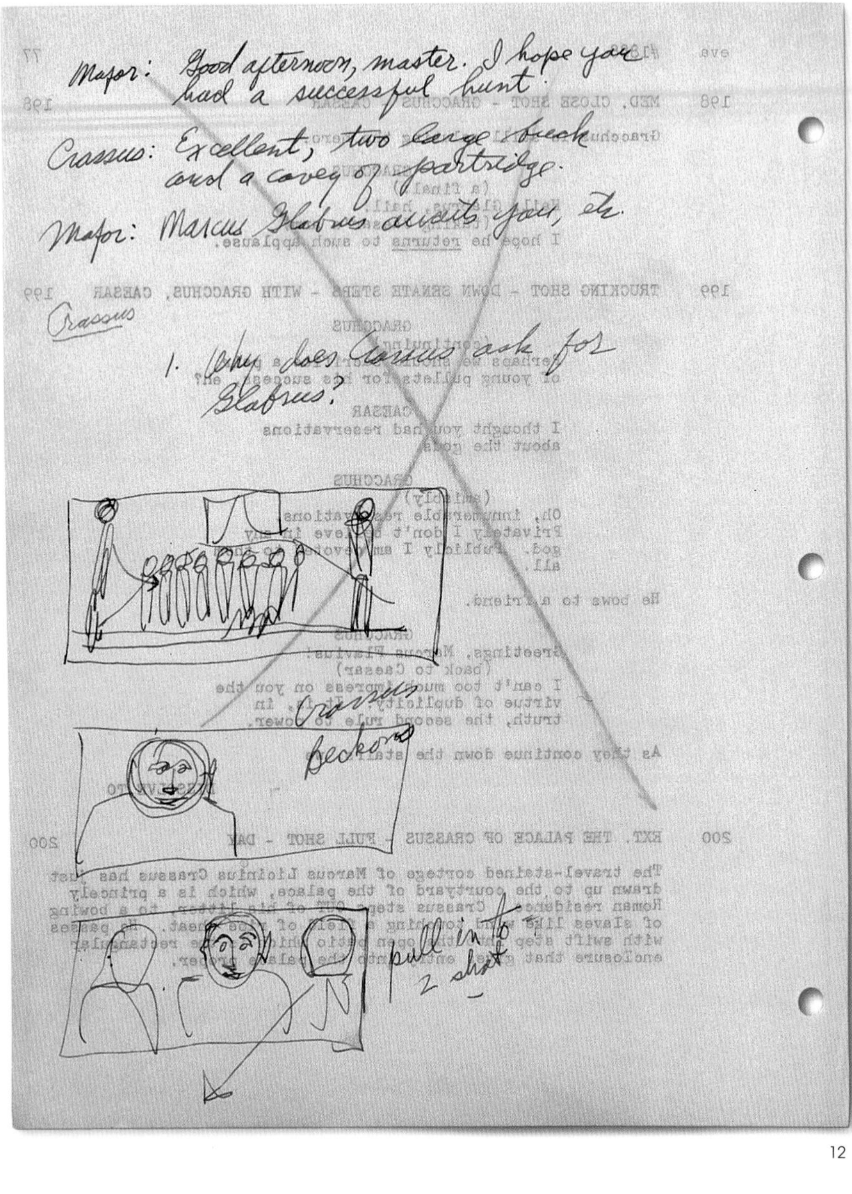
Major: Good afternoon, master. I hope you had a successful hunt.
Crassus: Excellent, two large buck and a covey of partridge.
Major: Marcus Glabrus awaits you, etc.
Crassus
1. Why does Crassus ask for Glabrus?
Crassus beckons
pull into 2 shot

appears overhead as they reach the top of the wall and then drop to the other side.

This sequence demonstrates Kubrick's assured handling not only of the widescreen frame, with which he had never worked before, but also of color, with which his experience was limited to his 1953 short documentary, *The Seafarers*. Regarding the widescreen ratio, Kubrick told me that he was never unduly concerned about composing shots in this format. "The first thing you do is make sure you have the action in the front of the frame blocked out properly," he said, "and then what is taking place on either side and in the background of the shot will almost take care of itself."

As Spartacus and his men latch onto the spear-pointed gate, which they are climbing like a ladder to reach the top of the wall, the camera looks down on them in their grubby slave vesture, which is the same muddy color as the earth below. When they go over the top, the camera turns upward to give them the brilliant blue sky, symbol of the freedom they have just won, as a background. The camerawork here was obviously calculated to take advantage of the vast expanse of space provided by the widescreen and employ it as a backdrop against which the action is being played.

Spartacus marshals the fugitives into an army of crusaders, fighting for freedom from Roman oppression. He eventually recruits more escaped slaves as he and his slave army travel across Italy, including Varinia (who escaped from her captors), and Antoninus (Tony Curtis), who becomes his best friend. The circumstances of Antoninus's joining Spartacus's revolt is depicted in a thought-provoking sequence.

Lounging in the splendor of his villa, which recalls the luxurious château in which the generals lived in *Paths of Glory*, Crassus receives a gift of slaves from the governor of Sicily. One slave, Antoninus, strikes Crassus's fancy. "You shall be my body servant," Crassus informs him. It is a matter of historical record that Roman generals indulged their proclivities for young specimens of their own sex as well as for members of the opposite sex. In a subsequent scene Crassus is being bathed by Antoninus. Both men are nearly naked, and Crassus says to Antoninus, "Do you consider the eating of oysters to be moral, and the eating of snails to be immoral? ... Of course not. It is all a matter of taste.... And taste is not the same as appetite, and therefore not a question of morals.... My taste includes both snails and oysters." Antoninus has not missed the meaning of Crassus's remarks, for he disappears during the following scene while the general, whose back is turned, gives him a grandiose speech about the power of Rome.

Vito Russo comments in his book *The Celluloid Closet*, on which the documentary of the same name was based, "Antoninus's fear of being homosexually involved with Crassus causes him to slip away" and join Spartacus and the other slaves in revolt.[8] After the film's premiere engagements, Universal cut the seduction

12 ***Since he did not have total control over the film, Kubrick's efforts to improve the script, seen here with his handwritten notes, were not as successful as he had hoped.***

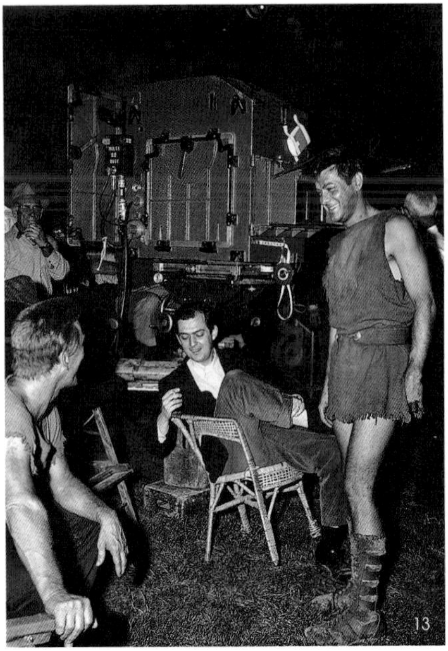

scene between Crassus and Antoninus from the film. The industry censor was apparently having second thoughts about the scene, since it maintained that homosexuality was a taboo topic for Hollywood films.

Meanwhile the wily Crassus persuades Julius Caesar (John Gavin) and the Senate to allow him to quell the slave revolt in order to display the might of Rome to all the world. He really intends to win fresh laurels as a conquering hero by destroying Spartacus, who is already a legend among the populace. "What is good for Crassus is good for Rome" is the extent of his political philosophy. In order that Crassus can quash the rebellion, the Senate concedes to him what amount to almost dictatorial powers—much to the consternation of Gracchus (Charles Laughton), his perennial enemy in the Senate. As the narrator told us in the film's spoken prologue, "The age of the dictator was at hand, waiting in the shadows for the event to bring it forth."

Kubrick focuses on Spartacus's slave army in a montage sequence, picturing them at rest in one of their temporary camping sites; the army includes not only fighting men, but their growing families. At one point his camera moves silently across the endless rows of sleeping slaves in a night scene, pausing on a couple sleeping in each other's arms, children curled up together, et cetera. Kubrick focuses on individuals in the welter of people that make up the numberless army of slaves, in order to personalize the epic scenes in the film. Also depicted here is the idyll between Varinia and Spartacus, who marry and are expecting a child.

The scenes involving masses of extras portraying either the slave army or the Roman army were shot on location. Some of them were filmed in Spain and others on the grassy hillsides of William Randolph Hearst's estate in San Simeon, which was

13 ***Kirk Douglas, Kubrick, and Tony Curtis.***
14 ***The relationship between Kubrick and Douglas (seen here with producer Ed Lewis) was tense, as Douglas was not only the star of the film but also its executive producer. Kubrick told Terry Southern in 1962, "[***Spartacus is***] *the only picture I've worked on where I was employed – and in a situation like that the director has no real rights, except the rights of persuasion… and I've found that's the wrong end of the lever to be on. First of all, you very often fail to persuade, and secondly, even when you do persuade, you waste so much time doing it that it gets to be ridiculous."****

the model of Xanadu, Charles Foster Kane's estate in Orson Welles's *Citizen Kane* (1941).

When Spartacus learns that Crassus plans to crush the slave revolt under the iron heel of Rome, he exhorts his crusaders: "(The Romans) hope to trap us here, against the sea.... We have no choice but to march against Rome herself and end this war the only way it could have ended: by freeing every slave in Italy.... I'd rather be here, a free man among brothers... than to be the richest citizen of Rome."

As the Roman army begins its advance across the battlefield toward the slave army, Kubrick photographs them in extreme long shot in order to encompass the entire formation. The director holds his camera steady and still, to let the enormity of the almost limitless force which the slaves are facing sink into the audience's consciousness. Kubrick once again takes full advantage of the widescreen.

As in his filming of the key battle scene in *Paths of Glory*, Kubrick's camera seems to be everywhere at once, burrowing into the bloody pileups of combatants who fight furiously, until at the end of the day the carnage is complete and the slaves have been defeated. Corpses, heaped one on another, mutely testify to the brutal battle that has just ended. This shot of the dead brings to mind the image of the battlefield casualties in D. W. Griffith's *The Birth of a Nation* (1915), which its director labeled "war's peace."

Crassus rummages around among the bodies in a fruitless effort to find Spartacus's corpse, while a tribune announces that the surviving slaves will be spared crucifixion if they will identify their leader's whereabouts. In what is one of the most moving scenes in any Kubrick film, Antoninus, who has been sitting next to Spartacus, stands up and shouts, "I am Spartacus!" and is joined by a whole host of his comrades who stand up and utter the same cry. Crassus realizes that his hopes to make an example of Spartacus have been frustrated.

Gracchus knows that Crassus's victory spells his defeat. Summoned to the Senate, he sits sullenly in the darkened, almost empty chamber as Crassus snarls, "The enemies of the state are known. Arrests are in progress.... (L)ists of the disloyal have been compiled." There is little doubt that this statement was inspired by Dalton Trumbo's bitter personal experiences with HUAC. "Where does my name appear on the list of disloyal enemies of the state?"

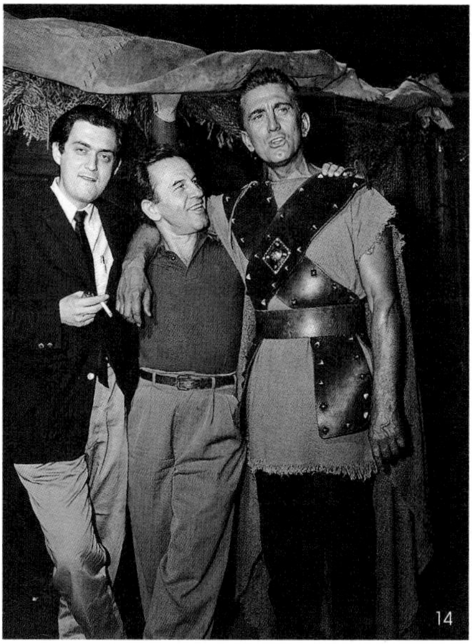
14

166 — by Gene D. Phillips

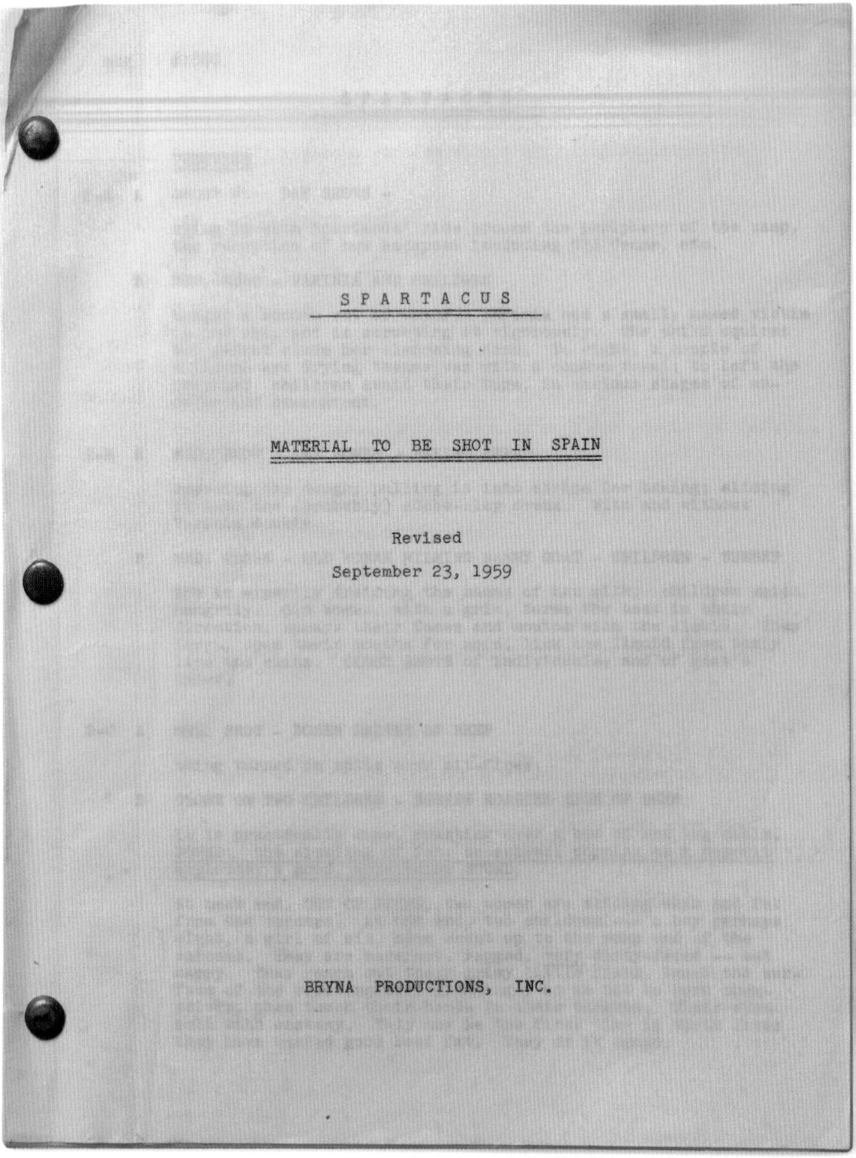

S P A R T A C U S

MATERIAL TO BE SHOT IN SPAIN

Revised

September 23, 1959

BRYNA PRODUCTIONS, INC.

mdg #1888

SPARTACUS

VESUVIUS

2-A A GROUP #1: DAY SHOTS -

tying in with Spartacus' ride around the periphery of the camp, the reception of new escapees including Old Crone, etc.

B MED. SHOT - VARINIA AND CHILDREN

beside a wooden vat of water. Varinia has a small, naked victim in the vat, and is scrubbing it vigorously. The child squirms but cannot elude her cleansing hand. To right, a couple of children are drying themselves with a common towel; to left the unwashed children await their turn, in various stages of undress and discontent.

2-B A MED. SHOT - TEN WOMEN - BAKING BREAD

kneading the dough; pulling it into strips for baking; sliding it into the (probably) adobe-clay ovens. With and without Varinia double.

B MED. CLOSE - OLD WOMAN MILKING NANNY GOAT - CHILDREN - SUNSET

She is expertly draining the nanny of her milk; children watch hungrily. Old Woman, with a grin, turns the teat in their direction, sprays their faces and mouths with the liquid. They laugh, open their mouths for more, lick the liquid from their lips and chins. CLOSE SHOTS of individuals, and of goat's udder.

2-C A MED. SHOT - DOZEN HALVES OF BEEF

being turned on spits over pit-fires.

B CLOSE ON TWO CHILDREN - BESIDE ROASTED SIDE OF BEEF

It is practically done, roasting over a bed of hot log coals. SOUND: the sizzling of fat; occasional popping as a deposit explodes; a good, nourishing SOUND.

At neck end, OUT OF SCENE, two women are slicing skin and fat from the carcass. At OUR end, two children --- a boy perhaps eight, a girl of six, have crept up to the rump end of the carcass. They are barefoot, ragged, very dirty-faced -- but happy. They reach out their grimy little fists, touch the surface of the roasting beef glancingly so as not to burn themselves, then touch their hands to their tongues. Their eyes roll with ecstasy. This may be the first time in their lives they have tasted good beef fat. They do it again.

16

15–16 ***The shooting script for the scenes filmed in Spain.***

Gracchus inquires, already sure of the answer. Crassus grandly responds that he intends to let Gracchus live as long as he is willing to help acclimate his former followers to the new regime.

The slaves who survived the battle are condemned to be crucified outside the gates of the city. "Could we have won?" Antoninus muses as he and Spartacus sit shackled, awaiting their turn to die. "Just by fighting them, we won something," Spartacus answers. "If just one man says: 'No, I won't,' Rome begins to fear. And we were tens of thousands who said 'no.' That was the wonder of it" Spartacus finally gives his identity away to Crassus, who forces Spartacus and Antoninus to fight to the death, proclaiming that the victor will be crucified; to spare him the fate of crucifixion, Spartacus kills his friend. Now secure in his final victory over the slave leader, Crassus orders that after Spartacus is crucified, there is to be "no grave for him, no marker. His body is to be burned and his ashes to be scattered in secret."

Batiatus brings Varinia and her newborn baby, whom Crassus had found in the battlefield and taken into his home, to Gracchus, who gives them all senatorial passes to leave the city, along with articles of freedom for her and the child. Gracchus wants to spite Crassus, who saw Varinia and the child as part of the "spoils of victory." Gracchus takes his leave of Varinia by saying, "I'm going on a journey too."

Once he is alone, he picks up a dagger and walks slowly down a corridor

away from the camera, a diminishing figure like that of General Mireau as he made his last exit near the end of *Paths of Glory*. In both cases a formerly powerful man is pictured as metaphorically reduced in stature by Kubrick's canny camera placement. Gracchus goes through a doorway and draws a curtain behind him. The curtain has closed on his career and his life.

Before leaving the city, Varinia takes her baby to the foot of Spartacus's cross and looks up at him. "This is your son," she says. "He is free." Spartacus looks down, his symbolic identification as a crucified Christ figure now complete, and repeats the one word, "free," as his head falls back against the cross in death. "He'll remember you, Spartacus, because I'll tell him who his father was and what he dreamed of," Varinia says. Then she gets into the cart that Batiatus has waiting for her, and they drive down the avenue lined with crosses which leads them beyond the gates of Rome.

Spartacus is ultimately defeated by the superior forces of Rome, but the empire is already weakening from within, as evidenced by the skullduggery that generals and senators like Crassus practice throughout the movie in an effort to use the crisis that Spartacus has precipitated to their own political advantage. Now that the age of the dictator has arrived, the Romans have in effect enslaved themselves to the despot Crassus, in exchange for his delivering them from Spartacus.

17 ***Kubrick lies behind the camera, relaxing between shots.***

In representing the rebellious slaves as a concretization of mankind's efforts to resist dehumanization throughout human history, *Spartacus* fits thematically into Kubrick's total canon of films better than some commentators on his work are prepared to admit: one can look back to *Paths of Glory* or forward to *Dr. Strangelove*. Moreover, *Spartacus* has a thematic

"It all really just came down to the fact there are thousands of decisions that have to be made, and that if you don't make them yourself, and if you're not on the same wavelength as the people who are making them, it becomes a very painful experience, which it was."

— SK/1968 (to Charles Kohler/*East Village Eye*)

affinity with Kubrick's other pictures, in its portrayal of an apparently foolproof plan that fails in the end—it is the might of the Roman army that is decisive in bringing about Spartacus's downfall. Hence *Spartacus* is more than a marginal film in Kubrick's career; indeed, at 196 minutes, it is the longest film he ever made. With *Spartacus* Kubrick proved once and for all that he could handle commercial subjects with distinction.

Furthermore, the reviewers of the finished film later paid court to the director's success in raising *Spartacus* above the level of the average spear-and-sandal epic; and Peter Ustinov, Russell Metty, and Alexander Golitzen won Academy

18

Awards for the movie. In addition, critics pointed to the staggering battle scenes, Alex North's stunning underscore, and to the standout performances of Laurence Olivier and Charles Laughton, as well as Peter Ustinov.

North (*A Streetcar Named Desire*) was nominated for an Oscar for his score. He was engaged to compose the score before Kubrick replaced Mann as director, so Kubrick could not call upon Gerald Fried, who provided the music for Kubrick's first four features. "For *Spartacus*," writes Lee Tsiantis, "North attempted to capture the feeling of pre-Christian Rome, using contemporary musical techniques.... North researched music of the period and unearthed unorthodox instruments such as the dulcimer in a quest for exotic tone color." Kubrick encouraged North in this endeavor, so "North used a large brass section to evoke the barbaric quality of the times. He withheld the violins until the film's love story blossomed" between Varinia and Spartacus. The love theme was delicately orchestrated, demonstrating North's lyric gifts.[9]

In *A Life in Pictures*, Peter Ustinov states, "The great virtue of the film is that it was the only epic of that scale that didn't have Jesus," taking place as it did in pre-

18–19 ***"I work with the editor right through until the film is ready for negative cutting. On* Spartacus, *my talented and patient film editor, Bob Lawrence, slaved seven days a week with me for about six months in the cutting room." –SK/1960 (to Charles Reynolds/*Popular Photography*)***

Christian Rome. Ustinov's remark is less facetious than it at first might appear. What he is really saying is that *Spartacus* is a good Roman spectacle because it omits all the clichés associated with that genre: Christian martyrs devoured by lions in the arena, chariot races, and orgies of scantily clad dancing girls. To that extent, the young Kubrick had outdone Cecil B. De Mille (*The Sign of the Cross*), the scion of the Hollywood costume epic, in making an inventive historical movie.

Spartacus was shortened from its original 196 minutes to 184 minutes for a 1967 reissue. According to Dawn Sova, there had been complaints from reviewers when the film was first released that the violence in the battle scenes "was too gruesome... so some of the bloodiest violence was elminated."[10] But the missing footage was restored under Kubrick's personal supervision for the 1991 release of the movie on home video. Among the restored footage was the suggestive scene between Crassus and Antoninus. However, when the soundtrack was to be reinserted in the video version, it was discovered that it had not survived for the scene in question. Tony Curtis redubbed his dialogue and Anthony Hopkins read the late Laurence Olivier's lines for the scene.

There is little doubt that Ridley Scott's *Gladiator* (2000) was inspired by Kubrick's *Spartacus*. There are several parallels between the two films, with Russell Crowe in the latter movie playing a rebellious slave who, like Spartacus, becomes a champion gladiator. The scenes in the school for gladiators and those in which the hero bests his opponents in the arena all recall *Spartacus*.

Yet Kubrick did not remember the film with any great satisfaction. Perhaps the most significant thing about the movie in terms of Kubrick's career as a whole is that his experience in making the picture served to strengthen his resolve to safeguard his artistic independence in making future films.

"I tried to forget that this film was costing millions and that we had all the extras we wanted, and just thought in terms of what each scene was about and how the characters would honestly behave."

— SK/1960 (*Look*)

Kubrick and Douglas never were reconciled. "He'll be a fine director some day," Douglas said afterward, "if he falls on his face just once. It might teach him how to compromise."[11] Elsewhere Douglas added that some directors are talented, some directors are bastards, and that Stanley Kubrick was a talented bastard. But Kubrick was not interested in compromising his artistic vision. In order to ensure total control of his next film, *Lolita*, he joined forces once more with James B. Harris and together they acquired the rights to Nabokov's controversial novel.

Notes

1. Gene D. Phillips, "Dalton Trumbo," in *The Encyclopedia of Stanley Kubrick,* with Rodney Hill (New York: Checkmark, 2002): 373.
2. James Howard, *Stanley Kubrick Companion* (London: Batsford, 1999): 69.
3. Gene D. Phillips, James Howard, Chris Morash, Richard Hayes, "Stanley Kubrick: A Discussion," *Film and Film Culture 1* (2002): 29.
4. Peter Ustinov, *Dear Me: An Autobiography* (London: Heinemann, 1977): 159.
5. Paul Zimmerman, "Kubrick's Brilliant Vision," *Newsweek* (January 3, 1972): 78.
6. Peter Bogdanovich, "What They Say about Stanley Kubrick," *The New York Times Magazine* (July 4, 1999): 22.
7. Tony Curtis, *Tony Curtis: The Autobiography,* with Barry Paris (New York: William Morrow, 1993): 85.
8. Vito Russo, *The Celluloid Closet: Homosexuality in the Movies,* rev. ed. (New York: Harper and Row, 1987): 119–20.
9. Lee Tsiantis, "Alex North," in *International Dictionary of Films and Filmmakers: Writers and Production Artists,* ed. Grace Jeromski, rev. ed. (Detroit: St. James Press, 1997): 612.
10. Dawn Sova, *Forbidden Films: Censorship* (New York: Checkmark, 2002): 277–78.
11. Paul Duncan, *Stanley Kubrick* (Cologne: TASCHEN, 2003): 62.

Lolita

1962 / BLACK AND WHITE / 153 MINUTES
Distributed by METRO-GOLDWYN-MAYER

CAST
HUMBERT HUMBERT JAMES MASON
CLARE QUILTY PETER SELLERS
CHARLOTTE HAZE SHELLEY WINTERS
LOLITA HAZE SUE LYON
DICK GARY COCKRELL
JOHN FARLOW JERRY STOVIN
JEAN FARLOW DIANA DECKER
NURSE MARY LORE LOIS MAXWELL
PHYSICIAN CEC LINDER
MRS. STARCH SHIRLEY DOUGLAS
VIVIAN DARKBLOOM MARIANNE STONE
MISS LEBONE MARION MATHIE
MISS FROMKISS MAXINE HOLDEN
TOM JOHN HARRISON
CHARLIE COHN MAITLAND
SWINE BILL GREENE
LOUISE ISOBEL LUCAS
BEALE JAMES DYRENFORTH
LORNA ROBERTA SHORE
HOSPITAL ATTENDANT IRVIN ALLEN
REX CRAIG SAMS
ROY ERIC LANE
POTTS C. DENIER WARREN
BILL ROLAND BRAND
MONA FARLOW SUZANNE GIBBS
MAN TERENCE KILBURN

CREW
DIRECTED BY STANLEY KUBRICK
PRODUCED BY JAMES B. HARRIS
SCREENPLAY VLADIMIR NABOKOV, based on his novel *Lolita*
ORIGINAL MUSIC NELSON RIDDLE
"LOLITA" THEME BOB HARRIS, orchestrations by GIL GRAU
PRODUCTION SUPERVISOR RAYMOND ANZARUT
ART DIRECTOR BILL ANDREWS
ASSOCIATE ART DIRECTOR SIDNEY CAIN
DIRECTOR OF PHOTOGRAPHY OSWALD MORRIS B. S. C.
EDITOR ANTHONY HARVEY
PRODUCTION MANAGER ROBERT STERNE
ASSISTANT DIRECTOR RENE DUPONT
CAMERA OPERATOR DENYS N. COOP
CASTING JAMES LIGGAT
2ND UNIT DIRECTOR DENNIS STOCK
MAKEUP GEORGE PARTLETON
ASSISTANT EDITOR LOIS GRAY

Produced at Associated British Studios, Elstree, England.

Opposite *The tagline of the movie's poster, "How did they ever make a movie of Lolita?", refers to the well-known difficulty of getting such a risqué subject past the censors.*

How did they ever make a movie of
LOLITA ?
FOR PERSONS
OVER 18 YEARS
OF AGE
METRO-GOLDWYN-MAYER presents in association with SEVEN ARTS PRODUCTIONS JAMES B. HARRIS and STANLEY KUBRICK'S LOLITA
Starring JAMES MASON · SHELLEY WINTERS · PETER SELLERS as "Quilty" and Introducing SUE LYON as "Lolita"
Directed by STANLEY KUBRICK · Screenplay by VLADIMIR NABOKOV based on his novel "Lolita" Produced by JAMES B. HARRIS
Music composed and conducted by Nelson Riddle
Lolita Theme by Bob Harris
APPROVED BY THE PRODUCTION CODE ADMINISTRATION

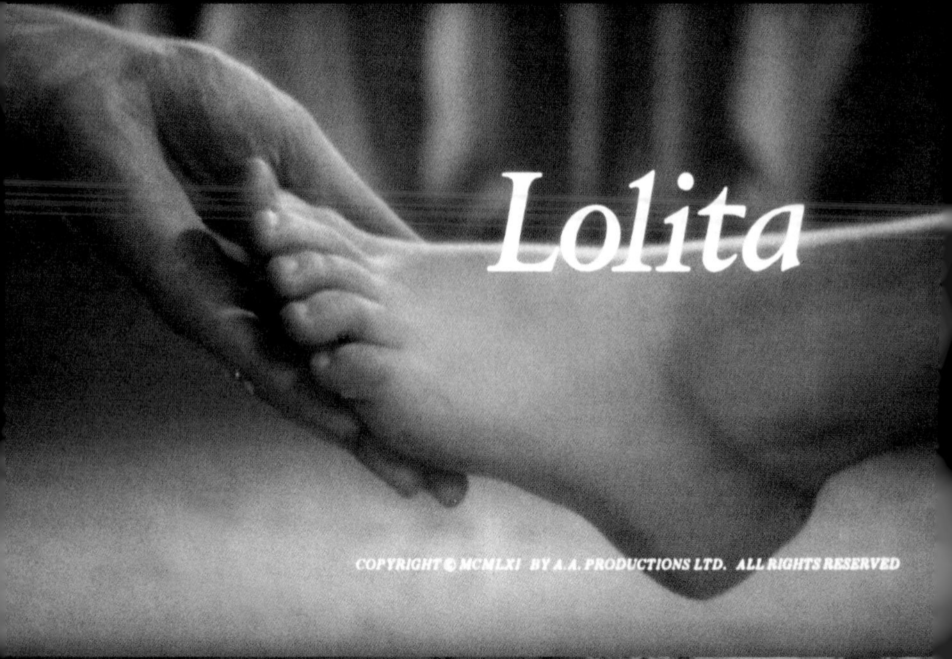
Lolita
COPYRIGHT © MCMLXI BY A.A. PRODUCTIONS LTD. ALL RIGHTS RESERVED

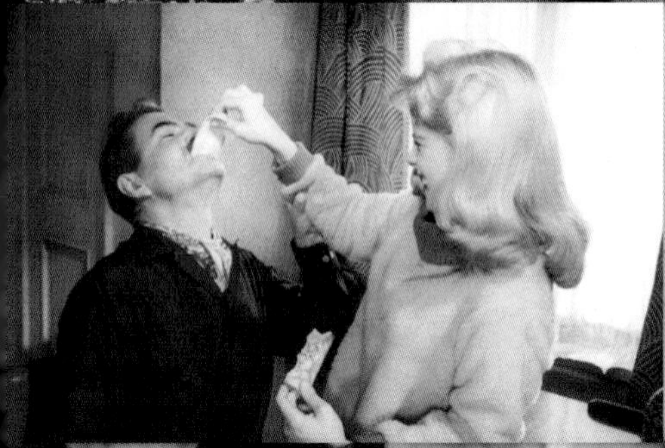
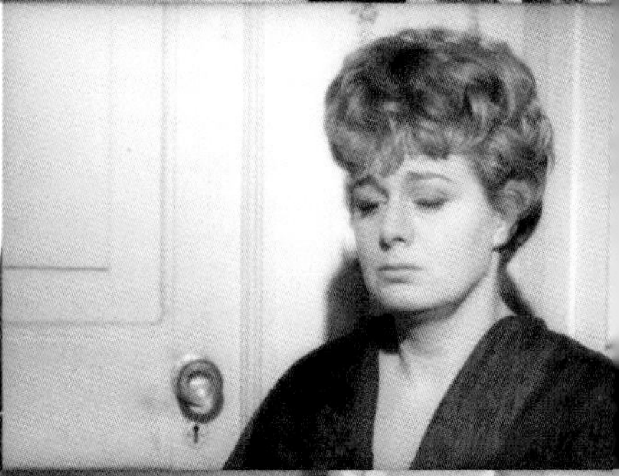

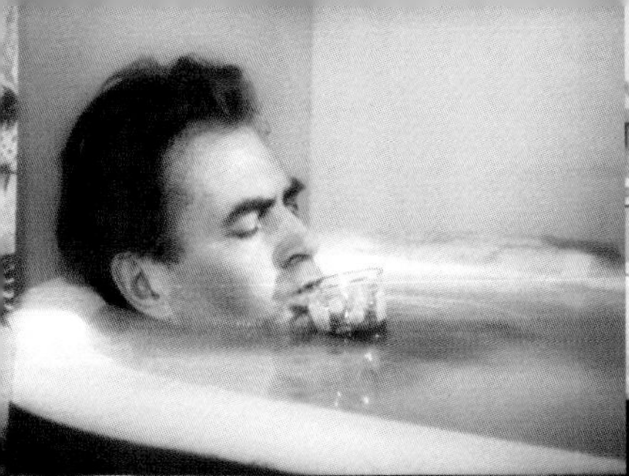

CAMP CLIMAX
FOR GIRLS
DRIVE CAREFULLY

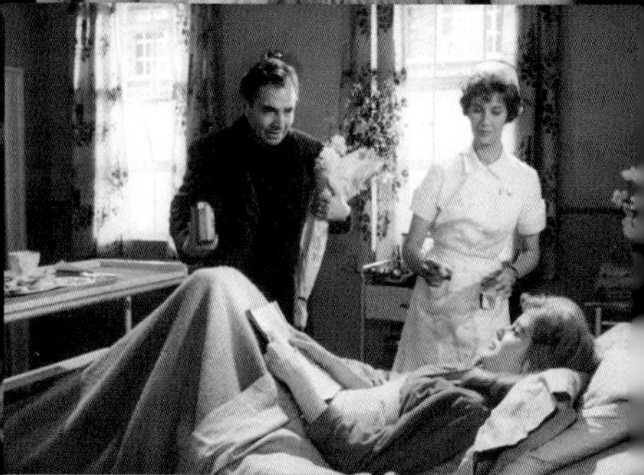

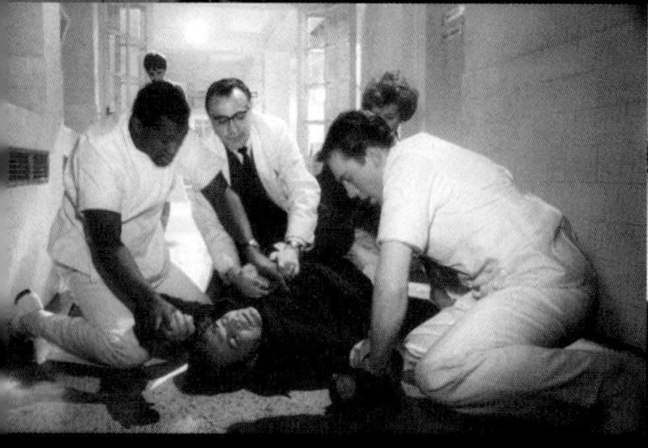

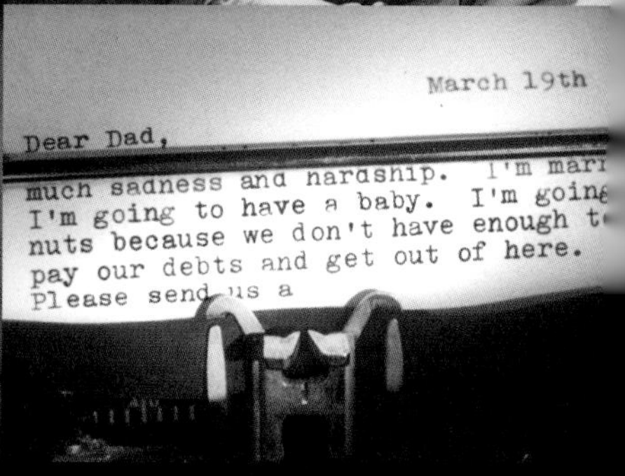
March 19th
Dear Dad,
much sadness and hardship. I'm mar
I'm going to have a baby. I'm going
nuts because we don't have enough t
pay our debts and get out of here.
Please send us a

Epilogue
Humbert Humbert died of
coronary thrombosis in prison
awaiting trial for the
murder of Clare Quilty.

01

Lolita

by Gene D. Phillips

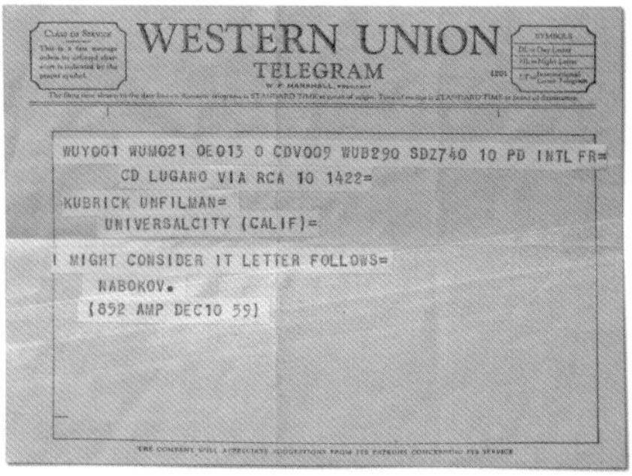
WESTERN UNION
TELEGRAM
W. P. MARSHALL, PRESIDENT

WUY001 WUM021 OE013 0 CDV009 WUB290 SDZ740 10 PD INTL FR=
CD LUGANO VIA RCA 10 1422=
KUBRICK UNFILMAN=
UNIVERSALCITY (CALIF)=
I MIGHT CONSIDER IT LETTER FOLLOWS=
NABOKOV.
(852 AMP DEC10 59)

03

To make *Lolita*, Kubrick moved to England, where he could more easily obtain financial backing; MGM had funds frozen there that they wanted to be used. When Kubrick and his partner, James B. Harris, announced that they had acquired the rights to Vladimir Nabokov's controversial novel, there was much speculation in the trade press as to how they would tackle a story that deals with the perverse love of an older man for a pubescent girl.

Part of their problem was rooted not so much in the novel itself, but in the sensational reputation the book had acquired since its publication, especially in the minds of those who had never read it. Despite Nabokov's credentials as a major novelist, the manuscript was originally rejected in 1954 by four American publishers, none of whom, he suspected, read it to the end. It was finally brought out in 1955 by the Olympia Press in Paris, which specialized in erotica. So Nabokov joined the ranks of James Joyce and other novelists who had to turn to a small Paris press when their work was turned down everywhere else.

When *Lolita* was first published, some critics thought it too explicit in dealing with sexual matters. Nabokov wrote to fellow-novelist Graham Greene at the time, commenting on the controversy surrounding the book: "My poor Lolita is having a rough time. The pity is that, if I had made her a boy, philistines might not have flinched."[1] Still, the novel found champions in literary circles when it was published in America and England in the late 1950s. In fact, Greene stoked serious interest in the book when he gave it a rave review in the London *Times*. Over the years Nabokov's novel has been recognized as the elegantly written, superb piece of fiction that it really is. At the time Kubrick undertook to film it, however, the book was still something of a *succès de scandale*.

The novel is narrated by Humbert Humbert (who has changed all the names in the story, including his own, "to protect the guilty"), as he commits the tale to his diary. He is a college professor who falls hopelessly in love with twelve-year-old Dolores Haze, known as Lolita to her friends. Humbert in the novel calls himself a "nympholept," a word by which Nabokov sought to suggest the term "lepidopterist," a butterfly specialist, something which Nabokov himself had been for years. The metaphor suggests that Humbert, in attempting to snare his butterfly, is enmeshed in the net

01 ***Kubrick with his leading nymphet, Sue Lyon.***
02 ***The director observes as Lyon is photographed on the set of the Hazes' backyard.***
03 ***Nabokov declined when Kubrick first asked him to write the screenplay for*** Lolita. ***In December 1959, Kubrick appealed to him to reconsider and received this telegram in reply.***

(1) OUTLINE FOR "LOLITA" AUGUST 24, 1959

1. DAY. EXT. COUNTRY ESTATE QUILTY. x-mas atmosphere
Six cars parked outside. Humbert's arrives. He enters.

2. INT. QUILTY HOUSE
Humbert kills Quilty. Exits house. **Plant loss of glasses and nearsighted.**

3. DAY. EXT. STATE PRISON

4. INT. DEATH ROW
Humbert is writing memoirs. <u>FLASHBACK TRANSITION</u>

5. DAY. EXT. SMALL TOWN (RAMSDALE) TRAIN STATION
Humbert exits train. No one meets him. Takes taxi.

6. DAY. EXT. RAMSDALE STREET. (HAZE'S BURNT HOUSE)
Puzzled, H. turns to find Haze car arrive. Haze explains missed him at train station. Late for faculty luncheon in Humbert's honor.

7. INT. HAZE CAR (PROCESS)
Warm reminicenses of past. Haze friend of family. Knew Humbert as a child. Produces photo of Annabele, had always meant to send it to him. Purpose was to show H. child picture. Hum strange reaction to A. prompts conversation hinting at romance. **Establish, Professor Haze must go to a "dry, sunny climate and must leave in the middle of the school term.**

8. EXT. DAY. RAMSDALE UNIVERSITY. CAR PULLS UP
see co-eds dig H.H. - turn heads

9. INT. FACULTY DINING ROOM.
Purpose of scene to introduce Clare Quilty; create a sense of reality that Humbert is really a teacher; comic minor characters; establish of rountie of Quilty's annual service to his alma mata, Ramsdale U, interrupting his Broadway & Hollywood writing career.

Football coach; Math head, 28, crew, steel glasses; Head of German dept; Head of Romance languages; faggy head of Art department; Dr. Quilty brother of Clare, Vivian Darkbloom, Mrs. Pratt of High school who "had to come"; Science dept.

They had begun to eat fearing that Humbert had missed the train. General awkwardness. People are introduced seated at the table. Only the people we are planting are given an introduction and make a reply, Mrs. Pratt, the Quilty's . Establish the play is over and Quilty is leaving town that day. Quilty treats Humbert with a certain patronizing defference. Humbert is familiar with Quilty's repitation.

04

himself and cannot possess the object of his obsession for long. Furthermore, the word *nympholepsy* had come to mean a frustrating attachment to an unattainable object, lending universal implications to Humbert's plight.

Nabokov's novel fairly begged to be committed to the screen, since he makes several references to cinema in the book. On one page Humbert muses, on watching Lolita play tennis, that he regrets that he had not immortalized her in segments of celluloid, which he could then run in the projection room of his mind. With so many cinematic references in the novel, it is not surprising that Kubrick engaged Nabokov to write the screenplay of *Lolita*. Kubrick vividly recalled his consternation when he received Nabokov's draft and discovered that it would run for several hours if all of its four hundred pages were filmed as they were written. Harris added that they could hardly *lift* the script, much less film it! They closeted themselves in an office for a month and drastically revised Nabokov's screenplay. The novelist later speculated that Kubrick finally used about 20 percent of his draft.

In addition to writing the first draft of the screenplay, Nabokov also participated in casting decisions. Kubrick placed Sue Lyon's photograph in a stack of pictures of young hopefuls who wanted to play Lolita and showed them to Nabokov; he singled out Lyon's photo, saying that she was undoubtedly the one girl to play Lolita. He also personally interviewed Shelley Winters and told Kubrick he was much impressed by her, because she would not make Charlotte Haze a harridan.

Principal photography took place at the Elstree studios on the outskirts of London, but locations were also employed. Thus Hillfield, a baronial mansion west of Elstree, served as the home of Clare Quilty, the rich playboy and TV personality.

Kubrick made further changes to the script in the course of shooting, because he had developed the habit over the years of encouraging his cast to improvise during the course of rehearsals (this procedure would prove particularly fortuitous in the case of *Dr. Strangelove*). Peter Sellers as Quilty does several comic impersonations in the course of the movie, as he endeavors to badger Humbert by various ruses into giving up Lolita to him. Although some critics later said that Kubrick seemed besotted with Sellers' abilities as a mimic, his brilliant flair for improvisation makes these scenes among the best in the movie.

Sellers' inclination to improvise in order to experiment with a variety of ways of handling a scene tested Shelley Winters' patience at times. When Sellers began improvising additional dialogue for a scene, she remembers, he at times seemed to her at least, if not to Kubrick, to be straying too far from the script. She thought he was "acting on a different planet. I never could connect with him." As a result, she found working with Sellers a stressful experience. Whenever she complained to Kubrick about Sellers, she says, he politely ignored

04 ***One of Kubrick's early outlines for the screenplay, showing drastic differences from the final version.***

her protests. "I never felt that anyone was listening to me," she concluded, "except the sound man" who was recording the dialogue.[2]

Kubrick thought Winters was too temperamental and became annoyed with her carping. Cinematographer Oswald Morris said, "Shelley Winters was difficult," and was nearly fired from the film. At one point an exasperated Kubrick said to Morris, "I think the lady's gonna have to go." This would have been a serious setback for the production schedule, "but he'd have got rid of her," Morris concludes, if he really thought it was necessary.[3] Kubrick kept Winters, reasoning that her character would disappear from the film halfway through.

James Mason felt that the rehearsal periods during shooting afforded the cast an excellent opportunity to explore the significance of each scene, although he also found the process wearing. Kubrick found that Sue Lyon had learned all her lines before filming started, Mason writes in his autobiography, *Before I Forget*, "and she had to be induced to think of the lines in a particular scene as something that came out of the feeling of the character in that scene. So we started improvising during rehearsals and forgot the lines we had learned and got to grips with the situation instead, finding that this helped us to understand much more quickly what each scene was basically about. She

05–06 ***Peter Sellers as Quilty in the film's opening scenes.***

made a considerable contribution to many of the scenes because she spoke the same language as the character she was playing."[4]

Kubrick had some distinguished collaborators behind the camera as well: director of photography Oswald Morris (*Our Man in Havana*), editor Anthony Harvey (*The L-Shaped Room*), and composer Nelson Riddle (*A Kiss Before Dying*). Each of them was much in demand in the industry.

Although Riddle wrote the underscore for *Lolita*, Kubrick asked him to incorporate a love theme into his score that had been composed by Bob Harris, James B. Harris's brother. When Kubrick first heard it, he said that he thought that this lush romantic theme, scored for piano and orchestra, would prove an ironic counterpoint to this caustic tale of an older man's infatuation with an underage girl. Riddle used the "Love Theme" in the opening credits and throughout the film. Still, Riddle composed a variety of themes of his own for the picture, including wall-to-wall ominous music in a minor key for the melodramatic sequences and the silly dance tunes that pour out of Lolita's transistor. This inane music reminds us that Lolita is only a kid, despite her sexual prowess.

The big problem with the movie, Harris explained to Jill Bernstein, was "how we were going to get this picture made, with the censorship restrictions" they would have to cope with. Kubrick and Harris were aware that the industry's censorship code forbade any explicit depiction of pedophilia. The film had to receive the industry censor's official seal of approval,

"If I have my way … [t]he audience will start by being repelled by this 'creep' who seduces a not-so-innocent child, but gradually, as they realize he really loves the girl, they'll find things aren't quite as simple as they seemed, and they won't be so ready to pass immediate moral judgment. I consider that a moral theme."

— SK/1960 (to Eugene Archer/*The New York Times*)

because most exhibitors would not book a movie that lacked the industry seal. So they promised Geoffrey Shurlock, the industry censor, at the outset that the relationship of Humbert and Lolita would be portrayed discreetly, and even leavened with some black humor. One way that Kubrick mollified the censor from the start was to cast fourteen-year-old Sue Lyon as Lolita, since he rightly assumed that Shurlock would not hear of Lolita being played by a girl of twelve, Lolita's age in the book. For the record, when filming began Sue Lyon was fourteen years and four months old; when the movie wrapped, she was fourteen years and nine months old.

It is obvious that at the time that Kubrick made *Lolita*, the freedom of the screen had not advanced to the point it has reached today. Shurlock insisted therefore that Kubrick be much less explicit in the film than Nabokov had been in his book in suggesting Humbert's sexual obsession for a nymphet. "I wasn't able to give much weight at all to the erotic aspect of Humbert's relationship in the film," Kubrick told me. "And because I could only hint at the true nature of his attraction to Lolita, it was assumed too quickly by filmgoers that Humbert was in love with her. In the novel this comes as a discovery at the end, when Lolita is no longer a nymphet."

Since the erotic aspect of the narrative had to be soft-pedaled, Kubrick decided to emphasize the black comedy inherent in the story. Pauline Kael writes in *I Lost It at the Movies*, "The surprise of *Lolita* is how enjoyable it is; it's the first new American comedy since those great days in the forties when Preston Sturges (*The Miracle of Morgan's Creek*) recreated comedy with verbal slapstick. *Lolita* is black slapstick and at times it's so far out that you gasp as you laugh."

Yet several critics questioned the casting of Sue Lyon in the title role, saying that she looked too old for the part and accusing Kubrick of copping out by giving the impression that Humbert was infatuated not with a twelve-year-old nymphet but with a teenager. "She was actually the right age for the part," Kubrick told me. "Lolita was twelve-and-a-half in the novel, and Sue was fourteen. I suspect that many people actually had a mental image of a nine-year-old."

Kael laid that objection definitively to rest in her notice: "Have reviewers looked at the schoolgirls of America lately? The

07 *This progress report, dated December 5, 1960, notes, "Shelley Winters still indisposed." Though her performance was ultimately superb, Winters had a stressful time during shooting, often arriving late and finding it difficult to work with James Mason and Peter Sellers.*

MR. JAMES B. HARRIS

DAILY PRODUCTION PROGRESS REPORT

REPORT No. STUDIO 6

PRODUCTION " LOLITA "

DATE Monday, 5th December, 1960.

Studio SHOOTING SCHEDULE	BEGIN	FINISH	TOTAL DAYS	DAYS TO DATE
ESTIMATED	26.11.	[illegible].3.61	66	6
ACTUAL	28.11.			

DIRECTOR STANLEY KUBRICK

WHERE WORKING (STUDIO — STAGE — SET — LOCATION) STAGE 5
Int./Ext. Haze House

TIME

CALL	8.30 am
1st SET UP COMPLETED	3.05 pm
LUNCH—FROM	12.45 pm
TO	1.45 pm
UNIT DISMISSED	6.05
* TOTAL HOURS (¼ hr. Night)	taken

SCRIPT SCENES

	SCRIPT NUMBER	SCRIPT MINUTES	EXTRA NUMBER	EXTRA MINUTES	RETAKES NUMBER	RETAKES MINUTES
PREVIOUSLY TAKEN	1	9.25				
TAKEN TO-DAY	1	2.35				
TAKEN TO DATE	2	12.00				
TO BE TAKEN	213					
TOTAL SCRIPT SCENES	215					

DAILY AVERAGE - SCREENTIME: 2.00

CONTRACT ARTISTES

NAME	W	Call	Diss
JAMES MASON (Arr: 7.40 Dep: 6.05)	6	8.00	6.00
SUE LYON (Arr: 8.20 Dep: 7.25)	3	8.00	6.00

(On the way to the Studio Sue Lyon decided to return to her flat to pick up something she forgot)

SHORT ENDS

Previous	5,040
Today	995 (740.255)
	6,035
Used Today	570
Todate	5,465

SMALL PARTS

NAME / DAILY RATE

REMARKS (continued)

Shelley Winters still indisposed, but Insurance Doctor informed us, through Mr. Geddes the Assessor, that she should be fit for work again tomorrow. However, we could carry on shooting without her to give her a chance to recover her strength.

STAND INS NAME	STAND INS RATE	CROWDS NUMBER	CROWDS RATE
2 @	4 2 4		

ACTION PROPS AND EFFECTS	SLATE NUMBERS	SCENE NUMBERS
Silent Wind. Transatlantic Crane & Crab Dolly on hire for run of production.	9 - 11.	43 completed.

B & W PICTURE — NEGATIVE FILM FOOTAGE — SOUND (Magnetic Transfer)

WASTE	RESERVE & N/G	PRINT	TOTAL		TOTAL	PRINT	RESERVE & N/G	WASTE
345	3,785	11,125	15,255	PREVIOUSLY USED	11,245	10,495	-	750
145	485	1,945	2,575	USED TO-DAY	2,060	2,060	-	-
490	4,270	13,070	17,830	TOTALS TO DATE	13,305	12,555	-	750

STILLS	PREVIOUSLY TAKEN	TAKEN TO-DAY	TAKEN TO DATE
B & W Rolls	13	2	15 Rolls
Colour	3		3 Rolls
5 x 4 B&W	36	-	36

REMARKS

* Rushes 6.00 - 7.25 p.m.

STATUS	DAYS	OVER
PREVIOUSLY REPORTED	5	2½
TO-DAY	1	
TO DATE	6	2½

SET UPS	
PREVIOUS	8
TO-DAY'S	3
TO DATE	11

	MAGNETIC FILM USED
Prev	14 Rolls
Today	1 Roll (15A)
Todate	15 Rolls

08

classmates of my fourteen-year-old daughter are not merely nubile; some of them look badly used." She complimented Kubrick and company for not dolling Sue Lyon up in childish clothes and pigtails, in which case she would have looked to be nine. "The facts of American life are that adolescents and even pre-adolescents wear nylons and makeup and two-piece-strapless bathing suits and have *figures*."[5] In effect, Kubrick opted for accuracy over the filmgoer's preconception of how Lolita should look.

On May 25, 1961, Shurlock granted the film industry's official seal of approval (seal #2000) to *Lolita*. But then Kubrick and Harris had to contend with the Legion of Decency, which rated the acceptability of films for its Catholic constituency. Nevertheless, in the absence of an industry rating system—which would not come into being until 1968—the Legion's ratings were followed by many non-Catholics. Consequently, studio bosses demanded that Kubrick and Harris avoid receiving a condemned rating for the picture from the Legion, which would damage the film's chances at the box office.

In Jan Harlan's documentary, Harris states that the Legion of Decency advised them that it was prepared to condemn the film on the basis of a couple of scenes which they were convinced were objectionable. So Kubrick and Harris accordingly arbitrated with the Legion to change the rating.

08 ***Shooting the scene in which Charlotte gives Humbert a tour of her house.***
09 ***Kubrick lines up the shot of Humbert climbing the stairs in pursuit of Quilty.***

Harris points to the scene in which Humbert, who has married Lolita's mother, Charlotte, just to be near her daughter, embraces Charlotte on the bed; he surreptitiously gazes beyond Charlotte to the picture of Lolita on the bedside night table. This implies that Humbert refers his sexual encounters with Charlotte to Lolita. Monsignor Thomas Little, the director of the Legion, maintained that this emphasized Humbert's obsession with the girl too blatantly. As Harris affirms in the documentary, "We agreed to change that" by simply reducing the number of times Humbert is shown looking at Lolita's photo. As a direct result of the modifications he and Kubrick made in the film at the behest of the Legion, *Lolita* was spared the condemned rating;

Msgr. Little, in concert with his advisory board, finally gave the Legion's blessing to the picture, with the condition that the movie's ads state that *Lolita* was "for persons over eighteen only."[6] In sum, by making concessions to the Legion, the picture was approved for mature audiences across the board. Yet some film historians still persist in asserting that the movie was condemned by the Roman Catholic Church, which is manifestly untrue.

When it came time to shoot the credit sequence of the movie, Oswald Morris had departed for another assignment. So Kubrick brought in lighting cameraman Gilbert Taylor to shoot it. The credits are superimposed on a shot of Humbert's hand caressing Lolita's foot as he begins to

10 ***Charlotte prepares to cut in on Quilty's dance***
11 ***Kubrick pretends to be Humbert during rehearsal.***

11

paint her toenails, thereby making a wry comment on the subservient nature of his infatuation with the young girl. The action is set against a background of satin drapes, and Taylor photographs the images in soft and delicate tones. Kubrick was so impressed with his work that he later hired Taylor to shoot his next picture, *Dr. Strangelove*.

"Music is one of the most important elements in a film, as is silence."

— SK/1960 (to Charles Reynolds/ *Popular Photography*)

After the credits there is a prologue in which Humbert arrives at Quilty's musty mansion for a decisive showdown with him about Lolita. Sellers' improvising on the set during rehearsals yielded some excellent bits of dialogue for this scene. In addition, this sequence firmly establishes the air of black comedy that permeates the picture. Humbert stumbles about among the cluttered rooms looking for Quilty, who begins to stir under the dust cover of one of the sheeted chairs in the living room, which is strewn with empty bottles and other remnants of previous festivities.

The disheveled Quilty, dressed in pajamas and slippers and trying vainly to cope with a hangover, wraps the sheet around himself like a toga and says with a lisp, "I am Spartacus; have you come to free the slaves?" This jibe at the unpleasant experience that making *Spartacus* had been for Kubrick must have given him some consolation. Quilty's frivolous and erratic behavior is in arch counterpoint to Humbert's single-minded, broken-voiced despair: "Do you recall a girl called Dolores Haze? Lolita?" Quilty eyes the gun Humbert points at him and, wrapped in the haze of a hangover, glides into an imitation of an old sourdough, reminiscent of countless sagebrush epics: "That's a durlin' little gun you got there, mister." Making every effort to ignore this horseplay, Humbert forces Quilty to read from a confession that he has penned for him. Quilty focuses his bleary eyes and reads, "Because you cheated me, because you took her at an age when young lads—" He halts when Humbert takes the paper from him, saying, "That was getting kinda smutty there."

Quilty sits down at a piano, like a composer in some forgotten Hollywood musical biography; he seeks to distract his tormentor by saying, "You look like a music lover to me. Why don't you let me play you a little thing I wrote last week." He launches into a Chopin polonaise. "The moon is blue and so are you," he sings. "She's mine tonight— *yours*, she's *yours* tonight...." Finally bedeviled beyond endurance, Humbert fires and Quilty runs up the grand staircase. Humbert follows his prey up the stairs, as Quilty scrambles behind a painting that is propped against the wall. The camera lingers on the painting as it fills up with bullet holes. The rest of the film will unfold in flashback.

12–13 ***Bert Stern's suggestive portraits of Sue Lyon as Lolita; most of the photos in this series were too risqué to be used for publicity purposes.***

Much critical ink has been spent over whether Kubrick should have transferred Quilty's murder from its place at the end of the novel to the opening of the film. Kubrick was aware that much of the interest in the novel centered around Humbert's machinations to possess Lolita. When Lolita later disappears and he tracks her down, Humbert learns that Quilty had snatched her from him after playing several grim tricks to get Humbert to relinquish his hold on the girl. By shifting Humbert's final encounters with Quilty to the beginning of the movie, Kubrick tips off the viewer that Quilty is the immediate architect of Humbert's ruin. The filmgoer thus has the satisfaction of being aware all along about Quilty's ingenious bamboozling of Humbert at every turn, and wonders when Humbert will realize what Quilty is up to. Hence the prologue works very well.

Nabokov framed the story with first-person narration. Kubrick, in turn, followed Nabokov's lead in the movie by having first-person narration at crucial moments—a technique he had not used since *Killer's Kiss.* Kubrick in this way reminds us in the course of the picture that the story is being told from Humbert's point of view, as he apparently reads to us from his diary.

After the prologue, the story proper gets under way with a title that reads "4 Years EARLIER." Humbert, acting as narrator, explains in voice-over how he came to meet Lolita. "Having recently arrived in America.... I had been appointed to a lectureship in poetry at Beardsley College,

Ohio, in the fall. Friends had given me several addresses in Ramsdale where lodgings were available for the summer."

Charlotte Haze, a bumptious, dowdy widow, guides Humbert on a tour of her house, wearing sexy skin-tight leotards, pretentiously waving a cigarette holder at him and calling him "Monsieur." In opening her campaign to win Humbert, she ever so casually mentions that she is a widow, pointing to a picture of her deceased husband (who looks like a younger Nabokov). Charlotte is a mixture of dime-store sophistication, woman's club energy, and sexual hunger. Her attempts at sophistication are sabotaged when she spies one of Lolita's discarded bobby socks. Her highbrow manner is demolished as she says to Humbert, "Excuse the soiled sock."

She recovers by leading Humbert into the back yard, where he sees Lolita for the first time and is utterly bedazzled. The girl lounges languidly in the sun in an abbreviated swimsuit, exuding a sex appeal beyond her years. Lolita, one critic has put it, is interested in Humbert the way a tigress is interested in its prey. Not knowing what he is in for, Humbert slyly leers at her and instantly agrees to move in with Lolita—and her mother.

At a high school dance that Humbert and Charlotte are chaperoning, Quilty, who has been a guest speaker at the school, puts in an appearance. "Hello *again*"—Charlotte greets him like an elephant in heat. She dances into his arms. Quilty grins knowingly, "Didn't you have a daughter with a lovely, lyrical, lilting name?" In retrospect, the viewer will later infer from this interchange that Quilty had seduced Charlotte to gain access to

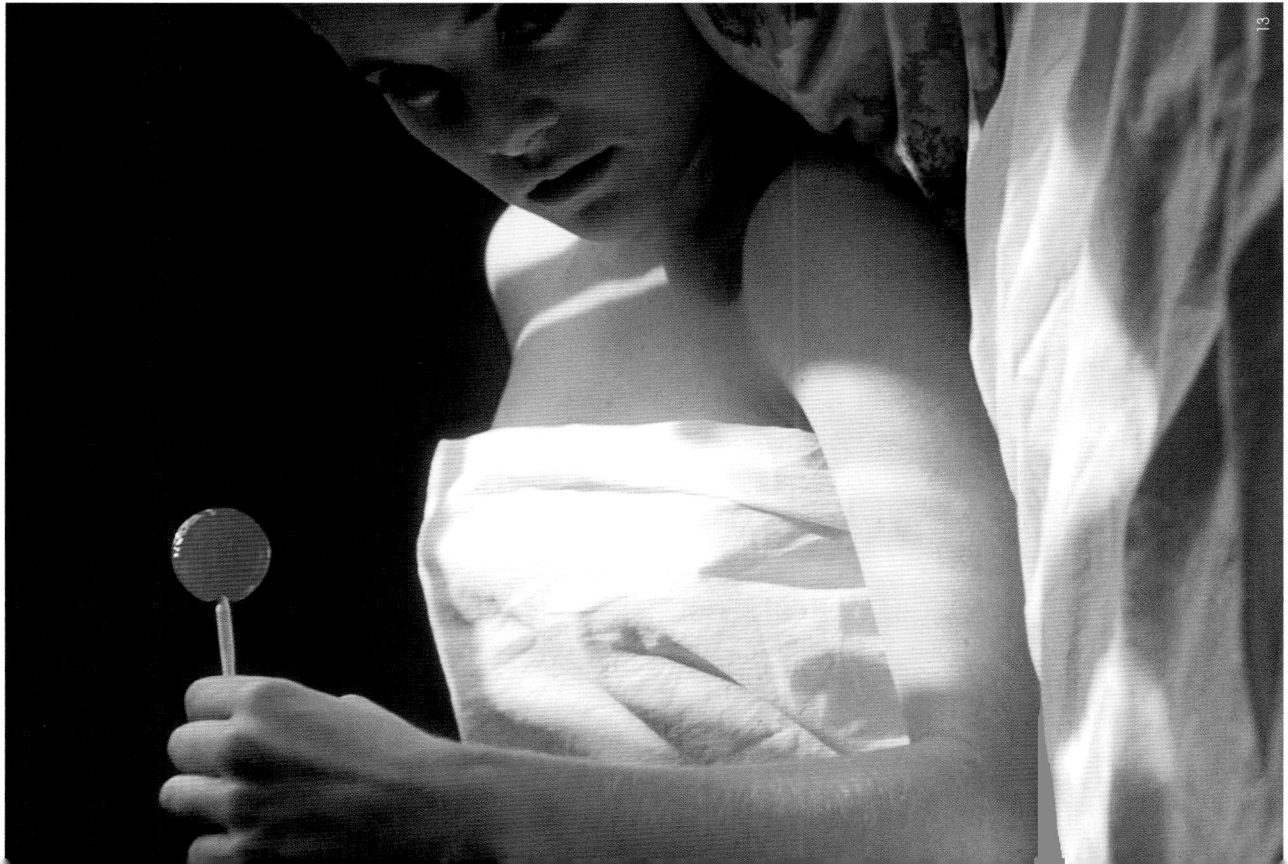
13

"One of the basic problems with the book, and with the film even in its modified form, is that the main narrative interest boils down to the question 'Will Humbert get Lolita into bed?' ... We wanted to avoid this problem in the film, and Nabokov and I agreed that if we had Humbert shoot Quilty without explanation at the beginning, then throughout the film the audience would wonder what Quilty was up to."

— SK/1970 (to Joseph Gelmis)

Lolita, just as Humbert will marry the hapless Charlotte for the same reason.

After the dance, Lolita goes off to a teen party, and Charlotte dragoons Humbert home for a cozy supper. She slips into a seductive gown with a leopard-skin design. Then she switches on some Latin music supplied by Nelson Riddle, which has an emphatic beat. Winters did some improvising of her own at this point. "Stanley didn't really tell me to make it a sexy dance," she remembers. "I decided to flirt with Mason while I was dancing, and Kubrick said, 'That's it.'"[7]

Charlotte steers Humbert into a corner, passionately protesting her love for him. Lolita picks just this moment to return from the party, and Humbert is saved from submitting to his landlady's blandishments. He gracefully bows out. Tears of frustration in her eyes, Charlotte puts the bottle of champagne back into the ice bucket and begins to weep.

In this scene Shelley Winters demonstrates her ability to make us laugh at Charlotte's frowsy gentility and dreams of youthful romance; at the same time she stirs our compassion for the young widow's vulnerability and loneliness. As she whimpers and cries at the end of the scene, we realize for the first time just how deeply the actress has made us understand Charlotte. In the novel Humbert suggests that Charlotte is like a foolish teenager herself, mooning over an inaccessible male who has given her the go-by.

In due course, Charlotte decides to send Lolita off to a summer camp so that she and Humbert can be alone. On the day that she drives Lolita off to camp, she leaves a note behind for Humbert, virtually proposing to him. Humbert understands that he will have to marry Charlotte if he is to remain in a position to carry out his designs on Lolita. He accepts his fate and the marriage takes place.

Humbert takes refuge in the bathroom at times, in order to commit his thoughts to his diary. When he emerges on one occasion, Charlotte is waiting for him in the bedroom. Pursuing Humbert's affections with the savagery of a cave woman, Charlotte embraces him on the bed. He slyly looks beyond his wife to a photograph of Lolita on the bedside table, referring his sexual encounters with Lolita's mother to the girl herself.

Charlotte then informs Humbert that she intends to send Lolita straight from camp on to boarding school, ending with the life sentence: "It's going to be me and you alone forever." He looks wistfully at the photo of Lolita, which now seems so desperately out of reach.

To his utter dismay, shortly afterwards Humbert discovers Charlotte in his study, busily prying into his diary. Now that she has learned from his diary his true motives in marrying her, Charlotte is beside herself with rage. Hysterically rushing out of the house and into the street, she is hit by a car. In the novel, at this point Humbert comments in an aside that it is impossible for him to relay to the reader the impact he felt at seeing his wife lying dead in the street after the accident. He is forced instead to describe the calamity in a succession of individual phrases—although his eyes took in the entire scene in a single flash of vision.

In the film, Kubrick shows the aftermath of the accident in a single image, just as Humbert himself first saw it: the milling crowd of neighbors, the distraught driver of the car, and finally the corpse underneath a blanket that the police have placed over it.

Nabokov compliments Kubrick for his direction of the following scene, in which Humbert, like an ex-convict savoring the first moments of parole, soaks dreamily in the bathtub, sipping a cocktail and gloating with a rotten smile over the realization that he is now rid of Charlotte and presumably has Lolita all to himself. Nabokov salutes "that rapturous swig of Scotch in the bathtub."[8]

Humbert drives to Camp Climax, the summer camp where Charlotte had stowed Lolita, to pick her up. In the course of the film, Quilty dons a variety of disguises in his efforts to badger Humbert into giving up Lolita. One of Quilty's impersonations occurs at this point. Because of Sellers' brilliant flair for impersonation, these scenes are among the best in the movie.

Editor Anthony Harvey told me that Kubrick favored long takes while photographing *Lolita*. An extended take, uninterrupted by cuts to other angles, enables an actor to give a sustained performance of a long speech and thus build steadily to a dramatic climax. Asked for an example, he cited one of Quilty's monologues, adding that Kubrick rarely interrupted these extended takes by the insertion of reaction shots, if the actor was giving a brilliant performance—as Sellers certainly was: "Stanley's great thing was, don't cut to a reaction shot; let the filmgoers imagine the reaction shot for themselves."

The scene that Harvey had in mind occurs when Humbert stops at a hotel with Lolita overnight, and it just so

14 ***Sellers, Mason, and Kubrick on the set of the hotel porch. In this scene, Quilty impersonates a police officer to intimidate Humbert.***
15 ***Humbert glances at the photo of Lolita on the nightstand as he kisses his bride, Charlotte. Though Charlotte was supposed to take off her robe before slipping into bed for this scene, Shelley Winters was unable to relax enough to produce an acceptable take, so she ultimately acted the scene with her robe on.***

16–17 ***Sellers was originally meant to play the part of the school psychologist in drag, but at the last minute, according to James B. Harris, he, Sellers, and Kubrick agreed that it was a "bit too broad (no pun intended)" to have Quilty impersonate a woman. The character of Dr. Zemph was thus invented on the spot.***

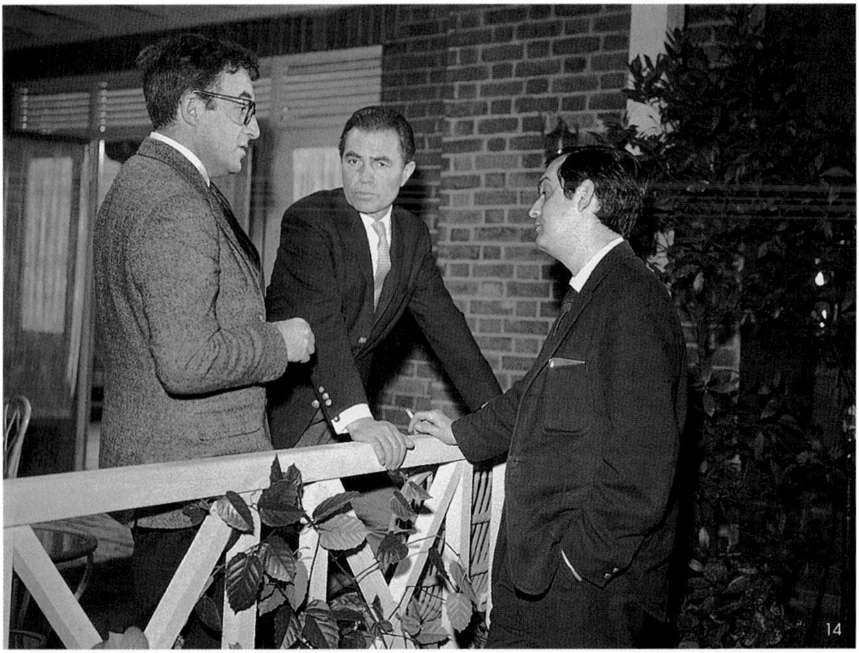
14

15

16

17

18

happens that Quilty has followed them there. He decides to utilize a crafty ploy in a jealous effort to discourage Humbert from bedding down Lolita that night. Impersonating a police detective, he introduces himself to Humbert on the shadowy hotel terrace, leaning on the railing with his back to Humbert so as not to be recognized. When Humbert, feigning nonchalance, asks the stranger whom he is with, the response is unnerving: "I am not really with someone, I am with you."

Kubrick continues the scene in an extended take. When Quilty says he's a state trooper, Humbert starts to bow out; Quilty continues, "No, you don't really have to go at all." He then launches into a seemingly casual but really coldly calculated monologue, in which he discusses, among other things, his having been arrested for "standing around on street corners," presumably looking for male companionship. Humbert does not know what to make of Quilty's stream of chatter, and finds it all the more threatening for that reason.

"I couldn't help noticing when you checked in tonight," Quilty observes. "It's part of my job. I said to myself, 'That's a guy with the most normal-looking face I ever saw in my life.' It would be great for two normal guys like us to get together and talk about—world events." Now Quilty bears down a bit more on his victim: "I noticed you had a lovely, pretty little girl with you.... You could have a lovely room, a bridal suite, for you and your lovely little girl." With that last thrust Humbert is completely undone by Quilty and hastily goes upstairs to his room.

The relevance of Quilty's monologues to the film as a whole has been questioned by some commentators, as if they were mere comic interludes. On the contrary, each of Quilty's comic turns grows out of the action and has a strong influence on what develops next. So here, as a result of his encounter with Quilty, Humbert scraps his elaborate plans to seduce Lolita that night.

In the morning, Lolita awakens Humbert and asks him coquettishly if he would like to play a game that she learned at Camp Climax. A look of lecherous anticipation crosses Humbert's face, and the scene fades. Very tactfully Kubrick has managed to get across to the audience that, in spite of all of Humbert's intricate plans to seduce Lolita, she has in effect finally seduced him.

Geoffrey Shurlock was particularly concerned about this seduction scene. Kubrick and Harris promised that Lolita would be attired in a heavy flannel nightgown and Humbert would be wearing pajamas and a bathrobe—there would be no suggestion of nudity between the underage girl and her stepfather in the scene as filmed. Richard Corliss comments on the action at this point that, "as an actress Lyon never editorializes; she never lets you see her disapproval of the character. She shows imagination and authenticity in all of Lolita's gestations: temptress, dominatrix, brat." He concludes, "Once she knows she has Humbert's undivided obsession, she tunes out and pursues a more elusive male, Quilty. It is a wonderful portrayal of the banality of lust."[9]

18 ***Kubrick cranes his neck behind Sue Lyon's back to watch James Mason's performance from the same angle as the camera.***

Afterward, as they continue their trip in the station wagon, Lolita insists on stopping to call her mother, who Humbert has not yet told Lolita is deceased. Just before shooting this scene, Kubrick called for a Coke and a bag of potato chips for Sue Lyon, in order to add just the right flavor of incongruity to the scene in which Humbert is forced to tell Lolita that her mother is dead—an example of how some nice touches occur to the director just before the cameras roll. When Humbert finally convinces the girl that Charlotte is dead, she stops munching and bursts into tears.

"Accompany us to Beardsley College," says Humbert, in voice-over, "where my lectureship in French poetry is in its second semester." By this time the relationship of stepfather and stepdaughter has become increasingly stormy. He is jealous of her younger male companions. When Humbert returns from class one afternoon, he finds an uninvited visitor awaiting him in his dark living room. When he switches on the light, Quilty, disguised as Dr. Zemph, the school psychiatrist, materializes like an apparition. He is wearing thick glasses and a mustache, and speaks with the smooth German accent which Sellers will call upon again in the title role of *Dr. Strangelove.*

Kubrick and director of photography Oswald Morris had a falling out over this scene. Like Russell Metty, the cinematographer on *Spartacus,* Morris got impatient with Kubrick for taking his time in rehearsing the cast and keeping the camera crew waiting. Furthermore, he was sometimes nettled, like Metty, when Kubrick personally supervised his work, because Morris was an experienced cameraman.

In setting up the scene, Kubrick instructed Morris, "Now I want the scene lit as though there's just one light bulb in the middle of the set." Fifteen minutes later, he came back and said, "What are all those lights? I told you just one light bulb." Morris replied, "It's basically and faithfully lit as if with one light bulb," but Morris had placed a couple more bulbs near the set, because he feared that otherwise the actors' faces would not be visible. Morris concludes, "It all got a bit boring, inquests about the lighting."[10]

Actually Kubrick had good reason for worrying about too much light in this scene. In it Quilty questions Humbert about the propriety of his relationship with his stepdaughter. He sits in Humbert's shadowy living room where only a slim shaft of light illuminates the scene. Kubrick's concern about seeing to it that the scene was dimly lit, as if by a single light bulb, was to make it credible for the viewer that Humbert would not see past Quilty's disguise and recognize the man whom he had encountered before at the school dance. Despite his differences with Kubrick, Morris's atmospheric lighting in this and other scenes in *Lolita* was a hallmark of the film's technical quality.

As the scene progresses, Dr. Zemph informs Humbert that the school board is growing suspicious of his relationship with his stepdaughter. With disarming illogic, Dr. Zemph winds up his spiel with the threat that *four* psychologists will have to come and inspect the home situation of Lolita. "I feel that you and I should do all in our power to stop that old Dr. Cudler and his quartet of psychologists from fiddling around in the home situation."

19

Humbert of course agrees. At his wit's end, he does not notice that, when Quilty prepares to light a cigarette, he has to lift his thick glasses furtively in order to see what he is doing. The clues are beginning to mount up for the viewer, if not for Humbert, that Lolita is involved with another older man. Quilty, writes Kael, "is the sneaky villain who dogs Humbert's trail and digs up every bone that Humbert ineptly tries to bury and presents them to him. Humbert can conceal nothing."[11]

19 ***Lolita in the hotel room she shares with Humbert after he picks her up from Camp Climax.***
20 ***Though many critics claimed that Sue Lyon was too old for the part of Lolita (she was fourteen when shooting completed), Harris and Kubrick were forced to give the impression that the character was no younger than fifteen to avoid being denied a Code Seal.***

Completely unhinged, Humbert is totally intimidated by Quilty's insinuations and eventually coaxes Lolita into taking a long trip with him around the country, away from the disapproving eyes of the school authorities, not to mention the neighbors.

In the course of the trip Lolita is spirited away from him by Quilty, according to a prearranged scheme he has secretly hatched with Lolita. The novel chronicles Humbert's fruitless efforts to find Lolita, but Kubrick wisely bypasses this episode and cuts immediately to Humbert receiving a letter from her, in which she asks him for money, because she and her husband are expecting a baby.

Following this lead, Humbert tracks down Lolita to a tawdry bungalow in a

A.A. PRODUCTIONS LTD.

INTER-OFFICE COMMUNICATION

TO: Stanley Kubrick

FROM: James B. Harris

DATE: December 6, 1960.

SYNOPSIS - QUIGLEY'S SUGGESTIONS
Page 83 to end

1. Page 85 - Objection to Swine's speech about three ladies in bed, one disguised as a man.

2. Page 85 - Thinks we are insulting police unnecessarily.

   (We can defend this very easily by explaining potential danger to Humbert with police present - not an insult).

3. Page 86 - Objection to Lolita's speech - the word is "incest". Suggests using word "adultery".

   (I believe he is right recommending making this change).

4. Page 87. - Objection to entire business with pills. Suggests we re-write to avoid implication of use of an aphrodisiac.

   (It's possible he missed insert of vitamin pill bottle which is on preceding page. Even so he may be right.)

5. Page 92. - Scenes 81E & 81F. Suggests we are very careful how we play this. He is worried that Humbert may appear like a beast and disgust audience.

   (Perhaps our description of Humbert pacing back and forth gave him this idea. However, he only suggests our being careful, which of course we will).

Contd...

slum. Wearing glasses, her hair askew, and six months pregnant, Lolita is no longer the sleek, sensual girl that Humbert had enshrined in his memory. Lolita provides a complete explanation of how Quilty manipulated Humbert, fitting all the pieces of the puzzle into place: "Do you remember Dr. Zemph?" she asks. "Remember Mother's old flame at the school dance? ... Do you remember the guy that you talked to at the hotel? ... It was Clare Quilty.... I had a crush on him ever since the times that he used to come and visit Mother... I guess he was the only guy I was ever really crazy about." Humbert is clearly destroyed by this, but Lolita, characteristically, does not notice. "(Quilty took me) to a dude ranch near Santa Fe.... He had such a bunch of weird friends staying there.... He promised to get me a studio contract, but it never turned out that way. And instead, he wanted me to cooperate

21 ***List of the film censor's objections to specific parts of the film, with advice from consultant Martin Quigley on how to ensure that the film would receive the MPAA Code Seal.***
22 ***Kubrick during the shooting of Lolita's confession to Humbert about her affair with Quilty.***
23 ***The director carefully observes as Sellers and Winters rehearse.***
24 ***Kubrick with Sue Lyon as the married, pregnant Lolita.***
25 ***Viewfinder in hand, Kubrick gives instructions for the scene in which Humbert first lays eyes upon Lolita.***
26 ***Kubrick took this photo of Lyon being primped by the makeup artist.***

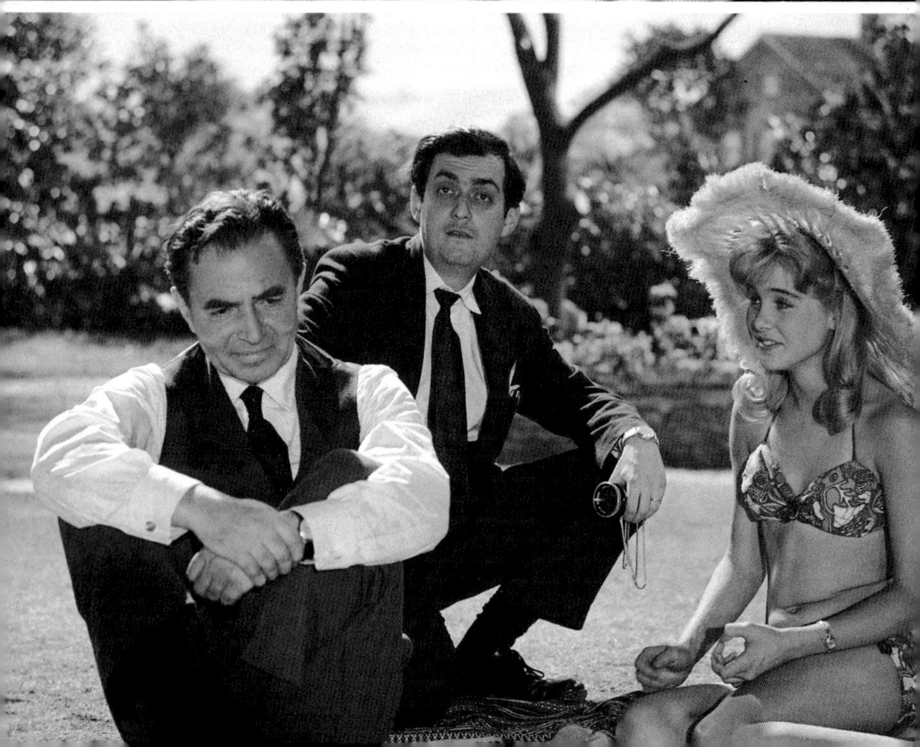

24

26

with the others in making some kind of a—you know, an art movie.... No, I didn't do it!" she snaps.

Lolita flares up for a second like her mother. Indeed, Lolita is already becoming a slatternly matron very much like her dead mother. Humbert realizes regretfully that he has helped to rob her of her youth. She adds that she met her husband Dick in Phoenix, where she was working as a waitress after Quilty abandoned her.

Lolita begins to understand that Humbert's sexual obsession with her has at last turned into genuine love. "It is this last encounter," Kubrick told me, "in which Humbert expresses his love for Lolita, who is no longer a nymphet but a pregnant housewife, that is one of the most poignant elements of the story." Humbert pleads with her to let him rescue her from her present shabby circumstances. But Lolita firmly declines his invitation. She has wrecked too many lives, and she will not hurt Dick, "who is very sweet." With that, Humbert, reduced to sobs, takes his leave.

He proceeds immediately to Quilty's mansion, intent on killing him, we now understand, not just because Quilty had lured Lolita away from him, but because Quilty had merely used her for a while and then coldly discarded her. Kubrick repeats footage from the prologue, and we see Humbert enter Quilty's lair searching for him. The film ends with a shot of the painting behind which Humbert had finally trapped Quilty, riddled with bullet holes. A printed epilogue informs us: "Humbert Humbert died of coronary thrombosis in prison awaiting trial for the murder of Clare Quilty."

The ending of *Lolita* is unique. I know of no other movie that creates as much compassion for the tragic end of its obsessed hero by employing a simply worded epitaph on the screen at the fade-out. One cannot help feeling somewhat sorry for a man who organized his entire life around the pursuit of a goal that would be short-lived in any event, the love of a nymphet who could not remain a nymphet for long. It is Humbert's recognition that he has used Lolita and must suffer for it, however, that humanizes him in our eyes to the point that he becomes worthy of whatever pity we wish to bestow on him. Commenting on the deeper implications of the novel, Nabokov stated, "*Lolita* is a tragedy.... Furthermore, this is at heart a novel of redemption. It is about a lust that matures, under fire, to love."[12]

In 1974, Nabokov published his version of the script, in which he retained some of the scenes that had been deleted. For example, Nabokov includes a scene in his scenario depicting the death of Humbert's mother, after she has been struck by lightning at a picnic: her specter floats upward, holding a parasol as she blows kisses to her family below. This is the kind of material that would have complicated further a film that eventually was to run a full two and a half hours in its final version.

When Nabokov finally saw *Lolita* at a private screening, as he recalls in his foreword to the screenplay, he found that it was a first-rate film, even though much of his version of the script had gone unused. He admitted that Kubrick's inventions

27 ***Kubrick's handwritten draft of the letter Lolita writes to Humbert.***

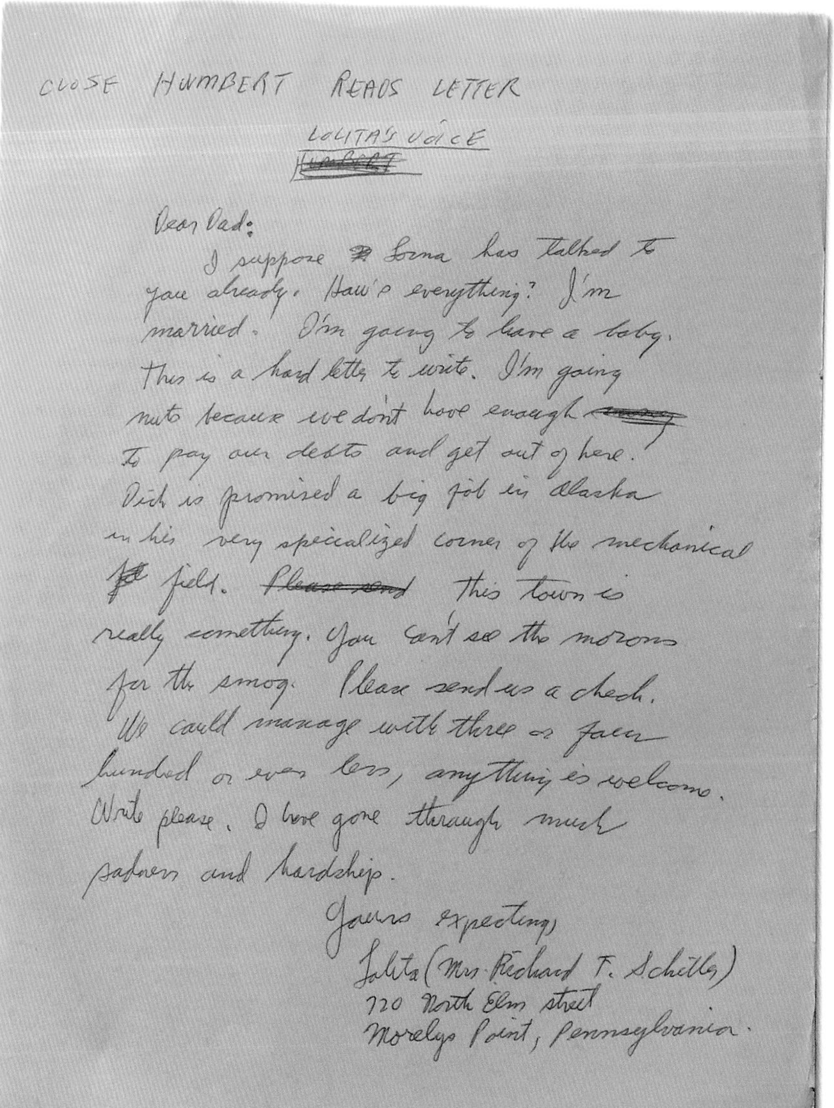
CLOSE HUMBERT READS LETTER

LOLITA'S VOICE

~~HUMBERT~~

Dear Dad:

I suppose ~~?~~ Lorna has talked to you already. How's everything? I'm married. I'm going to have a baby. This is a hard letter to write. I'm going nuts because we don't have enough ~~money~~ to pay our debts and get out of here. Dick is promised a big job in Alaska in his very specialized corner of the mechanical ~~f~~ field. ~~Please send~~ This town is really something. You can't see the morons for the smog. Please send us a check. We could manage with three or four hundred or even less, anything is welcome. Write please. I have gone through much sadness and hardship.

Yours expecting,

Lolita (Mrs. Richard F. Schiller)
720 North Elm street
Morelys Point, Pennsylvania.

were by and large "appropriate and delightful": Lolita childishly pulling on her sweater, during the scenes in which she and Humbert travel cross-country, is unforgettable. The killing of Quilty "is a masterpiece, and so is the death of Charlotte Haze." He confesses, "I am no dramatist; I'm not even a hack scenarist." On the one hand, he felt that only "ragged odds and ends of my script had been used." On the other hand, he realized that Kubrick's final shooting script was, after all, derived from his own screenplay, and that hence all of Kubrick's revisions of the script were not sufficient to erase his name from the credit titles as author of the screenplay. Still, he also admits that "infinite fidelity may be an author's ideal but can prove a producer's ruin," and so offers his published screenplay, "not as a pettish refutation of a munificent film, but purely as a vivacious variant on an old novel."[13]

"I think the most influential filmmakers for me have been (in no special order): Chaplin, De Sica, Bergman, Fellini, Hitchcock, Welles, and Ophüls."

— SK/1960 (to Charles Reynolds/ *Popular Photography)*

Lolita was the last film Kubrick made in association with James B. Harris, who went back to Hollywood and became a director himself, notably of *The Bedford Incident* (1965). Kubrick elected to stay on in England and make *Dr. Strangelove*, which expands his study of human folly in *Lolita* to cosmic proportions.

Notes

1. Gene D. Phillips, "Vladimir Nabokov," in *The Encyclopedia of Stanley Kubrick*, with Rodney Hill (New York: Checkmark, 2002): 259.
2. Gene D. Phillips, "Shelley Winters," in *The Encyclopedia of Stanley Kubrick*: 401.
3. James Howard, *Stanley Kubrick Companion* (London: Batsford, 1999): 80.
4. James Mason, *Before I Forget* (London: Hamish Hamilton, 1981): 250.
5. Pauline Kael, *I Lost It at the Movies* (New York: Boyars, 1994): 204.
6. Dawn Sova, *Forbidden Films: Censorship* (New York: Checkmark, 2001): 181.
7. Peter Bogdanovich, "What They Say about Stanley Kubrick," *The New York Times Magazine* (July 4, 1999): 22.
8. Vladimir Nabokov, "Foreword," *Lolita: A Screenplay* (New York: McGraw Hill, 1974): xiii.
9. Richard Corliss, *Lolita* (London: British Film Institute, 1994): 86.
10. Gene D. Phillips, "Oswald Morris," in *The Encyclopedia of Stanley Kubrick*: 22.
11. Kael: 206.
12. Phillips, "Vladimir Nabokov": 260.
13. Nabokov: ix, xii, xiii.

28 ***Tossing a football between takes.***

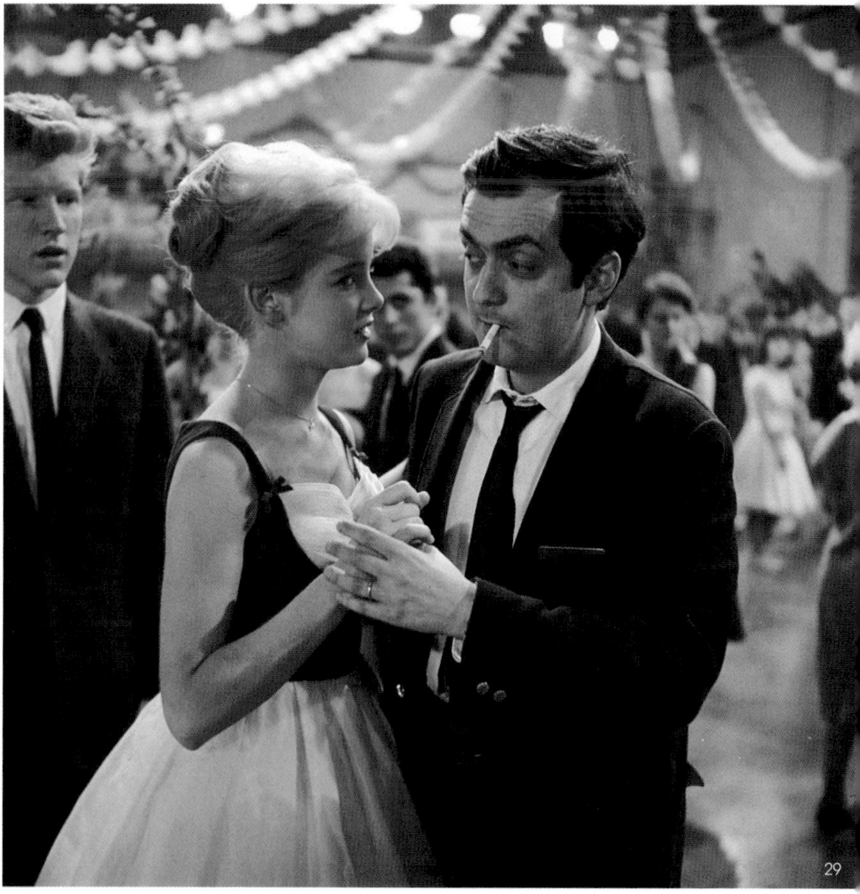
29

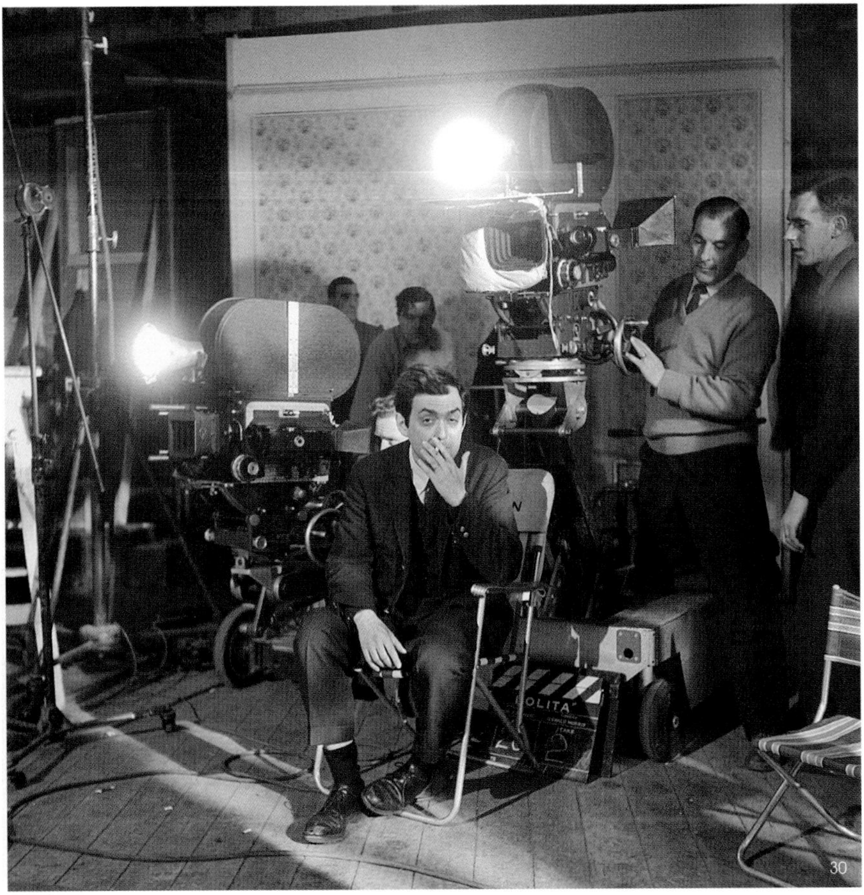

29 *Of Sue Lyon, Kubrick told* Look *magazine, "From the first, she was interesting to watch – even in the way she walked in for her interview, casually sat down, walked out. She was cool and non-giggly. She was enigmatic without being dull. She would keep people guessing about how much Lolita knew about life." (Jack Hamilton, 1962)*

30 *Kubrick deep in thought as the cameras are being prepared to shoot.*

An Interview with Stanley Kubrick

by Terry Southern

The following interview took place in the New York office of Harris-Kubrick Pictures in July 1962

What was it mainly that appealed to you in the novel *Lolita*?

Well, it's certainly one of the great love stories, isn't it? I think Lionel Trilling's piece in *Encounter* is very much to the point when he speaks of it as "the first great love story of the 20th century." And he uses as his criteria the total shock and estrangement which the lovers in all the great love stories of the past have produced on the people around them. If you consider *Romeo and Juliet, Anna Karenina, Madame Bovary, The Red and the Black,* they all had this one thing in common, this element of the illicit, or at least what was considered illicit at the time, and in each case it caused their complete alienation from society.

But then in the 20th century, with the disintegration of moral and spiritual values, it became increasingly difficult, and finally impossible, for an author to credibly create that kind of situation, to conceive of a relationship which would produce this shock and estrangement—so that what was resorted to, to achieve the shock value, was erotic description. Whereas Trilling felt that *Lolita* somehow did succeed, in the classic tradition, in having all the stormy passion and tenderness of the great love story as well as this element of the lovers being estranged from everyone around them. And, of course, Nabokov was brilliant in withholding any indication of the author's approval of the relationship. In fact, it isn't until the very end, when Humbert sees her again four years later, and she's no longer by any stretch of the definition a nymphet, that the really genuine and selfless love he has for her is revealed. In other words, this element of their estrangement, even from the author—and certainly, from the reader—is accomplished, and sustained, almost through to the very end.

After the script was finished you began casting—and I imagine you must have looked at quite a few young girls. Did you actually look for a girl who was between twelve and thirteen?

Well, she had to be between twelve and thirteen at the beginning, but between sixteen and seventeen at the end—I mean one girl who could play both parts—and we did look at quite a few young girls, some of them very young indeed. It was amazing how many parents would write in, you know, from Montana and so on, saying: "My daughter really is Lolita!"—that sort of thing. But we looked at them all, and of course, Sue Lyon was just one of them—but the moment we saw her, we thought "My God, if this girl can act" ... because she had this wonderful, enigmatic, but alive quality of mystery, but was still very expressive. Everything she did, commonplace things, like handling objects or crossing a room, or just talking, were all done in a very engaging way ... and, incidentally this is a quality which most great actors have, it's a strange sort of personal unique style that goes into everything they do—like when Albert Finney sits down in a chair and drinks a bottle of beer, and, well, it's just great

31 ***Shelley Winters warms up for the little dance she will do for Humbert.***

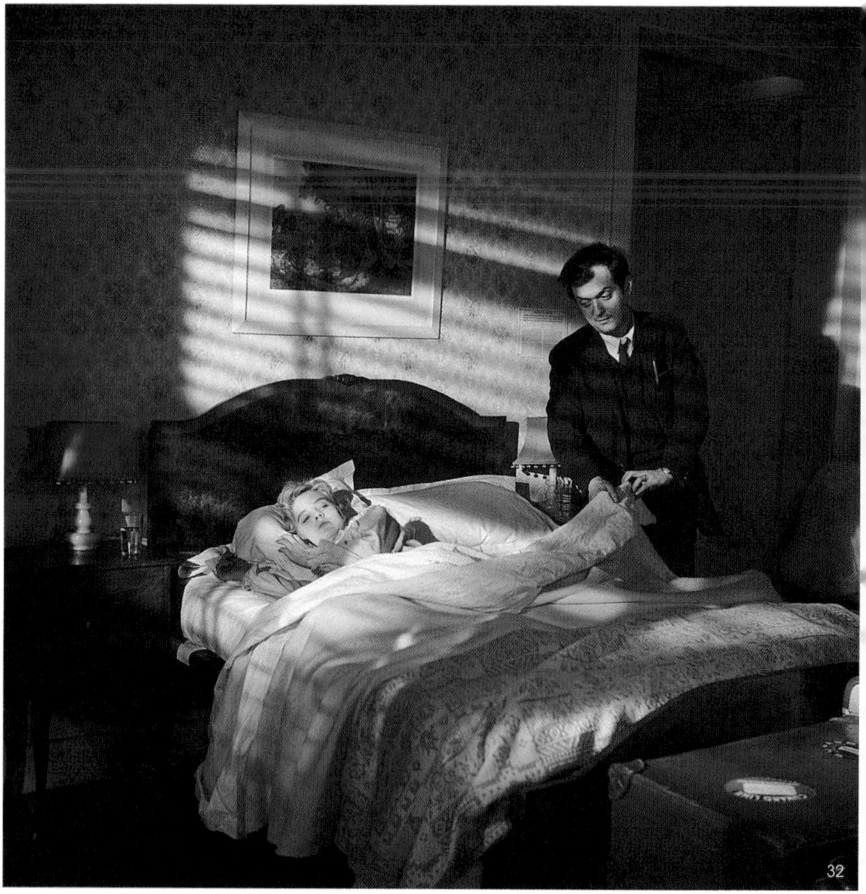

and you think "God, I wish I could drink a bottle of beer like that," or the way Marlon, you know, pushes his sunglasses on his forehead and just leaves them there instead of putting them in his pocket... and, well, they all have ways of doing everyday things that are interesting to watch. And she had this, Sue Lyon. But of course we still didn't know whether she could act. Then we did some scenes, and finally shot a test with Mason, and that was it. She was great.

And Mason, did he occur to you right away as the choice for Humbert?

Yes, I always thought he had just the right qualities for Humbert—you know, handsome but vulnerable... sort of easy-to-hurt and also a romantic—because that was true of Humbert, of course, that beneath that veneer of sophistication and cynicism, and that sort of affected sneer, he was terribly romantic and sentimental.

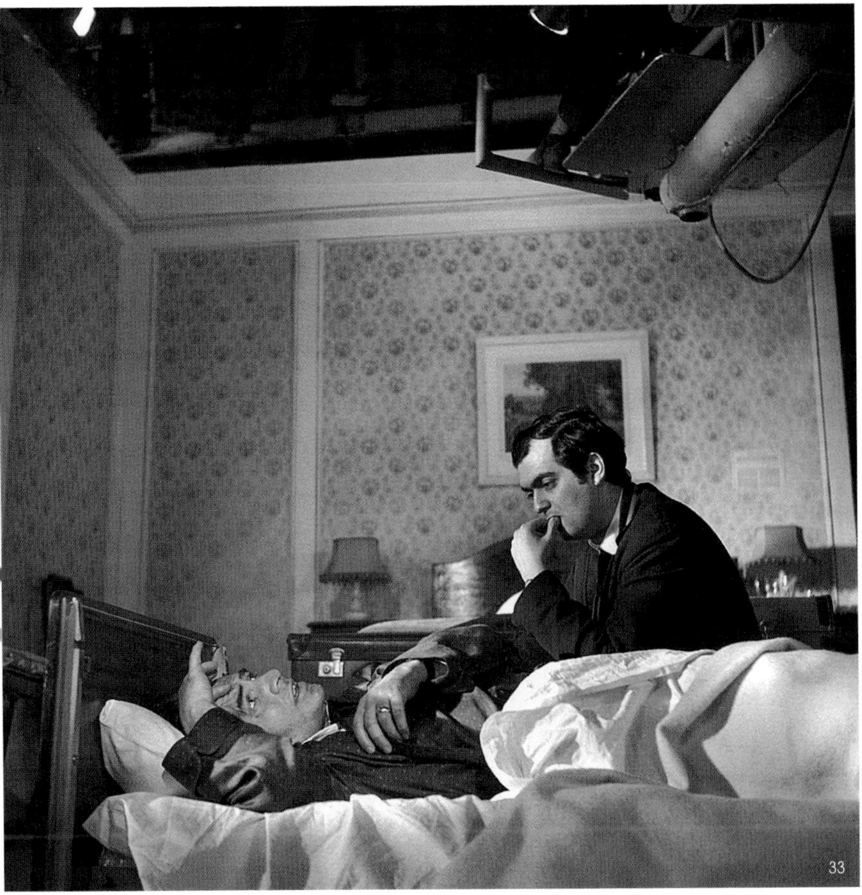

33

One of his big scenes, of course, is at the end, when Humbert finds Lolita again, and breaks down when he fails to persuade her to go away with him. This is a long and very complex scene—how long did it take to shoot it?

32 ***The director demonstrates how Humbert should try to sneak into bed with Lolita.***
33 ***Kubrick sits close to Mason as they work on a scene in the hotel room.***

We shot that for twelve days. One of the things I wanted to get there, as completely as possible, was this element of disparity, which you see in life but practically never in film, where two people meet after a long time and one of them is still emotionally involved and the other one is simply embarrassed—and yet she wants to be nice, but the words just sort of plunk down, dead, and nothing happens... just sort of total embarrassment and incongruity.

34

For the film, you greatly expanded, or at least developed, the role of Quilty, didn't you?

Yes, well, it was apparent that just beneath the surface of the story was this strong secondary narrative thread possible, because after Humbert seduces her in the motel, or rather after she seduces him, the big question has been answered, so it was good to have this narrative of mystery continuing after the seduction.

This role, the role of Peter Sellers as Quilty, and his disgusted recurrence throughout the film, seems unique. I don't recall any other instance in movies of such an elaborate combination of the comic-grotesque. Was this treatment derivative of something you had seen or read?

Well, that aspect of the picture interests me very much. I've always thought, for example, that Kafka could be very

35

unny, or actually is very funny—I mean ke a comic nightmare, and I think that ellers in the murder scene, and in fact in he whole characterization, is like some-hing out of a bad dream, but a funny ne. I'm very pleased with the way that came off and I think it opens up an avenue, as far as I'm concerned, of telling certain types of stories in ways which haven't yet been explored in movies.

Now, this is an erotic film—I mean, in the sense that sexual love is necessarily treated, and is sometimes in the foreground of a dramatic scene. Do you have any particular theories about the erotic?

Only that I think the erotic viewpoint of a story is best used as a sort of energizing

34 ***The producer-director duo of Harris-Kubrick Pictures.***
35 ***Kubrick, James B. Harris, and Sue Lyon on the set of the school dance.***

force of a scene, a motivational factor, rather than being, you know, explicitly portrayed. I thought, for instance, in *Les Amants,* when the guy's head slides down out of the frame, it was just sort of funny—though it shouldn't have been. When you're watching it with an audience it just becomes laughable. I think it's interesting to know how one person makes it known to another person that they want to make love, and it's interesting to know what they do after they make love, but while they're doing it, that's something else. It's such a subjective thing, and so incongruous to the audience that the effect is either one of vague embarrassment, or just the feeling of mischief on the part of the filmmaker.

In any case, since this was your own picture, there was no pressure on you to be overly prudent or anything like that?

None whatever. We had complete freedom about every aspect of the production.

You have some interesting double-entendre things in there—like this "Camp Climax" for girls, and lines like: "Wednesday she's going to have a cavity filled by your uncle, Ivor." Were there any objections to those?

No. And, of course, the general public is a good deal more sophisticated than most censors imagine—and certainly more so than these groups who get up petitions and so on can believe. After all, if a film is really obscene, it simply doesn't play in a theater, because the police of that city close it down—so that if a movie is playing, it's obviously not obscene. Prevailing law-enforcement takes care of that, so there's really no point in those petitions. It's a matter for the courts.

How do you account for this increased sophistication on the part of film audiences?

Well, for the past few years, they've been getting used to better and better movies.... Television was the best thing that ever happened to American movies because it knocked out this middle-of-the-road mediocrity type picture which had so long dominated the field.

What do you think of the techniques and stated philosophy of the French New Wave directors—Vadim, Resnais, Truffaut—and of the reigning Italian directors: Fellini, Antonioni, De Sica, etc.?

Statements of philosophy aside, they've made some superb films.

What do you feel would be the best training ground for a movie director: television, the stage, or still photography, as in your case?

I don't know—the main thing is to want to make a film bad enough to get some sweet, trusting, and insane friends or family to lend you the money to do so.

I understand that you often play music on the set, to help everyone get in a particular mood.

Yes, well, that was a device used, you know, by silent-film actors—they all had their own violinists, who would play for them during the takes, and even sort of direct them. And I think it's probably the easiest way to produce an emotion, which is really the actor's main problem—producing authentic emotion. We play it before the take, and if the dialogue isn't too important, during the take, and then post-synchronize the dialogue—it's amazing how quick this will work, and I mean making a movie is such

36 ***Extras stand next to Kubrick on the set of the car crash scene.***

a long, fragmented, dragging process, and you get into, say, about the ninth week, you're getting up every morning at 6:30, not enough sleep, probably no breakfast, and then at 9:15 you have to do something you feel about as far from doing as you possibly can.... So it's a matter of getting in the right mood—and music I've found is the best for this, and practically everyone can respond to some piece or other.

What were the pieces you used in making *Lolita*?

Well, there were a couple of bands of *West Side Story* that must have somehow been very important to Shelley Winters—we used those in her crying scene—and she would cry, very quickly, great authentic tears. And let's see, yeah, *Irma la Douce*, that would always floor Mason. And I've forgotten what Sue's was... a ballad by someone—not Elvis, but someone like that.

In making this film, do you feel you encountered any problems or considerations which were categorically different from those you've dealt with in other films?

Yes, I think the thing of gradually penetrating the surface of comedy which overlies the story into the, well, the ultimate tragic romance of it puts it in a category apart. And then, too, treatments of mood, subtleties and range of mood.... I mean *Lolita* is really like a piece of music, a series of attitudes and emotions that sort of sweep you through the story.

I'd like to ask you now about your general attitude towards filmmaking, other than what you've already indicated—first, what particular advantages do you feel that films have over other media of expression and communication?

Well, for one thing I think it is fairly obvious that the events and situations that are most meaningful to people are those in which they are actually involved—and I'm convinced that this sense of personal involvement derives in large part from visual perception. I once saw a woman hit by a car, for example, or right after she had been hit, and she was lying in the middle of the road. I knew that at that moment I would have risked my life if necessary to help her, whereas if I had merely read about the accident or heard about it, it could not have meant too much. Of all the creative media I think that film is most nearly able to convey this sense of meaningfulness; to create an emotional involvement and a feeling of participation in the person seeing it.

Do you feel you have some specific goal or direction as an artist?

In making a film, I start with an emotion, a feeling, a sense of a subject or a person or a situation. The theme and technique come as a result of the material passing, as it were, through myself and coming out of the projector lens. It seems to me that simply striving for a genuinely personal approach, whatever it may be, is the goal—Bergman and Fellini, for example, although perhaps as different in their outlook as possible, have achieved this, and I'm sure it is what gives their films an emotional involvement lacking in most work.

37 *Call sheet for the scene in which Humbert paints Lolita's toenails, indicating "supply of nail varnish and brush" as required props.*

CALL SHEET

STUDIO NO. 57.

PRODUCTION " LOLITA "

DATE TUESDAY, FEBRUARY 14TH 1961.

UNIT CALL 8.30 A.M.

WHERE WORKING STAGE 3.
INT. HUMBERT'S BEARDSLEY HOUSE BEDROOM

ARTISTE	CHARACTER	DRESSING ROOM	MAKE-UP	READY ON SET
JAMES MASON	HUMBERT	78	8.00	8.30
SUE LYON	LOLITA	-	8.00	8.30
STAND-INS:				
George Leach	for Mr. Mason	110	8.00	8.30
Pearl Hedgcock	" Miss Lyon	111	8.00	8.30

ESSENTIAL PROPS: Supply of nail varnish and brush, (N.B. Supply of nail varnish remover to be available.) Script of School Play.
Bath Towels.
All else as per Script and Breakdown.

LUNCH: 12.45 - 1.45 p.m.

RUSHES: 12.45 p.m. (Dubbing Theatre)

CANTEEN: Tea Trolley on Stage 3 at 9.30 a.m. and 3.30 p.m. for 60 People, please.

SCENE NUMBERS 101 DAY.
Next Set: INT. FIRST MOTEL (STAGE 5) Sc. No. 91.

RENE DUPONT
ASSISTANT DIRECTOR

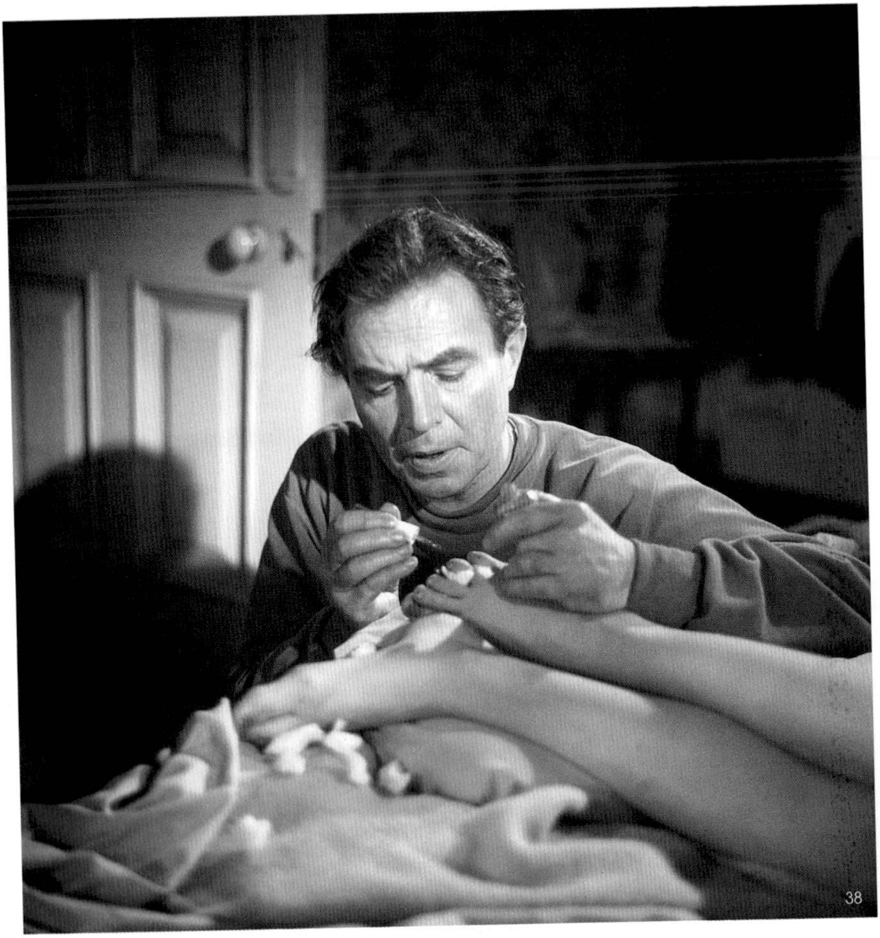

38

I understand that you cut and edit your own pictures—don't you feel there are experienced editors who could do this?

I feel that the director, or the film-maker as I prefer to think of him, is wholly responsible for the film in its completed form. Making a film starts with the germ of an idea, continues through script, rehearsing, shooting, cutting, music projection, and tax-accountants. The old-fashioned major-studio concept of a director made him just another color on the producer's palette—which also contained all the above "colors." Formerly, it was the producer who dipped into all the colors and blended the "masterpiece." I don't think it so surprising that it should now fall to the director.

Do you think that a young director, with new ideas, can get ahead in Hollywood making films the way he wants to —without creating enemies?

I don't think you make enemies by doing films the way you want to do them; I think you make enemies by being rude, tactless, and nasty to people.

You have won unreserved critical praise for at least three of your pictures. At thirty-three you have already directed one of the biggest pictures ever made. Will success spoil Stanley Kubrick?

Fifth Amendment.

38 ***Humbert gives Lolita a loving pedicure.***
39 ***Lolita lashes out against Humbert for refusing to let her attend the cast party after the school play.***

Dr. Strangelove, or: How I Learned to Stop Worrying and Love the Bomb

1964 / BLACK AND WHITE / 93 MINUTES
Distributed by COLUMBIA PICTURES

CAST
GROUP CAPTAIN LIONEL MANDRAKE, PRESIDENT MUFFLEY, AND DR. STRANGELOVE PETER SELLERS
GENERAL BUCK TURGIDSON GEORGE C. SCOTT
GENERAL JACK D. RIPPER STERLING HAYDEN
COLONEL BAT GUANO KEENAN WYNN
MAJOR T. J. "KING" KONG SLIM PICKENS
AMBASSADOR DE SADESKY PETER BULL
LIEUTENANT LOTHAR ZOGG, BOMBARDIER JAMES EARL JONES
MISS SCOTT TRACY REED
MR. STAINES JACK CRELEY
LIEUTENANT H. R. DIETRICH, D. S. O. FRANK BERRY
ADMIRAL RANDOLPH ROBERT O'NEIL
LIEUTENANT W. D. KIVEL, NAVIGATOR GLENN BECK
FRANK ROY STEPHENS
CAPTAIN G. A. "ACE" OWENS, CO-PILOT SHANE RIMMER
MEMBERS OF BURPELSON BASE DEFENSE CORPS HAL GALILI, LAURENCE HERDER, JOHN MCCARTHY
GENERAL FACEMAN GORDON TANNER
LIEUTENANT B. GOLDBERG, RADIO OPERATOR PAUL TAMARIN

CREW
DIRECTED AND PRODUCED BY STANLEY KUBRICK
SCREENPLAY STANLEY KUBRICK, TERRY SOUTHERN, and PETER GEORGE (based on the book *Red Alert* by Peter George)
ART DIRECTOR PETER MURTON
PRODUCTION MANAGER CLIFTON BRANDON
DIRECTOR OF PHOTOGRAPHY GILBERT TAYLOR
CAMERA OPERATOR KELVIN PIKE
FILM EDITOR ANTHONY HARVEY
PRODUCTION DESIGNER KEN ADAM
ASSOCIATE PRODUCER VICTOR LYNDON
CAMERA ASSISTANT BERNARD FORD
ASSISTANT DIRECTOR ERIC RATTRAY
SPECIAL EFFECTS WALLY VEEVERS
MAKEUP STUART FREEBORN
SOUND EDITOR LESLIE HODGSON
ASSISTANT EDITOR RAY LOVEJOY
ASSISTANT ADVISOR CAPT. JOHN CREWDSON
MUSIC LAURIE JOHNSON

Made at Shepperton Studios, England, by Hawk Films Ltd.

Opposite *Film poster.*

Peter Sellers • George C. Scott
in Stanley Kubrick's
Dr. Strangelove
Or:
How
I Learned
To
Stop
Worrying
And
Love
The
Bomb
the hot-line suspense comedy
also starring Sterling Hayden · Keenan Wynn · Slim Pickens and introducing Tracy Reed (as "Miss Foreign Affairs")
Screenplay by Stanley Kubrick, Peter George & Terry Southern Based on the book "Red Alert" by Peter George
Produced & Directed by Stanley Kubrick · A Columbia Pictures Release

STRANGELOVE
DR
OR:
HOW I
LEARNED
TO STOP
WORRYING
AND
LOVE THE
BOMB
U.S. AIR FORCE
U.S. AIR FORCE
COPYRIGHT (C) MCMLXIII HAWK FILMS LTD. ALL RIGHTS RESERVED

U.S.

PEACE IS OUR PROFESSION
LATERAL

U.S. AIR FORCE

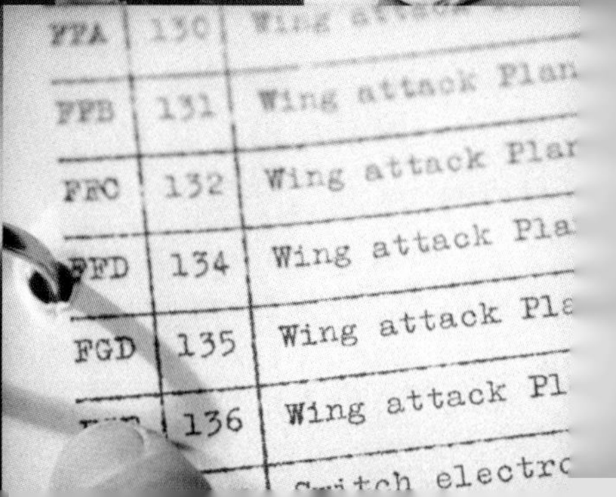
FPA 130
FPB 131 Wing attack Plan
FPC 132 Wing attack Plan
FFD 134 Wing attack Pla
FGD 135 Wing attack Pla
136 Wing attack Pl
Switch electro

TOP SECRET

AUTO DESTRUCT

NUCLEAR WARHEAD
HANDLE WITH CARE
Hi THERE!
NUCLEAR WARHEAD
HANDLE WITH CARE
DEAR JOHN

Dr. Strangelove, or: How I Learned to Stop Worrying and Love the Bomb

by Gene D. Phillips

n 1962, Kubrick acquired the screen rights to Peter George's *Red Alert* (1958), a novel about a psychotic general who orders his troop of B-52 bombers to launch a nuclear attack inside Russia. Kubrick then set about doing a serious adaptation of the book in collaboration with George; the film was set to be distributed by Columbia Pictures.

While Kubrick was working on the script, word got out that a film was being planned that was based on Eugene Burdick and Harvey Wheeler's novel *Fail-Safe* (1962), which was also about a nuclear attack on Russia. Max Youngstein, who had disliked *The Killing* when he was production chief at United Artists, was now in charge of his own independent production company and was producing *Fail-Safe*, to be directed by Sidney Lumet (*Long Day's Journey into Night*). Kubrick and George saw so many parallels between *Red Alert* and *Fail-Safe* as novels that Kubrick instigated a plagiarism suit on George's behalf against Burdick and Wheeler. His purpose was to tie up *Fail-Safe* in litigation and prevent Youngstein from making the film version.

There were undoubted similarities between the two books: each was about the launching of an unauthorized nuclear attack on Russia by the United States; each indicated that Russia had a nuclear device that would retaliate against such an unprovoked attack. "Both stories had War Rooms, military gadgetry, and officers and diplomats with stiff upper lips."[1] However, Kubrick failed to secure an injunction against the making of *Fail-Safe*, Lumet told me, and that enabled him to go ahead with his film.

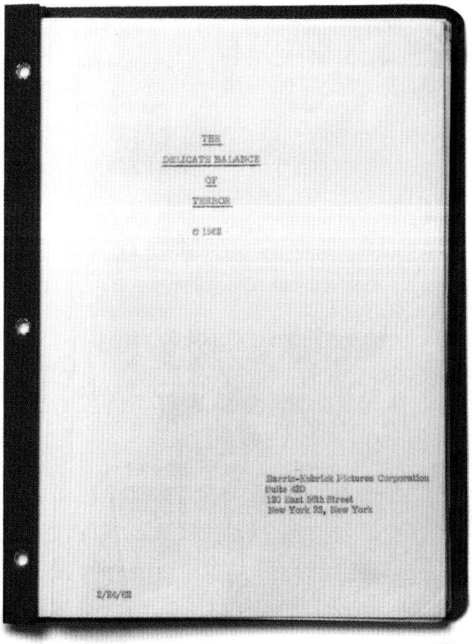

03

As he developed the script with George, Kubrick's approach to the material changed. He no longer saw *Dr. Strangelove* as a straightforward melodrama, which is precisely what *Red Alert* was. Furthermore, he did not find the ending of the novel congenial. In the book the bombing mission against Russia is aborted, so that the Russians' retaliatory device, the Doomsday Machine, is not unleashed on the United States. Hence the novel concludes with the hope that the world can remain at peace. Kubrick rather envisioned a decidedly pessimistic finale for the film.

01 ***The War Room.***
02 ***Kubrick during shooting of the Burpelson base exteriors.***
03 ***This early draft of the script, titled "The Delicate Balance of Terror," was a serious adaptation of Peter George's novel,*** **Red Alert.**

He told me, "My idea of doing it as a nightmare comedy came in the early weeks of working on the screenplay. I found that in trying to put meat on the bones and to imagine the scenes more fully, one had to keep leaving things out which were either absurd or paradoxical in order to keep it from being funny; and these things seemed to be close to the heart of the scenes in question." After all, he reasoned, what could be more absurd than two superpowers starting a nuclear conflict because of the actions of a lunatic in the high command? The only way to tell the story, he concluded, was as a black comedy, a dark satire.

Moreover, Kubrick was convinced that treating the concept of nuclear war as an outrageous joke would patently set *Dr. Strangelove* apart from *Fail-Safe* and prevent Lumet's film from stealing thunder from his own movie. Columbia Pictures eventually intervened and took over the distribution of *Fail-Safe*, in addition to *Dr. Strangelove*. The front office at Columbia wisely arranged to release *Dr. Strangelove* in January 1964; and, after it was played out in theaters, to distribute *Fail-Safe* the following October.

Peter George, who presumably consented to the transformation of his serious

04 ***Peter George on the set.***
05 ***After it was decided that the film would be written as a comedy, Kubrick labeled this previous draft "Serious version."***
06–08 ***Examples of screenplay drafts in various stages of evolution.***

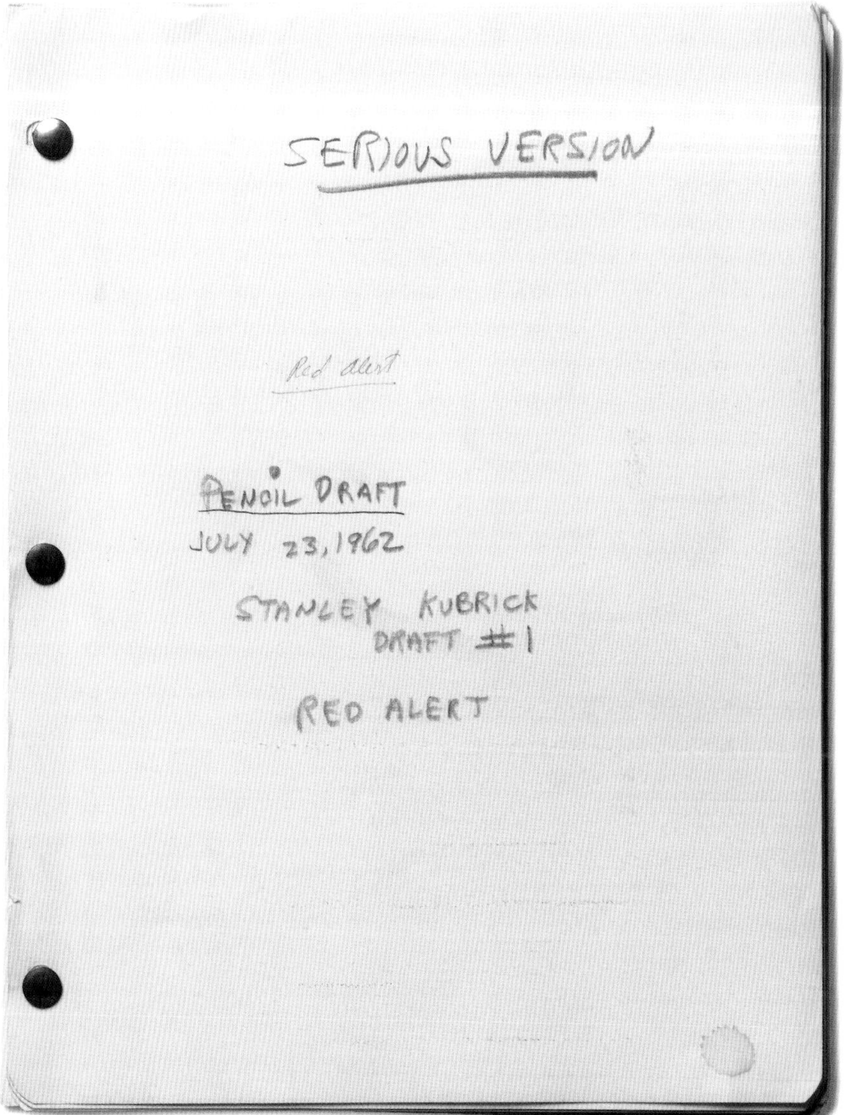
SERIOUS VERSION
Red alert
PENCIL DRAFT
JULY 23, 1962
STANLEY KUBRICK
DRAFT #1
RED ALERT

05

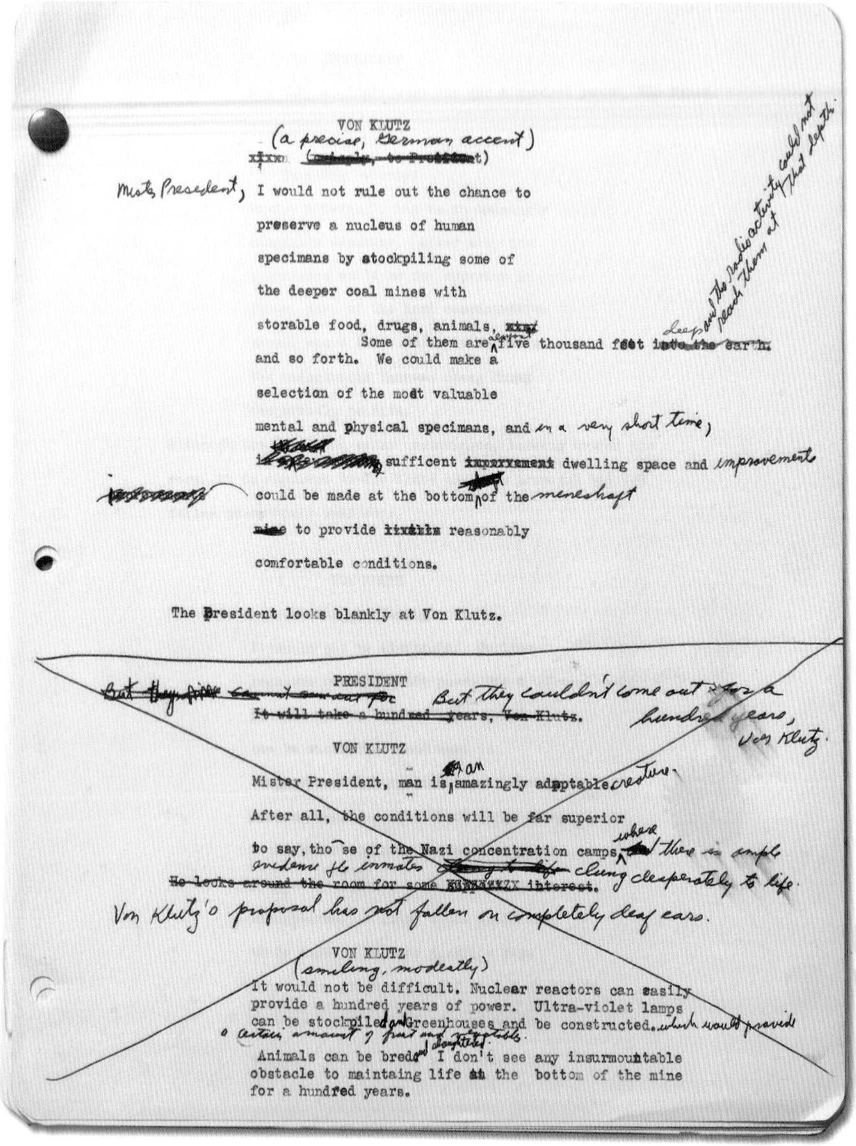

VON KLUTZ
(a precise, German accent)
~~(quickly, to President)~~

Mister President, I would not rule out the chance to preserve a nucleus of human specimans by stockpiling some of the deeper coal mines with storable food, drugs, animals, and so forth. Some of them are almost five thousand feet ~~into the earth~~ deep and the radio activity could not reach them at that depth. We could make a selection of the most valuable mental and physical specimans, and in a very short time, sufficent ~~improvement~~ dwelling space and improvements could be made at the bottom of the mineshaft ~~mine~~ to provide reasonably comfortable conditions.

The President looks blankly at Von Klutz.

PRESIDENT
~~It will take a hundred years, Von Klutz.~~
But they couldn't come out for a hundred years, Von Klutz.

VON KLUTZ
Mister President, man is an amazingly adaptable creature. After all, the conditions will be far superior to say, those of the Nazi concentration camps, where there is ample evidence the inmates clung desperately to life.

~~He looks around the room for some interest.~~
Von Klutz's proposal has not fallen on completely deaf ears.

VON KLUTZ
(smiling, modestly)
It would not be difficult. Nuclear reactors can easily provide a hundred years of power. Ultra-violet lamps can be stockpiled and Greenhouses and be constructed which would provide a certain amount of fruit and vegetables. Animals can be bred and slaughtered. I don't see any insurmountable obstacle to maintaing life at the bottom of the mine for a hundred years.

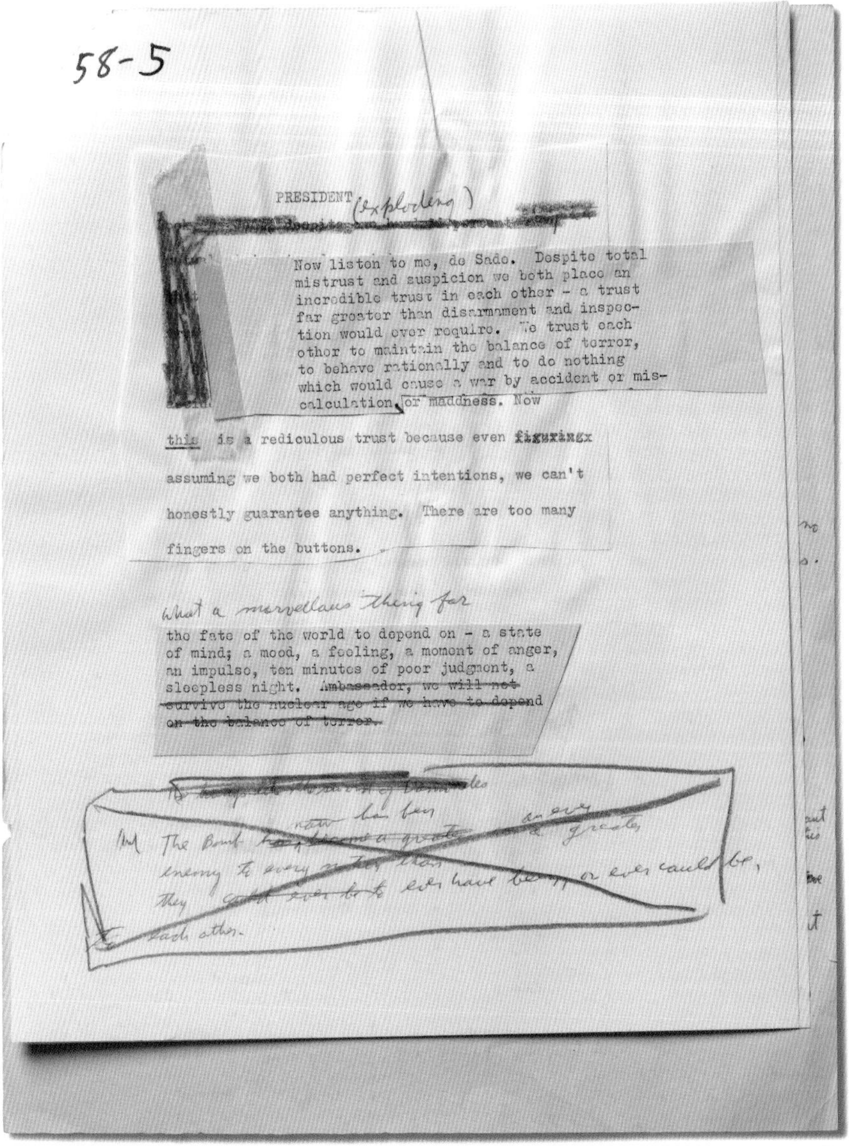

58-5

PRESIDENT (exploding)

[illegible]

Now listen to me, de Sade. Despite total mistrust and suspicion we both place an incredible trust in each other - a trust far greater than disarmament and inspection would ever require. We trust each other to maintain the balance of terror, to behave rationally and to do nothing which would cause a war by accident or miscalculation, or maddness. Now this is a rediculous trust because even ~~figuringx~~ assuming we both had perfect intentions, we can't honestly guarantee anything. There are too many fingers on the buttons.

What a marvellous thing for the fate of the world to depend on - a state of mind; a mood, a feeling, a moment of anger, an impulse, ten minutes of poor judgment, a sleepless night. ~~Ambassador, we will not survive the nuclear age if we have to depend on the balance of terror.~~

~~[illegible]~~

~~The Bomb now has been an even greater enemy to every nation than they ever have been, or ever could be, to each other.~~

26bb. INT B-52

The crew are lined up facing ~~MajorzTzJzDzKong~~ ~~the T.J. (Pilot)~~ ~~pilot~~ T.J. who holds six plastic packages ~~aboutzthezsizezof~~ ~~smallzxxzxzTXXXzChristmaszparcelszx~~ which look something like a boys christmas surprise parcel.

T.J.

Okay, boys, I'm supposed to hand these survival kits out before we get over enemy coast. In them you will find -

(he reads from printing on the side)

One .45 automatic, two boxes ammunition, four days concentrated emergency rations, one fishing line, and hooks, one pocket knife, one compass, one ~~issue~~x drug issue containing: anti-biotic, morphine, vitamin pills, pep pills, sleeping pills, tranquillizer pills, (A) one hundred dollars in ~~roux~~ Rubles, one hundred dollars in ~~gold~~ gold, four 21 jewels Swiss ~~wrist~~ watches, five gold plated fountain pens, ~~two~~ ten packs chewing gum, one issue propholayctics, three lipsticks, three pairs nylon stockings. ~~andzonez issuexprophalgctiesx~~

(A) one ~~coat~~ ~~one change~~ ~~and~~ menature combination Russian phrase books, and bible, ~~and~~

09

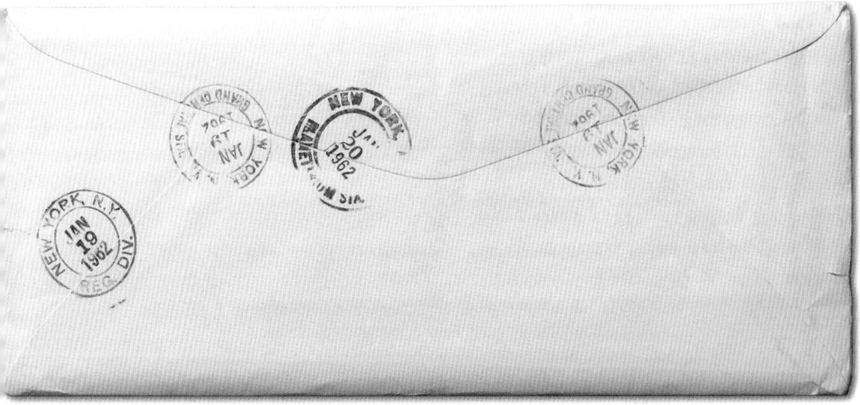

10

novel into a dark comedy, since he is listed in the screen credits as co-author of the script, committed suicide two years after the release of the film. Christiane Kubrick told me that George was "a very heavy drinker," and subject to fits of depression. His follow-up novel to *Red Alert*, entitled *Commander-1*, another tale of nuclear war, was not as well received as *Red Alert*, and it was not made into a film. It may be that he was convinced that he could not repeat the success of *Red Alert* and *Dr. Strangelove* that discouraged him to the point of taking his own life.

Once Kubrick had decided on a new concept for *Dr. Strangelove*, he brought over Terry Southern from America to lend his brand of irreverent black humor to the

09–10 ***This envelope, sent by Kubrick to himself on January 19, 1962, contained a description of his intended screenplay revisions for* Red Alert. *The act of sending oneself documents and preserving the postmarked, unopened envelopes is known as the "poor man's copyright."***

screenplay, and Peter George bowed out of the picture. During their period of collaboration, November-December, 1962, Kubrick would pick up Southern at his London hotel in his chauffeured limo at 5 a.m., and they would work on the script en route to Shepperton Studios. In Kubrick's old Bentley, they would work on separate little tables in the back seat. Kubrick's cynical humor, a vestige of his youth in the back streets of the Bronx and Greenwich Village, meshed with Southern's off-the-wall humor.

"As I kept trying to imagine the way in which things would really happen, ideas kept coming to me which I would discard because they were so ludicrous. I kept saying to myself: 'I can't do this. People will laugh.'"

— SK/1970 on why he decided to make *Dr. Strangelove* as a comedy (to Joseph Gelmis)

Some of the movie's best scenes are not in the book; furthermore, Kubrick and Southern departed from the novel's fundamentally sympathetic approach to the characters and retooled them into a gallery of grotesques. There is, for example, General Jack D. Ripper (General Quinten in the book), who initiates the attack on Russia; his mad motivation is his paranoid conviction that his diminishing sexual potency can be traced to an international Communist conspiracy to poison the drinking water.

One of the humorous elements of *Strangelove* is the collection of absurd names with which Kubrick and Southern have blessed their bizarre characters. Many of the names have sexual connotations, such as General Jack D. Ripper, named for the notorious sexual psychopath. Ripper reveals his fears of impotency to Captain Mandrake, who is named after the mandrake root, a plant that in mythic lore is said to encourage fertility. General Buck Turgidson's last name is made up of an adjective meaning swollen (referring in this case to the male member) and the word for male offspring. The bald Merkin Muffley's first name is a reference to female pubic hair. The two Russians' names are Ambassador de Sadesky and Premier Kissoff, and Colonel Bat Guano's last name is defined by Webster's dictionary as bird manure. And there is, of course, the weird scientist of the film's title, whose strange love of death and destruction, nurtured by a lifetime spent in perfecting instruments of destruction, enlivens him in a way that nothing else can.

Kubrick chose Sterling Hayden, who organized the ill-fated robbery as Johnny Clay in *The Killing*, to play General Ripper, the paranoid survivalist; George C. Scott to play General Turgidson, a right-wing Pentagon hawk; and Slim Pickens, whom he had cast in *One-Eyed Jacks* before quitting that picture, to play Major "King" Kong, a pilot who is more at home on a bucking bronco than on a B-52.

Peter Sellers plays not only the title role of the eccentric scientist, but also the President of the United States, Merkin Muffley, and Group Captain Lionel Mandrake,

11 ***Kubrick's brainstorms for the title of the film.***

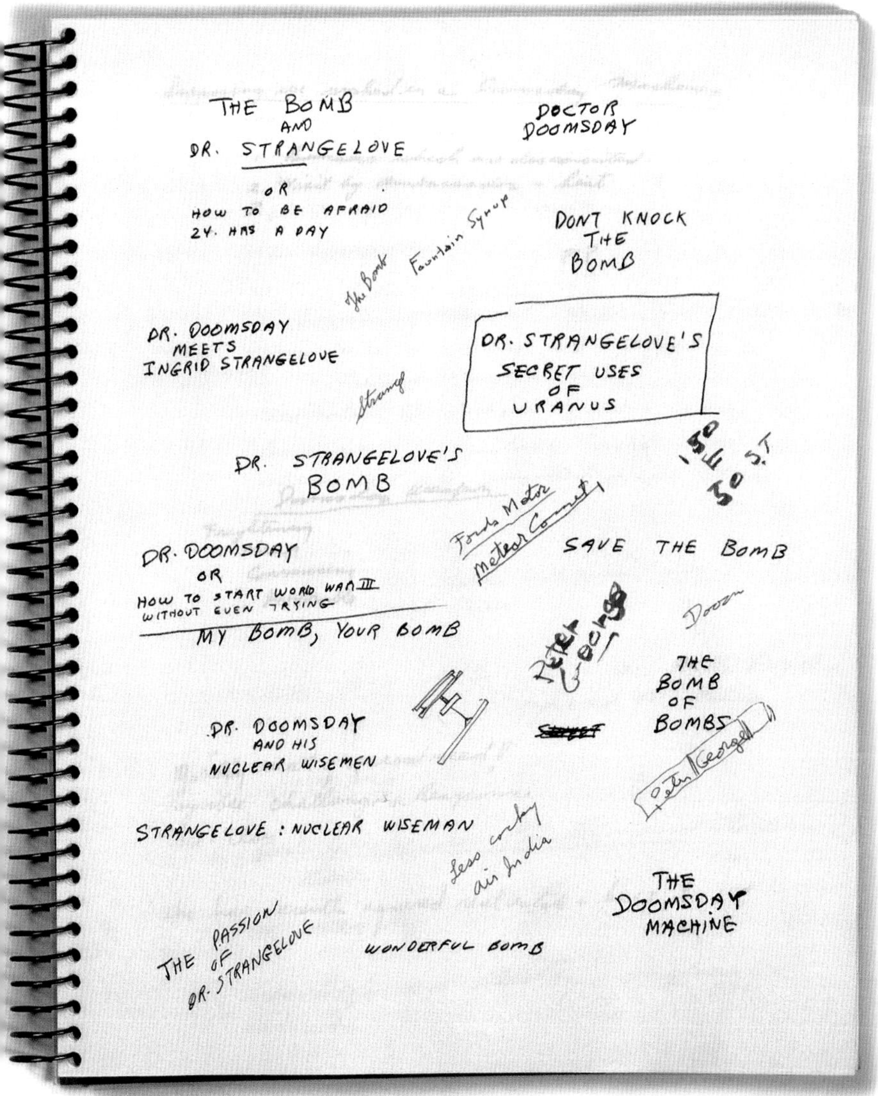
THE BOMB AND DR. STRANGELOVE OR HOW TO BE AFRAID 24. HRS A DAY
DOCTOR DOOMSDAY
DONT KNOCK THE BOMB
The Bomb
Fountain Syrup
DR. DOOMSDAY MEETS INGRID STRANGELOVE
DR. STRANGELOVE'S SECRET USES OF URANUS
Strange
DR. STRANGELOVE'S BOMB
Fords Motor
Meteor Comet
SAVE THE BOMB
DR. DOOMSDAY OR HOW TO START WORLD WAR III WITHOUT EVEN TRYING
MY BOMB, YOUR BOMB
Peter George
Doom
THE BOMB OF BOMBS
DR. DOOMSDAY AND HIS NUCLEAR WISEMEN
Peter George
STRANGELOVE : NUCLEAR WISEMAN
Less costly Air India
THE DOOMSDAY MACHINE
THE PASSION OF DR. STRANGELOVE
WONDERFUL BOMB

11

the British RAF officer who tries to dissuade General Ripper from his set purpose. Kubrick had also intended Sellers to play Major Kong, the commander of the only bomber to get through to its Russian target. Sellers hesitated to take the role of Kong, because he was uncertain that he could master Kong's Texas twang, but Kubrick remained adamant that he play it. Finally, Sellers accidentally injured his ankle, when he tripped while emerging from his limo, and begged off from doing Kong's scenes. Kubrick complied, but wondered if Sellers had suffered the fall "accidentally-on-purpose," to get out of playing a part he was not comfortable with. Kubrick was disappointed that Sellers declined to play the fourth part, since, in his view, that would have meant that almost everywhere the viewer looks, there is some version of Peter Sellers holding the fate of the world in his hands.

Nevertheless, as things stand, Sellers enacts the roles of the three men behind the scenes who are most deeply involved in trying to keep Major Kong from carrying out the mission that he has been led to believe by Ripper's orders is his duty. In any case, Slim Pickens gives the performance of his career as Kong, the good-natured, benighted Texan. As for Sellers' achievement in playing three parts in *Dr. Strangelove,* Kubrick commented that each of the roles required a singular talent. "I don't think anyone else can play the three roles as well. It's like having three different great actors" for the price of one.[2]

Besides a superior cast, Kubrick also had on hand some top-notch production artists: lighting cameraman Gilbert Taylor, who had filmed the title sequence of *Lolita;* film editor Anthony Harvey, who had also edited *Lolita;* production designer Ken Adam (*Dr. No*); and composer Laurie Johnson (*Tiger Bay*). The interiors were filmed at Shepperton Studios near London. To shoot exteriors for the attack on Burpelson Air Base, Kubrick used the grounds of Shepperton Studios, with the studio buildings themselves standing in for the complex of buildings at Burpelson. Ken Adam posted military propaganda signs on the outside of the buildings.

12 ***This photo by Weegee shows Peter Sellers as Major Kong; when he injured his ankle, Slim Pickens was hired to replace him in the role.***
13 ***These notes appear on the first page of the screenplay.***

Principal photography got underway on January 28, 1963, and finished on April 23. Kubrick, as usual, continued to revise the script while the film was in production, during what Kubrick termed "the crucial rehearsal periods." He would listen to all of the suggestions that the cast and crew had to offer, weigh them against his own ideas and finally decide on how the scene should be handled. "Stanley is a very quiet person and a brain picker," says Slim Pickens. "He surrounds himself with a bunch of bright people, and when anybody comes up with a bright idea, Stanley uses it."[3] This period of rehearsal is one of maximum tension and anxiety, Kubrick told me, "and it is precisely here where a scene lives or dies." The subsequent choice of camera angles, he believed, was relatively simple by comparison with the working out of the scene with the actors in rehearsal.

George C. Scott had gained the reputation of being a temperamental actor, along the lines of Charles Laughton, with whom Kubrick had to cope on *Spartacus*. But Scott's assessment of Kubrick was positive: "Kubrick most certainly is in command," he said afterward; "but he's so self-effacing, it is impossible to be offended by him. No pomposity, no vanity.... But he has a brilliant eye; he sees more than the camera (does)."[4]

Dr. Strangelove recalls *The Killing* because it shows how a supposedly foolproof plan of action can go awry, and once more Kubrick is telling a story that takes place in several places at once. Kubrick develops the parallel lines of action in *Dr. Strangelove* by cutting abruptly back and forth from one place to another in mid-scene. Consequently, the screenplay for *Dr. Strangelove* remains one of the most tightly knit, brilliantly constructed scripts ever devised. Only repeated viewings can indicate the subtlety and skill with which it has been put together.

Yet both Kubrick and Harvey were very disappointed with the first assemblage of the footage that Harvey created. Harvey had been gradually assembling the footage into a rough cut while Kubrick was shooting the movie,

GENERAL NOTES:

1. The story will be played for realistic comedy - which means the essentially truthful moods and attitudes will be portrayed accurately, with an occasional bizarre or super-realistic crescendo. The acting will never be so-called "comedy" acting.

2. The sets and technical details will be done realistically and carefully. We will strive for the maximum atmosphere and sense of <u>visual</u> reality from the sets and locations.

3. The Flying sequences will especially be presented in as vivid a manner as possible. Exciting backgrounds and special effects will be obtained.

and he finished his first cut shortly after filming was finished. Then Kubrick joined him to produce the director's cut of the film. When Harvey and Kubrick looked at Harvey's cut, they were depressed. "As with all first cuts," Harvey said, "you want to slit your throat, and everyone runs off in different directions looking for a knife!...

"As fewer and fewer people find solace in religion... I actually believe that they unconsciously derive a kind of perverse solace from the idea that in the event of nuclear war, the world dies with them. God is dead, but the bomb endures; thus, they are no longer alone in the terrible vulnerability of their mortality."

— SK/1968 (to Eric Nordern/*Playboy*)

I remember that I took the whole film apart, and we started with the first reel," and went through to the last "in minute detail." Harvey recalls, "Stanley and I put cards up on a big corkboard and rearranged them in many different ways until it looked like a more interesting way to cut it. We recut the whole film, the juxtaposition of placing one scene to another was totally different. When you've got the film on the Moviola editing machine, one so often does rearrange things—it was major in this case."[5]

The tone of the screenplay neatly straddles the line between straightforward realism and straight-faced farce. The flight deck of Major Kong's B-52, for example was constructed at Shepperton Studios in authentic detail in an area about the size of a packed linen closet. It is just this air of realism and the inexorable plausibility with which the story unfolds that led Columbia Pictures (at the behest of the State Department), to add a printed preface at the beginning of the film—after advising Kubrick that nuclear war was no laughing matter. It reads:

"It is the stated position of the United States Air Force that their safeguards would prevent the occurrence of such events as are depicted in this film. Furthermore, it should be noted that none of the characters portrayed in this film are meant to represent any real persons living or dead." The last sentence is more fiction than fact, because certain characters in the film were based on real persons. According to history professor Paul Boyer, Hayden's character was based on the head of the Strategic Air Command (SAC) during the 1950s. "The cigar-chewing Curtis LeMay provided an easily recognizable prototype for the film's fanatical General Jack D. Ripper. LeMay never met a bombing plan he didn't like." In 1957, he declared to a congressional committee charged with investigating U. S. military policy that, if a Soviet attack ever seemed likely, he planned to "knock the shit out of them before they ever got off the ground," and bomb them back into the Stone Age, according to Boyer. Reminded by the

14 ***Major Kong (Slim Pickens, right) and his co-pilot open the instructions for wing attack Plan R.***
15 ***Shooting the scenes of the interior of the B-52 bomber.***

14

15

Tribune

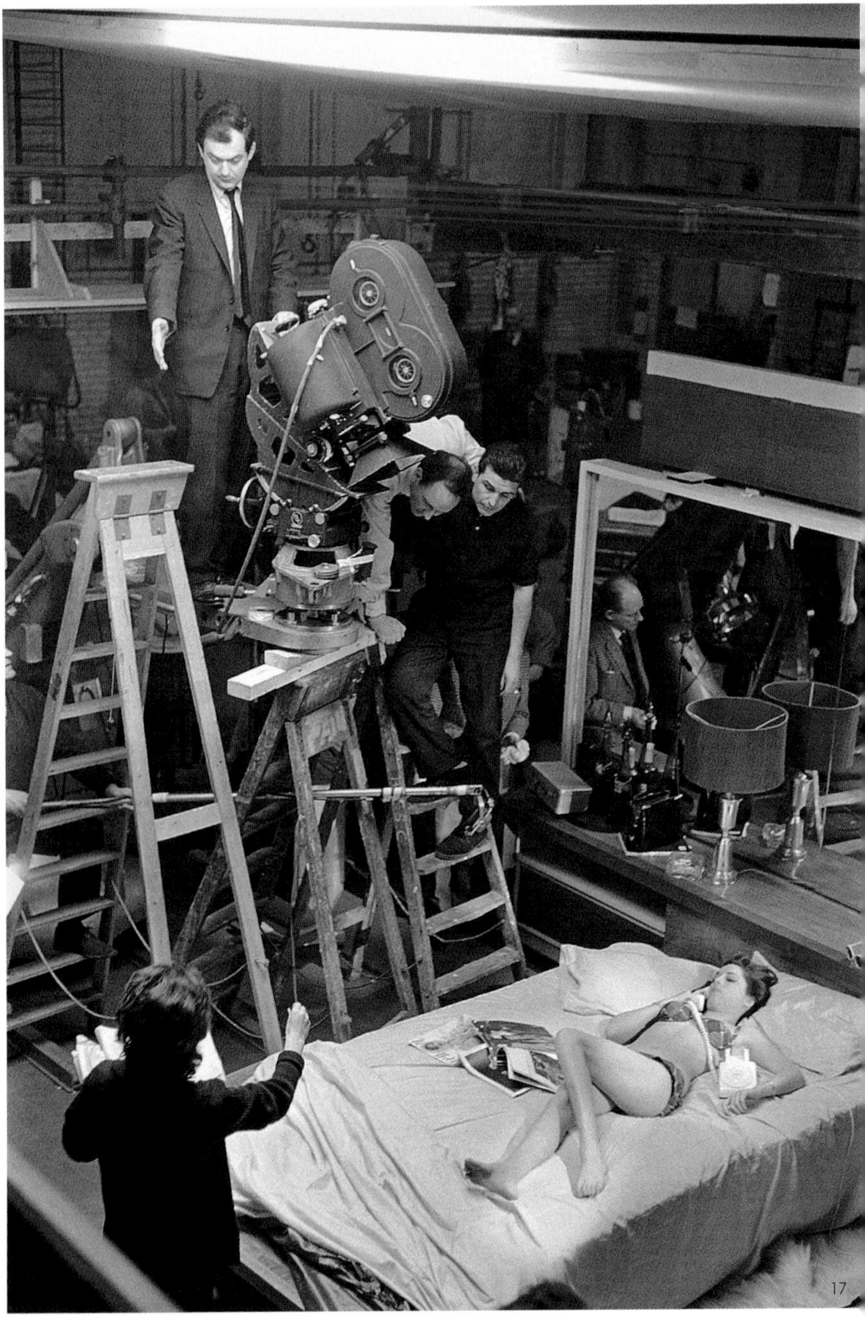

17

committee members that a preemptive first strike was not official government policy, he retorted, "No, it's not official policy; but it's my policy."

In addition, Dr. Strangelove, an ex-Nazi atomic scientist, Boyer continues, was based on Wernher von Braun, the former Nazi rocket scientist that headed America's space research program after the war. "This time I wanted to be on the winning side," von Braun said at the time.[6]

16 ***Tracy Reed (Miss Scott), Kubrick, and George C. Scott (General Turgidson).***
17 ***This overhead shot of Miss Scott, Turgidson's secretary/mistress, was not used in the film.***
18 ***Tracy Reed's lines were written on a board to assist her in the scene in which Miss Scott takes a call for Turgidson.***

Following the "official" disclaimer, an expanse of clouds is seen stretching across the screen with mountain peaks poking through in the distance. A narrator says, "For more than a year, ominous rumors had been privately circulating among high-level Western leaders that the Soviet Union had been at work on what was hinted to be the ultimate weapon, a Doomsday device. Intelligence sources traced the site of the top-secret Russian project to the perpetually fog-shrouded wasteland below the Arctic peaks of the Zhokhov islands. What they were building, or why it should be located in such a remote and desolate place, no one could say."

The picture will be more than half over before further reference is made to the Doomsday machine, which will in the

19

end reduce the world to the trackless waste pictured in the very opening image of the film.

The credit sequence begins with a close-up of the nose of a plane protruding proudly toward the camera like an erect penis. To the strains of "Try a Little Tenderness," which Laurie Johnson chose to play softly in the background, a nuclear bomber is refueled in mid-flight by a tanker aircraft. This symbolic coupling sets the tone for the sexual metaphors that are spread throughout the movie, underscoring the obsessions of various characters, chiefly General Ripper.

Ripper informs Group Captain Lionel Mandrake, a British RAF officer, that Burpelson Air Base is being put on Condition Red. "It looks like we are in a shooting war. My orders are to seal the base tight." Holed up in his office, Ripper resembles nothing so much as Adolf Hitler in his bunker during the last days of the Third Reich.

The narrator, in his last appearance on the sound track, explains that in order to guard against the possibility of surprise attack, SAC maintains a force of planes airborne twenty-four hours a day, spread out from the Persian Gulf to the Arctic Ocean. "But they all have one geographic factor in common. They are all two hours from their targets inside Russia."

19 ***Peter Sellers (as President Muffley), Weegee, and Peter Bull (Ambassador de Sadesky).***
20 ***Kubrick examines Weegee's special blimp housing, used to silence his camera for shooting on the set.***

20

Hence Ripper has placed the planes in his command on "Plan R," according to which they will all proceed to bomb their specifically allotted targets within the Soviet Union.

Inside one of the bombers, Major King Kong receives the instructions to proceed to his target inside Russia. Kong dramatically opens the book of instructions labeled "Plan R," clamping on his trusty ten-gallon hat like a cowboy in some forgotten Western epic, just as the insistent strumming of "When Johnny Comes Marching Home" commences on the sound track. This melody, as adroitly orchestrated by Laurie Johnson, will continue to be heard in every one of the flight deck scenes, its incessant snare drum accompaniment building tension in a manner akin to Ravel's *Bolero*.

The phone in General Turgidson's bedroom is answered by bikini-clad bombshell Miss Scott (Tracy Reed, the daughter of film director Carol Reed). Miss Scott, the general's full-time secretary and part-time mistress, informs Turgidson (who is "indisposed") that he has an emergency phone call. After taking the call, he tells her with forced nonchalance that he is going to "mosey down to the War Room" to see what is going on.

At Burpelson the guards and enlisted men listen tensely to Ripper's proclamation of the red alert over the public-address system. In several shots of the men, the SAC motto can be seen posted prominently in the background: "Peace is our profession." This banner also appears on the wall behind General Ripper as he sits at his desk making his speech. Ripper, who has severe sexual hang-ups, is here shown sporting a phallic symbol in his hand: a huge cigar.

Mandrake bursts into Ripper's office; standing at attention, he formally demands that Ripper give him the code prefix by which he can radio the bomber wing to turn back from their Russian targets. Ripper pulls a gun on Mandrake and locks his office door. He then attempts in an extended, complicated monologue to explain to Mandrake his reasons for implementing Plan R. Sterling Hayden remembers that this, his first day of filming, was torture; he found that he could not handle the technical jargon in his lines. "I was nervous, scared, did forty-eight takes," he continues. "I was utterly humiliated." He expected Kubrick to explode at him; instead, Kubrick was gentle and calmed him. He told Hayden, "The terror on your face may yield just the quality we want; and if it doesn't, the hell with it. We'll shoot the thing over." Comments Hayden, "He was beautiful. A lot of directors like to see an actor wallow. Stanley wasn't one of them."[7] At any rate, when Ripper finishes his speech, Mandrake is seen as a tiny figure photographed in long shot—helplessly standing alone, as he realizes that he is imprisoned with a lunatic.

Kubrick, commenting on this scene, said that there was in fact a serious threat that a psychotic figure somewhere in the command structure could start a war. Even if it involved only a limited exchange of nuclear weapons, he maintained, it

21 ***The director performs a pie-throwing test.***
22–25 ***The raucous pie fight scene that was cut from the film.***

could devastate large areas. "I'm not assured that somewhere in the Pentagon or Red Army upper echelons there does not exist the real-life prototype of General Jack D. Ripper."[8] He was implicitly denying the statement in the printed prologue of the film, imposed on him by the studio, that the events portrayed in the movie could not occur.

We now get our first glimpse of Ken Adam's stunningly designed War Room, a murky, cavernous place which cinematographer Gilbert Taylor has skillfully filled with looming shadows. President Muffley sits at a vast circular table with his advisors, reminiscent of King Arthur and his Knights of the Round Table. Overhead is a round bank of lights that bathes the men below in an eerie glow. They are surrounded by darkness, like the conspirators planning the robbery in *The Killing*. This threatening darkness often hovers over Kubrick's characters, as they futilely endeavor to keep it from overwhelming them.

Buck Turgidson gleefully informs the president that things have already gotten to the point where the only possible recourse is to back Ripper's attack with an all-out nuclear offensive against the Russians, before they can retaliate. The president—who is not quite the simpleton that some critics have made him out to be—counters sensibly that it is the avowed policy of the United States never to strike first with nuclear weapons and that General Ripper's action was not in

22

2

23

25

26

28

27

29

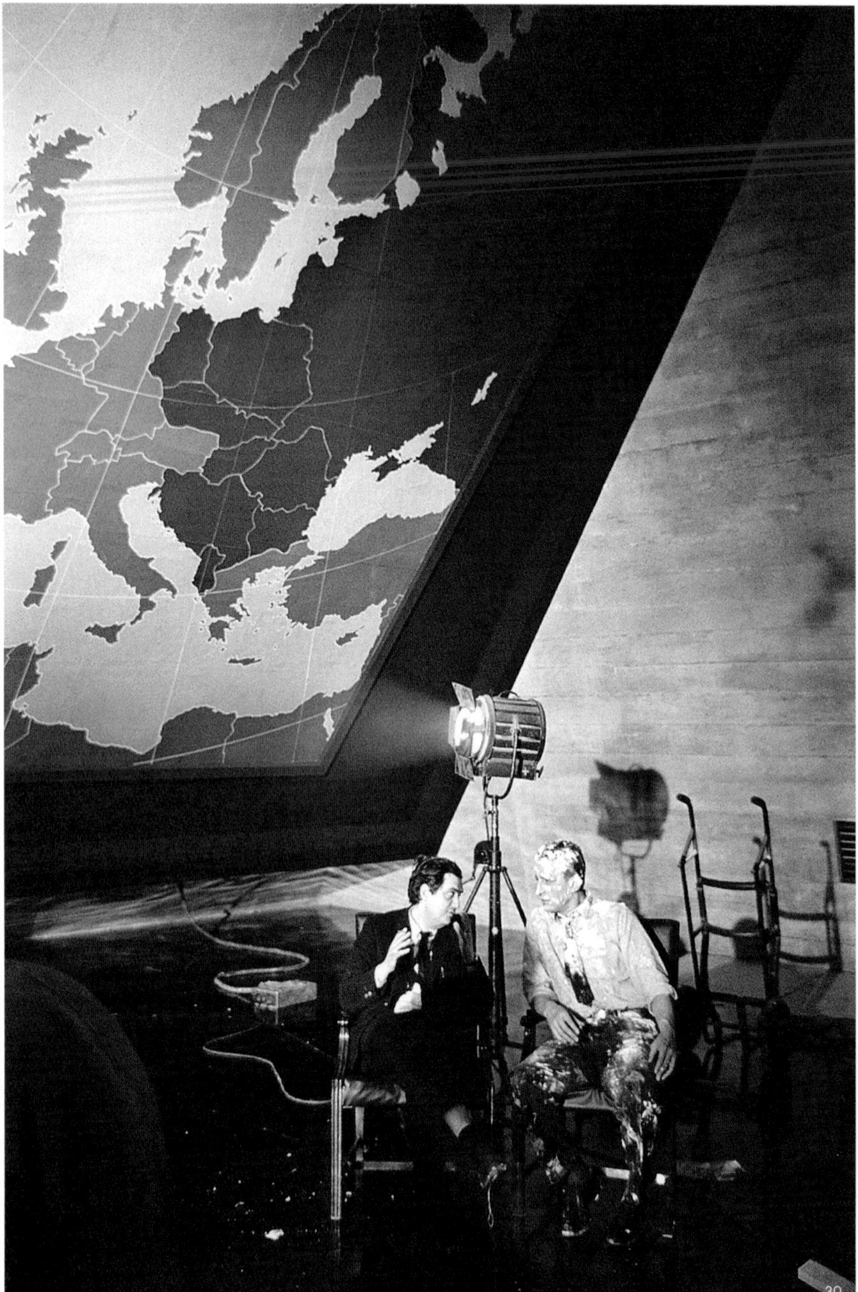

30

line with national policy. This statement makes clear why Kubrick told me that Muffley "was the one sane man in the War Room." Moreover, the president contends, there are still other alternatives to the acts of aggression proposed by Turgidson.

Scott often complained at the time of the film's release that Kubrick directed him to play the role over the top, and then chose Scott's most overwrought and manic takes for the final cut of the movie. As a result, he felt that in this and some other scenes in the movie he came across as a fast-talking, blithering buffoon— frowning, grimacing, and yelping as he fences verbally with the president.

Roger Ebert emphatically disagrees, contending that Scott gave the best performance in the movie: "I found myself paying special attention to the tics and twitches, the grimaces and eyebrow arching, the sardonic smiles.... Scott's sandpaper voice slips from whiplash harshness to silky persuasion" as the occasion demands. All the while he clutches to his breast a military volume entitled *World Targets in Megadeaths.* Kubrick endorsed

26–34 ***Images from the pie fight scene. Kubrick told Joseph Gelmis in 1970, "[A]fter a screening of* Dr. Strangelove *I cut out a final scene in which the Russians and Americans in the War Room engage in a free-for-all fight with custard pies. I decided it was farce and not consistent with the satiric tone of the rest of the film."***
28 ***Kubrick's wife, Christiane, throws a pie as Weegee photographs.***

Scott's facial grimaces, Ebert concludes, because the actor never allows the plastic facial movements to slide into mugging or overacting.[9]

Turgidson forges on in his diatribe to the president, respectfully maintaining that the president must support Ripper's nuclear attack on Russia before the Russians can retaliate. Robert Brustein applauds the manner in which Scott delivers his speech at this point, "in a fine frenzy of muscle-flexing pugnacity — stuffing his mouth with wads of chewing gum and flashing an evil smile as he outlines his plan to obliterate the 'Commie punks' entirely."[10]

"I'm not saying we wouldn't get our hair mussed," Turgidson concedes, displaying a rather mild disdain for the casualties involved that recalls General Mireau planning the suicide attack in *Paths of Glory*. "I'm saying ten to twenty million people killed— tops—depending on the breaks." Muffley nonetheless orders a detachment of soldiers to invade Burpelson Air Base and force General Ripper to phone him. He still favors negotiation over Turgidson's preemptive air strike.

The Russian ambassador, Alexei de Sadesky (Peter Bull) is summoned to the War Room, and the president then phones the Russian premier, Dimitri Kissoff. What follows is a brilliant comic monologue in which Sellers once again proves, as he did in *Lolita*, that he is the master of improvisation and of black comedy. Kubrick said that Sellers was always at his best in dealing with grotesque and horrifying

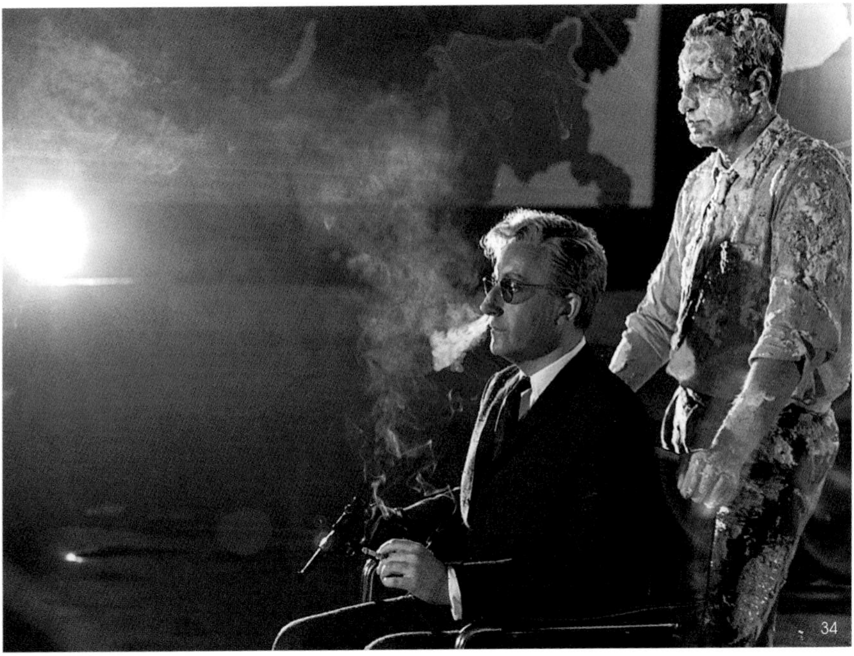

34

circumstances which other actors would not think playable at all. This makes him the perfect ally for the director, of whom Alexander Walker has written, "Comedy, for Kubrick, makes it possible to deal with issues that would be unbearable in any other form."[11]

President Muffley attempts to explain the critical state of affairs to Premier Kissoff, who unfortunately happens to be drunk. "Now then, Dimitri, one of our base commanders went a little funny in the head, and did a silly thing.... He ordered his planes to attack your country.... Well, can you imagine how *I* feel about it?!"

The president goes on to say that the bombers will not reach their objectives for another hour, and this statement is accompanied by a shot of their positions on the "Threat Board." Then Muffley haltingly offers to give to the Russian air staff a complete rundown on the targets for which the B-52s are aiming, along with their flight plans and defense systems. "If we can't recall them in time," he says, dreading the sound of his own words, "we are just going to have to help you destroy them." Sellers' monologue was shot in a single long take.

At this point Dr. Strangelove comes forward in his wheelchair to enter the discussion. He is Kubrick's vision of man's final capitulation to the machine: he is more of a robot than a human being, his mechanical arm spontaneously saluting Hitler (his former employer), his mechanical hand, gloved in black, at one point trying to strangle the flesh and blood that still

remains in him. His arm and hand, Sellers commented, take on a life of their own.

Kubrick told me that Dr. Strangelove is reminiscent of Dr. Rotwang, the deranged scientist in Fritz Lang's *Metropolis* (1926). Dr. Strangelove's prosthesis was inspired by Rotwang's mechanical arm and black-gloved hand. Sellers found the inspiration for Dr. Strangelove's high-pitched German accent from photojournalist Weegee (Arthur Fellig), who was stills photographer on the set. Kubrick, an admirer of Weegee since he was himself a young photojournalist in New York, had invited him to take stills on the set during shooting.

Now de Sadesky reveals that if one U.S. bomber reaches its Russian target, the Russians' retaliatory Doomsday machine will be set off automatically, and "a Doomsday shroud — a lethal cloud of radioactivity ... will encircle the earth for ninety-three years." Turgidson remarks that the Angel of Death is hovering over them, and the camera focuses on Dr. Strangelove, immersed in dark shadows. He asks the Russian envoy why the Doomsday device was kept a secret, since it was meant to be a deterrent to nuclear attack. "The premier was going to announce

35 ***Peter Sellers (as Group Captain Mandrake), Sterling Hayden (General Jack D. Ripper), and Kubrick on the set of Ripper's office.***
36 ***Kubrick demonstrates for Keenan Wynn how to shoot the Coke machine.***
37 ***Kubrick sets up a shot of Slim Pickens astride the bomb.***
38 ***Finding just the right angle for a shot of Hayden and Sellers.***

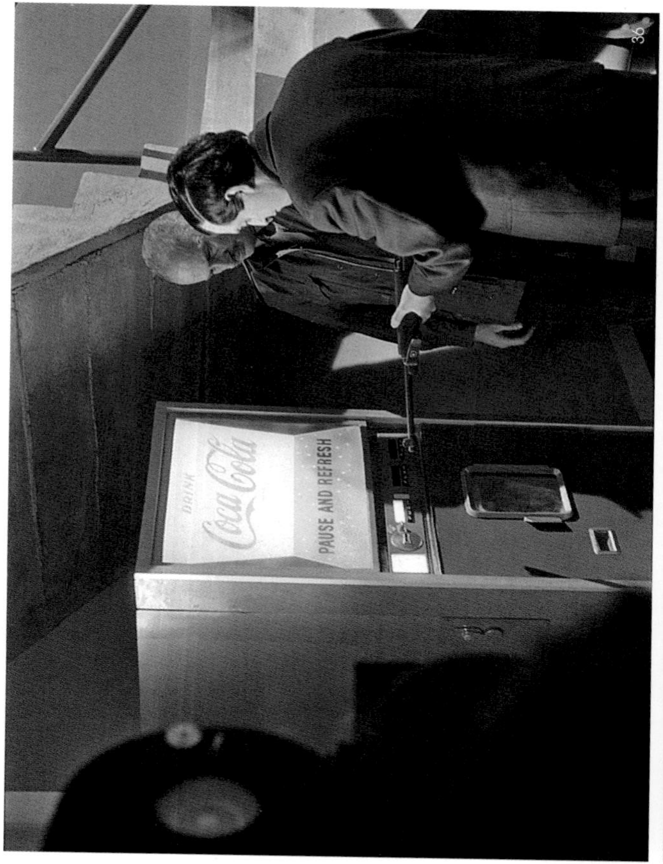

36

37

"The fact that it has not been used on people deliberately or accidentally since World War II is a bit like an airline with a perfect twenty-year safety record. One has to admire such a performance but it can't last forever."

—SK/1965 (asked to comment on the atomic bomb for *The Sunday Times Magazine*)

it at the Party Congress on Monday," de Sadesky replies laconically; "he loves surprises." At one point a disagreement between Turgidson and de Sadesky threatens to turn into a brawl and the president admonishes them, "Please, gentlemen, you can't fight here; this is the War Room." (When Ronald Reagan became president, he supposedly asked to be shown the War Room—not realizing that it was a fictional invention.)

Kubrick originally included a scene in the film in which the War Room personnel engage in a free-for-all with cream pies from the buffet table. Kubrick devoted five days to shooting this sequence, Ken Adam told Michel Ciment. "It was a very brilliant sequence, with a *Hellzapoppin* kind of craziness. Undoubtedly one of the most extraordinary pie battles ever filmed. The characters were hanging from chandeliers and throwing pies which ended up by covering the maps of the General Staff. Shooting lasted a week, and the sequence ended with the President of the United States and the Soviet ambassador sitting on what was left of the pies and building 'pie castles' like children on a beach."[12] In shooting the pie fight, which involved thirty actors, many of them in military dress, the participants heaved one thousand pies a day at each other.

After watching this segment with an audience, Kubrick decided to delete it completely from the final print of the picture because "it was too farcical and not consistent wit the satiric tone of the rest of the film," he told me. This was a wise decision, since the humor in *Dr. Strangelove* is mostly of the tongue-in-cheek variety, not slapstick.

Anthony Harvey recalls that, at one point in the pastry-throwing scene, the president is hit with a pie. One of the generals says, "Our beloved president has been struck down in his prime." In the wake of the assassination of President John F. Kennedy, that line would have proved unacceptable. But, as things turned out, the whole scene was scuttled.

Meanwhile, back at the base, Ripper learns that Burpelson is being invaded by a battery of troops. In the depths of his psychosis, Ripper thinks that the Russian army has taken over his citadel, rather than the American soldiers dispatched by the president. Mandrake futilely tries to reason with him, but the general only lumbers on, in the grip of his madness; "I happen to believe in a life after this one, and I know I'll have to answer for what I have

39–41 ***Slim Pickens was suspended on wires for the shots of Major Kong riding the bomb.***

40

done—and I think I can." Having relinquished his cigar, Ripper takes yet another phallic symbol in hand, a loaded pistol, and retreats to the bathroom, where he blows his brains out, as if he were subconsciously aping Adolf Hitler to the last. Brustein sums up Hayden's performance by commenting that it is deliciously mad: "his eyes fanatically narrowed, his teeth clenched on a large cigar, as he drawls to Mandrake his motivation for his irrational actions."[13]

When Mandrake endeavors to reach the president in order to inform him about the recall code he has discovered in Ripper's crazed notes, he finds that he lacks the correct change for the coin telephone—the only phone left operating on the base—and that the White House will not accept a collect call! He demands that Colonel Bat Guano (Keenan Wynn) fire into a Coca-Cola machine in order to obtain the necessary money.

Col. Guano, who seems to be as paranoid as General Ripper ever was, tells Mandrake, "I think you're some kind of deviated prevert (sic). I think General Ripper found out about your preversion (sic), and that you were organizing some kind of mutiny of preverts (sic)." Nevertheless, to humor Mandrake, Guano reluctantly agrees to shoot into the Coke machine, ruefully reminding him that it is he who will have to answer to the Coca-Cola Company. But he warns that, when Mandrake makes the call in the phone booth, he had better not "try any perversions in there, or I'll blow your head off!" This has become one of the most frequently repeated lines from the film. In fact, one film historian nominated it as one of the all-time great movie lines in cinema history. After Guano blasts the machine, he bends down to scoop up the cascading coins and is squirted in the face with Coke by the vindictive machine.

Kubrick told Joseph Gelmis that "most of the humor in *Strangelove* arises from the depiction of everyday human behavior in a nightmarish situation, like ... the reluctance of the U.S. officer to let a British officer smash open a Coca-Cola machine for change to phone the president about a crisis on an air force base, because of his conditioning about the sanctity of private property."[14] Sterling Hayden, contemplating the film's theme of worldwide nuclear devastation, remarked to Keenan Wynn during rehearsal, "Wait till audiences see this one. They'll have nightmares." "That's what we're here for, isn't it?" answered Wynn quietly.[15]

Major Kong and his crew aboard the Leper Colony have survived an encounter they had with Russian fighter planes upon entering Soviet air space; the bomber has been damaged, not disabled. Kong reassures his crew, "Well, boys, we got three engines out, and we got more holes in us than a horse trader's mule. The radio's gone and we're leaking fuel; and if we were flying any lower we would need sleigh bells on this thing. But at this height the Rooskies won't spot us on no radar screen." However, the plane's radios have been damaged, preventing the recall message from getting through, and so the unstoppable Leper Colony inexorably reaches its Russian target. Major Kong manages to dislodge a bomb that has been stuck in its chamber, as he sits astride it, to unleash it on its target. As the bomb hurtles toward the earth, taking Kong along for the ride, it looks like a mighty symbol of potency clamped between his flanks, the immense phallic image recalling General Ripper's fear of impotency, which had triggered the bombing mission in the first place. "Slim Pickens, in an unforgettably funny and horrifying image, rides the bomb, rodeo-style, to Armageddon."[16] The screen turns a dazzling white as the bomb hits its target; and we return for the last time to the brooding shadows of the War Room.

At this moment of utter desolation, Dr. Strangelove speaks up. He is never at a

loss for a plan for the survival of himself and his colleagues, whatever may happen to humanity at large. He advises the president how key military and political figures and their descendants can survive in America's mine shafts for a century, until the nuclear fallout has finally dissipated: "With a ratio of ten women to every man, I estimate we could re-attain the present gross national product in twenty years." The doctor is teaching his listeners to "stop worrying and love the bomb" the way he does.

"*Can you imagine what might have happened at the height of the Cuban Missile Crisis if some deranged waiter had slipped LSD into Kennedy's coffee—or, on the other side of the fence, into Khrushchev's vodka? The possibilities are chilling.*"

—SK/1968 (to Eric Nordern/*Playboy*)

Turgidson asks with feigned detachment, "Doctor, wouldn't this necessitate the abandonment of the so-called monogamous sexual relationship?" Indeed it would, because the male survivors would have to breed many offspring. Life in the mine shaft, as pictured by Strangelove, would involve assembly-line sex, which is just the kind of mechanical process that would appeal to him.

Even in the midst of cosmic calamity, man remains true to his perverse inclinations. The Russian ambassador surreptitiously takes pictures of the Threat Board with a camera concealed in his pocket watch, seemingly oblivious of the fact that these photos will be of no earthly use now that life on the surface of the planet will be impossible for at least a century. And Turgidson, with his abiding paranoia about Russian conspiracies, begins yammering at the president that the Soviets may try "an immediate sneak attack to take over our mine shaft space. Mr. President, we cannot allow a mine shaft gap!"

Just at this moment Strangelove miraculously rises from his wheelchair. "Mein Führer," he exclaims, "I can walk!" Strangelove, with all his artificial limbs, we recall, is more a machine than a man. Therefore, once the Doomsday Machine has been detonated, he experiences a surge of energy, a sympathetic vibration as it were, with this ultimate and decisive triumph of the machine over mankind.

There follows a series of blinding explosions, while on the sound track we hear a popular ditty that Kubrick resurrected from World War II, "We'll meet again, don't know where, don't know when...." Kubrick told me that he used the original recording by Vera Lynn, which served not only to bring the song back to popularity but Ms. Lynn as well.

In the context of the film's ending, the song becomes an anthem of the millions who will be extinguished by the radioactive fallout precipitated by the Doomsday Machine. The singer fondly reflects that the survivors "will be happy to know that as you saw me go I was singing this song." This line recalls Dr. Strangelove's observation that the survivors will not be depressed by the loss of so many of their loved ones: "When they go down to the

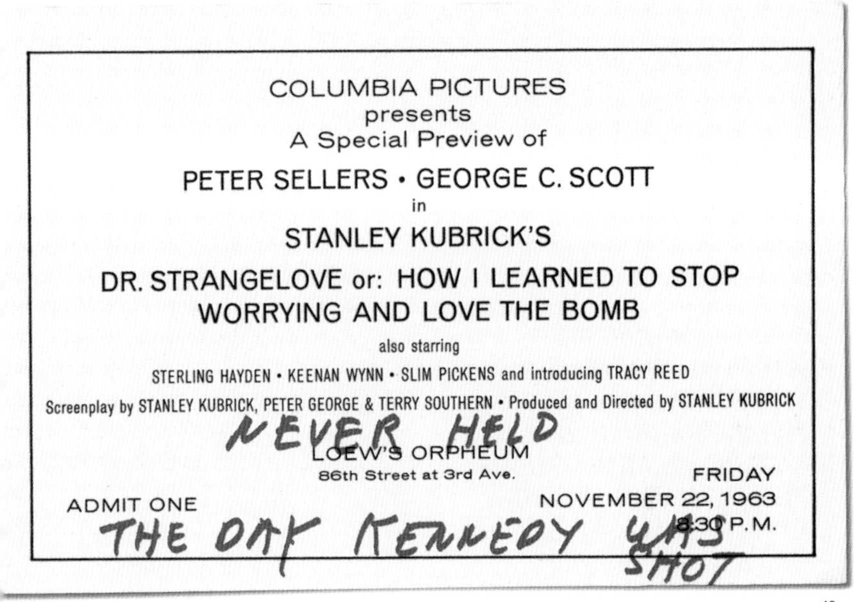
COLUMBIA PICTURES
presents
A Special Preview of
PETER SELLERS • GEORGE C. SCOTT
in
STANLEY KUBRICK'S
DR. STRANGELOVE or: HOW I LEARNED TO STOP WORRYING AND LOVE THE BOMB
also starring
STERLING HAYDEN • KEENAN WYNN • SLIM PICKENS and introducing TRACY REED
Screenplay by STANLEY KUBRICK, PETER GEORGE & TERRY SOUTHERN • Produced and Directed by STANLEY KUBRICK
NEVER HELD
LOEW'S ORPHEUM
86th Street at 3rd Ave.
FRIDAY
NOVEMBER 22, 1963
8:30 P.M.
ADMIT ONE
THE DAY KENNEDY WAS SHOT

42

mineshafts, everyone will be alive. The prevailing emotion afterward should be one of nostalgia for those left behind." Another verse speaks of the future, when the blue skies will drive the dark (radioactive) clouds away. This is illustrated by the vision of a distant sunset amid the black mushroom clouds now enveloping the earth.

Summing up the film, one can say that the humor Kubrick had originally intended to exclude from *Dr. Strangelove* provides some of its most meaningful moments. These moments, as devised for the revised screenplay, are made up of the incongruities, the banalities, and the misunderstandings that we are constantly aware of in our lives. On the brink of annihilation they become irresistibly absurd.

Pauline Kael, however, who adored the black comedy of *Lolita*, was not happy with *Dr. Strangelove*'s further foray into the same territory: "*Dr. Strangelove* opened a new movie era. It ridicules everything and everybody it showed," she wrote. "*Dr. Strangelove* was clearly intended as a cautionary movie; it meant to jolt us awake to the dangers of the bomb by showing us the insanity of the course we were pursuing. But artists' warnings about war and the dangers of total annihilation never tell us how we are supposed to regain control and *Dr. Strangelove*, chortling over madness, did not indicate any possibilities of sanity."[17]

Kubrick's own response to this kind of criticism was to point out that "in the

42 ***Kubrick noted on this invitation card the fact that the preview was cancelled because of President Kennedy's assassination.***

deepest sense I believe in man's potential and in his capacity for progress. In *Dr. Strangelove* I was dealing with the inherent irrationality in man that threatens to destroy him; that irrationality is with us as strongly today, and must be conquered. But a recognition of insanity doesn't imply celebration of it, nor a sense of despair and futility about the possibility of curing it."[18]

"In the context of imminent world destruction, hypocrisy, misunderstanding, lechery, paranoia, ambition, euphemism, patriotism, heroism, and even reasonableness can evoke a grisly laugh."

—SK/1971 (to Alexander Walker)

In *Dr. Strangelove,* then, Kubrick has turned the searchlight of satire on the "balance of terror" that the nuclear powers seek to maintain to hold each other in check. In so doing, Kubrick illuminated the common foibles of ordinary humanity as well—human flaws that are all the more obvious when they come to the surface in the context of a cosmic catastrophe. The unsettling theme that emerges from *Dr. Strangelove* is the plight of fallible man placing himself at the mercy of his infallible machines and bringing about his own destruction by this abdication of moral responsibility. As he told me, "I don't pretend to have the answers; but the questions are certainly worth considering."

Dr. Strangelove had absolutely no problems with the industry censor, which was a relief to Kubrick after the problems that *Lolita* had run into. Over the years it has been the recipient of some distinguished awards. When the AFI honored the best one hundred American films made during the first century of cinema in a TV special aired on July 16, 1998, *Dr. Strangelove* was included. In an earlier tribute, the film was selected by the Library of Congress as among those American films to be preserved in the permanent collection of the National Film Registry.

In addition, *Premiere* magazine, in a nationwide poll of its readership conducted in 2003, listed *Dr. Strangelove* as among the one hundred greatest films of all time. In a subsequent poll, published in 2004, *Premiere* picked the one hundred greatest movie characters of all time, among whom was counted Peter Sellers as Dr. Strangelove. "The wheelchair-bound, chain-smoking German with the dark glasses and the black-gloved hand, is ultimately one of the greatest comic mutations that Kubrick and Sellers—or anybody else for that matter—ever conceived."[19]

Perhaps the greatest accolade bestowed on the film is the result of the poll conducted by *Sight and Sound,* the London film journal, in 2002. *Dr. Strangelove* was chosen by an international panel of film professionals to be among the top ten films of all time. The recognition accorded to this film attests to its status as an enduring masterpiece.

Notes

1. Vincent LoBrutto, *Stanley Kubrick: A Biography* (New York: Da Capo, 1999): 243.
2. Elaine Dundy, "Stanley Kubrick and *Dr. Strangelove*," in *Stanley Kubrick: Interviews*, ed. Gene D. Phillips (Jackson: University Press of Mississippi, 2001):13.
3. Gene D. Phillips, "Slim Pickens" in *The Encyclopedia of Stanley Kubrick*, with Rodney Hill (New York: Checkmark, 2002): 289.
4. James Howard, *Stanley Kubrick Companion* (London: Batsford, 1999): 94.
5. John Gallagher, *Film Directors on Film Directing* (New York: Greenwood Press, 1989): 75.
6. Paul Boyer, "*Dr. Strangelove*," in *Past Imperfect: History According to the Movies*, ed. Mark Carnes (New York: Holt, 1995): 267–68.
7. Gene D. Phillips, "Sterling Hayden," in *The Encyclopedia of Stanley Kubrick*: 155.
8. Eric Nordern, "The *Playboy* Interview: Stanley Kubrick," *Playboy* (September 1968).
9. Roger Ebert, "Great Movies: *Dr. Strangelove*," *Chicago Sun-Times*, July 11, 1996.
10. Robert Brustein, "Out of This World," in *Perspectives on Stanley Kubrick*, ed. Mario Falsetto (New York: G. K. Hall, 1996): 137.
11. Alexander Walker, *Stanley Kubrick, Director* (New York: Norton, 1999): 156.
12. Michel Ciment, *Kubrick: The Definitive Edition* (New York: Faber and Faber, 2001): 208.
13. Brustein: 139.
14. Joseph Gelmis, "The Film Director as Superstar: Stanley Kubrick," in *Stanley Kubrick: Interviews*: 97.
15. Dundy: 9.
16. Glenn Kenny, et al., "The 100 Greatest Movies," *Premiere* 16, no. 7 (March, 2003): 78.
17. Pauline Kael, *Kiss Kiss Bang Bang* (New York: Bantam, 1969): 78.
18. Nordern: 68.
19. Glenn Kenny, et al., "The 100 Greatest Movie Characters of All Time," *Premiere* 17, no. 7 (April, 2004): 58.

How I Learned to Stop Worrying and Love the Cinema

by Stanley Kubrick

Published in Films and Filming,
June 1963

Finding a story which will make a film is a little like finding the right girl. It's very hard to say how you do it, or when you're going to do it. Some stories just come from a chance thing.

For instance, I had read *Paths of Glory* when I was fourteen years old. Regarding *The Killing,* I had seen the book mentioned in a column by Jimmy Cannon, a very good sports writer in the States. He said it was the most exciting crime novel he'd ever read. Just out of curiosity, I went into a bookshop and I bought it. I can't remember where I first heard about *Lolita. Dr. Strangelove* came from my great desire to do something about the nuclear nightmare. I was very interested in what was going to happen, and started reading a lot of books about four years ago. I have a library of about seventy or eighty books written by various technical people on the subject and I began to subscribe to the military magazines, the Air Force magazine, and to follow the US naval proceedings.

I was struck by the paradoxes of every variation of the problem from one extreme to the other—from the paradoxes of unilateral disarmament to the first strike. And it seemed to me that, aside from the fact that I was terribly interested myself, it was very important to deal with this problem dramatically because it's the only social problem where there's absolutely no chance for people to learn anything from experience. If it ever happens, there may be very little of the world left to profit by the experience. So it seemed to me that this was eminently a problem, a topic to be dealt with dramatically. This was the background to *Dr. Strangelove.* Then I was talking one day with Alastair Buchan from the Institute of Strategic Studies and he mentioned the novel *Red Alert* which was published in 1958. I read it and of course I was completely taken by it.

Now *Red Alert* is a completely serious suspense story. My idea of doing it as a nightmare comedy came when I was trying to work on it. I found that in trying to put meat on the bones and to imagine the scenes fully one had to keep leaving things out of it which were either absurd or paradoxical, in order to keep it from being funny, and these things seemed to be very real. Then I decided that the perfect tone to adopt for the film would be what I now call nightmare comedy, because it most truthfully presents the picture.

It is often difficult not to have a cynical view of human relationships. But I think that in a subject like this the cynicism should at least try to serve some constructive purpose. It seemed to me that, since this is a

"Just as man once viewed the earth as the true center of the Universe, he now views his nation as the moral center of the Universe.... Who will be our Galileo?"

—SK/Handwritten note ca.1962

43 ***Kubrick perched near the camera against the backdrop of the War Room maps.***

tragedy which has not yet occurred, any insight which could be provided, any sense of reality which could be given to it so that it didn't seem just an abstraction (which the nuclear problem is in most people's minds) was really quite useful. The paradoxes of deterrent have become so abstract, and so many euphemistic expressions have been thrown into it that I seriously doubt that the problem is at all real to anyone. This film presents a situation where a mad general launches his wing of bombers, and from then on everybody takes it quite seriously ... in this case a bit too late.

Kennedy made a speech where he said that 'the world is living under a nuclear Sword of Damocles which can be cut by accident, miscalculation or madness,' and in this case it's cut by madness. The story, in addition to making the possibilities seem real, shows the sub-theme of mutual interest between Russia and the United States in addition to their main theme of conflict. They have a great mutual interest in avoiding nuclear war, certainly avoiding the possibility of causing one inadvertently. You may want to be fatalistic about nuclear war, but not about *accidental* nuclear war. There was a very good analogy in one of the books I read of the type of mutual conflict/mutual interest situation where it gets similar to, say, a game where two men get on a train in different cars—they know the rules but they can't communicate. And the game is this: that if they both get off at the first station man A gets ten dollars and man B gets three dollars. If they both get off at the second station man B gets ten dollars and man A gets three dollars. But if they don't get off at the same station, in other words if they get off differently, neither one of them gets anything. So here you have a situation where you have mutual conflict and mutual interest and great chances for misunderstanding even under the circumstances where one side was willing to give a little more than the other, or than he was willing to take.

I work as hard as I possibly can on the script, usually spending six months, sometimes a year on it. But I always find that once you start working on a set, you get ideas that don't occur to you on paper. Certain things become clear which you thought were foggy—and vice versa. And lines either have to be cut or added. Thinking of the visual conception of a scene at script stage can be a trap that straitjackets the scene. I find it more profitable to just try to get the most interesting and truthful business going to support the scene, and then see if there's a way to make it interesting photographically. There's nothing worse than arbitrarily setting up some sort of visual thing that really doesn't belong as part of the scene.

If, by going on location you can pick up a great deal of atmosphere which you can't achieve in the studio, it's worth going outside. But I have found for myself and for most actors that I've worked with, that rather than being inspired by exterior location, it's very distracting. The presence of people across the street or just the general confusion of working on location can make the performance start evaporating because you don't have the concentration that you can get in a studio. But if atmosphere is tremendously important to a scene and it can't be

recreated, then it's worth doing. And it also depends where you go. If you go to some big old house in the country and it's quiet, well it's really no different to working in a studio. But it would be very unwise to try to do a sensitive and psychological scene in the middle of Piccadilly Circus.

In the studio the only people around are the crew. It all comes down to how much is the atmosphere worth and where is it? The actor's ability to create authentic emotion and to concentrate is usually helped by quiet, rather than by confusion and so on. It just depends what sort of a scene it is. If the scene takes place after the England-Scotland rugby match or something and there's pandemonium in Piccadilly Circus, then the confusion may help and it'll be good. But if it's a love scene between a couple on a relatively quiet night, but there's an awful lot of traffic going by, their concentration tends to evaporate.

My background as a stills photographer makes it much easier for me to find an interesting way to shoot something at the last minute and not have to worry about how to shoot it. I more or less feel that if a scene rehearses well and looks interesting, then you can find an interesting way to put it on the screen. But the important thing is to not start thinking of the camera too soon, because then you stop concentrating on what's happening and start worrying about how somebody

44 ***The round table with its halo of lights.***

45

will get from one place to another and what will happen then. There's a way to shoot any scene. So you work first on the content of the scene then on how you'll shoot it.

The one exception to this is what you might call a pure action scene, then all you are thinking of is cutting, angles, and how to make the action realistic. But in scenes which are essentially psychological and depend on dialogue, then the performance and truthful staging has to take precedence over just thinking about shots. If you have an interesting set there's an almost infinite number of ways to get an interesting shot. For instance, it's very hard to make shots within the war room set of *Dr. Strangelove* that are not interesting one way or the other.

45 ***Kubrick lines up and shoots a photo of George C. Scott.***
46 ***Sellers and Kubrick.***
47 ***In the War Room with Peter Sellers as President Muffley (background) flanked by military and government officials.***

46

47

2001: A Space Odyssey

1968 / COLOR / 139 MINUTES
Distributed by METRO-GOLDWYN-MAYER

CAST
DAVID BOWMAN KEIR DULLEA
FRANK POOLE GARY LOCKWOOD
DR. HEYWOOD FLOYD WILLIAM SYLVESTER
MOON-WATCHER DANIEL RICHTER
SMYSLOV LEONARD ROSSITER
ELENA MARGARET TYZACK
HALVORSEN ROBERT BEATTY
MICHAELS SEAN SULLIVAN
VOICE OF HAL 9000 DOUGLAS RAIN
MISSION CONTROL FRANK MILLER
POOLE'S FATHER ALAN GIFFORD
POOLE'S MOTHER ANN GILLIS
STEWARDESS PENNY BRAHMS
FLOYD'S DAUGHTER VIVIAN KUBRICK (uncredited)

CREW
DIRECTED AND PRODUCED BY STANLEY KUBRICK
SCREENPLAY STANLEY KUBRICK and ARTHUR C. CLARKE
SPECIAL PHOTOGRAPHIC EFFECTS DESIGNED AND DIRECTED BY STANLEY KUBRICK
SPECIAL PHOTOGRAPHIC EFFECTS SUPERVISORS WALLY VEEVERS, DOUGLAS TRUMBULL, CONPEDERSON, TOM HOWARD
PRODUCTION DESIGNERS TONY MASTERS, HARRY LANGE, ERNEST ARCHER
FILM EDITOR RAY LOVEJOY
WARDROBE HARDY AMIES

Opposite *Signed 1974 re-release poster.*

DIRECTOR OF PHOTOGRAPHY GEOFFREY UNSWORTH
ADDITIONAL PHOTOGRAPHY JOHN ALCO
FIRST ASSISTANT DIRECTOR DEREK CRACKNELL
SPECIAL PHOTOGRAPHIC EFFECTS UNIT COHN J. CANTWELL, BRYAN LOFTUS, FREDERICK MARTIN, BRUCE LOGAN, DAVID OSBORNE, JOHN JACK MALICK
CAMERA OPERATOR KELVIN PIKE
ART DIRECTOR JOHN HOESLI
SOUND EDITOR WINSTON RYDER
MAKEUP STUART FREEBORN
EDITORIAL ASSISTANT DAVID DE WILDE
SOUND SUPERVISOR A. W. WATKINS
SOUND MIXER H. L. "DICKIE" BIRD
CHIEF DUBBING MIXER J. B. SMITH
SCIENTIFIC CONSULTANT FREDERICK I. ORDWAY III
ASSOCIATE PRODUCER (PRE-PRODUCTION AND MAIN-UNIT) VICTOR LYNDON
ASSISTANTS TO MR. KUBRICK ANTHONY FREWIN, ANDREW BIRKIN
FRONT PROJECTION SUPERVISOR TOM HOWARD
"DAWN OF MAN" CHOREOGRAPHY DANIEL RICHTER
MR. RICHTER'S ASSISTANTS ADRIAN HAGGARD, ROY SIMPSON
EXPLOITATION DESIGNER, MODEL DESIGNER CHRISTIANE KUBRICK

Filmed in Super Panavision (70 mm).

Made at MGM British Studios Ltd, Borehamwood, England.

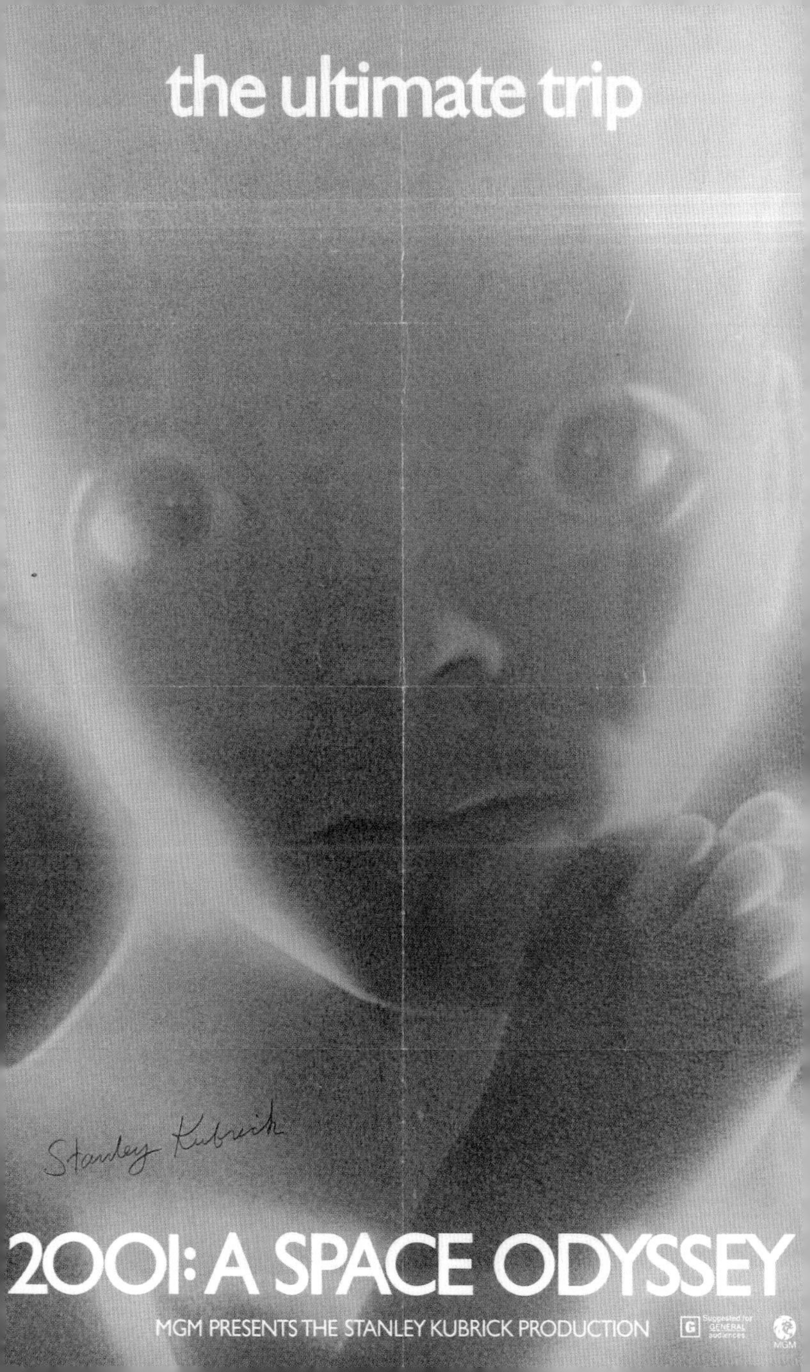
the ultimate trip
Stanley Kubrick
2001: A SPACE ODYSSEY
MGM PRESENTS THE STANLEY KUBRICK PRODUCTION
G
Suggested for GENERAL audiences
MGM

001: A SPACE ODYSSE
© MCMLXVIII by Metro-Goldwyn-Mayer Inc. All rights in this Motion Picture Reserved Under International Conventions

THE DAWN OF MAN

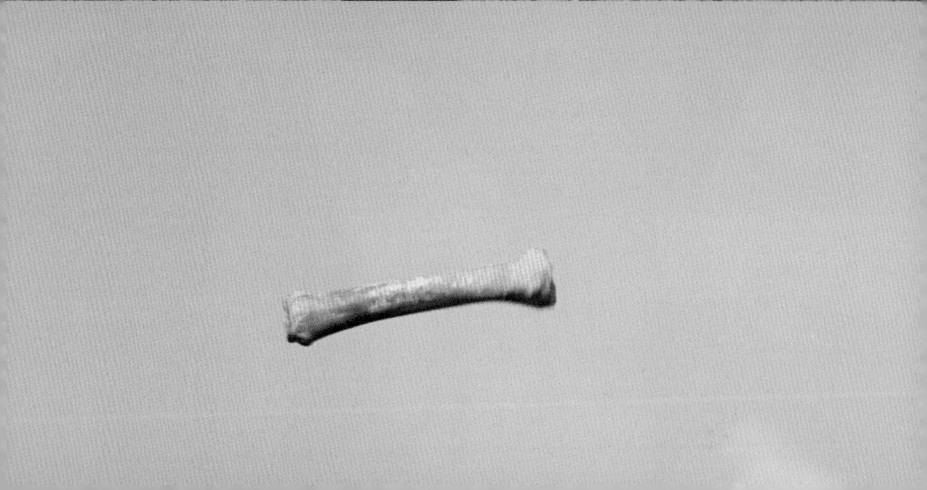

CAUTION
WEIGHTLESS
CONDITION
CAUTION
WEIGHTLESS
CONDITION

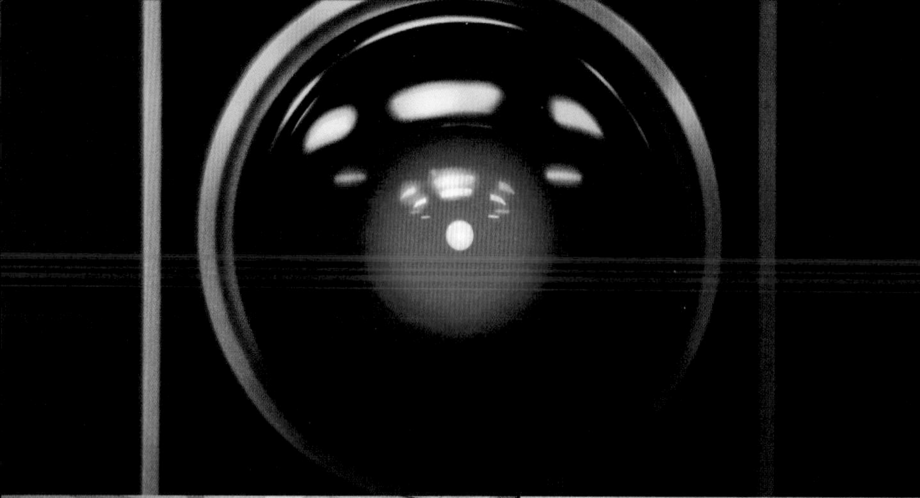

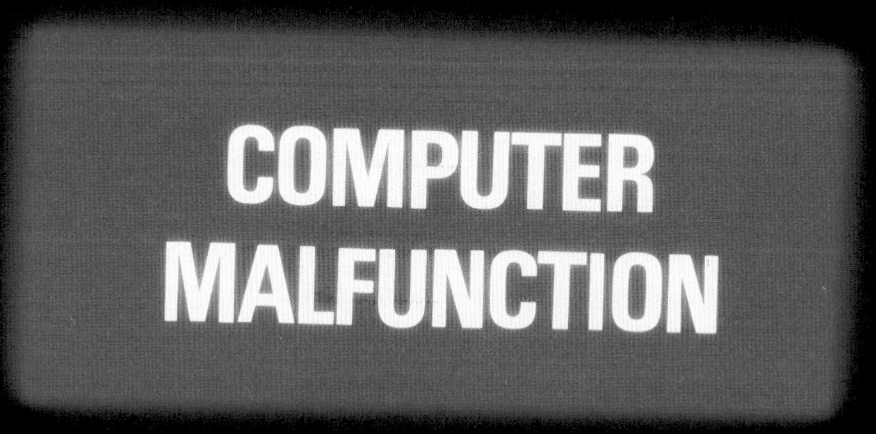
COMPUTER
MALFUNCTION

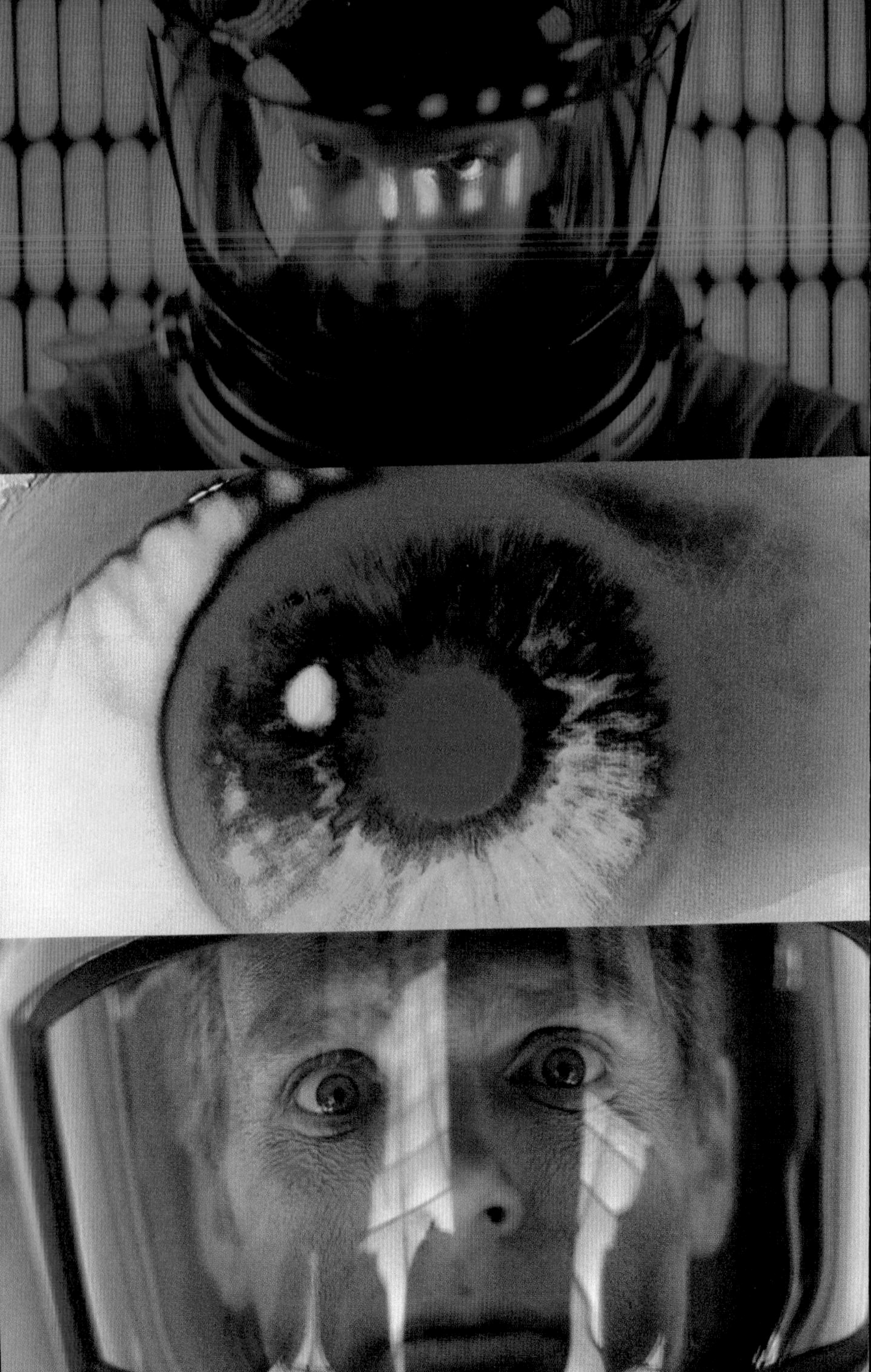

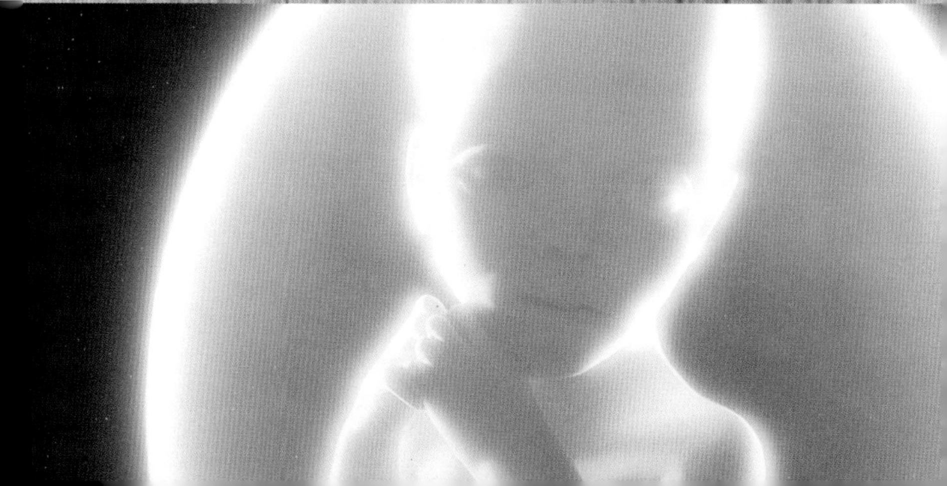

A SPACE ODYSSEY
680-1
DATE

Outline

by Carolyn Geduld

01 ***Keir Dullea as David Bowman in the replica hotel suite.***
02–03 ***Dr. Heywood Floyd (William Sylvester) meets with Smyslov (Leonard Rossiter) and the other Russian scientists on Space Station 5. "The interior of the space station was a giant curved set over three hundred feet long, and sloping up at one end to nearly forty feet. It may be noticeable that in the long shot of two men approaching the camera from the far end, their pace is slightly awkward, and th was due to the very steep slope at that end of the set." – Douglas Trumbull (***American Cinematographer, ***June 1968)***

03

From Filmguide to 2001: A Space Odyssey *by Carolyn Geduld (Indiana University Press, 1973)*

A gigantic pockfaced moon, glorified by Richard Strauss's *Also Sprach Zarathustra,* drifts down the cavernous Cinerama screen. Sunrise appears on the Earth-crescent hanging above in the sky. So begins the cinematic purple-prose of *2001: A Space Odyssey*, a film in four episodes:

(1) "The Dawn of Man." This title, appearing after the view of sunrise beyond the moon and after the credits, brings us directly to Earth. In silence, we continue with shots taking us from sunrise to sunset on a forbidding primordial half-desert, where a tribe of apes lives a kind of minimal existence among a herd of gentle tapirs. One ape (Daniel Richter), called Moon-Watcher in the script, singles himself out as the leader when the mock ferocity

HAWK FILMS LTD. "2001: A SPACE ODYSSEY"

ROLL I "CONT"

SLATE: 126 TEST: DATE: 1-9-67.

TITLE: DAWN OF MAN

LENS ON CAMERA: TAKE I :- 35M/M, TAKE 2:- 100M/M, 200M/M, 135M/M

~~LENS ON PROJECTOR:~~

STOP: TAKE I :- 2.8, TAKE 2:- 2.8(100M/M), 4(200M/M), 4(135M/M).

SPEED: 24 F.P.S.

PRINT LIGHT: TAKE I - 12, TAKE 2:- 14(100M/M), 10(200M/M), 10(135M/M).

MAG: 116

FOOTAGE LOADED: 1000' CONT

EMULSION: 948-142-5.

CAMERA NO: M013.

~~DISTANCE TO MIRROR CAMERA:~~

~~DISTANCE TO MIRROR PROJECTOR:~~

FOCUS POINTS:

~~FILTERS PROJECTOR:~~

FOOT CANDLES: TOP LIGHT :- 225 F/C, KEY :- 1,5K + SUN GUN :- 400 F/C

LIGHTING INFORMATION: - ON 5K :- FULL BLUE, ON SUN GUN ½ BLUE.

TAKE I :- 5 SUN GUNS = 200 F/C, TAKE 2 :- (100M/M) 3 SUN GUNS 150 F/C,

~~ON PROJECTOR:~~ - (200M/M) 5 SUN GUNS 200 F/C, (135M/M) 5 SUN GUNS 200 F/C.

LENS TO:

CAMERA HEIGHT: (NOTE ALL SUN GUNS (EX KEY LIGHT) ARE REFLECTED OF WHITE BOARD)

ROLL NO.	SLATE	(TEST)	COUNTER	FOOTAGE	PRINT
I	126	1	250	110	P
(CONT)	"	2	470	220	P

(NO PROJECTOR PICTURE ON THIS SHOT.)

04

of his screams discourages a rival tribe from using the territorial waterhole.

After an ominous night, the awakening apes find that an unnatural object has appeared in their den. It is an outsized black rectangular monolith, made more mysterious by György Ligeti's unearthly requiem slowly swelling in the background. After Moon-Watcher cautiously fingers the monolith, the whole tribe, spellbound, gathers around to caress it as the sun rises "magically" over its roof.

Some time after, we find Moon-Watcher foraging as usual near the broken skeleton of some large, horned animal when—an interrupting shot of the monolith suggests—a new idea enters his consciousness. Tentatively, he picks up one of the larger bones and tries to use it as a cudgel. His efforts become more and more vigorous, and while Strauss's triumphant music drowns out all natural sound, associative shots of a falling tapir—the ape-man's first kill—are intercut. Later, at the water-hole, the tribe, armed with bones, kills the weaponless leader of the rivals. Moon-Watcher, victorious, tosses his bone high in the air, and as it comes down, it changes—

(2)—into a man-made satellite orbiting in space four million years later. Rotating to the strains of Johann Strauss's *The Blue Danube,* we see the satellite's companions in space: Earth; a wheel-shaped space station; and the space ship *Orion,* bringing Dr. Heywood Floyd (William

04 ***Camera sheet from a "Dawn of Man" scene. Between shots, the ape-actors used sticks to keep the masks' mouths open.***
05 ***Lenses of various focal lengths were tested using miniature apes and a maquette of the "Dawn of Man" set.***
06 ***Ape-actors on the waterhole set for the "Dawn of Man" sequence.***

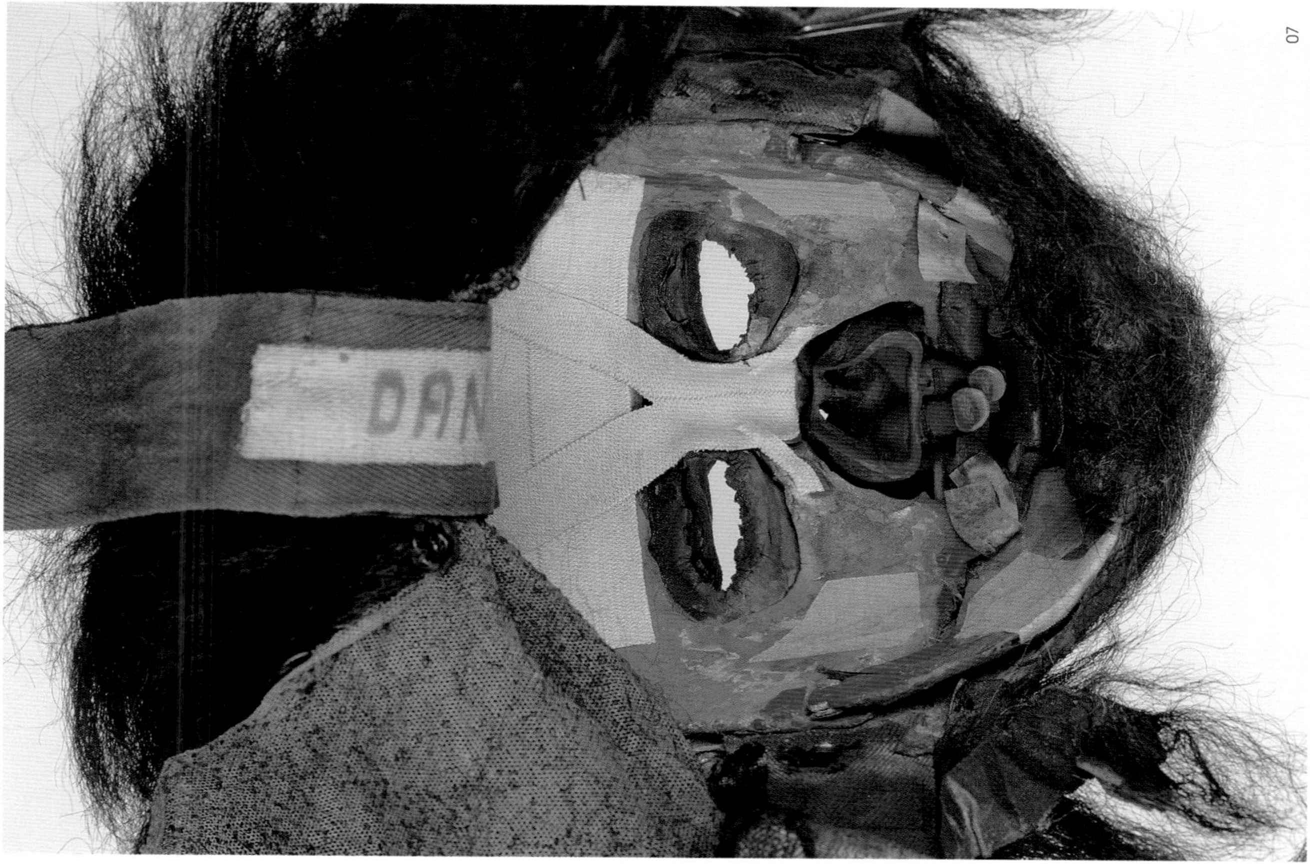

07

09

Sylvester), the chairman of the U.S. National Council of Astronautics, from Earth. The docking of *Orion* and the station completed, Dr. Floyd is cleared by "voice print identification" and waits in the passenger lounge for a connecting flight to the moon. There, he phones his daughter "Squirt" (Vivian Kubrick, the director's daughter) and chats briefly with a party of Russian scientists, who unsuccessfully press for an explanation of the mystery at the American moon-base in the crater Clavius.

The Blue Danube accompanies the spherical space vehicle *Aries* from the space station to the moon, where Dr. Floyd attends a briefing at Clavius to discuss the top secret object discovered near the base. As Ligeti's *Lux Aeterna* is heard, Dr. Floyd and his colleagues — Halvorsen (Robert Beatty) and Michaels (Sean Sullivan) — travel to the site in a moon bus and talk fleetingly about the strange "rock," recently excavated, that seems to have been "deliberately buried" four million years before. At the excavation, we find another monolith and again hear Ligeti's requiem. Immediately after Dr. Floyd circles and warily touches it, the monolith emits a shrill noise, causing the whole party to fall back, stunned.

10

(3) "Jupiter Mission: 18 months later." The adagio from Khatchaturian's *Gayaneh Ballet Suite* introduces the spaceship *Discovery* and her crew of six: three hibernating scientists, two astronauts — Mission Commander Dave Bowman (Keir Dullea) and his deputy Frank Poole (Gary Lockwood) — and a talking computer addressed as HAL (Douglas

07–08 ***The head-mask of Moon-Watcher costume worn by Dan Richter. "[A]bout a year was spent trying to develop a makeup which would look convincing, because I'd never seen ape characters presented realistically in a film.... The body problem was partially solved by finding dancers and mimes with extremely narrow hips and skinny legs.... And the head problem was solved by making a very intricate headpiece. This had a sub skull under it, to which elastics were attached, just as muscles are attached in the human skull, so that when mouths opened the lips curled, and with little toggle switches that the people could work with their tongues, you could control left-side snarl, right-side snarl, etc." – SK/1968 (to Charles Kohler,*** **East Village Eye*****)***

09 ***Putting the finishing touches on the Hilton reception desk.***

10 ***Kubrick took this photo of Dan Richter (Moon-Watcher) wearing an early prototype of the ape costume.***

Rain as HAL's voice). Deep in space, the two on-duty astronauts cope with boredom by jogging, sketching, playing chess with HAL, and monitoring a prerecorded interview with the BBC. From the interview, we learn details about the hibernators, HAL's responsibilities (overseeing the entire operation of the mission) and his "personality," and the ship's destination—Jupiter. A sinister note enters the uneventful ship routine when HAL, ostensibly preparing a psychology report on the crew, points out some incongruities about the nature of the mission. Suddenly, he interrupts the conversation with news of the imminent failure of the AE-35 unit—a component of *Discovery*'s communications network located on the antenna outside of the ship. Bowman uses a spherical "pod"—a vehicle designed for extra
vehicular activity—to replace the uni
which, it is discovered, appears to be i
perfect condition. This possible error i
judgment raises the question of HAL's reli
ability. The two astronauts step into
soundproofed pod to discuss the contin
gency of disconnecting the computer
without realizing that HAL can still see
them and is able to read their lips. Mean
while, they plan to return the supposedl
defective unit to the antenna as a cross
check on HAL's accuracy.

11-12 ***The set of Space Station 5 was lit from above with hundreds of powerful lights and was consequently so bright that the actors wore sunglasses between takes.***

An intermission follows, and then we re-
ırn to the film to find Poole leaving *Discov-*
ry in the pod and subsequently space-
'alking to the antenna. At this point, a
apid series of shots reveals that HAL has
aken control of the pod and used its me-
hanical claws to sever Poole's air hose.
owman, helmetless in a second pod, tries
'ithout success to rescue his colleague,
nly to find that HAL refuses to let him back
ırough the pod-bay door. While the com-
uter "murders" the three hibernating
cientists, Bowman enters the emergency
ir-lock and uses his pod's explosive bolts to
last himself through the vacuum to safety. Back inside the ship, he enters HAL's weightless "logic memory center" and painstakingly disconnects the still-conscious computer. Immediately after, a prerecorded briefing is spontaneously projected on a nearby screen: Dr. Floyd reveals the true purpose of the mission, known only to HAL—to follow an alien radio signal sent to Jupiter by the monolith found on the moon.

(4) "Jupiter and Beyond the Infinite." Ligeti's music, heard throughout much of the last episode, reveals a third monolith, seen floating in the Jovian system, brightened by the Jupiter sunrise. As Bowman rushes toward it in his pod, he "falls" into

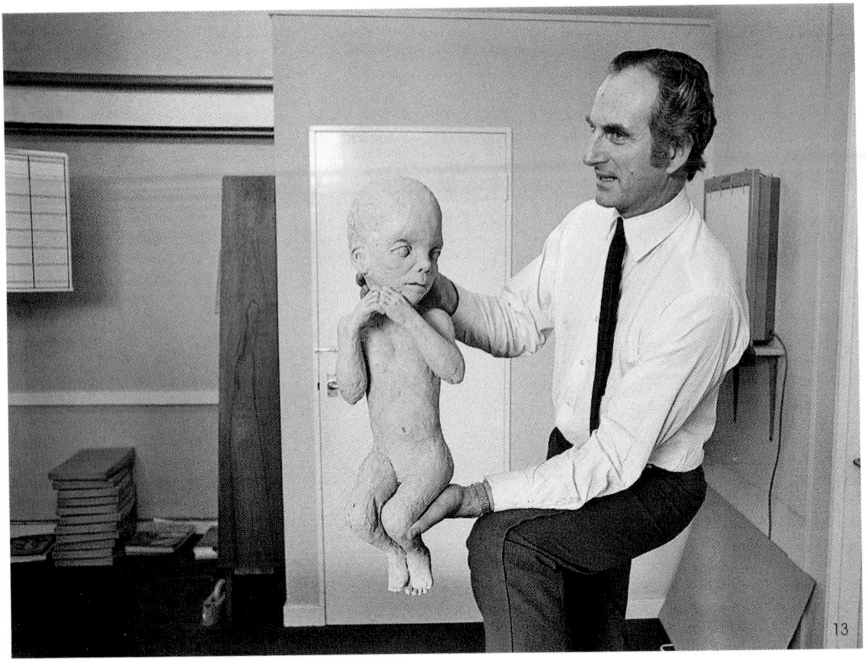

what scriptwriter Arthur C. Clarke calls the Star Gate, a time-warp represented by "psychedelic" color effects which takes Bowman on an alarming journey to an uncanny room resembling an elegant 18th-century-style bed chamber. There, Bowman, already mysteriously aged, is transformed again into an even older man who accidentally breaks his wine glass while dining. The accident signals his third transformation into an ancient bed-ridden version of himself. As the dying Bowman reaches up and tries to touch it, a fourth monolith appears, enveloping his bed in a strange fog. Out of this comes a huge fetal infant-*in-utero*, the Star Child, who is last seen floating between Earth and the moon as *Also Sprach Zarathustra* welcomes him in the background.

13 ***Production designer Tony Masters holding the Star Child, modeled by Liz Moore.***
14 ***Camera sheet from the Star Child sequence.***

HAWK FILMS LTD. "2001: A SPACE ODYSSEY"

SLATE: SJA417-2-3 TEST: DATE: 11-9-67

TITLE: STAR CHILD

LENS ON CAMERA: 135 M/M. + 4 GAUZES

LENS ON PROJECTOR:

STOP: 2.8

SPEED: 24 F.P.S

PRINT LIGHT:

MAG: 21 | MAG 112.

FOOTAGE LOADED: 840 S/E CONTD | 1000 N/R.

EMULSION: 948-143-9. | 948-141-18

CAMERA NO: 7013

~~DISTANCE TO MIRROR CAMERA:~~

~~DISTANCE TO MIRROR PROJECTOR:~~

FOCUS POINTS: CHILD 8'8"

~~FILTERS PROJECTOR:~~

FOOT CANDLES: 700 F/C FROM 3/4 BACK (2 NOK + 1/4 BLUE, 1 CAM RIGHT, 1 CAM L)

OTHER LIGHTING INFORMATION: 25 F/C FRONT FILL (BASHER + 1/4 BLUE)

AMPS ON PROJECTOR:

LENS TO: BABY 8'8"

CAMERA HEIGHT: 3'10"

BABY'S FEET TO FLOOR = 4'9½

CAMERA VERTICAL ~~HORIZONTAL~~

ROLL NO.	SLATE	(TEST)	COUNTER	FOOTAGE	PRINT
1 CONTD	47	2.	790	390	P
	50' WASTE				
2.	47	3.	350	350	P.

1/60 @ 5.6 + 4 GAUZES

15

16

15–19 ***The replica hotel suite at the end of the film was lit entirely through the floor. "Possibly one of the most unusual aspects of the live action photography on the interior sets of*** **2001** ***is that almost all lighting was an actual integral part of the set itself, and additional lighting was used only for critical close-ups." – Douglas Trumbull*** **(American Cinematographer,** ***June 1968)***

20 ***Director of photography Geoffrey Unsworth shows a test Polaroid to Keir Dullea.***
21 ***"Journey Beyond the Stars" film-story draft. "[I]t was written as a fifty-thousand-word prose 'thing,' looking more like a novel than anything else. This was the basis of the screenplay." – SK/1968 (to Charles Kohler,*** **East Village Eye*****)***

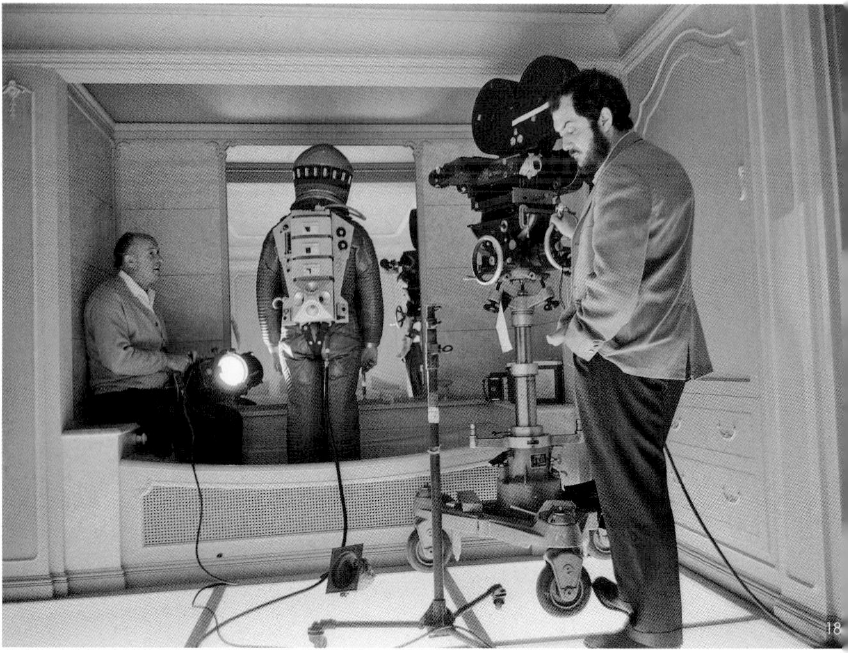

"Dear Mr. Clarke: It's a very interesting coincidence that our mutual friend Caras mentioned you in a conversation we were having about a Questar telescope. I had been a great admirer of your books for quite a time and had always wanted to discuss with you the possibility of doing the proverbial 'really good' science-fiction movie. My main interest lies along these broad areas, naturally assuming great plot and character: 1. The reasons for believing in the existence of intelligent extra terrestrial life. 2. The impact (and perhaps even lack of impac in some quarters) such discovery would have on Earth in the near future. 3. A space-probe with a landing and exploration of the Moon and Mars.… [W]ould you consider … coming [to New York] with a view to a meeting, the purpose of which would be to determine whether an idea might exist or arise which would sufficiently interest both of us enough to want to collaborate on a screenplay."

—SK in a letter to Arthur C. Clarke, March 31, 1964

HAWK FILMS-MGM 88
'2001 A SPACE ODYSSEY'
DIR. STANLEY KUBRICK
CAM GEOFF UNSWORTH
729-1
DATE TUE: 28-6-

19

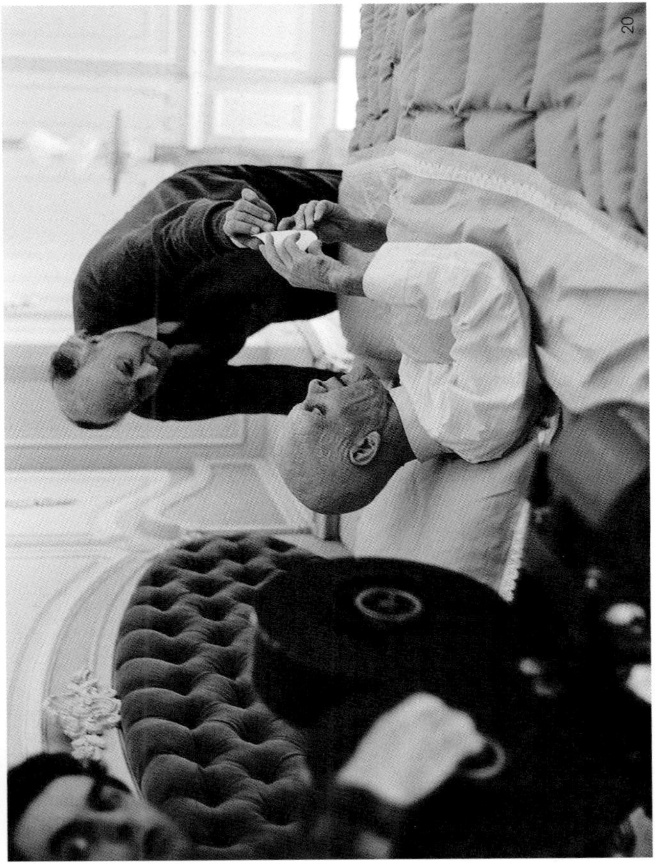

20

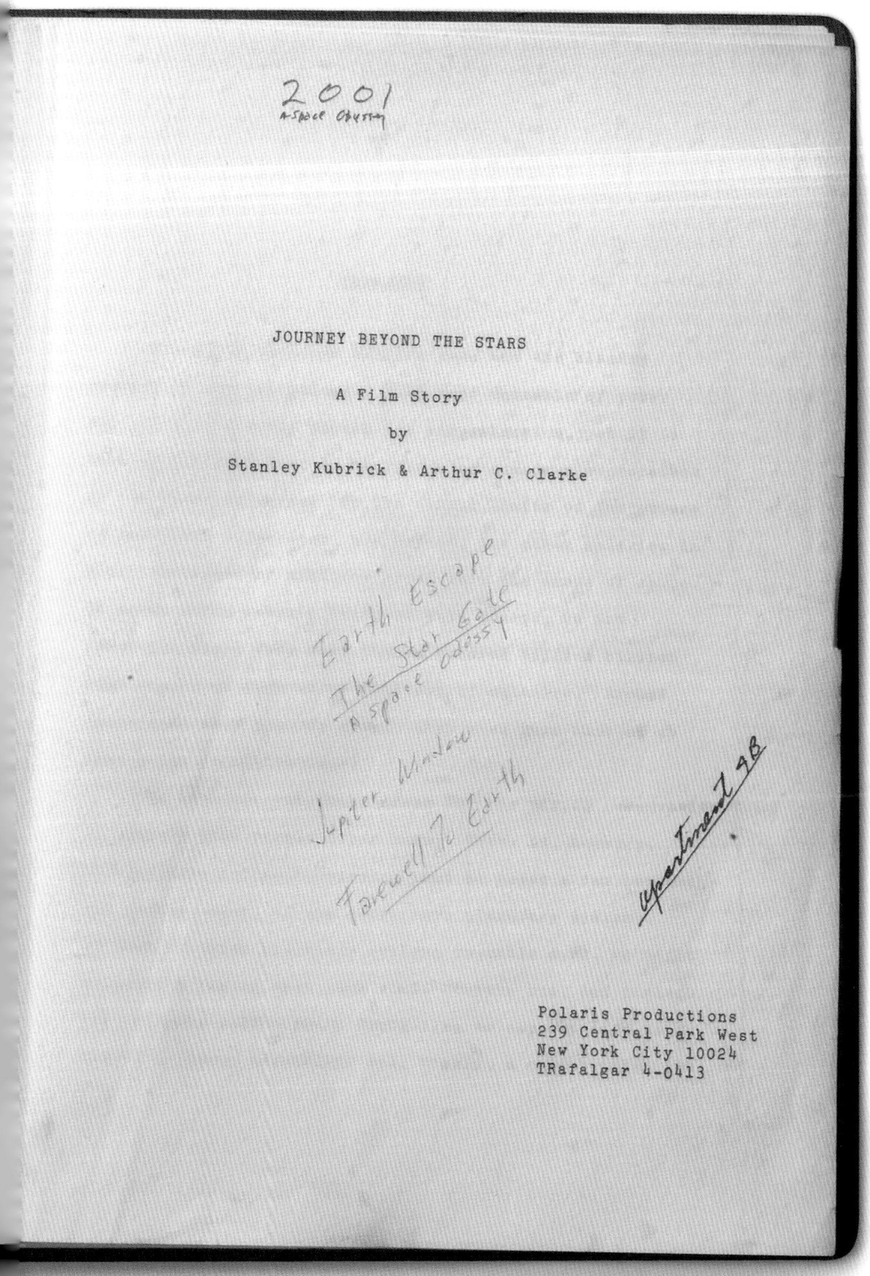

2001
A Space Odyssey

JOURNEY BEYOND THE STARS

A Film Story

by

Stanley Kubrick & Arthur C. Clarke

Earth Escape
The Star Gate
A Space Odyssey

Jupiter Window

Farewell To Earth

Apartment 9B

Polaris Productions
239 Central Park West
New York City 10024
TRafalgar 4-0413

The Production: A Calendar

by Carolyn Geduld

From Filmguide to 2001: A Space Odyssey *by Carolyn Geduld (Indiana University Press, 1973)*

1902

In France, George Méliès makes what is perhaps the first science-fiction film, *A Trip to the Moon,* a sixteen-minute production.

1926

Hugo Gernsback publishes the first American hard-core science-fiction magazine, *Amazing Stories,* creating a brand new kind of buff—the Space Opera fan.

1930s

First working automatic computers built. In 1930, Dr. Vannevar Bush completes the first general purpose analog computer at the Massachusetts Institute of Technology. In 1939, Dr. George R. Stibitz builds the first digital computer for Bell Telephone Laboratories in New York. *2001*'s HAL (for **H**euristically programmed **AL**gorithmic computer) is an advanced hybrid of these two original types of computers.

1948

Arthur C. Clarke writes his short story "The Sentinel." Superman, film's first Star Child, arrives from the planet Krypton in a Columbia movie serial based on the comic strip originally conceived by Jerry Siegel and Joe Schuster in 1938.

22 ***Arthur C. Clarke and Kubrick aboard the* Aries *lunar passenger ship. "[Clarke] has the kind of mind of which the world can never have enough, an array of imagination, intelligence, knowledge, and a quirkish curiosity which often uncovers more than the first three qualities." – SK/1970 (to Jerome Agel)***

1950s

High-water mark for science-fiction films. Directors like George Pal[1] and Byron Haskin in films like *Destination Moon* (1950) and *The Conquest of Space* (1955) ransack the special-effects departments in attempts to create authentic-looking space technology consistent with the scientific ideas of the day.

1960s

BBC televises a science-fiction serial with close affinities to *2001*—Nigel Kneale's *Quatermass and the Pit* (re-made in a film version by Hammer Film Productions as *Five Million Years to Earth* in 1967). In one episode, while excavating to enlarge the London underground, a five-million-year-old alien artifact is discovered. Near it lie the ape ancestors of man, whose skulls have been surgically modified to increase intelligence.

Universe, an award-winning twenty-eight-minute black-and-white animated documentary is produced by the National Film Board of Canada. It is to become the inspiration for *2001*'s panning shots of slowly revolving planets and moving stars in deep space. In 1965, Kubrick tries to hire *Universe*'s special effects team of Wally Gentleman, Herbert Taylor, and James Wilson. Wally Gentleman agrees to do a few months' preparatory work on *2001* before a sudden illness forces him to abandon the project.

1964

Spring. Kubrick contacts Clarke and asks him to collaborate on a sci-fi film.

April. Clarke leaves his home in Ceylon for his first meeting with Kubrick in New York.

Kubrick suggests the unorthodox procedure of writing a novel together before writing a script, a project that was to take two years to complete.

May. Kubrick agrees to use Clarke's "The Sentinel" as the central idea for the novel. The discovery of the alien artifact on the moon is to be the climax of the story. Meanwhile, Kubrick views every available science-fiction film.

July 31. *Ranger VII* sends close-up pictures of the moon back to Earth before crashing on the lunar surface.

August 6. "Female" computer called Athena written into novel.

November. Gathering of ideas of what is to be the "Dawn of Man" episode. This is intended to be a flashback interrupting the main story.

December 25. Clarke finishes the first fifty-thousand-word draft of the novel, which ends at the Star Gate sequence. Kubrick is able to sell the idea for a film based on this draft to MGM and Cinerama. The film's projected budget is $6 million.

1965

February 21. MGM press release announcing forthcoming production of a Kubrick film to be called "Journey Beyond the Stars."

March 18. Aleksei A. Leonov, a Russian astronaut, becomes the first man to "walk" in space.

Spring. Clarke revises novel. Kubrick begins to hire staff (thirty-five designers, twenty special-effects technicians, a total of 106 people) and cast for the production. "The

Sentinel" pyramid is changed to a black tetrahedron, then a transparent cube, finally a black rectangular block—the monolith.

April. Kubrick selects *2001: A Space Odyssey* as the new title for the film.

May. Clarke works on possible endings for the novel.

June 3. Ed White becomes the first American to "walk" in space, bettering Leonov's feat by twenty minutes.

June 14. *Mariner IV* comes within 6,200 miles of Mars and sends twenty-two photographs of the planet's surface back to Earth. Kubrick contacts Lloyds of London to price an insurance policy against Martians being discovered before the release of his film.

August. After a brief return to his home in Ceylon, Clarke joins Kubrick at the MGM studios in Borehamwood near London. There, sets are being built, the most meticulously detailed models ever made for a film are being constructed over a period of months, costumes are being designed and executed with an eye toward fashions thirty-five years in the future, and the ape makeup and costuming are being developed over the course of a year.

October 3. The final decision about the ending of the film is reached. Bowman will turn into an infant.

23 ***Shooting of* 2001 *began in December 1965 on the moon excavation set at MGM's Shepperton studio, near London.***
24-25 ***Kubrick's notes for the screenplay of* 2001.**

October 15. Kubrick decides that Bowman should be the only surviving member of *Discovery*'s crew.

December 29. First day of shooting in Shepperton studio near London, which is spacious enough to accommodate oversized sets. Kubrick films the scene in the moon excavation in the Tycho crater. The set is a huge 60 by 120 by 60 foot pit constructed on the second-largest stage in Europe. Background details of the lunar terrain and the miniature Earth in the sky are added a year later.

"The screenplay is the most uncommunicative form of writing ever devised."

—SK/1969 (to Maurice Rapf/*Action*)

1966

January. Production moves to the smaller Borehamwood studios. Kubrick films scenes on board *Orion*. Clarke finishes draft of novel, adding HAL's rebellion and alien hotel room to plot.

February 2. Makeup tests for Gary Lockwood and Keir Dullea, who remain in the studio for seven months of filming.

February 3. First soft landing on the moon by an unmanned Russian spacecraft.

February 4. Screening of "demonstration film" for Metro Goldwyn Mayer, consisting of a few completed scenes, including shots of the interiors of the space station and the moon shuttle. Mendelssohn's *Midsummer Night's Dream* and Vaughan Williams's *Antarctica Symphony* are used on the soundtrack.

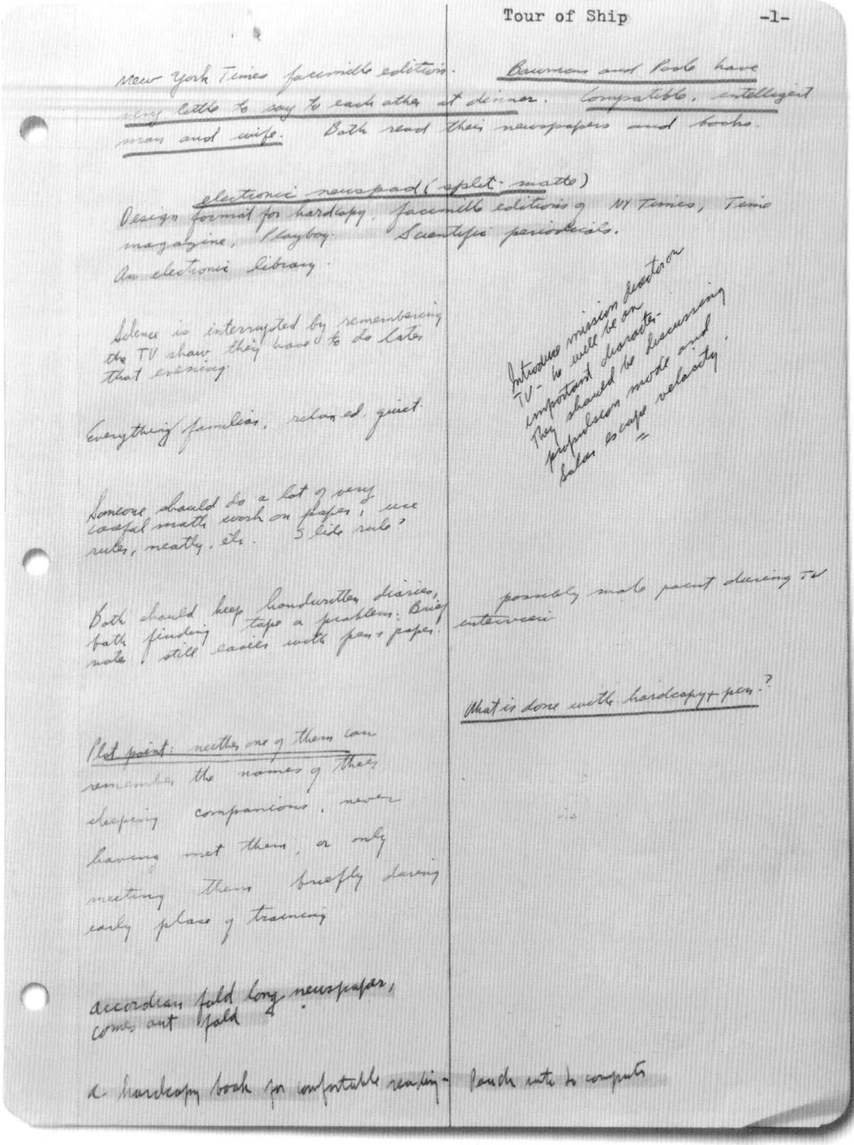

Tour of Ship -1-

New York Times facsimile edition. Bowman and Poole have very little to say to each other at dinner. Compatible, intelligent man and wife. Both read their newspapers and books.

electronic newspad (split-matte)

Design format for hardcopy, facsimile editions of NY Times, Time magazine, Playboy. Scientific periodicals.

An electronic library.

Silence is interrupted by remembering the TV show they have to do later that evening.

Introduce mission director on TV - he will be an important character. They should be discussing propulsion mode and Solar escape velocity.

Everything familiar, relaxed, quiet.

Someone should do a lot of very careful math work on paper, use rules, neatly, etc. Slide rule?

Both should keep handwritten diaries, both finding tape a problem. Brief note still easier with pen + paper. — possibly make point during TV interview

What is done with hardcopy + pen?

Plot point: neither one of them can remember the names of their sleeping companions, never having met them, or only meeting them briefly during early phase of training

accordian fold long newspaper, comes out fold 4.

a hardcopy book for comfortable reading - punch into computer

One evening (or whenever Poole's) sleep cycle is) he brings up a rumor he heard prior to departure. It is semi- serious

Rumour was that there was a secret aspect of the mission that only the sleepers knew, and that was why they were trained seperately and brought aboard already asleep.

The computer can be asked this directly. No.

Bowman pleasantly jokes about this fantastic possibility. Poole doesn't believe it — not really. It's like the rumors of high level CIA men being involved in Kennedy assassination. Somehow this gets into the idea of asking the computer who cannot lie.

They do as a joke (but obviously covering real interest) and the computer services mission. "Is there anything that has been witheld from mission?" The computer says "No."

There is a devilish, perverse (BY Poole + Bowman) humor about it. An eye watering, the imp of the perverse.

March–April. Shooting inside *Discovery*'s Ferris-wheel-shaped centrifuge. The Vickers Engineering Group builds a real one for the production at a cost of $750,000. The wheel is forty feet in diameter and rotates at three miles per hour. A closed-circuit television system enables Kubrick to direct the filming from outside the wheel. Inside, two kinds of camera setups are used: either the camera is attached to the set and rotates with it (used when the actors appear to be climbing the centrifuge walls) or the camera is secured to a small dolly which remains with the actors at the bottom of the rotating set (used when Poole jogs). Kubrick plans to put a Chopin waltz on the soundtrack during the astronauts' routine activities.

May. Clarke visits Hollywood to promote the film and placate worried MGM executives.

June. Clarke returns to Borehamwood. He tries unsuccessfully to convince Kubrick to allow publication of the novel before the release of the film.

June 2. First soft landing on the moon by an unmanned American spacecraft, *Surveyor I.*

December. Original target date for film's release.

1967

January–February. Composer Alex North records his music for *2001* in London, until Kubrick changes his mind about using an original score for the film. Most of the year is devoted to completing the film's exacting and complex special effects, a job taking more than eighteen months and costing $6,500,000 out of a total budget of $10,500,000.

1968

March 13. Kubrick returns to the United States. While the last special effects shots are still coming in, he edits the film. Several scenes are omitted, including the purchase of a bushbaby for Dr. Floyd's daughter, Squirt; routine activities on the moon; shots of the astronauts' families; shots of the ping-pong table, shower, and piano in *Discovery.* After a screening for the MGM executives in Culver City, California, Kubrick cuts the prologue and all voice-over narration from the film.

March 29. Screening of the film for *Life* magazine.

March 31, April 1. Washington press previews.

April. The discovery of a man-like jaw bone in southern Ethiopia pushes man's history back to the four million year mark.

April 1, 2. New York press previews of the film in Loew's Capital Cinerama Theater.

April 3. New York premiere in the Capital Theater.

April 4. Los Angeles premiere.

April 4, 5. Kubrick cuts nineteen minutes from the film's original running time of two hours and forty-one minutes, shortening scenes including "Dawn of Man," *Orion,* Poole jogging in *Discovery,* and Poole in the pod.

April 6. Final version released in New York in the Cinerama Theater on Broadway, sixteen months late and at a cost of $4,500,000 over the original budget of $6 million.

Early April. Kubrick edits the *2001* trailer.

July. Publication of Clarke's novel, *2001: A Space Odyssey.* The paperback edition sale exceeds one million copies.

December 21. *Apollo VIII* carries man into a moon orbit for the first time.

26

1969

April. Kubrick receives an Oscar for special effects; three British Film Academy awards for cinematography, art direction, and soundtrack; and the Italian film industry's David di Donatello award for the best film from the West.

July 20. Neil Armstrong and Edwin Aldrin walk on the moon.

Editor's Note

1. *Destination Moon* was directed by Irving Pichel, not George Pal, as this seems to imply.

26 ***"Macy's wasn't happy that it was cut," said Arthur C. Clarke, referring to the scene showing Heywood Floyd's video-phone purchase of a bushbaby from Macy's pet department. (to Jerome Agel/1970)***

27 ***"Several versions of the full-sized pod were used during the*** **Discovery** ***sequence. Three dummy pods were used in the pod bay, two of which had operational doors, but only roughly mocked-up interiors. A separate interior pod set was built which included all the instrumentation, controls, and read-out displays. Finally, a full-sized pod was built with completely motorized, articulated arms. It took ten or twelve men at long control consoles to simultaneously control the finger, wrist, forearm, elbow, and shoulder actions of the two pod arms, and the interior of that pod was a maze of servos, actuators, and cables." – Douglas Trumbull (*****American Cinematographer,** ***June 1968)***

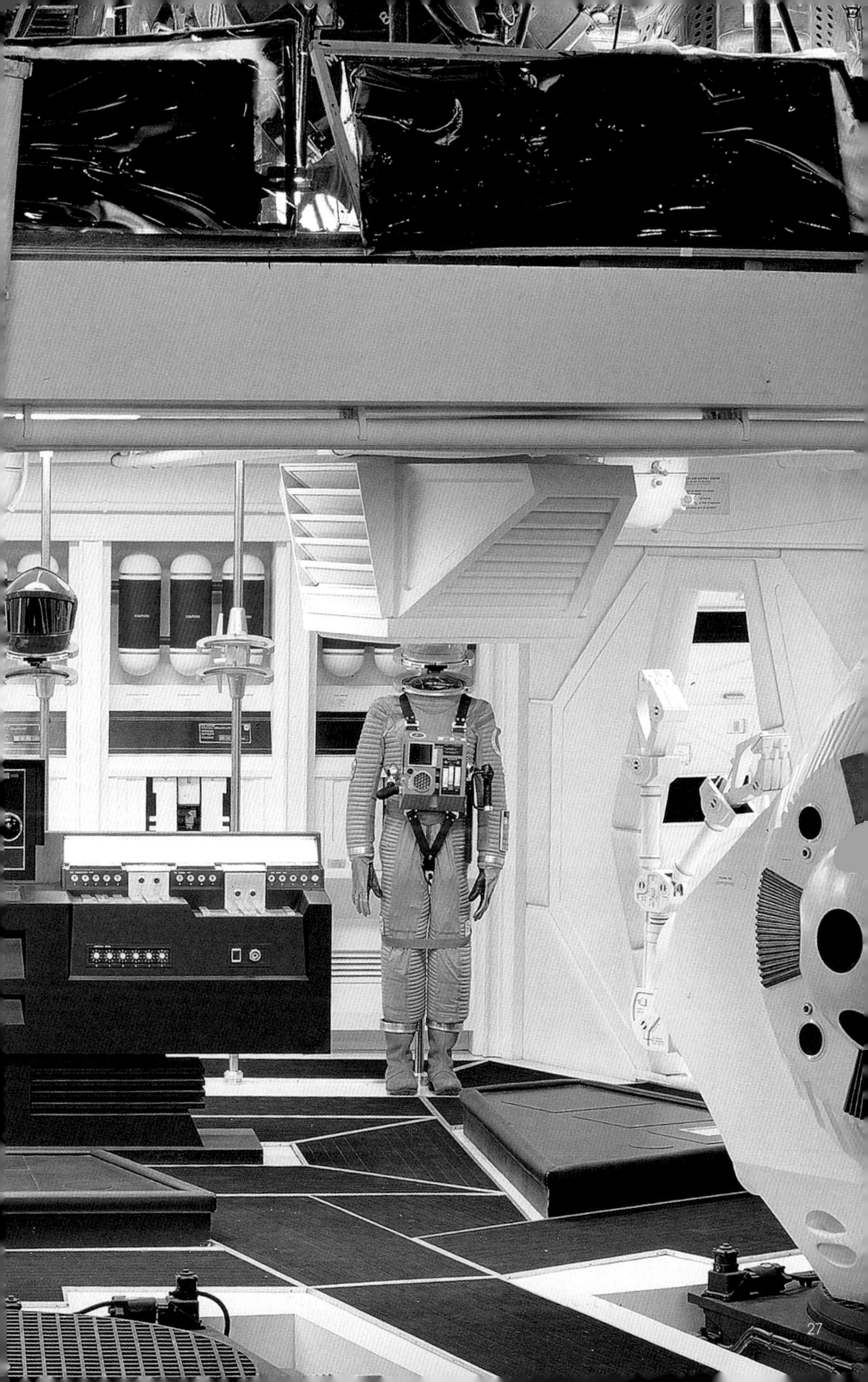

"The feel of the experience is the important thing, not the ability to verbalize or analyze it."

—SK/1968 (*BOOKS*)

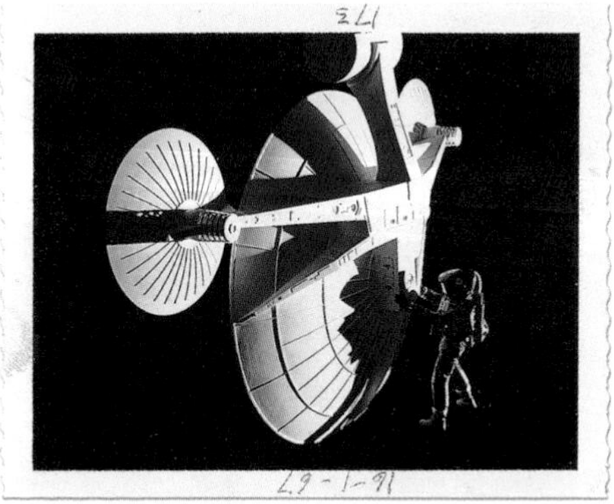

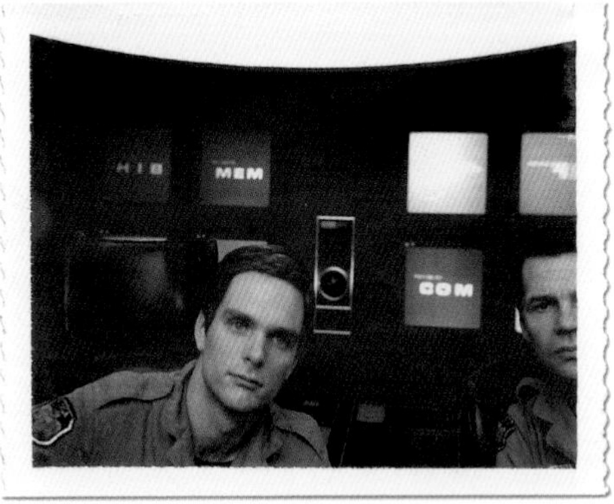

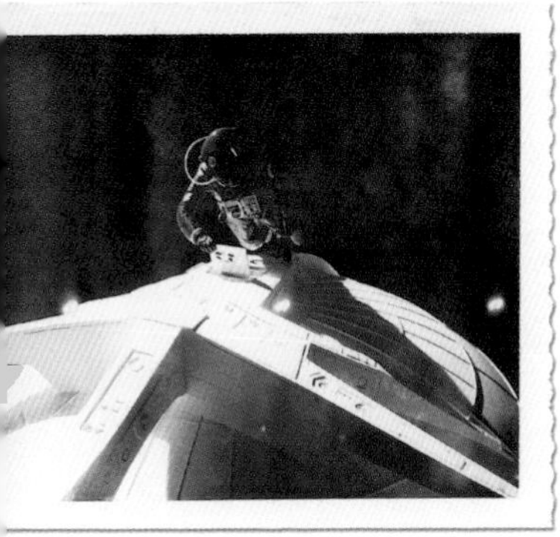

28-39

28-51 ***Continuity Polaroids.***

PANAVISION T 3
POLA SCR IN HELMET
POLA SC IN CAMERA
6500 F.C.

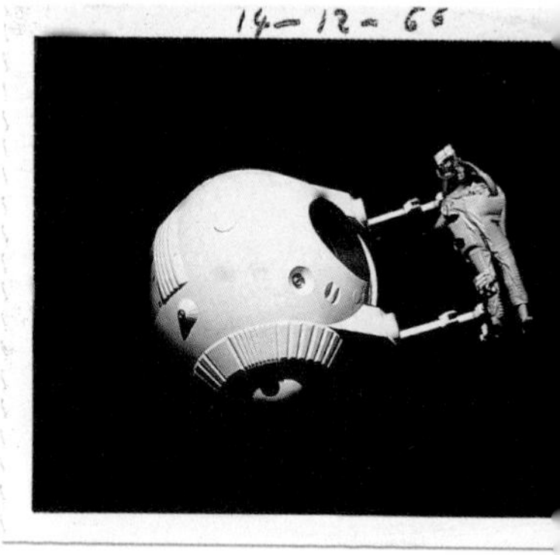
14-12-65

1/30 @ 5.6
100 F.C.

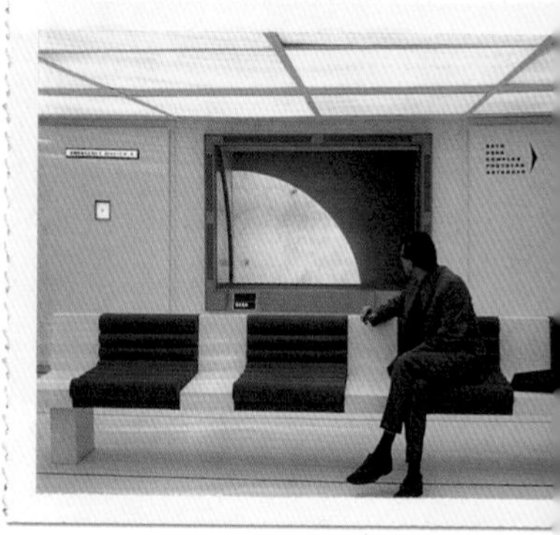

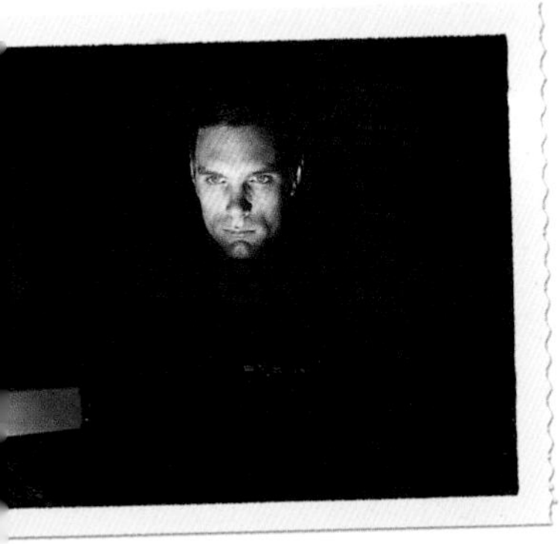

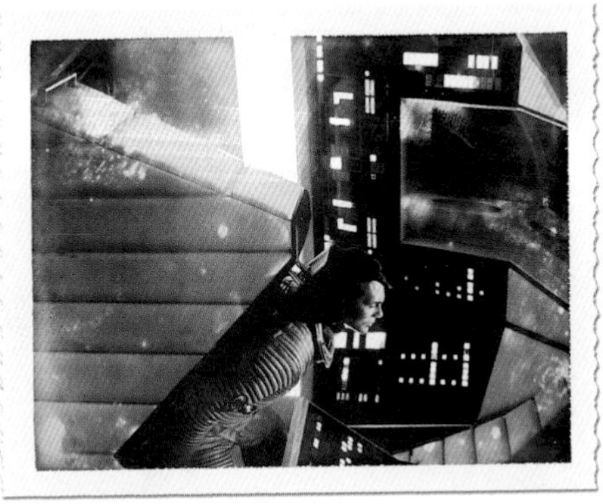

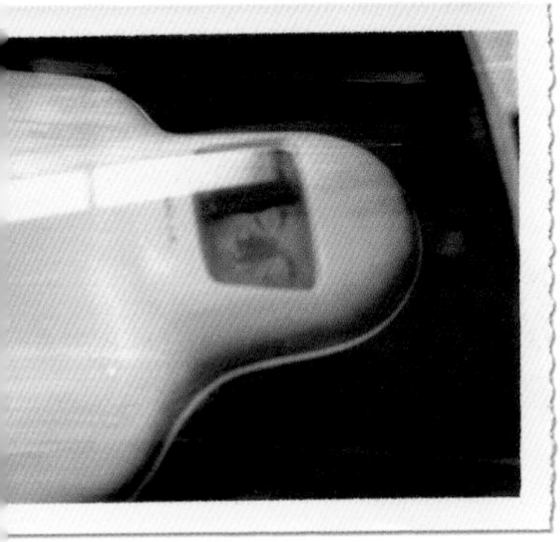

40–51

Stanley Kubrick and the Search for Extraterrestrial Intelligence

by Anthony Frewin

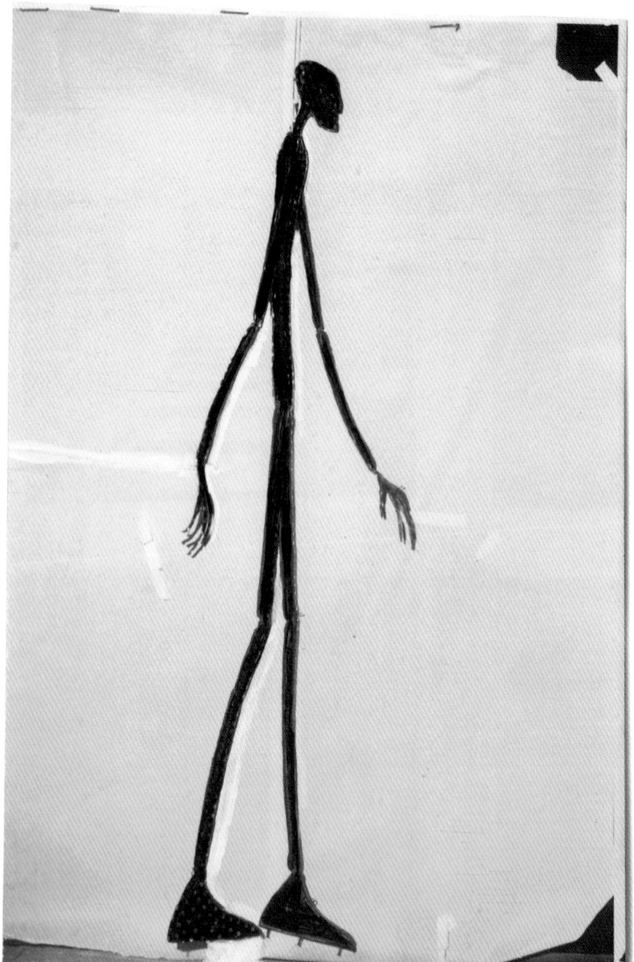

52

Stanley Kubrick had a problem when he began pre-production of *2001: A Space Odyssey* in 1965. In fact, he had many problems, but there was one particular problem, initially, anyway, that vexed him greatly: the public perception of science fiction or futuristic films. It may be difficult for anyone under the age of fifty to appreciate the fact that prior to *2001* science fiction in the cinema was something for Saturday morning kids' showings and the "B" film circuit. It was UFOs, flying saucers, little green men, "Mars Attacks," and Flash Gordon and Buck Rogers. It was the cinema engendered by the fantasy pulp magazines of the 1930s and 1940s and produced by the *schlockmeisters* of Hollywood's Poverty Row.[1] True, there may have been one or two exceptions in the history of the cinema, but these were largely forgotten in the popular imagination.[2]

Breaking this perception down, one came up with two issues in regard to *2001*: space travel and the idea of extraterrestrial life, the latter being one of the major themes of the film. The subjects were not taken seriously and could hardly be the basis of what is commonly known to the film industry's barkers and shills as a *major motion picture*.

SK felt that he needed primarily to establish that the question of extraterrestrial life *was* a legitimate subject for scientific investigation and the question *Are we alone?* was of the most profound importance to mankind. If he could do this, acceptance of the other issues would follow. Without doing this he feared that *2001* would be dismissed as just another romp in the galaxy, another space opera, the perfect accompaniment for popcorn.

SK's solution to this problem was simple. He would interview on film the most important scientists, theologians, astronomers, and philosophers who had confronted the problem of extraterrestrial life and "prefix" *2001: A Space Odyssey* with an introduction made up of edited clips from those interviews, much in the manner of Herman Melville collecting quotations on whales and whaling from various authorities at the beginning of *Moby Dick*. This was a direct and elegant way of setting the scene and letting the audience know that what was coming might be worthy of more than passing attention. To this purpose, SK carefully drew up a list of questions, researched those he wished to interview[3] and sent his associate, Roger Caras, hither and thither around the world in 1966 interviewing on 35 mm black-and-white film twenty-one scientists and others that he felt could contribute to the production.[4]

And while Caras was interviewing them he could also ask questions about artificial intelligence, the future of computing, the origin of life, and other matters that could contribute to an accurate portrayal of the year 2001 (SK was never one to miss an opportunity).

All of those interviewed were or have become major international figures in their fields and, to underscore their importance, several of them are included in David W. Swift's recent and much praised *SETI Pioneers: Scientists Talk about Their Search for Extraterrestrial Intelligence*.[5]

52 ***This Giacometti-inspired figure, affectionately called "Reddy Kilowatt," was one of the more promising ideas for depicting aliens.***

HAWK FILMS LTD. "2001: A SPACE ODYSSEY"

SLATE: SJA 426 TEST: DATE: 21-9-67

TITLE: ET MODEL.

LENS ON CAMERA: BUG EYE.

LENS ON PROJECTOR:

STOP: F. 22. + WEDGE F2 TO F64 IN HALF STOPS.

SPEED: 1½ FRAMES PER SECOND

PRINT LIGHT:

MAG: 2'

FOOTAGE LOADED: 1,000 N/R.

EMULSION: 979-221-12

CAMERA NO: 7013.

DISTANCE TO MIRROR CAMERA:

DISTANCE TO MIRROR PROJECTOR:

FOCUS POINTS: EYE

FILTERS PROJECTOR:

FOOT CANDLES: KEY = 4500 F/C FROM BARE ARC WITH WHITE FLAME CARBON. KEY IS CAMERA LEFT

OTHER LIGHTING INFORMATION: FILL = 2,000 F/C FROM. FROM BARE 5K - CAMERA LEFT.

AMPS ON PROJECTOR: FRONT FILL 30 BABY BASHER WITH 275 WATT LAMP.

LENS TO MODEL IS ½" AT IT'S CLOSEST FROM FRONT ELEMENT.

CAMERA HEIGHT: 5'8"

MODEL HEIGHT = 5'8" (EYE).

MOTORISED MOY.

MOVE LASTING. 8 MINS 48 SECS

L—R.

ROLL NO.	SLATE	(TEST)	COUNTER	FOOTAGE	PRINT
1	426	1	180	100	P.
		2.			

SHOT RUNS FOR 784 FRAMES.

To take a number of names at random: Aleksandr Ivanovich Oparin (1894–1980), the most important twentieth-century scientist to research the origins of life, wrote what has been described as the first and principal modern appreciation of the problem. Harlow Shapley (1885–1972) was a great American astronomer, an eloquent writer, and someone to whom we owe our understanding of the size and shape of our galaxy. B. F. Skinner (1904–1990) is widely known for his work on behavioral conditioning. Freeman J. Dyson (1923–) invented the Dyson sphere. Dr. Margaret Mead (1901–1978) was the author of *Coming of Age in Samoa* (1928) and other important contributions to anthropology. Frank D. Drake (1930–) is a pioneer of SETI and radio astronomy and the formulator of the Drake Equation. Fred Whipple might well be considered *the* great astronomer of the twentieth century.

As the production of *2001* fast approached completion in the summer of 1968 SK realized that the film would have to stand on its own two feet, that the interviews might in fact be a confusing distraction for the audience and, besides, with the picture already running to 160 minutes, there just was not enough time to include them. So, the cans of 35 mm film were consigned to the vaults.

SK's Key Texts

SK was a voracious and catholic reader from an early age. His interest in science fiction dated back to the 1930s when as a child he read pulp magazines such as *Amazing Stories* and *Astounding Stories* and similar, which were then plentiful on the newsstands of the Bronx. It is to this time that we must look for the ultimate origins of his wish to make a "really good" science-fiction film. However, he never really considered himself a science-fiction fan or buff. It was a genre that he was impatient with: he liked the *ideas* but he found the writing jejune and the characterization deplorable. He was the first to admit that science fiction was hardly a sub-set of *belles-lettres,* as it were, but there was such a thing as *standards.*

It would take a John Livingston Lowes[6] and a lifetime of diligent study to track down the sources and influences that resulted in SK making *2001* but what I would like to do here is list the volumes that SK read and discussed when I first went to work for him in September 1965.

SK thought the two "best" volumes on ETI were Carl Sagan and I. S. Shklovskii's *Intelligent Life in the Universe*[7] (1966) and Roger A. MacGowan and Frederick I. Ordway III's *Intelligence in the Universe* (1966). SK appreciated having Fred Ordway on hand as the in-house ETI expert to elucidate and elaborate points raised in the book (and much else besides). Both volumes have dated hardly at all and can still be highly recommended.

A good "once over," in SK's term, was the book by *The New York Times* science editor, Walter Sullivan. This was *We Are not Alone: The Search for Intelligent Life on Other Worlds* (1964, and subsequent editions)—again a volume that still stands up remarkably well.

SK liked the philosophic dimensions and the grandeur of the universe as

53 ***Test shot of one of several prototypes of extraterrestrials.***

written about in Harlow Shapley's *The View from a Distant Star: Man's Future in the Universe* (1963) and he found very provocative Arthur C. Clarke's *Profiles of the Future* (1962) and I. J. Good's *The Scientist Speculates* (1962); the latter he thought a "Catherine wheel of a book" with its wild and "partly baked" ideas (the subtitle) and Good's puckish preface, which consists of just one sentence which SK found very amusing: "The intention of this anthology is to raise more questions than it answers."

Finally, A. G. W. Cameron's *Interstellar Communication: The Search for Extraterrestrial Life* (1963) was an "early" anthology of some thirty-two scientific papers, some of which were hard going for us in civvy street, but which nonetheless suggested ideas to SK. This was also the volume that introduced SK to the work of Freeman J. Dyson, Philip Morrison, and Frank Drake, three of the scientists who were interviewed.

SK had an abiding interest in ETI and Artificial Intelligence (AI) right up until his death, reading the latest issues of *Scientific American* and getting advance copies of books by scientists such as Marvin Minsky and Hans Moravec.[8]

54 ***Dan Richter was covered with polka-dots and filmed against a light backdrop in this attempt to find a way to portray extra-terrestrials, the idea being that with the use of high-contrast film, only the black dots would be visible and if inverted, would give the effect of an alien made up of dots of light. Richter wrote that the result was like "looking at a person decked out in polka dots."* (Moonwatcher's Memoir, 2002)**

Notes

1. I may have spoken too soon. Science fiction in the cinema has returned to its pre-*2001* state. There seems to be some inverse law at work here: as the special effects have got better and better the films have got more and more banal. The SFX in, say, *Independence Day* (1996) or *Lost in Space* (1998) or *The Matrix Reloaded* (2003) are beyond anything any of us could ever have imagined when we were making *2001*, yet the story and content of these representative films is juvenile. Several people have pointed to *Contact* (1997), the film based on the Carl Sagan novel, as having breached the barriers, but I would not agree. It has the ponderous faux seriousness that one used to associate with Stanley Kramer. There is room in the cinema for intelligent, well-crafted hokum—Ridley Scott's *Alien* (1979) and its progeny are good examples—but where is the movie with the ambition and import of *2001*? Andrei Tarkovsky's *Solaris* (1972) comes to mind, but what else?
2. Two films preceding *2001* that one might consider as sharing its grandeur and ambition are Fritz Lang's *Metropolis* (1927) and Alexander Korda/William Cameron Menzies's, *Things to Come* (1936), with a screenplay by H. G. Wells from his novel. SK thought that *Metropolis*, despite its imaginative art direction and cinematic strengths, was, essentially, silly. None of us demurred. However, neither myself nor Arthur C. Clarke could convince SK of the merits of *Things to Come* which he considered politically simplistic and preachy, though he did admire the special effects. Interestingly, two of the *2001* special effects supervisors, the gentlemanly Tom Howard and Wally "Where's Wally?" Veevers, both began their careers working on *Things to Come* under Ned Mann, the SFX chief. Christopher Frayling's *Things to Come* (London: British Film Institute, 1995) is a useful little study of the film that does not shirk its political implications.

HAWK FILMS LTD. "2001: A SPACE ODYSSEY"

Roll I

SLATE: 414 DATE: 8-9-67

TITLE: Polka Dot Man

LENS: Zoom

STOP: 8

SPEED: 48 F.P.S

PRINT LIGHT: 10

MAG: 112

FOOTAGE LOADED: 415ft S/E

EMULSION: 451-14-1 (High Contrast)

CAMERA: 7013

LENS TO:

CAMERA HEIGHT:

CAMERA ANGLE:

LIGHTING INFORMATION:

5,10Ks + 25Ks

SLATE	TAKE	COUNTER	FOOTAGE	PRINT
414	1	400	400	P
		15ft Waste		

To Be Developed To Normal – Pos Gamma

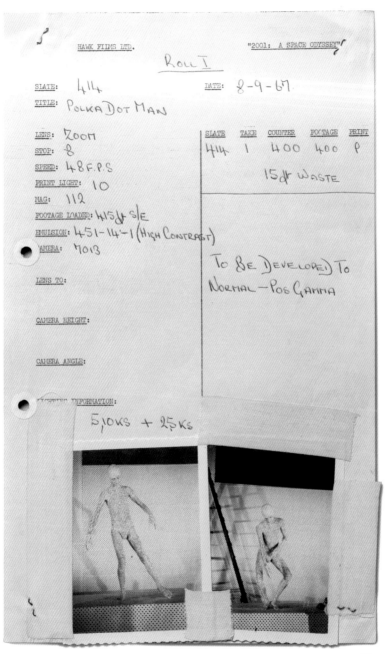

3. Principal input on names was from Fred Ordway, but Arthur C. Clarke and Jeremy Bernstein also contributed.
4. The letter of invitation was drafted by SK and went out under Caras's name. The 35 mm film would have been blown up to 70 mm by Technicolor in London for *2001*'s initial Cinerama release.
5. Tucson: University of Arizona Press, 1990.
6. John Livingston Lowes, *The Road to Xanadu: A Study in the Ways of the Imagination* (Boston: Houghton Mifflin, 1927). Over six hundred pages of literary detection on the sources and origins of Samuel Taylor Coleridge's *Kubla Khan* and *The Rime of the Ancient Mariner*. This, by the way, was a book that SK frequently dipped into. He admired not just the scholarship but the warmth of the scholarship and the cadences of Lowes's prose style and felt that a book such as this was "worth a thousand or more volumes of literary criticism with the words 'gender' or 'exegesis' in the title. The 'bull crit' stuff." Interestingly, SK also liked it because of the footnotes and once showed me what Lowes wrote in his preface, p. xii, "There are those who find the notes in a book more interesting than the text. I often do myself." Footnotes, SK said, were where the "real action" was, where the references were (and he liked references) and where the writer could abandon the sobriety of the main text and not mince his words.
7. Described by Stephen J. Dick as "the bible of scientific thought on extraterrestrial life." *The Biological Universe: The Twentieth-Century Extraterrestrial Life Debate and The Limits of Science* (Cambridge: Cambridge University Press, 1999): 289.
8. Marvin Minsky's *The Society of Mind* (New York; Simon and Schuster, 1986) and Hans Moravec's *Mind Children: The Future of Robot and Human Intelligence* (Cambridge, Mass.: Harvard University Press, 1988), both had a great influence on SK's conception of "A.I."

55 ***A page from the* 2001 *production notes. After unsuccessful attempts to find a convincing way of portraying extraterrestrials, Kubrick decided not to show them at all. "[W]e all discussed means of photographically depicting an extraterrestrial creature in a manner that would be as mind-boggling as the being itself. And it soon became apparent that you cannot imagine the unimaginable." – SK/1970 (to Joseph Gelmis)***

R E P L I C A   H O T E L   S U I T E

S y n o p s i s

Bowman finds himself in a replica of a normal, Earth-type hotel suite, and makes contact with the Extra-terrestrial beings.

C h a r a c t e r s

Bowman

Extra-terrestrials ?

C o s t u m e s

Bowman: Space-suit, and possibly a change of clothes into something provided for him by the Extra-terrestrials.

Extra-terrestrials ?

M a k e - u p

Bowman -- normal.

Extra-terrestrials ?

1.VI.65

Filming *2001: A Space Odyssey*

by Herb A. Lightman

MOONBUS (Neg 110) married to MOONSCAPE "Q" (T. 6)
(B. P. Sl. 837 - T. 2)

56

MOON BUS NEG. 268 B. P NO. 838 T. 1

57

Excerpts from an article published in American Cinematographer, *June 1968*

The Behind-the-scenes of a Great Film Adventure

I had heard about the elaborate "command post" which had been set up at Borehamwood during the production of *2001*. It was described to me as a huge, throbbing nerve center of a place with much the same frenetic atmosphere as a Cape Kennedy blockhouse during the final stages of Countdown.

"It was a novel thing for me to have such a complicated information-handling operation going, but it was absolutely essential for keeping track of the thousands of technical details involved," Kubrick explains. "We figured that there would be 205 effects scenes in the picture and that each of these would require an average of ten major steps to complete. I define a 'major step' as one in which the scene is handled by another technician or department. We found that it was so complicated to keep track of all of these scenes and the separate steps involved in each that we wound up with a three-man sort of 'operations room' in which every wall was covered with swing-out charts including a shot history for each scene. Every separate element and step was recorded on this history — information as to shooting dates, exposure, mechanical processes, special requirements and the technicians and departments involved. Figuring ten steps for two hundred scenes equals two thousand steps — but when you realize that most of these steps had to be done over eight or nine times to make sure they were perfect, the true total is more like sixteen thousand separate steps. It took an incredible number of diagrams, flow-charts and other data to keep everything organized and to be able to retrieve information that somebody might need about something someone else had done seven months earlier. We had to be able to tell which stage each scene was in at any given moment — and the system worked."

Smooth Trips for Star-voyagers

A recurring problem arose from the fact that most of the outer-space action had to take place against a starfield background. It is obvious that as space vehicles and tumbling astronauts moved in front of these stars they would have to "go out" and "come back on" at the right times — a simple matter if conventional traveling mattes were used. But how to do it a better way?

The better way involved shooting the foreground action and then making a 70 mm print of it with a superimposed registration grid and an identifying frame number printed onto each frame. The grid used corresponded with an identical grid inscribed on animation-type platens.

Twenty enlargers operated by twenty girls were set up in a room and each girl was given a five- or six-foot segment of the scene. She would place one frame at a time in the enlarger, line up the grid on the frame with the grid on her platen and then trace an outline of the foreground subject onto an animation cel. In another department the area enclosed by the outline would be filled in with solid black paint.

The cels would then be photographed in order on the animation stand to produce an opaque matte of the foreground action. The moving star background would also be shot on the animation stand, after which both the stars and the matte would be delivered to Technicolor Ltd. for the optical printing of a matted master with star background. Very often there were several foreground elements, which meant that the matting process had to be repeated for each separate element.

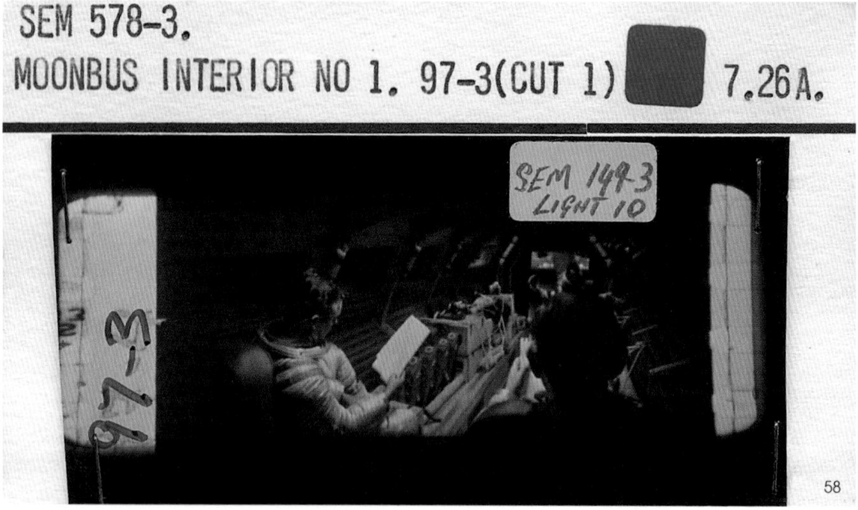

58

59

60

The Mechanical Monster With the Delicate Touch

In creating many of the effects, especially those involving miniature models of the various spacecraft, it was usually necessary to make multiple repeat takes that were absolutely identical in terms of camera movement. For this purpose a camera animating device was constructed with a heavy worm-gear twenty feet in length. The large size of this worm gear enabled the camera mount of the device to be moved with precise accuracy. A motorized head permitted tilting and panning in all directions. All of these functions were tied together with selsyn motors so that moves could be repeated as often as necessary in perfect registration.

For example, let us assume that a certain scene involved a fly-by of a spaceship with miniature projection of the interior action visible through the window. The required moves would be programmed out in advance for the camera animating device. A shot would then be made of the spaceship miniature with the exterior properly lighted, but with the window area blacked out. Then the film would be wound back in the camera to its sync frame and another identical pass would be made. This time, however, the exterior of the spacecraft would be covered with black velvet and a scene of the interior action would be front-projected onto a glossy white card exactly filling the window area. Because of the precision made possible by the large worm gear and the selsyn motors, this exact dual maneuver could be repeated as many times as necessary. The two elements of the scene would be exposed together in perfect registration onto the same original piece of negative with all of the moves duplicated and no camera jiggle.

Often, for a scene such as that previously described, several elements would be photographed onto held-takes photographed several months apart. Since light in space originates from a sharp single

56–59 ***Examples of index cards used by the special effects department.***
60 ***2001 slate.***

point source, it was necessary to take great pains to make sure that the light sources foiling on the separate elements would match exactly for angle and intensity.

Also, since the elements were being photographed onto the same strip of original negative, it was essential that all exposures be matched precisely. If one of them was off, there would be no way to correct it without throwing the others off. In order to guard against this variation in exposure very precise wedge-testing was made of each element, and the wedges were very carefully selected for color and density. But even with all of these precautions there was a high failure rate and many of the scenes had to be redone.

"We coined a new phrase and began to call these 're-don'ts'," says Kubrick, with a certain post-operative amusement. "This refers to a re-do in which you don't make the same mistake you made before."

Filming the Ultimate in Slow Motion

In the filming of the spacecraft miniatures, two problems were encountered which necessitated the shooting of scenes at extremely slow frame rates. First, there was the matter of depth-of-field. In order to hold both the forward and rear extremities of the spacecraft models in sharp focus, so that they would look like full-sized vehicles and not miniatures, it was necessary to stop the aperture of the lens down to practically a pin-hole. The obvious solution of using more light was not feasible because it was necessary to maintain the illusion of a single bright point light source. Secondly, in order to get doors, ports, and other movable parts of the miniatures to operate smoothly and on a large scale the motors driving these mechanisms were geared down so far that the actual motion, frame by frame, was imperceptible.

"It was like watching the hour hand of a clock," says Kubrick. "We shot most of these scenes using slow exposures of four seconds per frame, and if you were standing on the stage you would not see anything moving. Even the giant space station that rotated at a good rate on the screen seemed to be standing still during the actual photography of its scenes. For some shots, such as those in which doors opened and closed on the space ships, a door would move only about four inches during the course of the scene, but it would take five hours to shoot that movement. You could never see unsteady movement, if there was unsteadiness, until you saw the scene on the screen—and even then the

61

engineers could never be sure exactly where the unsteadiness had occurred. They could only guess by looking at the scene. This type of thing involved endless trial and error, but the final results are a tribute to MGM's great precision machine shop in England."

It's All Done With Wires —But You Can't See Them

Scenes of the astronauts floating weightlessly in space outside the *Discovery*—especially those showing Gary Lockwood tumbling off into infinity after he has been murdered by the vengeful computer—required some very tricky maneuvering. For one thing, Kubrick was determined that none of the wires supporting the actors and stunt men would show. Accordingly, he had the ceiling of the entire stage draped with black velvet, mounted the camera vertically and photographed the astronauts from below so that their own bodies would hide the wires.

61 ***"A 'control room,' constantly manned by several people and with walls covered by pert charts, flow diagrams, progress reports, log sheets, punch cards, and every conceivable kind of filing system, was used to keep track of all progress on the film." – Douglas Trumbull* (American Cinematographer, *June 1968)***

"We established different positions on their bodies for a hip harness, a high-back harness and a low-back harness," he explains, "so that no matter how they were spinning or turning on this rig—whether feet-first, head-first or profile—they would always cover their wires and not get fouled up in them. For the sequence in which the one-man pod picks Lockwood up in its arms and crushes him, we were shooting straight up from under him. He was suspended by wires from a track in the ceiling and the camera followed him, keeping him in the same position in the frame as it tracked him into the arms of the pod. The pod was suspended from the ceiling also, hanging on its side from a tubular frame. The effect on the screen is that the pod moves horizontally into the frame to attack him, whereas he was actually moving toward the pod."

To shoot the scene in which the dead astronaut goes spinning off to become a pin-point in space took a bit of doing. "If we had actually started in close to a six-foot man and then pulled the camera back until he was a speck, we would have had to track back about two thousand feet—obviously impractical," Kubrick points out. "Instead we photographed him on 65 mm film simply tumbling about

in full frame. Then we front-projected a six-inch image of this scene onto a glossy white card suspended against black velvet and, using our worm-gear arrangement, tracked the camera away from the miniature screen until the astronaut became so small in the frame that he virtually disappeared. Since we were rephotographing an extremely small image there was no grain problem and he remained sharp and clear all the way to infinity."

62 ***The Sausage Factory. "A few scenes show a miniature rear-projected image in the window of a spacecraft as the spacecraft is matted over an image of the moon. For this effect the foreground spacecraft was a still photograph mounted on glass and, using a bi-pack camera, the masters of the background image could be printed with a white backing behind the still photo – the photo silhouette producing its own matte. Then the photo and the rear-projected image could be shot as separate exposures onto the same negative. To produce exactly the same movement on each successive exposure, all movement drives and film advances were selsyn synchronized. The mammoth device designed to produce this effect we nicknamed the 'Sausage Factory,' because we expected the machine to crank out shots at a very fast rate. This turned out to be wishful thinking, however, and shooting became very painstaking and laborious work." – Douglas Trumbull*** **(American Cinematographer, *June 1968)***

63 ***A mock-up of the view of Discovery's antenna from the pod window, which was filmed separately and matted in.***

The same basic technique was used in the sequence during which the surviving astronaut, locked out of the mother ship by the computer, decides to pop the explosive bolts on his one-man pod and blast himself through the vacuum of space into the air-lock. The air-lock set, which appears to be horizontal on the screen, was actually built vertically so that the camera could shoot straight up through it and the astronaut would cover with his body the wires suspending him.

First a shot was made of the door alone, showing just the explosion. Then an over-cranked[1] shot of the astronaut was made with him being lowered toward the camera at a frame rate which made him appear to come hurtling horizontally straight into the lens. The following shot was over-cranked as he recovered and appeared to float lazily in the air-lock.

A Fascinating Ferris Wheel

2001: A Space Odyssey abounds in unusual settings, but perhaps the most exotic of them all is the giant centrifuge which serves as the main compartment of the *Discovery* spacecraft and is, we are told, an accurate representation of the type of device that will be used to create artificial gravity for overcoming weightlessness during future deep-space voyages.

Costing $750,000, the space-going "Ferris wheel" was built by the Vickers-Armstrong Engineering Group. It was thirty-eight feet in diameter and about ten feet in width at its widest point. It rotated at a maximum speed of three miles per hour and had built into it desks, consoles, bunks for the astronauts and tomb-like containers for their hibernating companions.

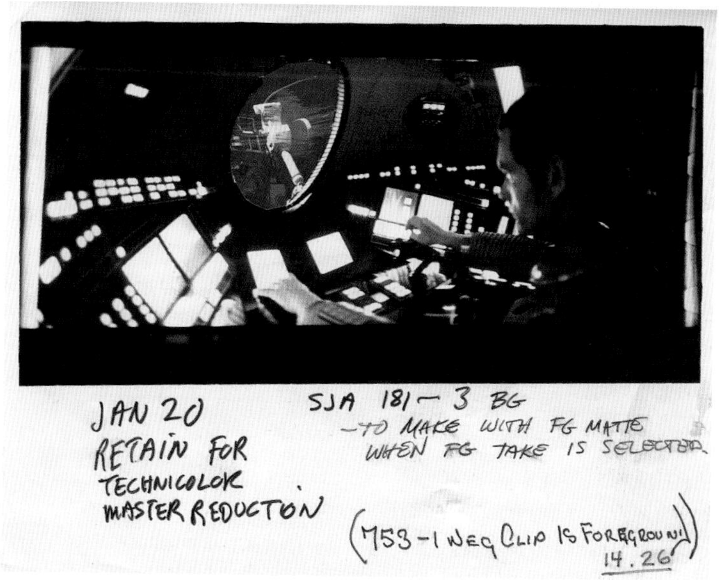

All of the lighting units, as well as the rear-projectors used to flash readouts onto the console scopes, had to be firmly fixed to the centrifuge structure and be capable of functioning while moving in a 360° circle. The magazine mechanisms of the Super-Panavision cameras had to be specially modified by Panavision to operate efficiently even when the cameras were upside down.

"Every child that sees the film—and I've spoken to twenty or thirty kids—knows that Doctor Floyd goes to the moon. You say, 'Well, how do you know?' and they say, 'Well, we saw the moon.' Whereas a number of people, including critics, thought he went to the planet Clavius. Why they think there's a planet Clavius I'll never know."

—SK/1969 (to Maurice Rapf/*Action*)

"There were basically two types of camera set-ups used inside the centrifuge," Kubrick explains. "In the first type the camera was mounted stationary to the set, so that when the set rotated in a 360° arc, the camera went right along with it. However, in terms of visual orientation, the camera didn't 'know' it was moving. In other words, on the screen it appears that the camera is standing still, while the actor walks away from it, up the wall, around the top and down the other side. In the second type of shot the camera, mounted on a miniature dolly, stayed with the actor at the bottom while the whole set moved past him. This was not as simple as it sounds because, due to the fact that the camera had to maintain some distance from the actor, it was necessary to position it about twenty feet up the wall—and have it stay in that position as the set rotated. This was accomplished by means of a steel cable from the outside which connected with the camera through a slot in the center of the floor and ran around the entire centrifuge. The slot was concealed by rubber mats that fell back into place as soon as the cable passed them."

Kubrick directed the action of these sequences from outside by watching a closed-circuit monitor relaying a picture from a small vidicon camera mounted next to the film camera inside the centrifuge. Of the specific lighting problems that had to be solved, he says:

"It took a lot of careful pre-planning with the Lighting Cameraman, Geoffrey Unsworth, and Production Designer Tony Masters to devise lighting that would look natural, and, at the same time, do the job photographically. All of the lighting for the scenes inside the centrifuge came from strip lights along the walls. Some of the units were concealed in coves, but others could be seen when the camera angle was wide enough. It was difficult for the cameraman to get enough light inside the centrifuge and he had to shoot with

64 ***Keir Dullea was suspended by a wire and lowered toward the floor for this shot of Bowman being blasted into the air-lock.***

64

his lens wide open practically all of the time."

Cinematographer Unsworth used an unusual approach toward achieving his light balance and arriving at the correct exposure. He employed a Polaroid camera loaded with *ASA* 200 black and white film (because the color emulsion isn't consistent enough) to make still photographs of each new set-up prior to filming the scene. He found this to be a very rapid and effective way of getting an instant check on exposure and light balance. He was working at the toe end of the film latitude scale much of the time, shooting in scatter light and straight into exposed practical fixtures. The ten thousand Pola-

65 ***The centrifuge was thirty-eight feet in diameter and rotated at a maximum speed of three miles per hour.***
66 ***Kubrick monitored scenes shot inside the centrifuge via closed-circuit television.***

66

roid shots taken during production helped him considerably in coping with these problems.

"Filmmaking" in the Purest Sense of the Term

To say that *2001: A Space Odyssey* is a spectacular piece of entertainment, as well as a technical tour de force, is certainly true, but there is considerably more to it than that.

In its larger dimension, the production may be regarded as a prime example of the *auteur* approach to filmmaking — a concept in which a single creative artist is, in the fullest sense of the word, the author of the film. In this case, there is not the slightest doubt that Stanley Kubrick is that author. It is his film. On every 70 mm frame his imagination, his technical skill, his taste, and his creative artistry are evident. Yet he is the first to insist that the result is a

67

group effort (as every film must be) and to give full credit to the 106 skilled and dedicated craftsmen who worked closely with him for periods of up to four years.

Among those he especially lauds are: screenplay co-author Arthur C. Clarke, Cinematographers Geoffrey Unsworth and John Alcott, and Production Designers Tony Masters, Harry Lange, and Ernie Archer. He also extends lavish praise to Special Effects Supervisors Wally Veevers, Douglas Trumbull, Con Pederson, and Tom Howard.

The praise, it would seem, is not all one-sided. *MGM*'s Post-production Administrator Merle Chamberlin worked with Kubrick for a total of twenty weeks, both in London and in Hollywood, on the final phases of the project. A man not given to rash compliments, Chamberlin has this to say of the endeavor: "Working with Stanley Kubrick was a wonderful experience—a tremendously pleasant and educational one. He knows what he wants and how to get it, and he will not accept anything less than absolute perfection. One thing that surprised me is his complete lack of what might be called 'temperament.' He is always calm and controlled no matter what goes wrong. He simply faces the challenge with incredible dedication and follows it through to his objective. He is a hard taskmaster in that he holds no brief for inefficiency—and it has been said that he knows nothing of the proper hours for sleeping—but he is a fantastic filmmaker with whom to work. I have been privileged to work very closely with David Lean on *Doctor Zhivago*, with John Frankenheimer

68

67 ***Kubrick in the special effects department, with Tony Masters (left), Arthur C. Clarke (third from right), and Fred Ordway (second from right).***
68 ***A special mount was designed to allow the camera to rotate smoothly on a 360-degree axis.***
69–70 ***In-flight entertainment scenes played on monitors aboard*** Aries. ***"A crew was dispatched to Detroit to shoot a sleek car of the future.... The exteriors were shot in 35 mm, but the interiors were shot without seats or passengers, as 4 x 5 inch Ektachrome transparencies. Using these as background plates for a normal rear-projection set-up, an actor and actress were seated in dummy seats and Kubrick directed the love scene. Shot on 35 mm, this was cut together with the previous exterior shots, and projected onto the TV screen using a first-surface mirror." – Douglas Trumbull (***American Cinematographer, ***June 1968)***

69

70

on *Grand Prix*, with Michelangelo Antonioni on *Blow-up* and with Robert Aldrich on *The Dirty Dozen*—all terrific people and wonderful filmmakers. But as a combination of highly skilled cinema technician and creative artist, Kubrick is absolutely tops."

From my own relatively brief contact with the creator of *2001: A Space Odyssey* I would say that this praise is not overstated, for Stanley Kubrick, Film Author, epitomizes that ideal which is so rare in the world today: Not merely "Art for the sake of Art" — but vastly more important, "Excellence for the sake of Excellence."

Editor's Note

1. This term is inconsistent with the effect being described; it's likely that the author meant to write "under-cranked" (i.e. fast motion).

71 ***"For long shots of the apparently weightless floating in mid-air, the pen was simply suspended on thin monofilament nylon strands. For the close-up reverse angle shots the entire end of the set was floated away, and an eight-foot diameter rotating glass was moved into position with the pen lightly glued to it. The stewardess merely had to pluck it off." – Douglas Trumbull*** **(American Cinematographer, *June 1968*)**

72 ***70 mm Panavision camera gate.***

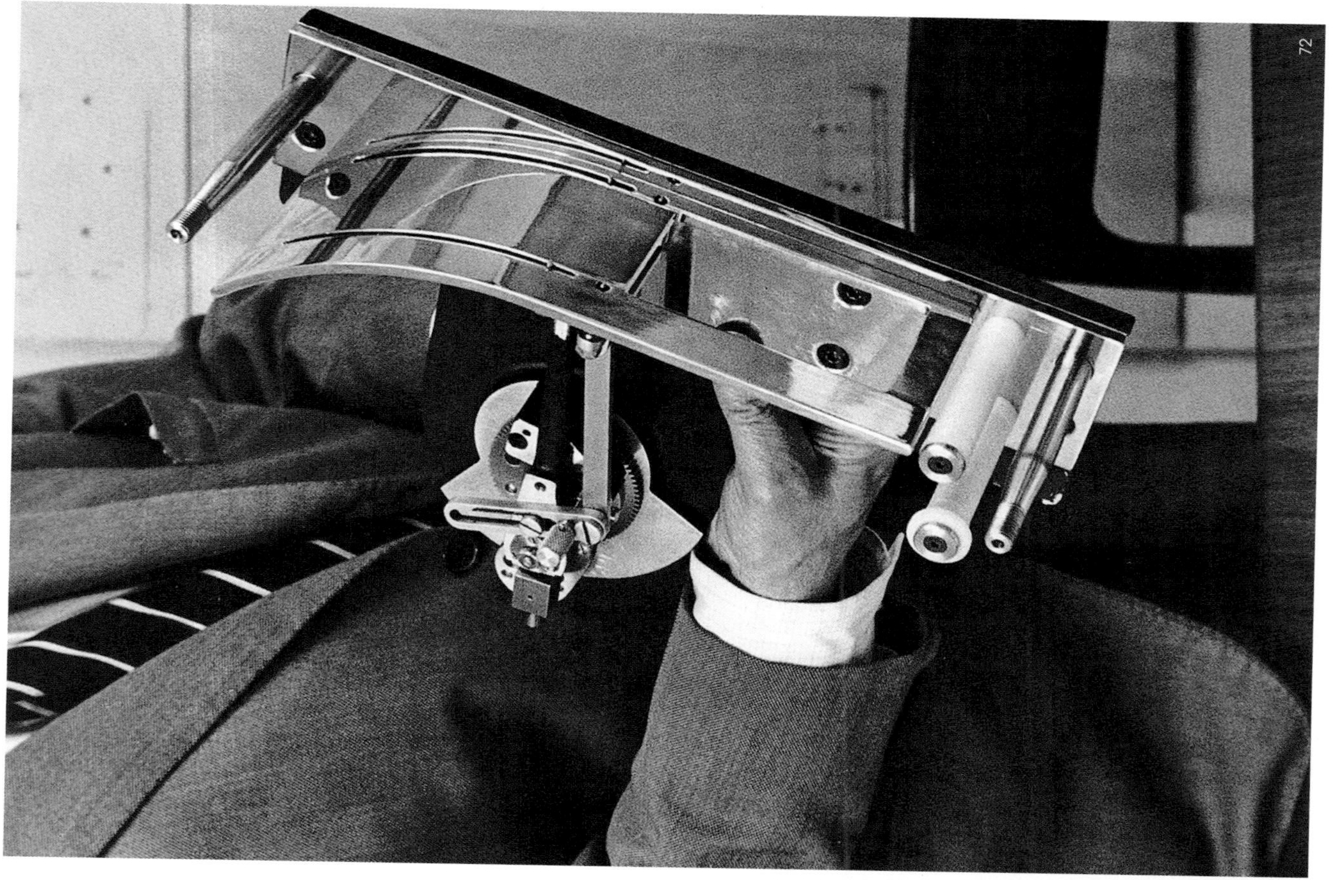

72

PASS No 1 + 2.

HAWK FILMS LTD. "2001: A SPACE ODYSSEY"

FRIDAY.

SLATE: SJA459-2. DATE: 27-10-67.

PASS No ONE + PASS No TWO.

TITLE: MIND BENDER

PROJ LENS = 110 m/m

LENS: 100 m/m.

STOP: 4

SPEED: 1/2 SEC.

PRINT LIGHT: 14.

MAG: 116

FOOTAGE LOADED: ~~[illegible]~~ 220' S/E.

EMULSION: 6-193-5.

CAMERA: 7013

SLATE	TAKE	COUNTER	FOOTAGE	PRINT
SJA 4592				

LENS TO: SHAFT OF TRIANGLE = 23'9"

DISTANCE BETWEEN MIRRORS = 7'4"

CAMERA HEIGHT: = 6 FT 1 1/4"

PROJ HAS 1,000 WATT BULB, (110 VOLTS)

- VARIAC SETTING = 120

CAMERA ANGLE: = 90° ON RIGHT.

" " = 2° TILT UP.

LIGHTING INFORMATION: 15 F/c ON WHITE TRIANGLE.

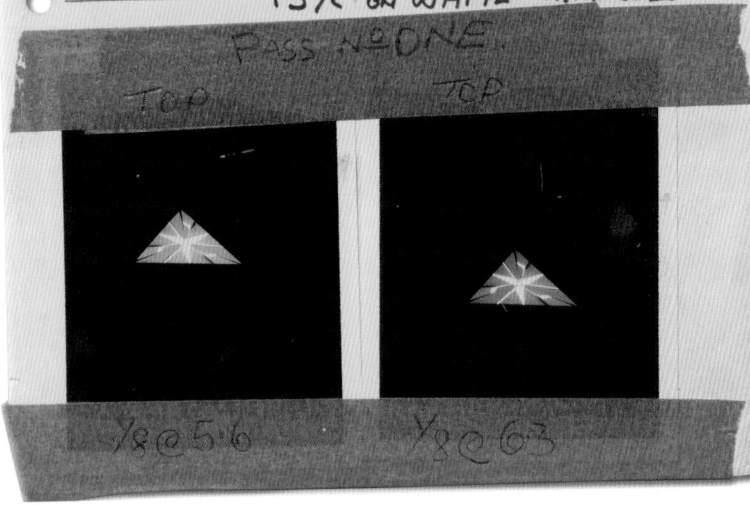

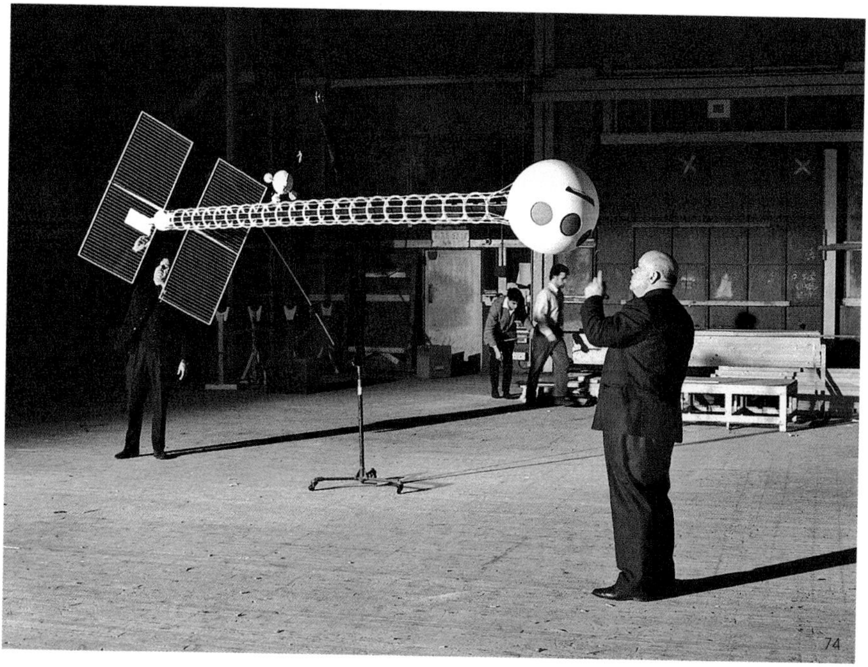

73 *The complex "Mindbender" effect, created for the Stargate sequence, was achieved by combining the slit-scan technique with projection onto multifaced screens. "SLIT-SCAN: This is a process wherein a single frame of film is exposed with the shutter open while the camera tracks in on a repeating track such as a worm gear towards an aperture which may be differently shaped such as a long narrow slit.... The movement of the aperture gives the motion and keeps the exposure sharp. Behind this slit, artwork of various types move, advancing themselves slightly on each frame. This gives the effect of great vanishing perspective and of motion travelling past the cameras." – "Exhibit A" of Hawk Films/MGM exclusivity and confidentiality contract.*

74, 76 *The small (fifteen-foot long) model of* Discovery *was filmed against a black backdrop for long shots (as opposed to the main, fifty-foot model used for close shots).*

75 *Index card referring to one of the techniques used for the Stargate sequence. "PURPLE HEARTS: This is a process where the color of normal photography is considered changed by making various high contrast master positives with incorrect colour filters. This technique represents a unique development in film effects and was developed at great time and expense by MGM." – "Exhibit B" of Hawk Films/MGM exclusivity and confidentiality contract.*

Fiction & Fact

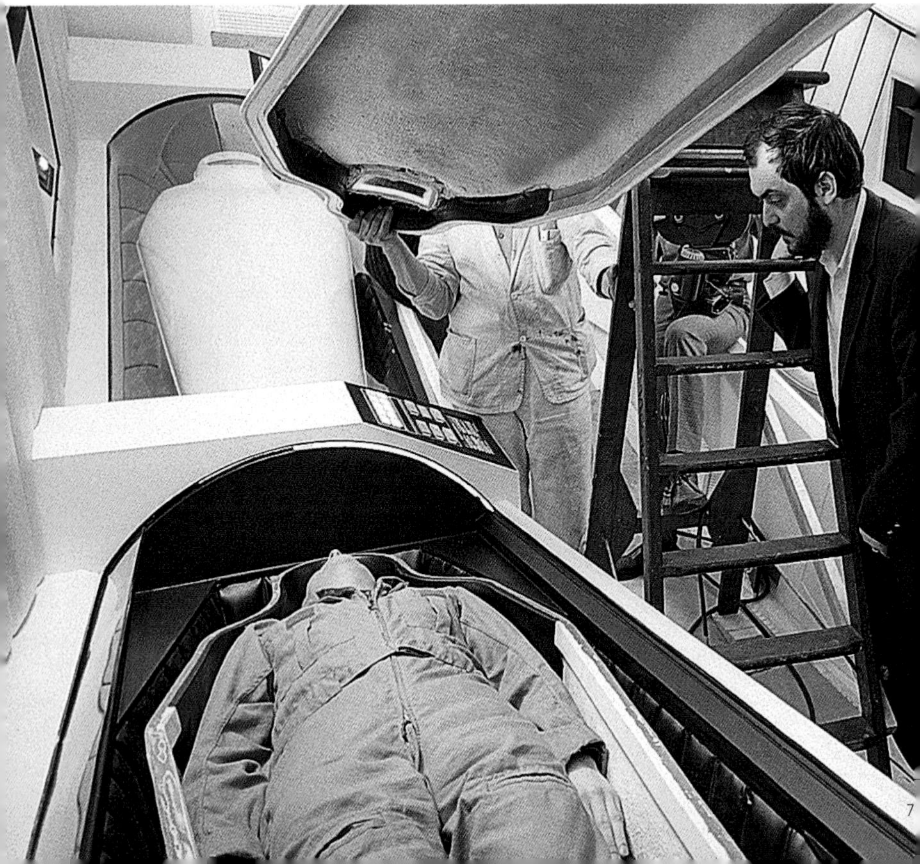

From "Facts for Editorial Reference"
(MGM publicity brochure, 1968)

2001: A Space Odyssey is above all a work of fiction—an epic adventure of the future encompassing all of the qualities that distinguish the most memorable motion pictures. The events in *2001*, how they happen, and the means by which they are accomplished appear as breathtaking fantasy when viewed through 1968 eyes. Yet it is in no sense a contradiction to say that *2001: A Space Odyssey* is equally a work of fact. Indeed, much of the excitement that unfolds on the Cinerama screen must be credited to the years of careful, intense preparation and research in the fields of aerospace technology, astronautics, biology, and cybernetics and astronomy by producer/director Stanley Kubrick and, in a sense, a lifetime of preparation by screenplay co-author Arthur C. Clarke. Everything in *2001: A Space Odyssey* can happen within the next three decades, and, in the opinion of the majority of the world's leading space authorities, most of the picture will happen by the beginning of the next millennium.

The world of the future in *2001: A Space Odyssey* begins in the present. And it begins on Earth. Right now, seven organizations, comprising major industrial firms, the United States Air Force, foundations, and universities, are spending more than $23 million a year for the sole purpose of prophesying the future. Knowing that technology has increased at a vastly accelerated pace in the past fifty years—we learned more in the past ten years than we did in the previous ten thousand—men in business, science, and education realize they must look a minimum of twenty years ahead as a matter of simple survival.

Their collective vision of life in the United States and the world at the turn of the millennium is overwhelmingly optimistic—fish bred and herded on ocean "farms"; crops of kelp and seaweed harvested and regenerated into nourishing food that could be made to taste like any natural food we choose—either of which could support a world population more than four times as large as the most pessimistic population forecasters predict will exist in the year 2000. The entire electrical requirements of the United States can be met by as few as a dozen nuclear generating stations located throughout the country.

Earthly transportation will include travel by ballistic rocket reducing the trip to any place on the globe to less than an hour. Household robots will perform most of the mundane chores that now bore a housewife, while she does her supermarket shopping by picture phone. The world of medicine will bear little resemblance to that of 1968; cancer, senility, mentally retarded children will no longer exist and artificial organs will be readily available.

These, then, are merely a few of the—not possibilities—but probabilities of Earthly life three short decades from now in the opinion of literally hundreds of hard-headed specialists and authorities in dozens of fields and professions.

In the same way that this futuristic vision of life on Earth is solidly grounded in

77 ***An actor lies in one of the hibernation chambers.***

present-day fact, the events of *2001: A Space Odyssey*, and the means by which these events happen, represent logical and highly realistic projections of current space technology:

1. Screen Fiction: Deep in space, a stewardess strolls down the aisle of a commercial spaceliner carrying a tray of food. Suddenly she turns and effortlessly walks up the wall, across the top of the spacecraft and passes through a doorway—completely "upside down."

Science Fact: Commercial space flights in the year 2001 will be making regular scheduled trips between Earth and the Moon. They will be spacious, luxurious craft with all of the comforts available in present-day airliners. One striking difference will be the complete absence of gravity. Although the interior of the craft is pressurized and has a breathable atmosphere permitting normal dress, one normal step in zero gravity would propel the stewardess into the air with no control over her movements. The simple solution to the problem is Velcro, an adhesive material which when attached to both the soles of the shoes and floor of the spacecraft permits near normal movement. In June 1966, United States astronaut Eugene Cernan left his space capsule to make his now famous space walk. He controlled his movements two hundred miles above the Earth by placing Velcro lined gloves against strips of Velcro on the outside of his Gemini 9 capsule.

"We are getting magnificent shots but everything is like a 106-move chess game with two adjournments."

—SK in a letter to Arthur C. Clarke, January 7, 1967

2. Screen Fiction: Mission Commander Dave Bowman (Keir Dullea), without his complete space suit and its life-giving oxygen and pressure systems, makes an emergency transfer from one spacecraft through the vacuum of outer space into a second space vehicle.

Science Fact: Until recently it has been generally believed that a human could not exist for any length of time in a complete vacuum. However, recent United States Air Force experiments have destroyed the myth of exploding astronauts. When chimpanzees and dogs were exposed to a vacuum for periods of up to two minutes, all of the animals survived without ill effects. In *2001* astronaut Bowman completes his transfer between the two vehicles in ten seconds, which is far from the apparent limit of human endurance under such conditions.

3. Screen Fiction: Throughout the nine-month journey toward Jupiter, three of the five crew members are kept in a state of complete artificial hibernation.

Science Fact: One of the many authorities consulted is Dr. Ormond G. Mitchell, professor of anatomy at New York University Medical Center, and one of the world's leading authorities on the subject of artificially induced hibernation. Dr. Mitchell's studies, conducted partially under a National Science Foundation grant, have led him to the firm conclusion that induced hibernation of humans for long periods of time is not only completely feasible but imminent.

4. Screen Fiction: HAL 9000 is an ultra-intelligent computer—a machine so sophisticated that it could only be manufactured by the computer that precedes it. HAL 9000 controls all systems aboard the interplanetary spaceship *Discovery*—it plots and maintains the ship's course, monitors the condition of all the *Discovery*'s thousands of working parts and automatically performs a multitude of additional functions. At the same time HAL 9000 can converse fluently with the human astronauts—which also means he can hear. HAL can see. With electronic "eyes" located throughout the spacecraft, nothing escapes his attention. HAL can think—literally. In fact, HAL 9000 is capable of emotional responses indistinguishable from those displayed by humans.

Science Fact: Computers are in their infancy. And yet after only twelve years of existence, these electronic "Model A's" are already exceeding the ability of humans in the performance of many functions formerly performed by man. According to Dr. Marvin Minsky, Professor of Mathematics at M. I. T., "... in thirty years we should have machines whose intelligence is comparable to man's. I think that when we get a machine as intelligent as humans, I feel quite sure that it will behave in every way as though it were conscious. By 2001, it should be very easy to make computers which appear to understand you and appear to converse with you." Dr. John Good of Trinity College, Cambridge, who also consulted with Stanley Kubrick, believes "... ultra-intelligent computers will be constructed within about the next thirty years ... and by an ultra-intelligent machine, I mean a machine that is capable of performing every intellectual activity somewhat better than any man."

Will this, then, be what life on this planet will be like a short thirty years from now? Most of us will see for ourselves. For it is also fact that: MOST OF THE PEOPLE NOW ALIVE ON THIS PLANET COULD LIVE TO SEE THE YEAR 2001!

78 ***Kubrick and production designer Tony Masters inside HAL's logic center.***

Music in *2001: A Space Odyssey*

by Gene D. Phillips

The opening image of *2001: A Space Odyssey* shows the Earth, moon, and sun in vertical alignment against a black sky. This shot is accompanied by the crashing opening chords of Richard Strauss's *Also Sprach Zarathustra*. Friedrich Nietzsche, the 19th-century philosopher, wrote the narrative fable that inspired Strauss's symphonic poem of the same name; in Nietzsche's fable, a 6th-century BCE Persian philosopher named Zoroaster (Zarathustra, in German) serves as a mouthpiece for Nietzsche: he propounds Nietzsche's theory of the superman—a heroic, life-affirming figure who aspires to greatness. In the course of his treatise, Nietzsche reflects that the distance between the ape and man is comparable to that between man and the superman. This remark is associated with the first episode in *2001*.

"It's simply an observable fact," Kubrick has said, "that all man's technology grew out of his discovery of the tool-weapon. There's no doubt that there is a deep emotional relationship between man and his machine-weapons, which are his children. The machine is beginning to assert itself in a very profound way, even attracting affection and obsession. Man has always worshiped beauty, and I think there's a new kind of beauty in the world."[1]

That beauty is marvelously evident in the first sequence in space, in which Space Station 5, which resembles a revolving Ferris wheel, spins gracefully on its way, orbiting two hundred miles above the Earth to the strains of *The Blue Danube* waltz. "It's hard to find anything much better than *The Blue Danube*," Kubrick comments, "for depicting grace and beauty in turning. It also gets about as far away as you can get from the cliché of space music."[2] As for the familiarity of Strauss's waltz, David Wishart responds that "*The Blue Danube* is a musical foray so familiar and so comfortable," that its "inherent gloriousness allays the piece from descending into the realms of Muzak" (the sort of music heard in elevators).[3] In addition, "the brilliant idea of using *The Blue Danube* not only invokes the music of the spheres with a deliciously buoyant humor," maintains Michel Ciment, "but adds a dash of Kubrick's characteristic nostalgia for a period when Johann Strauss's melody cradled revelers on board the Big Wheel in Vienna's Prater."[4]

As spaceship *Orion* docks at Space Station 5, which is a kind of "halfway house" for passengers on their way to the moon, a stewardess speaks the first words to be heard in the film, some thirty minutes after it has begun: "Here you are, sir. Main level, please." "See you on the way back," replies Dr. Heywood Floyd (William Sylvester). This is a fair sampling of the sparse, perfunctory type of dialogue that is used in the film. When some critics opined that the film needed more dialogue, Kubrick replied that he had tried to work things out so that anything important in the movie was transmitted through action rather than in dialogue scenes, which account for only forty-six minutes of the film's 139-minute running time. "There are certain areas of feeling and reality," Kubrick told *The New York Times*, "which are notably inaccessible to words. Non-verbal forms of expression such as music and painting can get at these

79 ***Kubrick cues up a track in his control booth for the scene of Poole (Gary Lockwood) jogging in the centrifuge.***

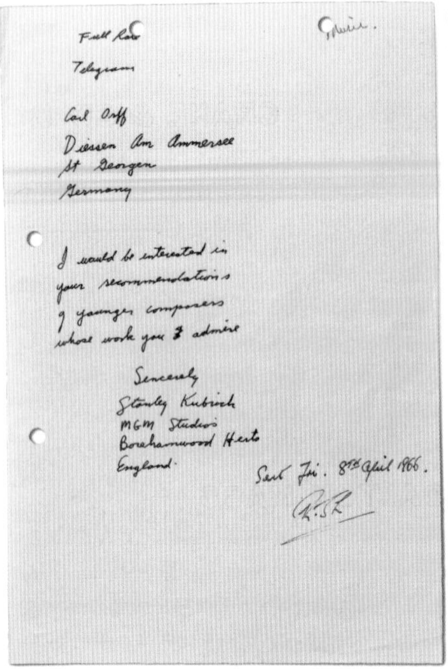

Full Rate

Telegram

Carl Orff
Diessen Am Ammersee
St Georgen
Germany

I would be interested in your recommendations of younger composers whose work you admire

Sincerely
Stanley Kubrick
MGM Studios
Borehamwood Herts
England.

Sent Fri. 8th April 1966.

Music.

80

areas, but words are a terrible straitjacket. It's interesting how many prisoners of that straitjacket resent its being loosened."[5]

There is a direct connection between the opening stanzas of Strauss's *Also Sprach Zarathustra* and the early scenes of Kubrick's film, states David Wishart: "Strauss's tone poem commences as does *2001*, with a sunrise—and the concept of a new dawn informs Kubrick's treatise; the film pivots on a series of dawnings, of new beginnings, of fresh enlightenments." Moreover, Strauss's opening motif, an ascending series of three notes (C-G-C), is known as the "World Riddle" theme, an especially appropriate introduction "for a labyrinthine film infused with mystery and enigma."[6] The opening chords of *Also Sprach Zarathustra* resonate on the soundtrack for the last time at the close of the movie, as the fetus of the Star Child floats through space, staring out at us, a look of wide-eyed expectation on its face. Michel Ciment affirms, "*2001* postulates the same progression as in Nietzsche's work, from ape to man, then from man to the Superman."[7]

During the long months of production, Kubrick had relied on temporary tracks of classical music to provide the proper atmosphere for the scenes that he was working on. When it came time to have a composer provide a background score for the film, Kubrick chose Alex North to write the underscore for the movie.

North had received an Academy Award nomination for *Spartacus* and subsequently composed the score for another Roman epic, *Cleopatra* (1963), for Joseph Mankiewicz. In December 1967, Kubrick phoned North with an offer to create the music for his science-fiction film *2001*. Kubrick pointed out that North would have to compose the score for the film without seeing a complete rough cut of the finished picture, because the complicated special effects would not be completed until the end of post-production. He told North to get started by creating a waltz to accompany scenes of spaceships in flight.

North flew to London, where the film was being made, and spent two days with Kubrick, who played the temporary music tracks he had used during the initial phase of editing the film, including works by Johann Strauss, Jr., Richard Strauss, and Aram Khatchaturian. Andrew Birkin, who worked on the special effects for the film,

80 ***Letter from Kubrick to composer Carl Orff.***

recalls that he played a recording of Strauss's *The Blue Danube* while he was screening some special effects footage with Kubrick. The director suddenly turned to him with a gleam in his eye and said, "Wait a minute. Could we actually use this for real? Am I crazy, or would this be a stroke of genius?" Birkin states that that was the first time Kubrick ever mentioned the possibility of retaining the temporary tracks for the movie's actual musical score on the sound track.[8]

As North recalls, "Kubrick was direct and honest with me concerning his desire to retain some of the 'temporary' music tracks which he had been using.... But I couldn't accept the idea of composing part of the score interpolated with other composers. I felt I could compose music that had the ingredients and essence of what Kubrick wanted and give it a consistency and homogeneity and contemporary feel."[9] North returned to London on December 24, 1967, to start work for recording his score on January 1, after having viewed and discussed with Kubrick the first hour of film for scoring. Kubrick arranged an apartment for him in Chelsea, on the banks of the Thames, and furnished him with a record player, tape machine, and the like.

North composed and recorded more than forty minutes of music in just two weeks, and then waited for the opportunity to look at the balance of the film and spot places for additional music. Kubrick even suggested over the phone certain emendations that could be made for a subsequent recording session. "After eleven tense days of waiting to see more film, in order to record in early February, I received word from Kubrick that no more score was necessary." Kubrick ultimately decided not to use any of North's score. "Well, what can I say? It was a great, frustrating experience," North concluded. He deemed the pre-recorded music of mostly classical composers that Kubrick had utilized on the soundtrack was "just not in keeping with the brilliant concept" of Kubrick's film.[10]

"Christiane heard a marvellous piece of music on the BBC, Requiem by Ligeti.... Christiane says that she thinks it would be marvellous for the film.... I would like you to find out how to get in touch with the composer in the event that Christiane is right and that the music is as marvellous as she says it is."

—SK in a letter to Jan Harlan, August 21, 1967

Because aficionados of North's music have vehemently protested Kubrick's scuttling North's score, Kubrick set the record straight in talking to Michel Ciment: "Why use music which is less good when there is such a multitude of great orchestral music available from the past and from our own time? When you're editing a film, it's very helpful to be able to try out different pieces of music to see how they work with the scene. When I had completed the editing of *2001: A Space Odyssey*, I had laid in temporary music tracks for almost all of the music that was eventually used in the film. Then, in the normal way, I engaged the services of a distinguished film composer to write the score. Although

(Alex North) and I went over the picture very carefully, and he listened to these temporary tracks... and agreed that they worked fine and would serve as a guide for the musical objectives of each sequence, he, nevertheless, wrote and recorded a score which could not have been more alien to the music we had listened to, and much more serious than that, a score which, in my opinion, was completely inadequate for the film."[11]

In 1993, North's score was issued by Varèse Sarabande in a recording by the National Philharmonic Orchestra, conducted by film composer Jerry Goldsmith. When one listens to the actual film score for *2001* alongside North's unused underscore, it is difficult to see how North's music would have been an improvement on the background music that Kubrick finally chose for the film. *The Blue Danube*, as used in the film, expresses the order and harmony of the universe, and possesses a flow and tranquility lacking in North's waltz for the same scene. While *Also Sprach Zarathustra* is awesome and fraught with foreboding brass statements that are overwhelmed by thunderous tympani, North's score employs brass and percussion and even chimes in a spirited theme that implies jubilation.

81 ***"We had a ping-pong table and a piano and a shower in the* Discovery*, but in the end they didn't seem worth putting into the film; one tries to tighten up wherever possible." –SK/1970 (to Jerome Agel)***
82 ***Kubrick used "temporary music" on the set during shooting.***

Frank Miller extols Kubrick for being the first film director "to create a best-selling score entirely pasted together from the classical canon."[12] The popularity of the recording of soundtrack music from *2001* makes it clear that the music chosen by Kubrick did catch the imagination of filmgoers. Indeed, Strauss's *Also Sprach Zarathustra* in particular has become as closely associated with *2001* as Rossini's *William Tell* Overture has with the Lone Ranger and the "Colonel Bogey" march has with *The Bridge on the River Kwai.*

Notes

1. Gene D. Phillips, *Major Film Directors of the American and British Cinema*, rev. ed. (Cranbury, N.J.: Associated University Presses, 1999): 134.
2. Gene D. Phillips, "Johann Strauss, Jr.," in *The Encyclopedia of Stanley Kubrick*, with Rodney Hill (New York: Checkmark, 2002): 360.
3. David Wishart, CD liner notes from *Music from the Films of Stanley Kubrick*, (New York: Silva Screen Records, 1999): 3.
4. Michel Ciment, *Kubrick: The Definitive Edition* (New York: Faber and Faber, 2001): 131.
5. William Kloman, "In 2001 Will Love be a Seven-Letter Word?" *The New York Times*, April 1, 1968, sec. 2:15.
6. Wishart, *Music from the Films of Stanley Kubrick*: 3.
7. Ciment: 128.
8. Gene D. Phillips, "Alex North," in *The Encyclopedia of Stanley Kubrick*: 268.
9. John Baxter, *Stanley Kubrick: A Biography* (New York: Carroll and Graf, 1997): 227.
10. Phillips, "Alex North": 268–69.
11. Ciment: 177.
12. Frank Miller, *Movies We Love: Classic Films* (Atlanta: Turner, 1996): 106.

82

Interpretations of *2001: A Space Odyssey*

by Margaret Stackhouse

Fifteen-year-old Margaret Stackhouse was a sophomore at North Plainfield High School in New Jersey when she wrote her reflections on 2001 *soon after the release of the film. Her teacher forwarded her text to Stanley Kubrick, who told Jerome Agel, "Margaret Stackhouse's speculations on the film are perhaps the most intelligent that I've read anywhere, and I am, of course, including all the reviews and the articles that have appeared on the film and many hundreds of letters that I have received. What a first-rate intelligence!" (Jerome Agel,* The Making of Kubrick's 2001, *New York: Signet, 1970)*

. **The monolith**—source of infinite knowledge and intelligence

A. Perfection represented in its shape; its color—black—could symbolize:

1. Evil and death, which result from man's misuse of knowledge;
2. The *incomprehensible*—man, with his limited senses, cannot comprehend the absence (perfect black) of color or light.

B. Its first appearance.

1. Movie implies that life has reached the stage when it is ready for inspiration, a divine gift, perhaps. (It is interesting that the apes are expectant, waiting for something.)
2. Maybe apes become men when this inspiration is given. (Question: Is man really a separate entity, with something (soul?) that no other form of life possesses, or is the difference merely in quantity (rather than quality) of intelligence? Is the evolution gradual and continuous or in defined levels? Does the difference in quantity become in fact this difference in quality?)
3. Inspiration is given:
   a. When men (apes) need it; or,
   b. When they seek it; or,
   c. At the whim of the force giving the gift; or,
   d. In various combinations of these three.
4. The purpose of the gift may be to allow man to create life-sustaining forces. (In this "cycle," he creates only death; interesting—death from death (bones).)
5. Its disappearance (after weapon is made)—Reasons:
   a. It is taken away in punishment for misuse of knowledge; or,
   b. It is no longer sought—apes (men) consider themselves masters now and try to continue on their own energies after the initial impulse. Maybe the monolith is always present, but is invisible to those who don't wish to see it or to whom it does not wish to be visible; or,
   c. It is taken away by the force that gave it, to prevent mortal understanding of everything.

C. Its second appearance (on Moon).

1. Reasons for appearance:
   a. Man is subconsciously seeking it again; or,
   b. It is needed to remind him of his insignificance; or,
   c. It is given as a new opportunity to create a meaningful existence for humanity.

83 ***Kubrick gives directions for the hotel bathroom scene.***

2. Men on Moon touch monolith in the same way that the apes did—this indicates no basic change in man's nature. Then, after touching it, they have the audacity to try to take photos—still conceited, still lacking in understanding of the gift.
3. From Moon, there is a strong magnetic field directed toward Jupiter (this is where man will go next). This indicates that man will still fail and will need monolith again when he reaches the next stage of exploration. Monolith is always beyond human scope—man is still reaching at death.
4. It is ironic that men on Moon believe that the monolith was made by a more advanced civilization. This to them is the ultimate—they can't comprehend that anything could be above the mortal level.

D. The monolith and infinity.
1. After HAL is made, man shows that once again he has refused, through ignorance and conceit, to take advantage of the chance to obtain superhuman intelligence. Maybe the system is slowing down and it is impossible for man to progress any further on his own energies.
2. Now he is given another chance—the monolith shows him infinity, perfect knowledge, and the beginning of the universe, but he can't comprehend it. Reasons for his being shown all this:
   a. It may be truly another chance for man; or,
   b. It may already be determined that he must die (maybe all people are shown perfect knowledge at death); or,
   c. Maybe perfect knowledge (represented by monolith) is always present, but our understanding of it will always be imperfect.

II. HAL

A. He is evil, but only because he reflects human nature.
B. His uneasiness about the mission implies that even the highest development of human intelligence is imperfect in ability to understand.
C. Man, trying to progress independently of divine aid, attempts, either consciously or unconsciously, to create life, in the form of HAL. This is not allowed. Man is reaching, or is being forced to reach, a limit in his ability to progress further.
D. Reasons for HAL's failure:
1. Eternal human error once again in evidence; or,
2. This may be a divine punishment; or,
3. God will not allow man to become subordinate to his own foolish creations.

E. The fact that man can overcome HAL's evil is optimistic; however, to do this he must destroy HAL, who is nearly a living being—again, the theme of death, futility. (This and triviality are shown in HAL's "song.")

III. The room (at end)

A. It is elegant, maybe to show man's cultural achievements, but it is sterile and silent—nothing has meaning without the spirit of the monolith. This is man's

84 ***Keir Dullea as the aging Bowman.***
85 ***The replica hotel bedroom.***

84

85

universe, that with which he is supposedly familiar, but even this is hostile to him.

B. Room could represent:
   1. All that man can comprehend (finite) of infinity. Even in this limited scope, he is confused; or,
   2. Man's cultural history, as men remember their past before they die; or,
   3. The trivia for which he relinquished the monolith (then at death he realizes his need for it); or,
   4. A reminder of man's failure to draw on past—it could contain more wisdom than the present. (Monkeys responded to the monolith better than modern man—race is slowly degenerating.)

C. In this room, man must die, because:
   1. He has reached his limit; or,
   2. He has failed too much; or,
   3. He has been shown infinity.

D. Question: Is his death (following degeneration) inevitable after being shown all knowledge, or is this experience still another chance to improve? Then, when man returns to trivia, perhaps this is the breaking point, the end of his opportunities.

E. Maybe he knows what is happening to him but is powerless to change it. The changes in the man may be a vision shown to him as punishment, or they may merely represent the various stages in the life of one man or of all men.

IV. The themes

A. Animalism and human failure
   1. Throughout picture, there is constant eating, made to appear revolting; also, exercising, wrestling.
   2. At end, goblet is broken. This may imply that man's failures will continue forever.
   3. Animal nature and conceit remain the same throughout. Will there never be any true progress? The monolith is always shown with sunrise and crescent. When first seen, this is a sign of hope, of a beginning; but the sun is never any higher except when man is shown infinity. This last fact may symbolize hope that, despite all his past failures, man will ultimately rise above animalism; or it may merely represent the perfect knowledge he cannot comprehend.
   4. There is a delicate balance between the animal and divine nature in man. We will never be permitted to go beyond a certain point (as individual and as a race).

B. Futility
   1. It is shown:
      a. In the rescue and subsequent release of Frank (after the struggle to catch him);
      b. In the meaningless talk—"People talking without speaking."
   2. Is all that we do in vain? Each person certainly dies without attaining all understanding. Will our race (history) also terminate and begin again, continually, with no progress ever made?

C. Whether the movie is terribly pessimistic or optimistic depends on the answer to the question, "Does the man at the end represent just our 'cycle' or all 'cycles' for eternity?"
   1. Pessimistic: Man may never become more "divine"—all chances for rebirth may be merely a mockery. Irony—no

matter how much man ruins his life, chances for improvement are always given. Since he will probably continue ruining his life for eternity, this may be the cruel tantalizing by some capricious god.

2. Optimistic: The preceding is impossible to believe if one assumes that there is some life-giving, life-sustaining force in the universe that is the source of absolute good. With this belief, one can hope that someday man will be able to use the divine inspiration offered him to propagate life-sustaining forces. Probably he will never be able to understand more, but he will use his understanding better. The sunrise, fetus, etc., seem to indicate this hope. Also, it seems that, despite human stupidity, new opportunities to become sublime are always given. Someday, perhaps, man will learn that he cannot truly "live" unless he accepts the gift, in the form of the monolith, that demands human subjugation to a divine force. Then he will not be required to create, and to experience, only death.

86–97 ***Panoramic photos taken by Kubrick with his prized Widelux camera.*** 86 ***shows a children's painting class on the moon base that was cut from the film.***

86

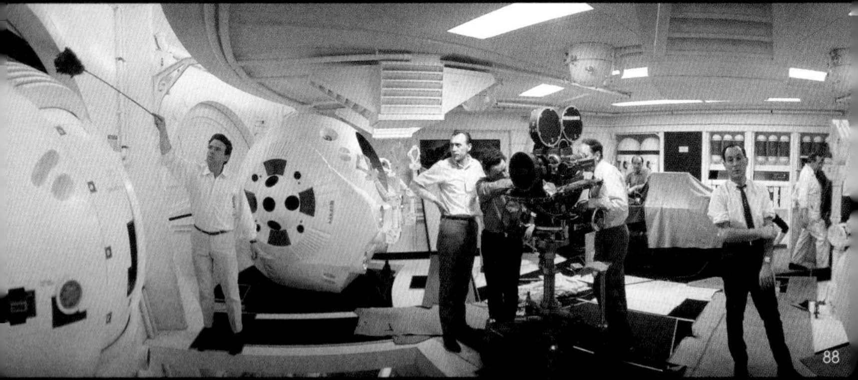

88

90

87

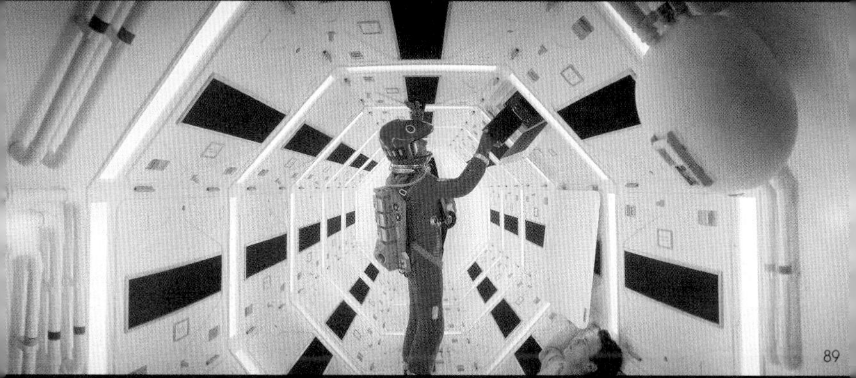
89

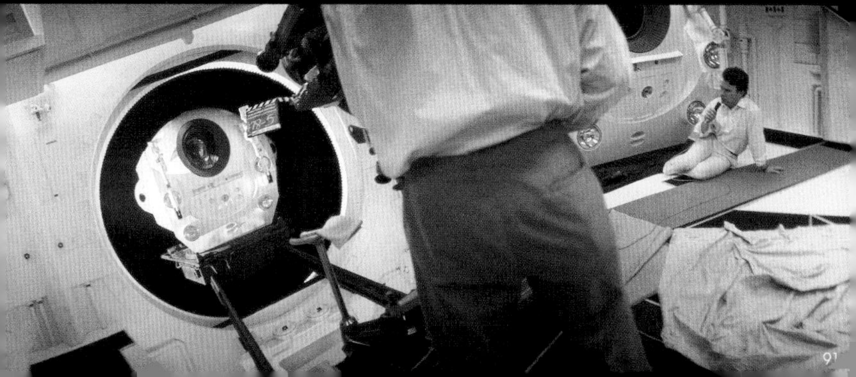
91

92

94

96

93

95

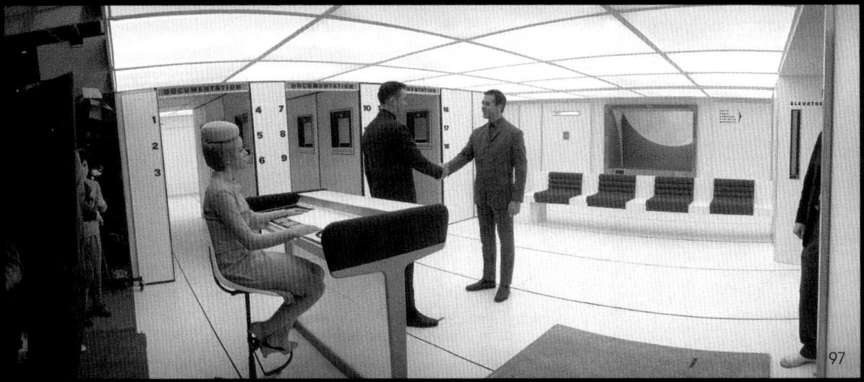

97

A Clockwork Orange

1971 / COLOR / 137 MINUTES
Distributed by WARNER BROS.

CAST
ALEX MALCOLM MCDOWELL
MR. ALEXANDER PATRICK MAGEE
DIM WARREN CLARKE
GEORGIE JAMES MARCUS
DELTOID AUBREY MORRIS
PRISON CHAPLAIN GODFREY QUIGLEY
MINISTER OF THE INTERIOR
ANTHONY SHARP
CHIEF GUARD MICHAEL BATES
DAD PHILIP STONE
MUM SHEILA RAYNOR
BILLY BOY RICHARD CONNAUGHT
MRS. ALEXANDER ADRIENNE CORRI
DR. BRODSKY CARL DUERING
PRISON GOVERNOR MICHAEL GOVER
CATLADY MIRIAM KARLIN
TOM STEVEN BERKOFF
TRAMP PAUL FARRELL
DR. BRANOM MADGE RYAN
CONSPIRATOR JOHN SAVIDENT
CONSPIRATOR MARGARET TYZACK
PSYCHIATRIST PAULINE TAYLOR
PETE MICHAEL TARN
LODGER CLIVE FRANCIS
STAGE ACTOR JOHN CLIVE

CREW
PRODUCED AND DIRECTED BY
STANLEY KUBRICK
SCREENPLAY STANLEY KUBRICK
(based on the novel by Anthony Burgess)
EXECUTIVE PRODUCERS
MAX L. RAAB and SI LITVINOFF
ASSOCIATE PRODUCER BERNARD WILLIAMS
ASSISTANT TO THE PRODUCER JAN HARLAN
LIGHTING CAMERAMAN JOHN ALCOTT
PRODUCTION DESIGNER JOHN BARRY
EDITOR BILL BUTLER
SOUND EDITOR BRIAN BLAMEY
ART DIRECTORS RUSSELL HAGG,
PETER SHEILDS
COSTUME DESIGNER MILENA CANONERO
SPECIAL PAINTINGS AND SCULPTURE
HERMAN MAKKINK, CORNELIUS MAKKINK,
LIZ MOORE, CHRISTIANE KUBRICK
CASTING JIMMY LIGGAT
ASSISTANT DIRECTORS DEREK CRACKNELL,
DUSTY SYMONDS
ASSISTANT EDITORS GARY SHEPHERD,
PETER BURGESS, DAVID BEESLEY
UNIT/PRODUCTION MANAGER
EDDIE FREWIN
PRODUCTION ASSISTANT
MARGARET ADAMS
ADDITIONAL PHOTOGRAPHY
STANLEY KUBRICK

Made at Pinewood Studios, London, England, at EMI-MGM Studios, Borehamwood, Herts, England, and on location in England by Hawk Films Ltd.

Opposite *Film poster.*

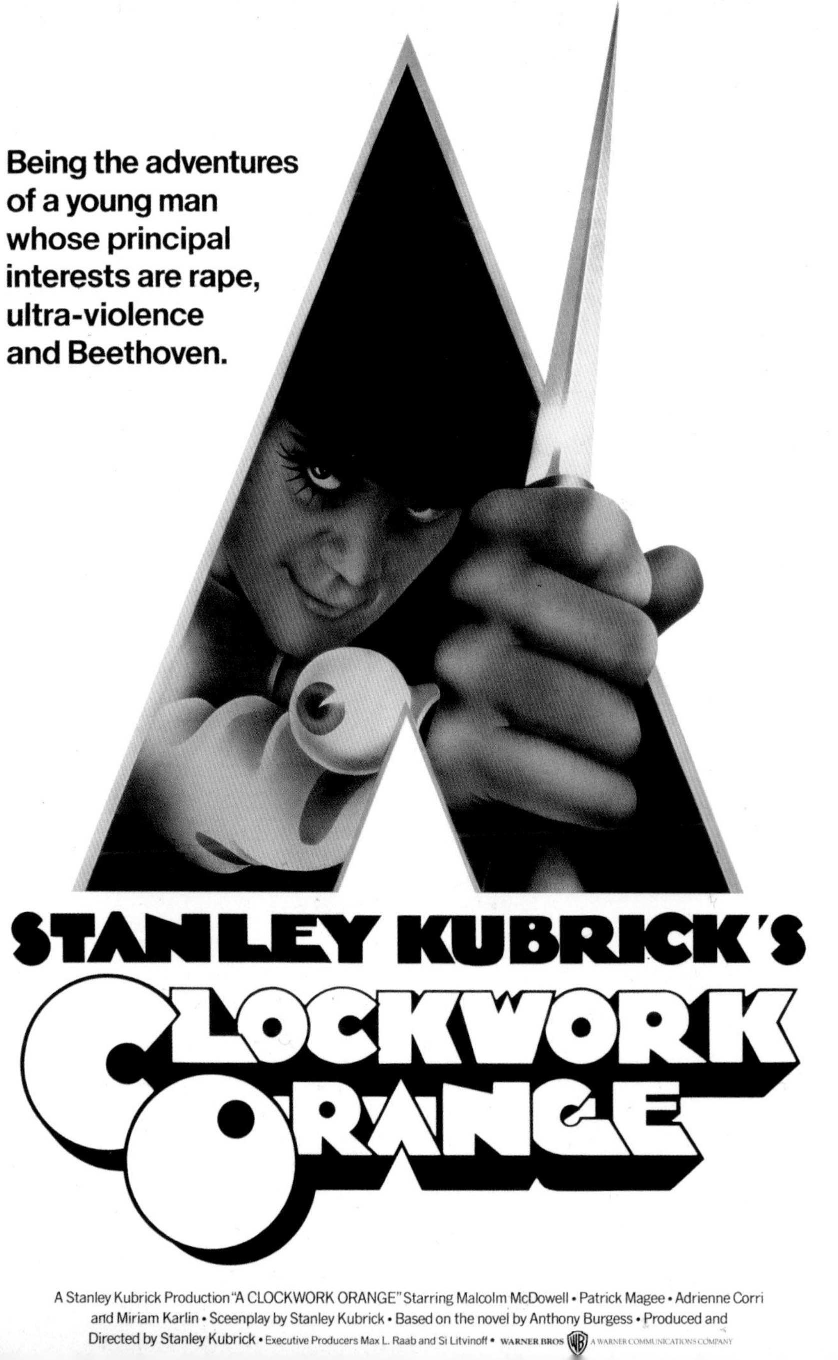
Being the adventures of a young man whose principal interests are rape, ultra-violence and Beethoven.
STANLEY KUBRICK'S
CLOCKWORK ORANGE
A Stanley Kubrick Production "A CLOCKWORK ORANGE" Starring Malcolm McDowell • Patrick Magee • Adrienne Corri and Miriam Karlin • Sceenplay by Stanley Kubrick • Based on the novel by Anthony Burgess • Produced and Directed by Stanley Kubrick • Executive Producers Max L. Raab and Si Litvinoff • WARNER BROS A WARNER COMMUNICATIONS COMPANY

A CLOCKWORK ORANGE

Moloko vellocet

Moloko vellocet

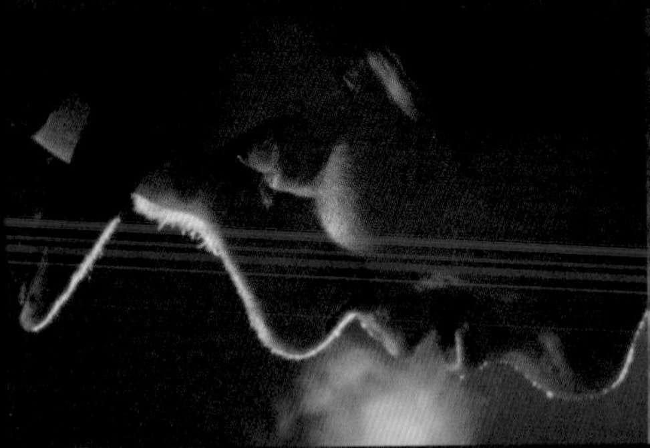

HOME
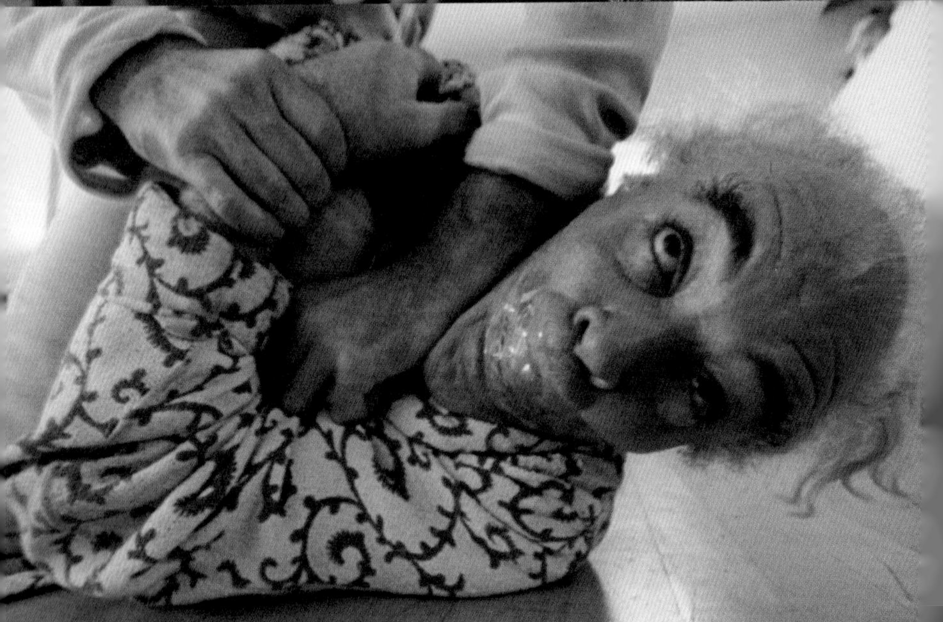

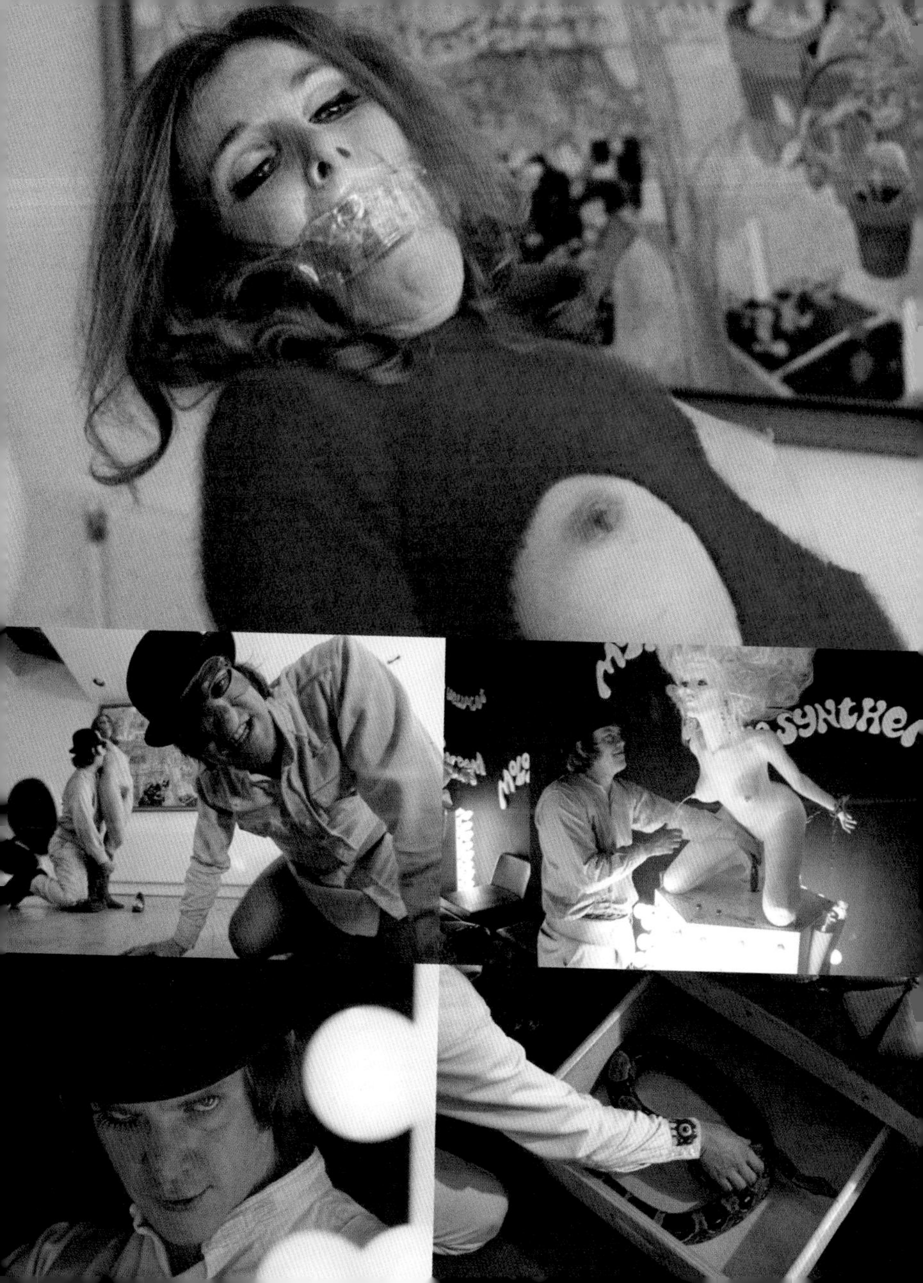

Murderer
freed: 'Science
has cure'

POLICE

STORM OVER
CRIME CURE' BOY

tors blame government
ientists for 'changing
Alex's nature'

By LOUIS CARAS
Mirror Political Editor

DOCTORS last night blamed secret laboratory experiments on criminals for causing Alex Burgess, the 'Cat-Woman Killer,' to attempt suicide.

Alex's body was found on Wednesday just two days after he had been released from jail, a "cured" man. He had undergone the Ludovico Technique.

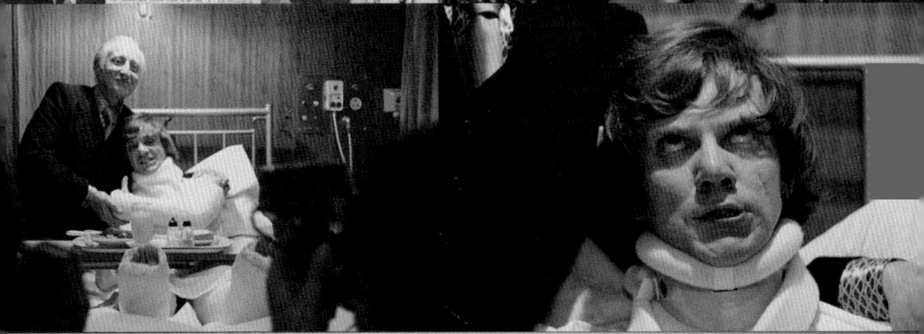

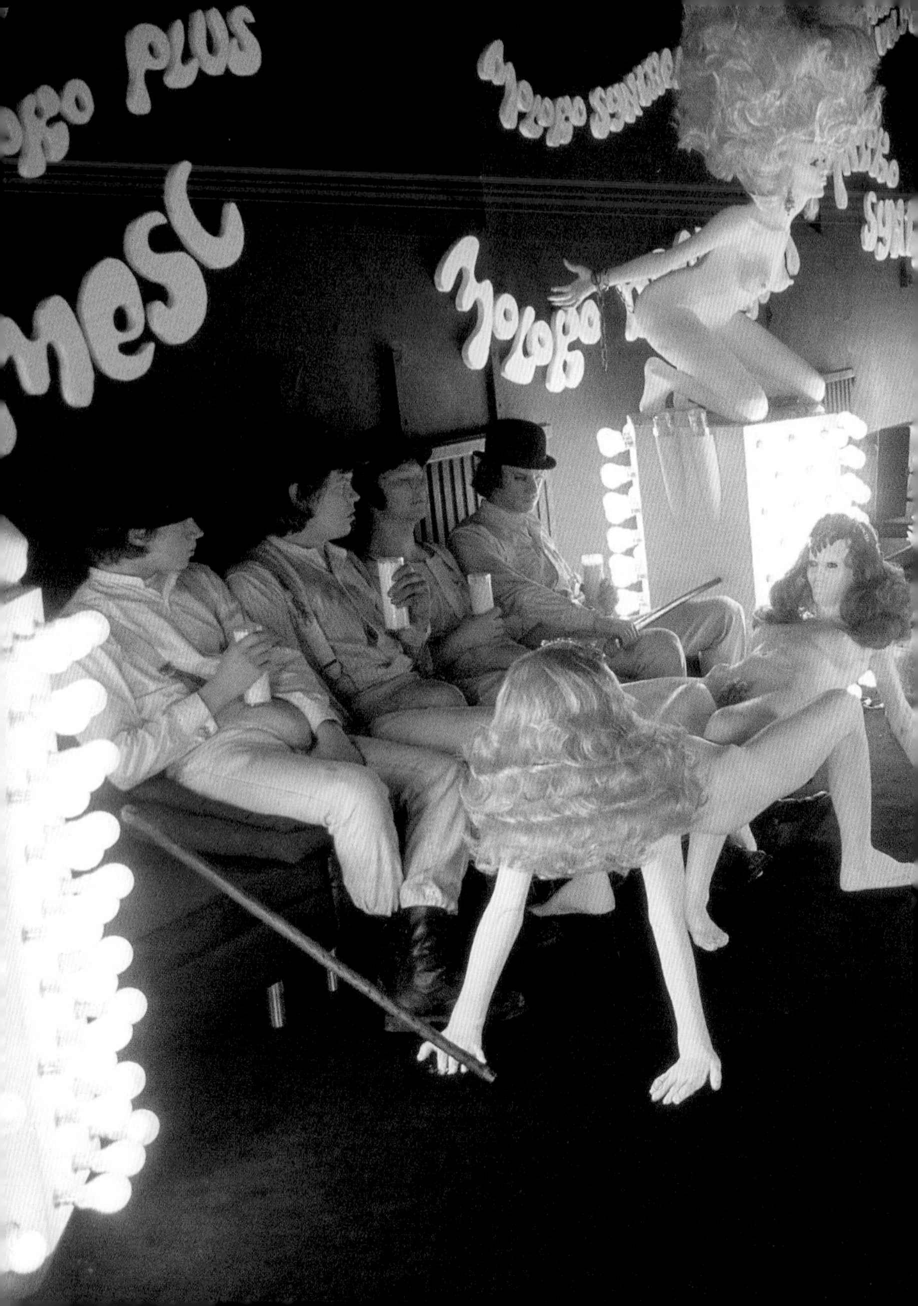
PLUS

MOLOKO VELLOCE
EXIT

A Clockwork Orange

by Michel Ciment

02

03

After finishing *2001: A Space Odyssey*, Stanley Kubrick turned to other projects, the first of which, "Napoleon," continued to obsess him for many years. To be produced—like *2001*—by MGM, it was abandoned because the major financial backing required for the production was not forthcoming; in addition, changes in MGM's management made the project even more problematic. Kubrick also gave some thought to a short novel by Arthur Schnitzler, *Rhapsody: A Dream Novel (Traumnovelle)*, whose potential had been spotted by his wife Christiane and which he brought to the screen some thirty years later as *Eyes Wide Shut*. But he was unable to develop a satisfactory screenplay for the Schnitzler and soon gave it up in favor of an Anthony Burgess novel recommended to him by his screenwriter for *Dr. Strangelove*, Terry Southern. This was *A Clockwork Orange*, on which Southern had taken out an option, adapting it for film with photographer Michael Cooper. Southern had then sold the rights to Si Litvinoff, his lawyer, and Litvinoff's partner, Max Raab. Kubrick signed a production deal with Warner Bros., with whom he was to work on all his remaining films, and bought the rights for $200,000 and a 50 percent share in all profits. "I was excited about everything about it," he said at the time, "the plot, the ideas, the characters and, of course, the language."

01 ***Kubrick mans the camera for this shot of the four droogs in the Korova Milkbar.***
02 ***Kubrick gave the film's clapboard as a gift to his parents.***
03 ***The director claps the clapboard to mark the start of a take.***

No great critical stir had greeted the publication of *A Clockwork Orange* in 1962. A difficult work for Burgess to write, it had a hideous autobiographical basis: his wife had been raped by U.S. deserters in London during World War II. The book formed part of a series of five novels written in quick succession by Burgess during a creative frenzy triggered by the discovery that he was suffering from a fatal brain tumor and had less than a year to live. In fact, he lived another twenty-five years.

This was the first film for which Kubrick wrote the screenplay single-handedly (*Barry Lyndon*, his next film, was the only other example of this). Of all the films that he made in Great Britain, these two are, paradoxically, the only ones whose cultural background is truly English. All the others, from *Lolita* to *Eyes Wide Shut*, are wholly American in both their settings and the nationality of most of their actors. The screenplays of both *A Clockwork Orange* and *Barry Lyndon* were, moreover, faithful adaptations of carefully structured narratives to which Kubrick made important but not radical changes. After working for four months—and using a computer for the first time, which enabled him to rearrange scenes digitally—he completed a first draft of the screenplay on May 15, 1970, using an unusual presentation: the action was described in the center of the page and the dialogue set out on either side. While shooting, from October 1970 to March 1971, Kubrick rewrote the dialogue extensively during long rehearsals with his actors and with Malcolm McDowell in particular.

A Clockwork Orange is set in England in the near future. The first scene takes place in the Korova Milkbar, where Alex (Malcolm McDowell) and his three *droogs*, Dim, Pete, and Georgie, imbibe hallucinatory drinks to stimulate their violent tendencies. They then attack a beggar and fight with their rivals, Billy-Boy and his gang.

"The central idea of the film has to do with the question of free-will. Do we lose our humanity if we are deprived of the choice between good and evil?"

—SK/1972 (to Michel Ciment)

Finally they raid the isolated house of a writer and politician, Mr. Alexander (Patrick Magee), raping his wife. Alex then returns home to listen to his favorite music, Beethoven's Ninth Symphony.

The next morning, while his parents are at work, Alex is visited by Deltoid, a social worker, and later has sex with two young women he meets in a record shop. Alex and his gang, of which he is the leader, invade the house of the Catlady, who manages to alert the police before Alex kills her. He is arrested and sentenced to fourteen years in prison, but after two years he agrees to undergo the "Ludovico" treatment, a form of shock therapy administered by the government in an attempt to reduce criminality. The treatment consists of showing him violent images, such as Nazi war crimes, in an attempt to condition him to react with nausea to his own violent or sexual impulses. He also develops a revulsion to Beethoven, the music played as these images are shown to him. Incapable of violence after this brainwashing, he is released from prison.

He discovers that a tenant has taken his place in his parents' house, is attacked by beggars, and is beaten up by his former *droogs* (now policemen), but is unable to retaliate. By chance, he finds refuge with Mr. Alexander, who had read about him in the newspaper. To avenge himself and embarrass the government, he pushes Alex to attempt suicide by making him listen to Beethoven's Ninth. But Alex survives and, after hospital treatment, is declared "cured" of his brainwashing. The Minister of the Interior (Anthony Sharp) offers him a lucrative job, allowing him to give free rein to his recrudescent violence. The film's last image shows Alex fantasizing that he is making love to a naked woman in the snow before a group of spectators. He crows, "I was cured all right."

In the original English edition of the novel, the last chapter finds Alex fully reintegrated into society and living a peaceful family life. Kubrick, who became aware of the extra chapter in the English edition after working on the adaptation, nevertheless chose to use the American edition's ending, which better suited his deep pessimism and biting irony.

04 ***A draft for the scene of Deltoid visiting Alex. Kubrick reordered the dialogue by giving each line a number.***

Scene 14 page 3 2.17.70

3. ~~Deltoid~~:Well, it's just a manner of speech from me to you that you watch out, little Alex, because next time, as you ~~xxxx~~ very well know, it's not going to be the corrective school anymore. Next time it's going to be the barry place and all my work ruined. If you have no consideration for ~~yourself~~ your horrible self you at least might have some for me, who have sweated over you. A big,black mark, I tell you in confidence, for everyone we dont reclaim.

2. Alex: I've been doing nothing I shouldn't , sir. The millicents have nothing on me,brother, sir I mean.

~~Deltoid: Just because the police haven't picked you up lately doesn't, as you very well know, mean you've not been up to some nastiness~~. There seems to have been a fair amount of assorted nastiness last night.

Silence

7. Deltoid:I'm warning you ~~it~~,little Alex, being a good friend to you as always, the one man in this sore and sick community who wants to save you from yourself.

8. Alex: I appreciate all that, sir, very sincerely.

~~Deltoid:Just watch it, that's all. INSERT 4~~

4. Alex: Nobody's got anything on me, sir. I've been out of the hands of the millicents for a long time now.

5. Deltoid: That's just what worries me. A bit too long of a time to be healthy. Do I make myself clear?

6. Alex : As an unmuddied lake, sir. Clear as an azure sky of deepest summer. You can rely on me, sir.

9. Alex gives him a nice, toothy smile.

Deltoid rises to go.

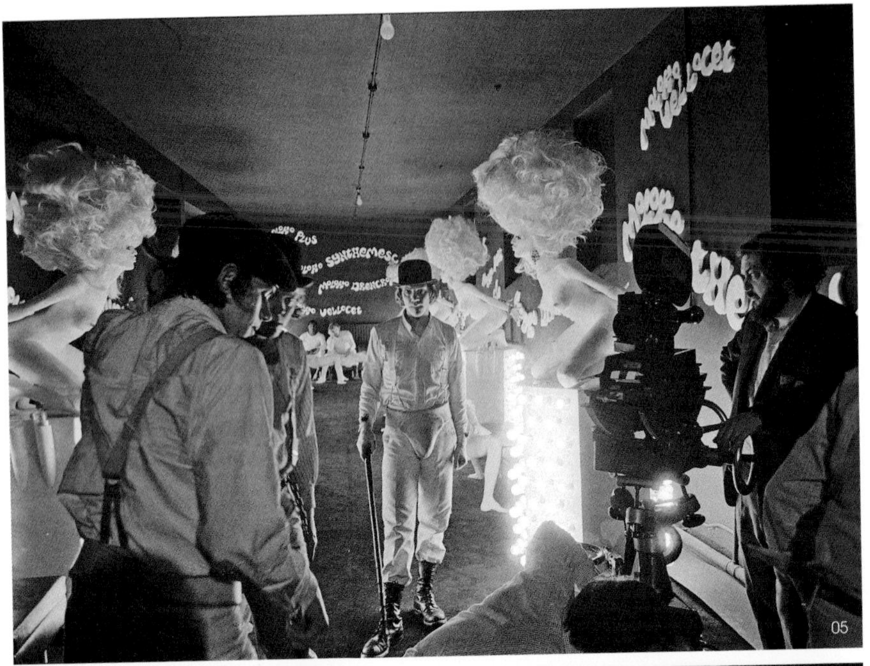

05

06

Considering the very slow, costly, and elaborate production of *2001: A Space Odyssey*, it is striking to note the small and extremely mobile crew used in *A Clockwork Orange* and the speed with which the film was made. For the first time since leaving the United States, Kubrick reverted to the methods of his earliest films, shooting for the most part in natural locations. Brunel University (later West London University) was the Ludovico medical center; the American drugstore on King's Road in Chelsea served as the location for the shopping center where Alex picks up the two young girls; the newly built Thamesmead area was used for the block of houses where Alex's parents live; South Norwood Library served as the auditorium where the press conference on Alex's treatment is held; the exterior of an Oxfordshire house was Mr. Alexander's home; and an old casino on Tagg's Island

05 ***Alex and* droogs *in the Korova Milkbar. Kubrick told* The Saturday Review, *"I had Malcolm McDowell in mind right from the third or fourth chapter of my first reading of the book. One doesn't find actors of his genius in all shapes, sizes, and ages." (to Penelope Houston, 1971)***

06 ***The director demonstrates how to serve a glass of milk-plus.***
07 ***The Milkbar under construction.***

was the setting for the gang-battle. But Kubrick was never dogmatic, and constructed three sets in a disused factory in Borehamwood near the old MGM studios: the Korova Milkbar, the admissions room of the prison, and the entrance hall of the Alexanders' house. The Alexanders' bathroom was constructed under a tent in the yard of the Oxfordshire house.

A sense of urgency and dazzling flexibility inspired the filming. Having worked as assistant and additional photographer on *2001*, John Alcott was chosen as the cinematographer, though Kubrick as usual retained absolute control of the visuals. Giving up the 70 mm of *2001*, he adopted the 35 mm 1.66:1 format in an effort to avoid the "pan and scan" technique used for television broadcast. For the long zoom pull-backs of which he was so fond, he used an aperture of f 20.1. Conversely, the widest aperture setting of f 0.95 allowed him to work with natural light until very late in the day (unlike the f 2 he had previously used). He also set up a wheelchair for the slightly elevated tight tracking shots in confined premises like the record shop visited by Alex and the prison visited by the Minister of the Interior. (This was one of his favorite stylistic techniques, much facilitated by the invention of Steadicam a few years later.) Often working with a hand-held camera—an Arriflex that cinematographer Haskell Wexler had tried out in his film *Medium Cool*—Kubrick could film within two meters of his actors and thus convey a striking impression of their physical proximity. (However, in *A Clockwork Orange* we also see Kubrick using experimental techniques rarely seen in his other films; for example, the orgy sequence was shot over twenty-eight minutes at two exposures a second, lasting a bare forty seconds on the screen, while conversely, the battle between Alex and his *droogs* was filmed in slow-motion.)

"A lot of the problems of the human condition derive from an awareness of our own mortality. This is the curse of intelligence and language. No other creature except man has to deal with it."

—SK/1972 (to Gene Siskel/*Chicago Tribune*)

The simple and straightforward techniques used for shooting were also applied to the soundtrack. Using miniature microphones worn by the actors, Kubrick recorded live sound and was a pioneer in post-production in using a new Dolby system to reduce or eliminate unwanted sounds.

A Clockwork Orange is, among Kubrick's films, the most directly linked to its period—to its fashions, anxieties, and social and political concerns; its astounding mix of realism and stylization allowed it to reflect the spirit of the times without ever becoming bogged down in naturalism.

08 ***Production designer John Barry's sketch for the milk-plus serving devices.***
09 ***Liz Moore sculpts a mannequin for the Milkbar. Kubrick told Michel Ciment, "To get the poses right for the sculptress who modeled the figures, John [Barry] photographed a nude model in as many positions as he could imagine would make a table. There are fewer positions than you might think."***

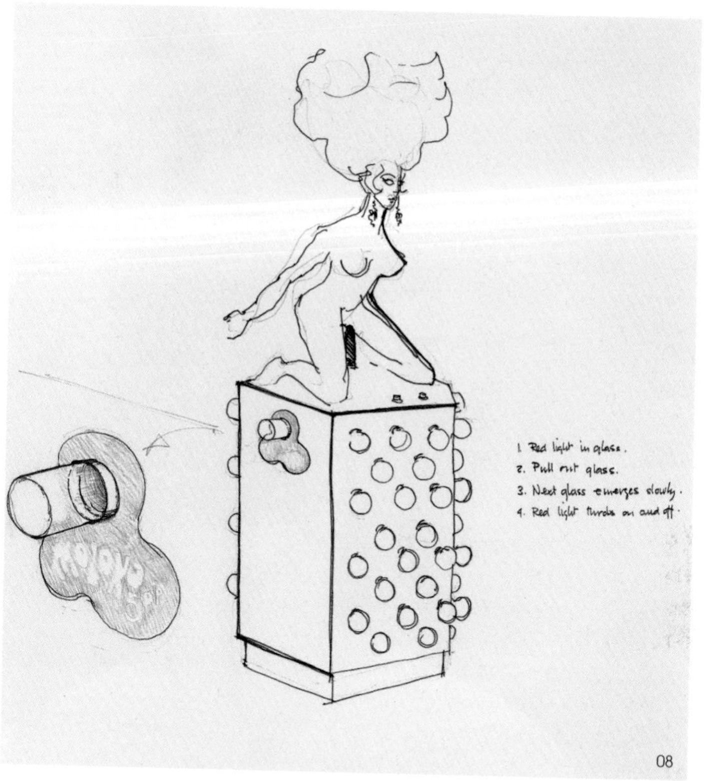
1. Red light in glass.
2. Pull out glass.
3. Next glass emerges slowly.
4. Red light throbs on and off.

08

09

10

11

12

Liz Jones, creator of the astral fetus in *2001*, collaborated with John Barry in the design of the Korova Milkbar, taking as inspiration the furniture-sculptures made by Allen Jones, featuring life-size effigies of fashion models, that Kubrick had seen in an exhibition. Two Dutch sculptors, Herman and Cornelius Makkink, created the four ceramic Christs (dancing as if in a musical comedy) that ornament Alex's room. The walls of the Alexanders' house and even those of the Catlady are decorated with contemporary paintings—including many by Christiane Kubrick, whose large canvas *Seedboxes* is clearly visible.

10–12 ***These photos of Malcolm McDowell's costume fittings were taken at Kubrick's home in Abbot's Mead.***

Similar care was invested in the costumes, notably Alex's. Working with Kubrick for the first time, Milena Canonero had the stylistic sensibility the director was looking for. The bowler hat, false eyelashes on one eye, white jump suit resembling a cricketer's uniform, and the rubber codpiece make Alex into a dandy—a parody of the elegant and sporty Englishman. They also distinguish him from the character described by Burgess, who had a crew cut and wore black tights and hobnailed boots.

Kubrick successfully appropriates Burgess's narrative through his sheer visual inventiveness, which makes the film a unique and personal creation. From this point of view, the choice of Malcolm McDowell was essential since he worked very

13 ***Michael Tarn (Pete, left) and Warren Clarke (Dim, right) model various types of hats being considered for their characters' costumes.***
14 ***During shooting of the prison chapel.***

13

actively with Kubrick on both his "look" and dialogue improvisation on the set. Kubrick had spotted McDowell in Lindsay Anderson's *If* (1968), in which he played a rebellious teenager. The two men formed a close friendship despite the fact that the filming proved very arduous for McDowell (his cornea was abraded in the scene in which a doctor administers eye-drops during the Ludovico treatment, his ribs were broken during the shooting of a public "re-education" lesson, and he was nearly drowned when his head was kept under water too long). Kubrick admired McDowell's vitality and humor, as well as the taste for extremity that he shared with Peter Sellers, Jack Nicholson, and Lee Ermey, setting him apart from another kind of actor favored by Kubrick: smooth and self-effacing types such as Keir Dullea, Ryan O'Neal, Matthew Modine, and Tom Cruise. Kubrick complemented McDowell with seasoned British stage and screen actors, a number of whom also went on to appear in *Barry Lyndon*: Patrick Magee, Philip Stone, Steven Berkoff, Godfrey Quigley, and Anthony Sharp. The scenes were created day-to-day as Kubrick improvised the action with his actors, taking as much time to rehearse as he deemed necessary.

"Although a certain amount of hypocrisy exists about it, everyone is fascinated by violence. After all, man is the most remorseless killer who ever stalked the earth."

—SK/1972 (to Paul D. Zimmermann/*Newsweek*)

He then spent six months editing, using two Steenbecks to select his shots as well as a Moviola. While making *2001*, Kubrick had discovered the possibilities afforded by existing music. Here he went further in this vein by asking the co-inventor of the Moog synthesizer, Walter Carlos (who subsequently underwent a sex-change to become Wendy Carlos), to compose electronic versions of Beethoven's Ninth, Rossini's *William Tell* Overture, and Purcell's *Music for the*

15–16 ***Malcolm McDowell sustained a corneal injury during the filming of the Ludovico treatment scene. Kubrick told*** Rolling Stone, ***"We used a piece of standard surgical equipment called a lidlock. It took courage and a local anesthetic for him to wear them. I can assure you he didn't like it at all and we never really got it finished the first time. He had to go back and face it again at the end. He had to do it. The scene wouldn't have been credible otherwise." (to Andrew Bailey, 1972) McDowell said recently, "Hey, listen, anything for art. Look what he did to my eyes." (interviewed for*** A Life in Pictures, ***2001)***

17 ***Kubrick films the reporters and the plastered legs of a stand-in.***

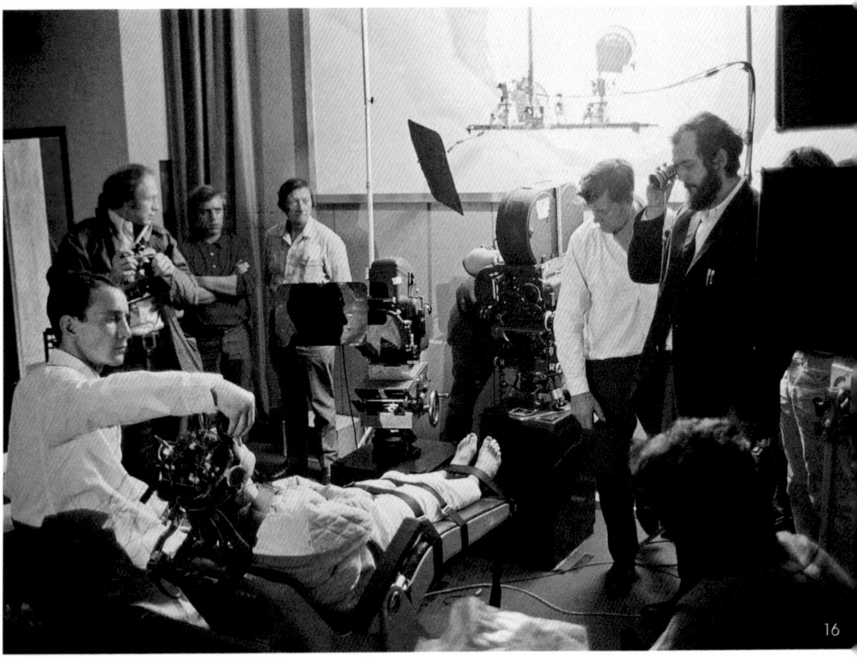

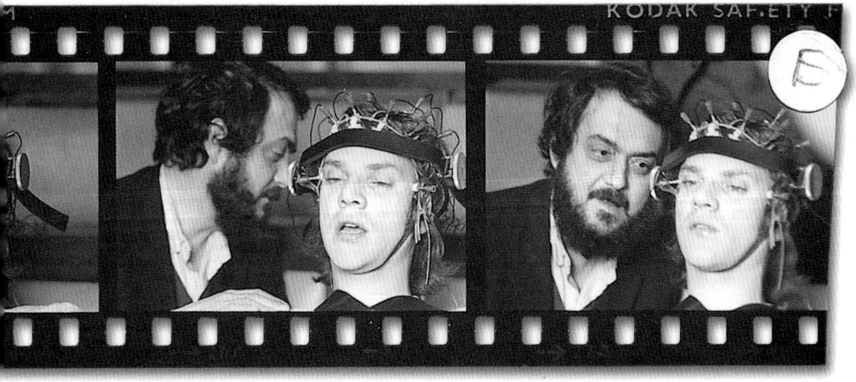

15

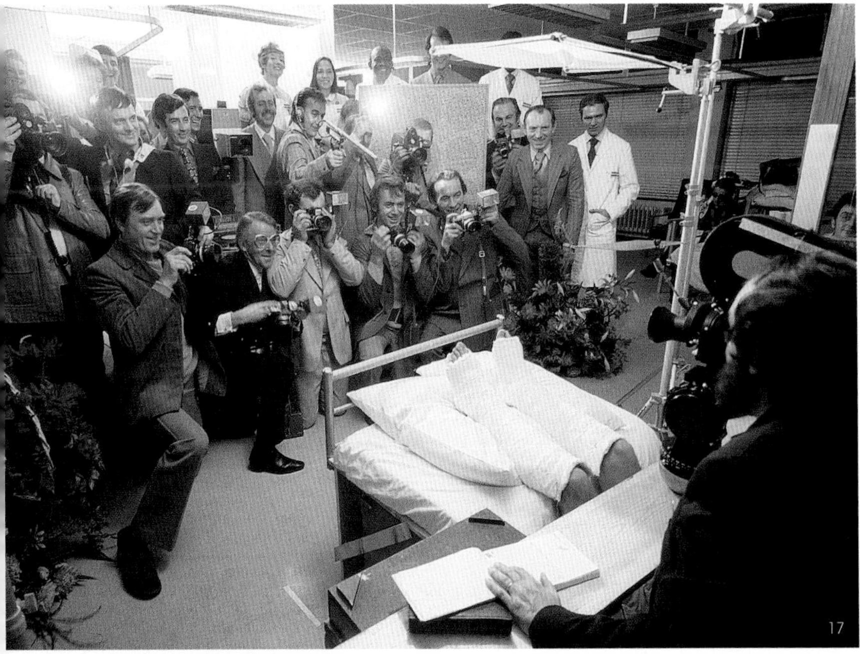

17

MURDER HUNT FOR 'CLOCKWORK' GANG

19

Funeral of Queen Mary. As in *2001*, Kubrick makes use of contrasting music and images: the Ninth Symphony's exaltation of joy and solidarity is divested of any moral content by Alex, who hears it simply as an expression of vitality, and Rossini's *Thieving Magpie* accompanies scenes of ultra-violence between the rival gangs.

Kubrick gained control of the publicity for the United States launch of the film, after a standoff with Warner Bros. marketing management, thanks to the support of producer John Calley and the assent of Warner Bros. president Ted Ashley; Kubrick maintained this control for all his subsequent films. Since he was already guaranteed the final cut, he was now in a position to manage every stage of the making of his film—though still subject to the decisions of the censors. These were most severe in the United States, where no cuts were requested but the film was X-rated when it was released on December 20, 1971. Quality films were rarely rated "X" but in the months previous to Kubrick's release, John Schlesinger's *Midnight Cowboy*, Sam Peckinpah's *Straw Dogs*, and Ken Russell's *The Devils* had all suffered this fate.

The film's English première took place on January 13, 1972, after it had been passed by the secretary of the British Board of Film Censors, John Trevelyan. Kubrick himself withdrew the film in England in 1974 after he became aware of copycat crimes committed by *droog* look-alikes and received threatening letters. *A Clockwork Orange* was finally re-released on March 17, 2000, having not been seen in England for more than a quarter of a century.

Evening Standard

LONDON LATEST

'Alex driven to suicide by scientists'

MINISTER IS ACCUSED OF INHUMAN CURE

55 boys searched by police

Demo jail sentences 'excessive'

Cricket fans want Springboks

Black rites witches

TRAWLERS IN TORBAY RACE

Protest over mobile X-rays

Go-ahead for 900 homes

Menace of poisoned water is growing

HOMES GET AWARD

Stockbroker fools staff

Ports may be oil terminals

GO TO TOWN...GO TO LYONS!

FLAMENCO

FOOD AND ENTERTAINMENT!

20

The critics were, as usual, divided. *A Clockwork Orange* won the New York Film Critics award, but Pauline Kael in *The New Yorker* wrote, "How can people go on talking about the dazzling brilliance of movies and not notice that directors are sucking up to the thugs in the audience?" Andrew Sarris echoed this in *The Village Voice*: "See *A Clockwork Orange* for yourself and suffer the damnation of boredom." Vincent Canby in *The New York Times* took the opposite view: "Brilliant, a tour de force of extraordinary images, words, music and feeling. *A Clockwork Orange* is so beautiful to look at and hear that it dazzles the senses and the mind." Derek Malcolm in *The Guardian* shared his enthusiasm, describing the film as "A chilling and mesmeric adaptation of the Anthony Burgess novel which could well become one of the seminal movies of the 70s." Kubrick's peers immediately recognized his genius: Fellini, of course, who had always admired him, and Buñuel as well, who wrote, "*A Clockwork Orange* is my current favorite. I was very predisposed against the film. After seeing it I realized it is the only movie about what the modern world really means."

A Clockwork Orange received a number of Oscar nominations—including Best Director, Best Adapted Screenplay, and Best Film Editing—though it was *French Connection* that swept the awards. Despite a flurry of nominations, it was the same story with the Golden Globe and British Academy of Film and Television Arts (BAFTA) awards. However, it was hugely

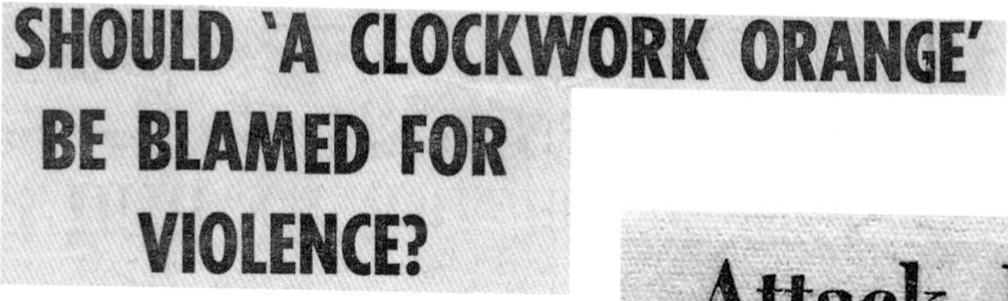
SHOULD 'A CLOCKWORK ORANGE' BE BLAMED FOR VIOLENCE?

21

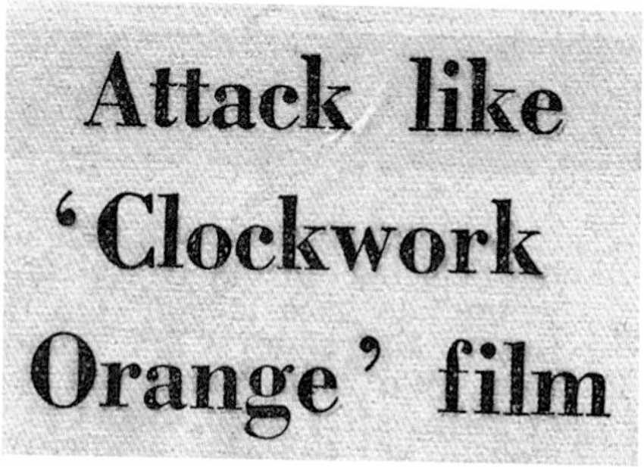
Attack like 'Clockwork Orange' film

22

18 *A strong backlight was used for the scene in which the droogs attack a homeless man.*
19, 21, 22 *British newspaper headlines reporting on* Clockwork *copycat crimes.*

20 *A prop newspaper picturing the Minister of the Interior (Anthony Sharp).*

successful with the public. By 1979, it had already earned forty million dollars at the box-office—having been made for a mere two million dollars.

The film is the third part of a futurist trilogy and the *allegro vivace* third movement of a symphony after the *allegro* of *Dr. Strangelove* and the *andante* of *2001*. These films, through a combination of huge box-office success, philosophical debates, and controversies over the aesthetics, cemented Kubrick's reputation as one of the great directors of his time. His independence, the audacity of his projects, and his technical brilliance made him a major influence for the young American filmmakers of the early 70s—from Coppola and Scorsese to Malick and Spielberg, the pillars of the Hollywood renaissance.

Kubrick was unsatisfied with *Lolita*, and *A Clockwork Orange* represented his successful attempt to translate an author's verbal genius and wordplay (Burgess's invented language, *nadsat*) to the screen while presenting an accomplished example of a cinematic first-person narrative, something he had attempted previously in *Lolita* and later repeated only in *Full Metal Jacket*. The publicity slogan for the film, "Being the adventures of a young

23 ***This scene taken from Burgess's book, in which the*** droogs ***attack a professor, was cut from the film.***

24 ***"I don't think I've ever had that much fun on a job…. The great thing that I think Stanley and I had in common… was a wicked sense of humor." – Malcolm McDowell (interviewed for*** A Life in Pictures, ***2001)***

man whose principal interests are rape, ultra violence and Beethoven," is reminiscent of chapter epigraphs in 18th-century novels, and provides a clue to the orientation of the film: it is a philosophical tale *à la* Voltaire, a picaresque narrative in the manner of Fielding. In this respect it resembles Kubrick's next movie, *Barry Lyndon*, based on a novel by Thackeray, which was itself inspired by Enlightenment novels. The adventures of Barry Lyndon resemble Alex's in their division into two parts, the "conquests" of the first part being annulled by the failures in the second. The symmetry of construction in *A Clockwork Orange* is very striking, with a number of sequences from the first part mirrored in the second: the drunken Irishman attacked by Alex later gets revenge, as does Mr. Alexander for the destroying of his home and the murder of his wife; Alex dominates his *droogs* in the first part and is beaten up by them in the second, when they have become policemen; Alex lives at his parents' house in the first part and finds his room is occupied by a stranger in the second, after his release from prison. This circularity is underlined by a number of visual motifs: bowler hat, billiard balls, eye lined by false eyelashes, the prisoners circling around the exercise yard, and

"To restrain man is not to redeem him."

—SK/1973 (to Gene D. Phillips)

women's breasts. The accompanying symmetry is present in the opening sequence in the bar, in the mirror-filled bathroom of the Alexanders' home, and in the checkered floor-tiles. The very title of the work, inspired by the Cockney expression "queer as a clockwork orange," conveys the duality between the mechanical (clockwork) and organic (orange).

Kubrick's position is far from Burgess's Christian vision. In Kubrick's dialectical perspective, the State cynically salvages Alex for its own purposes and employs society's worst members to reinforce its control. In this respect, the film is faithful to the libertarian character of its inspiration, echoing the aphorism "no gods, no masters." From *Paths of Glory* to *Full Metal Jacket* and from *Dr. Strangelove* to *A Clockwork Orange*—not to mention *Spartacus*, which was not even a Kubrick project—he always denounced the coercive power of politicians and the military and even of scientists, all of whom he perceived as forcing the individual to conform. Alex embodies our spontaneous resistance to those who attempt to make use of us. His behavior fills us with horror and his ethics are contemptible, but he is human nonetheless. Alex exercises his free will to do evil against a society that also does evil—in the name of morality. Kubrick implicates psychological conditioning as theorized by B. F. Skinner and reflects on the relationship between images and seeing.

25

The eye of Alex, actor and spectator of human decadence, as well as that of Mr. Alexander when he is forced to look on as his wife is raped, are the film's most striking manifestations of the power of sight. Moreover, Alex's own mental flashes are themselves steeped in Hollywood imagery: Alex as Roman centurion taking part in the flagellation of Christ, Alex as Dracula with dripping fangs, Alex as a biblical character surrounded by naked women and devouring grapes, and Alex violently beaten up as if in a Peckinpah movie. These film images are double-edged: they feed Alex's sadistic erotic fantasies, while for the State they serve as an instrument of surveillance and propaganda. Kubrick, criticizing the medium in which he works, has always favored distance over the character-identification basis of the Hollywood approach. But he knows the perverse power of cinema: the wide angle reverse traveling shots that he so favors are a manifestation of repulsion and also a sign of fascination. Kubrick also filled *A Clockwork Orange* with references to his own films: the close-up of Alex's eye that opens the film echoes the eye of the astral fetus in the last shot of *2001*; the two *devotchkas* in the drugstore (which is selling a record of the *2001* soundtrack) are Lolitas with their phallic lollipops. The two stereophonic speakers in the hospital room evoke the black monolith of *2001* as a prelude to Alex's regeneration, while the final vision of elegantly dressed aristocrats anticipates *Barry Lyndon*.

25–26 ***Shooting the music bootick scenes.***

In *A Clockwork Orange,* Kubrick, ever the orthodox Freudian, reaffirms the existence of the id and the dangers it represents, and is skeptical about the possibility of human progress. Alex, rising with his cane to bring his *droogs* into line, is filmed in slow-motion, from a low angle, like the ape of *2001* with his murderous bone-weapon. Violence is thus omnipresent, as is sexuality, which here is no longer subversive, as it was at the time of the surrealists, but is part of a fastidious and blasé celebration. Proof of this is found in the decoration of the Korova Milkbar with its statues offering the milk of artificial paradise, the phallic snake in Alex's room, the paintings and sculptures in the Catlady's home, and the obsession with breasts throughout the film. Homoeroticism also features in the sexual advances made by Deltoid to Alex, the latter's rectal examination by the chief warder, the emphasis on blows to Alex's testicles and penis (emphasized by his garments), and the rocking penis in the Catlady's house, whose décor is full of lesbian imagery.

Far from being a counterpoison to the excesses of nature, culture is impotent to constrain evil and even participates in it; Beethoven's music triggers Alex's destructive energies and is used in the very disturbing "curative" therapy he receives. Kubrick's outlook has never been as somber as it is in this film: hoodlums and police officers are interchangeable and the chief representative of the liberal opposition, who lives in luxury and despises the masses, is no better than the Minister of the Interior and his smooth-talking insincerity. Moreover, Mr. Alexander is in a sense Alex's double, sharing his name and his love of Beethoven (his doorbell sounds the opening theme of the Fifth Symphony) while resembling "Ludwig van" in his facial features and abundant mane of hair.

The negative dialectic of Kubrick's two most overtly comical films—the black farce of *Dr. Strangelove* and the biting satire of *A Clockwork Orange*—makes them the most powerful expression of a central theme in his work: the discontents of civilization.

References

Books

Burgess, Anthony, *A Clockwork Orange*. London: Heinemann, 1962; New York: Norton, 1963.

Ciment, Michel, Interview with Kubrick in *Kubrick: The Definitive Edition*. New York: Faber and Faber, 2001; Paris: Calmann Lévy, 1999.

McDougal, Stuart Y., *A Clockwork Orange*. Cambridge: Cambridge University Press, 2003.

Contemporary Articles

Benayoun, Robert, "Stanley Kubrick le libertaire." *Positif*, no. 139 (June 1972).

Bourge, Jean-Loup, "Les avatars du cercle." *Positif*, no. 136 (March 1972).

Canby, Vincent, "Orange, Disorienting but Human Comedy." *The New York Times*, January 9, 1972.

Houston, Penelope, and Philip Strick, "Interview with Stanley Kubrick." *Sight and Sound* (Spring 1972).

Hugues, Robert, "The Decor of Tomorrow's Hell." *Time* (December 27, 1971).

Kael, Pauline, "Stanley Strangelove." *The New Yorker* (January 1, 1972).

Sarris, Andrew, *The Village Voice* (December 30, 1971).

Strick, Philip, "Stanley Kubrick's Horrorshow." *Sight and Sound* (Winter 1971).

Letter to the Editor of *The New York Times*

by Stanley Kubrick

Published in The New York Times, *February 27, 1972*

"An alert liberal," says Fred M. Hechinger, writing about my film *A Clockwork Orange*, "should recognize the voice of fascism." They don't come any more alert than Fred M. Hechinger. A movie critic, whose job is to analyze the actual content of a film, rather than second-hand interviews, might have fallen down badly on sounding the "Liberal Alert" which an educationist like Mr. Hechinger confidently set jangling in so many resonant lines of alarmed prose.

As I read them, the image that kept coming to mind was of Mr. Hechinger, cast as the embattled liberal, grim-visaged the way Gary Cooper used to be, doing the long walk down main street to face the high noon of American democracy, while out of the Last Chance saloon drifts the theme song, "See what the boys in the backlash will have and tell them I'm having the same," though sung in a voice less like Miss Dietrich's than Miss Kael's. Alert filmgoers will recognize that I am mixing my movies. But then alert educationists like Mr. Hechinger seemingly don't mind mixing their metaphors: "Occasionally, the diverting tinsel was laced with some 'Grapes of Wrath' realism," no less.

It is baffling that in the course of his lengthy piece encouraging American liberals to cherish their "right" to hate the ideology behind *A Clockwork Orange*, Mr. Hechinger quotes not one line, refers to not one scene, analyzes not one theme from the film—but simply lumps it indiscriminately in with a "trend" which he pretends to distinguish ("a deeply anti-liberal totalitarian nihilism") in several current films. Is this, I wonder, because he couldn't actually find any internal evidence to support his trend-spotting? If not, then it is extraordinary that so serious a charge should be made against it (and myself) inside so fuzzy and unfocussed a piece of alarmist journalism.

Hechinger is probably quite sincere in what he feels. But what the witness feels, as the judge said, is not evidence—the more so when the charge is one of purveying "the essence of fascism."

"Is this an uncharitable reading of the film's thesis?" Mr. Hechinger asks himself with unwonted, if momentary doubt. I would reply that it is an *irrelevant* reading of the thesis, in fact an insensitive and inverted reading of the thesis, which, so far from advocating that fascism be given a second chance, warns against the new psychedelic fascism—the eye-popping, multimedia, quadrasonic, drug-oriented conditioning of human beings by other beings—which many believe will usher in the forfeiture of human citizenship and the beginning of zombiedom.

It is quite true that my film's view of man is less flattering than the one Rousseau entertained in a similarly allegorical narrative—but, in order to avoid fascism, does one have to view man as a *noble* savage, rather than an ignoble one? Being a pessimist is not yet enough to qualify one to be regarded as a tyrant (I hope). At least the film critic of *The New York Times*, Vincent Canby, did not believe so. Though modestly disclaiming any theories of initial causes and long range effects of films — a professional humility that contrasts very markedly with Mr. Hechinger's lack of the same — Mr. Canby nevertheless classified *A Clockwork Orange* as "a superlative example" of the kind of movies that "seriously attempt to analyze the meaning of violence and the social climate that tolerates it." He certainly did not denounce me as a fascist, no more than any well-balanced commentator who read "A Modest Proposal" would have accused Dean Swift of being a cannibal.

Anthony Burgess is on record as seeing the film as "a Christian Sermon" and lest this be regarded as a piece of special pleading by the original begetter of *A Clockwork Orange*, I will quote the opinion of John E. Fitzgerald, the film critic of *The Catholic News*, who, far from believing the film to show man, in Mr. Hechinger's "uncharitable" reading, as "irretrievably bad and corrupt," went straight to the heart of the matter in a way that shames the fumbling innuendos of Mr. Hechinger.

"In one year," Mr. Fitzgerald wrote, "we have been given two contradictory messages in two mediums. In print, we've been told (in B. F. Skinner's *Beyond Freedom and Dignity*) that man is but a grab-bag of conditioned reflexes. On screen, with images rather than words, Stanley Kubrick shows that man is more than a mere product of heredity and–or environment. For as Alex's clergyman friend (a character who starts out as a fire-and-brimstone spouting balloon, but ends up as the spokesman for the film's thesis) says: 'When a man cannot choose, he ceases to be a man.'

"The film seems to say that to take away man's choice is not to redeem but merely to restrain him; otherwise we have a society of oranges, organic but operating like clockwork. Such brainwashing, organic and psychological, is a weapon that totalitarians in state, church or society might wish for an easier good, even at the cost of individual rights and dignity. Redemption is a complicated thing and change must be motivated from within rather than imposed from without if moral values are to be upheld."

"It takes the likes of Hitler or Stalin, and the violence of inquisitions, pogroms and purges to manage a world of ignoble savages," declares Mr. Hechinger in a manner both savage and ignoble. Thus, without citing anything from the film itself, Mr. Hechinger seems to rest his entire case against me on a quote appearing in *The New York Times* of January 30, in which I said: "Man isn't a noble savage, he's an ignoble savage. He is irrational, brutal, weak, silly, unable to be objective about anything where his own interests are involved ... and any attempt to create social institutions based on a false view of the nature of man is probably doomed to failure." From this, apparently Mr.

27 ***The background for the driving scene was projected onto a screen in the studio.***

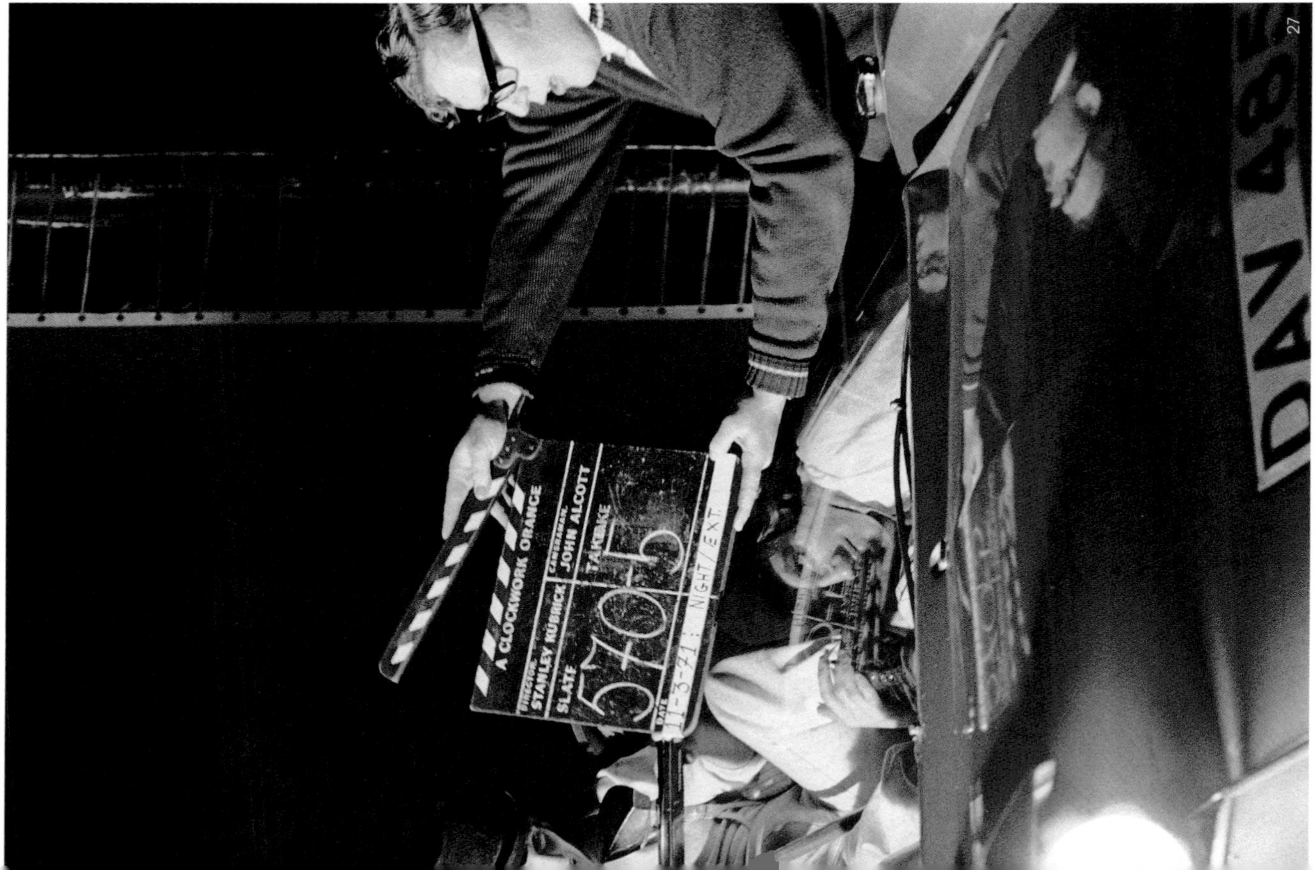
A CLOCKWORK ORANGE
DIRECTOR STANLEY KUBRICK
CAMERAMAN JOHN ALCOTT
SLATE 570
TAKE 5
DATE 11-3-71: NIGHT/EXT.
DAV 48
27

Hechinger concluded, "the thesis that man is irretrievably bad and corrupt is the essence of fascism," and summarily condemned the film.

Mr. Hechinger is entitled to hold an optimistic view of the nature of man, but this does not give him the right to make ugly assertions of fascism against those who do not share his opinion.

I wonder how he would reconcile his simplistic notions with the views of such an acknowledged anti-fascist as Arthur Koestler who wrote in his book *The Ghost in the Machine*, "The Promethean myth has acquired an ugly twist: the giant reaching out to steal the lightning from the Gods is insane.... When you mention, however tentatively, the hypothesis that a paranoid streak is inherent in the human condition, you will promptly be accused of taking a one-sided, morbid view of history; of being hypnotized by its negative aspects; of picking out the black stones in the mosaic and neglecting the triumphant achievements of human progress.... To dwell on the glories of man and ignore the symptoms of his possible insanity is not a sign of optimism but of ostrichism. It could only be compared to the attitude of that jolly physician who, a short time before Van Gogh committed suicide, declared that he could not be insane because be painted such beautiful pictures." Does this, I wonder, place Mr. Koestler on Mr. Hechinger's newly started blacklist?

It is because of the hysterical denunciations of self-proclaimed "alert liberals" like Mr. Hechinger that the cause of liberalism is weakened, and it is for the same reason that so few liberal-minded politicians risk making realistic statements about contemporary social problems.

The age of the alibi, in which we find ourselves, began with the opening sentence of Rousseau's *Emile*: "Nature made me happy and good, and if I am otherwise, it is society's fault." It is based on two misconceptions: that man in his natural state was happy and good, and that primal man had no society.

Robert Ardrey has written in *The Social Contract*, "The organizing principle of Rousseau's life was his unshakable belief in the original goodness of man, including his own. That it led him into the most towering hypocrisies, as recorded in the *Confessions*, is of no shaking importance; such hypocrisies must follow from such an assumption. More significant are the disillusionments, the pessimism, and the paranoia that such a belief in human nature must induce."

Ardrey elaborates in *African Genesis*: "the idealistic American is an environmentalist who accepts the doctrine of man's innate nobility and looks chiefly to economic causes for the source of human woe. And so now, at the peak of the American triumph over that ancient enemy, want, he finds himself harassed by the racial conflict of increasing bitterness, harrowed by juvenile delinquency probing championship heights."

Rousseau's romantic fallacy that it is society which corrupts man, not man who corrupts society, places a flattering gauze between ourselves and reality. This view, to use Mr. Hechinger's frame of reference, is solid box office but, in the end, such a self-inflating illusion leads to despair.

The Enlightenment declared man's rational independence from the tyranny of the Supernatural. It opened up dizzying and frightening vistas of the intellectual and political future. But before this became too alarming, Rousseau replaced a religion of the Supernatural being with the religion of natural man. God might be dead. "Long live man."

"How else," writes Ardrey, "can one explain—except as a substitute for old religious cravings—the immoderate influence on the rational mind of the doctrine of innate goodness?"

Finally, the question must be considered whether Rousseau's view of man as fallen angel is not really the most pessimistic and hopeless of philosophies. It leaves man a monster who has gone steadily away from his original nobility. It is, I am convinced, more optimistic to accept Ardrey's view that "... we were born of risen apes, not fallen angels, and the apes were armed killers besides. And so what shall we wonder at? Our murders and massacres and missiles and our irreconcilable regiments? For our treaties, whatever they may be worth; our symphonies, however seldom they may be played; our peaceful acres, however frequently they may be converted into battlefields; our dreams, however rarely they may be accomplished. The miracle of man is not how far he has sunk but how magnificently he has risen. We are known among the stars by our poems, not our corpses."

Mr. Hechinger is no doubt a well-educated man but the tone of his piece strikes me as also that of a well-conditioned man who responds to what he expects to find, or has been told, or has read about, rather than to what he actually perceives *A Clockwork Orange* to be. Maybe he should deposit his grab-bag of conditioned reflexes outside and go in to see it again. This time, exercising a little choice.

Modern Times: An Interview with Stanley Kubrick

by Philip Strick and Penelope Houston

Published in Sight and Sound, *Spring 1972*

How closely did you work with Anthony Burgess in adapting *A Clockwork Orange* for the screen?

I had virtually no opportunity of discussing the novel with Anthony Burgess. He phoned me one evening when he was passing through London and we had a brief conversation on the telephone. It was mostly an exchange of pleasantries. On the other hand, I wasn't particularly concerned about this because in a book as brilliantly written as *A Clockwork Orange* one would have to be lazy not to be able to find the answers to any questions which might arise within the text of the novel itself. I think it is reasonable to say that, whatever Burgess had to say about the story was said in the book.

How about your own contributions to the story? You seem to have preserved the style and structure of the original far more closely than with most of your previous films, and the dialogues are often exactly the same as in the novel.

My contribution to the story consisted of writing the screenplay. This was principally a matter of selection and editing, though I did invent a few useful narrative ideas and reshape some of the scenes. However, in general, these contributions merely clarified what was already in the novel—such as the Catlady telephoning the police, which explains why the police appear at the end of that scene. In the novel, it occurs to Alex that she may have called them, but this is the sort of thing that you can do in a novel and not in the screenplay. I was also rather pleased with the idea of "Singin' in the Rain" as a means of Alexander identifying Alex again towards the end of the film.

How did you come to use "Singin' in the Rain" in the first place?

This was one of the more important ideas which arose during rehearsal. This scene, in fact, was rehearsed longer than any other scene in the film and appeared to be going nowhere. We spent three days trying to work out just what was going to happen and somehow it all seemed a bit inadequate. Then suddenly the idea popped into my head—I don't know where it came from or what triggered it off.

The main addition you seem to have made to the original story is the scene of Alex's introduction to the prison. Why did you feel this was important?

It may be the longest scene but I would not think it is the most important. It was a necessary addition because the prison sequence is compressed, in comparison with the novel, and one had to have something in it which gave sufficient weight to the idea that Alex was actually imprisoned. The routine of checking into prison which, in fact, is quite accurately

28 ***"Do you know how many sticks, canes were broken [for the rape scene]? The poor prop man, he made balsa wood ones, he made rubber ones, with a piece of metal in the middle that bent when I hit her.... I went through fifty of them. And Stanley was going crazy because he could not believe the prop man couldn't figure out a way to make a practical stick that wouldn't hurt the poor girl, Adrienne Corri."* –*Malcolm McDowell (interviewed for* A Life in Pictures, *2001)***

presented in the film, seemed to provide this necessary weight.

In the book there is another killing by Alex while he is in prison. By omitting this, don't you run the risk of seeming to share Alex's own opinion of himself as a high-spirited innocent?

I shouldn't think so, and Alex doesn't see himself as a high-spirited innocent. He is totally aware of his own evil and accepts it with complete openness.

Alex seems a far pleasanter person in the film than in the book....

Alex makes no attempt to deceive himself or the audience as to his total corruption and wickedness. He is the very personification of evil. On the other hand, he has winning qualities: his total candor, his wit, his intelligence and his energy; these are attractive qualities and ones, I might add, which he shares with Richard III.

The violence done to Alex in the brainwashing sequence is in fact more horrifying than anything he does himself....

It was absolutely necessary to give weight to Alex's brutality, otherwise I think there would be moral confusion with respect to what the government does to him. If he were a lesser villain, then one could say: "Oh, yes, of course, he should not be given this psychological conditioning; it's all too horrible and he really wasn't that bad after all." On the other hand, when you have shown him committing such atrocious acts, and you still realize the immense evil on the part of the government in turning him into something less

than human in order to make him good, then I think the essential moral idea of the book is clear. It is necessary for man to have choice to be good or evil, even if he chooses evil. To deprive him of this choice is to make him something less than human—a clockwork orange.

But aren't you inviting a sort of identification with Alex?

I think, in addition to the personal qualities I mentioned, there is the basic psychological, unconscious identification with Alex. If you look at the story not on the social and moral level, but on the psychological dream content level, you can regard Alex as a creature of the id. He is within all of us. In most cases, this recognition seems to bring a kind of empathy from the audience, but it makes some people very angry and uncomfortable. They are unable to accept this view of themselves and, therefore, they become angry at the film. It's a bit like the king who kills the messenger who brings him bad news and rewards the one who brings him good news.

The comparison with Richard III makes a striking defense against accusations that the film encourages violence, delinquency and so on. But as Richard is a safely distant historical figure, does it meet them (sic) completely?

29 *Kubrick gets down on the floor to capture the attack on the Alexanders.*
30–31 *The shooting of scenes in the home of Mr. Alexander (Patrick Magee).*

KODAK
SAFETY FILM

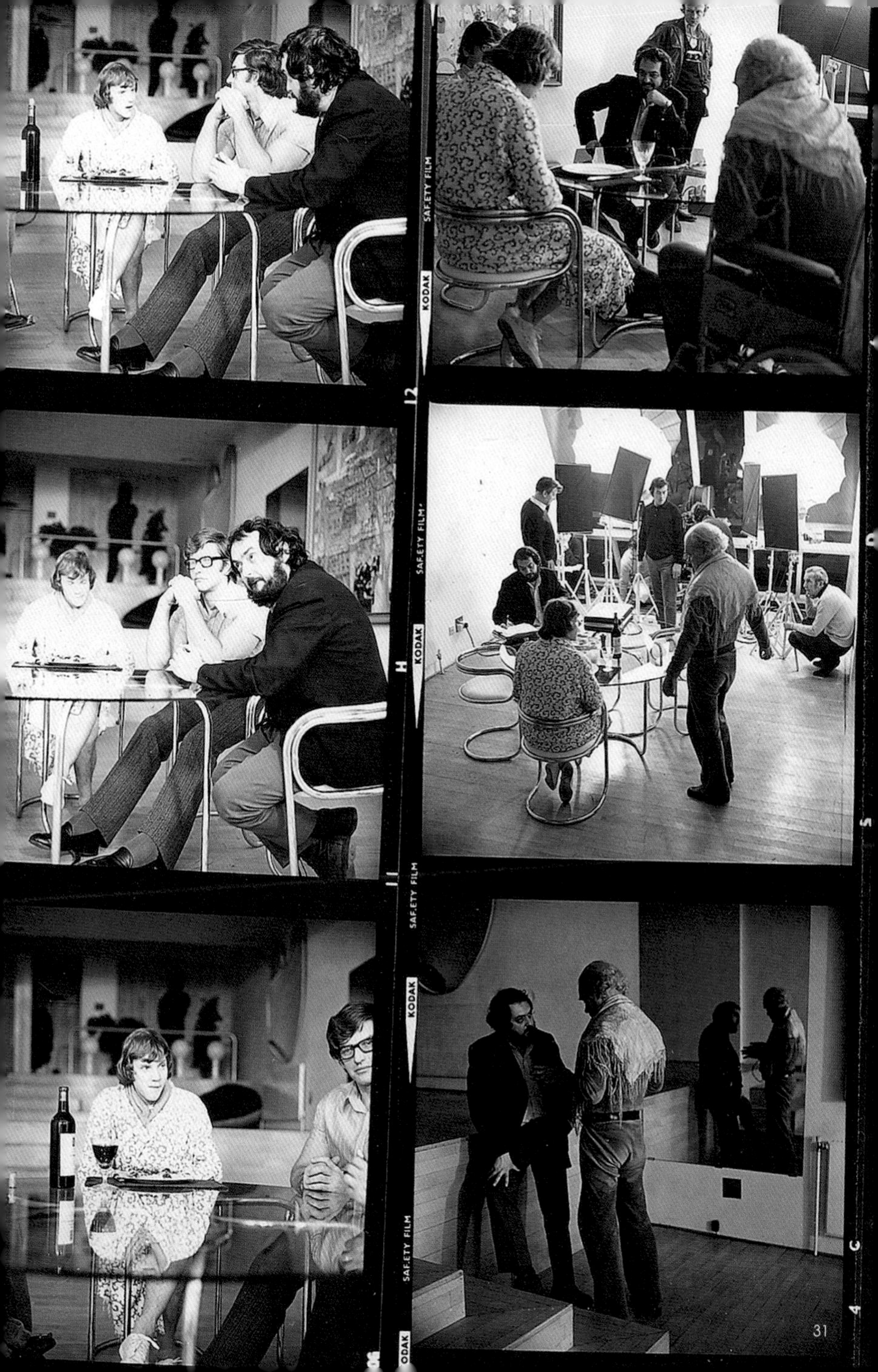
KODAK
SAFETY FILM

There is no positive evidence that violence in films or television causes social violence. To focus one's interest on this aspect of violence is to ignore the principal causes, which I would list as:

1. Original sin: the religious view.

2. Unjust economic exploitation: the Marxist view.

3. Emotional and psychological frustration: the psychological view.

4. Genetic factors based on the "Y" chromosome theory: the biological view.

5. Man—the killer ape: the evolutionary view.

To try to fasten any responsibility on art as the cause of life seems to me to have the case put the wrong way around. Art consists of reshaping life but it does not create life, or cause life. Furthermore to attribute powerful suggestive qualities to a film is at odds with the scientifically accepted view that, even after deep hypnosis, in a post-hypnotic state, people cannot be made to do things which are at odds with their natures.

Is there any kind of violence in films which you might regard as socially dangerous?

Well, I don't accept that there is a connection, but let us hypothetically say that there might be one. If there were one, I should say that the kind of violence that might cause some impulse to emu-

32 *Kubrick lining up a shot in the prison chapel.*
33 *This panoramic photograph of Gary Shepherd and the other assistant editors in the* Clockwork *editing room was taken by Kubrick with his beloved Widelux camera.*

"High standards of moral behavior can only be achieved by the example of right thinking people and society as a whole, and cannot be maintained by the coercive effect of the law. Or that of certain newspapers."

—SK/1972 (letter to the *Detroit News* protesting the newspaper's refusal to sell advertising space to films with an X-rating, including *A Clockwork Orange*)

late it is the "fun" kind of violence: the kind of violence we see in the Bond films or the *Tom and Jerry* cartoons. Unrealistic violence, sanitized violence, violence presented as a joke. This is the only kind of violence that could conceivably cause anyone to wish to copy it, but I am quite convinced that not even this has any effect. There may even be an argument in support of saying that any kind of violence in films, in fact, serves a useful social purpose by allowing people a means of vicariously freeing themselves from the pent up, aggressive emotions which are better expressed in dreams, or in the dreamlike state of watching a film, than in any form of reality of sublimation.

Isn't the assumption of your audience in the case of *A Clockwork Orange* likely to be that you support Alex's point of view and in some way assume responsibility for it?

I don't think that any work of art has a responsibility to be anything but a work of art. There obviously is a considerable controversy, just as there always has been, about what is a work of art, and I should be the last to try to define that. I was amused by Cocteau's *Orphée* when the poet is given the advice: "Astonish me." The Johnsonian definition of a work of art is also meaningful to me, and that is that a work of art must either make life more enjoyable or more endurable. Another quality, which I think forms part of the definition, is that a work of art is always exhilarating and never depressing, whatever its subject matter may be.

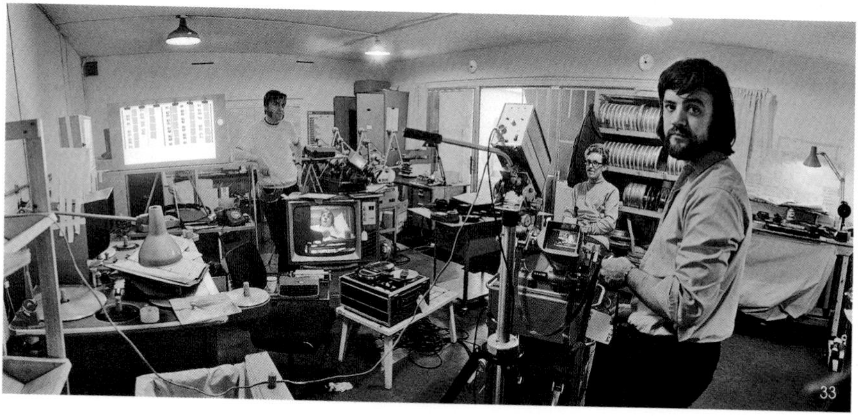

B2

In view of the particular exhilaration of Alex's religious fantasies, has the film run into trouble with clerical critics?

The reaction of the religious press has been mixed, although a number of superb reviews have been written. One of the most perceptive reviews by the religious press, or any other press, appeared in the *Catholic News* written by John E. Fitzgerald, and I would like to quote one portion of it: "In print we've been told (in B. F. Skinner's *Beyond Freedom and Dignity*) that man is but a grab-bag of conditioned reflexes. On screen with images rather than words, Stanley Kubrick shows that man is more than a mere product of heredity and/or environment. For as Alex's clergyman friend (who starts out as a fire-and-brimstone-spouting buffoon but ends up the spokesman for the film's thesis) says: 'When a man cannot choose, he ceases to be a man.'

"The film seems to say that to take away a man's choice is not to redeem but merely to restrain him: otherwise we have a society of oranges, organic but operating like clockwork. Such brainwashing, organic and psychological, is a weapon that totalitarians in state, church, or society might wish for an easier good even at the cost of individual rights and dignity. Redemption is a complicated thing and change must be motivated from within rather than imposed from without if moral values are to be upheld. But Kubrick is an artist rather than a moralist and he leaves it to us to figure what's wrong and why, what should be done and how it should be accomplished."

34 ***On location for the prison scenes.***
35–40 ***Philip Castle's poster artwork. A variation of*** 37 ***was the most common poster illustration, and*** 36 ***was used for some re-release posters.***

Your choice of lenses for the shooting of the film often gives it a subtly distorted visual quality. Why did you want that particular look?

It may sound like an extremely obvious thing to say, but I think it is worth saying nevertheless that when you are making a film, in addition to any higher purpose you may have in mind, you must be interesting; visually interesting, narratively interesting, interesting from an acting point of view. All ideas for creating interest must be held up against the yardstick of the theme of the story, the narrative requirements and the purpose of the scene; but, within that, you must make a work of art interesting. I recall a comment recorded in a book called *Stanislavski Directs*, in which Stanislavski told an actor that he had the right understanding of the character, the right understanding of the text of the play, that what he was doing was completely believable, but that it was still no good because it wasn't interesting.

Were you looking after the hand-held camera for the fight with the Catlady?

Yes, all of the hand-held camerawork is mine. In addition to the fun of doing the shooting myself, I find it is virtually impossible to explain what you want in a hand-held shot to even the most talented and sensitive camera operator.

To what extent do you rationalize a shot before setting it up?

There are certain aspects of a film which can meaningfully be talked about, but photography and editing do not lend themselves to verbal analysis. It's very much the same as the problem one has talking about painting, or music. The

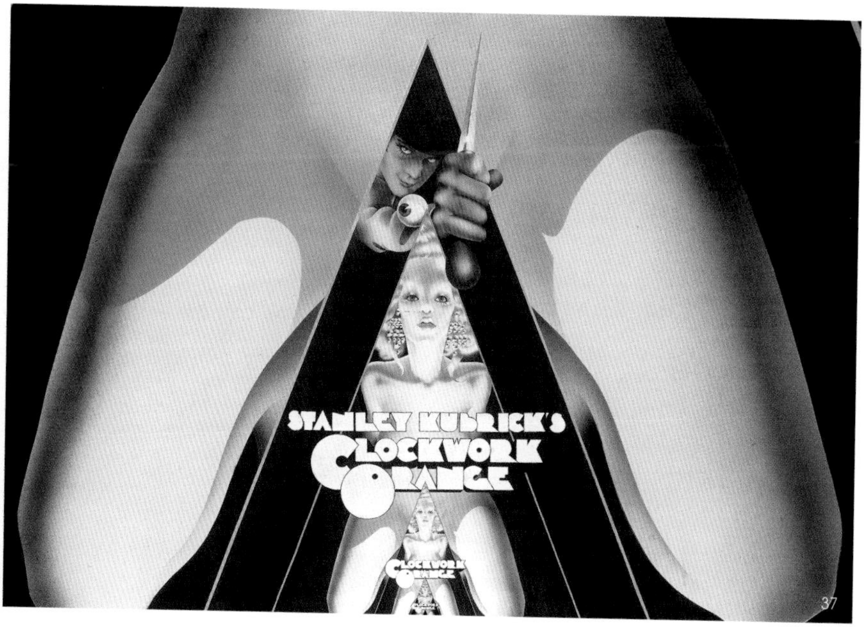

38

39

40

questions of taste involved and the decision-making criteria are essentially nonverbal, and whatever you say about them tends to read like the back of a record album. These are decisions that have to be made every few minutes during the shooting, and they are just down to the director's taste and imagination.

How did you come to choose the Purcell piece—*Music for the Funeral of Queen Mary*?

Well, this answer is going to sound a lot like the last one. You're in an area where words are not particularly relevant. In thinking about the music for the scene, the Purcell piece occurred to me and, after I listened to it several times in conjunction with the film, there was simply no question about using it.

The arrangements by Walter Carlos are extraordinarily effective....

I think that Walter Carlos has done something completely unique in the field of electronic realization of music—that's the phrase that they use. I think that I've heard most of the electronic and *musique concrète* LPs there are for sale in Britain, Germany, France, Italy, and the United States; not because I particularly like this kind of music, but out of my researches for *2001* and *Clockwork Orange*. I think Walter Carlos is the only electronic composer and realizer who has managed to create a sound which is not an attempt at copying the instruments of the orchestra and yet which, at the same time, achieves a beauty of its own employing electronic tonalities. I think that his version of the fourth

movement of Beethoven's Ninth Symphony rivals hearing a full orchestra playing it, and that is saying an awful lot.

There is very little post synchronization for the dialogue....

There is no post-synchronization. I'm quite pleased about this because every scene was shot on location; even the so-called sets that we built which were, in fact, built in a factory about forty feet off the noisy High Street in Borehamwood, a few hundred yards from the old MGM Studio. Despite this, we were able to get quite acceptably clean soundtracks.

With the modern equipment that's available today in the form of microphones, radio transmitters and so forth, it should be possible to get a usable soundtrack almost anywhere. In the scene where the tramp recognizes Alex who is standing looking at the Thames, next to the Albert Bridge, there was so much traffic noise on the location that you had to shout in order to be heard, but we were able to get such a quiet soundtrack that it was necessary to add street noise in the final mix to make it realistic. We used a microphone the size of a paper clip, and it was secured with black tape on the tramp's scarf. In several shots you can see the microphone, but you don't know what you are looking at.

In concentrating on the action of the film, as you do, isn't there a danger that the lesser characters may appear rather one-dimensional? The danger of everything that you do in a film is that it may not work, it may be boring, or bland, or stupid....

When you think of the greatest moments of film, I think you are almost always involved with images rather than scenes, and certainly never dialogue. The thing a film does best is to use pictures with music, and I think these are the moments you remember. Another thing is the way an actor did something: the way Emil Jannings took out his handkerchief and blew his nose in *The Blue Angel*, or those marvelous slow turns that Nikolai Cherkassov did in *Ivan the Terrible*.

How did you manage the subjective shot of Alex's suicide attempt?

We bought an old Newman Sinclair clockwork mechanism camera (no pun intended) for fifty pounds. It's a beautiful camera and it's built like a battleship. We

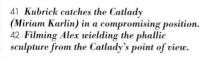

41 ***Kubrick catches the Catlady (Miriam Karlin) in a compromising position.***
42 ***Filming Alex wielding the phallic sculpture from the Catlady's point of view.***

made a number of polystyrene boxes which gave about eighteen inches of protection around the camera, and cut out a slice for the lens. We then threw the camera off a roof. In order to get it to land lens first, we had to do this six times and the camera survived all six drops. On the final one, it landed right on the lens and smashed it but it didn't do a bit of harm to the camera. This, despite the fact that the polystyrene was literally blasted away from it each time by the impact. The next day we shot a steady test on the camera and found there wasn't a thing wrong with it. On this basis, I would say that the Newman Sinclair must be the most indestructible camera ever made.

How much planning do you do before you start to shoot a scene?

As much as there are hours in the day, and days in the weeks. I think about a film almost continuously. I try to visualize it and I try to work out every conceivable variation of ideas which might exist with respect to the various scenes, but I have found that when you finally come down to the day the scene is going to be shot and you arrive on the location with the actors, having had the experience of already seeing some scenes shot, somehow it's always different. You find out that you have not really explored the scene to its fullest extent. You may have been thinking about it incorrectly, or you may simply not have discovered one of the variations which now in context with everything else that you have shot is simply better than anything you had previously thought of. The reality of the final moment, just before shooting, is so powerful that all previous analysis must yield before the impressions you receive under these circumstances, and unless you use this feedback to your positive advantage, unless you adjust to it, adapt to it and accept the sometimes terrifying weaknesses it can expose, you can never realize the most out of your film.

How do you usually work when you get to the reality of the final moment?

Whenever I start a new scene, the most important thing in my mind is, within the needs of the theme and the scene, to make something happen worth putting on film. The most crucial part of this comes when you start rehearsals on a new scene. You arrive on the location, the crew is standing around eating buns and drinking tea, waiting to be told what to do. You've got to keep them outside the room you're rehearsing in and take whatever time is necessary to get everything right, and have it make sense. There's no way to define what this process consists of. It obviously has to do with taste and imagination and it is in this crucial period of time that a film is really created. Once you know you've got something worthwhile, the shooting becomes a matter of recording (improving if you can) what you have already done in rehearsal. Whatever problems exist during the actual shooting are not the kind of problems that worry me. If the actor isn't getting it right, well, he'll get it right eventually. If the camera operator spoils a shot, it can be done again. The thing that can never be changed, and the thing that is the make or break of a picture, are those few

43–44 *This scene, in which the droogs steal the sports car that they drive to the Alexanders' home, was not used in the film.*

"One of the most dangerous fallacies which has influenced a great deal of political and philosophical thinking is that man is essentially good, and that it is society which makes him bad. Rousseau transferred original sin from man to society, and this view has importantly contributed to what I believe has become a crucially incorrect premise on which to base moral and political philosophy."

—SK/1972 (to Bernard Weintraub/*The New York Times*)

SCRIPT NOTES REGARDING SCENE No. 3 *used to be Duke of New York - Petrol Station.

The boys have a stolen car.

Alex should have a big bunch of keys.

Smashing windows.

Activity of breaking the car and stealing a car.

Starting a fire in the petrol station.

Two pedestrians run away while they see the gang approaching them from a far distance already.

Marble Arch tunnel.

Two lady police women.

19 November 1970

hours you spend alone in the actual place with the actors, with the crew outside drinking their tea.

Sometimes you find that the scene is absolutely no good at all. It doesn't make sense when you see it acted. It doesn't provide the necessary emotional or factual information in an interesting way, or in a way which has the right weight to it. Any number of things can suddenly put you in a position where you've got nothing to shoot. The only thing you can say about a moment like this is that it's better to realize it while you still have a chance to change it and to create something new, than it is to record forever something that is wrong. This is the best and the worst time: it is the time you have your most imaginative ideas, things that have not occurred to you before, regardless of how much you've thought about the scene. It's also the time when you can stand there and feel very dumb and unhappy with what you're seeing, and not have the faintest idea of what to do about it.

Do you very consciously favor a particular style of shooting?

If something is really happening on the screen, it isn't crucial how it's shot. Chaplin had such a simple cinematic style that it was almost like *I Love Lucy*, but you were always hypnotized by what was going on, unaware of the essentially non-cinematic style. He frequently used cheap sets, routine lighting and so forth, but he made great films. His films will probably last longer than anyone else's. You could say that Chaplin was no style and all content. On the other hand, the opposite can be seen in Eisenstein's films, who is all style and no content or, depending on how generous you want to be, little content. Many of Eisenstein's films are really quite silly; but they are so beautifully made, so brilliantly cinematic, that, despite their heavily propagandistic simplemindedness, they become important. Obviously, if you can combine style and content, you have the best of all possible films.

Do you have a preference for any one aspect of the whole filmmaking process?

I think I enjoy editing the most. It's the nearest thing to some reasonable environment in which to do creative work. Writing, of course, is very satisfying, but, of course, you're not working with film. The actual shooting of a film is probably the worst circumstances you could try to imagine for creating a work of art. There is, first of all, the problem of getting up very early every morning and going to bed very late every night. Then there is the chaos, confusion and frequently physical discomfort. It would be, I suppose, like a writer trying to write a book while working at a factory lathe in temperatures which range from 95 to negative 10 degrees Fahrenheit. In addition to this, of course, editing is the only aspect of the cinematic art that is unique. It shares no connection with any other art form: writing, acting, photography, things that are major aspects of the cinema, are still not unique to it, but editing is.

How long did the editing take on *Clockwork Orange*?

The editing up to the point of dubbing took about six months, working seven days a week.

Do you ever have problems cutting out your own material?

45

46

When I'm editing, I'm only concerned with the questions of "Is it good or bad?" "Is it necessary?" "Can I get rid of it?" "Does it work?" My identity changes to that of an editor. I am never concerned with how much difficulty there was to shoot something, how much it cost and so forth. I look at the material with completely different eyes. I'm never troubled losing material. I cut everything to the bone. When you're shooting, you want to make sure that you don't miss anything and you cover it as fully as time and budget allow. When you're editing, you want to get rid of everything that isn't essential.

How much support coverage do you shoot?

There's always a conflict between time, money, and quality. If you shoot a lot of coverage, then you must either spend a lot of money, or settle for less quality of performance. I find that when I'm shooting a scene where the acting is primarily important, I shoot a lot of takes but I don't try to get a lot of coverage from other angles. I try to shoot the scene as simply as possible to get the maximum performance from the actors without presenting them with the problem of repeating the performance too many times from different angles. On the other hand, in an action scene, where it's relatively easy to shoot, you want lots and lots of angles so that you can do something interesting with it in the cutting room.

45–46 ***Another scene filmed but not used, in which three ladies in a café provide an alibi for the*** **droogs** ***when the police question them about a robbery.***

Do you direct actors in every detail, or do you expect them to some extent to come up with their own ideas?

I come up with the ideas. That is essentially the director's job. There is a misconception, I think, about what directing actors means: it generally goes along the lines of the director imposing his will over difficult actors, or teaching people who don't know how to act. I try to hire the best actors in the world. The problem is comparable to one a conductor might face. There's little joy in trying to get a magnificent performance from a student orchestra. It's difficult enough to get one with all the subtleties and nuances you might want out of the greatest orchestra in the world. You want to have great virtuoso soloists, and so with actors. Then it's not necessary to teach them how to act or to discipline them or to impose your will upon them because there is usually no problem along those lines. An actor will almost always do what you want him to do if he is able to do it; and, therefore, since great actors are able to do almost anything, you find you have few problems. You can then concentrate on what you want them to do, what is the psychology of the character, what is the purpose of the scene, what is the story about? These are things that are often muddled up and require simplicity and exactitude.

The director's job is to provide the actor with ideas, not to teach him how to act or to trick him into acting. There's no way to give an actor what he hasn't got in the form of talent. You can give him ideas, thoughts, attitudes. The actor's job is to create emotion. Obviously, the actor may have some ideas too, but this is not what his primary responsibility is. You can make a mediocre actor less mediocre, you can make a terrible actor mediocre, but you cannot go very far without the magic. Great performances come from the magical talent of the actor, plus the ideas of the director.

The other part of the director's job is to exercise taste: he must decide whether what he is seeing is interesting, whether it's appropriate, whether it is of sufficient weight, whether it's credible. These are decisions that no one else can make.

You made what might seem some unusual casting choices for your last two films—how do you find the actors you want?

Well, that really comes down to a question of taste, doesn't it? A lot of pictures are cast by producers and their decisions are frequently based on proven success rather than unproven hints at talent. Many producers aren't willing to decide whether an actor who is unknown and who has done very little work is really good. I have nothing against people of proven talent, but sometimes there may be no one in that category who is right for the part.

Do you enjoy working with different actors? With a few exceptions—Peter Sellers, for instance—you haven't often used the same actor twice, unlike a lot of directors who obviously prefer to build up a sort of stock company of people who know their work.

I don't really think in those terms. I try to choose the best actors for the parts, whether I know them or not. I would avoid actors who have reputations for being destructive and neurotic but, other than that, there is no one whom I would not consider using for a part.

The only thing that is really important in your relationship with actors is that they must know that you admire them, that you admire their work, and there's no way to fake that. You must really admire them or you shouldn't use them. If they know that you admire their work, which they can sense in a thousand different ways, it doesn't really matter what you think of each other or what you say to them, or whether you are terribly friendly or not. The thing they care about is their work. Some actors are very amusing and pleasant and always cheerful. They are, of course, more pleasant to have around than those who are morose, vacant, or enigmatic. But how they behave when you're not shooting has very little to do with what happens when the camera turns over.

You made *Clockwork Orange* initially because you had to postpone your Napoleon project. How do you see the Napoleon film developing?

First of all, I start from the premise that there has never been a great historical film, and I say that with all apologies and respect to those who have made historical films, including myself. I don't think anyone has ever successfully solved the problem of dealing in an interesting way with the historical information that has to be conveyed, and at the same time getting a sense of reality about the daily life of the characters. You have to get a feeling of what it was like to be with Napoleon. At the same time, you have to convey enough historical information in an intelligent, interesting, and concise way so that the audience understands what happened.

Would you include Abel Gance's *Napoleon* in this verdict?

I think I would have to. I know that the film is a masterpiece of cinematic invention and it brought cinematic innovations to the screen which are still being called innovations whenever someone is bold enough to try them again. But on the other hand, as a film about Napoleon, I have to say I've always been disappointed in it.

Did you think of *Clockwork Orange* as being in any way a form of relaxation between two very big films?

I don't think in terms of big movies, or small movies. Each movie presents problems of its own and has advantages of its own. Each movie requires everything that you have to give it, in order to overcome the artistic and logistic problems that it poses. There are advantages in an epic film, just as there are disadvantages. It is much easier to do a huge crowd scene and make it interesting than it is to film a man sitting at a table thinking.

Barry Lyndon

1975 / COLOR / 185 MINUTES
Distributed by WARNER BROS.

CAST
BARRY LYNDON RYAN O'NEAL
LADY LYNDON MARISA BERENSON
CHEVALIER DE BALIBARI PATRICK MAGEE
CAPTAIN POTZDORF HARDY KRÜGER
LORD LUDD STEVEN BERKOFF
NORA BRADY GAY HAMILTON
BARRY'S MOTHER MARIE KEAN
GERMAN GIRL DIANA KOERNER
REVEREND RUNT MURRAY MELVIN
SIR CHARLES LYNDON FRANK MIDDLEMASS
LORD WENDOVER ANDRE MORELL
HIGHWAYMAN ARTHUR O'SULLIVAN
CAPTAIN GROGAN GODFREY QUIGLEY
CAPTAIN QUIN LEONARD ROSSITER
GRAHAM PHILIP STONE
LORD BULLINGDON LEON VITALI
YOUNG BULLINGDON DOMINIC SAVAGE
DAVID MORLEY BRYAN LYNDON
NARRATOR MICHAEL HORDERN
LORD HALLAM ANTHONY SHARP

CREW
WRITTEN FOR THE SCREEN, PRODUCED AND DIRECTED BY STANLEY KUBRICK (based on the novel by William Makepeace Thackeray)
MUSIC ADAPTED AND CONDUCTED BY LEONARD ROSENMAN
EXECUTIVE PRODUCER JAN HARLAN
ASSOCIATE PRODUCER BERNARD WILLIAMS
PRODUCTION DESIGNER KEN ADAM
DIRECTOR OF PHOTOGRAPHY JOHN ALCOTT
COSTUME DESIGNERS ULLA-BRITT SØDERLUND, MILENA CANONERO
EDITOR TONY LAWSON
HAIRSTYLES AND WIGS LEONARD
ART DIRECTOR ROY WALKER
ASSISTANT TO THE PRODUCER ANDROS EPAMINONDAS
ASSISTANT DIRECTOR BRIAN COOK
SOUND EDITOR RODNEY HOLLAND
ASSISTANT EDITOR PETER KROOK
SECOND UNIT CAMERAMAN PADDY CAREY
CAMERA OPERATORS MIKE MOLLOY, RONNIE TAYLOR
FOCUS PULLER DOUGLAS MILSOME
CAMERA ASSISTANTS LAURIE FROST, DODO HUMPHREYS
PRODUCTION MANAGERS DOUGLAS TWIDDY, TERENCE CLEGG
ASSISTANT DIRECTORS DAVID TOMBLIN, MICHAEL STEVENSON
GAMBLING ADVISER DAVID BERGLAS
HISTORICAL ADVISER JOHN MOLLO
FENCING COACH BOB ANDERSON

Lenses for candlelight photography made by Carl Zeiss, West Germany, adapted for cinematography by Ed DiGiulio.

Made on location in England, Eire, and Germany by Hawk Films Ltd, and re-recorded at EMI Elstree Studios Ltd, England.

Opposite *Original poster.*

BARRY LYNDON
A
a film by
STANLEY KUBRICK
starring
RYAN O'NEAL
and
MARISA BERENSON
with
PATRICK MAGEE
GAY HAMILTON
HARDY KRUGER
DIANA KOERNER
LEONARD ROSSITER
MARIE KEAN
Based on the novel by
WILLIAM MAKEPEACE THACKERAY
Executive Producer
JAN HARLAN
from Warner Bros
A Warner Communications Company
Soundtrack album available on Warner Bros Records K56189

BARRY LYNDON

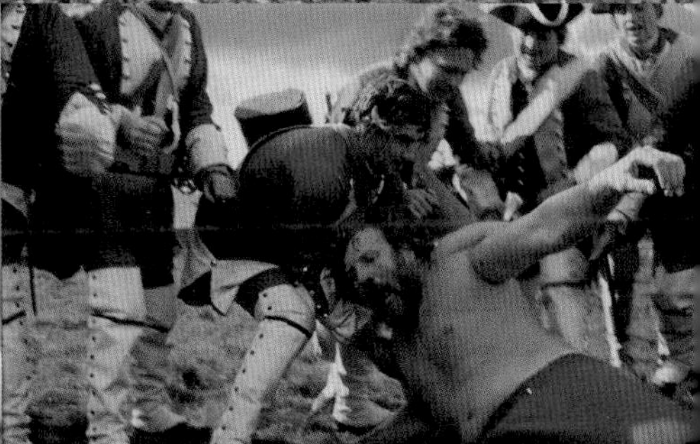

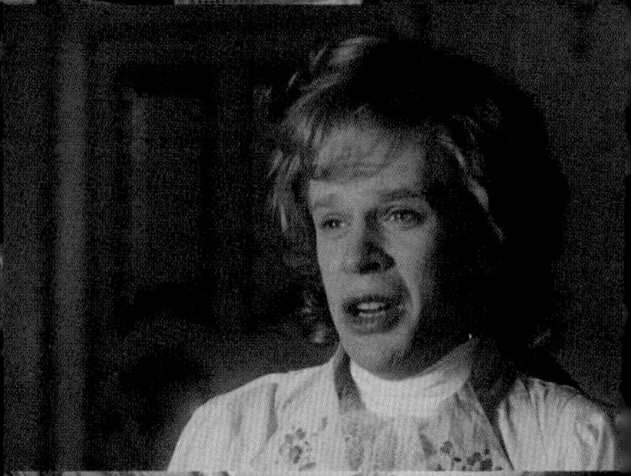
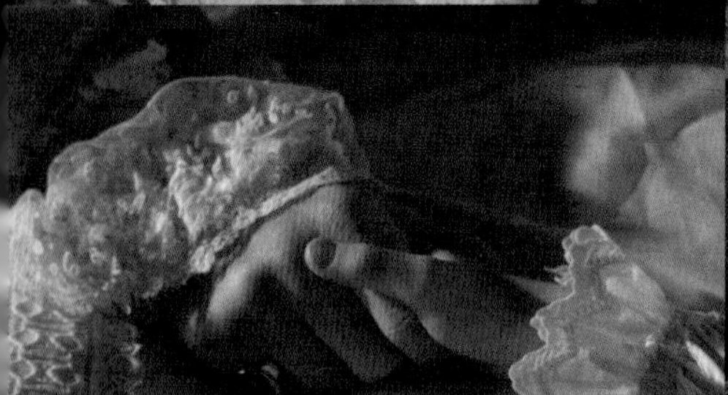

01

Barry Lyndon

by Rodney Hill

"The most important parts of a film are the mysterious parts—beyond the reach of reason and language."

—SK/1976 (to John Hofsess/*The New York Times*)

"There is such a total sense of demoralization if you say you don't care. From start to finish on a film, the only limitations I observe are those imposed on me by the amount of money I have to spend and the amount of sleep I need. You either care or you don't, and I simply don't know where to draw the line between those two points."
—Stanley Kubrick

03

The extent to which Stanley Kubrick cared about producing quality films is made manifest in every frame of *Barry Lyndon*. By some accounts it is Kubrick's least understood and most under-appreciated work (though that distinction may now belong to *Eyes Wide Shut*); but for those who admire Kubrick's films, *Barry Lyndon* stands among his most beautiful and arguably most perfect cinematic achievements, rivaled (and perhaps eclipsed) only by *2001: A Space Odyssey*. It also pointedly contradicts charges from Kubrick's detractors that his films lack any emotional substance, and its title character, despite his faults, is among the most fully and sympathetically drawn in the Kubrick canon.

According to Paul Duncan, Stanley Kubrick stumbled upon William Makepeace Thackeray's second novel, *The Memoirs of Barry Lyndon, Esq.*, by chance.[1] (Like most of Thackeray's major works, it had been published first in a monthly serial form; its original 1844 title, *The Luck of Barry Lyndon*, was changed when it appeared in two volumes in 1852.) "Kubrick does not know what drew him to this tale of a scoundrel's rise and fall," said *Time* magazine in 1975. "Beyond noting that he has always enjoyed Thackeray, he does not try to explain his choice: 'It's like trying to say why you fell in love with your wife—it's meaningless.'"[2]

In studio-issued publicity, Kubrick repeated his reluctance to pin down what it was that drew him to the novel: "That's the hardest question to answer about any film I've done. Really, it comes down to one's affection for the material.... The only really important thing about any work of art is that it be relevant to human life, and have some element of truth."[3]

Willem Hesling points out Thackeray's tendency to confront his reader "with the foolishness, weakness, and wickedness of human nature, the injustice of society and the fickleness of fate," all themes that have surfaced throughout Kubrick's *oeuvre*. Furthermore, Thackeray declines

01 ***Ryan O'Neal, as Barry Lyndon, with Kubrick, who said of him, "He was the best actor for the part.... In retrospect, I think my confidence in him was fully justified by his performance, and I still can't think of anyone who would have been better for the part." (to Michel Ciment, 1976)***
02 ***Location photograph of the film's opening duel scene, with the figures drawn in and lines marking the edge of frame.***
03 ***The director arranging Ryan O'Neal and Diana Koerner for the shot of their parting kiss.***

to moralize overtly in his satiric approach to the foibles of the middle and upper classes.[4] Clearly Kubrick shared such a reluctance to offer obvious moral stands in his films, opting to raise more questions than he answered.

Part I begins in 18th-century Ireland, as Barry's father is killed in a duel. Young Barry Redmond (Ryan O'Neal) falls in love with his cousin, Nora Brady (Gay Hamilton), who seems to be toying with the naive lad's heart. Nora turns her affections to an English officer, Captain Quin (Leonard Rossiter), and soon they announce their engagement. A jealous Barry challenges Quin to a duel, and Nora's brothers engineer a scheme by which Barry mistakenly thinks he has killed Quin; believing he will be punished for murder, Barry flees to Dublin. On the way, he is robbed of his horse and money and must join the English army to make a living. He eventually escapes his duties by stealing the uniform, papers, and horse of a lieutenant. Posing as a diplomatic courier, Barry encounters a Prussian regiment led by Captain Potzdorf (Hardy Krüger); the latter discovers Barry's ruse and forces him to join the Prussian army. In battle, Barry saves Potzdorf's life and later receives a citation and monetary reward.

"[I]f my earlier films seem more verbal than the later ones, it is because I was obliged to conform to literary conventions. Then, after some success, I was given greater freedom to explore the medium as I preferred. There'll be no screenplay of* Barry Lyndon *published, because there is nothing of literary interest to read."

—SK/1976 (to John Hofsess/*The New York Times*)

Potzdorf introduces Barry to his uncle, the minister of police; they send him to Hungary to spy on the Chevalier de Balibari (Patrick Magee), an Irishman suspected of being a spy for Austria. Barry meets the Chevalier but cannot betray him, as he is overwhelmed emotionally by the encounter with a fellow countryman, the first he has seen since leaving home. They escape Prussia and become gambling partners, and on one of their excursions Barry sets his sights on Lady Lyndon (Marisa Berenson). She is accompanied by her elderly, ailing husband, Sir Charles Lyndon (Frank Middlemass), their young son, Lord Bullingdon (Leon Vitali), and Lady Lyndon's spiritual advisor, the Reverend Runt (Murray Melvin), who is also Bullingdon's tutor. Lady Lyndon falls in love with Barry, to the consternation of Sir Charles, whose sudden death brings a close to Part I.

As Part II begins, Barry Redmond and Lady Lyndon are wed, but it soon becomes apparent that Barry does not love her. They have a son, Bryan, but Barry continues his philandering, practically right under his wife's nose. Lord Bullingdon, now roughly ten years old, defies Barry to the

04 ***Kubrick with Leonard Rossiter as Captain Quin.***
05 ***Against a backdrop of extras in English military dress, Kubrick with Godfrey Quigley as Captain Grogan (seated).***

04

05

110 NIGHT INT GAMBLING ROOM

Lord Ludd at play flanked by 2 lovely ladies. He is losing.

Barry (o.s.): How have we had the best blood, and the brightest eyes, too, of Europe throbbing around the table as I and the Chevalier have held the cards and the bank against some terrible player, who was matching some thousands out of his millions against our all which was there on the baize!

Barry cheats – how?

Barry (o.s.): Among such fellows it was diamond cut diamond. What you call fair play would have been a folly. The Irish gentlemen would have been fools, indeed, to appear as pigeons in such a hawk's nest. None but men of courage and genius could live and prosper in a society where every one was bold and clever; and here the chevalier and I held our own; ay, and more than our own.

Lord Ludd asks for paper + ink to write promissory note

Barry (o.s.): We always played on parole with anybody; any person, that is, of honour and noble lineage. We never pressed for our winnings or declined to receive promissory notes in lieu of gold.

point of insulting him. On one such occasion, Barry whips him with a cane.

Seven years later, Barry is spending the Lyndon fortune rather freely, hosting parties and other entertainments in pursuit of a peerage. Bryan has become something of a spoiled brat, and when he distracts Bullingdon from his studies once too often, the elder brother (now a young man) gives him a spanking. Barry sees this and whips Bullingdon again with a cane. Humiliated, Bullingdon vows to kill him one day.

During a harpsichord concert given by Lady Lyndon, Lord Bullingdon brings Bryan in, wearing Bullingdon's shoes, which clomp noisily and disrupt the music. Barry loses control and attacks Bullingdon in front of the distinguished guests, resulting in a brawl. After the incident, Bullingdon leaves home, and Barry is considered a social pariah.

When Bryan, the only remaining person whom Barry genuinely loves, dies from a horseback-riding accident, Barry is thrown into a state of depression. The family fortune continues to dwindle, and Lady Lyndon attempts suicide. Bullingdon returns to save his mother from ruin. He challenges Barry to a duel and wounds him in the leg, which must be amputated. Bullingdon sends Graham (Philip Stone), the family's secretary, to offer Barry an annuity on the condition that he leave England permanently, which he does. The final scene shows Lady Lyndon, looking pale and devoid of emotion, signing Barry's pension check.

06 ***Page from one of the numerous drafts of Kubrick's adaptation of Thackeray's novel.***

Stanley Kubrick said, "One thing that makes *Barry Lyndon* accessible in movie terms is that you don't have to destroy the essential qualities of the story by compression. Though a great deal had to be cut out, it still survives as a film."[5]

Thackeray's novel is told from Barry's point of view, as he recalls events in a journal from a prison cell decades later, in 1814. Kubrick replaced Barry's recollections with a more detached, third-person omniscient narration, read splendidly by Michael Hordern.

"People like Barry are successful because they are not obvious—they don't announce themselves."

—SK/1975 (to Duffy and Schickel/*Time*)

Kubrick's screenplay follows the same general chronology as the novel, but it simplifies the events by reducing the historical span covered, combining certain characters and actions, omitting or modifying certain episodes, and by inventing a few new ones. For example, Barry's seduction of Lady Lyndon in the film takes place with a few suggestive glances and a kiss on a balcony; and after a single confrontation with Barry, Sir Charles is dead, allowing the marriage to take place after a year of mourning. In the novel, however, Sir Charles clings to life for two years after his wife and Barry meet, and even after Sir Charles's death, Lady Lyndon continues to evade Barry for another three years.[6]

Kubrick also reconceptualized the character of Lord Bullingdon consider-

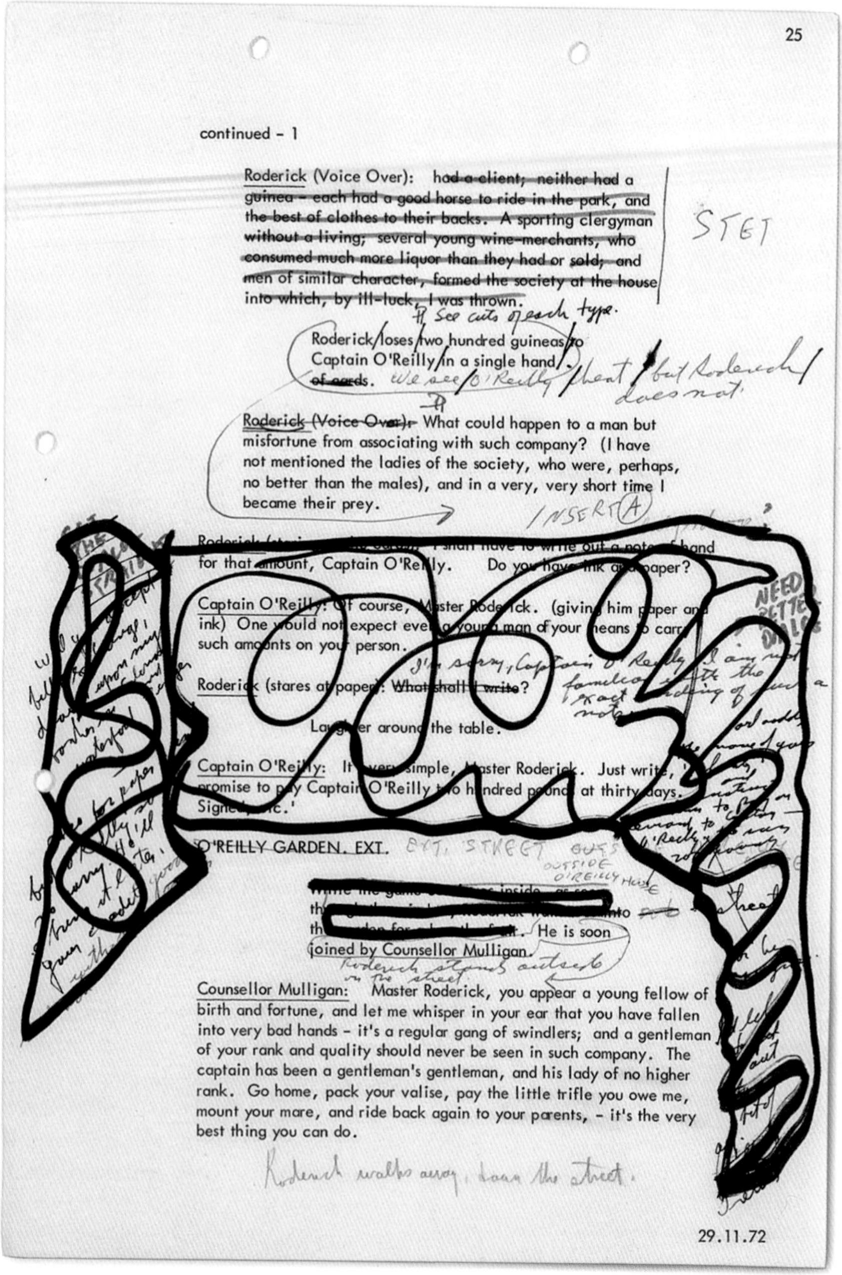

25

continued - 1

Roderick (Voice Over): had a client; neither had a guinea - each had a good horse to ride in the park, and the best of clothes to their backs. A sporting clergyman without a living; several young wine-merchants, who consumed much more liquor than they had or sold; and men of similar character, formed the society at the house into which, by ill-luck, I was thrown.

STET

¶ See cuts of each type.

Roderick loses two hundred guineas to Captain O'Reilly in a single hand of cards. We see O'Reilly cheat but Roderick does not.

Roderick (Voice Over): What could happen to a man but misfortune from associating with such company? (I have not mentioned the ladies of the society, who were, perhaps, no better than the males), and in a very, very short time I became their prey.

INSERT (A)

Roderick (stari... I shall have to write out a note of hand for that amount, Captain O'Reilly. Do you have ink and paper?

Captain O'Reilly: Of course, Master Roderick. (giving him paper and ink) One would not expect even a young man of your means to carry such amounts on your person.

Roderick (stares at paper): What shall I write?

I'm sorry, Captain O'Reilly, I am not familiar with the exact wording of such a note.

Laughter around the table.

Captain O'Reilly: It's very simple, Master Roderick. Just write, 'I promise to pay Captain O'Reilly two hundred pounds at thirty days. Signed, etc.'

NEED BETTER DIALOG

O'REILLY GARDEN. EXT. EXT. STREET OUTSIDE O'REILLY HOUSE

[redacted]. He is soon joined by Counsellor Mulligan.

Roderick stands outside on the street.

Counsellor Mulligan: Master Roderick, you appear a young fellow of birth and fortune, and let me whisper in your ear that you have fallen into very bad hands - it's a regular gang of swindlers; and a gentleman of your rank and quality should never be seen in such company. The captain has been a gentleman's gentleman, and his lady of no higher rank. Go home, pack your valise, pay the little trifle you owe me, mount your mare, and ride back again to your parents, - it's the very best thing you can do.

Roderick walks away, down the street.

29.11.72

ably. Thackeray's Bullingdon, a much braver young man than Kubrick's, crosses the Atlantic to fight against the American "rebels" and is thought to have been killed in battle. Years later he resurfaces to find Lady Lyndon in Bath, about to give in once more to Barry's charms. Bullingdon turns Barry over to the police for his immense debts, and thus Barry ends his days in a London debtors' prison. Kubrick invented entirely the two dramatically decisive scenes with Bullingdon: the harpsichord concert and the duel.

Other interesting differences concern Barry's mother and the Chevalier. In the novel, Mrs. Barry does not play such a central role in the later drama as she does in the film (it is she, in Kubrick's version, who tries to take over the household and who pushes Barry to try to get a title for himself, ultimately leading to his ruin). In Thackeray's story, the handsome Chevalier de Balibari (an Italianization of "Bally Barry") turns out to be Barry's long-lost uncle. Perhaps Kubrick thought such a connection would seem overly melodramatic in the film, requiring too much explanation. For the film's purposes, it is enough to establish a feeling of kinship between Barry and his fellow Irishman.[7]

For the title role, Kubrick said he never envisioned anyone other than Ryan O'Neal. He had been "tremendously impressed" with O'Neal in *What's*

07 ***An example of Kubrick's unflinching script editing.***
08 ***Ryan O'Neal and Kubrick.***

Up Doc? (Peter Bogdanovich, 1972) and other films. Kubrick elaborated: "He's got qualities as an actor that had never been used. And strangely enough, Ryan's emotional acting—when the going gets heavy in *Barry Lyndon*—is almost easier for him than anything else. The character also had to be physically attractive, incredibly charming."[8] A modeling sensation of the 1970s, Marisa Berenson studied acting at Wynn Handman's school and with method-acting master Lee Strasberg; but her first film role came about quite by chance. She and Helmut Berger were frequent guests of Luchino Visconti. One evening, Visconti casually mentioned that Berenson would be perfect for a role in *Death in Venice* (1971), as the wife of Dirk Bogarde's character. Her next role, as the German heiress in *Cabaret* (Bob Fosse, 1972), caught the attention of Stanley Kubrick. Without even meeting her, Kubrick offered Berenson the female lead in *Barry Lyndon*. She characterized the experience as: "Hard work! I've never worked so hard in my life! (Kubrick is) such a perfectionist. He pushed people until they almost couldn't take it anymore." She told Andy Warhol in *Interview*, "I love (Kubrick). He's really wonderful. He has a

09 ***Executive producer Jan Harlan photographs Marisa Berenson (Lady Lyndon) with costume designer Milena Canonero in the background.***
10 ***Kubrick with production designer Ken Adam, who had previously worked with him on* Dr. Strangelove.**

marvelous sense of humor. He's very shy, especially with women, and very introverted.... On the set he's not at all tyrannical with his actors; he's always very calm."[9]

Kubrick found "a tragic sense about her," pointing out that the kind of silent presence she achieves in *Barry Lyndon* requires a special kind of talent. "Marisa shares a quality with all the greatest film actresses, who don't have to move or do too much. They project a certain stillness on the outside, yet you know what they're feeling and thinking."[10]

In supporting roles, Kubrick used a few "alumni" from previous films. Leonard Rossiter, who appeared briefly as a Russian scientist in *2001: A Space Odyssey*, creates the memorable character of

"Filmmaking violates the old adage that what is wanted is a system designed by geniuses which can be run by idiots. It has always been the other way around with films."

—SK/1971 (to Alexander Walker)

Captain Quin, Barry's rival for the hand of Nora Brady. His second, Captain Grogan, is portrayed by Godfrey Quigley, who played the unforgettable prison chaplain in *A Clockwork Orange*. That film also featured Patrick Magee (Mr. Alexander, the writer), who plays the Chevalier de Balibari, and Philip Stone (Alex's dad), who portrays Lady Lyndon's secretary, Graham (and who would find his signature role as Grady in Kubrick's next film, *The Shining*).

11

Production began in the autumn of 1973 and lasted for eight and a half months, with 250 shooting days.[11] Originally budgeted at $2.5 million, *Barry Lyndon*'s price tag eventually reached $11 million;[12] and to coin a phrase, every penny appears up on the screen, thanks in large part to Kubrick's use of existing castles, manor houses, and other locations. Cahir Castle, near Waterford, stands in as part of Prussia, where Barry has been coerced into the army of Frederick the Great; the stone walls and towers of Kells served as the assembly point for the English "Redcoats"; and Carrick-on-Suir was used as the background for the sequences of Barry in the English militia. The interiors of Dublin Castle were adapted to resemble a posh hotel and a casino. One of the most difficult location problems was to find a number of period buildings situated close enough to each other that they could pass for a main thoroughfare in 18th-century Prussia. Eventually, Potsdam (then in East Germany) provided the solution.

When the production shifted to England, a variety of stately homes was used to portray the lives of high society and the aristocracy. They included Castle Howard, in the north of England, and Wilton House, near Salisbury, for scenes at Lady Lyndon's estate. Barry's wedding to Lady Lyndon

11 ***Production design sketch.***
12 ***For the shots of the British army marching into battle, three cameras were moved simultaneously along eight hundred feet of dolly tracks.***

was filmed at the chapel at Longleat, seat of the Marquess of Bath. Some of the battle scenes were filmed near Bath, Somerset; and other locations include Corsham Court, Wiltshire, and the tithe barn at Glastonbury Abbey. All in all, Ken Adam's team (including Stanley and Christiane Kubrick's daughter, Katharina) spent approximately six months on location scouting and arranging for all the facilities and cooperation essential for the prolonged shooting.[13]

In addition to locations, costumes lent a crucial air of authenticity to the production; all told, the costuming phase lasted eighteen months. Milena Canonero, who had designed the costumes on *A Clockwork Orange*, supervised every detail of the wardrobes, including jewelry and wigs. The garments had to be not only in correct period style but also naturally integrated in the characters' "daily lives." Basic costume designs came from paintings and printed illustrations of the period. The designers also procured a rich haul of authentic 18th-century garments from various collectors in England; some of these were copied stitch by stitch. Canonero and Ulla-Britt Søderlund designed, cut, assembled, and dyed the dozens of principal costumes, representing virtually every social class in England and Ireland.[14]

Some 250 soldiers from the Irish Army appeared in the film, reenacting the maneuvers, skirmishes, and full-scale battles of the Seven Years' War. Their costumes, representing the armies of

12

15

14

16

England, Prussia, and France, were designed with the help of renowned historian John Mollo, an expert in military uniforms.[15]

Production designer Ken Adam told *American Cinematographer*: "Stanley had my continuity sketch artist do hundreds of sketches using various lenses on groups of soldiers, to see how they would look through a 50 mm or wide-angle lens. We also experimented with having the first line of infantry in proper uniforms, the second line in paper uniforms, the third line as cutouts, and so on.... I always felt that he put such a great amount of effort into the attack and defense sequences because he was thinking of *Napoleon*, and this approach would have been of vital importance on that project."[16] Adam saw his design work on *Barry Lyndon* as being "much more reproductive than imaginative.... We did enormous amounts of research. That's why it was never that exciting to me as a designer, even though I won the Academy Award for it.... We studied every painter of the period, photographed every detail we could think of; bought real clothes of the period, which, incidentally, were almost invariably too small.... There were enormous challenges too, such as the house of Lady Lyndon. That was like a jigsaw puzzle, a combination of about ten or eleven stately homes in England."[17]

The sheer lushness of *Barry Lyndon* owes a great deal to the brilliant cinematography of John Alcott, for which he won an Academy Award as well as an award for outstanding cinematography from the National Society of Film Critics. Arguably it is the crowning achievement of his career. Alcott strove to create the feeling of natural light throughout, although he did use some artificial lighting, contrary to the

17

myth that has grown up around the picture. Taking his cues from the way the natural light actually fell on a setting, Alcott would simulate that effect with a combination of natural light and lighting units, to achieve a filmable level of illumination. In a few cases, he used virtually no natural light at all, as with the scene in the dining room when Bryan asks if Barry has bought him a horse.

Hold on opening frame 15 ft. then start pan – 8 seconds for effect to enter + exit the frame
tighten up gradually on zoom
Just enough empty f.g. field out of shot but no more than that
Blue frame represents static shot

The fact of using only actual locations presented rather unique cinematographic challenges, as Alcott told *American Cinematographer.* With what he rated as the most difficult scene to shoot in *Barry Lyndon,* a complex set of problems arose due to the combination of natural and artificial light, as well as the nature of the location. The scene in the restaurant, where Barry gets the cold shoulder from Wendover, "involved a 180-degree pan, and what made it difficult were the fluctuations in the weather outside," Alcott said. "There were many windows, and I had lights hidden behind the brick-work and beaming through the windows. The outside light was going up and down so much that we had to keep changing things to make sure the windows wouldn't blow out excessively.... What complicated it further was that this was one of those stately houses that had the public coming

13 ***Marisa Berenson in her role as Lady Lyndon.***
14 ***From left: Marie Kean (Barry's mother), David Morley (Bryan), Leon Vitali (Lord Bullingdon), and Murray Melvin (Reverend Runt).***
15 ***Kubrick prepares to shoot a scene of Barry and his family playing croquet.***
16 ***From left: Andre Morell (Lord Wendover), Marisa Berenson, Ryan O'Neal, and Anthony Sharp (Lord Hallam).***
17 ***Kubrick's instructions for a landscape shot.***

18

19

through and visiting at the same time we were shooting."[18]

Barry Lyndon makes extensive (and astonishing) use of the zoom lens, even though Alcott generally preferred prime lenses. (He felt that many cinematographers misused the zoom, simply as a means to speed up production by not having to change lenses.) Most camera setups in *Barry Lyndon* are stationary, but on the handful of occasions when the camera moves, it does so elaborately and to stunning effect. The battle sequence involved an eight-hundred-foot track, with three cameras moving simultaneously along as the troops advanced.

All of the candlelit scenes were done entirely without artificial light, by candlelight and reflectors alone, necessitating the development of custom lenses. Alcott told *American Cinematographer*, "Kubrick located three 50 mm f 0.7 Zeiss still-camera lenses, which were left over from a batch made for NASA. We had a nonreflex Mitchell BNC which was sent over to Ed DiGiulio to be reconstructed to accept this ultra-fast lens."[19] DiGiulio wondered why Kubrick wanted special lenses developed, when there were already lenses that would suffice for candlelit scenes, provided that artificial fill light was used. He said Kubrick told him "that he was not doing this just as a gimmick, but because he wanted to preserve the natural patina and feeling of these old castles at night as they actually were."

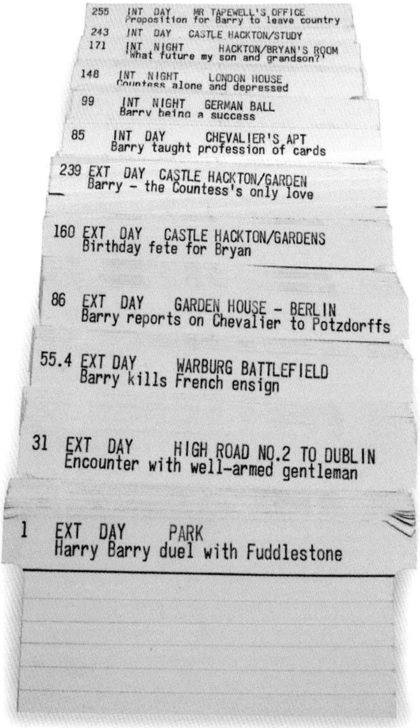

255 INT DAY MR TAPEWELL'S OFFICE
Proposition for Barry to leave country
243 INT DAY CASTLE HACKTON/STUDY
171 INT NIGHT HACKTON/BRYAN'S ROOM
'What future my son and grandson?'
148 INT NIGHT LONDON HOUSE
Countess alone and depressed
99 INT NIGHT GERMAN BALL
Barry being a success
85 INT DAY CHEVALIER'S APT
Barry taught profession of cards
239 EXT DAY CASTLE HACKTON/GARDEN
Barry - the Countess's only love
160 EXT DAY CASTLE HACKTON/GARDENS
Birthday fete for Bryan
86 EXT DAY GARDEN HOUSE - BERLIN
Barry reports on Chevalier to Potzdorffs
55.4 EXT DAY WARBURG BATTLEFIELD
Barry kills French ensign
31 EXT DAY HIGH ROAD NO.2 TO DUBLIN
Encounter with well-armed gentleman
1 EXT DAY PARK
Harry Barry duel with Fuddlestone

20

DiGiulio continued, "The addition of any fill light would have added an artificiality to the scene that he did not want. To achieve the amount of light he actually needed in the candlelight scenes, and in order to make the whole movie balance out properly, Kubrick went ahead and push developed the entire film one stop — outdoor and indoor scenes alike."[20]

One problem with these custom-fitted lenses was that they had virtually no depth of field at such low light levels. Alcott had

18 ***The director with Marisa Berenson and O'Neal, preparing for the scene of Bryan's funeral.***
19 ***Kubrick performing a hand-held shot.***
20 ***A note card system was used to organize the scenes (yellow cards for interior, blue for exterior).***
21 ***Ryan O'Neal, Kubrick, and art director Roy Walker.***

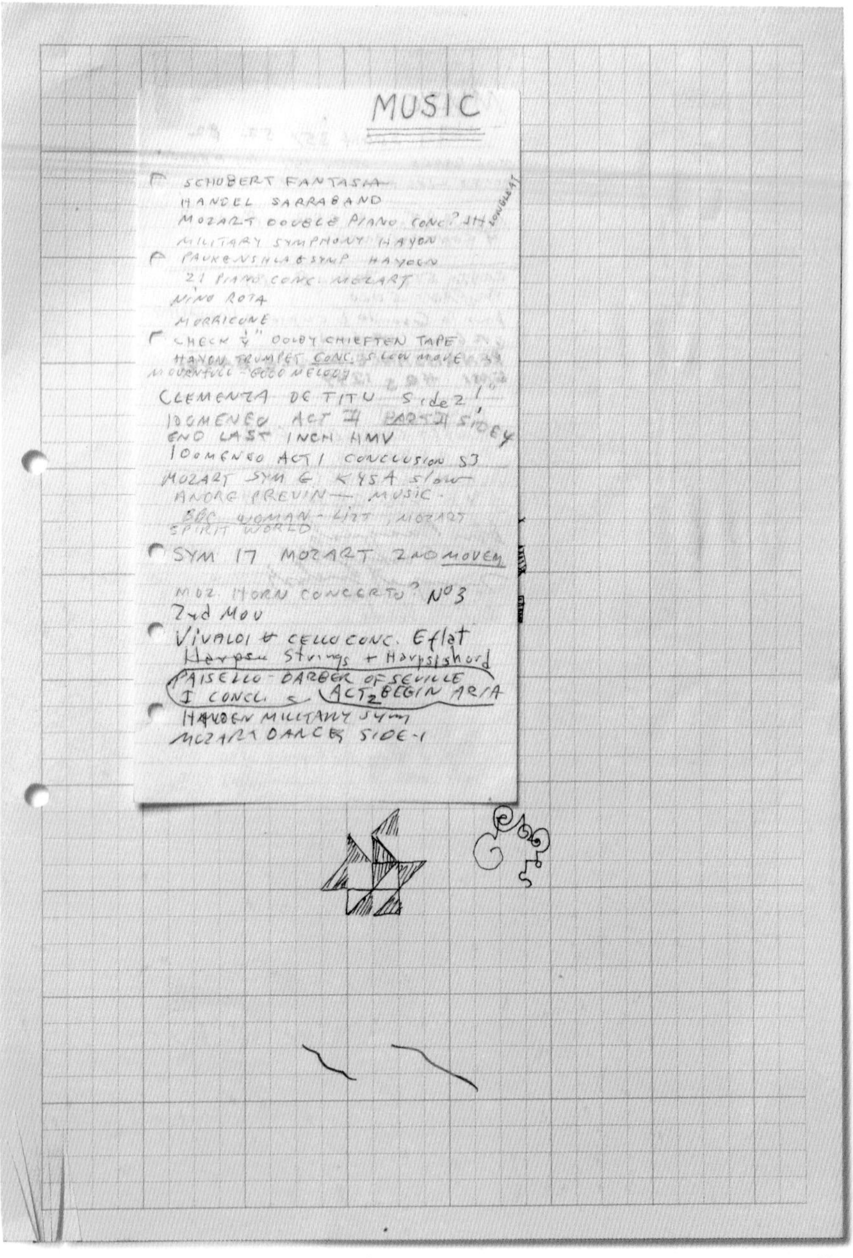
MUSIC

SCHUBERT FANTASIA
HANDEL SARRABAND
MOZART DOUBLE PIANO CONC? 1H LONGLEAT
MILITARY SYMPHONY HAYDN
PAUKENSHLAGSYMP HAYDN
21 PIANO CONC MOZART
NINO ROTA
MORRICONE
CHECK ¼" DOLBY CHIEFTEN TAPE
HAYDN TRUMPET CONC. SLOW MOVE 33
MOURNFULL - GOOD MELODY
CLEMENZA DE TITU Side 2 1"
IDOMENEO ACT II PART II SIDE 4
END LAST INCH HMV
IDOMENEO ACT I CONCLUSION S3
MOZART SYM G K454 slow
ANDRE PREVIN — MUSIC.
BBC WOMAN - LIZT, MOZART
SPIRIT WORLD
SYM 17 MOZART 2ND MOVEM
MOZ. HORN CONCERTO? No 3
2nd MOV
VIVALDI + CELLO CONC. Eflat
Harpsu Strings + Harpsishord
PAISELLO - BARBER OF SEVILLE
I CONCL. ACT 2 BEGIN ARIA
HAYDEN MILITARY SYM
MOZART DANCES SIDE-1

to gauge the lenses' focal settings by doing hand tests from two hundred feet down to four feet. He and Douglas Milsome came up with an elaborate system using closed-circuit video with a grid placed over the TV screen to mark the range within which actors could move and still remain in focus.

When asked to what extent Kubrick collaborated on cinematography, Alcott told Michel Ciment: "He knows exactly what he wants. If he were not a director, he would probably be the greatest lighting cameraman in the world. On the set, he works at the camera and you can learn a lot from working with him.... He is, in his heart of hearts, a photographer, and he likes getting the best possible effects out of a camera."[21]

Kubrick also clearly liked getting the best possible performances out of his actors, even if it meant doing thirty takes or more. While some performers have resented his methods, others such as Ryan O'Neal, Leon Vitali, and Murray Melvin appreciated them on *Barry Lyndon*. O'Neal wrote in his diary at the time, "God, he works you hard. He moves you, pushes you, helps you, gets cross with you, but above all he teaches you the value of a good director." He told *Time* magazine,

22 ***Among Kubrick's notes for* Barry Lyndon *was this list of music he considered using for the film; ultimately, the soundtrack, a mixture of original and adapted works orchestrated by Leonard Rosenman, won an Academy Award.***
23 ***Shooting the gambling scenes entirely by candlelight.***

23

H.M. Customs & Excise
Kings Beam House
Mark Lane
London EC3

July 6th, 1973

Dear Sirs:

Cinema Products of Los Angeles have constructed a special BNC camera, which is owned by Osprey Films Inc, 9777 Wilshire Boulevard Beverly Hills, Calif. 90212. This camera is the only camera in the world able to use a 50 mm f 0.7 Zeiss Planar lens, this lens being the 'fastest' in the world. The work on this camera has taken months and everything is now completed. Osprey Films Inc. are willing to rent this camera to us for a special candlelight motion picture photographic sequence in August 1973. We will be shooting the film in England, using this camera and will be returning the camera after the production is completed.

The same applies to an Arriflex 2C which was specially altered by Cinema Products to take ultra fast aspheric lenses, namely the Canon 55 mm f 1.2 and the Canon 24 mm lens f 1.4.

Please grant us temporary import under the terms of your notice, Number 209.

Yours faithfully,
for and on behalf of
HAWK FILMS LTD.

Jan Harlan

Re: MITCHELL BNC CAMERA No. 332
ZEISS PLANAR LENS SERIAL NO. 2584566
ARRIFLEX 2C Serial No. 13049

"Stanley brought out aspects of my personality and acting instincts that had been dormant. I had to deliver up everything he wanted, and he wanted just about everything I had."[22]

Leon Vitali (Lord Bullingdon), who went on to become Kubrick's personal assistant and casting director, told *American Cinematographer*: "I can't understand why an actor complains when a director wants to do more takes, because it's just an opportunity to do different things, and to give the scene another slant.... If it wasn't clicking for some reason, we'd all go to his caravan and work on the scene. He'd say, 'Well, how would you say this? How would you do this?' All the time, he was probing you to find what it was you were trying find."[23]

Murray Melvin (Reverend Runt) would seem to agree. "Stanley (was) a great believer in the man. *You* have to do it." On the subject of multiple takes, Melvin added, "I knew he had seen (i.e., liked) something I had done. But because he was a good director, he wouldn't tell me what it was. Because if someone tells you you've done a good bit, then you know it and put it in parentheses and kill it. The better actor you were, the more he drew out of you."[24]

As with all of Kubrick's mature work, the music in *Barry Lyndon* plays a crucial role in establishing mood. For the sake of stylistic verisimilitude, most of the music comes from the period, with compositions ranging from Bach ("Concerto for Two Harpsichords and Orchestra in C Minor, BWV 1060"), to Mozart ("March from *Idomeneo*"), to Frederick II of Prussia ("Hohenfriedberger March"). Some pieces were reorchestrated by Leonard Rosenman, as was the case with Handel's "Sarabande" (originally written for piano), used as a recurring theme with variations throughout the film.

Rosenman's adapted score in *Barry Lyndon* helps to propel the action, define character, reveal psychological subtext, and provide a subtle link between characters and the audience—tasks not usually fulfilled by a stand-alone classical piece. From the first note, over the Warner Bros. logo, the "Sarabande" theme establishes a tone of majestic melancholy that defines the overall mood of the film. Perhaps the most outstanding instance where Kubrick puts Rosenman's musical arrangement to pointed dramatic effect occurs during the duel between Barry and Lord Bullingdon. Dialogue is kept to a minimum in what may be the film's most dramatically charged scene. A simple, ominous, bass and tympani duet offers a variation on "Sarabande," creating an almost unbearable, fatalistic tension, as Barry's world is shattered unexpectedly.

In addition to the period classical music, *Barry Lyndon* features traditional Irish airs performed by the internationally recognized folk group The Chieftains. In the first scene in which Barry appears, playing cards with his cousin Nora, the tune "Women of Ireland" conveys the exquisite, delicate tenderness Barry feels for Nora, where words would fail. Like many scenes throughout the film, this one uses

24 ***Letter from executive producer Jan Harlan to British customs, regarding import of the BNC camera custom-mounted with the f 0.7 Zeiss lens used to shoot the candlelit scenes.***

dialogue sparingly, and the music speaks volumes about the palpable emotion in the scene.[25]

Kubrick's contract with Warner Bros. not only gave him final cut on *Barry Lyndon*, but the studio also afforded him the freedom to take an entire year for post-production. John Calley, then production chief at Warner Bros., explained: "It would make no sense to tell Kubrick, 'OK, fella, you've got one more week to finish the thing.' What you would get then is a mediocre film that cost say, eight million dollars, instead of a masterpiece that cost eleven million. When somebody is spending a lot of your money, you are wise to give him time to do the job right."[26]

Much of the critical opinion at the time held that Kubrick had indeed done the job right. *Variety* found that "casting, concept and execution are all superb."[27] A cover story in *Time* called it, "Overwhelming ... an uncompromised artistic vision ... an art-film spectacle — something few directors since Griffith and Eisenstein have brought off," citing a "greatness that time alone can, and probably will, confirm." *Playboy* heralded it as "one of the most breathtakingly beautiful films of all time ... a classic." The *New York Post* raved: "Brilliant.... Even (Kubrick) has never before made a film quite so audacious.... Its aching beauty will wipe you out."[28]

Winner of the British Academy Award for direction and four Oscars (cinematography, production design, adapted music, and costumes), the film also received Academy Award nominations for best picture, direction, and screenplay. The National Board of Review named it the best film of the year (tied with *Nashville*) and Kubrick best director (tied with Robert Altman).

Praise was not universal, however, and some critics were harshly dismissive, finding the film detached, slow, and antihumanist. Initially it was a financial failure (except in France), but in time (as is the case with all of Kubrick's films) it has made a profit, thanks largely to the video (and now DVD) market.

On the eve of the film's release, according to *Time*, Kubrick was "armored in the serene belief that whatever judgment the public passes on his new movie ... he has fulfilled the director's basic ideal, which is to shoot 'economically and with as much beauty and gracefulness as possible.'"[29]

Some critics and audiences have accused *Barry Lyndon* of being cold, detached, and lacking emotion and humanity. Furthermore, they found its hero to be unsympathetic — even despicable and incapable of love. However, the protagonist, for all his faults, demonstrates his capacity for genuine love and compassion at several important points in the film.

The whole story is set in motion because of Barry's intense (though foolish) love for Nora Brady. His passion (so admired by Captain Grogan) propels him blindly into the duel with Quin, after which

25 ***Patrick Magee, left, as the Chevalier de Balibari. Regarding Kubrick's penchant to have actors perform takes repeatedly, Magee told*** Time, ***"The catch-words on the set are 'Do it faster, do it slower, do it again.' Mostly, 'Do it again.'" (to Duffy and Schickel, 1975)***
26 ***Ryan O'Neal and Hardy Krüger (Captain Potzdorf) with Kubrick.***

25

26

played the same game herself: clearly, she married the repugnant Sir Charles for his fortune.

The great love of Barry's life is his son, Bryan, for whom he proves himself capable of sacrifice and folly. In an ironic twist of fate, by trying to please his son with the gift of a horse, Barry inadvertently causes his death. The loss of Bryan is as devastating for Barry as it is for Lady Lyndon.

Despite his faults, Barry demonstrates an admirable level of character at key points in the film. When Potzdorf (who had forced him back into service) is wounded in battle, Barry could easily leave him to die (and perhaps escape the Prussian Army), but he saves him. Similarly, in the final duel, after Bullingdon's pistol misfires, Barry has the chance to kill him and to be rid of a pesky enemy; but from some combination of basic humanity, a misguided sense of "honor," and perhaps even some modicum of love for Lady Lyndon, Barry fires into the ground. This turns out to be a serious error of judgment, as Bullingdon takes advantage of the situation and shoots Barry.

The worst that can be said of Barry is that he is greedy, naive, and unaware of when he has gone too far. He overreaches his station in life and tragically fails to anticipate the wrath that the upper class (in the person of Bullingdon) will exact upon him. (Herein lies a curious

he must go on the road. When Barry meets Grogan again in the English army, their friendship deepens, and Grogan's death comes as a serious emotional blow. It is difficult to imagine a scene with more tenderness than the one in which Barry cradles the dying Grogan in his arms. Similarly, Barry's instant affinity for the Chevalier de Balibari is expressed in a genuine outpouring of emotion, which reveals the loneliness the hero has felt being so long away from home.

It is true, of course, that Barry does not love his wife. He has married her for her money and station, a fact that becomes immediately apparent (to her and to the audience) as he blows smoke into her face in the scene following their wedding. However, Lady Lyndon had

27 ***For this shot of Barry post-amputation, O'Neal's leg was folded up into a sling.***
28 ***Patrick Magee being prepared for the scene of the Chevalier and Barry Lyndon's first meeting.***
29 ***From left, Murray Melvin, Jan Harlan, and Kubrick.***

28

29

30

31

32

33

parallel to *Eyes Wide Shut*: both Barry and Bill Harford foolishly step into situations that are "out of their league," but Barry is able to "gate-crash" in high society for several years, whereas Bill Harford cannot even manage it for an evening; curiously, each is "expelled" by a character portrayed by Leon Vitali.) By the end of the film, Barry is a broken man, having lost virtually everyone he ever loved, and one cannot help but feel considerable sympathy for the character.

Still, scholars such as Hesling point out that Kubrick's visual style distances the viewer from the type of cliché romance, heroism, and solemnity sometimes associated with historical epics. The narrator's often ironic, contrapuntal commentary contributes to this distancing effect. While one hardly could call *Barry Lyndon* Brechtian, some of the effects are the same: the viewer is allowed some emotional remove to ponder the intellectual dimensions of the film. This also results in a more universal story: it is not simply concerned with the "psychologically realistic" portrayal of complex, individual 18th-century characters, but rather with "types" that can find some resonance with modern audiences.

Furthermore, for both Thackeray and Kubrick, fate is a far more important driving force in the story than individual will. In the novel, Barry complains, "Alas! We are the sport of destiny."[30] Kubrick's narrator engages in occasional foreshadowing, as with Bryan's death and Barry's downfall, and other stylistic elements further contribute to the sense of fatalism. Notably, the repeated use of the slow zoom-out serves not only to distance the viewer from the events being portrayed but also to situate the characters within a larger universe, where their quarreling and conniving seem trivial and futile. As Hesling points out, the film "sketches life as a treacherous game no one is able to control and in which a chance occurrence or a wrong move can be fatal...."[31]

With time, *Barry Lyndon* has taken on the status of an acknowledged classic. Even some reviewers who misunderstood the film initially have revised their opinions of it. Notable among these is *Variety*'s Todd McCarthy. In 2001, he wrote: "I can think of just one instance of having completely reversed my opinion of a film that I had previously weighed in on in print—Stanley Kubrick's *Barry Lyndon*. On first viewing, its overall point and meaning eluded me, and I was not able to appreciate anything beyond its pictorial and musical qualities; it was only on second viewing that its staggering, Stroheimesque stature as a corrosive contemplation of the foolishness of most human endeavor became abundantly clear."[32]

Also with the benefit of hindsight, J. Hoberman wrote in 2000: "*Barry Lyndon* could be considered Kubrick's masterpiece. At the very least, this cerebral action film represents the height of his craft ... the loveliest of Stanley Kubrick films ... the saddest of swashbucklers and the most melancholy of bodice-rippers.... After a decade of adaptations from Jane Austen, Henry James, and Thomas Hardy, Kubrick's oddest project seems twenty years ahead of its time. *Barry Lyndon* is the movie Miramax would most want to release, albeit polished by Tom Stoppard and cut by ninety minutes."[33] Sadly, in the absence of Stanley Kubrick, neither Miramax nor anyone else will have the chance to release a film like *Barry Lyndon* ever again.

Bizarre accounts in the mainstream press have relentlessly portrayed Stanley Kubrick as a cold, calculating, misanthrope; but his films, when fully reflected upon, belie that notion. Consider the profound, cosmic anticipation at the end of *2001: A Space Odyssey* (1968). Steven Spielberg has referred to the Star Child's appearance as, "the greatest moment of optimism and hope for mankind that has ever been offered by a modern filmmaker."[34] Consider also the final scene of *Paths of Glory* (1957), in which the battle-worn French soldiers are moved to tears by the simple song of a frightened, young German girl (Susanne Christian, a.k.a. Christiane Kubrick). The tragic human frailty of *Barry Lyndon* belongs firmly in this tradition. As "a melancholy lamentation on time elapsing and the loss of innocence,"[35] it remains perhaps Kubrick's strongest, most defiant response to those who misjudge his work.

30 ***Mealtime in the British army.***
31 ***Kubrick with his wife, Christiane.***
32 ***Second and third from left: Katharina and Vivian Kubrick, two of Stanley's daughters, appeared as extras.***
33 ***On the subject of the duel between Bullingdon and Barry, Kubrick told Michel Ciment: "The setting was a tithe barn which also happened to have a lot of pigeons nesting in the rafters .... The sounds of the pigeons added something to this, and, if it were a comedy, we could have had further evidence of the pigeons." He was referring, presumably, to the pigeon droppings that caused the crew to wear hats during the shooting of this scene.***

34

35

36

Notes

1. Paul Duncan, *Stanley Kubrick: Complete Films* (Cologne: TASCHEN, 2003): 145. (Thackeray's first novel, *Catherine*, appeared in 1839.)
2. Martha Duffy and Richard Schickel, "Kubrick's Grandest Gamble: Barry Lyndon," *Time* (December 15, 1975). Reprinted in Gene D. Phillips, ed., *Stanley Kubrick: Interviews* (Jackson: University Press of Mississippi, 2001): 162.
3. Warner Bros. Studios, pressbook for Barry Lyndon, 1975.
4. William Hesling, "Kubrick, Thackeray and The Memoirs of Barry Lyndon, Esq." *Literature/Film Quarterly*, vol. 29 no. 4 (2001): 266–7.
5. Ibid.
6. Philippe Pilard, *Synopsis: Barry Lyndon/Stanley Kubrick* (Paris: Editions Nathan, 1990): 43–4.
7. Ibid: 46–7.
8. Warner Bros.
9. Quoted in Rodney Hill, "Berenson, Marisa," in Gene D. Phillips and Rodney Hill, *The Encyclopedia of Stanley Kubrick* (New York: Checkmark, 2002): 30.
10. Warner Bros.
11. Duffy and Schickel: 161; Pilard: 17.
12. Pilard: 18.
13. Warner Bros.
14. Ibid.
15. Hill, "Mollo, John," in Phillips and Hill: 225.
16. Ron Magid, "Quest for Perfection," *American Cinematographer* (October 1999).
17. Quoted in Hill, "Adam, Ken," in Phillips and Hill: 1.
18. Quoted in Hill, "Alcott, John," in Phillips and Hill: 9.
19. Ibid.
20. Quoted in Jay S. Beck, "DiGiulio, Ed," in Phillips and Hill: 78.
21. Michel Ciment, *Kubrick: The Definitive Edition* (New York: Faber and Faber, 2001): 213.
22. Duffy and Schickel: 169.
23. Magid.
24. Duffy and Schickel: 166.
25. Beck, "The Chieftains," in Phillips and Hill: 45.
26. Duffy and Schickel: 167.
27. *Variety* (December 17, 1975).
28. Warner Bros.; Duffy and Schickel: 160.
29. Duffy and Schickel: 168.
30. Quoted in Hesling: 270.
31. Hesling: 276.
32. Todd McCarthy, "Some films are worth a second look," *Variety* (October 11, 2001).
33. J. Hoberman, "Endless Summer," *Village Voice* (April 19–25, 2000).
34. Steven Spielberg, "Foreword," in Christiane Kubrick, *Stanley Kubrick: A Life in Pictures* (London: Bulfinch Press, 2002).
35. Hesling: 276.

34 ***The fistfight scene.***
35 ***Ryan O'Neal and Kubrick both looking pensive, with focus-puller Douglas Milsome on the right.***
36 ***Godfrey Quigley and Ryan O'Neal rehearse.***

Interview with Stanley Kubrick

by Michel Ciment

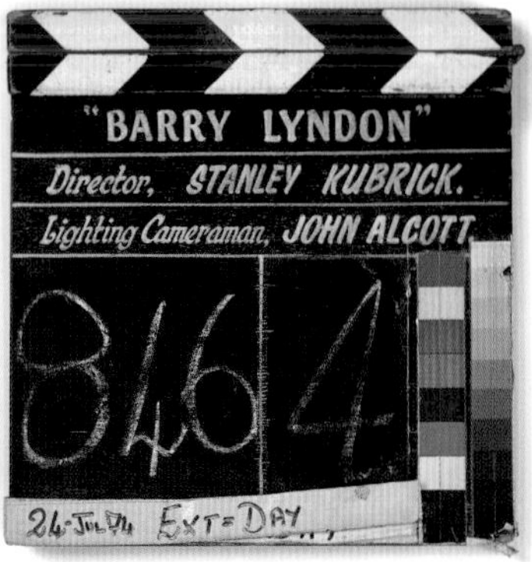

37

38

Excerpts from a 1976 interview published in Kubrick: The Definitive Edition *by Michel Ciment*

...Your last three films were set in the future. What led you to make an historical film?

...Since I am currently going through the process of trying to decide what film to make next, I realize just how uncontrollable is the business of finding a story, and how very much it depends on chance and spontaneous reaction. You can say a lot of "architectural" things about what a film story should have: a strong plot, interesting characters, possibilities for cinematic development, good opportunities for the actors to display emotion, and the presentation of its thematic ideas truthfully and intelligently. But, of course, that still doesn't really explain why you finally chose something, nor does it lead you to a story. You can only say that you probably wouldn't choose a story that doesn't have most of those qualities.

Since you are completely free in your choice of story material, how did you come to pick up a book by Thackeray, almost forgotten and hardly republished since the 19th century?

I have had a complete set of Thackeray sitting on my bookshelf at home for years, and I had read several of his novels before reading *Barry Lyndon*. At one time, *Vanity Fair* interested me as a possible film but, in the end, I decided the story could not be successfully compressed into the relatively short time-span of a feature film. This problem of length, by the way, is now wonderfully accommodated for by the television miniseries, which, with its ten- to twelve-hour length, presented on consecutive nights, has created a completely different dramatic form. Anyway, as soon as I read Barry Lyndon I became very excited about it. I loved the story and the characters, and it seemed possible to make the transition from novel to film without destroying it in the process. It also offered the opportunity to do one of the things that movies can do better than any other art form, and that is to present historical subject matter. Description is not one of the things that novels do best but it is something that movies do effortlessly, at least with respect to the effort required of the audience. This is equally true for science-fiction and fantasy, which offer visual challenges and possibilities you don't find in contemporary stories.

There is very little introspection in the film. Barry is open about his feelings at the beginning of the film, but then he becomes less so.

At the beginning of the story, Barry has more people around him to whom he can express his feelings. As the story progresses, and particularly after his marriage, he becomes more and more isolated. There is finally no one who loves him, or with whom he can talk freely, with the possible exception of his young son, who is too young to be of much help. At the same time I don't think that the lack

37 ***The clapboard.***
38 ***Kubrick smiles for the camera as director of photography John Alcott (right) surveys the weather conditions.***
39 ***Kubrick shooting the fistfight between Barry Lyndon and Toole (Pat Roach) with a hand-held camera. The close-range shots in this scene recall his early work on*** **Day of the Fight** ***and*** **Killer's Kiss.**

"I don't like doing interviews. There is always the problem of being misquoted or, what's even worse, of being quoted exactly, and having to see what you've said in print."

—SK/1976 (to Michel Ciment)

of introspective dialogue scenes are any loss to the story. Barry's feelings are there to be seen as he reacts to the increasingly difficult circumstances of his life. I think this is equally true for the other characters in the story. In any event, scenes of people talking about themselves are often very dull.

In contrast to films which are preoccupied with analyzing the psychology of the characters, yours tend to maintain a mystery around them. Reverend Runt, for instance, is a very opaque person. You don't know exactly what his motivations are.

But you know a lot about Reverend Runt, certainly all that is necessary. He dislikes Barry. He is secretly in love with Lady Lyndon, in his own prim, repressed, little way. His little smile of triumph, in the scene in the coach, near the end of the film, tells you all you need to know regarding the way he feels about Barry's misfortune, and the way things have worked out. You certainly don't have the time in a film to develop the motivations of minor characters.

Lady Lyndon is even more opaque.

Thackeray doesn't tell you a great deal about her in the novel. I found that very strange. He doesn't give you a lot to go on. There are, in fact, very few dialogue scenes with her in the book. Perhaps he meant her to be something of a mystery. But the film gives you a sufficient understanding of her, anyway.

In the first part of *A Clockwork Orange*, we were against Alex. In the second part, we were on his side. In this film, the attraction/repulsion feeling towards Barry is present throughout.

Thackeray referred to it as "a novel without a hero." Barry is naive and uneducated. He is driven by a relentless ambition for wealth and social position. This proves to be an unfortunate combination of qualities which eventually leads to great misfortune and unhappiness for himself and those around him. Your feelings about Barry are mixed but he has charm and courage, and it is impossible not to like him despite his vanity, his insensitivity, and his weaknesses. He is a very real character who is neither a conventional hero nor a conventional villain.

The feeling that we have at the end is one of utter waste.

Perhaps more a sense of tragedy, and because of this the story can assimilate the twists and turns of the plot without becoming melodrama. Melodrama uses all the problems of the world, and the difficulties and disasters which befall the characters, to demonstrate that the world is, after all, a benevolent and just place.

In many ways, the film reminds us of silent movies. I am thinking particularly of the seduction of Lady Lyndon by Barry at the gambling table.

That's good. I think that silent films got a lot more things right than talkies. Barry and Lady Lyndon sit at the gaming table and exchange lingering looks. They do not say a word. Lady Lyndon goes out on the balcony for some air. Barry follows her outside. They gaze longingly into each other's eyes and kiss. Still not a word is spoken. It's very romantic, but at the same time, I think it suggests the empty attraction they have for each other that is to disappear as quickly as it arose. It sets the stage for everything that is to follow in their relationship. The actors, the images, and the Schubert worked well together, I think.

Did you have Schubert's Trio in mind while preparing and shooting this particular scene?

No, I decided on it while we were editing. Initially, I thought it was right to use only 18th-century music. But sometimes you can make ground-rules for yourself which prove unnecessary and counterproductive. I think I must have listened to every LP you can buy of 18th-century music. One of the problems which soon became apparent is that there are no tragic love-themes in 18th-century music. So eventually I decided to use Schubert's Trio in E Flat, Opus 100, written in 1828. It's a magnificent piece of music and it has just the right restrained balance between the tragic and the romantic without getting into the headier stuff of later Romanticism.

You are well known for the thoroughness with which you accumulate information and do research when you work on a project. Is it for you the thrill of being a reporter or a detective?

I suppose you *could* say it is a bit like being a detective. On *Barry Lyndon*, I accumulated a very large picture file of drawings and paintings taken from art books. These pictures served as the reference for everything we needed to make clothes, furniture hand props, architecture, vehicles, etc. Unfortunately, the pictures would have been too awkward to use while they were still in the books and I'm afraid we finally had very guiltily to tear up a lot of beautiful art books. They were all, fortunately, still in print which made it seem a little less sinful. Good research is an absolute necessity and I enjoy doing it. You have an important reason to study a subject in much greater depth than you would ever have done otherwise, and then you have the satisfaction of putting the knowledge to immediate good use.

The designs for the clothes were all copied from drawings and paintings of the period. None of them were designed in the normal sense. This is the best way, in my opinion, to make historical costumes. It doesn't seem sensible to have a designer interpret, say, the 18th century, using the same picture sources from which you could faithfully copy the clothes. Neither is there much point sketching the costumes again when they are already beautifully represented in the paintings and drawings of the period. What is very important is to get some actual clothes of the period to learn how they were originally made. To get them to look right you really have to make them the same way. Consider also the problem of taste in designing clothes, even for today. Only a handful of designers seem to have a sense of what is striking and beautiful. How can a designer, however brilliant, have a feeling for the clothes of another period which is equal to that of the people and the designers of the period itself, as recorded in their pictures? I spent a year preparing *Barry Lyndon* before the shooting began and I think this time was very well spent. The starting point and *sine qua non* of any historical or futuristic story is to make you believe what you see.

The danger in an historical film is that you lose yourself in details, and become decorative.

The danger connected with any multi-faceted problem is that you might pay too much attention to some of the problems to the detriment of others, but I am very conscious of this and I make sure I don't do that.

Why do you prefer natural lighting?

Because it's the way we see things. I have always tried to light my films to simulate natural light; in the daytime using the windows actually to light the set, and in night scenes the practical lights you see in the set. This approach has its problems when you can use bright electric light sources, but when candelabras and oil lamps are the brightest light sources which can be in the set, the difficulties are vastly increased. Prior to *Barry Lyndon*, the problem has never been properly solved. Even if the director and cameraman had the desire to light with practical light sources, the film and the lenses were not fast

40

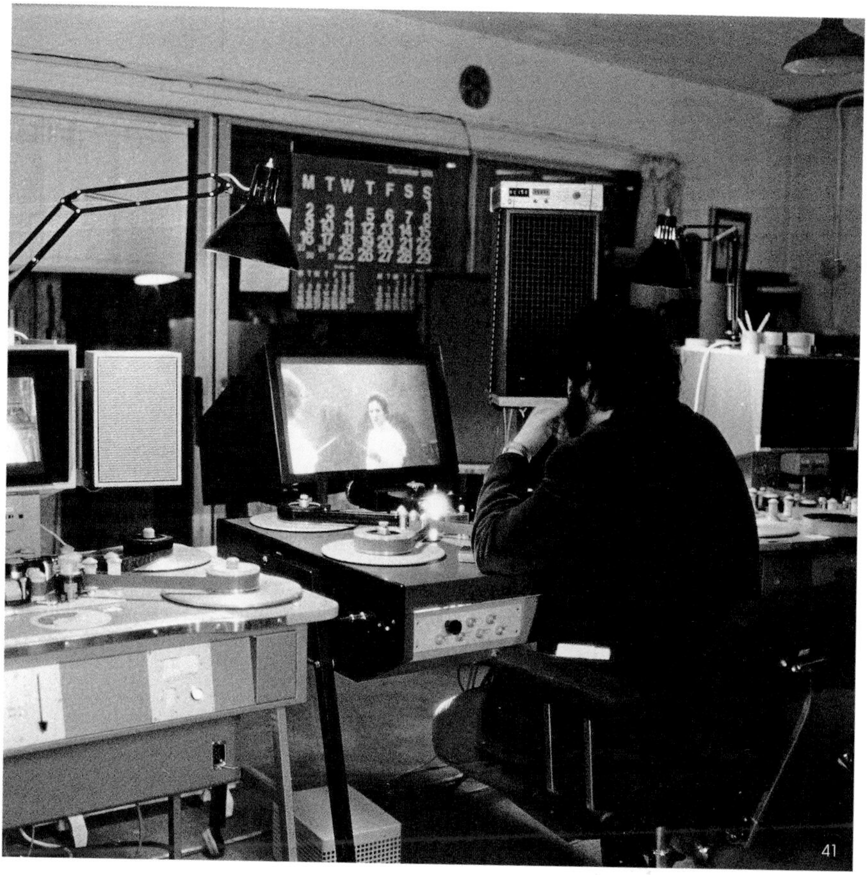

40 *Testing a tracking shot with a viewfinder and a wheelchair.*
41 *One of Kubrick's garages at his home in Abbot's Mead was turned into an editing room to cut the film. Kubrick told Gene D. Phillips, "When I'm editing, my identity changes from that of a writer or a director to that of an editor. I am no longer concerned with how much time or money it costs to shoot a given scene. I cut everything to the bone and get rid of anything that doesn't contribute to the total effect of the film."*

enough to get an exposure. A 35 mm movie camera shutter exposes at about 1/50 of a second, and a useable exposure was only possible with a lens at least 100 percent faster than any which had ever been used on a movie camera. Fortunately, I found just such a lens, one of a group of ten which Zeiss had specially manufactured for NASA satellite photography. The lens had a speed of f 0.7 and it was 100 percent faster than the fastest movie lens. A lot of work still had to be done to it and to the camera to make it useable. For one thing, the rear element of the lens had to be 2–5 mm away from the film plane, requiring special modification to the rotating camera shutter. But with this lens it was now possible to shoot in light conditions so dim that it was difficult to read. For the day interior scenes we used either the real daylight from the windows, or simulated daylight by banking lights outside the windows and diffusing them with tracing paper taped on the glass. In addition to the very beautiful lighting you can achieve this way, it is also a very practical way to work. You don't have to worry about shooting into your lighting equipment. All your lighting is outside the window behind tracing paper, and if you shoot towards the window you get a very beautiful and realistic flare effect.

42 ***Continuity Polaroids of the scene in which Lord Bullingdon (Leon Vitali) challenges Barry Lyndon.***

3-6-74
3-6-74
3-6-74
4-6-74
TAKE 3
4-6-74
X

The Shining

1980 / COLOR / 145 MINUTES
Distributed by WARNER BROS.

CAST
JACK TORRANCE JACK NICHOLSON
WENDY TORRANCE SHELLEY DUVALL
DANNY DANNY LLOYD
HALLORANN SCATMAN CROTHERS
ULLMAN BARRY NELSON
GRADY PHILIP STONE
LLOYD JOE TURKEL
DOCTOR ANNE JACKSON
DURKIN TONY BURTON
YOUNG WOMAN IN BATH LIA BELDAM
OLD WOMAN IN BATH BILLIE GIBSON
WATSON BARRY DENNEN
FOREST RANGER 1 DAVID BAXT
FOREST RANGER 2 MANNING REDWOOD
GRADY DAUGHTER LISA BURNS
GRADY DAUGHTER LOUISE BURNS
NURSE ROBIN PAPPAS
SECRETARY ALISON COLERIDGE
POLICEMAN BURNELL TUCKER
STEWARDESS JANA SHELDON
RECEPTIONIST KATE PHELPS
INJURED GUEST NORMAN GAY

CREW
PRODUCED AND DIRECTED BY STANLEY KUBRICK
EXECUTIVE PRODUCER JAN HARLAN
SCREENPLAY STANLEY KUBRICK and DIANE JOHNSON (based upon the novel by Stephen King)
DIRECTOR OF PHOTOGRAPHY JOHN ALCOTT
PRODUCTION DESIGNER ROY WALKER
EDITOR RAY LOVEJOY
PRODUCTION MANAGER DOUGLAS TWIDDY
ASSISTANT DIRECTOR BRIAN COOK
COSTUME DESIGNER MILENA CANONERO
STEADICAM OPERATOR GARRETT BROWN
HELICOPTER PHOTOGRAPHY MACGILLIVRAY FREEMAN FILMS
PERSONAL ASSISTANT TO THE DIRECTOR LEON VITALI
ASSISTANT TO THE PRODUCER ANDROS EPAMINONDAS
ART DIRECTOR LES TOMKINS
MAKEUP TOM SMITH
CAMERA OPERATORS KELVIN PIKE, JAMES DEVIS
FIRST UNIT FOCUS (ALSO LIGHTING) DOUGLAS MILSOME
2ND UNIT PHOTOGRAPHY DOUGLAS MILSOME, MACGILLIVRAY FREEMAN FILMS
ASSISTANT DIRECTORS TERRY NEEDHAM, MICHAEL STEVENSON
CASTING JAMES LIGGAT
LOCATION RESEARCH JAN SCHLUBACH, KATHARINA KUBRICK, MURRAY CLOSE

Made by Hawk Films Ltd at EMI Elstree Studios Ltd., England.

Opposite ***Lobby card showing Saul Bass's artwork.***

A MASTERPIECE OF MODERN HORROR
THE SHINING
Stanley Kubrick
A STANLEY KUBRICK FILM
STARRING
JACK NICHOLSON SHELLEY DUVALL "THE SHINING" WITH SCATMAN CROTHERS
BASED ON THE NOVEL BY STEPHEN KING
SCREENPLAY BY STANLEY KUBRICK & DIANE JOHNSON
PRODUCED AND DIRECTED BY STANLEY KUBRICK
EXECUTIVE PRODUCER JAN HARLAN
PRODUCED IN ASSOCIATION WITH THE PRODUCER CIRCLE CO.
R RESTRICTED
UNDER 17 REQUIRES ACCOMPANYING PARENT OR ADULT GUARDIAN
From Warner Bros. A Warner Communications Company
©Warner Bros. Inc. 1980 All Rights Reserved.

THE SHINING

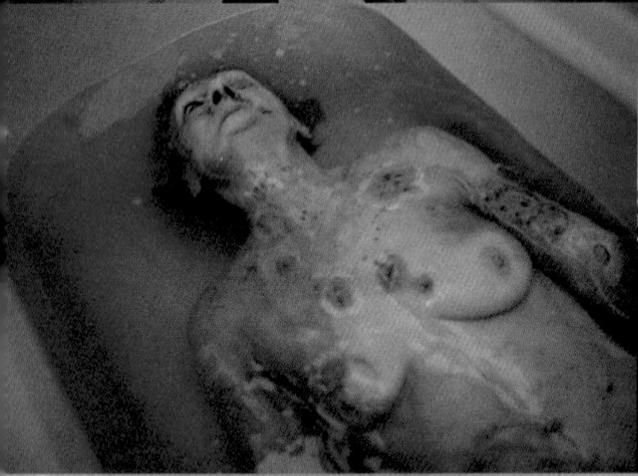

REDRUM

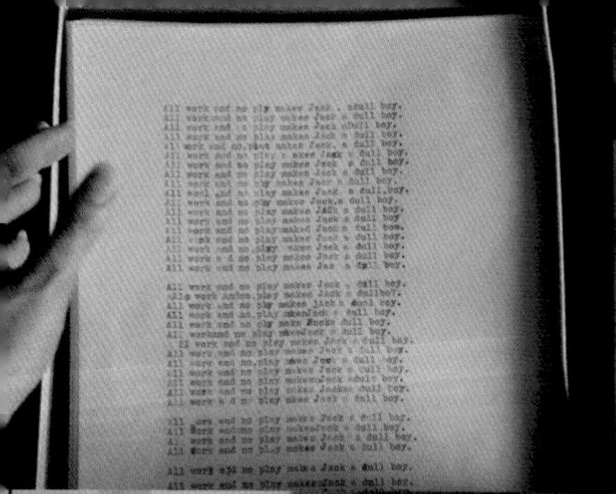

The Gold Room

JIM BEAM
WALKER
25

The Shining

by Rodney Hill

I sent my soul through the invisible, some letter of that afterlife to spell: and by and by my soul returned to me and answered, "I myself am Heaven and Hell."
—The Rubáiyát of Omar Khayyám

"The problem in writing stories of this kind is to prevent the reader from ever being reminded of historical existence, for, if he once thinks of real people whose passions are interrupted by a need for lunch or whose beauty can be temporarily and mildly impaired by the common cold, the intensity and timelessness become immediately comic."

—Passage underlined by SK in W. H. Auden's essay on the writings of Edgar Allan Poe, above which he wrote, "Shining partially refutes this." (*Forewords and Afterwords* by W. H. Auden, London: Faber and Faber, 1973: 210–11)

If each of Stanley Kubrick's films can be said to have a central theme dealing with the Jungian duality of man, then *The Shining* has it in spades. Departures from Stephen King's 1978 novel abound in Kubrick's transformation of the supermarket bestseller into a formidable work of cinematic art. Perhaps the most important in this regard is the shift away from King's Manichean conflict between the innocent child, Danny, and the absolute, external evil of the Overlook Hotel, in favor of an inner conflict waged within the character of Jack Torrance—between his own god and devil, his own heaven and hell—a losing battle that has been going on for quite some time as the film begins.

To emphasize this grand-scale, inner struggle between darkness and light, Kubrick's Overlook is full of dual imagery: symmetry, mirrors, and doubling of characters—Danny/Tony, two ghostly little girls, two women in room 237 (the seductive siren and the horrible old hag), two ghostly servants (Lloyd and Grady), indeed two Gradys (Charles and Delbert), and finally two Jacks (the one who is there when the film takes place, and the one who has "always" been there). Jack's ultimate surrender to his evil impulses is brought about by a number of temptations: alcohol, adultery, violence, and most of all, status, all at the expense of his responsibility to care for his family.

Like each of Kubrick's films, *The Shining* finds resonance with all of the others. Michel Ciment has brilliantly pointed out that *The Shining* and *Eyes Wide Shut* constitute a matched pair—doubles of each other, if you will—one a horrific vision of what happens when a man is cooped up with his family for too long, cut off from the outside world entirely, the other an equally bizarre nightmare about what happens when a man ventures too far outside the protective structure of the family.[1] *The Shining* also finds a good deal of kinship with many other Kubrick films in its dual status as a complex work of art, both structurally and aesthetically, and a

01 ***Left to right: Joe Turkel (Lloyd), Kubrick, and Jack Nicholson (Jack Torrance). "Jack's performance here is incredibly intricate, with sudden changes of thought and mood.... In this particular scene Jack produced his best takes near the highest numbers."***
–SK/1980 (to Michel Ciment)
02 ***The Grady sisters surprise Danny in the games room.***

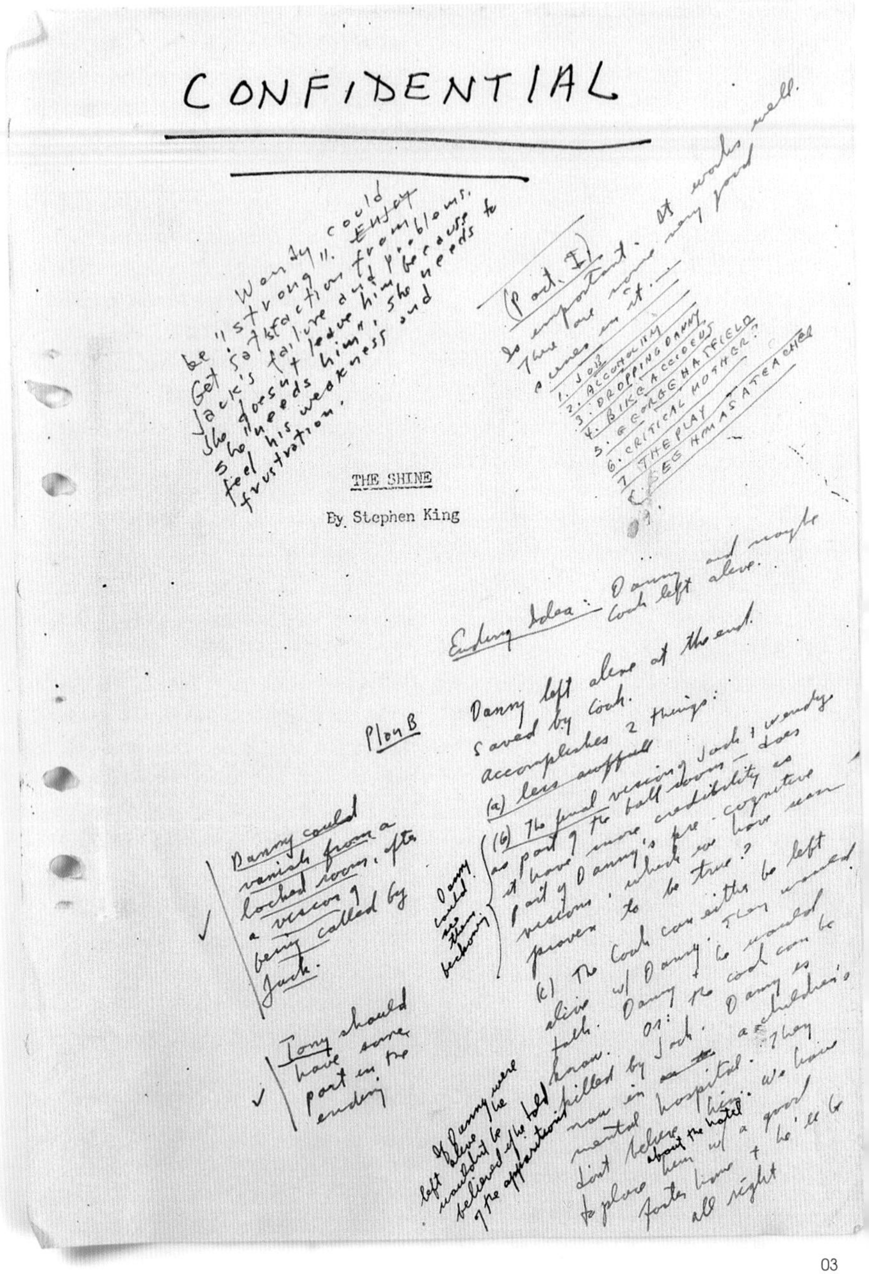
CONFIDENTIAL

Wendy " could be " strong " . Enjoy
Get satisfaction from blows.
Jack's failure and problems.
She doesn't leave him because
she " needs him " . She needs to
feel his weakness and
frustration.

(Part I)
So important. It works
There are some very good
scenes in it. —
1. JOB
2. ALCOHOLISM
3. DROPPING DANNY
4. BIKE ACCIDENTS
5. GEORGE HATFIELD
6. CRITICAL MOTHER?
7. THE PLAY
8. SEES HIM AS A TEACHER

THE SHINE

By Stephen King

Ending Idea: Danny and maybe Cook left alive.

Plan B

Danny left alone at the end.
saved by Cook.
accomplishes 2 things:
(a) less awful
(b) The final visions Jack & Wendy as part of the ball room — does it have more credibility as part of Danny's pre-cognitive visions, which we have seen proven to be true?
(c) The Cook can either be left alive w/ Danny. They would talk. Danny & he would know. Or: the cook can be killed by Jack. Danny is now in ~~a~~ a children's mental hospital. They don't believe him about the hotel. We have to place him w/ a good foster home & he'll be all right.

Danny could see them beckoning.

✓ Danny could vanish from a locked room, after a vision of being called by Jack.

✓ Tony should have some part in the ending

If Danny were left alive he wouldn't be believed if he told of the apparitions.

03

Only the wind spoke back, gusting more strongly this time, scattering leaves across the sloping roof below his window. Some of them slipped into the raingutter and came to rest there like tired dancers.

Danny...Danneee...

He started at the sound of that familiar voice and craned out the window, his small hands on the sill. With the sound of Tony's voice the whole night seemed to have come silently and secretly alive, whispering even when the wind quieted again and the leaves were still and the shadows had stopped moving. He thought he saw a darker shadow standing by the bus stop a block down, but it was hard to tell if it was a real thing or an eye-trick.

Don't go, Danny... Tony

Then the wind gusted again, making him squint, and the shadow by the bus stop was gone...if it had ever been there at all. He stood by his window for

(a minute? an hour?)

some time longer, but there was no more. At last he crept back into his bed and pulled the blankets up and watched the shadows thrown by the alien streetlight turn into a sinuous jungle filled with flesh-eating plants that wanted only to slip around him, squeeze the life out of him, and drag him down into a blackness where one sinister word flashed in red: (green fire last time)

REDRUM.

wouldn't it look like

REDRUM

MURDER

special effect

REDRUM

NOT LIKE THAT.

member of that most maligned of species: the genre film.

At least a decade prior to filming *The Shining*, Stanley Kubrick had expressed an interest in horror and (as with his approach to science-fiction with *2001: A Space Odyssey*) in making a superior work in that genre. John Baxter writes, "As early as 1966, he'd told a friend he would 'like to make the world's scariest movie.'"[2] Diane Johnson, co-scenarist on *The Shining*, told *The New York Times* that Kubrick saw "a certain amount of intellectual challenge in doing a horror film right."[3] Apparently Warner Bros. was also keen to have him work in horror: according to Baxter the studio had offered Kubrick the chance to direct *The Exorcist* and later *The Exorcist II*, both of which he declined.

In 1977, John Calley (then Warner production chief) sent Kubrick galley proofs of Stephen King's novel, *The Shining*, a project that was brought to the studio by an independent production company, the Producers Circle. Although Kubrick said he had "always been interested in ESP and the paranormal," it was King's plot that attracted him most: "I thought it was one of the most ingenious and exciting stories of the genre I had read."[4]

Johnson guesses that the story attracted Kubrick because of its "psychological underpinnings." She adds, "A father threatening his child is compelling. It's an archetypal enactment of unconscious rage."[5]

Ultimately, though, Kubrick was reluctant or perhaps unable to say precisely what drew him to the project, as he told Ciment: "There is no useful way to explain how you decide what film to make. In addition to the initial problem of finding an exciting story ... you have the added problem of its being sufficiently different from the films you have already done."

For Kubrick, one way of dealing with the latter consistently was always to start with an existing story, a strategy he followed for all of his films after *Killer's Kiss*. This allowed him to judge the story more objectively than if he had written it himself. As he explained to Ciment: "If you read a story which someone else has written, you have the irreplaceable experience of reading it for the first time. This is something which you obviously cannot have if you write an original story."

For months after finishing *Barry Lyndon*, Kubrick read voraciously in search of material for his next project. He discovered the novels of Diane Johnson, particularly *The Shadow Knows*. He and Johnson met a few times, and Kubrick learned that she was teaching a course on the Gothic novel at U.C. Berkeley. Thus, he told Ciment, "When *The Shining* came up she seemed to be the ideal collaborator, which, indeed, she proved to be."

03 ***Kubrick received galleys of Steven King's*** **The Shining** ***(working title "The Shine") before it was published, and covered them with notes.***
04 ***Making notes in the galleys of King's book, Kubrick noted how "REDRUM" would appear in mirrored writing.***

05 ***Left to right: Leon Vitali (seated), Lisa and Louise Burns (Grady daughters), Vivian Kubrick (with camera), Shelley Duvall (Wendy Torrance), Garrett Brown (wearing Steadicam apparatus), and Kubrick.***
06 ***Kubrick's daughter Vivian (background) films as Lisa and Louise Burns prepare to shoot.***

05

06

(Kubrick chose not to read the screenplay that King had already written; Vincent LoBrutto characterizes Kubrick's relationship with King as similar to the one he had with Anthony Burgess on *A Clockwork Orange*: Kubrick did not want the author involved in the adaptation process.)[6]

Starting their collaboration in June 1977, Kubrick and Johnson discussed King's book for a full month without writing anything at all, asking such questions as, "Is Jack a nice man?" "Does Wendy love him?" "What kind of clothes would she wear?" In order to understand Gothic horror more fully and seriously, they also discussed such works as *Jane Eyre, Wuthering Heights,* and the stories of Edgar Allan Poe. In addition, both read Bruno Bettelheim's treatise on the fairy tale, *The Uses of Enchantment,* as well as Freud's essay on the uncanny. Johnson later explained, "We read Freud a lot. In his essay on the uncanny, Freud says specific things about why eyes are scary and why inanimate objects like puppets are scary in their animate shapes. We talked about the role of memory and wish in making you afraid...." Then each individually came up with a short plot outline. They compared notes, shuffled scenes around, and then wrote a more fleshed-out outline. According to Johnson, "The writing was secondary to knowing who the characters were, what the events were, and the exact function of every scene. Stanley kept saying, 'When you know what's happening in a scene, the words will follow.'" Together, Kubrick and Johnson wrote several drafts of the screenplay, and the process of revision continued through preproduction and into production.[7] Janet Maslin hailed the result as a "shrewd and economical screenplay," adding that "most of their alterations in the story, which has been changed and improved considerably, have the effect of letting it run deeper."[8]

"I think we tend to be a bit hypocritical about ourselves. ... We are capable of the greatest good and the greatest evil, and the problem is that often we can't distinguish between them when it suits our purpose."

—SK/1980 (to Michel Ciment)

Kubrick and Johnson were concerned about how to approach the ghosts in the story. Were they to be real ghosts, or hallucinations brought on by mental disturbances? And Johnson points out a third, more complex possibility: "The psychological states of the characters can create real ghosts who have physical powers. If Henry VIII sees Anne Boleyn walking around the bloody tower, she's a real ghost, but she's also caused by his hatred."

Jack Torrance (Jack Nicholson), a former schoolteacher and aspiring writer, has traveled from Vermont to Colorado along with his wife, Wendy (Shelley Duvall)

07 ***"I believe that Jack is one of the best actors in Hollywood, perhaps on a par with the greatest stars of the past like Spencer Tracy and Jimmy Cagney.... Jack is particularly suited for roles which require intelligence. He is an intelligent and literate man, and these qualities are almost impossible to act."***
–SK/1980 (to Michel Ciment)

All work and no play makes Jack a dull boy. All work and no play makes Jack a dull boy. All work and no play makes Jack a dull boy. All work and no play makes Jack a dull boy. All work and no play makes Jack a dull boy. All work and no pla makes Jack a dull boy ¾. A ll work and no play m kes Jack a dull boy.

All work and no play makes Jack a dull boy. All work and no play makes Jack a dull boy. All work and no play mak s Jack a dull boy. All work and no play makes Jack a dull boy. All work and no play makes Jack a dullboy. All work and no play makes Jack a dullboy. All work and no play makes Jack a dull boy. All work and no play makes Jack a dull boy. All work and no play makes Jack a dull boy. All work and no play makes Jack a dull boy. All work and no play makes Jack a dull boy. All work and no play makes Jack a dull boy. All work and no play makes Jack a dull boy. All work and no play makes Jack a dull boy. All work and no play makes Jack a dull boy.

All work and no play makes Jack a dull boy. All work and no play makes Jack a dull boy. All work and no play makes Jack a dull boy. All work and no play makesJack a dull boy. All work and no play makes Jack a dull boy. All work and no play makes Jack a dull boy. All work and no play makes Jacka dull boy. All work and no play makes Jack a dull boy. All work and no play makes Jack a dull boy. All work and no play makes Jack a dull boy. All work and no play makes Jack a dull boy. All work and no play makes Jack a dull boy. all work and no play makes Jack a dull boy. All work and no play makes Jack a dull boy. Alo work and no play makes Jack a dullboy. All work and no play makes Jack a dull boy. All work and no play makes Jack a dull boy. All work and no play makes Jack a dull boy. All work and no play makes Jack a dull boy. All work and no play makes Jack a dull boy. All work and no play makes Jack a dull boy. All work and no play makes Jack a dull boy. All w rk and no play makes Jacka dullboy. All work and no play makes Jack a dull bo.y. All work and no play makes Jack a dull boy.

All work and no play makes Jack a dull boy. All work and no play mak es Jack a dull boy. Allwork and no play makes Jack a sdullboy. all work and no play makes Jack a dull boy. All work and no play makes Jack a dull boy. All work and no play makes Jack a dull boy. All work and no play makes Jack a dull boy. All work and no play makes Jack a dull boy. All work and no play makes Jack a dull boy. All wor kand no play makes Jack a dullboy.

and their five-year-old son, Danny (Danny Lloyd). He takes a job as winter caretaker at the Overlook Hotel, nestled high up in the Rocky Mountains, despite the fact that the hotel was the scene of a multiple murder and suicide perpetrated by a previous caretaker named Grady (Philip Stone) ten winters earlier.

Unbeknownst to his parents, Danny possesses limited psychic powers that manifest themselves through a voice that he calls "Tony" (Wendy thinks that Tony is simply an "imaginary friend"). Through Tony, Danny glimpses a few horrific images of the Overlook (including two girls in blue party dresses, presumably Grady's daughters), but he is unable to discuss his fears with Wendy other than to express mild misgivings. We learn that Tony's first appearance coincided with an "accident" in which a drunken Jack dislocated Danny's shoulder.

The family arrives at the Overlook on "closing day," as the regular staff is packing up and leaving. The manager, Stuart Ullman (Barry Nelson) shows them around, pointing out various aspects of the hotel's storied past, its famous hedge maze, etc., as well as practical information like how to use the Sno-Cat should they need to get down the mountain in the snow.

Left alone in the games room, Danny is startled when the two girls from his

08 ***One of hundreds of typed pages from Jack's manuscript.***
09 ***Filming the model of the maze as focus-puller Douglas Milsome (far left) looks on.***

09

earlier vision appear suddenly. Later, he meets the head chef, Dick Hallorann, who also has psychic powers, an ability Hallorann calls "shining." He tells Danny that some places "shine" like people, and that the Overlook is such a place. Out of the blue, Danny asks about room 237, and Hallorann replies that there is nothing there, though he warns Danny sharply to "stay out!"

A month passes, and Jack suffers from writer's block and also grows impatient and irritable with Wendy. Danny's psychic flashes grow more and more realistic and disturbing, as he sees images of the two girls' bloody corpses lying next to an axe. Despite Hallorann's warning, Danny remains fascinated with room 237, but he cannot enter the locked room.

Jack has brief moments of "shining" himself, as when he gazes at a scale model of the hedge maze and sees the tiny figures of Wendy and Danny walking around in it. Jack's dissatisfaction with his family begins to veer toward malice, and his distraction from his writing veers toward dementia. (Jack's "manuscript" consists of hundreds of typed pages of the phrase, "All work and no play makes Jack a dull boy," repeated over and over). As the winter snowstorms set in and phone lines go down, the Torrance family becomes more and more isolated.

10 ***Father and daughter behind their cameras. In addition to shooting the documentary*** **Making "The Shining,"** ***Vivian Kubrick also appeared as an extra in the ballroom party scene.***

At the same time, the Overlook's ghostly manifestations grow more and more "real," as they begin to seduce Jack and to menace Danny. Jack encounters a bartender, Lloyd (Joe Turkel) who enables him to slip back into his alcoholism, as well as a waiter named Grady (Philip Stone), a sort of alternate incarnation of the former caretaker who had murdered his wife and daughters. Grady encourages Jack to "deal with" Danny and Wendy in "the harshest possible way." Both Danny and Jack have disturbing encounters with the rotting corpse of a hideous old woman in room 237. Danny reports to Wendy that she tried to strangle him; when Jack goes to investigate, the presence in room 237 first appears to him as a sexy, nude, young woman. As they embrace, Jack sees her true form in a mirror, and he recoils in horror, fleeing the room. Yet, he tells Wendy that he saw nothing there.

Meanwhile, in his Miami apartment, Hallorann picks up images of these events, a kind of "distress call" from Danny. Unable to reach the Torrances by phone, he flies to Denver, rents a Sno-Cat, and heads for the Overlook.

When Jack finally does turn into a real threat, Wendy manages to fight him off and lock him in a pantry, but he escapes with Grady's intervention. Meanwhile, the horrified Danny has retreated entirely into the personality of Tony, who screams warnings to Wendy of Jack's impending attacks.

Jack starts chopping his way into the family's apartment with an axe. Danny manages to escape out the bathroom window, but Wendy can't fit through. Just as Wendy seems doomed, they hear Hallorann's Sno-Cat approaching.

Jack kills Hallorann and continues his murderous pursuit of Danny, chasing him into the hedge maze, easily following his footprints in the snow. Realizing this, Danny backtracks so that his footprints appear to stop abruptly; he then runs out of the maze and into Wendy's arms. They head down the mountain in the Sno-Cat. Unable to find his way out, Jack freezes to death in the maze. The final scene of the film ends on a close-up of a photo, depicting a smiling Jack with dozens of revelers at the Overlook's July 4th ball of 1921, suggesting that Jack has "always been there."

From the start, Stanley Kubrick envisioned Jack Nicholson for the role of Jack Torrance. The two had met a few years earlier, when Kubrick wanted him to star in *Napoleon*. Kubrick told Michel Ciment

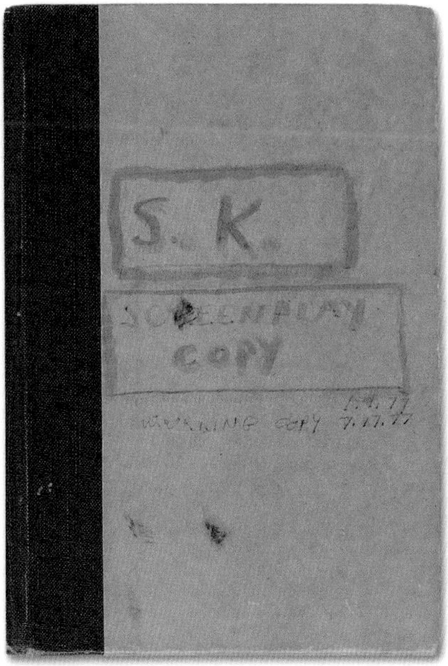

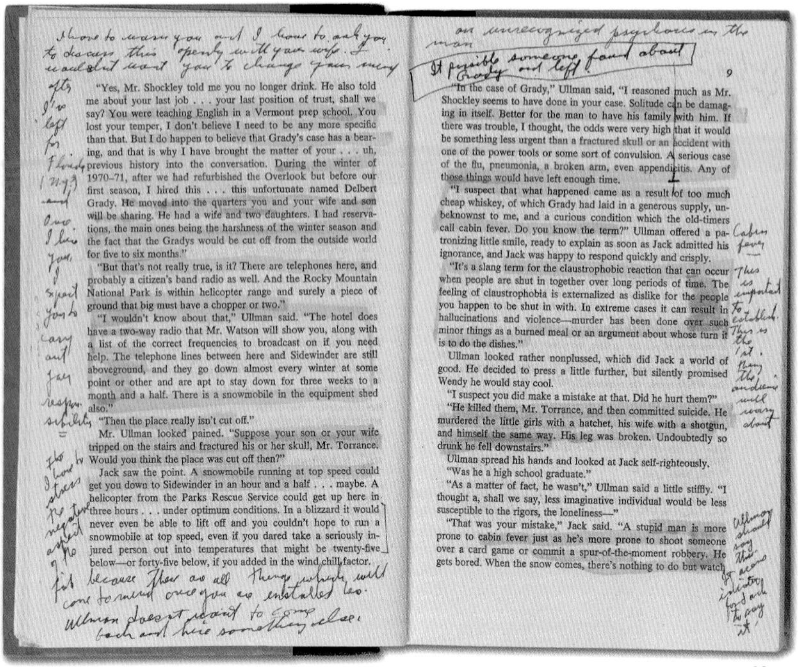
"Yes, Mr. Shockley told me you no longer drink. He also told me about your last job . . . your last position of trust, shall we say? You were teaching English in a Vermont prep school. You lost your temper, I don't believe I need to be any more specific than that. But I do happen to believe that Grady's case has a bearing, and that is why I have brought the matter of your . . . uh, previous history into the conversation. During the winter of 1970–71, after we had refurbished the Overlook but before our first season, I hired this . . . this unfortunate named Delbert Grady. He moved into the quarters you and your wife and son will be sharing. He had a wife and two daughters. I had reservations, the main ones being the harshness of the winter season and the fact that the Gradys would be cut off from the outside world for five to six months."

"But that's not really true, is it? There are telephones here, and probably a citizen's band radio as well. And the Rocky Mountain National Park is within helicopter range and surely a piece of ground that big must have a chopper or two."

"I wouldn't know about that," Ullman said. "The hotel does have a two-way radio that Mr. Watson will show you, along with a list of the correct frequencies to broadcast on if you need help. The telephone lines between here and Sidewinder are still aboveground, and they go down almost every winter at some point or other and are apt to stay down for three weeks to a month and a half. There is a snowmobile in the equipment shed also."

"Then the place really isn't cut off."

Mr. Ullman looked pained. "Suppose your son or your wife tripped on the stairs and fractured his or her skull, Mr. Torrance. Would you think the place was cut off then?"

Jack saw the point. A snowmobile running at top speed could get you down to Sidewinder in an hour and a half . . . maybe. A helicopter from the Parks Rescue Service could get up here in three hours . . . under optimum conditions. In a blizzard it would never even be able to lift off and you couldn't hope to run a snowmobile at top speed, even if you dared take a seriously injured person out into temperatures that might be twenty-five below—or forty-five below, if you added in the wind chill factor.

9

"In the case of Grady," Ullman said, "I reasoned much as Mr. Shockley seems to have done in your case. Solitude can be damaging in itself. Better for the man to have his family with him. If there was trouble, I thought, the odds were very high that it would be something less urgent than a fractured skull or an accident with one of the power tools or some sort of convulsion. A serious case of the flu, pneumonia, a broken arm, even appendicitis. Any of those things would have left enough time.

"I suspect that what happened came as a result of too much cheap whiskey, of which Grady had laid in a generous supply, unbeknownst to me, and a curious condition which the old-timers call cabin fever. Do you know the term?" Ullman offered a patronizing little smile, ready to explain as soon as Jack admitted his ignorance, and Jack was happy to respond quickly and crisply.

"It's a slang term for the claustrophobic reaction that can occur when people are shut in together over long periods of time. The feeling of claustrophobia is externalized as dislike for the people you happen to be shut in with. In extreme cases it can result in hallucinations and violence—murder has been done over such minor things as a burned meal or an argument about whose turn it is to do the dishes."

Ullman looked rather nonplussed, which did Jack a world of good. He decided to press a little further, but silently promised Wendy he would stay cool.

"I suspect you did make a mistake at that. Did he hurt them?"

"He killed them, Mr. Torrance, and then committed suicide. He murdered the little girls with a hatchet, his wife with a shotgun, and himself the same way. His leg was broken. Undoubtedly so drunk he fell downstairs."

Ullman spread his hands and looked at Jack self-righteously.

"Was he a high school graduate."

"As a matter of fact, he wasn't," Ullman said a little stiffly. "I thought a, shall we say, less imaginative individual would be less susceptible to the rigors, the loneliness—"

"That was your mistake," Jack said. "A stupid man is more prone to cabin fever just as he's more prone to shoot someone over a card game or commit a spur-of-the-moment robbery. He gets bored. When the snow comes, there's nothing to do but watch

12

that he considered Nicholson to be "one of the best actors in Hollywood, perhaps on a par with the greatest stars of the past like Spencer Tracy and Jimmy Cagney." This particular stroke of casting pleased Janet Maslin of *The New York Times*, who wrote: "Nicholson's Jack is one of his most vibrant characterizations, furiously alive in every frame and fueled by an explosive anger."

What attracted Kubrick to Shelley Duvall was her "eccentric quality." He said it made her believable as the type of woman who would marry Jack and put up with him, unlike the more attractive and self-reliant Wendy of King's novel. Kubrick had seen and admired all of Duvall's previous films, including *Nashville* and *Three Women*.

For the role of Danny, Kubrick wanted a non-professional, so Warner Bros. ran ads in Chicago, Denver, and Cincinnati, soliciting headshots. A list was made of about 5,000 boys who looked right for the part, and Kubrick's assistant, Leon Vitali, videotaped interviews with all of them. Kubrick looked at the tapes, and eventually the number was narrowed down to five youngsters who could have played Danny. In his discussion with Michel Ciment, Kubrick expressed his thorough pleasure with the job that young Danny Lloyd did in the film.

According to John Baxter, Jack Nicholson helped Scatman Crothers to get the part of Hallorann. They had worked together previously on *One Flew Over the*

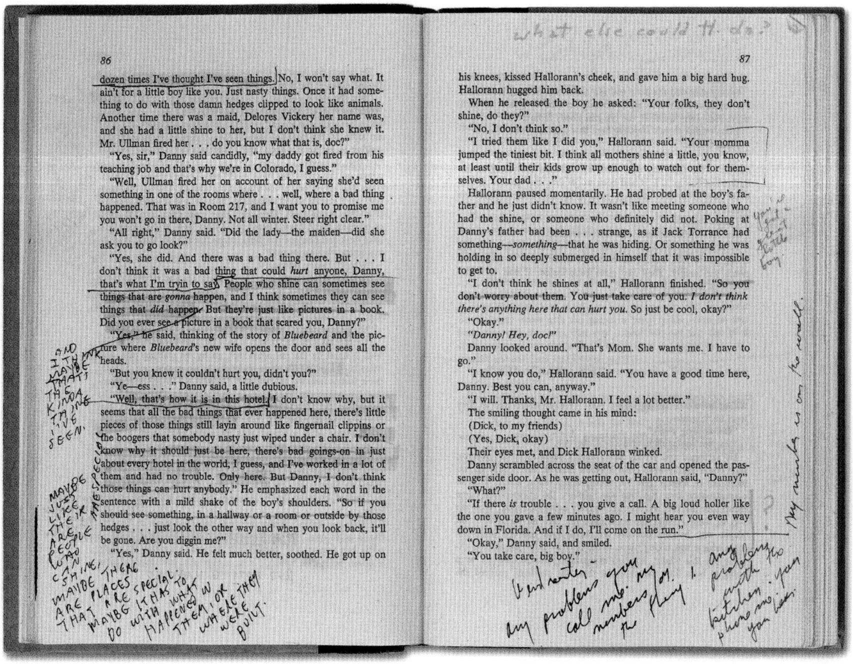

86

dozen times I've thought I've seen things. No, I won't say what. It ain't for a little boy like you. Just nasty things. Once it had something to do with those damn hedges clipped to look like animals. Another time there was a maid, Delores Vickery her name was, and she had a little shine to her, but I don't think she knew it. Mr. Ullman fired her . . . do you know what that is, doc?"

"Yes, sir," Danny said candidly, "my daddy got fired from his teaching job and that's why we're in Colorado, I guess."

"Well, Ullman fired her on account of her saying she'd seen something in one of the rooms where . . . well, where a bad thing happened. That was in Room 217, and I want you to promise me you won't go in there, Danny. Not all winter. Steer right clear."

"All right," Danny said. "Did the lady—the maiden—did she ask you to go look?"

"Yes, she did. And there was a bad thing there. But . . . I don't think it was a bad thing that could *hurt* anyone, Danny, that's what I'm tryin to say. People who shine can sometimes see things that are *gonna* happen, and I think sometimes they can see things that *did* happen. But they're just like pictures in a book. Did you ever see a picture in a book that scared you, Danny?"

"Yes," he said, thinking of the story of *Bluebeard* and the picture where *Bluebeard*'s new wife opens the door and sees all the heads.

"But you knew it couldn't hurt you, didn't you?"

"Ye—ess . . ." Danny said, a little dubious.

"Well, that's how it is in this hotel. I don't know why, but it seems that all the bad things that ever happened here, there's little pieces of those things still layin around like fingernail clippins or the boogers that somebody nasty just wiped under a chair. I don't know why it should just be here, there's bad goings-on in just about every hotel in the world, I guess, and I've worked in a lot of them and had no trouble. Only here. But Danny, I don't think those things can hurt anybody." He emphasized each word in the sentence with a mild shake of the boy's shoulders. "So if you should see something, in a hallway or a room or outside by those hedges . . . just look the other way and when you look back, it'll be gone. Are you diggin me?"

"Yes," Danny said. He felt much better, soothed. He got up on

AND I THINK MAYBE THAT'S THE KINDA THING I'VE SEEN.

MAYBE JUST LIKE THERE ARE PEOPLE WHO CAN SHINE, THERE MAYBE ARE PLACES THAT ARE SPECIAL. MAYBE IT HAS TO DO WITH WHAT HAPPENED IN THEM, OR WHERE THEY WERE BUILT.

what else could H. do?

87

his knees, kissed Hallorann's cheek, and gave him a big hard hug. Hallorann hugged him back.

When he released the boy he asked: "Your folks, they don't shine, do they?"

"No, I don't think so."

"I tried them like I did you," Hallorann said. "Your momma jumped the tiniest bit. I think all mothers shine a little, you know, at least until their kids grow up enough to watch out for themselves. Your dad . . ."

Hallorann paused momentarily. He had probed at the boy's father and he just didn't know. It wasn't like meeting someone who had the shine, or someone who definitely did not. Poking at Danny's father had been . . . strange, as if Jack Torrance had something—*something*—that he was hiding. Or something he was holding in so deeply submerged in himself that it was impossible to get to.

"I don't think he shines at all," Hallorann finished. "So you don't worry about them. You just take care of you. *I don't think there's anything here that can hurt you.* So just be cool, okay?"

"Okay."

"Danny! Hey, doc!"

Danny looked around. "That's Mom. She wants me. I have to go."

"I know you do," Hallorann said. "You have a good time here, Danny. Best you can, anyway."

"I will. Thanks, Mr. Hallorann. I feel a lot better."

The smiling thought came in his mind:

(Dick, to my friends)

(Yes, Dick, okay)

Their eyes met, and Dick Hallorann winked.

Danny scrambled across the seat of the car and opened the passenger side door. As he was getting out, Hallorann said, "Danny?"

"What?"

"If there *is* trouble . . . you give a call. A big loud holler like the one you gave a few minutes ago. I might hear you even way down in Florida. And if I do, I'll come on the run."

"Okay," Danny said, and smiled.

"You take care, big boy."

13

Cuckoo's Nest and other films. Crothers had never heard of Kubrick and was baffled by the director's working methods. Still, in an interview for Vivian Kubrick's behind-the-scenes documentary on *The Shining*, a tearful Crothers expressed his gratitude for being a part of the film and a fondness for the "beautiful people" involved.

All of the film's interiors (including inside of the hedge maze) were shot in Elstree and Pinewood Studios, just outside London. For the establishing shots of the Overlook, a second unit led by Douglas Milsome filmed the Timberline Lodge in Mt. Hood, Oregon. Other second-unit locations included Glacier National Park in Montana, Yosemite National Park in California, Bretton Woods in New Hampshire, and locations in Colorado. A section of the Timberline Lodge exterior was recreated on the back lot at Elstree, as was the hedge maze exterior.

Filming began in May 1978. The shoot was scheduled to last 17 weeks but went on for 14 months and an estimated 200 shooting days, with a budget reported between $13 million and $19 million.[9] According to *The New York Times*, *The Shining* was "filmed with an excess of secrecy.... No outsider (was) allowed on the set, nor (were) any interviews permitted with Mr. Kubrick or with his actors."[10]

11–13 ***Kubrick's work copy of Stephen King's book.***

Since the Overlook Hotel is essentially a central character in the story, its conception and design were key. Production designer Roy Walker sent a team (including Kubrick's daughter Katharina) around the U.S. to photograph hotels that seemed suitable for the story. Then Walker and Kubrick spent weeks going through the photos and making selections for the various rooms. The Colorado Lounge, with its Navajo motifs, is based heavily on the Ahwahnee Lodge in Yosemite Valley. Other particular inspirations include a Frank Lloyd Wright men's room in an Arizona hotel (the basis of the red men's room where Jack's encounter with Grady takes place). Kubrick told Ciment, "I wanted the hotel to look authentic rather than like a traditionally spooky movie hotel. The hotel's labyrinthine layout and huge rooms, I believed, would alone provide an eerie enough atmosphere."

Further contributing to the eerie atmosphere is the then-innovative (and therefore visually arresting) use of the Steadicam. While other films of the mid-1970s had utilized Garrett Brown's invention for specific effects, *The Shining* was the first film to use the new technology extensively.[11] Kubrick described the Steadicam's effect as being "like a magic carpet. The fast, flowing camera movements in the maze would have been impossible to do without the Steadicam.... Most of the hotel set was built as a composite, so that you could go up a flight of stairs, turn down a corridor, travel its length and find your way to still another part of the hotel. It mirrored the kind of camera movements that took place in the maze. In order to fully exploit this layout it was necessary to have moving camera shots without cuts, and of course the Steadicam made that much easier to do."[12]

Another technological innovation that Kubrick employed for *The Shining* was a video-assist system. An elaborate network of antennas was built into the walls of the sets to pick up transmissions from a video camera mounted so as to approximate the framing of the Arriflex-BL. Not only did this allow instant video playback of a scene, but it also enabled Kubrick to monitor performances in the hedge maze and other scenes involving fast-moving characters. *Shining* cinematographer John Alcott told Ciment: "Video makes for better technical coordination between the camera, the actors' movements and the sets. For *The Shining*... video was used as a means of judging the performances and the composition of the image."

According to Alcott, the technical crew on *The Shining* was rather small. Although there was a large special effects team, particularly for the snow scenes, normally there were no more than ten crewmembers on the set.[13] Such an economical production mode allowed Kubrick to indulge in such luxuries as extended shooting schedules and high shooting ratios.

According to Elstree Studios, it is reported that Kubrick shot more than 1.3 million feet of film on *The Shining*, with a shooting ratio of 102:1, compared to the typical 5:1 to 15:1. Some insight into Kubrick's penchant for lots of takes may

14 ***Philip Stone and Jack Nicholson reading between takes.***
15 ***Shooting the killing of Hallorann.***

14

15

be found in remarks by editor Gordon Stainforth: "Typically, Nicholson's first take would be absolutely brilliant. Then the thing would start to get stale after about ten takes. Then you can see he's almost marking time, so he doesn't get exhausted. Then he's going right over the top.... Stanley tended to go for the most eccentric and rather over-the-top ones."[14]

Other scenes, however, are characterized by rather ordinary performances that might even be termed flat. Kubrick saw this sort of tone as essential in dealing with the fantastic, as he told Michel Ciment: "... in fantasy you want things to have the appearance of being as realistic as possible. People should behave in the mundane way they normally do. You have to be especially careful about this in the scenes which deal with the bizarre or fantastic details of the story."

So, arguably Kubrick's penchant for multiple takes helped him to draw out a duality of performance styles from his actors: exceedingly ordinary on the one hand, over the top on the other. This runs parallel to what Kubrick termed the "psychological misdirection" of *The Shining*, which allows the audience to believe for a time that all the events have rational, psychological explanations, only to con-

16 ***Kubrick with Philip Stone (Grady).***
17 ***An excerpt from Kubrick's editing notebooks, in which he often doodled and jotted down thoughts and ideas.***
18 ***Two cameras were rolled up tracks on the stairs to capture Shelley Duvall's performance in tight and wide shots simultaneously.***

firm later an unquestionably supernatural presence in the story.

The supernatural mood of the film is enhanced tremendously by what Janet Maslin called a "stunningly effective score." For the opening title music, Wendy Carlos and Rachel Elkind re-orchestrated the centuries-old *Dies Irae* theme for synthesizer and voices. Initially, Kubrick asked Carlos and Elkind to score the entire film, but he used their music only in a few other places. For the bulk of the film, Kubrick used pre-existing recordings, most of which come from the Polish composer Krzysztof Penderecki. Additionally, several scenes use Béla Bartók's "Music for Strings, Percussion, and Celesta," and one piece by György Ligeti was also used. For the party in the Gold Room and for the end credits, Kubrick chose a 1920s dance tune, "Midnight, the Stars, and You," performed by the Ray Noble orchestra. Much of Carlos and Elkind's music for the film remains unreleased, but one additional piece can be heard in Vivian Kubrick's documentary.

As with all of his films, Stanley Kubrick supervised the editing of *The Shining*. Furthermore, his contract with Warner Bros. gave him final cut. Thus, the job of the editors was simply to execute the cuts as Kubrick envisioned them. After the initial theatrical release, a number of changes were made under Kubrick's supervision. During the first weeks of the theatrical run, Kubrick eliminated a two-minute scene at the end in which Ullman visits Wendy and Danny in the hospital. Before its London

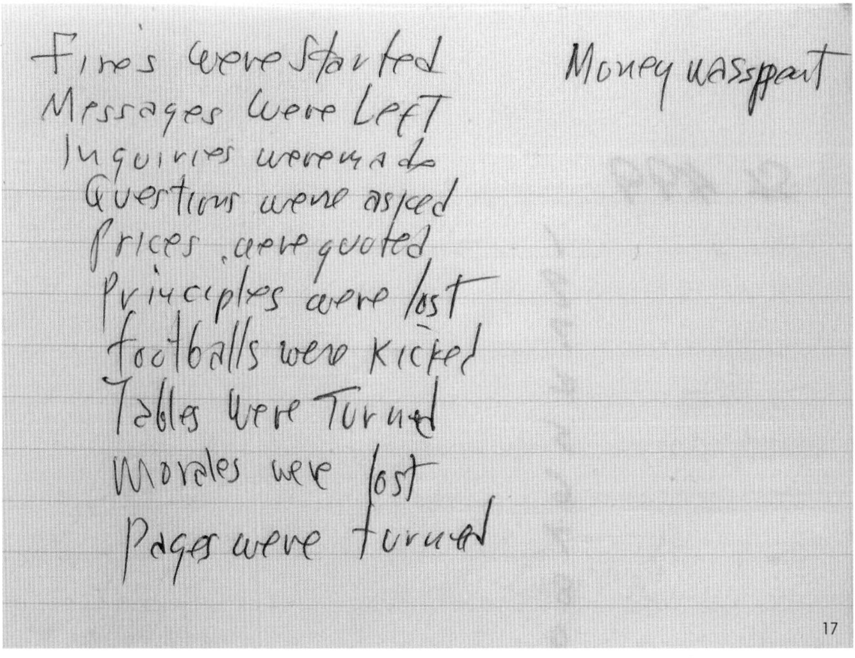
Fire's were Started
Messages were Left
Inquiries were made
Questions were asked
Prices were quoted
Principles were lost
footballs were kicked
Tables were Turned
Morales were lost
Pages were turned
Money was spent
17

opening, the film was preview-tested, and further cuts were made for UK and Australian theaters, resulting in the elimination of nearly thirty minutes of footage. Most notable among the cuts are an early scene with a pediatrician (Anne Jackson) examining Danny and scenes showing Hallorann's journey back to the hotel. While most of the other cuts do not significantly alter the content of the story, they do result in a different rhythm, especially in some transitions. One other change was made for the ABC-TV airing of the film: in the scene in room 237, video blurring was used to obscure some nudity—the only time Kubrick ever made such a change in order to get a network television broadcast for one of his films.

Advance publicity for *The Shining* included poster art by the legendary Saul Bass, who had revolutionized motion picture credit sequences and poster design in the 1950s, and had also designed the titles for *Spartacus*. Bass's design for the theatrical poster employed a pointillist image of a child's horrified face, trapped in the giant black letters of the title, all against a rich golden background. A tagline across the top of the poster proclaimed the film "a masterpiece of modern horror." Subsequent versions of the poster and ad campaign kept a smaller-scale version of Bass's title treatment without the boy's face, adding Jack Nicholson's leering "Here's Johnny" expression and Shelley Duvall's horrified reaction to his axe.

In May 1980, *The Shining* was released in a "step" pattern, opening on eleven screens and expanding to 750 within a few weeks. In its first week, the film broke house records in six of its eleven venues. Indeed, *The Shining* ranks as Stanley Kubrick's biggest commercial success according to *Variety*'s "Champs List," with $30.9 million in theatrical rentals.[15] That figure corresponds to a domestic box-office gross of $44 million, placing the film at #9 among the top-ten grossing films of 1980.

Predictably, the initial critical response to *The Shining* was mixed. Tim Cahill noted in a 1987 article that some reviewers saw a falling off of quality in *The Shining*, though a critical reevaluation was in process. "This seems to be typical of (Kubrick's) critical reception," he added.[16] *Variety* editor Todd McCarthy seems to agree: "*The Shining* was seriously misunderstood as an off-target horror film by most critics when it first came out, but has subsequently risen in many observers' estimations."[17] Also in *Variety*, Richard Natale and Leonard Klady observe in hindsight: "*The Shining*... turned out to be more highly praised in later years than at the time of release.... (Kubrick's) work seemed to take on greater weight as the years went by, thanks to the quality of his craftsmanship and the universality of his themes."[18]

"I wanted the hotel to look authentic rather than like the traditionally spooky movie hotel. The hotel's labyrinthine layout and huge rooms, I believed, would alone provide an eerie enough atmosphere.... It seemed to me that the perfect guide to this approach could be found in Kafka's writing style. His stories are fantastic and allegorical, but his writing is simple and straightforward, almost journalistic."

—SK/1980 (to Michel Ciment)

Of course, a few reviewers at the time responded quite positively to Kubrick's

19 ***The facade of the Overlook, based on the Timberline Lodge, was created on the back lot of the Elstree Studios.***
20 ***A photograph of the Timberline Lodge in Mt. Hood, Oregon, which served as the model for the Overlook and was also filmed by a second unit for the approach shots. Among Kubrick's instructions for the crew is the reminder to frame for a 1.85:1 aspect ratio but to "protect" the full 1.33:1 frame; this reflects his policy, for his last three films, of simultaneously composing widescreen for theatrical release and full frame for television.***

18mm
208
LIGHTS
LIGHTS
310/312
In order to accurately get the central path curve, you have to se
set up the shots and put stakes in the ground sp that the curve as seen through the ground
glass corresponds to what is drawn. THERE IS NO OTHER WAY
TO DO IT REPEAT NO OTHER WAY excercise the greatest care as the compositional
effect of a different pat
be BAD BAD BAD

1-1:85
IGNORE WHAT LOOKS LIKE A CENTRAL PATH JUST HAVE THE SNOW SMOOTHLY AND
ROUNDLY CHANGE ITS DIRECTIO UP THE SLOPE AT ABOUT THE
POSITION OF THE WHAT IS DRAWN AS A CENTRAL PATH
THE FRAME IS EXACTLY 1-1:85 Obviously you compose for that
but protect the full 1-1:33 area.
226
MAKE SURE IT DOESN'T WIND UP LOOKING LIKE A SNOW PLOW DID IT
After you push the snow around the wind and fresh snow fall should keep it from looking plowed
2 Trees could cover the poles

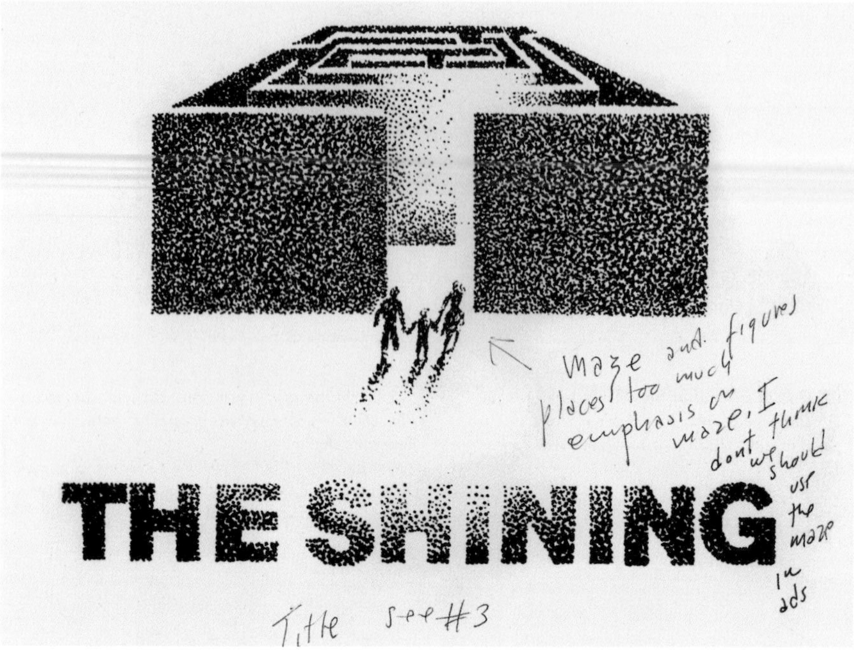

maze and figures places too much emphasis on maze, I dont think we should use the maze in ads
THE SHINING
Title see #3

21

PS. I would like to suggest it is a film of terror (and the supernatural)
a must
if possible

film, among them Janet Maslin of *The New York Times*. She called it, "spellbinding… gloriously diabolical," adding that it "unfolds at a leisurely pace almost as playful as it is hair-raising. Meticulously detailed and never less than fascinating, *The Shining* may be the first movie that ever made its audience jump with a title card that simply says 'Tuesday.'"[19]

Back on Kubrick's side of the Atlantic, two critics in *Sight and Sound* pointed out the levels of complexity in the film. P.L. Titterington suggested that "something very different from what one had expected is being attempted," and that, "within hours of the screening, it can happen that the sequences and the experiences begin to rearrange themselves, and a completely different way of looking at the film starts to emerge."[20] Paul Mayersberg adds, "To take *The Shining* at its face value is a mistake. It has no face, only masks… *The Shining* belongs firmly in the tradition of *The Turn of the Screw* and *The Beast in the Jungle*."[21]

21 ***One of several of Saul Bass's proposals for the poster, with Kubrick's comments. Above: further suggestions from Kubrick to Bass.***

22–23 ***Many of the sets were directly based on location scouting photographs of actual hotels, such as these.***
24 ***The set of the Overlook's Colorado Lounge, based on the interior of the Ahwahnee Hotel in Yosemite National Park.***

(A) As the chase progresses, the hotel comes to life; lights, music, etc

61

The scene that follows will be

a ~~Now follows~~ ~~the~~ terrifying, and suspensefull

deadly hide and seek. Danny desperately tries to elude the murderous Halloran by now an appaling firgure of savagery, smashing at the walls of ~~corridors~~ ~~anything~~ in sigh with an axe, snarling, shrieking , foaming and chocking.

snarling

grunting

frenzied

animal like

panting

foaming and chocking with frenzied rage

shrieking bellowing roaring

maniacally

At the same time, Wendy, armed with the knife, frantically searches through the hotel for Danny. (A)

The cimax occurs/in the large lounge when Wendy intervenes at the last moment and is able to kill Halloran in a bizarre and utterly unexpected ~~fashion~~ way. She rushes out of the room with Danny. The camera ~~stays~~ does not follow her and holds for a few seconds on the empty room. Then it begins to slowly move toward ~~the~~ Jack's work table. The scrapbook stil; lies open on it, Jack's scrapbbok still lies open. It is open to the page of ~~the~~ with glossy photo posed ~~group photograph~~ , taken in the crowded ballroom,

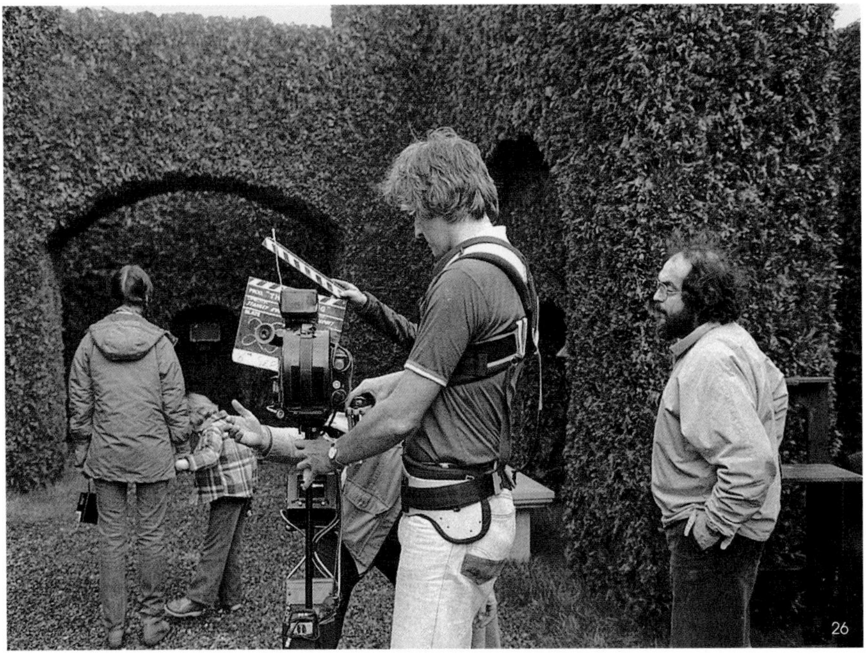

Conversely, most of the negative criticism at the time stemmed from the fact that *The Shining* was not the film that reviewers were expecting. In the *New Yorker*, Pauline Kael complained that the film denied her the kind of shadowy, spooky atmosphere she wanted from the horror genre. Of course it comes as no surprise that Kael panned *The Shining*, as she had similarly misunderstood other Kubrick masterpieces including *2001: A Space Odyssey* and *A Clockwork Orange*. While one may give Kael a measure of credit for consistency (she stubbornly injects a few jabs at the "foolishness" of *2001* into her *Shining* review), arguably such writings call into question the very function and legitimacy of popular "criticism" and entertainment "journalism."

Some of the most outspoken criticism of Kubrick's film came from Stephen King, who felt that Kubrick lacked a basic understanding of the horror genre. When King wrote a teleplay based on *The Shining*, made as a mini-series in 1997, his well-known dislike for the film prompted the requirement that King not make public comparisons between the two versions, as a condition of Kubrick's giving up

25 ***In an early version of the script, Hallorann was to become maniacal upon arriving at the hotel, attempting to murder Danny.***
26 ***Garrett Brown (center) filming Wendy and Danny's walk through the maze.***

27

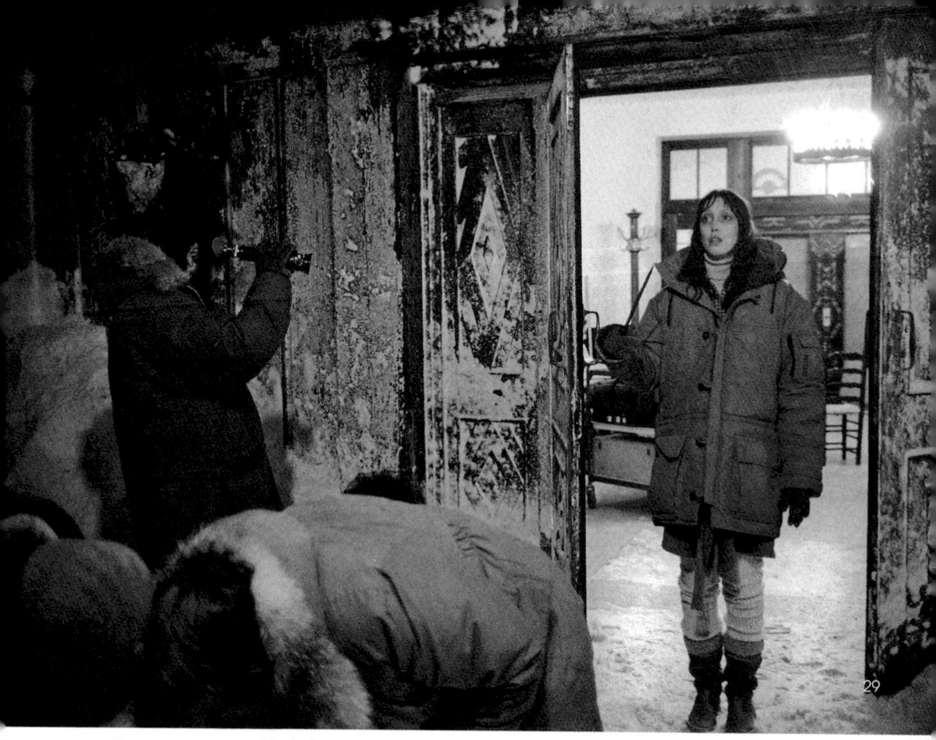

29

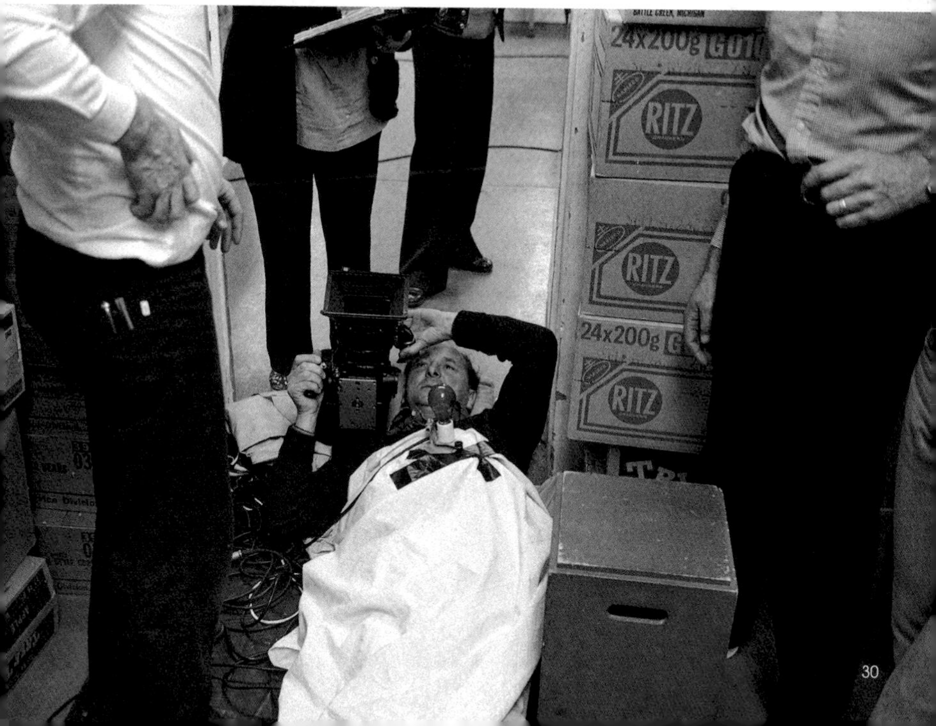

30

exclusive screen rights. Anyone who has seen King's preferred version—or any of the films that he himself has directed, for that matter—may be the judge of who has displayed a better understanding of horror films, King or Kubrick.

Hated by some, Stanley Kubrick's *The Shining* has proved an inspiration to others. For instance, Dominik Moll—whose film *With a Friend Like Harry* (2000) was an international art-house hit—became so fixated with film as a university student that, according to *Variety*, he would view *The Shining* repeatedly, with notepad in hand.[22] The entertainment industry press has also noted *The Shining*'s direct influence on other recent films, including *One Hour Photo* (2002) starring Robin

27 ***Kubrick with nephew Manuel Harlan and daughter Vivian.***
28 ***Kubrick frames Joe Turkel with his viewfinder.***
29 ***"The wonderful thing about Shelley is her eccentric quality – the way she talks, the way she moves, the way her nervous system is put together." – SK/1980 (to Michel Ciment)***
30 ***Camera operator Kelvin Pike lay on the floor with a light bulb on his chest to film Jack Nicholson leaning against the locked door of the pantry.***
31 ***Director of photography John Alcott with Kubrick.***
32 ***Garrett Brown was hired to operate his invention, the Steadicam, which was most notably used in the maze scenes and for shots of Danny riding through the hotel's corridors.***

32

33

Williams, Larry Fessenden's *Wendigo* (2001), and *Jericho Mansions* (2003).

Among the many miracles of Stanley Kubrick's films, especially his mature works, are that they function on so many different levels, have such longevity, and

"In all things mysterious —never explain."

—SK/1980, quoting H. P. Lovecraft (to John Hofsess/*Int'l Herald Tribune*)

can be appreciated by a wide range of audiences. Such is the case with *The Shining*. Its appeal to general audiences is evident from its box-office returns, while more serious film aficionados might more fully appreciate Kubrick's narrative structure and aesthetic mastery. Furthermore, upon repeated viewings, the full richness of *The Shining* begins to emerge, revealing ideas that operate on a grand scale, themes involving America, capitalism, and history.

A few superb book-length analyses of Kubrick's work have appeared, including Alexander Walker's *Stanley Kubrick: Director* and Thomas Allen Nelson's book, *Kubrick: Inside a Film Artist's Maze*. Their arguments are too detailed to summarize here, but we might note just a few observations. The Overlook Hotel arguably stands in for modern America: built on the suffering of others (the Indian burial ground, Grady's racist slur of "Nigger cook," etc.), it co-opts the very cultures that it has displaced (the "authentic" Navajo designs, originally imbued with mythical meanings, have been relegated to the status of mere background décor). In this light, certain lines of dialogue take on added significance, as when Halloran tells Danny: "A lot of things have happened in this particular hotel, over the years, and not all of 'em was good." Jack's downfall takes place largely because he has so readily "sold out" his family responsibilities in favor of financial responsibilities, and therein lies the true "selling of the soul." This is a theme to which Kubrick returns in *Eyes Wide Shut*, specifically with the character of Nick Nightingale, who has moved thousands of miles away from his wife and children, to "go where the work is."

On an even grander scale than "America" and "capitalism," though, *The Shining* seems to be about history and humanity's relation to it. The ability to "shine" may be likened to

33 ***Filming the scene in which Wendy finds the lounge full of cobwebs and skeletons.***
34–35 ***Executive producer Jan Harlan sent this letter and picture to Kubrick in 1976 to inform him of the invention of the Steadicam, a hand-held camera device that would be used on*** The Shining ***and all of Kubrick's subsequent films. Garrett Brown (left), the Steadicam's inventor, is pictured with a prototype of the device.***

SUITE 918
EXECUTIVE LIFE BUILDING
9777 WILSHIRE BOULEVARD
BEVERLY HILLS, CALIFORNIA 90212

10. Feb. 76

ED DI GIULIO CAMERA BRACKET

Dear Stanley,

I saw this new contraption for hand-held shots in action. It's just terrific. Enclosed a photograph of one of the prototypes. The whole secret is a perfect balance of the camera and the arm AND a spring ~~loaded~~- tension arm which separates the body movement from the camera to an astonishing degree. The operator can run and the camera moves through the air as if held on a string from above. I saw a roll of film this morning shot by Haskel where the operator sits on a crane - the crane comes down the the ground, the operator gets of the seat and walks away, no cut. Not only will this thing safe a lot of money and time by avoiding tracks, but you could do shots and think of shots which would not enter your mind otherwise. You see, I am sold on that thing, although it costs $ 30,000.--. Ed will be in London on Feb 25 for 4 hours and I told him to send you that roll of film which I saw. I promised him that you will send it back to him within a few days. He will just arrange with someone that the roll is delivered to you.

Ed will be in Copenhagen in 2 weeks and I have asked him to see Mr. Jakobsen and find out for himself what ~~the~~ is happening. I assume that Jakobsen has not contacted you in the meantime.

best Jan

34

35

36

historical awareness, the ability to "see things that happened a long time ago" and to predict their effects on the present and future. Here, Tony's reminder that Danny's shining is "just like pictures in a book" seems particularly salient. It is Danny's willingness to heed impressions from the past and to speculate on the future that ultimately saves him and Wendy, as they get Tony's warnings of "redrum" just in time to evade the axe-wielding Jack. By contrast, Jack willfully ignores the troubling nature of his episodes of "shining," especially the incidents in room 237, which he should take as grave warnings; but to acknowledge them as such would be to abandon his ambitious quest for status within the world of the hotel. Put simply, those who are unaware of history are doomed to repeat it, just as Jack seems doomed to a fate similar to Grady's.

Finally, like history, Kubrick's film *Shining* provides us with an incomplete, troubling puzzle. Not only are some of the pieces missing, but what pieces we do have do not always fit together. This welcome challenge gives us all the more reason to venture back into *The Shining's* mazes, time and time again.

37

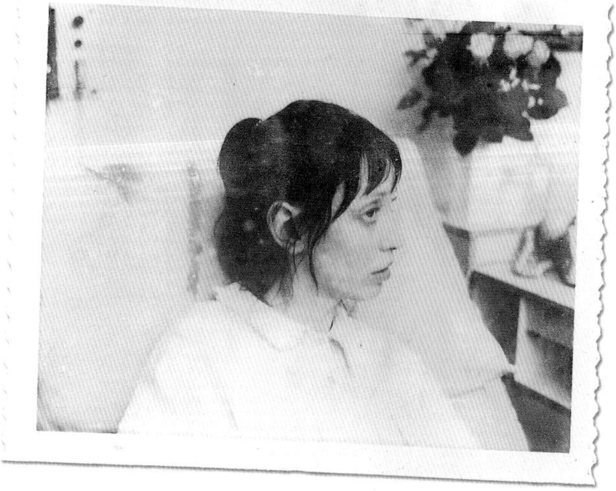

38

Notes

1. Introductory speech by Michel Ciment given before screening of *The Shining* at the Museum of Modern Art, New York, 2000.
2. John Baxter, *Stanley Kubrick: A Biography* (New York: Carroll & Graf), 1997: 296.
3. Aljean Harmetz, "Kubrick Films 'The Shining' In Secrecy in English Studio," *The New York Times*, November 6, 1978.
4. Michel Ciment, *Kubrick: The Definitive Edition* (New York: Faber and Faber, 2001): 181.
5. Harmetz.
6. Quoted in Rodney Hill, "King, Stephen," in Gene D. Phillips and Rodney Hill, *The Encyclopedia of Stanley Kubrick* (New York: Checkmark, 2002): 189.
7. Harmetz; Ciment.
8. Janet Maslin, "The Shining," *The New York Times*, May 23, 1980: C8.
9. Michael Fleming, "Kubrick Pic in Home Stretch," *Variety* (June 23, 1997).
10. Harmetz.
11. Elstree Studios website: www.elstree.co.uk/shining.html.
12. Ciment, Kubrick: 189.
13. Ibid: 216.
14. Baxter: 317.
15. *2001* is also on the "Champs List," with $26 million in theatrical rentals as of 1997.
16. Tim Cahill, "The Rolling Stone Interview: Stanley Kubrick," *Rolling Stone* (August 27, 1987). Reprinted in Gene D. Phillips, ed., *Stanley Kubrick: Interviews* (Jackson: University Press of Mississippi), 2001: 191.
17. Todd McCarthy, "More to Kubrick than first meets the eye," *Variety*, (July 16, 1999).
18. Richard Natale and Leonard Klady, "Stanley Kubrick Dies," *Variety*, (March 8, 1999).
19. Maslin.
20. P. L. Titterington, "Kubrick and 'The Shining,'" *Sight and Sound* 50, no. 2 (1981): 117–21.
21. Paul Mayersberg, "The Overlook Hotel," *Sight and Sound* 50, no. 1 (1980–81): 54–57.
22. "Ten to Watch 2001: Directors," *Variety* (variety.com January 16, 2001).

36–38 ***Continuity Polaroids showing the final scene that was cut from the film, in which Wendy recovers in the hospital and is visited by Ullman.***

39

42

43

39–45 ***Continuity Polaroids.***
46 ***Self-portrait with daughter Vivian on the men's restroom set, with, from left, focus-puller Douglas Milsome, Jack Nicholson, and continuity supervisor June Randall.***

40

41

45

44

Full Metal Jacket

1987 / COLOR / 116 MINUTES
Distributed by WARNER BROS.

CAST
PVT. JOKER MATTHEW MODINE
ANIMAL MOTHER ADAM BALDWIN
PVT. PYLE VINCENT D'ONOFRIO
GUNNERY SGT. HARTMAN LEE ERMEY
EIGHTBALL DORIAN HAREWOOD
RAFTERMAN KEVYN MAJOR HOWARD
PVT. COWBOY ARLISS HOWARD
LT. TOUCHDOWN ED O'ROSS
LT. LOCKHART JOHN TERRY
CRAZY EARL KIERON JECCHINIS
PAYBACK KIRK TAYLOR
DOORGUNNER TIM COLCERI
DOC JAY JOHN STAFFORD
POGE COLONEL BRUCE BOA
LT. CLEVES IAN TYLER
T.H.E. ROCK SAL LOPEZ
DONLON GARY LANDON MILLS
DA NANG HOOKER PAPILLON SOO SOO
SNOWBALL PETER EDMUND
V. C. SNIPER NGOC LE
MOTORBIKE HOOKER LEANNE HONG
ARVN PIMP TAN HUNG FRANCIONE

CREW
DIRECTED AND PRODUCED BY STANLEY KUBRICK
SCREENPLAY STANLEY KUBRICK, MICHAEL HERR, and GUSTAV HASFORD (based on the novel *The Short-Timers* by Gustav Hasford)
EXECUTIVE PRODUCER JAN HARLAN
CO-PRODUCER PHILIP HOBBS
ASSOCIATE PRODUCER MICHAEL HERR
ASSISTANT TO THE DIRECTOR LEON VITALI
DIRECTOR OF PHOTOGRAPHY DOUGLAS MILSOME
PRODUCTION DESIGNER ANTON FURST
EDITOR MARTIN HUNTER
SOUND EDITORS NIGEL GAIT, EDWARD TISE
SPECIAL EFFECTS SUPERVISOR JOHN EVANS
SPECIAL EFFECTS SENIOR TECHNICIANS PETER DAWSON, JEFF CLIFFORD, ALAN BARNARD
CASTING LEON VITALI
1ST ASSISTANT DIRECTOR TERRY NEEDHAM
2ND ASSISTANT DIRECTOR CHRISTOPHER THOMSON
PRODUCTION MANAGER PHIL KOHLER
UNIT PRODUCTION MANAGER BILL SHEPHERD
PRODUCTION CO-ORDINATOR MARGARET ADAMS
COSTUME DESIGNER KEITH DENNY
MONTAGE EDITING ENGINEER ADAM WATKINS
VIDEO OPERATOR MANUEL HARLAN
CAMERA ASSISTANT JASON WRENN
ART DIRECTORS ROD STRATFOLD, LES TOMKINS, KEITH PAIN
TECHNICAL ADVISOR LEE ERMEY
ART DEPARTMENT RESEARCH ANTHONY FREWIN
STEADICAM OPERATORS JOHN WARD, JEAN-MARC BRINGUIER
ASSISTANTS TO THE PRODUCER EMILIO D'ALESSANDRO, ANTHONY FREWIN

Filmed on location and at Pinewood Studios, Iver, Bucks.

IN VIETNAM
THE WIND
DOESN'T BLOW
IT SUCKS
BORN
TO
KiLL
Stanley Kubrick's
FULL
METAL
JACKET
WARNER BROS PRESENTS STANLEY KUBRICK'S FULL METAL JACKET
STARRING
MATTHEW MODINE ADAM BALDWIN VINCENT D'ONOFRIO LEE ERMEY DORIAN HAREWOOD ARLISS HOWARD
KEVYN MAJOR HOWARD ED O'ROSS SCREENPLAY BY STANLEY KUBRICK MICHAEL HERR GUSTAV HASFORD
BASED ON THE NOVEL THE SHORT-TIMERS BY GUSTAV HASFORD CO PRODUCER PHILIP HOBBS EXECUTIVE PRODUCER JAN HARLAN PRODUCED AND DIRECTED BY STANLEY KUBRICK
WARNER BROS
A WARNER COMMUNICATIONS COMPANY

FULL METAL JACKET

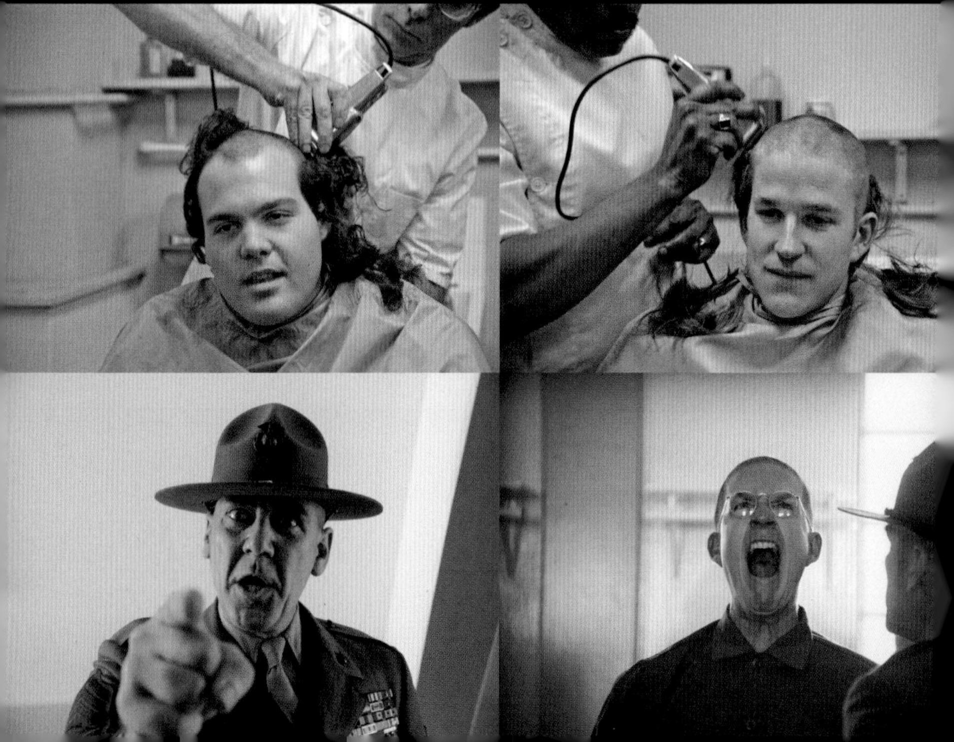

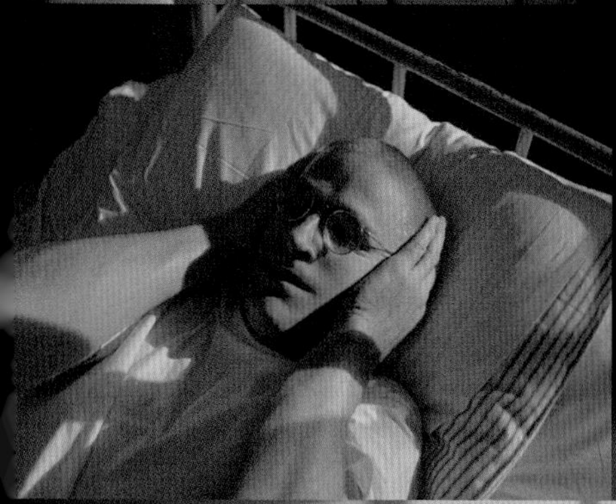

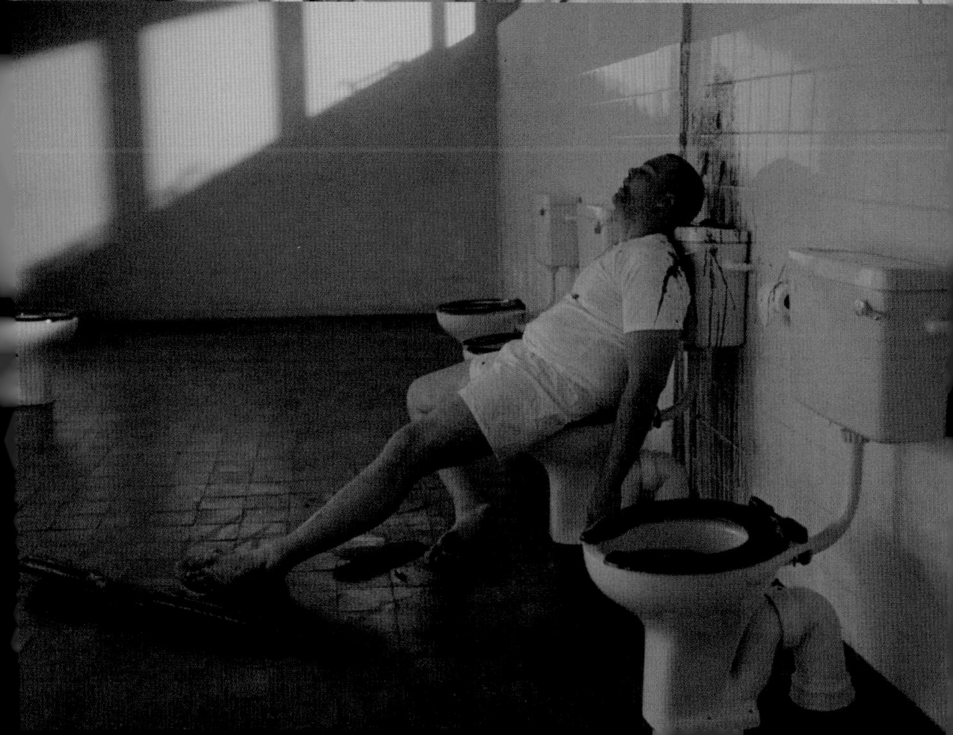

KILL

PROD: FULL METAL
STANLEY KUBRICK
SLATE
242
16-10-85

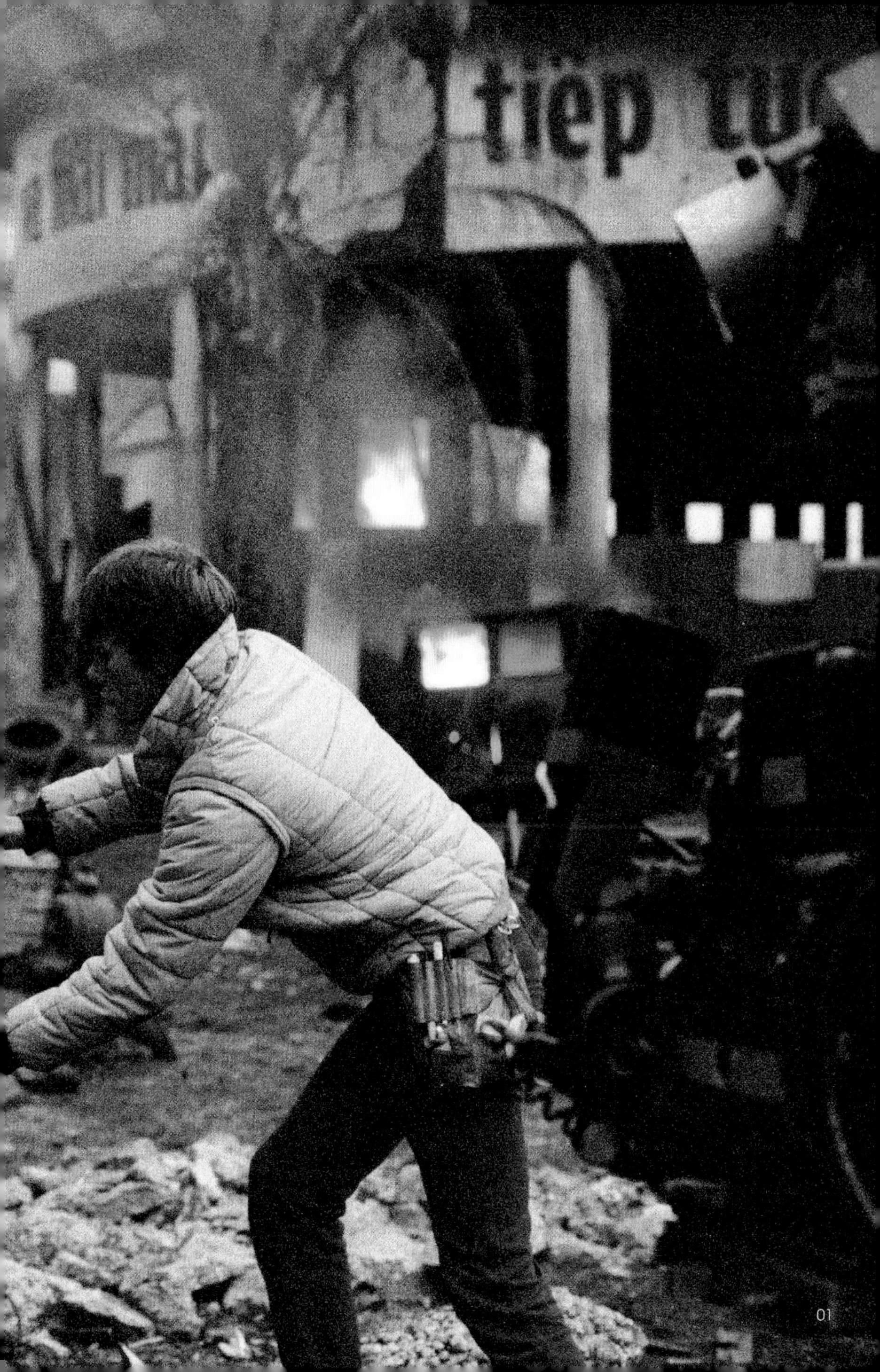
tiep

Full Metal Jacket

by Rodney Hill

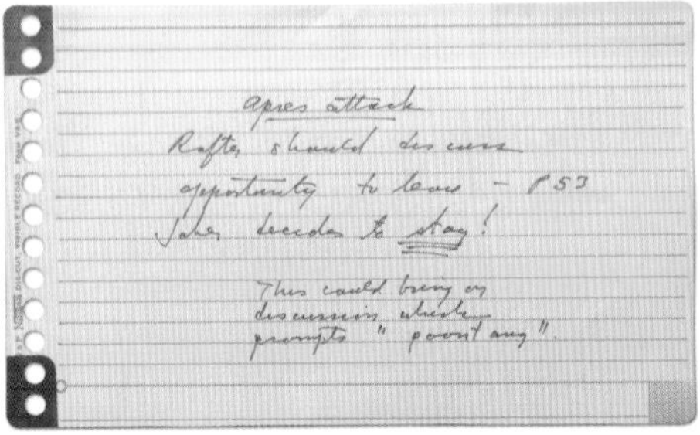

02

"As they expressed it in Vietnam, 'Yea, Though I walk through the Valley of the Shadow of Death, I will fear no Evil, for I am the Evil.' And the Fear, they could have added."

—Michael Herr

"I don't blame the grunts for their cynical view of the war.... They were unprepared culturally for the situation they were put into, and the language barrier didn't help. Neither did the fact that every man and woman and child might have been a V. C. When they got there, they quickly realized the war was hopeless, that the people back home were being given a false picture of the war. There is no question in my mind that their innocence and courage were misused."

—Stanley Kubrick

Anyone seeking a "statement" about the Vietnam War from Stanley Kubrick need look no further than the comments above, which he made to Gene Siskel at the time of *Full Metal Jacket*'s theatrical release in 1987. The movie itself certainly offers no clear political "message" about the war, either pro or con, and in many ways it is much more a "Kubrick film" than it is a "Vietnam movie." Actually, Michael Herr's observation noted above gives a clearer insight into the Kubrickian themes of *Full Metal Jacket*—albeit in an abstruse fashion—chief among them being the Jungian duality of man. As Paul Duncan has suggested, the conundrum of *Full Metal Jacket* lies in the questions of whether or not its main character will become a killer and if, in doing so, he will lose his humanity.[1]

"I like the lack of a readily discernable moral attitude which is so familiar in a war story."

—SK/Handwritten notes on Hasford's book, white lined paper

For Stanley Kubrick, the hardest part of directing was searching for a good tale that could sustain the imagination. He told Siskel, "The fact that each of the last three films has taken about five years has been because it is so hard to find something I think is worth doing. I didn't set out to do a Vietnam film. I don't work that way. A good story suitable for making into a film is so rare, subject matter is secondary."[2]

Still, according to Michael Herr, as early as 1980 Kubrick was thinking about returning to the subject of war. "He had a strong feeling about a particular kind of war movie that he wanted to make, but he didn't have a story."[3] On the subject of war in general, Kubrick told Gene Siskel: "It obviously is emotionally intense and offers great visual possibilities. And it's full of irony, depending on the war."[4]

Kubrick learned of Gustav Hasford's novel, *The Short-Timers*, in *Kirkus Reviews*, which he read regularly when searching

01 ***Camera assistant Jason Wrenn marks the start of a take.***
02 ***Screenplay notes written on a special hole-punched note card, one of many examples of the unusual stationery Kubrick collected and used.***
03 ***Kubrick with daughter Anya.***

for a story. After an initial pass through the book, he reread it almost immediately. He savored its "economy of structural statement" and sought to transfer that quality to the screen "quite literally, because the dialogue is so almost poetic in its carved-out, stark quality."[5] Furthermore he admired "its sense of uncompromising truth." He told Siskel, "The book offered no easy moral or political answers; it was neither pro-war nor antiwar. It seemed only concerned with the way things are. There is a tremendous economy of statement in the book, which I have tried to retain in the film."[6]

Co-scenarist Michael Herr first met Stanley Kubrick in the spring of 1980, through their mutual friend, David Cornwell (a.k.a. spy novelist John le Carré). Herr later recalled, "We talked about many things that night, but mostly about war and movies.... During the next three years, we talked on the telephone. I think of it now as one phone call lasting three years, with interruptions. The substance was single-minded: the old and always serious problem of how you put into a film or a book the living, behaving presence of what Jung called the Shadow, 'the most accessible of archetypes, and the easiest to experience.'"[7]

Herr had read *The Short-Timers* in galleys in 1979 and found it brilliant, so when Kubrick asked him to collaborate on a screen adaptation, he was more than willing. Herr describes the writing process in terms quite similar to Diane Johnson's experience with *The Shining*: "Stanley wrote

a detailed treatment of the novel. We met every day for a month and talked. We broke the treatment down into scenes, with a titled filing card for each scene.... I wrote the first-draft screenplay from this, in prose form. The pages, if any, went out by car every afternoon, followed in the evening by a phone call.... When I finished the draft, he rewrote it, and I rewrote that. Gus came to London and wrote. Stanley rewrote all through shooting."[8]

Kubrick described the process of adaptation as: "almost a matter of code-breaking, of breaking the work down into a structure that is truthful, that doesn't lose the ideas or the content or the feeling of the book. And fitting it all into the much more limited time frame of a movie. And as long as you possibly can, you retain your emotional attitude, whatever it was that made you fall in love in the first place. You judge a scene by asking yourself, 'Am I still responding to what's there?' ... It's an intuitive process, the way I imagine writing music is intuitive. It's not a matter of structuring an argument."[9]

04 *D'Onofrio, Modine, and Howard.*
05 *From left: Arliss Howard (Cowboy), Matthew Modine (Joker), and Vincent D'Onofrio (Gomer Pyle) between takes of boot camp training scenes.*
06 *Kubrick edited* Full Metal Jacket *using Montage (his room-sized machine, imported from the US in 1986, was the first digital editing system used in the UK). This "Montage storyboard" printout shows in and out edit points for the scene in which Pyle kills Hartman.*

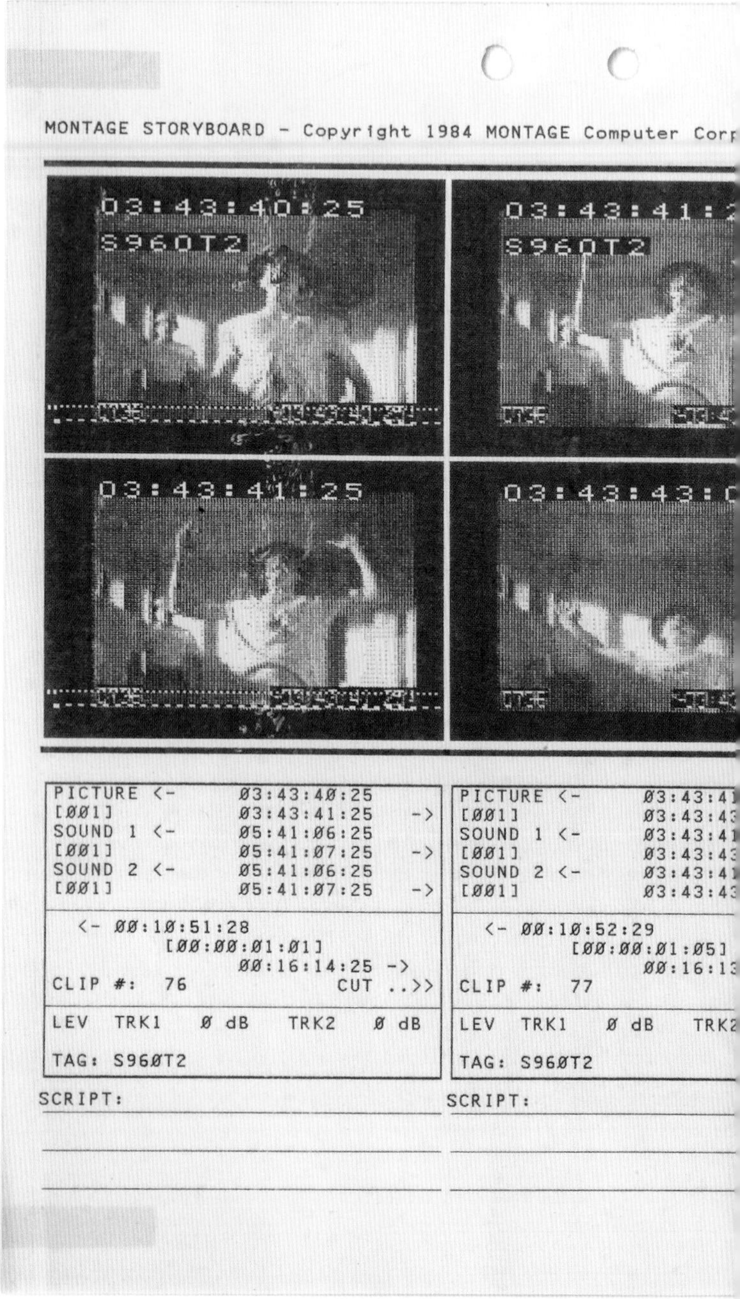
MONTAGE STORYBOARD - Copyright 1984 MONTAGE Computer Corp

PICTURE <- Ø3:43:4Ø:25 [ØØ1] Ø3:43:41:25 -> SOUND 1 <- Ø5:41:Ø6:25 [ØØ1] Ø5:41:Ø7:25 -> SOUND 2 <- Ø5:41:Ø6:25 [ØØ1] Ø5:41:Ø7:25 ->	PICTURE <- Ø3:43:4 [ØØ1] Ø3:43:4 SOUND 1 <- Ø3:43:4 [ØØ1] Ø3:43:4 SOUND 2 <- Ø3:43:4 [ØØ1] Ø3:43:4
<- ØØ:1Ø:51:28 [ØØ:ØØ:Ø1:Ø1] ØØ:16:14:25 -> CLIP #: 76 CUT ..>>	<- ØØ:1Ø:52:29 [ØØ:ØØ:Ø1:Ø5] ØØ:16:1 CLIP #: 77
LEV TRK1 Ø dB TRK2 Ø dB TAG: S96ØT2	LEV TRK1 Ø dB TRK2 TAG: S96ØT2

SCRIPT:

SCRIPT:

16-APR-1987 15:13:55 Page ØØ2Ø of ØØ59

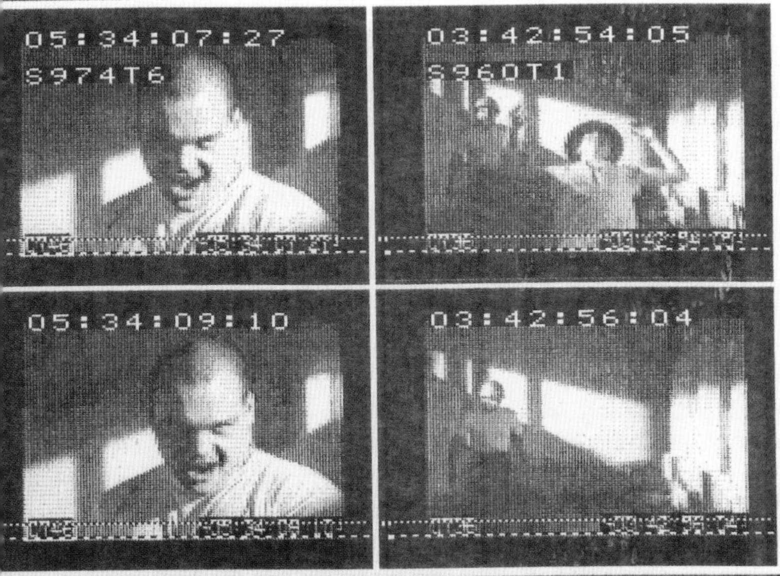

ICTURE <- Ø5:34:Ø7:27 ØØ1] Ø5:34:Ø9:1Ø -> OUND 1 <- SILENCE SILENCE -> OUND 2 <- SILENCE SILENCE ->	PICTURE <- Ø3:42:54:Ø5 [ØØ1] Ø3:42:56:Ø4 -> SOUND 1 <- SILENCE SILENCE -> SOUND 2 <- SILENCE SILENCE ->
<- ØØ:1Ø:54:Ø4 [ØØ:ØØ:Ø1:14] ØØ:16:12:Ø6 -> LIP #: 78 CUT ..>>	<- ØØ:1Ø:55:18 [ØØ:ØØ:Ø2:ØØ] ØØ:16:1Ø:Ø6 -> CLIP #: 79 CUT ..>>
EV TRK1 Ø dB TRK2 Ø dB	LEV TRK1 Ø dB TRK2 Ø dB
AG: S974T6	TAG: S96ØT1

RIPT:

SCRIPT:

On Parris Island, S. C., Gunnery Sgt. Hartman (Lee Ermey) molds a fresh crop of Marine recruits into killing machines before they are to ship out to Vietnam. One bumbling, overweight recruit whom Hartman nicknames "Private Gomer Pyle" (Vincent D'Onofrio) seems particularly ill-suited for the harsh drill instructor's brand of boot camp training. His squad leader, Private Joker (Matthew Modine), tries to help Pyle, to little avail. Joker's best friend, Cowboy (Arliss Howard), and the other recruits lose patience with Pyle when Hartman begins to punish all of them for his mistakes. Joker reluctantly joins the rest of the platoon in a dreadful act of violence against Pyle, intended to "motivate" him to shape up. From then on, Pyle's mental state deteriorates even as his discipline seems to soar. Finally Pyle snaps, shoots Hartman dead, and puts a bullet through his own head.

"I like the lack of info about Joker's life before he joined the marines."

—SK/Handwritten notes on Hasford's book, white lined paper

The story abruptly jumps ahead to Vietnam, where Joker is stationed in Da Nang as a combat correspondent (essentially writing propaganda) for *Stars and Stripes* and has befriended Rafterman (Kevyn Major Howard), a photographer for the paper. In the wake of the 1968 Tet offensive, they meet up with Cowboy's squadron, led by Lt. Touchdown (Ed O'Ross). On a patrol in Hue, Touchdown is killed, leaving Cowboy as squad leader. When two members of the squad are wounded by a sniper shooting from inside a bombed-out building, the gung-ho Animal Mother (Adam Baldwin) insists on going in to save them, against Cowboy's orders. The two wounded men die, and the sniper also kills Cowboy. Out for vengeance, Joker finds the sniper, who turns out to be a young Vietnamese woman; he fumbles his rifle as he tries to shoot her, and Rafterman guns her down just before she can kill Joker. Wounded and suffering, she begs the soldiers to kill her. Joker shoots her out of mercy—his first and only "kill" of the film.

The first act of *Full Metal Jacket* follows *The Short-Timers* fairly closely.[10] Some departures from Hasford's book include a couple of key changes in the film's ending. In the novel, Joker is forced to kill Cowboy, who is mortally wounded and being used as bait by the sniper. Joker then finds himself in command, as the remains of the squad move on. In the film, other characters are used as bait by the sniper, who subsequently shoots Cowboy. Then Joker must decide whether or not to kill the sniper; and it seems that Animal Mother will emerge as the new squad leader.

While Kubrick retained a good deal of the dialogue he so admired from Hasford's book, Lee Ermey improvised approximately 50 percent of his dialogue as Hartman.[11] This places Ermey among a select few performers whom Kubrick allowed such freedom of input, including Peter Sellers and Jack Nicholson.

07 ***Kubrick's notes covering a script page from the sniper's death scene.***

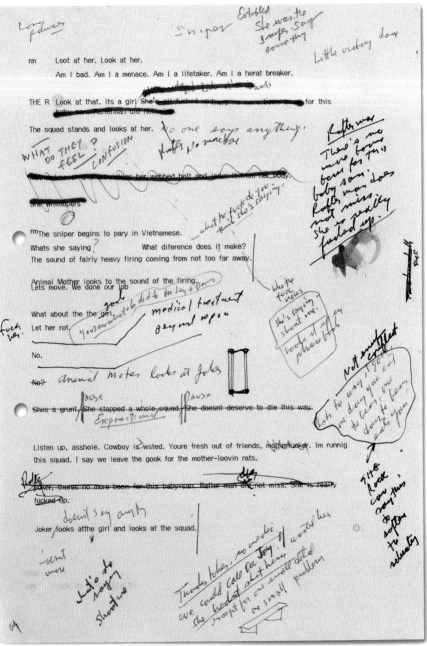

Long pduces

Sniper Establed She was the sniper. Say some thing

Little victory dance

rm Loot at her. Look at her.

Am I bad. Am I a menace. Am I a lifetaker. Am I a herat breaker.

[redacted] words

THE R Look at that. Its a girl She[redacted] for this [redacted]

The squad stands and looks at her. No one say anything.

WHAT DO THEY FEEL? CONFUSION

Rafter man no more boo

Rafter was There's no more boom for this baby san. Rafter man does not miss. She is really fucked up.

[redacted] her webbed belt and jerks it from her body.

[redacted]

rm The sniper begins to pary in Vietnamese.

— what the fuck do you think she's saying

Whats she saying?   What diference does it make?

The sound of fairly heavy firing coming from not too far away.

Animal Mother looks to the sound of the firing.
Lets move. We done our job

What about the the ~~girl~~ gook. you sound want to be died to Doc Jay + Donny

medical treatment beyond hope

fuck her.

Let her rot.

Who the fuck knows

She's saying shoot me.

looks it up in phrase book

No.

~~No?~~ Animal Mother looks at Joker

pause   pause

~~Shes a grunt. She stopped a whole squad. She doesnt deserve to die this way.~~

Expositional

Not smart conflict

Thats the way it goes on day you eat the bear, one day the bear eats you

Listen up, asshole. Cowboy is wsted. Youre fresh out of friends, ~~motherfucker~~. Im runnig this squad. I say we leave the gook for the mother-loovin rats.

~~Rafter Joker, theres no more boom for this baby-san. Rafter man did not miss. She is really fucked up.~~

9th Rock Cow tries say this to soften the situation

doesn't say anything

Joker looks atthe girl and looks at the squad.

doesnt move

that's she saying shoot me

Thanks Joker, no medic we could call Doc Jay if she hadnt shot him. except for one small detail one small problem

watch her

08 *Kubrick discusses a scene with Lee Ermey (seated).*
09 *Shooting the television crew shooting the war.*
10 *Matthew Modine (left) with Kubrick and nephew Manuel Harlan (right), who worked as video operator.*
11 *"Matthew Modine was perfect for the part. He's a combination of sensitivity and macho virility. If Gary Cooper and Henry Fonda had a baby – it would be Matthew Modine." – SK/1987 (to Michel Ciment)*
12 *The scene in which Joker and Rafterman arrive at the outskirts of Hue.*
13 *Dorian Harewood (Eightball) speaks to the camera for the combat interview segment.*
14 *Kubrick on the abandoned gasworks outside London that his crew partially demolished: "It looks absolutely perfect, I think. There might be some other place in the world like it, but I'd hate to have to look for it. I think even if we had gone to Hue, we couldn't have created that look." (to Lloyd Grove/*Washington Post, *1987)*

Initially, Kubrick had hired Ermey (a Vietnam veteran and former drill instructor) as a technical military advisor, a position he had also held on Francis Ford Coppola's *Apocalypse Now* (1979) as well as *The Boys in Company C* (1978) and *Purple Hearts* (1984). Ermey told the New York *Daily News*: "I got terribly excited when Stanley called me. He was not offering me the role. They actually had a contract with another actor to play the part, but I went to London with the intent of going after the role, and once there, I continued to pursue it."

When Ermey first asked for the part, Kubrick told him that he wasn't vicious enough. Not to be put off so easily, Ermey began to humiliate the young men who were auditioning for the roles of the recruits. Kubrick was so impressed that he gave him the role of Hartman, calling him a "super-intimidator."[12]

Initial casting efforts on *Full Metal Jacket* took a similar tack as on *The Shining*: Warner Bros. issued an open call for young men to send in videotapes to audition for roles as Marine recruits. However, some of the major roles were cast in a more conventional manner. Kubrick knew he wanted Matthew Modine to play Private Joker, having seen him in Alan Parker's *Birdy* (1984), a performance he loved.

Vincent D'Onofrio landed the role of Private Pyle based on several videotaped auditions and an audio tape that he mailed to Kubrick. He originally learned of the part through his friend Matthew

10

12

11

13

Modine. He later recalled, "I rented a home video camera, found a green stoop that resembled an army barracks, put on an army cap and green fatigues, and did a monologue about a rookie cop, except that I left out all of the lines about cops. I sent it off and got a call right back." Kubrick said of this particular bit of casting: "Pyle was the hardest part to cast in the whole movie. I wanted to find new faces. We received about three or four thousand videotapes."[13]

"Problems.... We don't know if Joker gets out alive.... I love the Homeric honesty when Joker says I never felt so alive.... To be crude, there is no dramatic pay-off, not in plot, character or idea. It just ends."

—SK/Handwritten notes on Hasford's book, white lined paper

To fit the part of the overweight, self-conscious Private Pyle, the normally physically fit D'Onofrio put on more than sixty pounds, of which he said: "Physical transformation is part of being an actor.... That's how I was trained, the same way as DeNiro and Duvall, and the people who change themselves when they do things. The emotion can come, but the physicalness is very important. The secret is to put yourself totally in the circumstances of your character."[14]

Cinematographer Douglas Milsome said of D'Onofrio's performance in the powerful murder-suicide scene: "D'Onofrio flashes what people are now referring to as the 'Kubrick crazy stare.' Stanley has a stare like that which is very penetrating and frightens the hell out of you sometimes. I gather he's able to inject that into his actors as well."[15]

When Adam Baldwin's agents approached him about the possibility of working with Kubrick, he jumped at the chance. "I had always been a huge fan of Stanley's ever since I saw *A Clockwork Orange*," he said. Add to that the fact that Baldwin self-identifies as "one of those bleeding-heart liberals"; so he was also attracted to the story's themes. "War is for fools," he told *Interview*. "If I had been eighteen when the Vietnam War began, I wouldn't have fought"—not exactly the words one would expect from Baldwin's character, the bloodthirsty, somewhat reactionary Animal Mother, who seems to be a kind of Rambo parody. "There were guys like that," he explained to *The New York Times*, "and they had to be portrayed.... There were guys like that who believed in the war, and once they got over there, it was a whole different thing."[16]

Like many who worked with Kubrick, Baldwin found the experience to be grueling but ultimately rewarding, as he told the *Hollywood Reporter*: "I spent ten months working fifteen-hour days, six days a week, logging through dirt and rubble, with bombs going off and everything. It

15 ***Draft of the script. In this version, Animal Mother was to cut off the sniper's head and toss it through a hole in the wall, and the final scene was to show the death of Joker intercut with glimpses of him as a child, pretending to be shot down.***

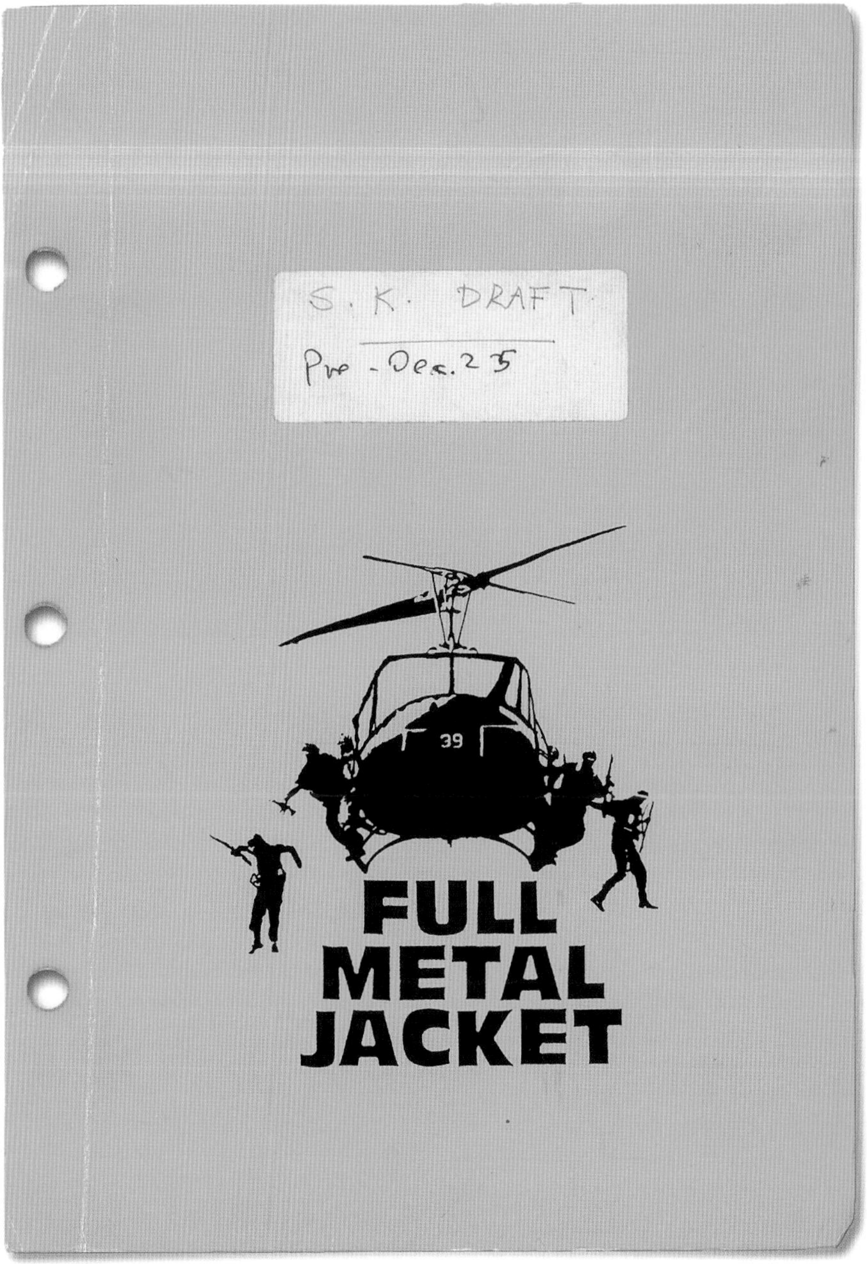
S.K. DRAFT
Pre-Dec. 25
39
FULL
METAL
JACKET

was long and hard, but it was great. I'd do it again in a second."[17]

Filming locations included England's Isle of Dogs and Epping Forest, as well as the Bassingbourn military barracks in Cambridgeshire, which served as the Parris Island boot camp. A second unit shot some footage of military parades surreptitiously, on location at Parris Island.

The film's most impressive location was an abandoned 1930s gasworks in Beckton, a town on the Thames that was transformed into the bombed-out city of Hue. This same location had been used for the film of *Nineteen Eighty-Four* (1984), among others. Kubrick told *Rolling Stone*: "We worked from still photographs of Hue in 1968. And we found an area that had the same 1930s functionalist architecture. Now, not every bit of it was right, but some of the buildings were absolute carbon copies of the outer industrial areas of Hue.... It had been owned by British Gas, and it was scheduled to be demolished. So they allowed us to blow up the buildings. We had demolition guys in there for a week, laying charges. One Sunday, all the executives from British Gas brought their families down to watch us blow the

16 ***This boot camp training scene was not used in the film.***

17 ***This page included in a draft of the screenplay describes Kubrick's intention to cast young actors in the roles of the recruits. During the casting process, however, he came to realize that eighteen-year-olds in general didn't have the maturity required to be great actors, and was thus forced to scrap his original idea and cast actors in their twenties.***

p 27 barrel (?)
p 48 Hershey

NOTE

The average age of Joker and the other Marine grunts in this story is 18 (high school seniors), as, indeed, it was in Vietnam.

Contrary to the general habit in war films of accommodating important actors who are the wrong age by casting everyone else older than they should be, in this film the young Marines will be played by 18 year-olds.

Parris Island 24 - 30
Tet to Big attack 53 - 60
Big attack

place up. It was spectacular. Then we had a wrecking ball there for two months, with the art director telling the operator which hole to knock in which building.... We brought in palm trees from Spain and a hundred thousand plastic tropical plants from Hong Kong."[18] If Kubrick had had to build sets from the ground up for the scenes in Hue, the film's $17 million budget would have been exceeded several times over.

After designing Neil Jordan's *The Company of Wolves* in 1984, Anton Furst got a call from Stanley Kubrick, who had liked that film's look. Kubrick appreciated Furst's references to Doré, Samuel Palmer, Bruegel, and other artists, and asked him to do the production design on *Full Metal Jacket*. Furst later recalled his two years of working with Kubrick as being exhilarating, instructive, and exhausting, "like being suspended in a black hole of high thought and creativity." He told *The Face*: "Stanley is hard work. But if you're absolutely up front and honest about the possibility of fucking up and you *tell* him, then I've never met anyone easier. Stanley doesn't travel; everything comes to him, so there was no question of visiting Vietnam. Therefore when he told me we'd be creating Vietnam in England, my reaction was, 'Great, we can do it better!' ... because we could blow the bloody thing up. Go for broke. I don't think you could fault it in terms of looking like Vietnam.... We had *huge* amounts of research material."[19]

The over-all look of *Full Metal Jacket*, which Siskel describes as "harshly lit barracks and urban daylight," owes as much to the cinematography as to the production design. Douglas Milsome, who had been John Alcott's camera assistant on *A Clockwork Orange* and *The Shining*, "graduated" to become Kubrick's cinematographer on *Full Metal Jacket*. Milsome said of the experience: "I've actually had a much harder time working with a lot less talented people than Stanley Kubrick. He's a drain because he saps you dry, but he works damn hard himself and expects everybody else to.... You eat, drink, and sleep the movie, and you're under contract to Stanley body and soul. But he allows you the time to get everything absolutely right, which is what I find so rewarding."[20]

One thing Milsome learned from Kubrick and Alcott was the ability to disguise lighting instruments as either natural light sources or practical lights in the set. For the opening scene of *Full Metal Jacket*, in which the camera tracks backwards through the barracks in front of Hartman, we eventually see the full 360 degrees of the set. This was achieved much in the same way that the Overlook Hotel lobby was lit in *The Shining*: banks of lights were placed outside the barracks windows, and the intense light streaming in was made to appear as sunlight. No other light was used in the scene.

Always the innovator, Kubrick was notorious for modifying existing equipment to suit his needs, using it in ways that had not occurred to anyone before. Milsome de-

18–19 ***Mock-ups of the barracks and latrine sets. The latter was the only set that was not realistic, with its rows of toilets facing each other. Kubrick commented, "We did that as a kind of poetic license. It just seemed funny and grotesque." (to Lloyd Grove/*****Washington Post*****, 1987)***

18

19

scribes a rather unusual "dolly" that was used in the battle scenes of both *Barry Lyndon* and *Full Metal Jacket* (in the latter, the dolly was used in conjunction with the Steadicam, for the sake of repeatability of camera movement). For tracking across uneven terrain, a traditional dolly simply would be too shaky, so Kubrick had his crew modify a camera car, removing the engine to make it lighter. Thus, six grips could push the car quite easily, and it delivered a remarkably smooth ride across the uneven ground.[21]

"I suppose the single improvement one might hope for the world, which would have the greatest effect for good, would be an appreciation and acceptance of this Jungian view of man by those who see themselves as good and externalize all evil."

—SK/1987 (to Gene Siskel/*Chicago Tribune*)

Shooting, which began in August 1985, ran longer than expected: until September 1986. One reason the production ran over schedule was that it had to shut down for five months after Lee Ermey sustained severe injuries in an automobile accident.

By this time, Stanley Kubrick was notorious for often requiring large numbers of takes from his actors. He explained to *Rolling Stone*: "It happens when actors are unprepared.... If actors have to think about the words, they can't work on the emotion. So you end up doing thirty takes of something. And still you can see the concentration in their eyes; they don't know their lines." By contrast, Kubrick noted that, "Lee Ermey, for instance, would spend every spare second with the dialogue coach, and he always knew his lines. I suppose Lee averaged eight or nine takes. He sometimes did it in three. Because he was prepared."[22]

Even so, Ermey found himself occasionally breaking up during takes with the younger actors. "I would get in their noses and yell: 'YOU MISERABLE PIECE OF SHIT! DID YOUR PARENTS EVER HAVE ANY CHILDREN THAT LIVED?!' The kids would look at me so pitifully that it was tough not to laugh. I had my moments where I'd break down and giggle, and so would they." To cure Ermey of his laughing problem, Kubrick had Leon Vitali throw tennis balls at him while he rehearsed his lines. This went on for days, until Ermey could do the lines perfectly without being distracted. The result is a brilliant, chilling performance, so intensely real that Ermey paralyzed some of his co-stars with fear. "It was terrifying to those actors. My objective was intimidation. No one had ever invaded their private space; no one had ever put his head close to them. The first time I came up to Vincent, all he had to say was 'Yes, sir,' and 'No, sir,' and he was so shocked he blew his lines three or four times." To maintain this atmosphere of tension, Kubrick kept Ermey from rehearsing with the other actors and from socializing with them during off time.[23]

Of course another important tool Kubrick used to achieve tension in the film was editing, a process which he supervised entirely and which took ten months.[24]

His editor on *Full Metal Jacket*, Martin Hunter, told *American Cinematographer* about an important lesson he learned from Kubrick: "to impart the intended emotion of the scene, it's crucial that the reactions be precisely correct." Hunter went on to say: "Many (directors) believe that reactions are something you pick up at the end of a scene; they'll just run the camera and say, 'That'll do,' which is not the best way to do it. (Stanley) would shoot take after take of people who were only observers in the scene, and didn't have any dialogue. Then, as we were cutting it, he'd comb through the material exhaustively. I remember saying to him once, 'Stanley, would you ever consider looking at a couple of takes and picking a reaction shot that works, and not bother to look at the others?' He looked at me in some shock and replied, 'I'd never think of doing that. So much work has gone into it so far, why not take it to its conclusion?'"[25]

20 ***Matthew Modine with Lee Ermey, who was originally hired as military advisor and convinced Kubrick to cast him in the role of the drill sergeant. Kubrick told* Rolling Stone, *"I'd say 50 percent of Lee's dialogue, specifically the insult stuff, came from Lee. [He] came up with, I don't know, 150 pages of insults. Off the wall stuff: 'I don't like the name Lawrence. Lawrence is for faggots and sailors.'" (to Tim Cahill/1987)***

Kubrick applied the same kind of assiduity in selecting the film's music. For the first time, he made extensive use of preexisting pop songs such as "Chapel of Love," "Wooly Bully," and The Rolling Stones' "Paint

it Black." Kubrick and co. sifted through *Billboard* magazine's Top-100 list for each year between 1962 and 1968, looking for songs that would play well with particular scenes. The most memorable musical moments of the film occur with Nancy Sinatra's recording of "These Boots are Made for Walking," Tom T. Hall's twangy "Hello Vietnam," and the manic "Surfin' Bird," which Kubrick found to be "an amazing piece." He told *Rolling Stone,* "What I love about the music in that scene is that it suggests post-combat euphoria ... the pleasure one has read described in so many accounts of combat.... The choices weren't arbitrary."[26]

Additionally, *Full Metal Jacket* features a good deal of original music, composed by Kubrick's youngest daughter, Vivian. Perhaps to sidestep distracting accusations of nepotism, she used the pseudonym "Abigail Mead," a pun on the longtime Kubrick home known as Abbot's Mead. Vivian Kubrick performed the haunting score herself, on a Fairlight music computer. The *Washington Post* characterized her music as, "ingenious ... bleating, beating, moaning, metallic, as if machine guns could sing."[27] Vivian also shot a documentary of the making of *Full Metal Jacket,* as she had for *The Shining,* but it was never completed.

21 ***The director hands a Polaroid he has just taken to an assistant.***

In the final scene, Joker and the remnants of the squad march through a fiery, nighttime landscape that one might reasonably term "hellish," singing the theme song from Disney's *Mickey Mouse Club*—a song that appears in Hasford's novel, but not at the end. In his choice to feature the song prominently as the film's coda, Kubrick achieves what Janet Maslin called "the kind of heavy irony that would sink anyone else, and that in his hands becomes bone-chilling."[28]

The final scene's irony taps into the idea of Jungian duality that permeates the film. This theme finds its most concrete incarnation in the juxtaposition of Joker's peace symbol pin and his combat helmet, on which he has handwritten the slogan, "Born to Kill." Early in the second act, a colonel confronts Joker in the field, asking whether the seemingly conflicting message is "some kind of sick joke," or if not, what it is supposed to mean. Joker replies that he was trying to say "something about the duality of man... the Jungian thing." The perturbed and possibly confused colonel retorts with a question: "Whose side are you on, son?" to which Joker responds blankly, "Our side, sir." This brief exchange is laden with appropriately double meanings: born/kill; peace/combat; whose side of the Jungian duality is Joker on? Our side; i.e., the two sides are of the same coin. Significantly, an image of Joker's helmet, prominently featuring the peace symbol pin, the words "born to kill," and a supply of bullets in their "full metal jackets," was used as the key artwork for the film's initial poster and ad campaigns, created by Philip Castle.

As was often the case with Kubrick's films, the initial critical response to *Full Metal Jacket* was somewhat mixed, but with time its reputation has solidified. As *Variety* points out, "*Jacket* was different from all other movies on the Vietnam War and eventually became as definitive and persuasive a statement about the nature of war as (Kubrick's) earlier *Paths of Glory*."[29]

While Gene Siskel, writing in the *Chicago Tribune*, did not find *Full Metal Jacket* to be among Kubrick's best work, he did offer praise for the film: "the humor in *Full Metal Jacket* is so raw, its horror so unflinching, that seeing it reminds one that Kubrick's near-best work is more adult, more complex and more audacious than the movies of virtually any other filmmaker today." Siskel's main disappointment with the film came in the ending, which he said leaves us "wanting more." Given the old show-biz adage that one should "always leave 'em wanting more," this hardly seems a major fault.

Siskel's one-time television partner, Roger Ebert, was not so generous in his review for the *Chicago Sun-Times*. He wrote: "Kubrick seems to want to tell us the story of individual characters, to show how the war affected them, but it has been so long since he allowed spontaneous human nature into his films that he no longer knows how.... The movie's climax, which Kubrick obviously intends to be a mighty moral revelation, seems phoned in from earlier war pictures."[30] Like a few other critics at the time, Ebert falls into the seductive trap of trying to outsmart Kubrick and the movie, first making erroneous assumptions about Kubrick's "obvious" intentions and then attempting to demonstrate that the film fails to achieve them. In fact,

22

Kubrick never offered a "mighty moral revelation" in this or any other film. Indeed, he professed in an interview with *Rolling Stone*: "I have no easy answers to offer."[31]

Fortunately, other prominent critics at the time did respond quite positively, while acknowledging the film's dark point of view. Janet Maslin in *The New York Times* called it "Kubrick's most sobering vision... infinitely more troubling and singular than the one set forth in Oliver Stone's *Platoon*." In the *Washington Post*, Desson Howe hailed it as "the most eloquent and exacting vision of the war to date."[32] Also in the *Washington Post*, Rita Kempley offered one of the most astute contemporary reviews of *Full Metal Jacket*, likening its first act to "a boot camp opera, the Parris Island Follies, a drill instructor's aria sung to a chorus of grunts."

Another rave came from Brian Baxter, in *Films and Filming*: "The opening images of this audacious and powerful movie are as disturbing and 'experimental' as any you are likely to see in the commercial cinema.... Relentless.... Startling... a sparse and brilliant screenplay... (I had to see it twice in the space of a week to get to grips with it).... One realizes long after the film has ended just how deeply one has been scarred by the images of humiliation and the horrors of war.... It is a work that demands concentration and a form of stamina alien to audiences in these days of pap and cinematic trash."[33]

Kubrick himself was pleased with *Full Metal Jacket* (which incidentally was a financial success and among the year's top-twenty grossing films, at $46.4 million). He told *The New York Times*: "I'm happy with the picture. My films have all had varying critical opinion and it's always been subsequent critical reaction that settles the scores.... The only thing I can think of is that everybody's always expecting the last movie again, and they're sometimes angry—I mean some critics—often put off because they're expecting something else."[34]

By this time, Kubrick had grown weary of some of the bizarre stories about him that had appeared in the press over the years; so he took the opportunity to clear up a few things in a 1987 interview with Gene Siskel: "There's so much misinformation about me. The stories get more elaborate as they're repeated in the papers. I've read that I wear a football crash helmet in a car, and I don't allow my driver to go over thirty miles per hour. Well, I drive a white Porsche 928S. It's a lot of fun to drive. I don't wear a football helmet or any other helmet, and I don't have a driver.... Practically everything I read about me is grotesquely wrong. The only 'story' about me

22 **Full Metal Jacket** ***clapboard.***

that's true is that I don't like to fly. I'm not a recluse. I lead a relatively normal life, I think. But this stuff has been written and rewritten so often it takes on a life of its own."[35]

The disturbing vision put forth in *Full Metal Jacket* provided even more grist to the mill that had been churning out a processed image of Kubrick the misanthrope. In response, he told Siskel: "You don't have to make Frank Capra movies to like people. Capra presents a view of life as we all wish it really were. But I think you can still present a darker picture of life without disliking the human race. And I think Frank Capra movies are wonderful. And I wish life were like most any one of them. And I wish everybody were like Jimmy Stewart. But they're not."[36]

Notes

1. Paul Duncan, *Stanley Kubrick: Complete Films* (Cologne: TASCHEN, 2003): 175.
2. Gene Siskel, "Candidly Kubrick," *Chicago Tribune*, June 21, 1987. Reprinted in Gene D. Phillips, ed., *Stanley Kubrick: Interviews* (Jackson: University Press of Mississippi, 2001): 177–88.
3. Michael Herr, "Foreword," in Stanley Kubrick, Michael Herr, and Gustav Hasford, *Full Metal Jacket: The Screenplay* (New York: Alfred A. Knopf, 1987): v.
4. Siskel: 187.
5. Francis Clines, "Stanley Kubrick's Vietnam War," *The New York Times*, June 21, 1987. Reprinted in Gene D. Phillips, ed., *Stanley Kubrick: Interviews* (Jackson: University Press of Mississippi, 2001): 171–76.
6. Siskel: 180.
7. Herr: v.
8. Herr: vi.
9. Tim Cahill, "The Rolling Stone Interview: Stanley Kubrick," *Rolling Stone* (August 27, 1987). Reprinted in Gene D. Phillips, ed., *Stanley Kubrick: Interviews* (Jackson: University Press of Mississippi, 2001): 196.
10. Duncan: 170.
11. Cahill: 197.
12. Quoted in Rodney Hill, "Ermey, Lee," in Gene D. Phillips and Rodney Hill, *The Encyclopedia of Stanley Kubrick* (New York: Checkmark, 2002): 104.
13. Quoted in Rodney Hill, "D'Onofrio, Vincent," in Phillips and Hill: 81.
14. Ibid.
15. Ibid.
16. Quoted in Hill, "Baldwin, Adam," in Phillips and Hill: 17.
17. Ibid.
18. Cahill: 194–95.
19. Quoted in Hill, "Furst, Anton," in Phillips and Hill: 130.
20. Ron Magid, "Quest for Perfection," *American Cinematographer* (October 1999).
21. Hill, "Milsome, Douglas," in Phillips and Hill: 253.
22. Cahill.
23. Quoted in Hill, "Ermey": 103.
24. Lloyd Rose, "Stanley Kubrick, at a Distance," *Washington Post*, June 28, 1987: F1.
25. Magid.
26. Cahill: 193.
27. Rita Kempley, "Full Metal Jacket," *Washington Post*, June 26, 1987.
28. Janey Maslin, "Inside the 'Jacket': All Kubrick," *The New York Times*, July 5, 1987.
29. Richard Natale and Leonard Klady, "Stanley Kubrick Dies," *Variety*, March 8, 1999.
30. Roger Ebert, "Full Metal Jacket," *Chicago Sun-Times*, June 26, 1987.
31. Cahill: 203.
32. Desson Howe, "Full Metal Jacket," *Washington Post*, June 26, 1987.
33. Brian Baxter, "Full Metal Jacket," *Films and Filming* (October 1987): 35–36.
34. Clines: 174.
35. Siskel: 178.
36. Ibid.: 187.

Eyes Wide Shut

1999 / COLOR / 159 MINUTES
Distributed by WARNER BROS.

CAST
DR. WILLIAM HARFORD TOM CRUISE
ALICE HARFORD NICOLE KIDMAN
VICTOR ZIEGLER SYDNEY POLLACK
NICK NIGHTINGALE TODD FIELD
MARION MARIE RICHARDSON
DOMINO VINESSA SHAW
MILICH RADE SHERBEDGIA
DESK CLERK ALAN CUMMING
HELENA HARFORD MADISON EGINTON
ROZ JACKIE SAWIRIS
ILONA LESLIE LOWE
VICTOR ZIEGLER'S SECRETARY MICHAEL DOVEN
GAYLE LOUISE TAYLOR
NUALA STEWART THORNDIKE
HARRIS RANDALL PAUL
MANDY JULIENNE DAVIS
SANDOR SZAVOST SKY DUMONT
LISA LISA LEONE
LOU NATHANSON KEVIN CONNEALY
CARL THOMAS GIBSON
JAPANESE MAN 1 TOGO IGAWA
JAPANESE MAN 2 EIJI KUSUHARA
MILICH'S DAUGHTER LEELEE SOBIESKI
MYSTERIOUS WOMAN ABIGAIL GOOD
TALL BUTLER BRIAN W. COOK
RED CLOAK LEON VITALI

CREW
PRODUCED AND DIRECTED BY STANLEY KUBRICK
SCREENPLAY STANLEY KUBRICK and FREDERIC RAPHAEL (inspired by Arthur Schnitzler's *Traumnovelle*)
EXECUTIVE PRODUCER JAN HARLAN
CO-PRODUCER BRIAN W. COOK
ASSISTANT TO THE DIRECTOR LEON VITALI
DIRECTOR OF PHOTOGRAPHY LARRY SMITH
PRODUCTION DESIGNERS LES TOMKINS, ROY WALKER
EDITOR NIGEL GALT
COSTUME DESIGNER MARIT ALLEN
PRODUCTION MANAGER MARGARET ADAMS
ASSISTANT TO STANLEY KUBRICK ANTHONY FREWIN
CASTING DENISE CHAMIAN, LEON VITALI
1ST ASSISTANT DIRECTOR BRIAN W. COOK
2ND ASSISTANT DIRECTOR ADRIAN TOYNTON
3RD ASSISTANT DIRECTORS BECKY HUNT, RHUN FRANCIS
SOUND RECORDIST EDDIE TISE
SUPERVISING SOUND EDITOR PAUL CONWAY
RE-RECORDING MIXERS GRAHAM V. HARTSTONE, MICHAEL A. CARTER, NIGEL GALT, TONY CLEAL
LOCATION MANAGERS SIMON MCNAIR SCOTT, ANGUS MORE GORDON
LOCATION RESEARCH MANUEL HARLAN
SUPERVISING ART DIRECTOR KEVIN PHIPPS

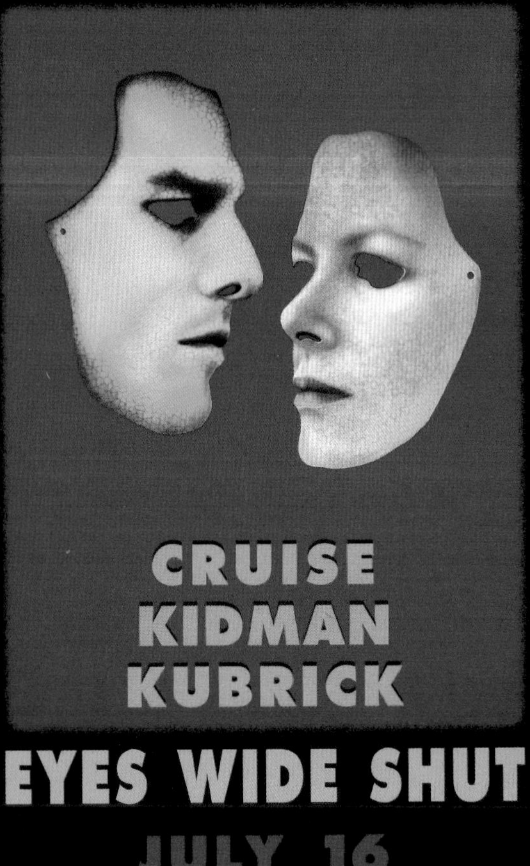

ART DIRECTOR JOHN FENNER
ORIGINAL PAINTINGS CHRISTIANE KUBRICK, KATHARINA HOBBS
SET DECORATORS TERRY WELLS SNR, LISA LEONE
FIRST ASSISTANT EDITOR MELANIE VINER CUNEO
AVID ASSISTANT EDITOR CLAUS WEHLISCH
STEADICAM OPERATORS ELIZABETH ZIEGLER, PETER CAVACIUTI
CAMERA OPERATOR MARTIN HUME

Made at Deluxe Pinewood Studios and on UK locations in Norfolk and The Home Counties.

EYES WIDE SHUT

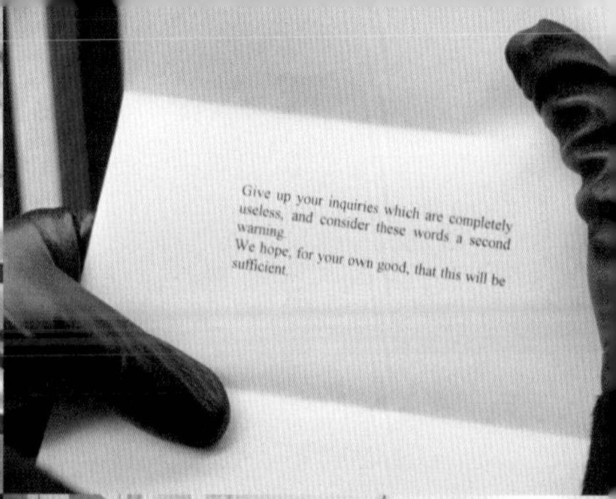
Give up your inquiries which are completely useless, and consider these words a second warning.
We hope, for your own good, that this will be sufficient.

SPECIAL
LUCKY

Eyes Wide Shut

by Rodney Hill

02

"I can believe anything provided that it is quite incredible."

—Oscar Wilde

"From that chamber, and from that mansion, I fled aghast."

—Edgar Allan Poe

Without exception, Stanley Kubrick's films since the mid-1960s have been misunderstood at first, at least to some degree, only to be re-evaluated later as masterpieces. Perhaps the most underestimated of all of them is his brilliant, final achievement, *Eyes Wide Shut*, based on Arthur Schnitzler's 1926 novella, *Traumnovelle* (*Dream Story*). Audiences and critics who were expecting "the sexiest movie ever made," or perhaps a star vehicle suitable for Saturday-night diversion, did not know what to make of this complex, ambiguous treatise on fidelity, desire, and the necessary evils of deception in marriage and in society—a film brought to us by a director who was not only an artisan at the top of his craft, but also one of the major artists of the 20th century.

According to Kent Lambert, Stanley Kubrick first became aware of Arthur Schnitzler's work thanks to his second wife, Ruth Sobotka.[1] Kubrick's affinity for Schnitzler also may have developed partly from his admiration for the films of Max Ophüls, whose *La Ronde* (1950) is based on a Schnitzler novel and is close to the original in terms of tone, setting, and themes.[2] In a 1960 interview, Kubrick expressed his esteem for the Viennese author: "It's difficult to find any writer who understood the human soul more truly and who had a more profound insight into the way people think, act, and really are, and who had a somewhat all-seeing point of view—sympathetic if somewhat cynical."[3]

Also in 1960, Kubrick discussed his desire to make a film "of a contemporary story that really gave a feeling of the times, psychologically, sexually." It is unclear whether Kubrick was actually thinking of adapting Schnitzler to the screen at this point, but indeed several of his plays and novels deal with erotic encounters, problematic relationships, and the often enormous differences between love and desire. The characters may seem on the surface to lead graceful, charming, and respectable lives, but ultimately they are morally and emotionally empty and doomed.[4] Schnitzler's thematic debt to his fellow Austrian and contemporary, Sigmund Freud, must also have attracted Kubrick, whose other films (especially *The Shining* and *Full Metal Jacket*) clearly take on aspects of Freudian psychology. In a 1971 interview, Kubrick specifically mentioned his interest in *Traumnovelle*, which he would eventually bring to the screen nearly thirty years later as *Eyes Wide Shut*.[5]

Page 593 ***This proposal for the film's poster, designed by Katharina Kubrick Hobbs and Christiane Kubrick, was rejected in favor of a design more clearly showing the film's two stars.***
01 ***Shooting the masked party scenes on location at Elveden Hall in Norfolk. Kubrick's longtime assistant, Leon Vitali, who had played Lord Bullingdon in*** Barry Lyndon, ***played "Red Cloak" in addition to his roles as Kubrick's assistant and casting director.***
02 ***Tom Cruise, Kubrick, and Julienne Davis (as the corpse) with director of photography Larry Smith (right).***

In November 1994, Stanley Kubrick began working with scenarist and novelist Frederic Raphael on a screen adaptation of *Traumnovelle*. Perhaps what made the director interested in Raphael were the scripts he had written for John Schlesinger: *Darling* (1965, Oscar for best screenplay), which deals with the decadence of modern society, and *Far from the Madding Crowd* (1967), an adaptation of a literary classic.[6]

"[Traumnovelle] *is a difficult book to describe—what good book isn't? It explores the sexual ambivalence of a happy marriage, and it tries to equate the importance of sexual dreams and might-have-beens with reality. All of Schnitzler's work is psychologically brilliant, and he was greatly admired by Freud....*"

—SK/1972 (to Michel Ciment)

Raphael initially found *Traumnovelle* to be rather dated, and he told Kubrick that it would be difficult to transpose the story from late-19th-century Vienna to modern-day New York. When Kubrick asked why he thought so, Raphael replied that relations between men and women—issues such as jealousy, attraction, fidelity, and roles within a marriage—had changed considerably since Schnitzler's time. Kubrick disagreed; and upon further reflection Raphael changed his mind.[7]

Still, the shifts in time and place did present significant challenges, as Raphael told *Pitch Weekly*: "The trick was to re-imagine all the elements, not just translate bits of Germanic elements into more American dialogue. The very air... the furniture, the reference points, all those things had to be changed. It's like a transplant. If the heart doesn't pump, it doesn't matter how nifty you have put the stitches. The point is: Do the people come to life? Once you've done that, everything else will come to life, too. I'm glad to say it was a bit tough, because otherwise somebody else could have done it easily."[8]

Kubrick and Raphael wrote four drafts of the screenplay, working at Kubrick's residence, Childwickbury House, and also by phone and fax, from autumn 1994 until early 1996. Raphael complained that Kubrick wanted the authorial stamp on the project to be all his. Kubrick was not so interested in Raphael's dialogue (even though he admired its sharpness); rather, he saw the script only as a blueprint for shooting the film, which would be his own artistic creation.[9]

Eyes Wide Shut begins as Dr. Bill Harford (Tom Cruise) and his wife, Alice (Nicole Kidman), prepare to attend a

03 ***Kubrick's notation of the asking price for the film rights to Arthur Schnitzler's*** **Traumnovelle** ***(then known as*** **Rhapsody** ***in English).***
04 ***Immediately after completing*** **A Clockwork Orange,** ***Kubrick planned to begin working on a screen adaptation of*** **Traumnovelle** ***but eventually decided that he wasn't ready to tackle the project.***
05–06 ***Some of the scenes showing Tom Cruise (as Bill Harford) walking the New York City streets were filmed in a studio using back projection.***

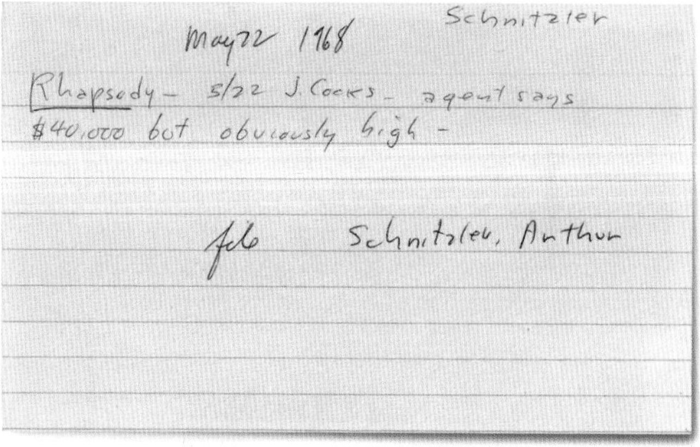

May 22 1968 Schnitzler

Rhapsody – 5/22 J. Cocks – agent says $40,000 but obviously high –

file Schnitzler, Arthur

03

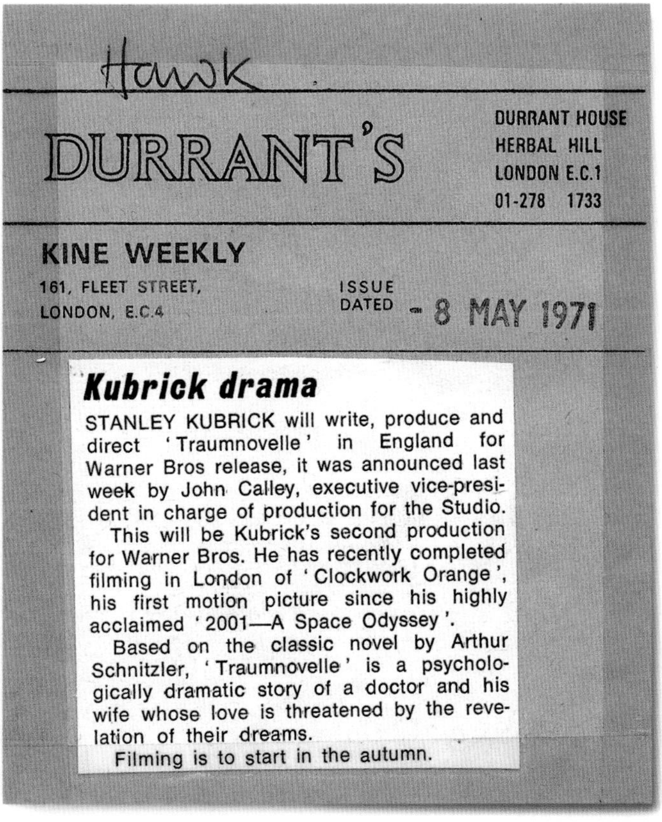

Hawk

DURRANT'S

DURRANT HOUSE
HERBAL HILL
LONDON E.C.1
01-278 1733

KINE WEEKLY
161, FLEET STREET,
LONDON, E.C.4

ISSUE DATED – 8 MAY 1971

Kubrick drama

STANLEY KUBRICK will write, produce and direct 'Traumnovelle' in England for Warner Bros release, it was announced last week by John Calley, executive vice-president in charge of production for the Studio.

This will be Kubrick's second production for Warner Bros. He has recently completed filming in London of 'Clockwork Orange', his first motion picture since his highly acclaimed '2001—A Space Odyssey'.

Based on the classic novel by Arthur Schnitzler, 'Traumnovelle' is a psychologically dramatic story of a doctor and his wife whose love is threatened by the revelation of their dreams.

Filming is to start in the autumn.

04

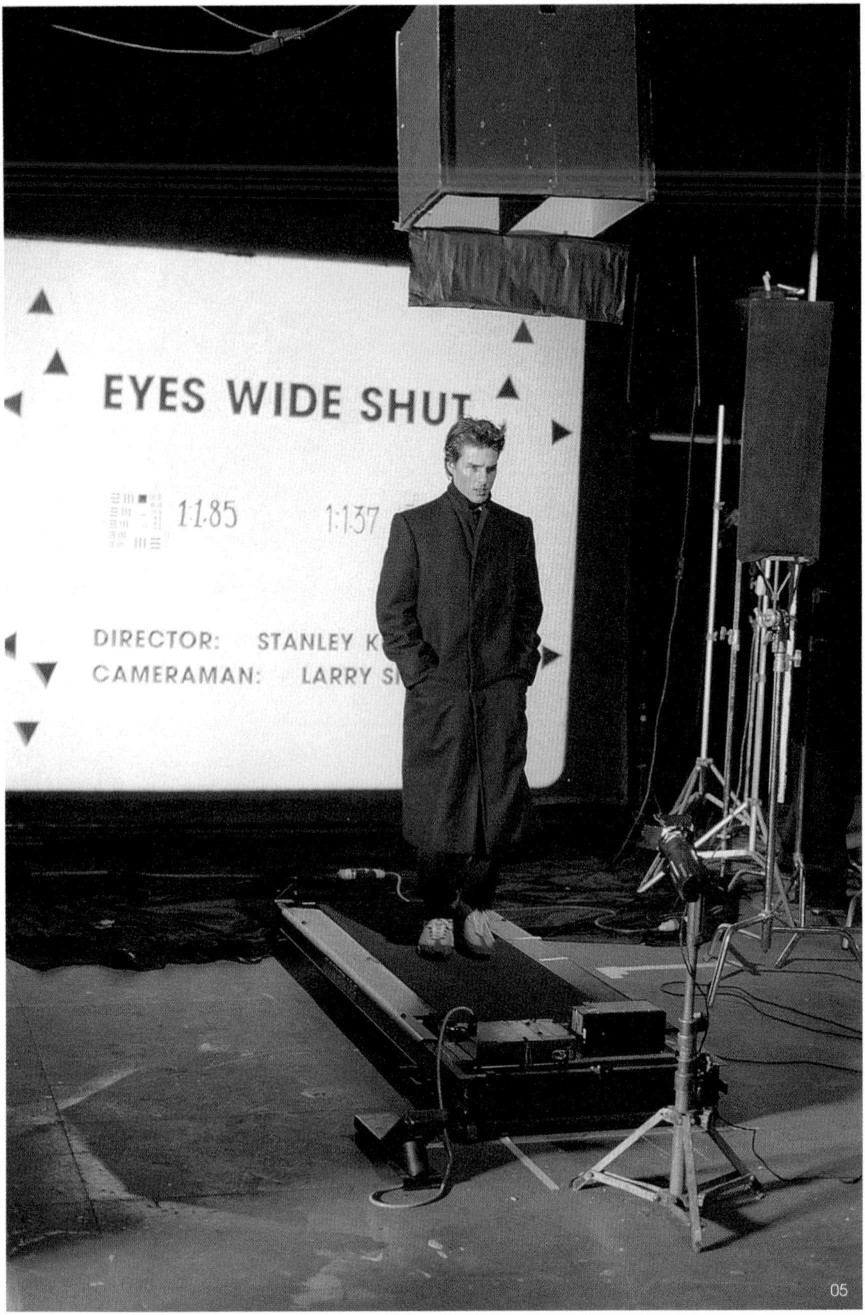

05

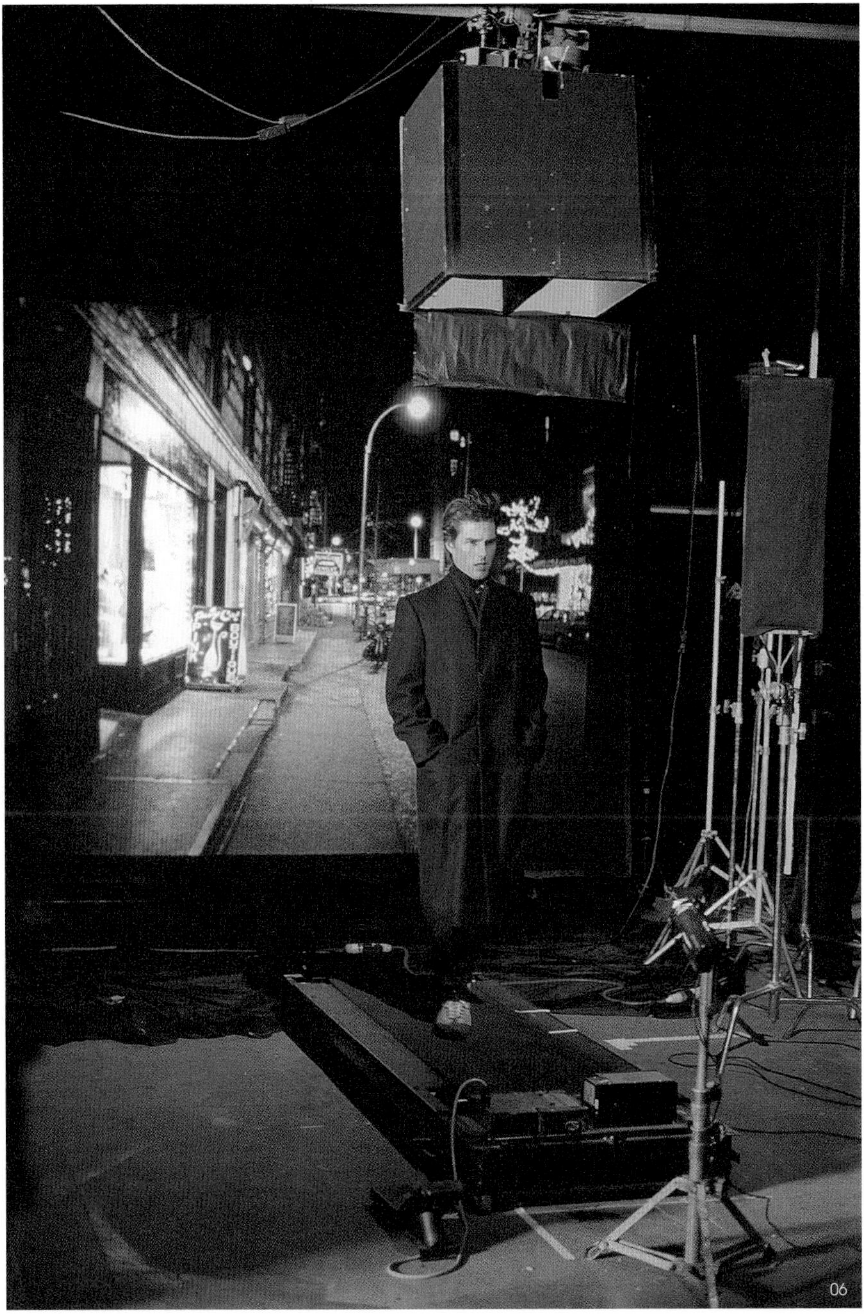

06

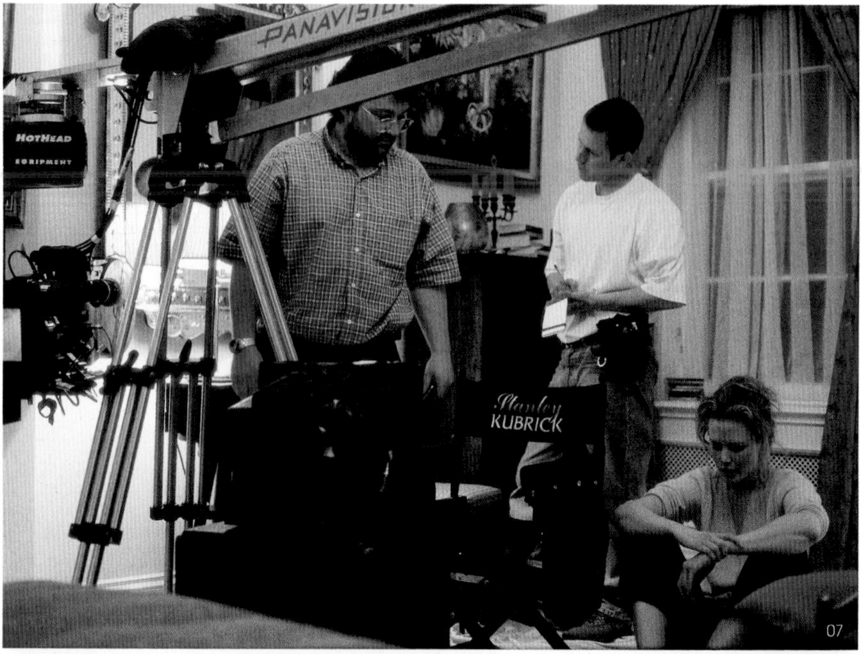

07

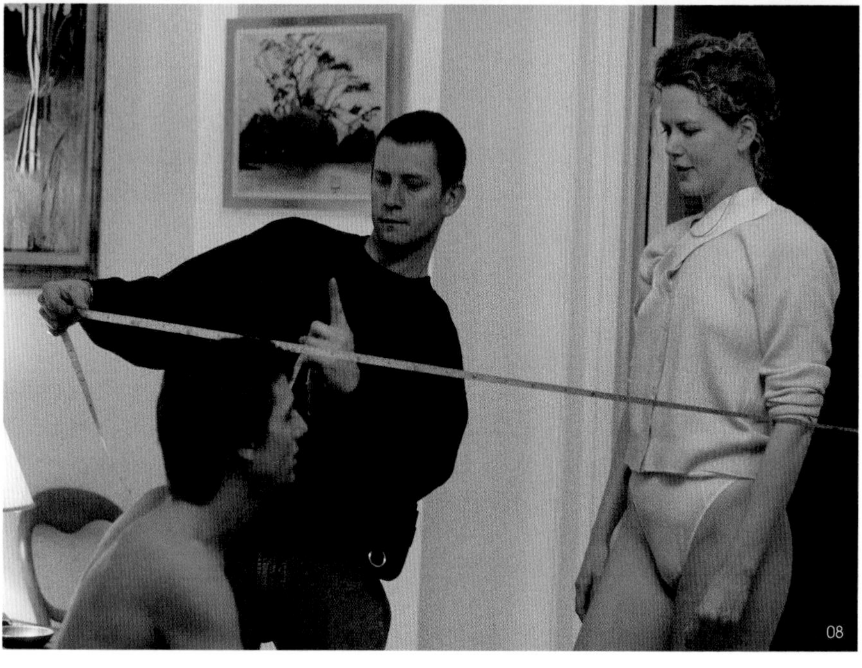
08

lavish Christmas party thrown by one of Bill's most prominent patients, multimillionaire Victor Ziegler (Sydney Pollack). At the party, Bill recognizes an old friend from medical school, Nick Nightingale (Todd Field), who is playing piano with the hired band. During the evening, both Bill and Alice are pursued (doggedly at times) by members of the opposite sex, but they manage to keep everything at the level of flirtation. Bill is called upstairs to assist Victor in reviving a prostitute named Mandy (Julienne Davis) who has passed out from a heavy dose of heroin and cocaine.

A couple of nights later, Bill and Alice are smoking pot and talking about their encounters at the party, and the discussion escalates into an argument. Alice seems perturbed that Bill never gets jealous of her, perhaps feeling that he takes her for granted. She tells him of a time on holiday when she saw a handsome young naval officer and was so tempted that she would have given up everything for just one night with him, if he would have had her.

Just then the phone rings, and an agitated Bill learns that one of his patients has died; he must go put in an appearance. During the visitation, Marion (Marie Richardson) the daughter of the deceased, blurts out a confession of love for Bill and kisses him unexpectedly. He tries to calm her down and makes a hasty retreat.

07 ***Nicole Kidman (Alice Harford) prepares for the bedroom confession scene.***
08 ***"In my life now there's pre-*****Eyes Wide Shut *****and post-*****Eyes Wide Shut*****, because of what Stanley taught me." –Nicole Kidman (interviewed for *****A Life in Pictures*****, 2001)***
09 **Eyes Wide Shut *clapboard.***

Wandering the streets of New York and plagued by thoughts of his wife with the naval officer, Bill meets a prostitute named Domino (Vinessa Shaw), and he is about to have sex with her when Alice calls his cell phone to check in. Bill pays Domino and leaves without consummating their transaction. Remembering that

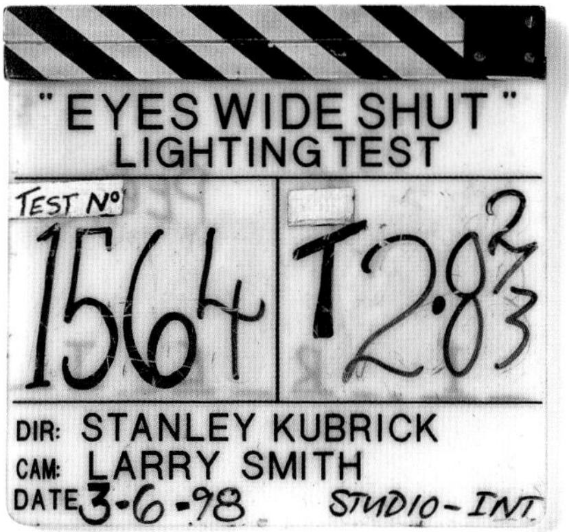

09

Nick Nightingale's band is playing in Greenwich Village, Bill decides to go hear them. After the last set, Nick tells him about his upcoming gig later that night, at a private party involving "such women" as he would not believe. Bill persuades Nick to give him the password for entry, "Fidelio," and Nick also tells him he will need to be in costume.

Even though it is now very late at night, Bill goes to a costume shop he believes to be owned by a former patient. Answering the door in his bathrobe, the new owner, Milich (Rade Sherbedgia) rents Bill the proper costume and mask, "for a price." As Bill is about to leave, they hear a noise, and Milich discovers two

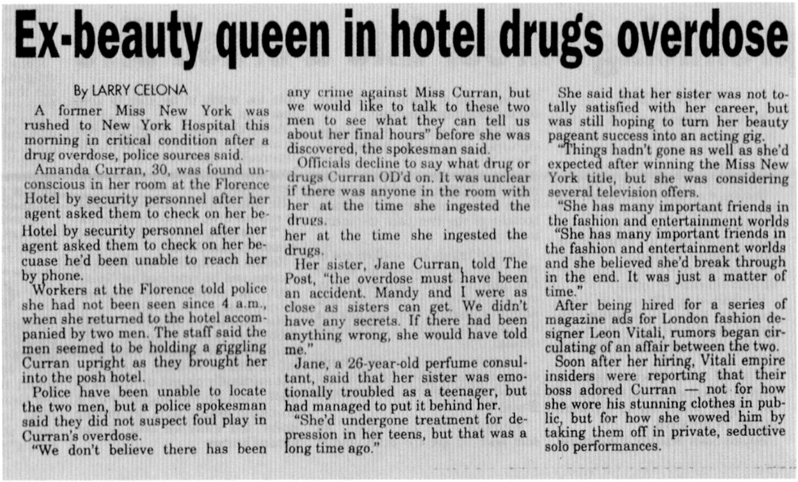

Ex-beauty queen in hotel drugs overdose

By LARRY CELONA

A former Miss New York was rushed to New York Hospital this morning in critical condition after a drug overdose, police sources said.

Amanda Curran, 30, was found unconscious in her room at the Florence Hotel by security personnel after her agent asked them to check on her be-
Hotel by security personnel after her agent asked them to check on her becuase he'd been unable to reach her by phone.

Workers at the Florence told police she had not been seen since 4 a.m., when she returned to the hotel accompanied by two men. The staff said the men seemed to be holding a giggling Curran upright as they brought her into the posh hotel.

Police have been unable to locate the two men, but a police spokesman said they did not suspect foul play in Curran's overdose.

"We don't believe there has been any crime against Miss Curran, but we would like to talk to these two men to see what they can tell us about her final hours" before she was discovered, the spokesman said.

Officials decline to say what drug or drugs Curran OD'd on. It was unclear if there was anyone in the room with her at the time she ingested the drugs.
her at the time she ingested the drugs.

Her sister, Jane Curran, told The Post, "the overdose must have been an accident. Mandy and I were as close as sisters can get. We didn't have any secrets. If there had been anything wrong, she would have told me."

Jane, a 26-year-old perfume consultant, said that her sister was emotionally troubled as a teenager, but had managed to put it behind her.

"She'd undergone treatment for depression in her teens, but that was a long time ago."

She said that her sister was not totally satisfied with her career, but was still hoping to turn her beauty pageant success into an acting gig.

"Things hadn't gone as well as she'd expected after winning the Miss New York title, but she was considering several television offers.

"She has many important friends in the fashion and entertainment worlds
"She has many important friends in the fashion and entertainment worlds and she believed she'd break through in the end. It was just a matter of time."

After being hired for a series of magazine ads for London fashion designer Leon Vitali, rumors began circulating of an affair between the two.

Soon after her hiring, Vitali empire insiders were reporting that their boss adored Curran — not for how she wore his stunning clothes in public, but for how she wowed him by taking them off in private, seductive solo performances.

10

Japanese men, nearly nude and wearing women's wigs, cavorting with his underage daughter (Leelee Sobieski); Milich vows to turn the men over to the police. The scantily clad daughter clings to Bill suggestively in response to her father's anger.

On the long cab ride out to the mysterious party, Bill fantasizes about Alice and the naval officer. When he arrives at the Long Island mansion, he states the password and gains admittance. Once inside, he sees that, like him, all of the guests are masked and wearing dark cloaks. He witnesses a ritual conducted by an ominous figure cloaked in red (Leon Vitali) during which several masked, nude women begin pairing off with guests. One of them escorts Bill from the room and then warns him that he is in danger and must leave at once. They are separated, and Bill wanders around the mansion, observing room after room of nude couples involved in various sex acts. The woman tries to warn him again, but Bill is brought before "Red Cloak" and dozens of assembled guests. When Bill is unable to reply correctly to a trick question about the "password for the house," he is ordered to unmask and remove his clothes. The woman who tried to warn him suddenly appears and offers herself in his place. Bill is released with a stern warning that he is to forget all about what he has seen, or there will be severe consequences for him and his family. At the end of the scene, a man in a long-beaked mask takes the woman's arm and leads her away, presumably to be punished for Bill's behavior.

Shaken, Bill arrives home at 4 a.m. Alice tells him of a nightmare she has just had, in which she has sex with dozens of

10 ***The article Bill reads in the* New York Post, *visible on-screen only momentarily.***
11 ***Kubrick with Tom Cruise on the costume shop set.***
12 ***The masked party actresses cover up between takes.***

11

12

13

men while Bill watches. In the dream, she wants to humiliate him, so she laughs as hard as she can. She weeps as she describes the dream to her stunned and disgusted husband.

"[A]s he moves deeper into this strange world he thinks back with affection to the stable world of his everyday realities.... [H]e feels the orderly social reality to which he belongs is some kind of monstrous sham...."

—Passages on the subject of *Traumnovelle*'s protagonist underlined by SK in *Arthur Schnitzler: A Critical Study* (Oxford: Martin Swales, 1971)

The next day, Bill tries to come to terms with what happened the night before. He returns the costume (having forgotten the mask), and the shop-owner implies clearly that for a price, Bill may enjoy the pleasures of his daughter. Nick Nightingale has vanished, whisked away from his hotel by two thugs at 5 a.m. Curious, Bill drives out to the mansion on Long Island and is met at the gate by a stone-faced servant who wordlessly hands him an envelope addressed to him by name, offering a "final warning." Back in New York City, Bill returns to Domino's apartment, but she is not in, and her roommate informs him that Domino has been diagnosed HIV-positive. As he leaves, Bill realizes he is being followed. He sees a newspaper item about a former beauty queen found dead in a hotel, and he thinks it may be the woman who saved him. Examining her body at the morgue, Bill is visibly moved as he stares into her lifeless eyes, trying to determine for sure if it is the same woman.

Victor Ziegler summons Bill to his house and after a bit of small talk reveals that he was present at the house on Long Island. In what seems to be an altogether duplicitous monologue, he tells Bill that all the sinister aspects of the night before were just an act, intended to frighten him and to make sure he would not return. Counter to

14

DREAM SEQUENCE — 'EYES WIDE SHUT'
I SEE THIS AS AN UNDULATING LANDSCAPE OF WRITHING BODIES THAT APPEAR TO GROW OUT OF THE MEADOW

15

these reassurances, though, in thinly-veiled, menacing tones, Ziegler warns Bill that he has stepped way out of line, not only in intruding on the party of the über-elite in the first place, but now in his attempts to investigate. He says that if Bill knew the names of the masked revelers, he wouldn't "sleep so well." Ziegler admits that the girl in the morgue was Mandy, the one who saved Bill, but he insists that she died of an accidental overdose. "Somebody died. It happens all the time. But life goes on; it always does, until it doesn't. But you know that."

Devastated, Bill returns home and finds Alice asleep in bed with his mask from the orgy lying on the pillow next to her. Bill breaks down and says that he will confess everything to her. After staying up all night talking and crying, they take their daughter Christmas shopping the next day. Alice tells Bill that they are lucky to have survived their dark adventures, whether dreamed or real, and that the one thing they have to do as soon as possible is to "fuck."

Interestingly, *Traumnovelle* has at least one important quality in common with Anthony Burgess's novel *A Clockwork Orange* (1962): it is short enough to allow a reasonably faithful screen adaptation. Indeed, the screenplay sticks close to the novella in its overall shape and in most of the key scenes: Alice's (in the book, Albertina's) confession to Bill (Fridolin in the book) about her intense sexual desire for the blond sailor she saw on holiday; Bill's close call with the HIV-positive prostitute (who in the book has syphilis); his chance meeting with Nick Nightingale (in the novella Nachtigall, German for "Nightingale"); his subsequent gate-crashing of the masked orgy and the mysterious woman who sacrifices herself to save him; Alice's recounting her terrible nightmare in which she wants to humiliate

13–15 ***Kubrick commissioned drawings by Chris Baker ("Fangorn") to help him visualize ways of portraying Alice's dream sequence. It was ultimately decided not to show Alice's dream but to simply film her telling it.***

him; Bill's visit to the morgue to view the woman's body; his final confession to Alice. Additionally, a good deal of dialogue is directly translated from Schnitzler, as with Alice's confession, the orgy, and the couple's reconciliation at the end. Gene D. Phillips points out the extent to which Kubrick and Raphael remain faithful to their source material, as is particularly illustrated in the orgy scene. In the film as well as the book, the participants wear masks and monastic garb and are presided over by a sinister, scarlet-clad figure resembling a cardinal. The proceedings blend Roman Catholic iconography and ritual with the feeling of a blasphemous black mass.[10] Aside from the period and locale, the major changes in the film are the addition of the Ziegler character and the inclusion of the opening party scene (which is only discussed after the fact by the couple in the book).

Tom Cruise was already one of the biggest movie stars in the world when Stanley Kubrick hand-picked him for *Eyes Wide Shut*; furthermore Cruise had several first-class performances to his credit, including demanding roles in Neil Jordan's

16 ***This was one of several "family idyll" scenes that were shot but not used in the film.***
17 ***Kidman preparing for the scene in which Alice tells Bill her dream. China balls were covered with gels to provide a strong blue hue.***

"I don't think there was very much in **Eyes Wide Shut** ***that was realistic, or that was intended to be realistic."***
– Sydney Pollack (interviewed for **A Life in Pictures,** ***2001)***

film of Anne Rice's *Interview with the Vampire* (1994), Oliver Stone's *Born on the Fourth of July* (1989) and Barry Levinson's *Rain Man* (1988). Sydney Pollack, who had directed Cruise in *The Firm* (1993), put Kubrick directly in touch with him.[11]

Kubrick specifically wanted a husband and wife to play Bill and Alice Harford, so Cruise and Nicole Kidman were his top choices. Kidman had already co-starred alongside Cruise in *Days of Thunder* (1990) and *Far and Away* (1992); and her reputation as a serious actress had solidified with such films as Gus van Sant's *To Die For* (1995). Both stars signed open-ended contracts, under which they agreed to work on the film until Kubrick released them, however long that might be.[12] Under Kubrick's direction, both Cruise and Kidman deliver what some critics consider among their finest, most nuanced performances.

In the role of Victor Ziegler, Sydney Pollack replaced Harvey Keitel, who had a conflicting commitment that prevented him from finishing the film. Roger Ebert called Pollack "the key supporting player, as a confident, sinister man of the world, living in old-style luxury, deep-voiced, experienced, decadent."

Another casting change came about when Kubrick needed to re-shoot some scenes between Bill and Marion, the grieving woman who declares her love for him. Jennifer Jason Leigh originally played that role, but because of scheduling conflicts she was not able to return for the re-takes. She was replaced by Marie Richardson, a

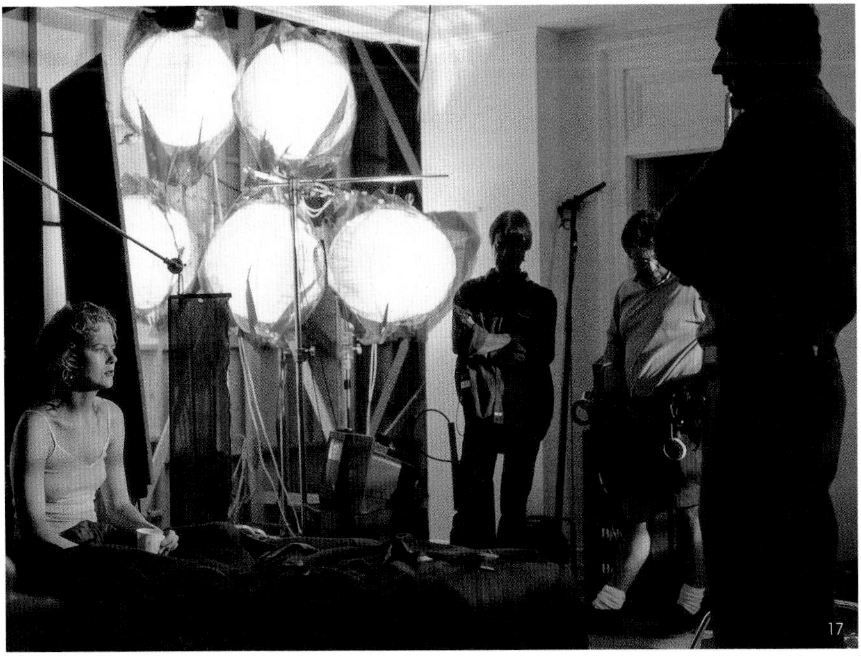

17

18

prominent actress in Swedish films and television.[13]

In the brief but unforgettable role of "Red Cloak," Kubrick cast his longtime associate Leon Vitali, who played the adult Lord Bullingdon in *Barry Lyndon*. After that film, Vitali returned to work for Kubrick in 1976 as the director's assistant, participating in every stage of pre-production, production, and post-production on *The Shining*, *Full Metal Jacket*, and *Eyes Wide Shut*.[14]

For a year prior to the start of shooting, Manuel Harlan (son of executive producer Jan Harlan) traveled around England photographing possible locations. (He then became the unit stills photographer on the production, the first person to hold that position on a Kubrick film since *2001: A Space Odyssey*.)[15] The Long Island mansion where the orgy takes place is an amalgam of interiors and exteriors of a few different locations: Highclere Castle in Hampshire, Elveden Hall in Norfolk, and

18 ***Tom Cruise, Kubrick, and Sydney Pollack (Victor Ziegler) rehearsing the billiard room scene, which was scheduled for four days' shooting and ended up taking seven weeks.***
19 ***"I saw Stanley go to lunch and come back in and say, 'Who's been messing with the lights?' and the cameraman would say, 'Nobody's touched the lights, Stanley'... 'Measure it, it's a quarter of a stop darker in here.' They'd measure it [and] it's a quarter of a stop darker.... It's like the princess and the pea."***
–Sydney Pollack (interviewed for* A Life in Pictures*, 2001)

Mentmore, a former Rothschild retreat in Buckinghamshire. Other locations include Thetford Forest in Norfolk; Chelsea & Westminster Hospital in London; Hamleys toy shop in London's Regent Street; Hatton Garden in London; Knebworth House in Stevenage, Hertfordshire; the Lanesborough Hotel, London; and Madame Jo-Jo's of Soho. Second-unit footage was shot in New York City for various establishing shots, notably an Upper East Side mansion that supplied the exterior of the Ziegler home.[16]

Most of the film's New York City streets were created at Pinewood Studios in Iver Heath, Buckinghamshire. So was the Harfords' apartment, which was based on the New York flat where the Kubrick family lived in the early 1960s.[17]

According to cinematographer Larry Smith, Kubrick obsessed over every visual element in every frame of *Eyes Wide Shut,* from furniture and props to the color of walls and other objects. "Stanley would tell the production designers and set dressers exactly what types of lamps, chairs, or decor he wanted, and he always preferred using the best materials—he wouldn't use paper and wood if it was possible to do it with plaster, cement or brick. If we didn't like the color of the walls or something else in the scene, he'd have them changed."[18]

Naturally, as a life-long photographer, Kubrick applied the same level of detailed scrutiny to the film's cinematography and processing. According to Chester Eyre, the head of operations at Deluxe Laboratories,

20

Kubrick "had his own ideas about what each picture should look like, and what he was trying to achieve with it. He had a fixed idea about the color of each sequence, and he would strive with (us) to obtain that color, even if it had no relation to the preceding sequence. He was always focused on the mood that could be achieved with a certain color. In the case of *Eyes Wide Shut*, Stanley actually supplied us with information about the red, green and blue (timing) lights. He would look at what had been shot the previous day, mentally adjust the colors, write the specifications on the camera sheets he gave to us, and then request certain color combinations that he'd devised with Larry Smith on the set. Normally, it's left to the laboratory to assess the color of the negative. A filmmaker might ask us to print something a certain way—say, dark and red—but Stanley was asking for specific combinations of colors."[19]

To light the sets, Kubrick stuck mainly with his usual strategy of using "practicals," i.e., lights that appear in the diegetic world of the film, such as table lamps, streetlights, and Christmas lights. Kubrick and Smith also tested a litany of different film stocks before settling on one that had been phased out by Kodak; as a courtesy to Kubrick, Kodak offered to supply as many rolls of the discontinued film stock as needed for the project.

Because of the relatively limited amount of light supplied by practicals, and also to achieve a certain visual effect, Kubrick decided to push-develop the entire film. In other words, he and Smith shot at light levels that normally would be considered too low; then in processing, the lab left the film in the developing bath longer, essentially "overprocessing" it to bring out the images. Eyre explained in *American Cinematographer*: "That created several advantages for (Kubrick): he could work with less light and obtain a particular mood. Force-developing in that way is very unusual, and it's normally done as a last resort if the filmmakers are losing their light and are desperate to get a shot. On this picture, though, it was a deliberate strategy that was designed to get a special look.... Lab people always worry when things are done in a non-standard manner, and at first we were all surprised that he wanted to do it. However, once we began seeing the results and the quality of the negative, we understood what he was trying to do. If you look at the night scenes in particular, they have terrific exposure and depth, as well as very good blacks."[20]

The effects of the push-developing are particularly evident in the scenes of Ziegler's Christmas party, lit almost exclusively by strands of Christmas lights. For fill, Smith occasionally used a lightweight, portable "China ball," with a dimmer-controlled 200-watt bulb, or an additional small curtain of the holiday lights. He described the result as a warm glow with "a slightly surreal edge."[21]

Principal photography began in November 1996 and lasted until January 31, 1998. Then, in April 1998, Kubrick called some cast members back for reshoots. With fifty-two weeks of filming, *Eyes Wide Shut* became the longest shoot on record for a major studio production, a distinction

20 ***Abigail Good as the "Mysterious Woman."***

previously held by *Lawrence of Arabia.*[22] Larry Smith points out that Kubrick's reputation for long shoots and multiple takes, although accurate, was often misconstrued as extreme, eccentric perfectionism. "We did occasionally do lots of takes, but it was more often due to a logistical problem than acting issues. Stanley didn't do take after take because he enjoyed it or wanted to drive everyone crazy—the scene was either right or it wasn't right, and whatever kept it from being right had to be eliminated. It might be something very subtle, like an ashtray facing the wrong way, but Stanley had a phenomenal eye for small details."[23]

"I think that it spoils a great deal of the pleasure of the film for anyone who happens to have been unfortunate enough to have read what the filmmaker 'has in mind.'"

—SK/1971 (to Alexander Walker)

Nicole Kidman's "take" on repeating scenes several times was: "He taught me you can do the same thing over and over again, many different ways, and discover something different every single take. It's a lot like working on the stage, actually."[24]

Tom Cruise observed: "He doesn't waste time; he's not indulgent.... He takes his time. It takes him a long time to find a good story and something that he's interested in. He just works on the script and

21

22

keeps working on it.... (But) it's very relaxed on the set. And he's got a wonderful sense of humor. There are a lot of misconceptions about Stanley."[25]

According to all reports, the version of *Eyes Wide Shut* released internationally is Stanley Kubrick's final cut, the version he showed to his family, Tom Cruise and Nicole Kidman, and Warner Bros. executives just days before his death in March 1999. He had spent almost a year in post-production on the film.

In order to meet a contractual agreement to deliver an R-rated film and to avoid making any actual cuts to Kubrick's work, digital hooded figures were added in the orgy scene, obscuring the most suggestive sexual imagery. Critics around the U.S. decried the MPAA's insistence on changing the film, but given the necessity to obtain an "R" rating, the digital figures may have been the lesser evil—certainly preferable to re-editing Kubrick's work. As Katharina Kubrick Hobbs explained, there was no way anyone was going to make cuts to that film after Stanley Kubrick had finished it.[26] Furthermore, Tom Cruise declared that anyone who intended to alter Kubrick's cut would have to answer to him. Weighing in on the controversy in *Variety*, Todd McCarthy wrote that the "difference in impact between the two versions is negligible, and actually seeing

21 ***Christiane Kubrick took this picture of her husband peeking into the mock-up of the New York set.***
22 ***On the set of the costume shop.***
23 ***Kubrick lines up a shot of Cruise.***

what the MPAA considers NC-17-worthy makes the (group's) nit-picking seem absurd, especially given the gruesomely graphic violence to which it routinely applies R ratings."[27]

A less-publicized controversy arose in relation to some of the film's original music, composed by Jocelyn Pook for the ritual and orgy scenes. At one point, the score incorporates a prominent Hindu scriptural quote. In a protest letter to Warner Bros., the American Hindus Against Defamation pointed out, "When (Tom Cruise) enters a large room where several sex acts are taking place, the background music subsides and the shloka (scriptural recitation) from Bhagwad Gita, one of the most revered Hindu scriptures, is played out. The shloka is: 'Parithranaya Saadhunam Vinashaya cha dushkrithaam Dharmasamsthabanarthaya Sambhavami yuge yuge ...' which means 'For the protection of the virtuous, for the destruction of the evil and for the firm establishment of Dharma (righteousness), I take birth and am incarnated on Earth, from age to age.'" In the *Journal of Religion and Film*, Robert Castle argues that the inclusion of this text need not be read as careless or offensive. Nonetheless, for the international theatrical release as well as

24 ***A whole block of a New York City street was constructed at Pinewood Studios, north of London. Here, Steadicam operator Elizabeth Ziegler films as Bill is propositioned by a prostitute named Domino (Vinessa Shaw).***
25 ***Kubrick peers through his viewfinder at Rade Sherbedgia (costume shop owner Milich) and Leelee Sobieski (Milich's daughter).***

for all video and DVD releases, the music was changed.[28]

Other striking music used on the soundtrack includes selections from György Ligeti's *Musica Ricercata no. 2* (1953), performed on piano by Kubrick's nephew, Dominic Harlan, at key dramatic points throughout the film. Dmitri Shostakovich's "Waltz 2" from his *Jazz Suite no. 2* (1938) opens and closes the picture; and Chris Isaak's haunting "Baby Did a Bad Bad Thing" (1995) accompanies a brief lovemaking scene between Cruise and Kidman.

Upon finishing the film, Stanley Kubrick told family members and close business associates that *Eyes Wide Shut* was the best work of his career.[29] John Calley (former head of production at Warner Bros.) told *Variety* that the last time he spoke to Kubrick, shortly before his death, the director was ecstatic about the film. "He was so excited because (Warner executives) had seen his film and they loved it. Nicole and Tom had seen it and they loved it," Calley said. "I've never heard him as excited about a film."[30]

When *Eyes Wide Shut* opened in mid-July 1999, it was the number one film at the box-office that week. Informal reports suggested that audiences were predominantly over twenty-five, with slightly more women than men. Box-office appeal for the film clearly was concentrated in the major cities. *Variety* reported that Kubrick had selected the release date himself, after analyzing reams of box-office data provided by Warner Bros.[31]

25

The international release of the film was primed by its prestigious opening-night slot at the 1999 Venice Film Festival. Kubrick generally did not show his films at festivals, as he preferred to premiere them for the U.S. public; but Venice had always shown an affinity for Kubrick and indeed had presented him a Career Golden Lion in 1997. His long-time executive producer, Jan Harlan, said, "I don't think we thought of this at the time it was first offered to us, but Venice is the ideal launch. It is the perfect opening for Europe, and though it's unusual for one of Stanley's films to open this way, it is best for his final film."[32] Indeed the strategy seems to have paid off, as the film was an international box-office success, surpassing $155 million.[33]

As was typical, only a handful of American critics seemed to appreciate *Eyes Wide Shut* at first. They included Richard Schickel of *Time* and Glenn Kenny of *Premiere*, both of whom proclaimed it a "masterpiece." Janet Maslin, of *The New York Times*, declared, "Mr. Kubrick left one more brilliantly provocative tour de force as his epitaph." In the *Chicago Tribune*, Michael Wilmington raved, "The great filmmaker's last feature is a spellbinder, provocatively conceived, gorgeously shot and masterfully executed."[34] Alexander Walker called it "an astonishing work" that reveals "a humanity that this director's detractors have insisted he did not possess."[35]

On the other end of the critical spectrum, *Eyes Wide Shut* met with a great deal of hostility and consternation. Ever ready to bash Stanley Kubrick, even beyond the grave, Pauline Kael came out of retirement to dismiss Kubrick's swan song as a "piece of crap."[36] More than a few critics complained that Ziegler's long dialogue scene around the red billiard table explains too much; but it only *seems* to explain everything, and in fact it explains nothing conclusively. Ziegler's "performance" is unconvincing, pointing up the unreliability of all he says and reinforcing his corrupt nature, which has already been established.[37] Critics like Kael failed to recognize the film's keenly sophisticated exploration of the emotional and psychological complexities of a marriage and a couple's relation to the outside world. Instead, negative reviews faulted the film for not being what the reviewers had expected: a quasi-pornographic, erotic thriller.

Some audiences and critics seemed to miss the dreamlike qualities of the film and the story altogether, offering such banal observations as that the street scenes are obviously not really in New York. But like all of Kubrick's mature films, *Eyes Wide Shut* operates on multiple thematic and aesthetic levels, and its richness begins to emerge on second, third, and subsequent viewings. Both Schnitzler's novella and Kubrick's film navigate the treacherous, gray area between waking life and dreams, between "reality" and fantasy, between actions and desires, between fidelity and deception, between the conscious and the unconscious. It is through such murky waters that some of the very best literature and films—like *Traumnovelle* and *Eyes Wide Shut*—can take us, if we only allow them to do so.

26 ***Cruise, Kubrick, and Kidman celebrate Kidman's last day of shooting.***

27 ***Pollack and Kubrick on the set of Ziegler's bathroom, with a painting by Christiane Kubrick.***
28 ***Kubrick with clapper-loader Craig Bloor.***
29 ***Alan Cumming (hotel clerk) with Kubrick.***
30 ***The party scenes in Ziegler's mansion were lit almost entirely by wall lamps, Christmas lights, and other "practicals" (i.e. lights appearing in the scene).***
31 ***The decoration of the New York street sets, down to the most minute of details, was based on extensive research.***

Notes

1. Kent Lambert, "Sobotka, Ruth," in Gene D. Phillips and Rodney Hill, *The Encyclopedia of Stanley Kubrick* (New York: Checkmark, 2002): 338.
2. Gene D. Phillips, "Schnitzler, Arthur," in Phillips and Hill: 306.
3. Quoted in Rodney Hill, "Traumnovelle," in Phillips and Hill: 371.
4. Phillips: 306.
5. Phillips, "Eyes Wide Shut," in Phillips and Hill: 105.
6. Phillips, "Raphael, Frederic," in Phillips and Hill: 295.
7. Frederic Raphael, *Eyes Wide Open: A Memoir of Stanley Kubrick* (New York: Ballantine, 1999).
8. Dan Lybarger, "'It's only a movie: an interview with Frederic Raphael," *Pitch Weekly* (July 22–28, 1999).
9. Phillips, "Raphael": 298.
10. Ibid.: 296.
11. Phillips, "Pollack, Sydney," in Phillips and Hill: 291.
12. Phillips, "Kidman, Nicole," in Phillips and Hill: 178.
13. *Variety* (April 27, 1998).
14. "Vitali, Leon," in Phillips and Hill: 395.
15. Phillips, "Harlan, Manuel," in Phillips and Hill: 144.
16. http://www.wheredidtheyfilmthat.co.uk
17. Phillips, "Kubrick, Christiane," in Phillips and Hill: 194.
18. Stephen Pizzello, "A Sword in the Bed," *American Cinematographer* (October 1999).
19. Ibid.
20. Ibid.
21. Ibid.
22. Phillips, "Kidman": 178.
23. Pizzello.
24. Quoted in Phillips, "Kidman."
25. Quoted in "Cruise, Tom," in Phillips and Hill: 69.
26. Katharina Kubrick Hobbs, interview with Rodney Hill, New York (June 2001).
27. Todd McCarthy, "MPAA shuts 'Eyes' for 65 seconds," *Variety* (July 12, 1999).
28. Robert Castle, "The Dharma Blues," *Journal of Religion and Film* (April 2002).
29. Kubrick Hobbs.
30. Dan Cox, "'Eyes' sheds tear," *Variety* (March 8, 1999).
31. *Variety* (July 19, 1999).
32. Robert Koehler, "Kubrick's Lido connection," *Variety* (August 20, 1999).
33. http://www.indelibleinc.com/kubrick/films/ews/
34. Quoted in Phillips, "Eyes Wide Shut": 107.
35. Quoted in Todd McCarthy, "Kubrick friend gives first eyes-wide 'Shut' review," *Variety* (June 23, 1999).
36. Quoted in Koehler.
37. Phillips, "Eyes Wide Shut": 106.

28

30

CHECK OUT TIME
12:00 NOON
PERSONAL IDENTIFICATION
MUST BE PRESENTED UPON
CHECK IN
CREDIT POLICY
CASH OR CREDIT CARDS
NO PERSONAL CHECKS

29

Phone
CHEESE SHOP
boro
ICHES
Don't
Litter
Put It
Here

31

Projects

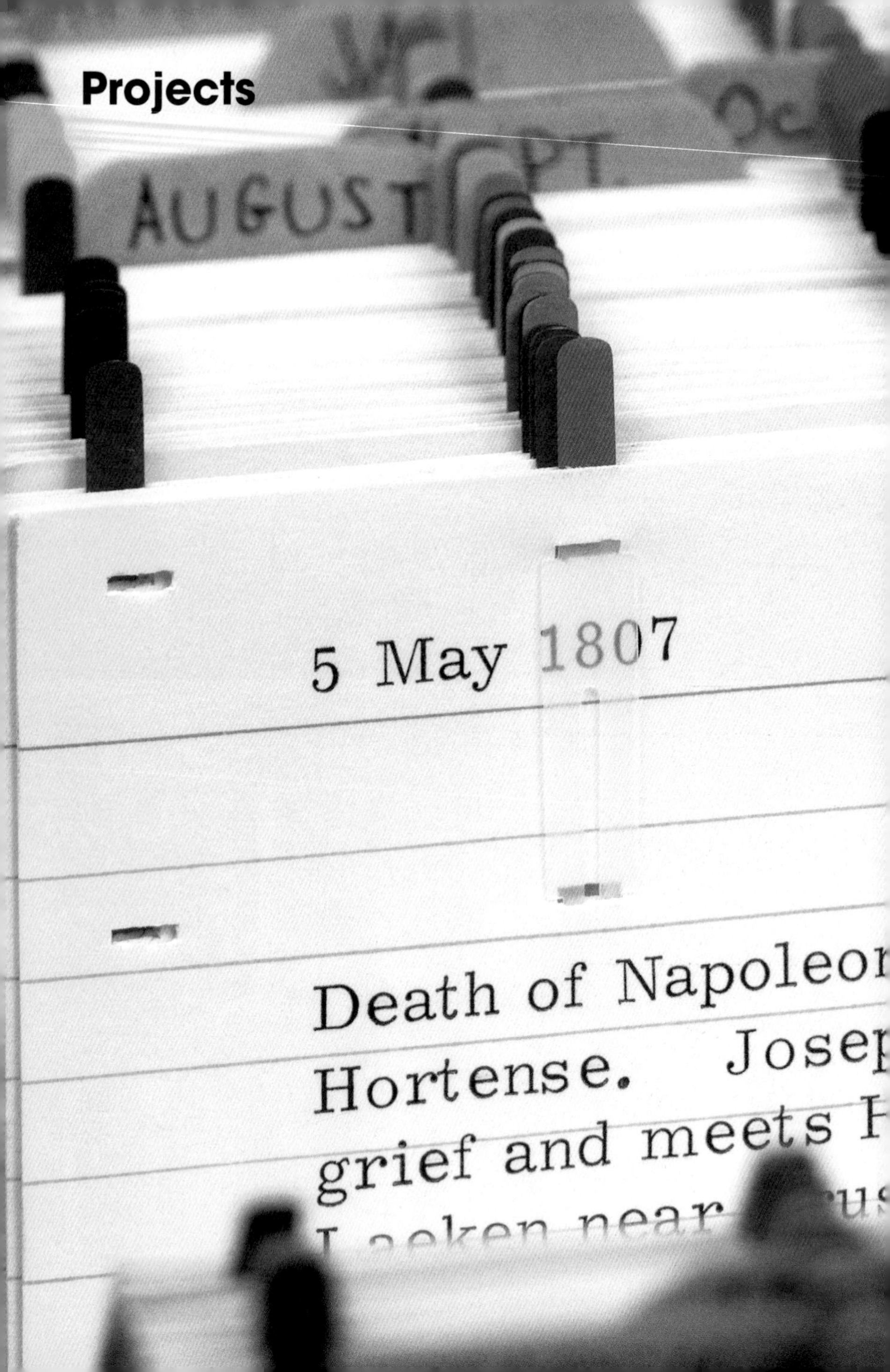
AUGUST
5 May 1807
Death of Napoleo
Hortense. Jose
grief and meets
Laeken near

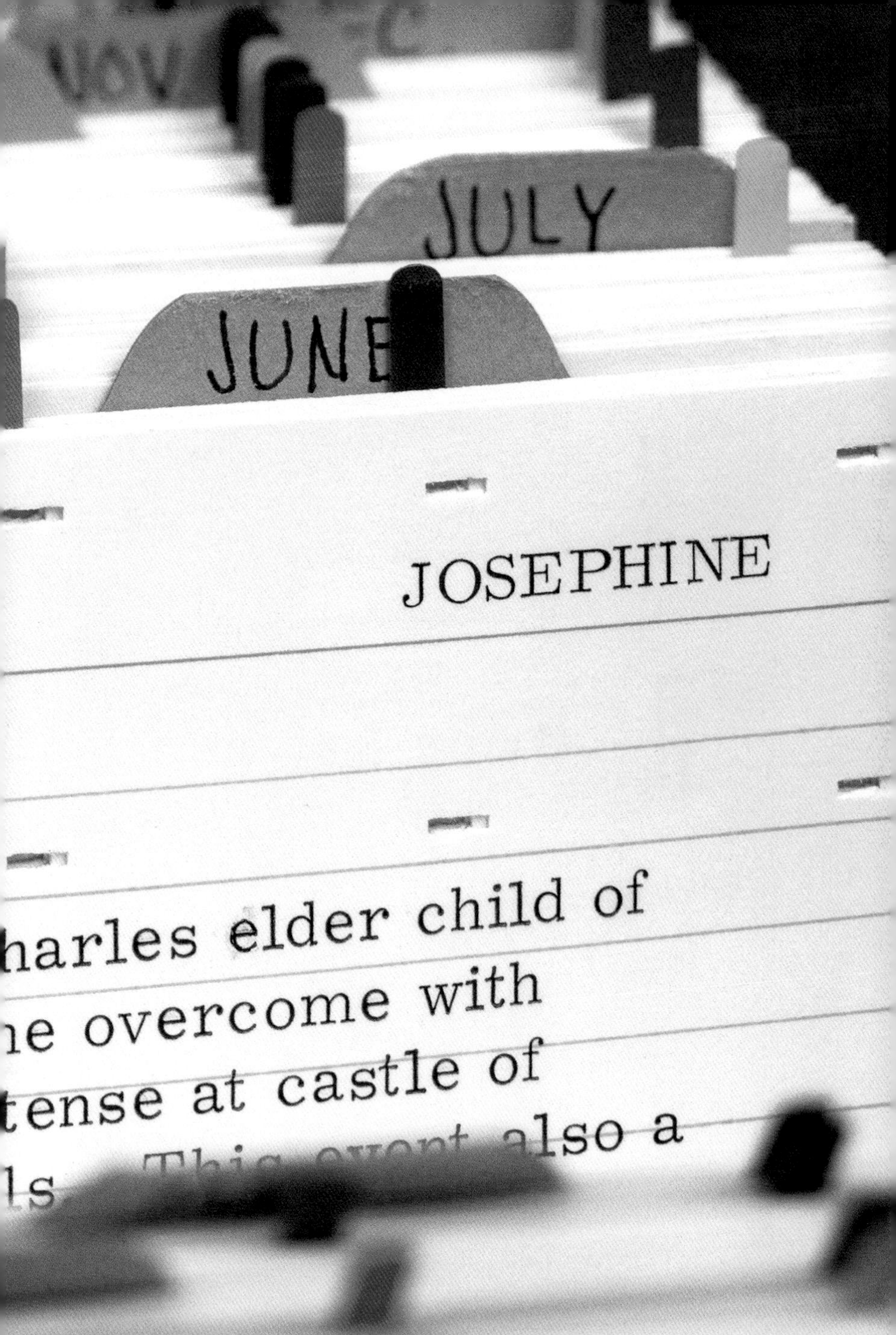
JULY
JUNE
JOSEPHINE
harles elder child of
ne overcome with
tense at castle of
ls also a

The Epic That Never Was: Stanley Kubrick's "Napoleon"

by Gene D. Phillips

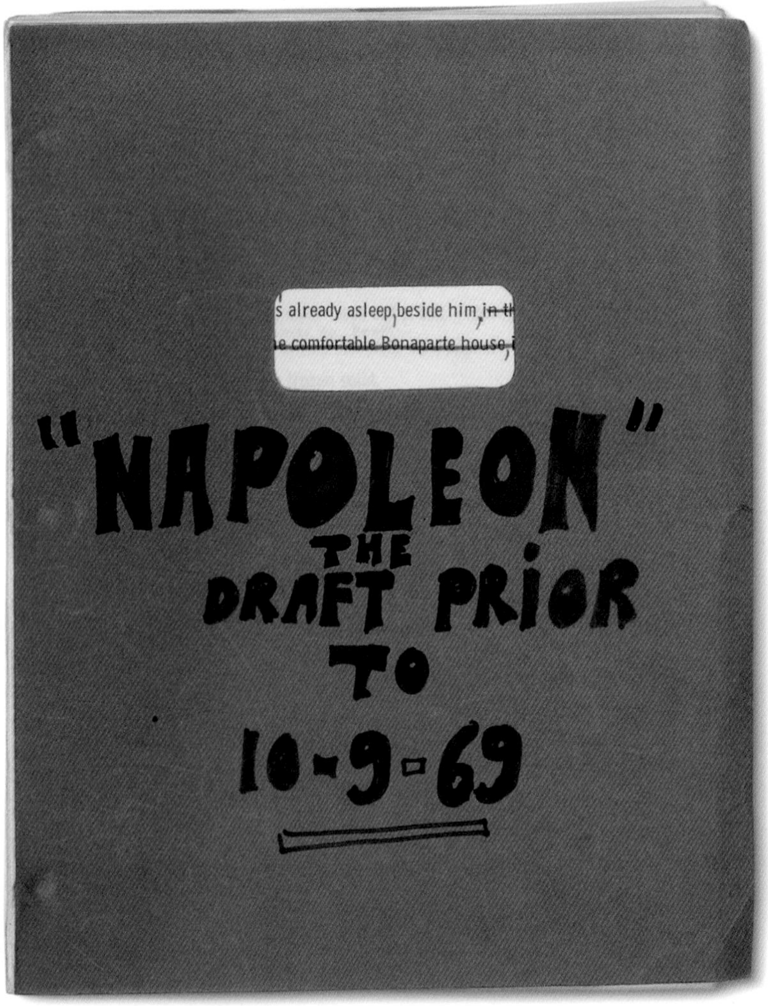

There are certain subjects that attract great filmmakers, such as the Promethean Conqueror or the Man of Destiny, Pauline Kael has written. Great directors will not settle for less than great subjects. "So it's no accident that Stanley Kubrick wanted to do a 'Napoleon.'"[1] Indeed, it was after Kubrick's *2001: A Space Odyssey* (1968) caught on with audiences and garnered favorable reviews around the country that Kubrick convinced MGM, which had released *2001*, to provide seed money for script development and a bevy of research assistants for his projected movie about Napoleon.

When Joseph Gelmis asked Kubrick why he wanted to make a film about Napoleon, Kubrick replied: "To begin with, he fascinates me. His life has been described as an epic poem of action. His sex life was worthy of Arthur Schnitzler. He was one of those rare men who move history and mold the destiny of their own times and of generations to come—in a very concrete sense, our own world is the result of Napoleon, just as the political and geographic map of postwar Europe is the result of World War II. And, of course, there has never been a good or accurate movie about him. The sheer drama and force of Napoleon's life is a fantastic subject for a film biography. Forgetting everything else and just taking Napoleon's romantic involvement with Josephine, for example, here you have one of the great obsessional passions of all time.... So this will not be just a dusty historic pageant."[2]

In discussing his Napoleon project with me after his interview with Gelmis, Kubrick noted that Napoleon once hazarded that his life would make a great novel. "I'm certain he would have said 'film' if movies had existed at the time." Kubrick's film was designed to capture all aspects of the man as soldier, statesman, and emperor.

Kubrick's interest in Napoleon dated back to his youth; but once he began gearing up to make the film, he gave himself a crash course in the history of Napoleon and his times. He explained to Gelmis: "The first step has been to read everything I could get my hands on about Napoleon, and totally immerse myself in his life. I guess I must have gone through several hundred books on the subject, from contemporary nineteenth-century English and French accounts to modern biographies. I've ransacked all these books for research material and broken it down into categories on everything from his food tastes to the weather on the day of a specific battle, and cross-indexed all the data in a comprehensive research file. In addition to my own reading, I've worked out a consultant arrangement with Professor Felix Markham of Oxford, a history don who has spent the past thirty-five years of his life studying Napoleon and is considered one of the world's leading Napoleonic experts."[3]

Kubrick secured the rights to Markham's biography of Napoleon and made it the basis for his screenplay. In May 1968, he sent a production assistant, Andrew Birkin (now a writer-director himself), on an expedition to photograph the sites associated with Napoleon's life for the use of the set designers. While on his research trip, Birkin was armed with a letter from André Malraux, the French Minister of Culture, which authorized him to visit and photo-

02 ***Kubrick's 167-page treatment.***

03

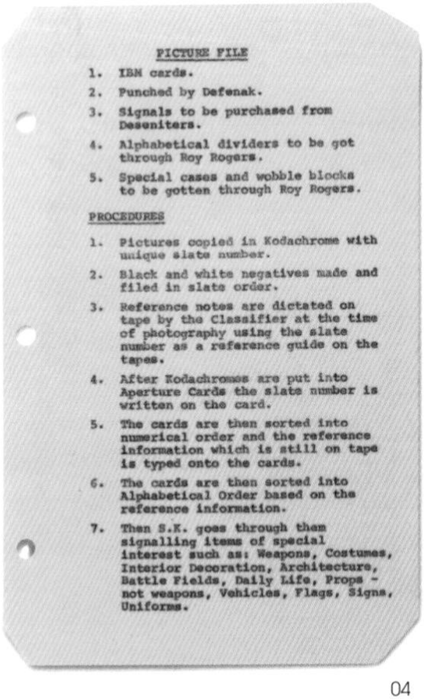

PICTURE FILE

1. IBM cards.
2. Punched by Defenak.
3. Signals to be purchased from Deseniters.
4. Alphabetical dividers to be got through Roy Rogers.
5. Special cases and wobble blocks to be gotten through Roy Rogers.

PROCEDURES

1. Pictures copied in Kodachrome with unique slate number.
2. Black and white negatives made and filed in slate order.
3. Reference notes are dictated on tape by the Classifier at the time of photography using the slate number as a reference guide on the tapes.
4. After Kodachromes are put into Aperture Cards the slate number is written on the card.
5. The cards are then sorted into numerical order and the reference information which is still on tape is typed onto the cards.
6. The cards are then sorted into Alphabetical Order based on the reference information.
7. Then S.K. goes through them signalling items of special interest such as: Weapons, Costumes, Interior Decoration, Architecture, Battle Fields, Daily Life, Props - not weapons, Vehicles, Flags, Signs, Uniforms.

04

05

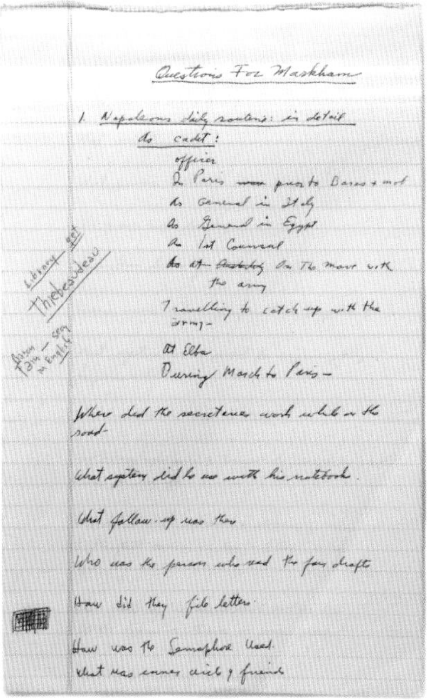
Questions For Markham

1. Napoleon's daily routine: in detail
As cadet:
officer
In Paris
As General in Italy
As General in Egypt
As 1st Consul
On the move with the army
Travelling to catch up with the army -
At Elba
During March to Paris -

Where did the secretaries work while on the road -

What system did he use with his notebook.

What follow-up was there

Who was the person who read the fair draft

How did they file letters

How was the Semaphore used
What was inner circle of friends

06

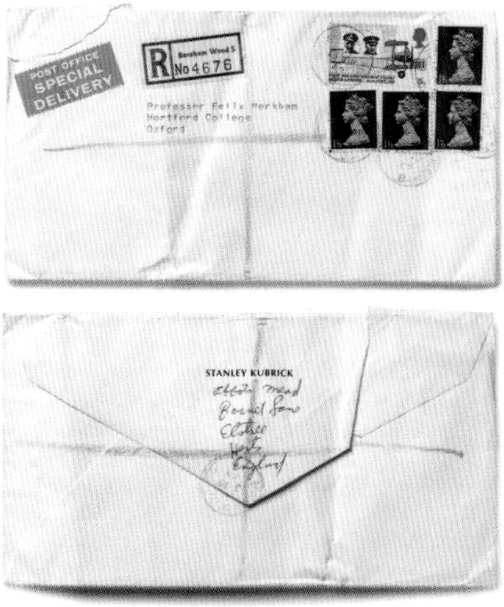

07

graph historical sites like the Palace at Versailles and to examine the hallowed relics of the emperor in various museums.

By June of 1968, Kubrick had twenty Oxford graduate students summarizing countless Napoleon biographies for Kubrick's ready reference. They built up a biographical file of the fifty principal historical figures in the film, listing on index cards the highlights of each person's life. Cinematographer John Alcott, who had discussed the Napoleon movie with Kubrick, said that Kubrick's research was so extensive that "he could tell you virtually where Napoleon was every day of his life, as well as everybody who was in his entourage" on any given occasion.[4]

Kubrick composed a full-scale screenplay, dated September 29,1969. He often employed a narrator in his films, and in the case of "Napoleon" the narrator was essential, for the narration had to impart to the audience the historical background of the events. In his screenplay it is clear that Kubrick aimed to downplay the heroics

01, 03 ***Kubrick's Napoleon file cabinet, with cards detailing, day by day and year by year, every known fact relating to Napoleon and his whereabouts and activities.***
04 ***Description of Kubrick's Napoleon picture files.***
05 ***One of the many metal drawer-boxes that made up the Napoleon picture files.***
06 ***Kubrick's notes for a discussion to be held with Felix Markham, the Oxford historian who was the director's Napoleon consultant. Among the questions listed are such specific queries as "what system did he use with his notebooks" and "how did they file letters."***
07 ***An envelope from one of many letters sent from Kubrick to Markham.***

Problems:

1. who is Napoleon
2. English
3. How does N. talk
4.

and to depict Napoleon "as more of a man, with all his male feelings, and less as a crusading hero," as Darryl Mason writes. "Kubrick wanted the audience to find out what it was like to be Napoleon, on and off the battlefield." If Kubrick's script portrayed his hero "making countless charges, it also detailed the behind-the-scenes preparations for a battle."[5]

As Kubrick told me: "It is difficult to make a film about a historical figure that presents the necessary historical information and at the same time conveys a sense of the day-to-day reality of the characters' lives. Most people don't realize, for example, that Napoleon spent most of his time on the eve of battle immersed in paperwork. You want the audience to get the feeling of what it was like to be with Napoleon." Kubrick, in short, wanted to present the past as a vivid present when he made a historical film, to portray the past as it was to the people living it.

Kubrick's screenplay begins with Napoleon's youth, which was spent in a military academy; he was a proud, fierce youngster who made little effort to get along with his fellow students; and they, in turn, felt antipathy towards him. In fact, when an older student tries to bully him, the young Napoleon simply tells him to "fuck off"—not once, but twice.[6] As he sits alone reading a history book in his room, he muses, voice-over on the soundtrack, "Life is a burden for me.... It is very difficult, because the ways of those with whom I live, and probably always shall live, are as different from mine as moonlight is from sunlight."

It is noteworthy that a couple of scenes from Napoleon's early life, such as his encounter with a prostitute and his presence at an orgy, are forerunners of scenes in Kubrick's last film, *Eyes Wide Shut*. Like Dr. Bill Harford in *Eyes Wide Shut*, Napoleon meets a good-hearted young streetwalker who treats him kindly. And, like Bill Harford, Napoleon attends a wild party given by a wealthy, powerful man for his decadent coterie, which seems like a rehearsal for the orgy in *Eyes Wide Shut*. Kubrick writes in a stage direction that some couples copulate while the guests coolly look on, but the young Napoleon, "still the provincial, can scarcely believe his eyes." Indeed, Kubrick very perceptively describes Napoleon's manner of conversing with the cynical, world-weary guests at the party as "speaking with the uncomfortable yet determined manner that shy but willful people often exhibit."

One reason that Napoleon turns away from the couples disporting themselves before the other guests is that he prefers to feast his eyes on Josephine de Beauharnais, an attractive young widow. It is love at first sight. Kubrick asked Markham during one of their consultations if it was true that Josephine was "part of a pretty swinging set," and if it would be "a smear on Josephine" to portray her as attending orgies of this kind. Markham replied in a fairly cagey manner, saying that Josephine was "obviously pretty permissive," and that such events were fashionable at the time; she was "keeping in with the influential rich." Accordingly, Kubrick places her at just such an orgy in the screenplay.

At any rate, after a whirlwind courtship, Napoleon and Josephine are wed. Nevertheless, when the first wave of passion subsides, both Napoleon and Josephine stray from the path of marital fidelity. When Napoleon, as Commander-in-Chief of the French Army waging war in Italy, is away at the front, Josephine betrays him with Captain Hippolyte Charles. The adulterous pair is shown frolicking in the very same oval bedroom where Napoleon and Josephine had made love earlier in the film. The bedroom is completely encircled with floor-to-ceiling mirrored panels, which multiply the images of the lovers for "maximum erotica," as Kubrick notes in a stage direction.

08 ***Kubrick had custom stationery created with separate spaces for questions and replies, which he used to send queries and requests to Markham.***
09 ***A letter from Kubrick to Markham reflecting the long process of researching and writing the script.***

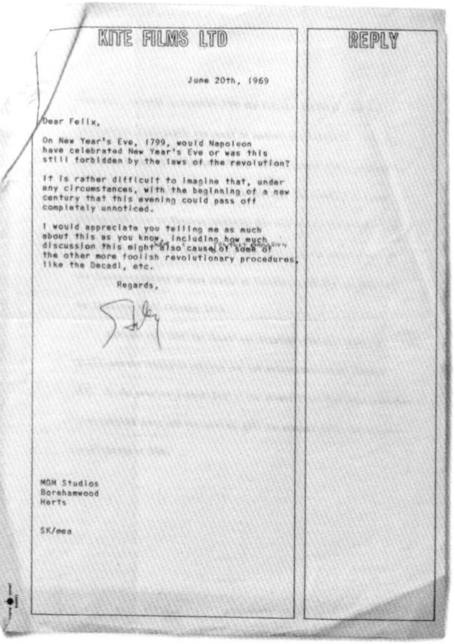

KITE FILMS LTD | REPLY

June 20th, 1969

Dear Felix,

On New Year's Eve, 1799, would Napoleon have celebrated New Year's Eve or was this still forbidden by the laws of the revolution?

It is rather difficult to imagine that, under any circumstances, with the beginning of a new century that this evening could pass off completely unnoticed.

I would appreciate you telling me as much about this as you know, including how much discussion this might also cause, of some of the other more foolish revolutionary procedures, like the Decadi, etc.

Regards,

Stanley

MGM Studios
Borehamwood
Herts

SK/mea

08

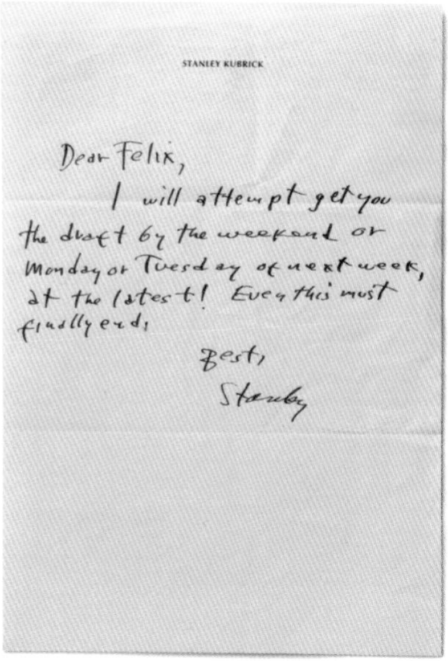

STANLEY KUBRICK

Dear Felix,

I will attempt get you the draft by the weekend or Monday or Tuesday of next week, at the latest! Even this must finally end,

Best,

Stanley

09

This montage is accompanied, with Kubrickian irony, by a voice-over in which Napoleon declares, in a series of excerpts from his love letters to his wife while he is in Italy, how he longs for her. Speaking of his feelings for her, which seem to smack more of lust than of love, he says in part, "You have inspired in me a limitless passion, and an intoxication that is degrading." Josephine's dalliance with the captain turns into a long-term affair, which Napoleon inevitably learns about; but he chooses to ignore it, at least for a while. (After his coronation, Napoleon is seen being unfaithful to Josephine, perhaps in revenge.)

Still, it is with Napoleon the warrior and ruler that the script is chiefly concerned. Early in the screenplay, just before Napoleon engages in battle with the enemy on an Italian battlefield, he reflects in voice-over: "There is no man more cautious than I am when planning a campaign. I exaggerate all the dangers, and all the disasters that might occur.... Once I have made up my mind, everything is forgotten, except what leads to success."

Napoleon enjoys phenomenal success on the battlefield; moreover, as the narrator points out, in governing France, he proves his "brilliant legislative, administrative, and organizational powers." Napoleon is finally rewarded by being crowned Emperor of the French. Referring to how the French Revolution destroyed the monarchy, Napoleon states, "I found the crown lying in the gutter and I picked it up." At the coronation ceremony he actually takes the crown not from the gutter but from the hands of the Pope, who is about to put it on his head, and with characteristic bravado places it on his own head.

"But the egotism which governed his actions ... if in a great measure it favoured the success of his enterprises, did him in the end much more evil than good; as it instigated his most desperate enterprises, and was the source of his most inexcusable actions."

—Passage marked by SK in Walter Scott's *The Life of Napoleon Bonaparte*, vol. IX, Edinburgh, 1827: 319

When it becomes apparent that Josephine will not produce an heir,

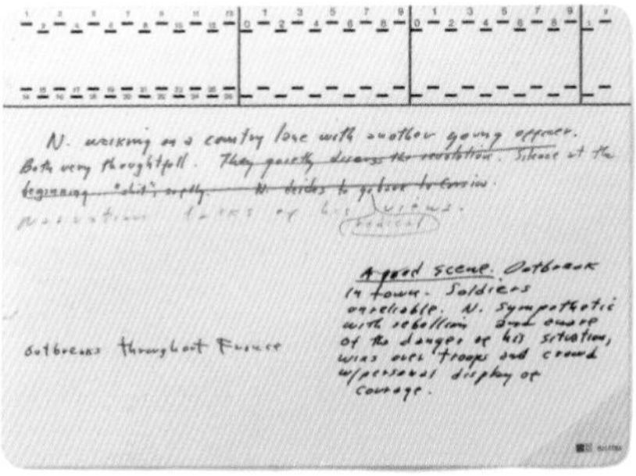

10

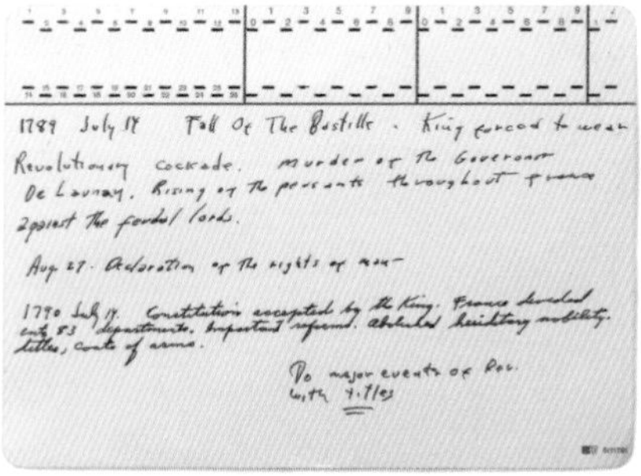

11

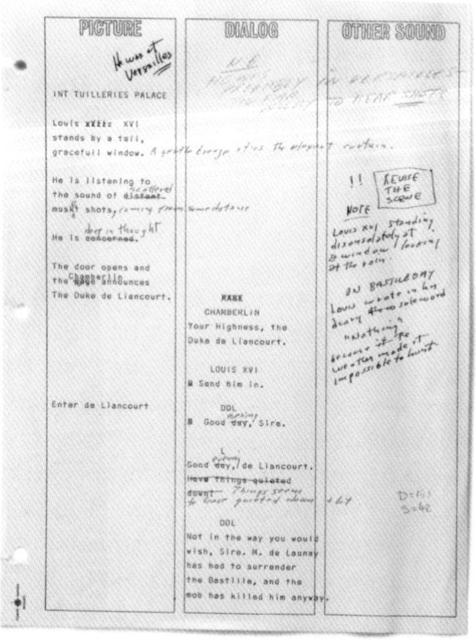
PICTURE | DIALOG | OTHER SOUND

He was at Versailles

INT TUILLERIES PALACE

Louis XVI stands by a tall, gracefull window. A gentle breeze stirs the elegant curtain.

He is listening to the sound of scattered musket shots, coming from some distance

He is deep in thought

The door opens and the Chamberlin announces The Duke de Liancourt.

CHAMBERLIN
Your Highness, the Duke de Liancourt.

LOUIS XVI
Send him in.

Enter de Liancourt

DDL
Good evening, Sire.

L
Good evening, de Liancourt. Have things quieted down?

DDL
Not in the way you would wish, Sire. M. de Launay has had to surrender the Bastille, and the mob has killed him anyway.

!! REVISE THE SCENE

NOTE
Louis XVI standing disconsolately at window looking at the rain.

ON BASTILLE DAY Louis wrote in his diary the one word "Nothing" because the weather made it impossible to hunt.

12

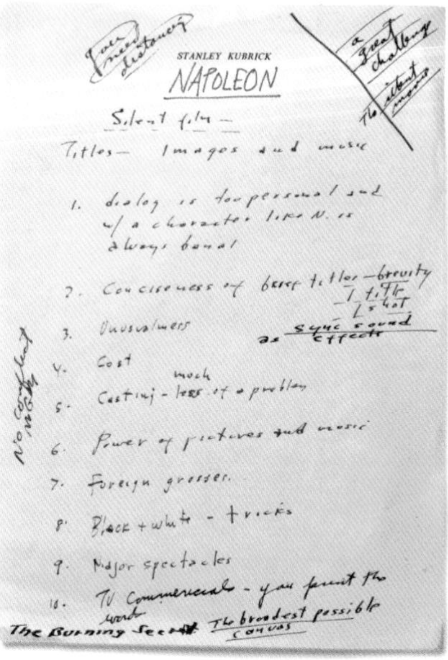
STANLEY KUBRICK
NAPOLEON

Silent film –
Titles – Images and music

1. dialog is too personal and w/ a character like N. is always banal
2. Conciseness of brief titles – brevity
3. Unusualness as sync sound effects
4. Cost
5. Casting – much less of a problem
6. Power of pictures and music
7. Foreign grosses.
8. Black + white – tricks
9. Major spectacles
10. TV Commercial – you found the word

The Burning Secret
The broadest possible canvas

No conflict
a great challenge

13

Napoleon publicly proclaims, "I have lost all hopes of having children by my beloved wife, the Empress Josephine. It is this consideration which induces me to … consult only the good of my subjects, and to desire the dissolution of our marriage." Privately he admits to his brother Joseph that he is fed up with Josephine's unfaithfulness: "My wife is a slut," he snaps; "while a man may want a slut for his mistress, he does not want her for his wife." Napoleon then marries the Archduchess Marie-Louise of Austria, who gives birth to a sickly son destined to die in his youth.

Meanwhile, friction between France and Russia grows steadily worse, and Napoleon decides to mount an invasion of Russia with his Grand Army, which combines the forces of France and her allies. Kubrick accompanies "an impressive shot of the Grand Army on the march" with the narrator's ironic observation that Napoleon had accumulated a mass of soldiers "of uneven quality" who constituted an army that was something less than grand. Still, Napoleon's superior numbers enable his troops to overrun Russia at the outset of the campaign.

Czar Alexander orders his retreating troops to destroy the cities that they have lost to the French and leave behind them nothing but a desert waste. As a result, a French cavalry patrol finds Moscow "a ghost town, deserted, lifeless, a city of the dead." To make matters worse, Napoleon's Grand Army is not prepared for the savage Russian winter. In an earlier scene

10–11 ***Screenwriting notes.***
12 ***Another example of Kubrick's custom stationery. This type of page, used to write the draft of the screenplay, featured separate boxes for "picture," "dialog," and "other sound."***
13 ***A page of notes and ideas for "Napoleon."***

"It took 33 days to destroy the armies of Prussia.... Perhaps it's like this: the greatest chess masters still cannot defeat the worst player in less than a certain number of moves. To a casual observer it might appear that the potzer is holding his own—but there has never really been a contest."

—SK/Handwritten notes in the margin of his "Napoleon" treatment of November 1968

Napoleon had quipped that "the first rule of warfare is that you must wear long underwear; you can never conjure up brilliancies with a cold bottom." Napoleon's little joke proves to be a grim foreshadowing of the disastrous Russian campaign. His soldiers, comments the narrator laconically, "were not bred to endure such cold," and they are transformed into "a starving, feverish mob without purpose. General Famine and General Winter, rather than Russian bullets, would conquer the French."

Kubrick brilliantly dramatizes the plight of the French forces by staging a scene in a Russian village in which several soldiers cram themselves into a cramped little house. He describes how they nail the doors shut to keep other troops from squeezing into the already overcrowded quarters, "virtually condemning them to death during the sub-zero night." Suddenly a fire accidentally breaks out inside the house, but the soldiers boarded up inside cannot get out in time to escape the conflagration. As they burn to death inside, the soldiers to whom they had denied entry "crowd as close as they can to the flames to warm themselves, or cook bits of

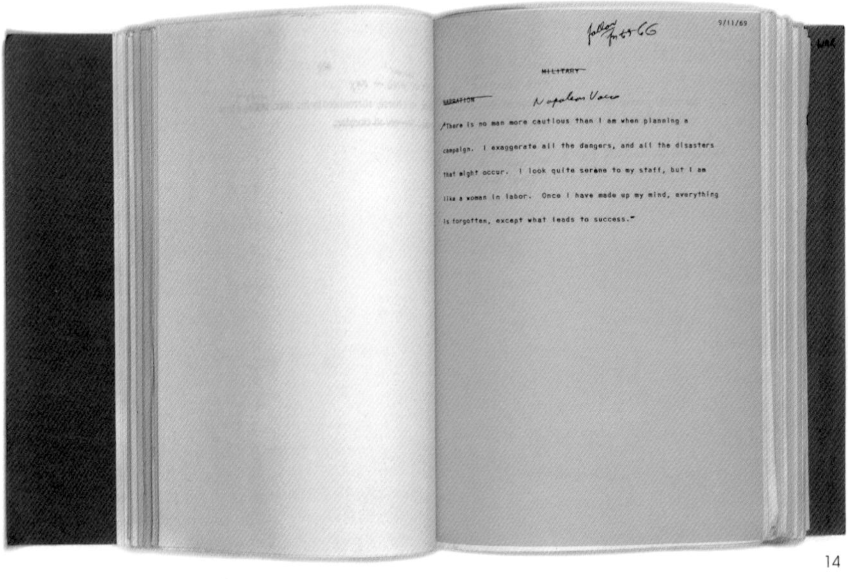

14

horse flesh on the points of their swords." And so Napoleon's once-grand army continues its "1,000 mile march into oblivion."

Kubrick told Michel Ciment that the Russian campaign was a catastrophe because, according to the old adage, Napoleon had arrogantly bitten off more than he could chew: "From the start, Napoleon ignored the evidence which suggested the campaign would be a costly disaster. He gambled on his military magic and lost."[7]

"In defeat," the narrator intones, "Napoleon would be punished by the Kings of Europe"; he is forced to abdicate and is exiled to the tiny island of Elba. "But in ten months' time ... this most reckless of all gamblers (would come) back into the game for a final, breathtaking spin of the wheel." Napoleon set sail from Elba in February 1815, with a force of French soldiers, in order to re-establish himself as ruler of France.

On June 18, 1815, with an army that had swelled to 74,000, Napoleon faced the Duke of Wellington and his British army, along with their allies, on the battlefield of Waterloo, near Brussels. Kubrick depicts the battle in meticulous detail. By mid-afternoon, "An incredible stalemate has developed in the battle. Dead men and horses are everywhere." At 7:30 p.m. Napoleon made his final assault on Wellington's forces. "When this failed, the French morale cracked.... Wellington put in his cavalry, and the French army broke in panic and ran." Wellington had won the day and Napoleon had met his Waterloo. He was exiled again, this time to the remote island of St. Helena in the South Atlantic.

Kubrick fashions a touching deathbed scene for Napoleon. As he lies dying,

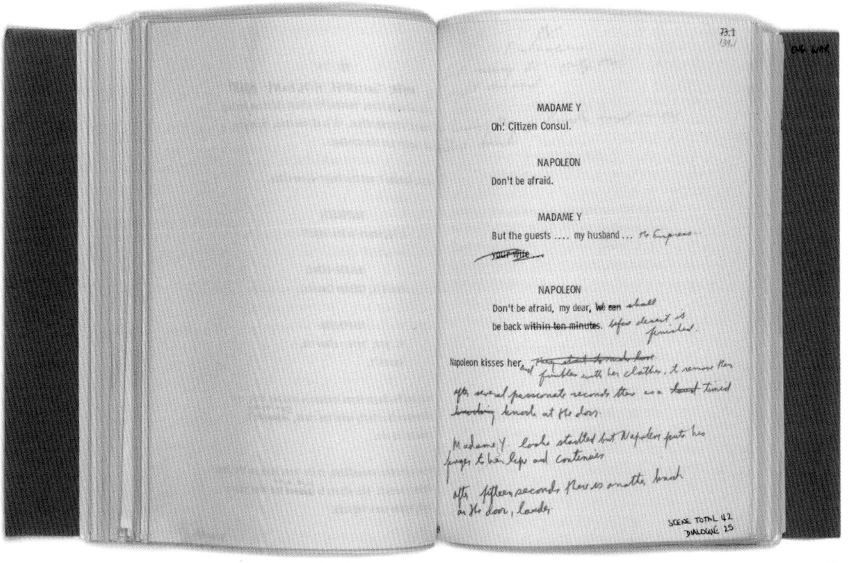

14–15 ***An example of one of the many screenplay drafts.***

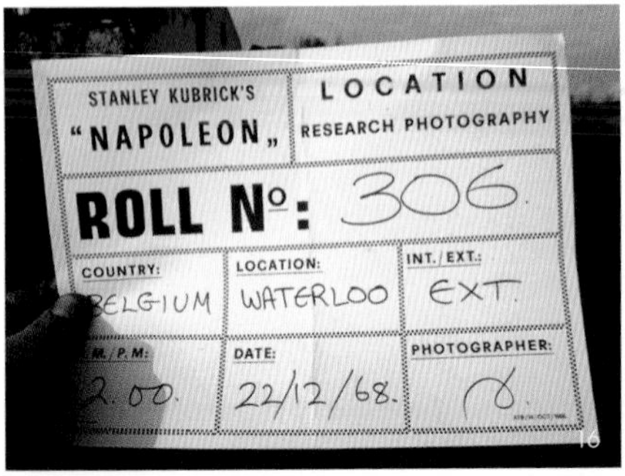

16

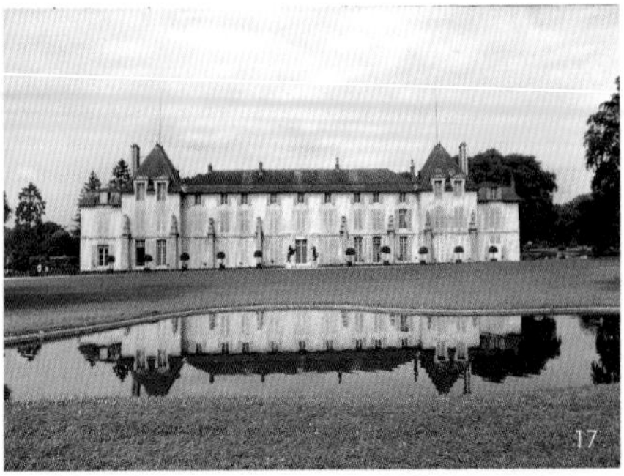
17

18

19

Napoleon recalls Josephine, recounting a dream in which she assured him that they would never be parted again. The film script closes with his death.

While working on the screenplay, Kubrick had drawn up a set of production notes, dated November 22, 1968. Like Napoleon planning a military campaign, Kubrick mapped out his strategy for filming a huge historical epic. He said to Gelmis, "We're now in the process of deciding the best places to shoot, and where it would be most feasible to obtain the troops we need for battle scenes. We intend to use a maximum of forty thousand infantry and ten thousand cavalry for the big battles, which means that we have to find a country which will hire out its own armed forces to us—you can just imagine the cost of fifty thousand extras over an extended period of time." In discussing the battle scenes, Kubrick said that he envisioned them as "a vast tableau where the formations moved in an almost choreographic fashion. I want to capture this reality on film, and to do so it's necessary to re-create all the conditions of the battle with painstaking accuracy."

"It's obviously a huge story to film, since we're not just taking one segment of Napoleon's life, military or personal, but are attempting to encompass all the major events of his career. I haven't set down any rigid guidelines on length; I believe that if you have a truly interesting film, it doesn't matter how long it is—providing, of course, you don't run on to such extremes that you numb the attention span of your audience."[8] Still, he added, if a film

16–22 ***Location research photographs:***
16 ***Cards such as this one were photographed at the beginning of each roll of film.***
17 ***Malmaison, Napoleon and Josephine's chateau near Paris.***
18 ***Bathroom at Malmaison.***
19 ***Venice bedroom.***
20 ***Waterloo.***
21 ***Romania.***
22 ***Josephine's bedroom at Malmaison.***

is sufficiently interesting, an audience will watch it for three hours, which is the length he had decided upon for "Napoleon."

When I first discussed the project with him, Kubrick said that he planned to use "authentic locations on the Continent, where many buildings and sites dating from Napoleon's time still are preserved. The battle scenes can be done in places like Yugoslavia, Hungary, and Romania, where arrangements can be made to enlist the services of the regular army for shooting," in the same way that he employed a corps of German policemen in *Paths of Glory* (1957).

Kubrick records in his production notes, which he appended to the screenplay, "We have received bids from Romania to provide up to a maximum of thirty thousand troops a day at two dollars per man, though it is unlikely that we will ever exceed fifteen thousand men on the largest day."

"Most of the interiors of a period film can be shot in mansions and castles that are still preserved in Europe, where the furniture and decor are already there," he explained to me. "You only have to move in your cast and crew and get to work." He mentions in the production notes that he had already arranged to rent these historical locations for as little as three hundred fifty dollars a day, whereas building all of the sets in a studio would cost a king's ransom.

Kubrick planned to begin principal photography in the winter of 1969, shooting battle scenes on location; he estimated that all of the exteriors would be completed in two or three months. After that he figured that shooting the interiors would take another three or four months. Furthermore, he writes in his production notes that he had discovered special photographic lenses that would enable him to continue shooting at exterior locations right into the evening, long after daylight had faded. He also found a way to shoot interiors lit solely by candlelight. This marked another decided advance in cinematography, since no scene in a motion picture had ever been lit with so little illumination before. He could accomplish this by using an extremely sensitive lens, originally developed by the aerospace industry for photographing the instrument panel on a spaceship. Even when making a costume picture, Kubrick was quick to adopt the latest technical developments in other fields to cinema. He would eventually utilize this technique in *Barry Lyndon*.

Although there had been various films about Napoleon over the years, such as Henry Koster's *Désirée* (1954), with Marlon Brando as the great dictator, the acknowledged classic film about Napoleon was French director Abel Gance's four-hour silent epic, *Napoléon* (1927), which left Kubrick unimpressed. In fact, he thought the film overrated, as he told Gelmis: "I've tried to see every film that was ever made on the subject, and I've got to say that I don't find any of them particularly impressive. I recently saw Abel Gance's movie, which has built up a reputation among film buffs over the years, and I found it really terrible. Technically he was ahead of his time and he introduced inventive new film techniques — in fact Eisenstein credited

23–26 ***Costume studies.***

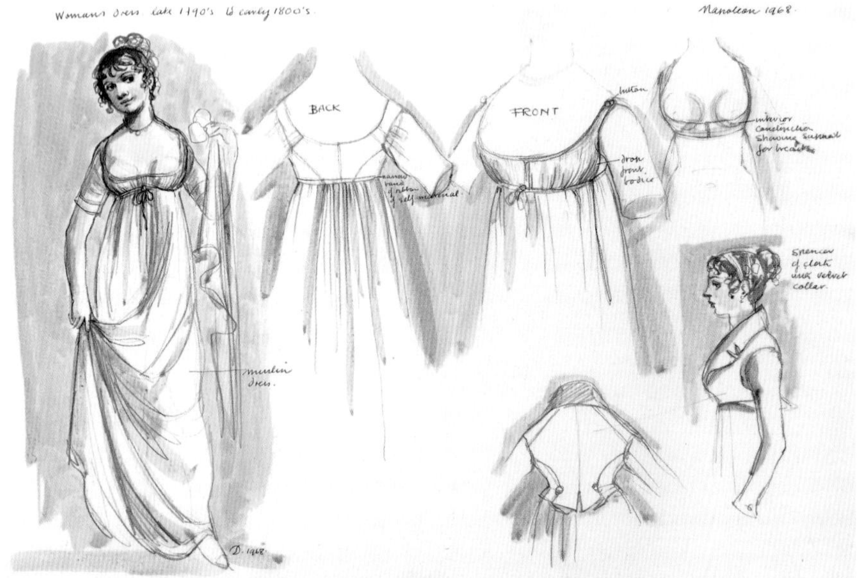

23

24

25

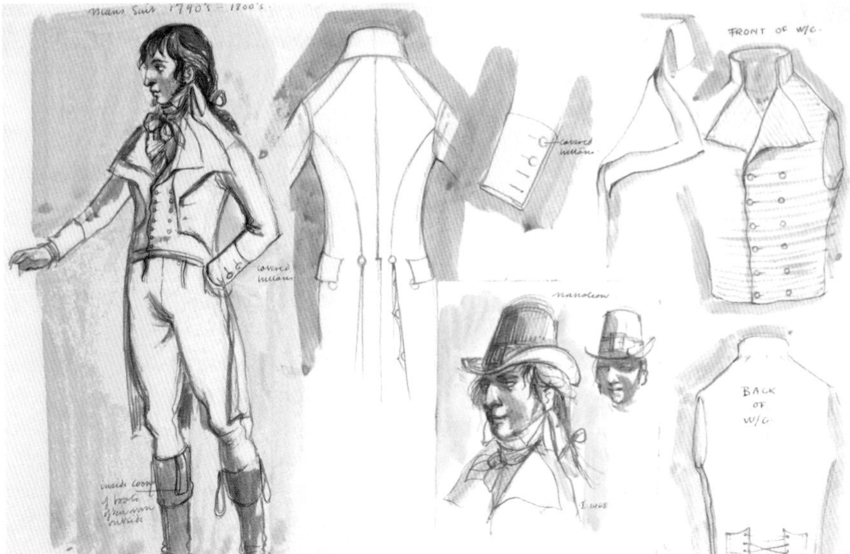

26

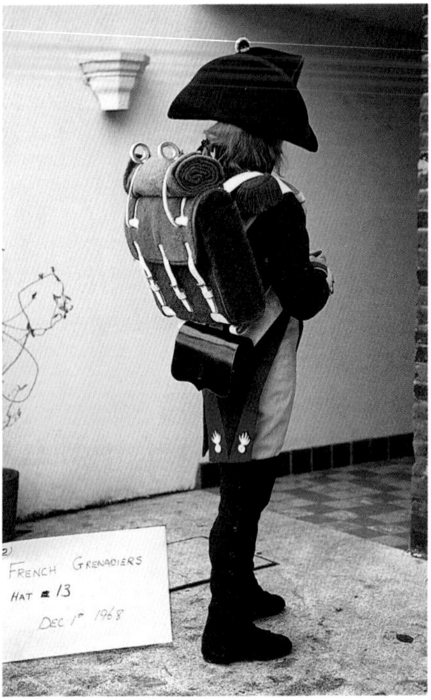

27

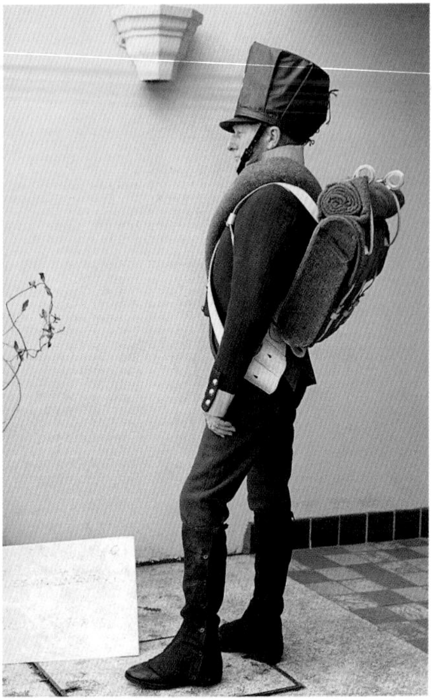

28

him with stimulating his initial interest in montage—but as far as story and performance goes it's a very crude picture."

Gance's film was re-released theatrically in 1981 to fresh acclaim, but Kubrick never changed his mind about it. To begin with, Gance covers only the early life of Napoleon (he intended to make a second film covering the rest of Napoleon's life but never did). Gance's movie focuses in particular on the period of the French Revolution, which in actual fact took place before Napoleon became a major force in French history. The film concludes with Napoleon's Italian campaign, when he was just rising to power in France. In order to encompass Napoleon's entire life, Kubrick's script compresses the period covered in Gance's film into the first third of his script, which allows him to carry on Napoleon's story all the way to Waterloo and St. Helena.

When I asked Kubrick why he thought Gance's picture crude, he replied that, among other things, he did not like Gance's approach to the staging of elaborate scenes filled with the proverbial cast of thousands. For example, in filming a banquet scene Gance tended to overload the frame with too much sumptuous decor and too many extras in fancy dress. As a result, a scene that Gance intended to be filled with rich visual detail would simply look cluttered. Similarly, Gance's crowd scenes, such as those portraying the mobs rioting during the French Revolution, are not compelling—they are just a lot of peo-

29

30

ple milling around. By contrast, Kubrick always took pains to carefully arrange the actors and the extras in a big scene in such a way as to achieve balance in composition within the frame. Kubrick had already proved with *Spartacus* that he could direct a historical spectacle with distinction and did not see Gance's *Napoléon* as much competition for his intended film.

At all events, in July 1968, MGM and Kubrick had jointly announced that Kubrick was to make "Napoleon." But by the time Kubrick delivered his script and production notes in September 1969, the studio had lost interest in the project. Kubrick told me that MGM had initially agreed to back the project "before the lights went out in Hollywood," in the wake of the failure of several large-scale productions, such as the Julie Andrews vehicle *Star!* (1968) and the Barbra Streisand vehicle *Hello, Dolly!* (1969). It seemed that king-size period pictures were going out of fashion at the time.

Furthermore, Robert O'Brien, who was president of MGM when Kubrick made *2001* and had been favorable to the project, was replaced in 1969 by Louis Polk, an executive who came to MGM with experience in the cereal industry. Polk had no interest in committing the studio to a historical spectacle; with that, Kubrick had to disband his research team. Then, in 1971, the Russians released *Waterloo*, a solemn

27–30 ***Examples of military uniforms photographed for Kubrick's reference.***

Napoleon film by Kubrick

NEW YORK, Saturday. — Metro - Goldwyn - Mayer announced today that it is planning a spectacular based on the life of Napoleon Bonaparte entitled Napoleon. It will be written, produced and directed by Stanley Kubrick of 2001 fame. —*Reuter*.

31

epic about Napoleon starring Rod Steiger. This lackluster Russian film was a heavy-handed pageant which garnered a cool critical reception and sank without a trace, and that made it unadvisable for Kubrick to make another movie about Napoleon at that time.

Kubrick had turned his attention to filming *A Clockwork Orange* (1971), derived from the novel by Anthony Burgess. After the film was released, Kubrick and Burgess discussed their mutual interest in Napoleon one night over dinner. Their discussion prompted Burgess to write his next novel, *Napoleon Symphony*, a reference to Beethoven's Third Symphony, which Beethoven had originally composed in honor of Napoleon, though he ultimately became disenchanted with Napoleon's lust for power and renounced his dedication of the symphony to him. So the symphony became known simply as the *Eroica* (heroic) Symphony. Burgess wrote the novel in the hope that Kubrick would make it the basis of his film. But it was not to be.

Jan Harlan, Kubrick's brother-in-law, who served as executive producer for all of Kubrick's films from *Barry Lyndon* onward, started out as a production assistant for the director on "Napoleon." Asked why Kubrick never got around to filming "Napoleon," he told me that, after *A Clockwork Orange*, Kubrick got interested in *Barry Lyndon*, another costume drama. "So 'Napoleon' drifted away," he concluded; "life goes on."

In "Napoleon" one finds resonances of a theme that has reasserted itself in

KUBRICK & MGM CALL IT QUITS

STANLEY KUBRICK will not be making his film on the life of Napoleon for MGM.

Announcing this last night, MGM stated that Kubrick retains control of the project and is making new financing and distribution arrangements for the film's scheduled start in September.

Two other Napoleon films have been announced — "The Battle Of Waterloo," to be made by Dino de Laurentiis and Segei Bondarchuk, and Bryan Forbes' look at Napoleon's family life.

32

31 ***Clipping from*** **The Evening Standard,** ***July 20, 1968.***
32 ***Clipping from*** **Daily Cinema,** ***January 1, 1969.***
33 ***After completing*** **A Clockwork Orange** ***and turning his attention back to Napoleon, Kubrick drafted this proposal, in which he wrote: "It's impossible to tell you what I'm going to do except to say that I expect to make the best movie ever made."***

much of Kubrick's best work. Kubrick has frequently shown in his films how human error and chance insinuate themselves into the most well-organized endeavors, to frustrate their implementation and final success. Spartacus is ground under by the superior military tactics and political corruption of the Romans; modern technology turns against its human instigators when their brainwashing techniques backfire in *A Clockwork Orange*. Barry Lyndon's lifelong schemes to become a rich nobleman ultimately come to nothing. In this list of failures Napoleon Bonaparte easily finds his place, in that his defeat was brought about by causes that all of his meticulous advance work did not foresee and could not cope with, as when the Russian winter destroyed his Grand Army.

The question arises as to whether or not Kubrick ever considered turning over his "Napoleon" script to another director, as he had considered collaborating with Steven Spielberg on "A.I." (Spielberg released his version, *Artificial Intelligence: A.I.*, in 2001). But Kubrick never expressed any intention that he might have someone else direct "Napoleon." "He wrote the script himself and oversaw the massive research and preparation for the project," writes Scott Brake, "and 'Napoleon' was obviously intended to be all Kubrick."[9] Jan Harlan concurs: "He never offered 'Napoleon' to anybody else; the script was his baby," he told me. Thus Kubrick aficionados are left to visualize in their own imaginations what might have been an extraordinary epic film from an extraordinary director.

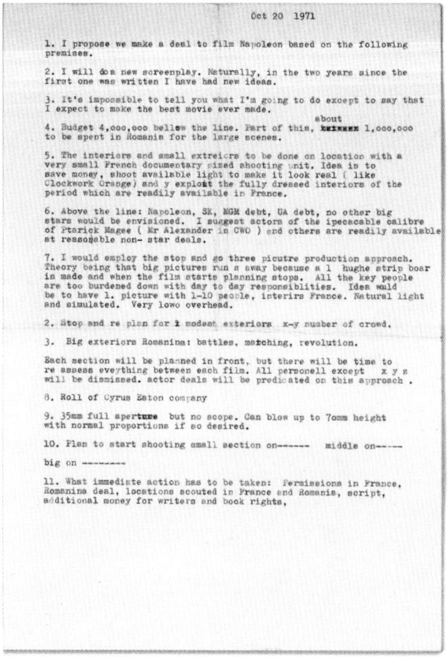

Oct 20 1971

1. I propose we make a deal to film Napoleon based on the following premises.

2. I will do a new screenplay. Naturally, in the two years since the first one was written I have had new ideas.

3. It's impossible to tell you what I'm going to do except to say that I expect to make the best movie ever made.

about
4. Budget 4,ooo,ooo bellow the line. Part of this, xxxxxx 1,ooo,ooo to be spent in Romania for the large scenes.

5. The interiors and small extreicrs to be done on location with a very small French documentary sized shooting unit. Idea is to save money, shoot available light to make it look real (like Clockwork Orange) and y exploit the fully dressed interiors of the period which are readily available in France.

6. Above the line: Napoleon, SK, MGM debt, UA debt, no other big stars would be envisioned. I suggest actors of the ipecacable calibre of Ptarick Magee (Mr Alexander in CWO) and others are readily available at reasonable non- star deals.

7. I would employ the stop and go three picutre production approach. Theory being that big pictures run s away because a 1 hughe strip boar is made and when the film starts planning stops. All the key people are too burdened down with day to day responsiblities. Idea wuld be to have 1. picture with 1-10 people, interirs France. Natural light and simulated. Very lowo overhead.

2. Stop and re plan for modest exteriors x-y number of crowd.

3. Big exteriors Romanina: battles, marching, revolution.

Each section will be planned in front, but there will be time to re assess eveything between each film. All personell except x y z will be dismissed. actor deals will be predicated on this approach .

8. Roll of Cyrus Eaton company

9. 35mm full aperture but no scope. Can blow up to 7omm height with normal proportions if so desired.

10. Plan to start shooting small section on------ middle on-----

big on --------

11. What immediate action has to be taken: Permissions in France, Romanina deal, locations scouted in France and Romania, script, additional money for writers and book rights,

33

Notes

1. Pauline Kael, *For Keeps* (New York: Dutton, 1996): 882.
2. Joseph Gelmis, "Stanley Kubrick: The Film Director as Superstar," in *Stanley Kubrick: Interviews*, ed. Gene D. Phillips (Lexington: University Press of Mississippi, 2001): 84.
3. Ibid.: 85.
4. Michel Ciment, *Kubrick: The Definitive Edition* (New York: Faber and Faber, 2001): 213.
5. Darryl Mason, "The Greatest Movie Stanley Kubrick Never Made," *Salon*, "Arts and Entertainment" (October 4, 2000): 5.
6. Stanley Kubrick, "Napoleon: A Screenplay" (1969).
7. Ciment: 197.
8. Gelmis, in Phillips: 83–85.
9. Scott Brake, "Script Review of Stanley Kubrick's Napoleon," *Film Face* (July 10, 2000): 3.

Stanley Kubrick's "A. I."

by Alison Castle

34 ***Painting of the entrance to Rouge, by Chris Baker.***

artificial intelligence *(noun): the capability of a machine to imitate intelligent human behavior (as reasoning, learning, or the understanding of speech).*

—Merriam-Webster Unabridged Dictionary

Stanley Kubrick once called the computer "one of man's most beautiful inventions."[1] On Arthur C. Clarke's recommendation, he bought a Hewlett Packard electronic calculator in 1970 (when such items were not only revolutionary but wildly expensive) and began using an IBM time-share computer (connected to a mainframe in London) that same year. Always looking for more efficient ways to organize and access information, he was delighted to be able to replace card catalogs with computers that could store text and perform keyword searches. Progressing to a WANG word processor in the early 1970s and a Philips model a few years later, he

34

became convinced that his entire staff could benefit from computer technology and in the early 1980s bought IBM "green screen" desktops for his employees. In 1984, he purchased his first laptop computer, religiously upgrading to each new model thereafter. Kubrick was the first person in the United Kingdom to use digital film editing equipment, importing a room-sized Montage machine from the United States in 1986 to edit *Full Metal Jacket*.

Artificial intelligence was a subject of enduring fascination for Kubrick, who became interested in the topic in the 1960s and made it a central theme of his 1968 film *2001: A Space Odyssey*. An avid reader of *Scientific American* and the writings of experts such as Hans Moravec and Marvin Minsky, Kubrick was convinced that with the prospects afforded by artificial intelligence and technology, computers would eventually surpass human beings. In 1971, he told Alexander Walker, "One of the fascinating questions that arise in envisioning computers more intelligent than men is at what point machine intelligence deserves the same consideration as biological intelligence.... You could be tempted to ask yourself in what way is machine intelligence any less sacrosanct than biological intelligence, and it might be difficult to arrive at an answer flattering to biological intelligence."[2]

"The next time you come here you will see an IBM, on-line, time-sharing terminal connected to an IBM 360 computer—cost 83£ per month plus 10/- per 3440 characters storage per month. It is fantastic!!"

—SK/1970 in a letter to Arthur C. Clarke, Feb. 13

Though *2001*'s supercomputer, HAL, developed homicidal behavior in an attempt to preserve itself from extinction, Kubrick believed that freethinking computers were not necessarily a menace to humanity: "If the computer acted in its own self-interest, there would never be the conflict often anticipated. For it is difficult to conceive any high level of intelligence acting less rationally than man does."[3] That humans, for all their intellectual capabilities, are ultimately governed by their emotions was a major theme throughout Kubrick's work, and was a principal reason for his fascination with Napoleon: how is it that a man can reach a level of intelligence as that of Napoleon, and yet allow impulses such as greed, jealousy, and impetuosity to cause his downfall?

That computers could someday attain levels of intelligence higher than man's, *without* the vulnerability inherent in human intelligence, was a possibility that in many ways Kubrick saw as an exciting and even positive prospect. But if computers were both smarter and more rational than humans, what, if any, would be man's redeeming quality? In the absence of religious explanation, what importance would human life hold when compared to, for example, highly advanced robots that looked, acted, and moved like humans yet were intellectually and physically superior in every possible way? In response to this line of questioning, Kubrick focused on the reductive yet fundamental notion of "real," in the sense expressed by the robot character David, to flesh out what it is that gives humans their spark. What it means to be "real," and how this intangible idea gives meaning to human life, is at the heart of Stanley Kubrick's "A.I."

In 1982, after spending years looking for what he called a "good story" about artificial intelligence, Stanley Kubrick optioned the rights to Brian Aldiss's short story "Super-Toys Last All Summer Long." Written in 1969, "Super-Toys" centers around David, an android boy struggling to deal with his feelings for his human "mother," Monica; while he thinks he feels genuine love for her, she cannot love him back, and interprets his reticence as "his verbal communication center ... giving trouble." Disturbed by the thought that he is somehow different from his human parents, David asks his teddy bear "You and I are real, Teddy, aren't we?" The bear, which "specialize(s) in comfort," replies that they are indeed. At the end of the story, Monica learns that she has won the parenthood lottery after four years of waiting. David, who had been her companion during that time, will presumably be overshadowed by the arrival of the "real" child.

Kubrick hired Aldiss to develop "Super-Toys" into a screenplay. He presented the writer with a copy of Carlo Collodi's *Pinocchio* on their first day of work together, suggesting that the theme of Pinocchio's quest to become a real boy, with the help of the Blue Fairy, should be incorporated into the storyline. Aldiss's aversion to the fairy-tale theme ultimately led to a stalemate and the two parted ways. Kubrick continued working on the project alone but, reasoning that the special effects required to create an android character would improve over the following years, postponed the project and made *Full Metal Jacket* instead.

In 1988, Kubrick's interest was renewed and the option on "Super-Toys" was exercised and paid for. After briefly working with writer Bob Shaw on the treatment, Kubrick hired science-fiction writer Ian Watson in the spring of 1990. They worked together throughout that year, Watson's

35

35 ***Chris Foss's sketches.***

36

most significant contribution being the character Gigolo Joe, a male sex robot that meets up with David on his journey. Ultimately, Kubrick was not satisfied with Watson's writing and ended the collaboration. The following year the project was put on hold and Kubrick turned his attention to a screen adaptation of Louis Begley's Holocaust novel, *Wartime Lies*. When that project was cancelled in late 1993, Warner Bros announced that Kubrick's next film would be "A.I." (as the "Super-Toys"-*Pinocchio* project was now known).

A brief collaboration with author Sara Maitland did not produce a satisfactory script, so in May 1994 Kubrick put together an eighty-seven-page treatment, appropriating contributions from previous collaborators and incorporating his own additions. It was with this that he began pre-production on "A.I."

Stanley Kubrick's treatment contains explicit vestiges of "Super-Toys" and overt references to *Pinocchio*. The story begins in the year 2200. The ice caps have been melted due to the greenhouse effect and many cities are under water. Henry and Monica, who live just outside New York City, are struggling to deal with the fact that their son, Martin, is being maintained in a cryogenic sleep until a cure can be found for his illness. Depressed and lonely while her husband is away on a business trip, Monica visits a psychiatrist who suggests that she look into buying a product that has just come on the market: a robot child that can be programmed to love. Monica convinces Henry to buy it — for twenty thousand "newbucks" ("the price of a luxury car"). David, as the child robot is named, happily joins the family, befriending Martin's robot teddy bear, Teddy. To complete the imprinting — the

36 ***Artist Chris Foss was commissioned to paint this rendition of New York under water.***

process that irrevocably causes David to love his owner—Monica speaks the series of words written in the instruction manual; within a few days, she notices that the "child" has become very attached to her. Just as in Aldiss's story, David begins to have doubts about Monica's love for him, and about whether or not he is "real." Having been read *Pinocchio*, David asks his "Mommy" if the Blue Fairy can make him into a real boy, like Pinocchio.

Monica is unable to understand why she cannot feel anything more than fondness for David, who so desperately wants her to love him. When her son is suddenly cured and brought home, she pays less and less attention to David, and after a few incidents (David sneaks into her bedroom at night and cuts off a lock of her hair and later accidentally causes Martin to fall and hurt himself) finally decides to give him up. Since the imprinting is permanent, David cannot be reprogrammed; he can only be disassembled and used for spare parts. Though she is unable to love him, Monica cannot bear the thought of David being junked, so she takes him, along with Teddy, to a remote forest. To give the inconsolable robot some hope, she tells him to find the Blue Fairy so she can make him a real boy. Then she drives off.

Thus begins David's odyssey. Before long, he wanders his way into danger, as he is chased by Lord Johnson Johnson the Third, a "rich lunatic human" on his way to the Heavy Flesh Festival in a gondola suspended from a moon-like dirigible; Johnson is, as a military robot informs David, "hunting robot the hard way, to challenge himself." Soon enough, David is caught up in the net with the other captured robots, including Gigolo Joe, a love-robot on the run for a murder he didn't commit. When the Moon-Blimp is shot down by a military robot, Gigolo Joe grabs David and Teddy for cover and runs off to hide in a derelict building. David tells Joe of his quest to find the Blue Fairy to become a real boy. Joe, thinking he could become a real man, decides to take David to Rouge to begin the search for her.

Hitchhiking a ride from a robot driving a truckload of coffins, they narrowly escape being caught at a checkpoint and finally arrive in the city of Rouge, heading straight for a Mr. Know shop. For twenty newbucks per hour, Mr. Know answers questions by consulting a vast database of world information. David inquires about the Blue Fairy; among the topics Mr. Know produces is "Project Pinocchio," begun fifty years earlier at the nearby Nichols Robotics Institute. The short-lived project involved a study group of Mark-6 robots that were asked to determine whether or not they could become real human beings. "The real purpose behind the experiment was to see how the robots would react when something they greatly desired proved impossible to achieve—would they construct irrational belief systems in the way human beings had developed religion?" The robots initially decided that being human, and thus mortal, was not preferable to being a robot. However, they mused, "A robot might live forever, yet what was the worth of its existence? Robots had created no art, nor had they made any scientific discovery. No robot was a creator. No robot was a genius.... What was their immortality worth, when the spark, the genius, was absent?" Finally, they concluded, "if a robot could become human, he would know what had been denied to him. Joy and desire and love, genius, imagination, spirit."

So the robots began the experiment in earnest, but after six months an accidental neutron explosion took place near the institute, killing all human personnel. Abandoned thereafter, the institute lies in a radiation wasteland known as the Zero-zone. With no other viable leads, Joe manages to steal an amphibicopter to fly David and Teddy to the Zero-zone, hoping to learn of the Blue Fairy's whereabouts. They crash at the outer limits of the Zero-zone and continue the journey on foot, through the decrepit terrain inhabited only by mutants and strange animals: "That night, red eyes glowed in the darkness, the owners keeping their distance. Unseen creatures gibbered and gobbled as if brutal incomprehensible conversations were occurring underwater. The forest itself seemed to mumble slow, vegetable words." As they near the site of the explosion, the vegetation changes, becoming "increasingly iridescent as though the leaves were covered in fish scales.... What might have once been a bull lumbered by.... Its hide was lizard-green, sparkling, crocodilian. Its horns branched like coral." The land is described as "at once sick and lovely, hectic with a quiet voluptuous brittle fever." The handful of pages dedicated to describing the Zero-zone is full of rich turns of phrase, such as "gilded rococo spires arose... like petrified stretched people reaching skinnily towards the sky" and "gauzy mists, pastel miasmas wreathed many of the jeweled structures in the town of glittering coral."

"Complex robots will sometimes get into trouble on their own initiative."

—Passage highlighted by SK in *Mind Children: The Future of Robot and Human Intelligence* (Hans Moravec, Harvard University Press, 1988)

David, Teddy, and Joe are slowly making their way through this unearthly land when a huge, skeletal robot appears. Kubrick writes, "Sequence to be written where Joe and the creature fight and destroy each other, and David and Teddy escape." Continuing on, David and Teddy finally reach the institute, where they find petrified human remains: "Gemmed skeletons sat at desks and table panels, as if locked into bizarre ormolu thrones like dead knights awaiting a magical trumpet call." From the ruins emerge several robots, whom David asks about Project Pinocchio. They explain to him that after the explosion, they continued their research and had made a great breakthrough: they had discovered the riddle that would lead them to the "transfiguring phenomenon, Our Lady of Indigo." Other robots had set off on the journey to solve the riddle but had never returned. When David asks to take the journey, the robots tell him the riddle: "Go to the city of death? / Go to the life awaiting you / Go to the end of the world? / Go to the wheel is in the water." The robots find and repair the amphibicopter and send David off to the place they interpret as the city of death: New York.

Kubrick describes the fate of his hometown with poetic, melancholy language: "abandoned eroded buildings reared from the wind-whipped waters. Jagged ziggurats, steep little islands of debris, marked where once-proud structures had succumbed to hurricanes and seaquakes.... Though the city appeared dead, it was not inert. It groaned. It wailed. Wind passing through the myriad empty glassless windows played eerie music in the buildings as though those were organ pipes of stone.... A tormented, inhuman symphony played forever."

David navigates the amphibicopter through the city, finally arriving at the tip of a wheel peeking out of the water. He repeats the last line of the riddle and decides he has found the wheel to which it refers. Hoping to find Our Lady of Indigo under the water, he submerges the amphibicopter and, turning on the floodlights, proceeds to the ocean floor. A defunct robot appears before them, seeming to wave its arms; it is apparently a robot from the institute that made it this far and lodged its feet in a giant clam. David guides the amphibicopter to an arched entrance resembling the mouth of a whale. Deep inside the immense beast, the floodlights fall upon a man sitting at a table: David has arrived at the ruins of a Pinocchio funhouse at Coney Island. Turning away from the whale, David sees that the floodlights fall upon a plastic figure of a young lady with blue hair; at the same moment, the Ferris wheel, which has been progressively becoming more and more unstable in the violent seas, finally topples and traps the amphibicopter underneath it. Thinking that he has finally found the Blue Fairy, David calls out to the plastic figure in front of him, begging her to turn him into a real boy. He continues to pray to

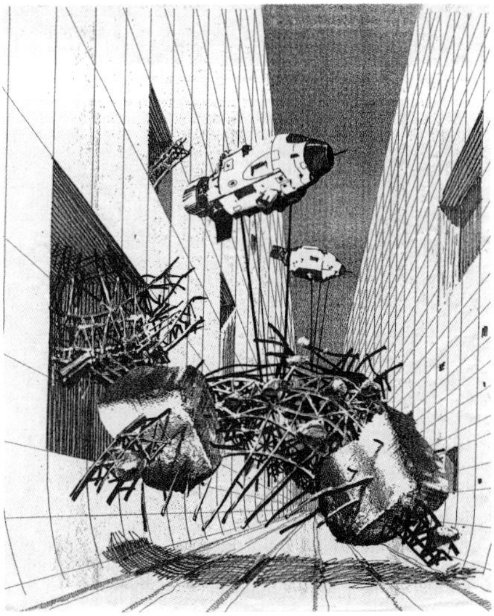

37

her for hundreds of years after the floodlights dim, until he eventually stops moving and just stares ahead, while around them the ocean slowly freezes. "Thus two thousand years pass by."

In the space of four centuries, all humans and animals became extinct, ravaged by the new ice age brought on by genetically engineered algae that was used to reverse global warming. "Only the robots remained from a dead past—man's children. By now the domestic servants and supertoys had evolved to superintelligences, incalculably greater than their human creators." Attempting to find reasons for their own existence in the absence of the humans that created them, the robots erected complex and ambitious projects to find life or meaning in the distant reaches of the universe. Their attempts were futile. "Human beings had created a million explanations of the meaning of life and of the world in works of

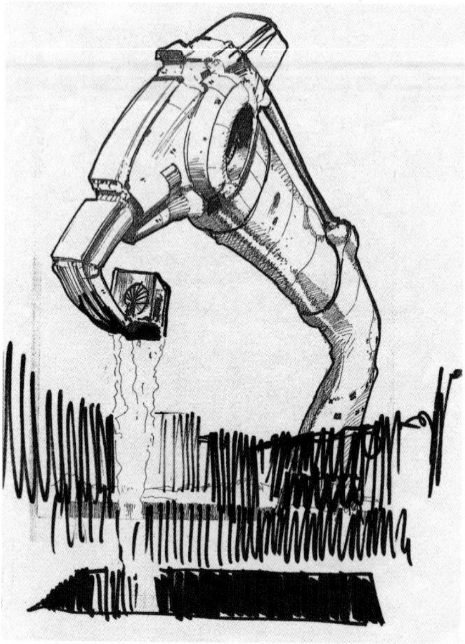

38

philosophy, in art, in poetry, in mathematical formulae. Surely human beings must be the key to the meaning of existence?"

The robots eventually developed a process that allowed them to recreate humans from surviving DNA; inexplicably, the men and women they resurrected only lived for one day, "slipping into final darkness" as they fell asleep on the first night. During the few hours that the robots spent with each "resurrectee" (a Kubrick neologism), they tried to glean meaning from human existence, "a bittersweet drug, the source, almost, of a soul."

One day, some two thousand years after it was trapped by the Ferris wheel, the amphibicopter is uncovered by robots performing excavations in the ice. Upon discovering the two robots inside, a robot exclaims, "These robots are two thousand-year-old originals. They knew living people, when people crowded the Earth. What a treasure!"

A lock of Monica's hair that Teddy had kept in his pouch allows the robots to resurrect her. David soon finds himself with Monica in a virtual environment created from his memory to resemble exactly the house they had lived in. After an idyllic day, Monica finally falls asleep, telling David the words he has been waiting two millennia to hear: "I do love you, my sweet little boy. I have always loved you." Holding her in his arms as she sleeps, David hopes for a miracle. The next morning, his wish comes true: Monica wakes up. The robots search for an answer to why, for the first time, a resurrectee has survived more than one day: "Was it the love of a robot child? No other resurrectee had ever before had someone who loved them to hold onto them." The treatment ends as Monica waltzes around the room with David "as she had done the day of his imprinting."

Many drafts had been written prior to this one, and many more would have followed had the project advanced further. This unfinished treatment, incorporating bits and pieces contributed by the various collaborators, can only give us a hint of what Kubrick may have intended for "A.I." While he was working on the story, Kubrick commissioned the work of illustrators including Chris Baker ("Fangorn"), who produced hundreds of promising designs for the look of the film. Members of Industrial Light & Magic (the special effects company responsible for many of the digital effects in *Jurassic Park*) were brought in to test ways to portray partially submerged New York skyscrapers, and the results were encouraging. Kubrick was also heavily involved in testing the special effects that would be necessary to create a realistic-looking boy, and this turned out to be the Achilles' heel of effects technology; specialists such as Chris Cunningham (who later transformed Björk into a robot for the music video "All is Full of Love") were hired to explore the possibilities, but after seeing the results, Kubrick realized that the technology available at the time was not adequate (even today this would prove a difficult task). He decided that using a real child actor might be the only solution, but he worried that the length of time he would take to shoot the film, since he always took time to lavish attention on all the production details, would cause obvious differences in the boy's age to be noticeable throughout the movie.

He thus considered a possible collaboration with Steven Spielberg, whose mastery in directing special effects in films such as *Jurassic Park* (1993) had impressed him and who was capable of shooting a film in a fraction of the time it would take Kubrick, meaning that a young boy could be cast in the role of David and would not visibly age during the shooting. Spielberg was receptive to the idea and the two met to discuss the possibilities. Ultimately, they were unable to sort out how to collaborate and the idea was put on hold. Kubrick told his producer Jan Harlan at the time, "I think the ideal director for this may be Steven Spielberg. If I do it, it may be too stark. I may emphasize too much the philosophical side."[4]

37–38 ***Sketches by Chris Foss showing the excavation of the Ferris wheel.***

Hoping that technology would eventually allow David to be realistically portrayed using computer-generated imagery, Kubrick decided to postpone "A.I." and turn to a project he had been thinking about for over twenty years, Schnitzler's *Traumnovelle*. In 1995, Warner Bros. announced that a Kubrick film starring Nicole Kidman and Tom Cruise would begin shooting the following year, and that "A.I." would be Kubrick's subsequent project. As production of *Eyes Wide Shut* neared its end in late 1998 and early 1999, Kubrick began to turn his attention back to "A.I."

"Monica will consist of David's + Teddy's memories of her, and her DNA."

—Note written by SK in margin of *Mind Children: The Future of Robot and Human Intelligence* (Hans Moravec, Harvard University Press, 1988)

After Kubrick's death, Steven Spielberg wrote his own version of the film based on Kubrick's treatment and, with Jan Harlan as executive producer, completed *Artificial Intelligence: A.I.* in 2001. Chris Baker's drawings became an important starting point for the look of Spielberg's film, for which the illustrator was hired as conceptual artist. Whether or not Kubrick's "A.I." would have ultimately employed the same visual design is something we shall never know, though Spielberg's breathtaking special effects, especially for the scenes of New York under water, are a testament to Kubrick's reasons for wanting to work with him. The differences in the two directors' concepts

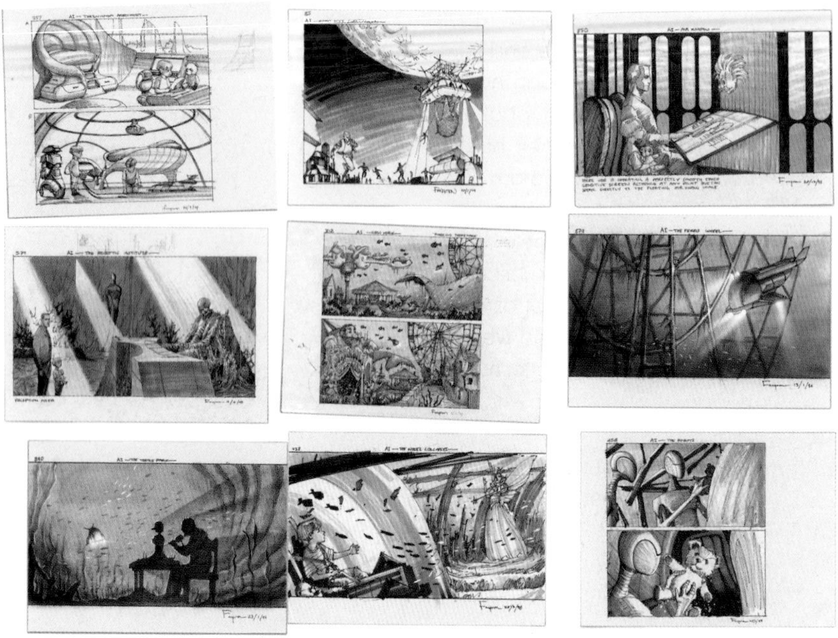

39

39 ***Examples of sketches made by Chris Baker ("Fangorn") between 1994 and 1996. Baker made hundreds of such drawings to provide Kubrick with visual ideas while he was working on the script.***

for the plot of the film are representative of their respective artistic sensibilities; Jan Harlan has pointed out that Spielberg brought out the human side of the story, whereas Kubrick had opined that his own vision was, perhaps, "too stark"—but, one might ask, for what? or whom?

Would Kubrick's David have indeed seen his "mother" successfully resurrected or would Kubrick have opted for a darker eventuality? He had expressed his dislike of the idea of a happy ending to Sara Maitland, telling her that he envisioned the film ending in the robots' failure to keep the resurrected Monica alive. The ending of his May 1994 draft of the treatment may reflect a change in this stance, or perhaps a desire to emphasize the powerful effect that love between a robot and a human could have. Did Monica's love for David make him, for all intents and purposes, a "real" boy? This would suggest that only the presence of humans, for all their fallibilities, could give meaning to the existence of robots. In Kubrick's future, however, people are long absent from an earth populated only by robots—each of which is searching for something only humans could possibly provide.

Like the 5th millennium robots in "A.I." that seek to discover the essence of man's soul, through his films Kubrick continually sought to pick out, amongst all of man's faults and atrocities, the elusive and volatile beauty of humanity. Though he describes a bleak future in which robots are "incalculably greater than their human creators," he centers the story around the robots' hopelessly futile quest to become human, to attain that indescribable quality that makes people "real." Was Kubrick suggesting that this vague concept of "real" (the spark, perhaps) is the closest we may ever come to finding a meaning for human life? Was he embracing—gasp—the human condition?

Though many called him a pessimist, Kubrick was, more precisely, a pragmatist; in a 1968 interview about *2001*, he beautifully summed up his view of man's plight: "However vast the darkness, we must supply our own light."[5]

Notes

1. Andrew Bailey, "A Clockwork Utopia," *Rolling Stone* (January 20, 1972): 16.
2. Alexander Walker, *Stanley Kubrick, Director* (New York: Norton, 2000): 32.
3. Ibid.: 187.
4. Channel 4 documentary *The Last Movie: Stanley Kubrick & Eyes Wide Shut.*
5. Eric Nordern, "The Playboy Interview: Stanley Kubrick," *Playboy* (September 1968): 195.

From *Wartime Lies* to "Aryan Papers"

by Jan Harlan

40 ***Costume fitting photographs of Johanna ter Steege, the Dutch actress Kubrick chose to play Tania.***

40

For decades, Stanley looked for material that might allow him to make a film about the Holocaust. He was not interested in a documentary, but wanted a dramatic structure that compressed the complex and vast information into the story of an individual that represented the essence of this man-made hell, if this was possible—and he was not sure that it was. Shakespeare succeeded brilliantly in reducing the essence of villainy in the characters of Iago and Richard III, but these were, of course, straightforward tales, simple by comparison to the enormity of the Holocaust.

At one point Stanley considered what he called "a soft option": a story set in the German film industry, using the day to day routine of Goebbels's propaganda machine as the setting in which the drama would unfold, but he never found a story that satisfied him. He liked Isaac Bashevis Singer's novels and short stories and suggested that I contact Singer and ask him to write an original screenplay for Stanley. This was in 1976. Singer lived in New York and had been surrounded for decades by refugees from the Nazi regime. Naively, we considered this reason enough for this wonderful writer to come up with what we were looking for. We imagined he would draw from all these experiences around him and combine them with the amply documented historical knowledge available and then streamline this knowledge through his skillful mind and pen into characters living out the horrific drama of Nazi persecution. My subsequent meeting with Isaac Bashevis Singer at his home in Manhattan culminated in a "moment of truth" that is as vivid before me now as it always was. After tea and the exchange of pleasantries, we came to the point of the visit and I told him how much Stanley liked his writing and that he hoped to persuade him to work on an original film treatment about the Holocaust. Isaac looked at us for some time in silence and then said that he felt very honored to be asked, but that he was not able to do this justice since—and I am quoting him literally—"I don't know the first thing about it." Back at the hotel I called Stanley in England and I told him Singer's answer. "I sure know what he means" was Stanley's only comment. He felt hurt, a bit chastised. Stanley decided it was unreasonable to suggest that only first-hand experience empowered a writer or artist to address this topic. But we knew also that this "topic" was unlike any other.

The search continued. In 1991 Stanley got very excited about Louis Begley's novel *Wartime Lies*. He was clearly in love with the story, the necessary prerequisite for him to undertake any preparation for a film. Here was a brilliantly written personal account seen through the eyes of a child, using autobiographical elements, translating these artistically and with the competence of a child's firsthand subjective experience into a horrendous testimony. The story follows Tania, a young Jewish woman, and her little nephew, Maciek, on the move through Poland, as they pretend to be Catholics in order to avoid betrayal and capture. They form a unique relationship as they struggle and try to blind their alien surroundings with "wartime lies" and "Aryan papers."

It was unthinkable to do this film in the U.K. and Stanley would have to go abroad. For Stanley, the very idea of having to

41

42

spend many months away from his home, and in a non-English speaking country, was troubling. It meant not just leaving his house, but also his children, his grandchildren, the animals, and the carefully developed infrastructure of his daily life. But he was so enthused by Begley's book and the idea of finally making this film that he was willing to accept this major change in his life.

Wartime Lies did not lend itself easily to a screenplay. Stanley worked on the drafts by himself and finally arrived at a treatment good enough for preparing a schedule and a budget. He proposed "Aryan Papers" to Warner Bros., but it was always clear that his script, like almost all of his scripts, was a suggested framework and that the depth of each scene had to be worked out in rehearsals—a slow process, but this was Stanley's way. I had witnessed this on prior films and later again in *Eyes Wide Shut*: it was a mixture of being well prepared and having a clear concept of certain images and the final film, but most of the details of the scenes and dialogues had still to be worked out. It meant being open for changes at all times, questioning everything that he had written so carefully himself. It was always a long way from the beginning of a scene to the final "thank you" that clinched it.

41–42 ***Kubrick's proof copy of* Wartime Lies*, with names of actresses, perhaps in consideration for the leading role, written on the first page.***

He knew he would change many details of his script, but at this stage "Aryan Papers" was only needed for the art department, for casting, wardrobe, etc. — the subtleties and hidden layers, the hallmark of all of Stanley's films, would come later. He was confident enough to go into full-blown pre-production.

Roy Walker was the production designer and Phil Hobbs the co-producer. An art director and a production manager were hired in Bratislava. Barbara Baum and her assistant worked at Stanley's house in England on the costumes, while I worked with Rick Senat, the lawyer in charge of Warner Bros. business affairs, to secure support from the various national and local authorities in Prague, Brno, and Bratislava. Phil Hobbs organized offices and looked for alternative "Polish Woods" in Denmark. Franz Bauer (art director of Edgar Reitz's much admired *Heimat*) and I traveled through Czechoslovakia and Hungary to look for locations. All of us took thousands of photographs and supplied Stanley daily with the gathered information via phone, fax, and courier. Johanna ter Steege was going to be our lead actress, playing Tania, and Joseph Mazzello was to play her nephew, Maciek. Then the doubts set in and the soul-searching turmoil began. Steven Spielberg had started his new production of *Schindler's List* near Krakow. Warner Bros. co-chief Terry Semel and Stanley realized that once more, our timing was most unfortunate. Stanley's previous film, *Full Metal Jacket*, had suffered at the box office because of *Platoon*, another Vietnam War film which had been released just before and had become a big hit. We were going to be in a similar situation again. It was then that Stanley and Terry agreed to postpone "Aryan Papers" in favor of "A.I."

I sometimes felt that this decision came as a relief for Stanley. But I also know that he was disappointed at having to put aside so much work and he was particularly sad not being able to work with Johanna ter Steege, since he was convinced that he had found an actress whose performance would catapult a new star to the forefront of international stardom and give this dark and serious film the needed "gloss." Stanley, in a letter to Barbara Baum, wrote: "I will keep you informed. All the work will not have been in vain." He did not know that the postponement was forever.

Chronology

Chronology

by Vincent LoBrutto

1928 Thursday, July 26: Stanley Kubrick born to Jacques and Gertrude (Perveler) Kubrick at the Lying-In Hospital in Manhattan.

1929 Kubrick Family resides at 21 Clinton Avenue in the Bronx.

1934 May 21: Barbara Kubrick, sister, born.
– Stanley Kubrick begins public school at P.S. 3 in the Bronx, New York.

1935 Scores above average on standard reading and intelligence tests.

1936 Due to poor school attendance records, Kubrick receives home instruction from January through June.
– September: he returns to P.S. 3 and his attendance is greatly improved.

1937 Kubrick family moves from Clinton Avenue apartment to houses on Grant Avenue in the Bronx, first at 1131, then 1135.

1938 June: Kubrick begins school at P.S. 90.

1940 Kubrick leaves P.S. 90 and spends the fall semester with Martin Perveler, his mother's brother, in California. It is his first trip to the land of Hollywood.

1941 Spends spring semester with his uncle in California.

02

03

- September: Kubrick returns to the Bronx, reentering P.S. 90 in the eighth grade.

1942 Kubrick family moves to 2715 Grand Concourse in the Bronx.
- Enters William Howard Taft High School.
- Poor attendance record at Taft, excellent one at the Loew's Paradise and RKO Fordham movie theaters, where he sees double features twice a week.

1943 February: takes Saturday morning children's art class at the Art Students League near Manhattan's Carnegie Hall.
- Kubrick is a percussionist in the Taft orchestra and plays drums in the school's swing band—Eydie Gormé is the vocalist.
- Kubrick becomes active in the Taft photography club. Uses Graflex camera lent to him by his father.

1944 Kubrick family now living on Shakespeare Avenue in the Bronx.
- Kubrick is photographer for the Taft newspaper and member of the Taft Review.

1945 Spring: Kubrick is reported to the attendance bureau for excessive absences.
- Receives low ratings in "Courtesy," "Dependability," and "Cooperation."
- Kubrick is a high school senior. His photograph of a newsvendor reacting to the

01 ***Stanley and Christiane Kubrick in Beverly Hills in 1960 with daughters Anya (left), Katharina (center), and newborn Vivian.***
02 ***Stanley Kubrick with his mother, Gertrude.***
03 ***With father, Jacques.***
04 ***Stanley, seen here taking a picture of his cousin, took up photography at a young age.***
05 ***Ten-year-old Stanley is seen holding his camera in this photograph taken by his father at a local airfield.***

04

05

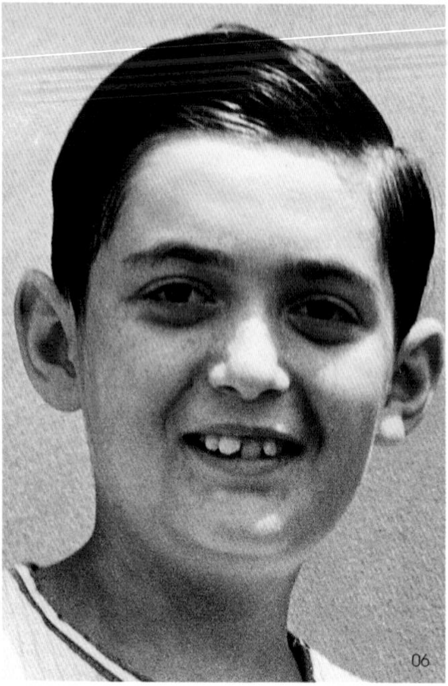
06

07

death of President Franklin Delano Roosevelt appears in the June 26th issue of *Look* magazine. He is paid $25.
– Kubrick family living in a private house at 1873 Harrison Avenue in the Bronx.
– Kubrick enters Herman Getter's art class at Taft and tells the teacher he is a photographer and doesn't paint or draw, to which Getter replies, "Well, that's art."

1946 Kubrick graduates from Taft High School, enrolls in evening classes at City College, and becomes a staff photographer for *Look*.

1947 Kubrick gets his pilot's license on August 15.

1948 May 11: Kubrick profiled in *Look* as a "two-year *Look* veteran."
– May 29: Kubrick marries Toba Etta Metz (1930) at a civil ceremony in Mount Vernon, New York. They had met as teenagers in the Bronx, when Kubrick was a senior at Taft and Toba was beginning her freshman year.
– The couple moves to 37 West 16th Street in Greenwich Village.

1949 *Look* publishes "Prizefighter," Kubrick's photo story on middleweight boxer Walter Cartier.
– Kubrick seeks financing for the screenplay, co-written with Howard O. Sackler, that would eventually become *Fear and Desire*.

1950 In his last year at *Look*, Kubrick continues publishing photo stories regularly.
– Kubrick directs his first film, *Day of the Fight*. The documentary is shot on location in New York, edited by Kubrick, and scored by friend Gerald Fried.

1951 Kubrick sells *Day of the Fight* to RKO-Pathé for $4,000, the largest sum ever paid by the company for a short, netting Kubrick a $100 profit and a $1,500 advance for a second short for the studio.
– April 26: *Day of the Fight* opens at the Paramount Theater in New York City.
– Directs the short documentary *Flying Padre*, a human-interest story, on location in Mosquero, in Harding County, part of northeastern New Mexico.
– Kubrick resigns from *Look* to pursue filmmaking career.
– He sets out to independently produce and direct a feature-length film.
– Raises nearly $10, 000 from friends, his father, and his uncle, Martin Perveler, who would be credited as associate producer.
– Kubrick's only steady income is the money he earns playing chess in Washington Square Park.
– *Fear and Desire* shot in 35 mm on location in the San Gabriel Mountains, a coastal river, and Azusa on the outskirts of Los Angeles. Kubrick edits the picture and soundtrack by himself in New York.

1952 Kubrick directs second unit for a television series on the life of Abraham Lincoln to be aired on the *Omnibus* series. On location in Hodgenville, Kentucky, Kubrick directs silent material establishing Lincoln's early years.
– Kubrick travels to New Salem, Illinois, and offers to help main director Norman Lloyd. After criticizing and offering the director suggestions, he is asked to leave and returns to New York.
– Kubrick spends most of his time at 1600 Broadway (a building housing various editing rooms, production companies, and other film-related businesses), where he learns about film technique from talking to technicians, salesmen, and craftspeople.
– He meets film editor Faith Hubley, who nurtures him with editing skills.
– Kubrick is a regular at the Museum of Modern Art's film program.

1953 Joseph Burstyn agrees to distribute *Fear and Desire*.
– March 26: *Fear and Desire* previewed in New York and praised by *Variety*.
– April 23: *Fear and Desire* receives a class B Classification from the Legion of Decency, due to a sexually suggestive scene depicting a tied-up woman and a soldier.
– *Fear and Desire* has a theatrical run at the Guild Theater in New York.

06–07 ***Stanley at about age thirteen.***
08 ***High school graduation portrait, 1946.***

– Kubrick commissioned by Seafarers' International Union to direct a short 16 mm industrial film. *The Seafarers*, produced by Lester Cooper Productions, is his first film in color.
– June: shooting takes place at the headquarters of the New York City Atlantic and Gulf District of the union.
– Kubrick begins to write his second feature film, *Killer's Kiss*.

1954 Kubrick raises $40,000 from friends and relatives to produce *Killer's Kiss*. The principal investor is Morris Bousel, a Bronx Pharmacist who is given a shared producer credit in second position despite alphabetical protocol.
– The film is shot on location in New York City, in a Greenwich Village loft, Wall Street, the streets of Times Square, the Theatre de

09 ***This portrait of Kubrick with his camera was probably taken by his father around 1946.***
10 ***Kubrick during his days as a photographer for*** **Look.**

Lys on Christopher Street, a mannequin factory, and Penn Station.

1955 January: Kubrick divorces Toba Metz and marries ballerina and choreographer Ruth Sobotka (1925–1967) in Albany, New York.

– Edits the picture and sound of *Killer's Kiss* at Titra Sound Studios.

– Kubrick sells *Killer's Kiss* to United Artists for worldwide distribution. The studio makes a profit on the film released on the bottom of a double bill. Kubrick does not break even but ultimately pays back his investors.

1956 Kubrick introduced to James B. Harris and they form Harris-Kubrick Pictures, opening an office on West 57th Street.

– Harris-Kubrick buys the rights to the novel *Clean Break* by Lionel White

– The screenplay, titled *The Killing*, is written by Kubrick and novelist Jim Thompson.

– United Artists puts up partial financing for *The Killing*. The remainder of the budget comes from Harris and an investment by his father.

– The production is mounted in California. Sets are built in the old Chaplin Studio. Designed by Ruth Sobotka, the sets include the betting area of a racetrack and several apartment interiors.

– *The Killing* is released by United Artists on May 20. The film is not a box office success but receives positive industry attention.

1957 Harris-Kubrick signs a deal with Dore Schary to write, produce, and direct a film in forty weeks for $75,000.

– Kubrick selects *Paths of Glory* by Humphrey Cobb as the project. Schary turns it down, calling it "downbeat antiwar stuff."

10

– In the MGM literary department Kubrick selects *The Burning Secret* by Stefan Zweig.
– Novelist Calder Willingham is asked by Harris-Kubrick to co-write the script.
– Despite MGM's rejection of *Paths of Glory*, Harris-Kubrick hires Jim Thompson to write the screenplay.
– Dore Schary is fired. MGM executive Benny Thaw cancels the Harris-Kubrick contract.
– Harris-Kubrick approaches United Artists with *Paths of Glory*. They will not accept the project without a rewrite or the commitment of a top star.
– Calder Willingham rewrites the Kubrick/Thompson screenplay.

12

Harris-Kubrick Pictures
250 NORTH CANON DRIVE • BEVERLY HILLS, CALIFORNIA • CRestview 4-7204

13

- Kirk Douglas accepts the lead role and signs Harris-Kubrick to a five-picture deal with his company, Bryna Productions.
- United Artists finances *Paths of Glory*.
- The film is shot on location in Munich, Germany.
- Kubrick marries Christiane Susanne Harlan (born in 1932), the German actress cast for the final scene of *Paths of Glory*. Christiane's daughter Katharina Christiane (born in 1953) is from her first marriage, to German actor Werner Bruhns.
- *Paths of Glory* is banned in France, on the Army and Air Force Military circuit in Europe, and Switzerland.
- Kubrick and Harris develop a television series about the exploits of a boy's school commandant. The project, based on Operation Mad Ball with Ernie Kovacs, was never realized.
- Kubrick develops *I Stole $16,000,000* with Jim Thompson based on a Bryna acquisition—it is the autobiography of Herbert Emerson Wilson, a safecracker who served twelve years in San Quentin. The project is not realized.

11 ***With second wife, Ruth Sobotka.***
12 ***Portraits of Kubrick and partner James B. Harris.***
13 ***Harris-Kubrick Pictures letterhead.***

1958 May 12: Kubrick signs on to direct a film based on *The Authentic Death of Hendry Jones* by Charles Neider, starring Marlon Brando and produced by his Pennebaker production company. He begins to work on the screenplay, originally written by Sam Peckinpah, with Brando and Calder Willingham. It is titled *One-Eyed Jacks*.
- Harris and Kubrick read Vladimir Nabokov's *Lolita* and agree they want to make the book into a film.
- Kubrick spends the summer in script conferences with Brando.
- Pre-production continues on Brando's Western—start date pushed back to September 15.
- November 21: Kubrick and Brando part ways, the latter taking over as director of *One-Eyed Jacks*.

1959 Kubrick family living at 316 South Camden Drive in Beverly Hills.
- February 13: director Anthony Mann fired from *Spartacus*. With the production underway since January 27, Kubrick is hired as director by Kirk Douglas, the film's star

and producer, and is given twenty-four hours to prepare.
- April 6: Anya Renata Kubrick born to Christiane and Stanley Kubrick.
- Harris-Kubrick purchases the rights to *Lolita*. They approach Nabokov about writing the screenplay, but he declines when he learns Humbert and Lolita may have to be secretly married to get the project past censors.
- Harris-Kubrick hires Calder Willingham to adapt *Lolita*, but the script is later rejected by Kubrick.
- Douglas learns that Harris-Kubrick is developing *Lolita*, and passes on it as part of their obligation to Bryna, convinced it will never be made due to the controversial content.
- December: Harris-Kubrick sends telegram to Nabokov imploring him to reconsider writing *Lolita* screenplay. Nabokov accepts.

1960 March 1: Nabokov and Kubrick meet in a Universal City Studios office to discuss screen adaptation of *Lolita*.
- March 9: Kubrick introduces Tuesday Weld to Nabokov as a posible Lolita—the author finds the actress unsuitable for the part.
- March 11: Kubrick sends Nabokov a rough outline of the scenes they had agreed upon for the first part of the novel.
- End of June: Nabokov has over a thousand index cards and a four-hundred-page typescript. Kubrick visits Nabokov to tell him his screenplay would make a seven-hour film.
- August 5: Vivian Vanessa Kubrick born to Christiane and Stanley Kubrick.
- September: Nabokov delivers short version of screenplay—accepted by Kubrick.
- September 15: Kubrick shows Nabokov photos of Sue Lyon, the young actress signed to play Lolita.
- Kubrick rewrites the Nabokov draft, though the author receives sole credit on the finished film.
- Harris-Kubrick turns down a Warner Bros. deal that does not give Kubrick the complete control he demands.
- October 19: *Spartacus* premieres at the Pantages Theater in Hollywood.

1961 May 25: *Lolita* receives code seal but the official certificate is pending to review of the finished film.
- Harris-Kubrick raises capital to put *Lolita* into production. Harris makes a deal

14 ***1954 headshot of Susanne Christian (stage name of Christiane Susanne Harlan).***
15 ***Christiane and Stanley Kubrick ca. 1959.***

with Eliot Hyman of Associated Artists for $1,000,000.
– James Mason agrees to play Humbert Humbert.
– Harris-Kubrick decides to make *Lolita* in England under the Eady plan, which allowed foreign producers to write off costs if 80 percent of the laborers were UK subjects.
– *Lolita* is produced at Elstree Studios in England.
– August 29: Harris is informed that there are four points of contention to be resolved before *Lolita* can be awarded a certificate of approval.
– After negotiations and re-cutting, *Lolita* is given a code seal.
– Fall: Harris-Kubrick released from contract with Kirk Douglas and Bryna Productions due to mutual artistic differences.

1962 The Kubrick family maintains addresses at 239 Central Park West and 145 East 84th Street in New York.
– Kubrick remains in England to prepare foreign versions of *Lolita* and to pursue the follow-up project of the Harris-Kubrick deal with Ray Stark and Seven Arts (formely Associated Artists).
– After battles with British censors and the Catholic Church, *Lolita*, Kubrick's first film produced entirely in England, is released by MGM in association with Seven Arts Productions, opening in New York on June 13.
– Kubrick, intrigued since 1958 with the threat of thermonuclear war, chooses it as the subject of his next film.
– Kubrick meets with Alastair Buchan, head of the Institute for Strategic Studies.

15

16

- Kubrick's Polaris Productions buys the motion picture rights to *Red Alert* by Peter George for $3,500.
- Kubrick and Peter George begin to work on a serious dramatic screenplay adaptation of *Red Alert*.
- Harris jokes to Kubrick about turning the project into a comedy or satire. They both agree to continue developing the film as a drama.
- Harris takes script to Eliot Hyman at Seven Arts and it is accepted as their second picture commitment.

1963 January 11: Kubrick sends a copy of the *Dr. Strangelove or: How I Learned to Stop Worrying and Love the Bomb* script to Geoffrey Shurlock of the Motion Picture Association of America (MPAA) to resolve any potential problems before shooting the film.
- February: Kubrick files a lawsuit to stop production of the motion picture adaptation of *Fail Safe*. Ultimately Columbia Pictures, which was distributing *Dr. Strangelove*, took over distribution of *Fail Safe* and released it in October of 1964, well after the December 1963 release of *Dr. Strangelove*.
- Kubrick tells *The New York Times* that Harris-Kubrick is working on *Dr. Strangelove* with Seven Arts. He describes the project as a satire.
- Harris decides to pursue a directorial career. Harris-Kubrick Pictures is amicably dissolved after almost ten years as a successful partnership.
- Kubrick learns about the manic comic gifts of writer Terry Southern through Peter Sellers and Bob Gaffney. He is brought onto the writing team along with Kubrick and George.
- Kubrick meets with production designer Richard Sylbert in New York coffee shops over a period of a month to plan if the film could be produced in New York. Sylbert convinces Kubrick it can't be done in the city or in America.

"No reviewer has ever illuminated any aspect of my work for me."

—SK/1972 (to Bernard Weintraub/ *The New York Times*)

16 ***On the set of* Lolita, *1961.***
17 ***Portraits, ca. 1961–62.***

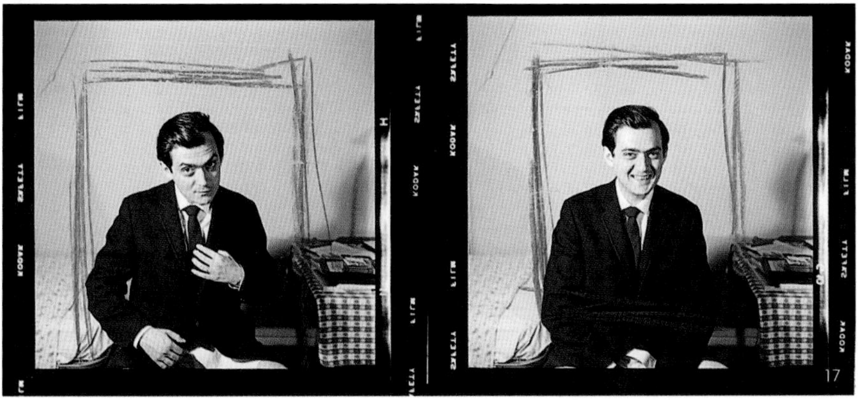
17

- Kubrick decides to produce *Dr. Strangelove* in England, at Shepperton Studios.
- He resides in Knightsbridge, London, during the production.
- Production designer Ken Adam designs and builds sets for the War Room, the B-52 interior, the military base offices and exterior, and a nuclear warhead missile.
- November 22: the first critics' screening of *Dr. Strangelove* is cancelled due to the assassination of President John F. Kennedy.

1964 January 2: *Dr. Strangelove* receives an MPAA Code Seal Certificate.
- *Dr. Strangelove, or: How I Learned to Stop Worrying and Love the Bomb* is released.
- Kubrick writes to Arthur C. Clarke about making a "'really good' science-fiction movie."
- April 23: Kubrick and Clarke meet at Trader Vic's in New York. The evening ends without discussion of a project.
- In their second meeting, after hours of spirited discussion on many topics, Kubrick officially asks Clarke to collaborate on a science-fiction film.
- Spring: Clarke and Kubrick meet for up to ten hours a day discussing ideas for the project.
- May 20: Clarke signs a formal contract with Kubrick that includes the sale of "The Sentinel" as well as six other short stories.
- Clarke begins to write the novel that will be adapted into the screenplay—both to be written in collaboration with Kubrick. Clarke begins work at Kubrick's Central Park West office, then moves to the Chelsea Hotel.
- End of August: the novel's three main characters begin to emerge—two astronauts and a computer.

18

19

- December 25: Clarke finishes first draft of the novel.

1965 Kubrick uses the manuscript of the novel to sell the film to MGM and Cinerama.
- February 23: in a press release, MGM announces its commitment to Kubrick's next film, whose working title is "Journey Beyond the Stars."
- April: Kubrick announces that the film will be produced in England.
- Spring: Clarke returns to his home in Ceylon to revise and expand the novel.

18 ***Playing chess on the set of* Dr. Strangelove, *1963.***
19 ***Polaroid taken during shooting of* 2001: A Space Odyssey.**

Kubrick interviews technicians, department heads, and actors.
- Massive research is underway. Kubrick and associates contact leading minds in the areas of space, science, and religion. Corporations working in a wide range of related topics to space flight are asked to share thoughts and plans for the next millennium.
- The special-effects team sets up offices designated "Santa's Workshop."
- December 26: Clarke completes first draft of the screenplay.
- December 29: first day of principal photography on *2001: A Space Odyssey*. Scenes concerning the TMA-excavation site where a monolith is discovered are shot.

1966 January 8: the *2001* production moves from Shepperton to MGM Studios in Borehamwood, north of London. Filming begins on sequences in which Dr. Floyd is transported to the space station.
– June: Clarke flies to MGM in Hollywood to screen demo reel with some completed scenes to appease the anxious studio executives.

1967 Kubrick and his special-effects team execute massive special-effects work.

"I have a wife, three children, three dogs, seven cats. I'm not Franz Kafka, sitting alone and suffering."

—SK/1972 (to Craig McGregor/*The New York Times*)

– Autumn: Kubrick shoots "The Dawn of Man" segment.
– December: composer Alex North flies to London to discuss the music for 2001.
– December 24: North returns to London to prepare recording the score.

1968 North records more than forty minutes of original music in a two-week period.
– Kubrick screens *2001* for MGM executives in Culver City, California. After the screening Kubrick deletes a prologue of experts discussing the possible existence of extraterrestrials and a voice-over narration.
– Kubrick abandons North's recorded music and scores the film with previously existing compositions, including Richard Strauss's *Also Sprach Zarathustra* and Johann Strauss's waltz *The Blue Danube*.

– March: Kubrick screens the first composite print of *2001*.
– Spring: Clarke is granted permission by Kubrick to publish the *2001: A Space Odyssey* novel simultaneously with the film's release.
– April 3: *2001: A Space Odyssey* opens in New York City, then in Hollywood the next day.
– April 5: Kubrick cuts seventeen minutes out of the original 156- minute version.
– Kubrick family living in a Gatsby-like mansion on Long Island, New York.
– Kubrick asks Bob Gaffney to come to England with him to work on his next project, on the life of Napoleon.

1969 Kubrick and his family move to Abbot's Mead, in England.
– Kubrick wins Academy Award for Best Special Visual Effects for *2001: A Space Odyssey*.
– Gaffney negotiates with the Romanian government for thirty-five thousand troops for the Napoleon project.
– Pre-production plans for "Napoleon" include massive amounts of flu vaccine to protect the large crew and military cast.
– Gaffney scouts Romania for locations.
– Kubrick conducts extensive research on Napoleon.

1970 Kubrick talks to Jack Nicholson about playing Napoleon.
– United Artists agrees to produce Kubrick's

20 ***Kubrick took this panoramic photo of his parents in their New Jersey apartment with his Widelux camera (early 1960s).***

21

"Napoleon" but recent losses of $45 million and a takeover by the Transamerica Corporation forces them to cancel Kubrick's three-hour epic.

- Kubrick looks into other possibilities for projects, including an adaptation of Arthur Schnitzler's *Traumnovelle*, which would eventually become the director's final film, *Eyes Wide Shut*.

- Kubrick decides to adapt Anthony Burgess's novel *A Clockwork Orange*.

- Warner Bros. signs on as the film's production company, paying Si Litvinoff and Max Raab $200 000 for the rights to the novel, for which they had originally purchased the rights from Burgess for a few hundred dollars.

- Kubrick's home in Abbot's Mead, thirty minutes outside of London, is his command center for developing the *Clockwork Orange* project.

- May 15: Kubrick completes first draft

screenplay adaptation of *A Clockwork Orange*.
- Winter: production begins on *A Clockwork Orange*. The film is shot on location in and around London.

1971 Winter: production of *A Clockwork Orange* is completed.
- Kubrick and his editor Bill Butler cut the film on the premises of the Kubrick estate.
- Jan Harlan, brother of Christiane, works on the film as assistant to the producer.
- Fall: Anthony Burgess screens the finished film and finds it a brilliant response to his novel.
- *A Clockwork Orange* receives an X rating from the MPAA.
- In England, the film is given a certificate by the British Board of Film Censors, rated restricted to audiences over eighteen.
- December 19: *A Clockwork Orange* premieres in New York and San Francisco.

1972 *A Clockwork Orange* nominated for best picture, Kubrick for best director and adapted screenplay, and Bill Butler receives a nod for editing. At the Academy Awards ceremony *The French Connection* wins in all of those categories.
- October: Kubrick withdraws *A Clockwork Orange* for sixty days to comply with the MPPA. Thirty seconds of footage in two scenes containing explicit sexual material is replaced with less objectionable shots. MPAA gives the new version an R rating and the film is re-released and allowed greater distribution, which had been withheld because of the former X rating.

1973 Warner Bros. informs *Variety* that Kubrick will be shooting a film starring Ryan O'Neal and Marisa Berenson in England, with principal photography to begin in May or June. Jan Harlan is the executive producer of the project.
- Violent crimes that copycat *A Clockwork Orange* begin to occur in the U.S. and the U.K.
- Kubrick contacts Ed DiGiulio of Cinema Products to find a way he can mount an f 0.7 Zeiss lens (intended for use by NASA) on a BNC Mitchell motion-picture camera to film scenes lit purely by candlelight. The lens, which was two stops faster than the super-speed lenses of the day, had a 50 mm barrel but no focusing mount. DiGiulio solved the problem by removing the camera's adjustable shutter and aperture plate and manufacturing a special

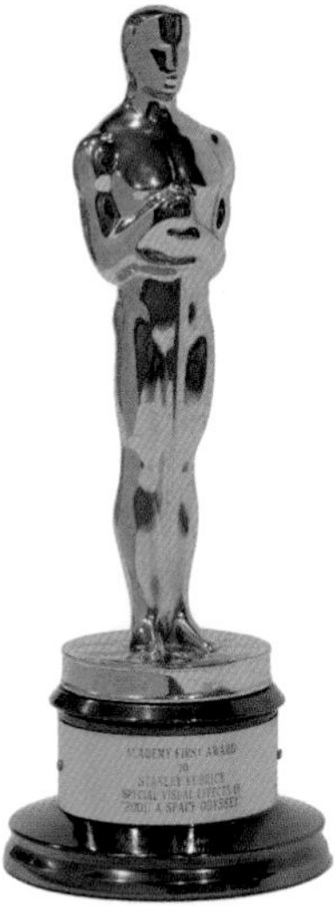

21 ***Daughters Katharina (left) and Vivian with one of the Olivier Mourgue-designed Djinn chairs used for the space station lounge in 2001.***
22 ***The only Oscar ever awarded to Kubrick, for Special Visual Effects in 2001.***

22

focusing mount which rendered the camera useless for any other purpose.

- Production designer Ken Adam is given the mandate by Kubrick to find actual locations for his adaptation of William Makepeace Thackeray's *The Luck of Barry Lyndon* within a ninety-minute radius of his home. Kubrick's title *Barry Lyndon* is kept secret, in fear that others could make a knockoff based on the book, which was in the public domain.

- Ken Adam scouts homes to create the scope of estates depicted in the film. He eventually convinces Kubrick to extend the search to Ireland. The director could not be convinced to shoot the sequences taking place in Germany on location. At the end of the production schedule, Kubrick finally dispatches a second unit crew to Potsdam and East Berlin to photograph castles and period streets.

- Kubrick and the art department engage in a massive research project on life in the eighteenth century.

- *Variety* erroneously speculates that Kubrick is shooting the previously announced project, Arthur Schnitzler's *Traumnovelle.*

1974 *Paths of Glory* is finally released in France.

- Concerned by violent copycat crimes linked to *A Clockwork Orange*, Kubrick pulls the film from distribution in England.

- After six months of shooting in Ireland,

23 ***Photograph by Stanley of two of his dogs in his*** **Clockwork Orange** ***editing room, 1971.***

filming is suspended and the company returns to England. The official reason given concerned lack of access to locations but reports from Dublin state the IRA made bomb threats to the production.

1975 Shooting resumes on *Barry Lyndon* in England. Kubrick had used the downtime to revise the script and production plans.
– December 18: *Barry Lyndon* premieres in New York City.

1976 *Barry Lyndon* underperforms in the U.S. but opens strongly throughout Europe.
– *Barry Lyndon* is nominated for a best-picture Oscar as well as Kubrick for best director. The film wins four Oscars: for adapted score, costumes, production design, and cinematography.
– February 10: Jan Harlan informs Kubrick of a new hand-held camera stabilizing device. The Steadicam was invented by Garrett Brown and developed with Ed DiGiulio of Cinema Products. Kubrick was shown a photograph of Brown with the prototype and told that the camera could move smoothly in any direction, making what were previously considered "impossible shots."

1977 Warner Bros. executive John Calley sends Kubrick the galleys for Stephen King's novel *The Shining*.
– Novelist Diane Johnson is chosen by Kubrick to work with him in adapting *The Shining* as his next film project.
– Kubrick in pre-production on film based on Stephen King's novel *The Shining*.
– During the FILM 77 exposition in London, Ed DiGiulio and Garrett Brown visit Kubrick at his home to show him the latest model of the Steadicam.
– Production designer Roy Walker tours American hotels and apartment buildings for research.
– King's Overlook Hotel is entirely built on a soundstage at EMI-Elstree Studios.

1978 Kubrick and Johnson adapt *The Shining*, working in England over a period of three months.
– May: production begins on *The Shining*, at the EMI-Elstree Studios. Jan Harlan is the executive producer.
– Vivian Kubrick films the documentary *Making "The Shining"*.

1979 Late January: a fire breaks out on the set, which is partially destroyed. It is partially rebuilt on another stage — production is set back by three weeks.
– April: production of *The Shining* at EMI-Elstree is completed.

1980 Kubrick purchases an old manor house on 172 acres in the exclusive estate of Childwickbury near St Albans, Herts, where the family still lives today.
– May 23: *The Shining* opens in New York.
– May 28: Kubrick orders that an epilogue to the film in which the hotel manager visits Wendy in the hospital be cut from all prints of the film.
– June 13: *The Shining* opens at 750 additional theaters across the U.S.
– Vivian Kubrick's *Making "The Shining"* is broadcast on BBC television.
– Kubrick contacts Michael Herr to discuss developing a war film.

1982 Arthur C. Clarke publishes *2010: Odyssey Two*. MGM strikes deal to film the sequel — Kubrick turns it down.
– Kubrick options the rights to Brian Aldiss's short story "Super-Toys Last All Summer Long" and hires the writer to work on a screen adaptation; the project is put

on hold when Kubrick turns his attention to Gustav Hasford's novel *The Short-Timers*.

1983 Director Peter Hyams approaches Clarke with interest in directing *2010*. He phones Kubrick, who gives him his approval—Hyams goes on to photograph and direct the sequel to *2001: A Space Odyssey*.

1984 March 10: Katharina Kubrick marries Philip Eugene Hobbs. Hobbs then becomes the co-producer of Kubrick's next film project, *Full Metal Jacket*. Jan Harlan is the executive producer.

"Shooting a movie is the worst milieu for creative work ever devised by man. It is a noisy, physical apparatus; it is difficult to concentrate—and you have to do it from eight-thirty to six-thirty, five days a week. It's not an environment an artist would ever choose to work in. The only advantage it has is that you must do it, and you can't procrastinate."

—SK/1970 (to Joseph Gelmis)

1985 Kubrick formally asks Michael Herr to collaborate on the screenplay adaptation of *The Short-Timers*. Hasford also works on the script.

- Kubrick, the production designer Anton Furst, and the design team research the Vietnamese city of Hue in 1968.

- Location scouts are sent to surrounding areas of London. The locations for the Parris Island boot camp and Vietnam sequences are found within a thirty-mile radius of Kubrick's base of operations.

- For the combat sequence, Kubrick selects a 1930s abandoned gasworks in the East London neighborhood of Beckton on the Thames. A demolition team blows up buildings and a wrecking ball is used to create the ruins of the Imperial City of Hue devastated in the Tet Offensive—the process takes seven weeks.

- April 23: mother, Gertrude Kubrick, dies in Los Angeles at age eighty-two.

- Summer: Shooting on *Full Metal Jacket* during extremely hot season in England, which provides just the right atmosphere to simulate Vietnam climate. The actors perform under difficult conditions in full army gear and are surrounded by dirt, rubble, gunfire, and explosions.

- October 19: father, Jacques Kubrick, dies in Los Angeles at age eighty-three.

- Fall: post-production on *Full Metal Jacket* begins.

- Vivian Kubrick composes the film's musical score under the name Abigail Mead.

1987 June 26: *Full Metal Jacket* opens in U.S. cinemas.

- The Academy of Motion Picture Arts and Sciences rejects Vivian's score for a possible nomination on the grounds that there was not a sufficient amount of original music to qualify.

- *Full Metal Jacket* receives one Oscar nomination, for best adapted screenplay.

1988 March: option to purchase rights to "Super-Toys" exercised and paid for.

- June: Kubrick receives two David di Donatello awards for *Full Metal Jacket*.

1989 Kubrick develops the "Super-Toys" project, briefly working with writer Bob Shaw on developing the story.

1990 Science-fiction writer Ian Watson is hired to collaborate on the script with Kubrick.

1991 Now known as "A.I.," the project is shelved when Kubrick concludes the special-effects technology necessary is not currently available.

1993 Jan Harlan secures the rights to Louis Begley's WWII Holocaust novel, *Wartime Lies,* for Kubrick.
– May: Kubrick in pre-production on a screen adaptation of *Wartime Lies*. Project is renamed "Aryan Papers."
– Young American actor Joseph Mazzello confirms he is about to work on a project with Kubrick.
– Location scouts go to Poland, Hungary, and Slovakia.
– Warner Bros. puts the project on their release schedule for Christmas 1994.
– Shooting schedule start date moved up to September or October.
– October: the *Hollywood Reporter* writes that the project is to be shot on location in and around Aarhus, Denmark.
– Start date moved to February 1994.
– November: Warner Bros. announces Kubrick's next film will be "A.I." The studio states that Kubrick would either produce and not direct "Aryan Papers," the adaptation of *Wartime Lies,* or direct it himself after completion of "A.I."
– Artist Chris Baker, known as "Fangorn," is hired to make illustrations of what the futuristic society of "A.I." might look like.

24 ***With Christiane, early 1970s.***

1994 Kubrick brings in writer Sara Maitland to work on "A.I."
– December: Frederic Raphael delivers the first draft of an adaptation of Arthur Schnitzler's novel *Traumnovelle*, which would become *Eyes Wide Shut*.

1995 March: Raphael delivers another draft.
– Summer: Kubrick talks with special-effects masters at George Lucas's Industrial Light and Magic and to effects experts at Quantel concerning "A.I."
– December: Warner Bros. press release announces that Kubrick's next film, *Eyes Wide Shut*, a story of jealousy and sexual obsession, will start filming in summer 1996, with a screenplay by Kubrick and Frederic Raphael and starring Tom Cruise and Nicole Kidman. Production of "A.I." is scheduled to follow.
– Raphael called to Childwickbury and asked to read Kubrick's rewrite of the project.

1996 Raphael revises the Kubrick draft.
– November 7: principal photography begins on *Eyes Wide Shut*. Locations include the Rothschild's country manor, Mentmore, London's Lanesborough Hotel, the mansion at Luton Hoo, and the Chelsea and Westminister Hospital in London, all being utilized for scenes taking place in and around Manhattan.
– New York City streets are built on the lot at Pinewood Studios in England.

1997 Kubrick receives the Director's Guild of America D. W. Griffith Award for Lifetime Achievement in film directing.
– September: Kubrick receives a Special Golden Lion Award at the Venice Film

25

26

Festival for his contribution to the art of cinema.

1998 May: Harvey Keitel, cast as Victor Ziegler, leaves the *Eyes Wide Shut* production and is replaced by Sydney Pollack, causing extensive re-shooting.
- Jennifer Jason Leigh, playing Marion Nathanson, is asked to re-shoot a scene but leaves the production because of a prior commitment. She is replaced by Marie Richardson.
- The original eighteen-week shooting schedule of *Eyes Wide Shut* stretches to fifty-two weeks over a period of fifteen months, during which Kubrick would close the production down for a week or two from time to time.
- *Eyes Wide Shut* announced to open in the autumn, later pushed back.

1999 March 7: Stanley Kubrick dies of a sudden massive heart attack six days after screening the final work print of *Eyes Wide Shut* for Warner Bros.
- The MPAA decides to give the film an NC-17 rating. Warner Bros. digitally alters the orgy sequences to obtain an R rating for U.S. distribution. The unaltered version of the film is released throughout Europe.
- July 16: *Eyes Wide Shut* opens.
- The Kubrick Collection is released on video and DVD by Warner Bros.

2000 Theatrical re-release of *Dr. Strangelove*.

25–26 ***With daughter Vivian.***
27 ***With Christiane, mid-1970s.***

- Theatrical re-release of *A Clockwork Orange* in Britain—first time film is officially shown since it was withdrawn by Kubrick in 1974.

2001 Kubrick documentary *Stanley Kubrick: A Life in Pictures*, directed by Jan Harlan, premieres at the Berlin Film Festival.
- Summer: *Artificial Intelligence: A.I.*, directed by Steven Spielberg, opens. Jan Harlan is the executive producer.
- *2001: A Space Odyssey* re-released.

2002 *Stanley Kubrick: A Life in Pictures* by Christiane Kubrick is published.

2004–2015 Several retrospectives of Kubrick's life and work open in galleries and museums worldwide, including the Deutsches Film Museum and Deutsches Architekturmuseum, Frankfurt am Main (2004); the Australian Centre for the Moving Image in Melbourne (2006); Palazzo delle Esposizioni in Rome (2007–2008); Cinémateque française in Paris (2011); Los Angeles County Museum of Art (2012–2013); and Museo da Imagem e do Som, São Paulo (2013–2014).

2016–2017 Kubrick exhibitions at the Contemporary Jewish Museum in San Francisco (June 30–October 30, 2016) and at Cineteca Nacional Mexico (December 1, 2016–March 31, 2017).

28 ***On the set of*** **The Shining.**
29 ***With one of his Golden Retrievers in his Childwickbury kitchen, mid-1980s.***
30 ***Christiane in her painter's apron and Kubrick with his camera, early 1970s.***

30

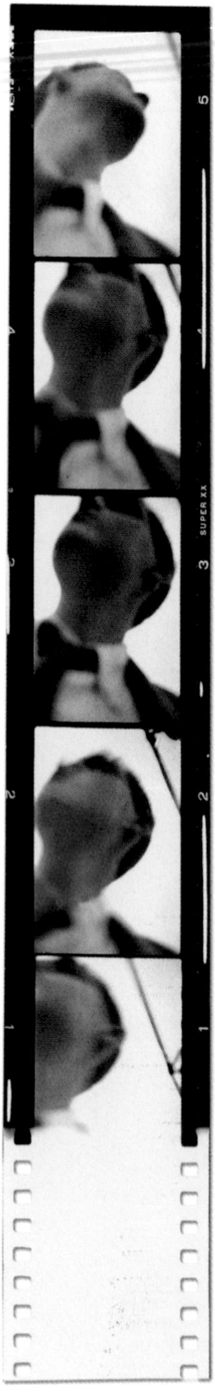

31

"Practically everything I read about me is grotesquely wrong.... I'm not a recluse. I lead a relatively normal life, I think. But this stuff has been written and rewritten so often it takes on a life of its own."

—SK/1987 (to Gene Siskel/*Chicago Tribune*)

32

35

34

36

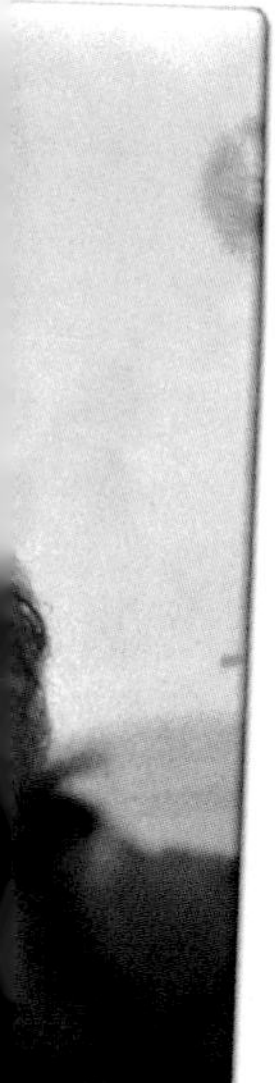

33

31–36 ***These self-portraits, taken over the years, appeared sporadically on rolls of film shot by Kubrick.***
37 ***On the set of*** **A Clockwork Orange.**

"Telling me to take a vacation from filmmaking is like telling a child to take a vacation from playing."

—SK/1972 (to Paul D. Zimmermann/*Newsweek*)

Bibliography

Published writings by Kubrick

- Letter to *L'Express*, March 5, 1959.
- "Director's Notes." *The Observer*, December 4, 1960.
- "Words and Movies." *Sight and Sound* (Winter 1960–61): 14.
- "How I Learned to Stop Worrying and Love the Cinema." *Films and Filming* (June, 1963): 12–13.
- Stanley Kubrick's *A Clockwork Orange*. New York: Ballantine Books, 1972.
- Letter to *The New York Times*, February 27, 1972.
- Letter to the *Detroit News*, April 9, 1972.
- *Full Metal Jacket* (with Michael Herr and Gustav Hasford). New York: Alfred A. Knopf, 1987.
- Introduction to Kieslowski and Piesiewicz's *Decalogue: 10 Commandments*. London: Faber and Faber, 1991.

Books about Kubrick

- Agel, Jerome, ed. *The Making of Kubrick's 2001*. New York: Signet, 1970.
- Bizony, Piers. *2001: Filming the Future*. London: Aurum Press, 1994.
- Ciment, Michel, ed. Stanley Kubrick, *La Biennale di Venezia*, Giorgio Mondadori, Venice-Milan, 1997.
- Ciment, Michel. *Kubrick: The Definitive Edition*. New York: Faber and Faber, 2001 and Paris: Calmann-Lévy, 1999.
- Coyle, Wallace. *Stanley Kubrick: A Guide to References and Resources*. Boston: G. K. Hall & Co., 1980.
- Crone, Rainer, and Petrus Graf Schaesberg. *Stanley Kubrick: Still Moving Pictures*. Munich: Schnell & Steiner, 1999.
- Deutsches Filmmuseum Frankfurt am Main. *Stanley Kubrick* (exhibition catalog). Frankfurt a. M., 2004.
- Duncan, Paul. *Stanley Kubrick*. Cologne: TASCHEN, 2003.
- Falsetto, Mario. *Stanley Kubrick: A Narrative and Stylistic Analysis*. Westport, CT: Praeger, 2001.
- Geduld, Carolyn. *Filmguide to 2001: A Space Odyssey*. Bloomington: Indiana University Press, 1973.
- Herr, Michael. *Kubrick*. New York: Grove Press, 2000.
- Jenkins, Greg. *Stanley Kubrick and the Art of Adaptation*. Jefferson, NC: McFarland and Company, 1997.
- Kagan, Norman. *The Cinema of Stanley Kubrick New Expanded Edition*. Oxford: Roundhouse, 1997.
- Kubrick, Christiane. *Stanley Kubrick: A Life in Pictures*. London: Bulfinch, 2002.
- LoBrutto, Vincent. *Stanley Kubrick: A Biography*. New York: Da Capo, 1999.
- Morel, Diane. *Eyes Wide Shut ou l'étrange labyrinthe*. Paris: Presses Universitaires de France, 2002.
- Nelson, Thomas Allen. *Kubrick: Inside a Film Artist's Maze*. Bloomington: Indiana University Press, 1982.
- Phillips, Gene D. *Stanley Kubrick: A Film Odyssey*. New York: Popular Library, 1977.
- Phillips, Gene D., ed. *Stanley Kubrick Interviews*. Jackson: University Press of Mississippi, 2001.
- Phillips, Gene D., and Rodney Hill. *The Encyclopedia of Stanley Kubrick*. New York: Checkmark Books, 2002.
- Richter, Dan. *Moonwatcher's Memoir: A Diary of 2001: A Space Odyssey*. New York: Carrol & Graf, 2002.

- Walker, Alexander, Sybil Taylor, and Ulrich Ruchti. *Stanley Kubrick, Director.* New York: Norton, 2000.

Films

- *Making "The Shining"* (Vivian Kubrick, 1980)
- *Stanley Kubrick: A Life in Pictures* (Jan Harlan, 2001)

Acknowledgements

Alison Castle would like to heartily thank: Jan Harlan and Christiane Kubrick; Anthony Frewin; Leon Vitali; Mark Smith, Tracy Crawley, Paula Murray (the Childwickbury support group); Katharina Kubrick Hobbs; Anya Kubrick Finney, Jonathan Finney; Mitch Mitchell; John Quartel; Maria Harlan; James B. Harris; Alexander Singer; Melanie Viner-Cuneo; Bernd Eichhorn, Tim Heptner; Maja Keppler, Hans-Peter Reichmann (Deutsches Filmmuseum); Vincent Staropoli

Jan Harlan and Christiane Kubrick would like to thank (in alphabetical order): Leith Adams; Paula Allen; Roger Arar; Jonathan Bader; Brad Ball; Louis Blau; Jeffrey Brauer; John Calley; Marlene Eastman; Iris Frederick; Con Gornell; Margarita Harder; Alan Horn; Brian Jamieson; Ivy Kwong; Jennifer Lewis; Barry Meyer; Steven Spielberg; Ron Suffrin; Amy Wollman

Afterword

Though this book is about the filmmaker Stanley Kubrick and his films, my afterword has to be about Stanley, my husband. When I married him, I knew I had embarked on a great and bold and romantic adventure. When he died I did not know how to live without him. I'm still not living without him. His voice is in my head, his image in my eyes. The long dialogue continues. I still follow his advice. I loved and admired the way he lived. He was never boring or ordinary. If I tell of the sensation of being on a journey down a huge river, the shores of the world in a haze, people will laugh at me for gushing in romantic clichés. But I'm only reflecting my memory with precision.

It is my great fortune that Stanley's love and care for his family had the same intensity that his films had.

Christiane Kubrick

Credits

Film scanning

Scanning of all 35 mm films: Prof. Mitch Mitchell, Kevin Wheatley/Cinesite (London)
Scanning of *2001* 70 mm: John Quartel/ Filmlight (London)
Scanning of *Spartacus* 70 mm: John Nicolard, Andrew Oran, Jose Parra, Vince Roth/Fotokem (Los Angeles)
Telecine transfers: Jon Compton, John Pegg, Lionel Runkel/Technicolor (London)
The lending of prints and interpositives was made possible by: Leon Vitali (negotiations), Brian Jamieson, Ned Price, and Steve Southgate (Warner Bros.); Jeffrey Brauer and Bob O'Neil (NBC Universal).

Text Credits

LOL Terry Southern, "An Interview with Stanley Kubrick": Copyright © 1962 by Terry Southern as an unpublished work. Copyright © 2005 by The Terry Southern Literary Trust. Reprinted by permission. All rights reserved.

DRS Stanley Kubrick, "How I Learned to Stop Worrying and Love the Cinema": Reprinted by permission of the Stanley Kubrick Estate.

2SO Herb A. Lightman, "Filming *2001*": Copyright © 1968 by *American Cinematographer Magazine*. Reprinted by permission. Carolyn Geduld, "Outline" and "The Production: A Calendar" from *Filmguide to 2001:* Copyright © 1973 Carolyn Geduld. Reprinted by permission of the author.

ACO Penelope Houston and Philip Strick, "Modern Times: An Interview with Stanley Kubrick": Copyright © 1972 by the British Film Institute. Reprinted by permission. Stanley Kubrick, letter to the editor of *The New York Times*: Reprinted by permission of the Stanley Kubrick Estate.

BLY Michel Ciment, excerpts from *Barry Lyndon* interview from *Kubrick*: Copyright © 1980 by Calmann-Lévy. English edition copyright © 1982 by HarperCollins Ltd. Reprinted by permission of Faber and Faber, Inc., an affiliate of Farrar, Straus and Giroux, LLC.

Image Credits

Unless otherwise noted, all material is courtesy of the Stanley Kubrick Estate. We regret that in some cases it was not possible to identify photographers and we apologize for any errors or omissions.

KKI Film frames reproduced by permission from MGM. Still photography by Alexander Singer except images 03 (unknown) and 10 (Stanley Kubrick).

KIL Film frames reproduced by permission from MGM. Stills photographer unknown. Additional photography by Stanley Kubrick.

POG Film frames reproduced by permission from MGM. Still photography by Lars Looschen.

SPA Film frames reproduced by permission from Universal Pictures. Still photography by William Read Woodfield. Additional photos by Stanley Kubrick and Christiane Kubrick.

LOL Film frames reproduced by permission from Warner Bros. Stills photographer unknown. Additional photos by Stanley Kubrick and Christiane Kubrick. Images 12–13 by Bert Stern.

DRS Film frames reproduced by permission from Columbia Pictures. Still photography by Bob Penn and Weegee. Additional photos by Stanley Kubrick and Christiane Kubrick.

2SO Film frames reproduced by permission from Warner Bros. Still photography by John Jay, Dmitri Kasterine, and Patrick Ward. Additional photos by Stanley Kubrick and Christiane Kubrick. Polaroids by Geoffrey Unsworth and Stanley Kubrick.

ACO Film frames reproduced by permission from Warner Bros. Still photography by Dmitri Kasterine. Additional photos by Jan Harlan, Stanley Kubrick, and Christiane Kubrick.

BLY Film frames reproduced by permission from Warner Bros. Still photography by Jan Harlan, Stanley Kubrick, and Christiane Kubrick.

SHI Film frames reproduced by permission from Warner Bros. Still photography by Jan Harlan and Stanley Kubrick except image 24 (Murray Close).

FMJ Film frames reproduced by permission from Warner Bros. Still photography by Jan Harlan and Stanley Kubrick.

EWS Film frames reproduced by permission from Warner Bros. Still photography by Manuel Harlan.

PRO Images 16, 17, 18, 19, 20, 22 Andrew Birkin. Image 21 Bob Gaffney. Felix Markham letters courtesy of Richard Markham.

The following photographs of archive material (Uwe Dettmar) are courtesy of the Deutsches Filmmuseum: EWK/p. 30; KKI/p. 41; KIL/p. 73; LOL/p. 175; DRS/p. 251; 2SO/p. 291; BLY/pp. 451, 474–75; SHI/p. 540; FMJ/p. 557; EWS/p. 593.

Imprint

EACH AND EVERY TASCHEN BOOK PLANTS A SEED!
TASCHEN is a carbon neutral publisher. Each year, we offset our annual carbon emissions with carbon credits at the Instituto Terra, a reforestation program in Minas Gerais, Brazil, founded by Lélia and Sebastião Salgado. To find out more about this ecological partnership, please check: *www.taschen.com/zerocarbon*
Inspiration: unlimited.
Carbon footprint: zero.

To stay informed about TASCHEN and our upcoming titles, please subscribe to our free magazine at *www.taschen.com/magazine*, follow us on Instagram and Facebook, or e-mail your questions to *contact@taschen*.com.

Hohenzollernring 53, D–50672 Köln
www.taschen.com

Original edition: © 2005 TASCHEN GmbH
English translation: Peter Snowdon

Printed in Slovenia
ISBN 978–3–8365–5582–1

CLOCKWORK ORANGE; PRIME PRINT FROM NEW INTERNEG
ROM NEW INTERNEG; YCM 9-99 REEL 3AB; DOLBY 5.1 STEREO
TERNEG; YCM 9-99 REEL 2AB; DOLBY 5.1 STEREO SOUNDTRACK
5.1 STEREO SOUNDTRACK
BARRY
BARRY
BARR
PRINT CONTINENTAL VERS.
"EYES W
"EYES WIDE SHUT"
F 8 TCOLOR 'P' PRINT
"EYES W
#2 of 8 TCOLOR 'P' PRINT
"EYES W

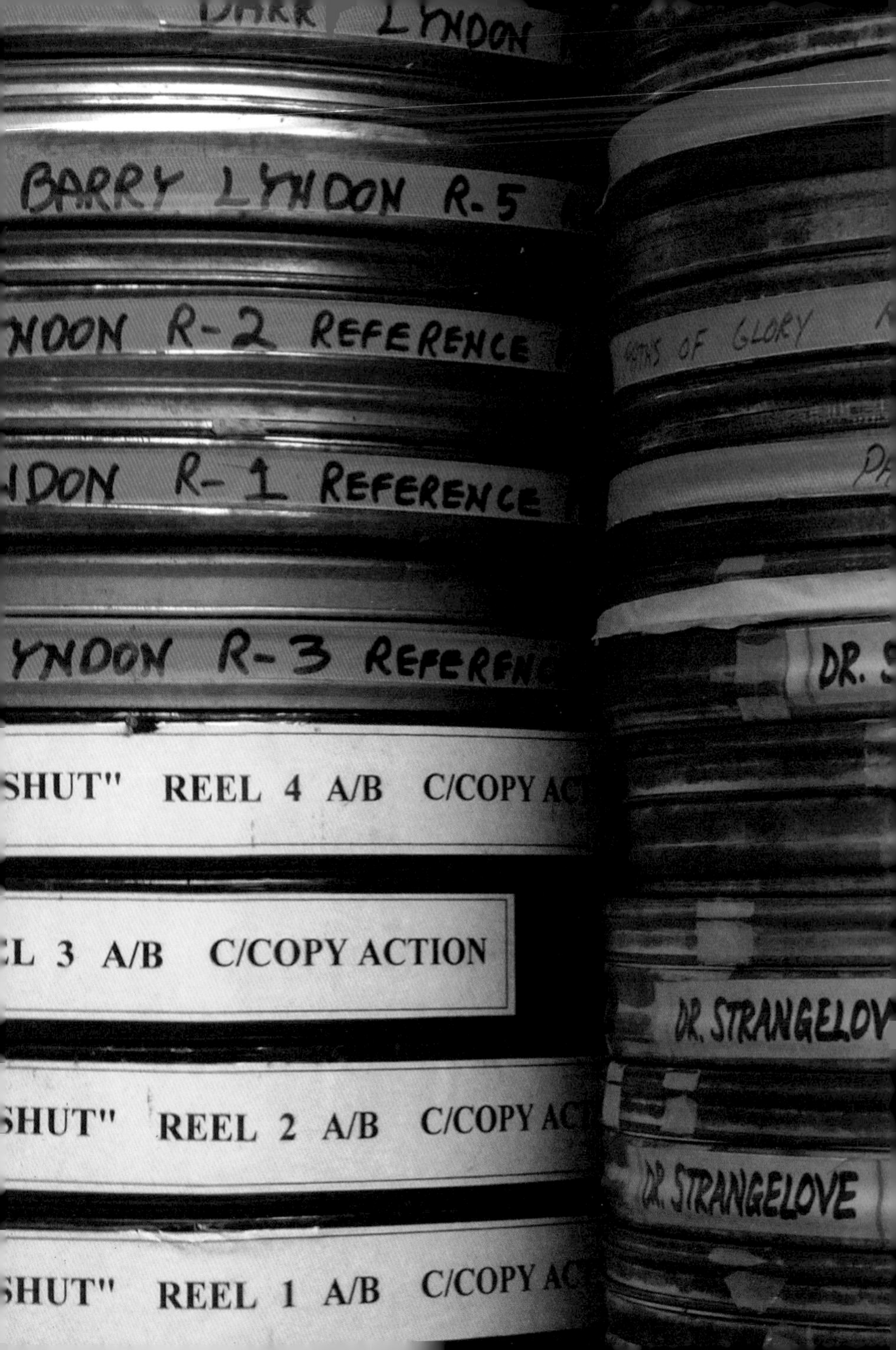
LYNDON
BARRY LYNDON R-5
NDON R-2 REFERENCE
OF GLORY
DON R-1 REFERENCE
YNDON R-3 REFEREN
DR. S
SHUT" REEL 4 A/B C/COPY AC
L 3 A/B C/COPY ACTION
DR. STRANGELOV
SHUT" REEL 2 A/B C/COPY AC
DR. STRANGELOVE
SHUT" REEL 1 A/B C/COPY AC